Handbook of Research on Synthesizing Human Emotion in Intelligent Systems and Robotics

Jordi Vallverdú
Universitat Autònoma de Barcelona, Spain

A volume in the Advances in Computational
Intelligence and Robotics (ACIR) Book Series

Managing Director:	Lindsay Johnston
Managing Editor:	Austin DeMarco
Director of Intellectual Property & Contracts:	Jan Travers
Acquisitions Editor:	Kayla Wolfe
Production Editor:	Christina Henning
Development Editor:	Erin O'Dea
Typesetter:	Cody Page
Cover Design:	Jason Mull

Published in the United States of America by
Information Science Reference (an imprint of IGI Global)
701 E. Chocolate Avenue
Hershey PA, USA 17033
Tel: 717-533-8845
Fax: 717-533-8661
E-mail: cust@igi-global.com
Web site: http://www.igi-global.com

Library of Congress Cataloging-in-Publication Data

CIP Data

Handbook of research on synthesizing human emotion in intelligent systems and robotics / Jordi Vallverdu, editor.
    pages cm
 Includes bibliographical references and index.
 ISBN 978-1-4666-7278-9 (hardcover) -- ISBN 978-1-4666-7279-6 (ebook) -- ISBN 978-1-4666-7281-9 (print & perpetual access) 1. Human-computer interaction. 2. Human engineering. 3. Robotics. I. Vallverdu, Jordi, editor.
 QA76.9.H85H363 2015
 004.01'9--dc23
                                        2014036854

This book is published in the IGI Global book series Advances in Computational Intelligence and Robotics (ACIR) (ISSN: 2327-0411; eISSN: 2327-042X)

British Cataloguing in Publication Data
A Cataloguing in Publication record for this book is available from the British Library.

For electronic access to this publication, please contact: eresources@igi-global.com.

Advances in Computational Intelligence and Robotics (ACIR) Book Series

ISSN: 2327-0411
EISSN: 2327-042X

MISSION

While intelligence is traditionally a term applied to humans and human cognition, technology has progressed in such a way to allow for the development of intelligent systems able to simulate many human traits. With this new era of simulated and artificial intelligence, much research is needed in order to continue to advance the field and also to evaluate the ethical and societal concerns of the existence of artificial life and machine learning.

The **Advances in Computational Intelligence and Robotics (ACIR) Book Series** encourages scholarly discourse on all topics pertaining to evolutionary computing, artificial life, computational intelligence, machine learning, and robotics. ACIR presents the latest research being conducted on diverse topics in intelligence technologies with the goal of advancing knowledge and applications in this rapidly evolving field.

COVERAGE

- Intelligent control
- Cognitive Informatics
- Computational Logic
- Algorithmic Learning
- Heuristics
- Adaptive and Complex Systems
- Robotics
- Neural networks
- Natural Language Processing
- Computer Vision

IGI Global is currently accepting manuscripts for publication within this series. To submit a proposal for a volume in this series, please contact our Acquisition Editors at Acquisitions@igi-global.com or visit: http://www.igi-global.com/publish/.

Titles in this Series

For a list of additional titles in this series, please visit: www.igi-global.com

Handbook of Research on Advancements in Robotics and Mechatronics
Maki K. Habib (The American University in Cairo, Egypt)
Engineering Science Reference • copyright 2015 • 993pp • H/C (ISBN: 9781466673878) • US $515.00 (our price)

Handbook of Research on Advanced Intelligent Control Engineering and Automation
Ahmad Taher Azar (Benha University, Egypt) and Sundarapandian Vaidyanathan (Vel Tech University, India)
Engineering Science Reference • copyright 2015 • 795pp • H/C (ISBN: 9781466672482) • US $335.00 (our price)

Handbook of Research on Artificial Intelligence Techniques and Algorithms
Pandian Vasant (Universiti Teknologi Petronas, Malaysia)
Information Science Reference • copyright 2015 • 873pp • H/C (ISBN: 9781466672581) • US $495.00 (our price)

Recent Advances in Ambient Intelligence and Context-Aware Computing
Kevin Curran (University of Ulster, UK)
Information Science Reference • copyright 2015 • 376pp • H/C (ISBN: 9781466672840) • US $225.00 (our price)

Recent Advances in Intelligent Technologies and Information Systems
Vijayan Sugumaran (Oakland University, USA & Sogang University, Seoul, Korea)
Information Science Reference • copyright 2015 • 309pp • H/C (ISBN: 9781466666399) • US $200.00 (our price)

Emerging Research on Swarm Intelligence and Algorithm Optimization
Yuhui Shi (Xi'an Jiaotong-Liverpool University, China)
Information Science Reference • copyright 2015 • 341pp • H/C (ISBN: 9781466663282) • US $225.00 (our price)

Face Recognition in Adverse Conditions
Maria De Marsico (Sapienza University of Rome, Italy) Michele Nappi (University of Salerno, Italy) and Massimo Tistarelli (University of Sassari, Italy)
Information Science Reference • copyright 2014 • 480pp • H/C (ISBN: 9781466659667) • US $235.00 (our price)

Computer Vision and Image Processing in Intelligent Systems and Multimedia Technologies
Muhammad Sarfraz (Kuwait University, Kuwait)
Information Science Reference • copyright 2014 • 312pp • H/C (ISBN: 9781466660304) • US $215.00 (our price)

Mathematics of Uncertainty Modeling in the Analysis of Engineering and Science Problems
S. Chakraverty (National Institute of Technology - Rourkela, India)
Information Science Reference • copyright 2014 • 441pp • H/C (ISBN: 9781466649910) • US $225.00 (our price)

www.igi-global.com

701 E. Chocolate Ave., Hershey, PA 17033
Order online at www.igi-global.com or call 717-533-8845 x100
To place a standing order for titles released in this series, contact: cust@igi-global.com
Mon-Fri 8:00 am - 5:00 pm (est) or fax 24 hours a day 717-533-8661

List of Contributors

Table of Contents

Section 4
Last Trends in Synthetic Emotions

Detailed Table of Contents

Section 1
Modeling Emotions

Chapter 1

Computational affective models are being developed both to elucidate affective mechanisms, and to enhance believability of synthetic agents and robots. Yet in spite of the rapid growth of computational affective modeling, no systematic guidelines exist for model design and analysis. Lack of systematic guidelines contributes to ad hoc design practices, hinders model sharing and re-use, and makes systematic comparison of existing models and theories challenging. Lack of a common computational terminology also hinders cross-disciplinary communication that is essential to advance our understanding of emotions. In this chapter the author proposes a computational analytical framework to provide a basis for systematizing affective model design by: (1) viewing emotion models in terms of two core types: emotion generation and emotion effects, and (2) identifying the generic computational tasks necessary to implement these processes. The chapter then discusses how these computational 'building blocks' can support the development of design guidelines, and a systematic analysis of distinct emotion theories and alternative means of their implementation.

Chapter 2

One way to evaluate cognitive processes in living or nonliving systems is by using the notion of "information processing". Emotions as cognitive processes orient human beings to recognize, express and display themselves or their wellbeing through dynamical and adaptive form of information processing. In addition, humans behave or act emotionally in an embodied environment. The brain embeds symbols, meaning and purposes for emotions as well. So any model of natural or autonomous emotional agents/systems needs to consider the embodied features of emotions that are processed in an informational channel of the brain or a processing system. This analytical and explanatory study described in this chapter uses the pragmatic notion of information to develop a theoretical model for emotions that attempts to synthesize some essential aspects of human emotional processing. The model holds context-sensitive and purpose-based features of emotional pattering in the brain. The role of memory is discussed and an idea of control parameters that have roles in processing environmental variables in emotional patterning is introduced.

This chapter proposes an emotional architecture organized around three pairs of antithetic universal symbols, or archetypes, derived from analytic psychology and anthropological accounts of mythical thinking. Their functions, relationships and interactions, on different levels of complexity within a dynamical system that mimics human emotional processes, are described by a formal model and a constructed ontology. The aim of the model is characterizing symbolic reasoning and figurative and analogue mechanisms of mental imagery associated with the internal representations of events. An automatic method for metaphor recognition and interpretation is proposed, targeting the identification of the proposed universal symbols in literary texts.

Emotion and social processes are evolutionarily intertwined. In this chapter, the authors present their TPR, TPR 2.0 and The Game of Emotions simulations along with the justification of necessary ideas in order to achieve the next level of research. This chapter describes a defense of the epistemological value of computer simulations for the analysis of emotions and social interactions. Finally, the elements of the model are described and defined with a sketch of the basic control algorithm.

    Saurabh K. Singh, Indian Institute of Technology Guwahati, India
    Shashi Shekhar Jha, Indian Institute of Technology Guwahati, India
    Shivashankar B. Nair, Indian Institute of Technology Guwahati, India

Emotion and memory have been two intermingled areas in psychological research. Although researchers are still fairly clueless on how human emotions or memory work, several attempts have been made to copy the dynamics of these two entities in the realm of robotics. This chapter describes one such attempt to capture the dynamics of human emotional memories and model the same for use in a real robot. Emotional memories are created at extreme emotional states, namely, very positive or happy events or very negative ones. The positive ones result in the formation of positive memories while the negative ones form the negative counterparts. The robotic system seeks the positive ones while it tries to avoid the negative ones. Such memories aid the system in making the right decisions, especially when situations similar to the one which caused their generation, repeat in the future. This chapter introduces the manner in which a multi-agent emotion engine churns out the emotions which in turn generate emotional memories. Results obtained from simulations and those from using a real situated robot described herein, validate the working of these memories.

    M.G. Sánchez-Escribano, Universidad Politécnica de Madrid, Spain
    Carlos Herrera, Universidad Politécnica de Madrid, Spain
    Ricardo Sanz, Universidad Politécnica de Madrid, Spain

Cognitive processes might be seen as reciprocal items and they are usually characterized by multiple feedback cycles. Emotions constitute one major source of feedback loops to assure the maintenance of well-being, providing cognitive processes with quantifiable meaning. This suggests the exploitation of models to improve the adaptation under value-based protocols. Emotion is not an isolated effect of stimuli, but it is the set of several effects of the stimuli and the relationships among them. This chapter proposes a study of the exploitation of models in artificial emotions, pointing out relationships as part of the model as well as the model exploitation method.

Section 2
The Body as a Space for Emotions

J. Lindblom, University of Skövde, Sweden
B. Alenljung, University of Skövde, Sweden

A fundamental challenge of human interaction with socially interactive robots, compared to other interactive products, comes from them being embodied. The embodied nature of social robots questions to what degree humans can interact 'naturally' with robots, and what impact the interaction quality has on the user experience (UX). UX is fundamentally about emotions that arise and form in humans through the use of technology in a particular situation. This chapter aims to contribute to the field of human-robot interaction (HRI) by addressing, in further detail, the role and relevance of embodied cognition for human social interaction, and consequently what role embodiment can play in HRI, especially for socially interactive robots. Furthermore, some challenges for socially embodied interaction between humans and socially interactive robots are outlined and possible directions for future research are presented. It is concluded that the body is of crucial importance in understanding emotion and cognition in general, and, in particular, for a positive user experience to emerge when interacting with socially interactive robots.

J. Vallverdú, Universitat Autònoma de Barcelona, Spain

Humans perform acts and imitate other humans' actions by innate mechanisms that imply the unconscious notion of innerbodiment. In this chapter, the author suggests a mechanistic method to capture, discretize and understand human actions, following a semi-supervised WOZ system that could allow robotic learning by imitation or even self-learning. A syntax and semantics basic model of human actions guide is provided as well as a philosophical analysis of the notion of action.

Carlos Herrera, Universidad Politécnica de Madrid, Spain
M.G. Sánchez-Escribano, Universidad Politécnica de Madrid, Spain
Ricardo Sanz, Universidad Politécnica de Madrid, Spain

Emotions are fundamentally embodied phenomena - but what exactly does this mean? And how is embodiment relevant for synthetic emotion? The specific role of embodied processes in the organisation of cognition and behaviour in biological systems is too complex to analyse without abstracting away the vast majority of variables. Robotic approaches have thus ignored physiological processes. At most, they hypothesise that homeostatic processes play a role in the cognitive economy of the agent – "gut feeling" is the embodied phenomenon to be modelled. Physiological processes play an actual role in the control of behaviour and interaction dynamics beyond information-processing. In this chapter, the authors introduce a novel approach to emotion synthesis based on the notion of morphofunctionality: the capacity to modulate the function of subsystems, changing the overall functionality of the system. Morphofunctionality provides robots with the capacity to control action readiness, and this in turn is a fundamental phenomenon for the emergence of emotion.

Section 3
Emotional Recognition and Implementation

Chapter 10

G. Shivakumar, Malnad College of Engineering, India
P.A. Vijaya, BNMIT, India

It is essential to distinguish between an imposter and a genuine emotion in certain applications. To facilitate this, the number of features is increased by incorporating physiological signals. Physiological changes in the human body cannot be pretended. Human emotional behavior changes the heart rate, skin resistance, finger temperature, EEG etc. These physiological signal parameters can be measured and included as the final feature vector. The network is to be trained considering all the feature points as inputs with a radial basis activation function at the hidden layer and a linear activation function at the output layer. The two physiological parameters galvanic skin response (GSR) and finger tip temperature (FTT) that are predominant in deciding the emotion of a person are considered in this chapter. The measurements made are transmitted to LabVIEW add-on card for further data processing and analysis. The results obtained are nearer to the reality with a good measure of accuracy.

Chapter 11

Gabriele Trovato, Waseda University, Japan
Atsuo Takanishi, Waseda University, Japan

Facial expressions are important for conveying emotions and communication intentions among humans. For this reason, humanoid robots should be able to perform facial expressions which represent their inner state in a way that is easy to understand for humans. Several humanoid robots can already perform a certain set of expressions, but their capabilities are usually limited to only the most basic emotions. It is necessary to consider a wider range of expressions and take advantage of the use of asymmetry. This chapter describes these aspects as well as insights about artificial emotions models, the mapping of human face into robotic face and finally the generation of facial expressions.

Chapter 12

O. Can Görür, Middle East Technical University, Turkey
Aydan M. Erkmen, Middle East Technical University, Turkey

This chapter focuses on emotion and intention engineering by socially interacting robots that induce desired emotions/intentions in humans. The authors provide all phases that pave this road, supported by overviews of leading works in the literature. The chapter is partitioned into intention estimation, human body-mood detection through external-focused attention, path planning through mood induction and reshaping intention. Moreover, the authors present their novel concept, with implementation, of reshaping current human intention into a desired one, using contextual motions of mobile robots. Current human intention has to be deviated towards the new desired one by destabilizing the obstinance of human intention, inducing positive mood and making the "robot gain curiosity of human". Deviations are generated as sequences of transient intentions tracing intention trajectories. The authors use elastic networks to generate, in two modes of body mood: "confident" and "suspicious", transient intentions directed towards the desired one, choosing among intentional robot moves previously learned by HMM.

Chapter 13

Reshma Kar, Jadavpur University, India

Amit Konar, Jadavpur University, India

Aruna Chakraborty, St. Thomas' College of Engineering and Technology, India

Several lobes in the human brain are involved differently in the arousal, processing and manifestation of emotion in facial expression, vocal intonation and gestural patterns. Sometimes people suppress their bodily manifestations to pretend their emotions. Detection of emotion and pretension is an open problem in emotion research. The chapter presents an analysis of EEG signals to detect true emotion/pretension: first by extracting the neural connectivity among selected brain lobes during arousal and manifestation of a true emotion, and then by testing whether the connectivity among the lobes are maintained while encountering an emotional context. In case the connectivity is manifested, the arousal of emotion is regarded as true emotion, otherwise it is considered as a pretension. Experimental results confirm that for positive emotions, the decoding accuracy of true (false) emotions is as high as 88% (72%), while for negative emotions, the classification accuracy falls off by a 12% margin for true emotions and 8% margin for false emotions. The proposed method has wide-spread applications to detect criminals, frauds and anti-socials.

Chapter 14

Reshma Kar, Jadavpur University, India

Anisha Halder, Jadavpur University, India

Amit Konar, Jadavpur University, India

Aruna Chakraborty, St. Thomas' College of Engineering and Technology, India

Atulya K. Nagar, Liverpool Hope University, UK

This chapter provides a novel approach to emotion recognition of subjects from the user-specified word description of their facial features. The problem is solved in two phases. In the first phase, an interval type-2 fuzzy membership space for each facial feature in different linguistic grades for different emotions is created. In the second phase, a set of fuzzy emotion-classifier rules is instantiated with fuzzy word description about facial features to infer the winning emotion class. The most attractive part of this research is to autonomously transform user-specified word descriptions into membership functions and construction of footprint of uncertainty for each facial feature in different linguistic grades. The proposed technique for emotion classification is very robust as it is sensitive to changes in word description only, rather than the absolute measurement of features. Besides it offers a good classification accuracy over 87% and is thus comparable with existing techniques.

Chapter 15

In this chapter, the authors explore social constructivist theories of emotion, which suggest that emotional behaviors are developed through experience, rather than innate. The authors' approach to artificial emotions follows this paradigm, stemming from a relatively young field called developmental or 'epigenetic' robotics. The chapter describes the design and implementation of a robot called MEI (multimodal emotional intelligence) with an emotion development system. MEI synchronizes to humans through voice and movement dynamics, based on mirror mechanism-like entrainment. Via typical caregiver interactions, MEI associates these dynamics with its physical feeling, e.g. distress (low battery or excessive motor heat) or flourishing (homeostasis). Our experimental results show that emotion clusters developed through robot-directed motherese ("baby talk") are similar to adult happiness and sadness, giving evidence to constructivist theories.

Chapter 16

Most computer models for the automatic recognition of emotion from nonverbal signals (e.g., facial or vocal expression) have adopted a discrete emotion perspective, i.e., they output a categorical emotion from a limited pool of candidate labels. The discrete perspective suffers from practical and theoretical drawbacks that limit the generalizability of such systems. The authors of this chapter propose instead to adopt an appraisal perspective in modeling emotion recognition, i.e., to infer the subjective cognitive evaluations that underlie both the nonverbal cues and the overall emotion states. In a first step, expressive features would be used to infer appraisals; in a second step, the inferred appraisals would be used to predict an emotion label. The first step is practically unexplored in emotion literature. Such a system would allow to (a) link models of emotion recognition and production, (b) add contextual information to the inference algorithm, and (c) allow detection of subtle emotion states.

Chapter 17

Socially interactive robots are expected to have an increasing importance in everyday life for a growing number of people, but negative user experience (UX) can entail reluctance to use robots. Positive user experience underpins proliferation of socially interactive robots. Therefore, it is essential for robot developers to put serious efforts to attain social robots that the users experience as positive. In current human-robot interaction (HRI) research, user experience is reckoned to be important and is used as an argument for stating that something is positive. However, the notion of user experience is noticeably often taken for granted and is neither described nor problematized. By recognizing the complexity of user experience the intended contributions can be even more valuable. Another trend in HRI research is to focus on user experience evaluation and examination of user experience. The current research paths of user experience of socially interactive robots are not enough. This chapter suggests that additional research directions are needed in order accomplish long-term, wide-spread success of socially interactive robots.

Section 4
Last Trends in Synthetic Emotions

Chapter 18

Diana Arellano, Filmakademie Baden-Wuerttemberg, Germany

Javier Varona, Universitat de les Illes Balears, Spain

Francisco J. Perales, Universitat de les Illes Balears, Spain

The question "What is the meaning of a smile?" could be easily answered with the sentence "it means happiness". But we can see in our daily lives that it is not always true. We also recognize that there is the context the one that makes us differentiate a happy smile from an embarrassed smile. The context is the framework that gives emotions a reason for happening because it describes what occurs around a person. Therefore, to create virtual characters, or agents that express emotions in a believable way it is necessary to simulate the context around them. The novelty of this chapter is the representation of context using ontologies, where context is seen not only as the events in the world, but also as that part of the character which allows them to react in one way or another, resulting in more believable emotional responses.

Chapter 19

Jai Galliott, The University of New South Wales, Australia

In this chapter the author considers the complex moral interplay between unmanned systems, emotion, and just war theory. The first section examines technologically mediated fighting and suggests that through a process of moral-emotional disengagement and emotional desensitisation, any pre-existing barriers to immoral conduct in war may be reduced. Having considered the impact on the long distance warrior's capacity or willingness to adhere to jus in bello norms, the author then examines the impact on the personal wellbeing of the operators themselves. Here, among other things, the author considers the impact of being simultaneously present in contrasting environments and argue that this, if nothing else, may lead to serious transgressions of just war principles. The fourth and final section asks whether we can eliminate or relieve some of these technologically mediated but distinctly human moral problems by further automating elements of the decision making process.

Unmanned aerial vehicles (UAVs), commonly known as drones, are a robotic form of military aircraft that are remotely operated by humans. Due to lack of situation awareness, such technology has led to the deaths of civilians through the inaccurate targeting of missile or gun attacks. This chapter presents the case for how a patented invention can be used to reduce civilian casualties through attaching an affect recognition sensor to a UAV that uses a database of strategies, tactics and commands to better instruct fighter pilots on how to respond while in combat so as to avoid misinterpreting civilians as combatants. The chapter discusses how this system, called VoisJet, can reduce many of the difficulties that come about for UAV pilots, including reducing cognitive load and opportunity for missing data. The chapter concludes that using UAVs fitted with VoisJet could allow for the reduction of the size of standing armies so that defence budgets are not overstretched outside of peacetime.

Preface

HUMANIZING MACHINES AS A FIRST STEP TOWARDS NEW COGNITION

The emotional flavour of all the spheres of human activities is a matter of fact, beyond any reasonable doubt for everyone interested on human cognition. Besides, emotional aspects can be also found as non-linguistic utterances that define the social domain of human life. From our bodies to social groups, emotions act as ways to regulate and model these exchanges. Emotions and feelings are basic regulators of human activity. In fact, they are the base of our interaction with the world: through pleasure, pain, hunger or fear, we create intentional dispositions, acting like homeostatic controls over our actions. From the basic emotions to complex ones, humans share a common nature to give sense to the world. Recent decades of scientific research on neurophysiology have shown how emotions are not simply a part of human activity, but a fundamental one. Emotional states had been historically banned in the territory of human rationality (Descartes and his "res cogitans" was the last and most convincing proponent of this approach). And evolutionary approaches to consciousness or studies of emotions have shown that the origin of consciousness, lying in the structure of the nervous system (which enables the data feedback loops, the cause of the emergence of consciousness) might be emotion (rather than perception) and that experienced sensations (i.e. *qualia*) inherently require someone to experience them. On the other hand, there are several kinds of studies of emotions in synthetic environments, such as affective computing or sociable robots. Some authors have also tried to develop computational models of artificial emotions or have drawn attention to the interesting phenomenon of emotions within artificial environments.

For the previous reason, this book covers an important area: how to recognize, model and implement emotions, from natural domains to artificial ones. Human-Robot Interaction (henceforth, HRI), for example, is one of the hottest topics in contemporary research: there is a necessity for a better understanding of how both can collaborate and share spaces and actions.

The potential readers of this publication can be classified under two main groups: active researchers (those implied actually into artificial emotions as well as related fields like AI, computing, robotics, philosophy, psychology, and so forth) and university students on these or general grades, because this book will not only provide an excellent frame for future researchers but tries at the same time to stimulate young and brilliant students towards the field of synthetic emotions. This publication also provides a solid conceptual frame for scientists and an opportunity for thinkers to develop new research lines for the future of the topic.

The book is organized following four sections, namely: 1) modeling emotions, 2) the body as a space for emotions, 3) emotional recognition and implementation, and 4) last trends in synthetic emotions. The first section is devoted to the modeling of emotions, a theoretical and computational process that implies a good conceptualization of all involved variables.

The first chapter of this section is authored by Eva Hudlicka and is titled "Computational Analytical Framework for Affective Modeling: Towards Guidelines for Designing Computational Models of Emotions". This is a very large chapter that provides a deep, exhaustive and perfect starting point for the analysis of emotional driving and the best ways to model it. Here, computational affective models are being developed both to elucidate affective mechanisms, and to enhance believability of synthetic agents and robots. Yet in spite of the rapid growth of computational affective modeling, no systematic guidelines exist for model design and analysis, and this lack of systematic guidelines contributes to *ad hoc* design practices, hinders model sharing and re-use, and makes systematic comparison of existing models and theories challenging. Lack of a common computational terminology also hinders cross-disciplinary communication that is essential to advance our understanding of emotions. In this chapter Hudlicka proposes a computational analytical framework to provide a basis for systematizing affective model design by: (1) viewing emotion models in terms of two core types: emotion generation and emotion effects, and (2) identifying the generic computational tasks necessary to implement these processes. Finally she discusses how these computational 'building blocks' can support the development of design guidelines, and a systematic analysis of distinct emotion theories and alternative means of their implementation.

Following to the long initial chapter, Alvandi's "Could Emotions Be Modelled Through Information Processing?" explores the cognitive notion of information processing in living or nonliving systems. According to the author, emotions as cognitive process orient human beings to recognize, express and display themselves or their wellbeing through dynamical and adaptive form of information processing. In addition, humans behave or act emotionally in an embodied environment. The brain embeds symbols, meaning and purposes for emotions as well. So any model of natural or autonomous emotional agents/systems needs to consider the embodied features of emotions that are processed in an informational channel of brain or a processing system. This chapter develops a theoretical model for emotions that attempts to synthesize some essential aspects of human emotional processing. The model will hold context-sensitive and purpose-based features of emotional pattering in the brain. The role of memory will be discussed and an idea of control parameters that have role in processing environmental variables in emotional patterning will be introduced.

The third chapter in this section, "Representing Emotions as Dynamic Interactions of Symbols: A Case Study on Literary Texts", by Băltoiu and Buiu tries a different approach for emotional modelization based on an emotional architecture organized around three pairs of antithetic universal symbols, or archetypes, derived from analytic psychology and anthropological accounts of mythical thinking. Their functions, relationships and interactions, on different levels of complexity within a dynamical system that mimics human emotional processes, are described by a formal model and a constructed ontology. The aim of the model is characterizing symbolic reasoning and figurative and analogue mechanisms of mental imagery associated with the internal representations of events. An automatic method for metaphor recognition and interpretation is proposed, targeting the identification of the proposed universal symbols in literary texts.

In the fourth chapter, "Emotions and Social Evolution: A Computational Approach," Casacuberta and Vallverdú sketch a new approach of emotional modeling that embraces techniques from computer sciences and integrates social simulations and evolutionary simulations based on emotional variables. Following the authors, the emotions and social processes are evolutionary intertwined. At the same time, in this chapter they present a new version of their simulation *The Game of Emotions* that justifies the necessary ideas in order to reach the next step of research. A defense of the epistemological value of computer simulations for the analysis of emotions and social interactions is described. Finally, the elements of the model are described as well as is defined a basic sketch of the basic control algorithm.

Singh, Jha and Nair suggest a different approach with "On Realizing Emotional Memories", where they explain that emotion and memory have been two intermingled areas in psychological research. Although researchers are still fairly clueless on how human emotions or memory work, several attempts have been made to copy the dynamics of these two entities in the realm of robotics. This chapter describes one such attempt to capture the dynamics of human emotional memories and model the same for use in a real robot. Emotional memories are created at extreme emotional states, namely, a very positive or happy event or a very negative one. The positive ones result in the formation of positive memories while the negative ones form the negative counterparts. The robotic system seeks the positive ones while it tries to avoid the negative ones. Such memories aid the system in making the right decisions especially when situations similar to the one which caused their generation, repeat in the future. This chapter introduces the manner in which a multi-agent emotion engine churns out the emotions which in turn generate emotional memories. Results obtained from simulations and those from using a real situated robot described herein, validate the working of these memories.

Finally, this first section is closed by Sánchez-Escribano, Herrera and Sanz's chapter, "The Exploitation of Models in Artificial Emotions", which considers that cognitive processes might be seen as reciprocal items and are usually characterized by multiple feedback cycles. Emotions constitute one major source of feedback loops to assure the maintenance of well-being, providing cognitive processes with quantifiable meaning. This suggests the exploitation of models to improve the adaptation under value-based protocols. Emotion is not an isolated effect of an stimuli, but it is the set of several effects of the stimuli and the relationships among them. This chapter proposes a study of the exploitation of models in artificial emotions, pointing out relationships as part of the model as well as the model exploitation method.

Section 2, "The Body as a Space for Emotions", contains three conceptual chapters devoted to the relationship between bodies and emotions, putting together contemporary research in cognitive sciences and artificial entities like computers or robots. The idea of embodied cognition and a naturalistic approach to emotional driving is a shared perspective for all chapters. First is "Socially Embodied Human-Robot Interaction: Addressing Human Emotions with Theories of Embodied Cognition", written by Lindblom and Alenljung. They show that a fundamental challenge of human interaction with socially interactive robots, compared to other interactive products, comes from them being embodied. The embodied nature of social robots questions to what degree humans can interact 'naturally' with robots, and what impact the interaction quality has on the user experience (UX). UX is fundamentally about emotions that arise and forms in humans through the use of technology in a particular situation. This chapter aims to contribute to the field of human-robot interaction (HRI) by addressing, in further detail, the role and relevance of embodied cognition for human social interaction, and consequently what role embodiment can play in HRI, especially for socially interactive robots. Furthermore, some challenges for socially embodied interaction between humans and socially interactive robots are outlined and possible directions for future research are presented. It is concluded that the body is of crucial importance in understanding emotion and cognition in general, and, in particular, for a positive user experience to emerge when interacting with socially interactive robots.

The second chapter, "Qualia Learning? Innerbodiment Construction and Machine Self-Learning by (Emotional) Imitation", written by Vallverdú goes one step beyond and constitutes a philosophical exercise of analysis on the meaning of being-from-a-body and how this is useful for better learning by

HRI. Humans perform acts and imitate other human's actions by innate mechanisms that imply the unconscious notion of innerbodiment. He suggests a mechanistic method to capture, discretize and understand human actions, following a semi-supervised WOZ system that could allow robotic learning by imitation or even self-learning. A syntax and semantics basic model of human actions guide is provided as well as a philosophical analysis of the notion of action.

The last chapter in this section, "The Embodiment of Synthetic Emotion" by Herrera, Sanchez-Escribano and Sanz, considers emotions as fundamentally embodied phenomena. But what exactly does this mean? And how is embodiment relevant for synthetic emotion? The specific role of embodied processes in the organisation of cognition and behaviour in biological systems is too complex to analyse without abstracting away the vast majority of variables. Robotic approaches have thus ignored physiological processes. At most, they hypothesise that homeostatic processes play a role in the cognitive economy of the agent – "gut feeling" is the embodied phenomenon to be modelled. Physiological processes play an actual role in the control of behaviour and interaction dynamics beyond information-processing. The authors introduce a novel approach to emotion synthesis based on the notion of morphofunctionality: the capacity to modulate the function of subsystems, changing the overall functionality of the system. Morphofunctionality provides robots with the capacity to control action readiness, and this in turn is a fundamental phenomenon for the emergence of emotion.

The third section of the book, "Emotional Recognition and Implementation," offers to the reader several techniques to capture emotions or to implement them into artificial devices. This process, from natural environments to artificial ones is at the core of most of contemporary interests in synthetic emotions. The chapter that opens this section "Investigation of Individual Emotions with GSR and FTT by Employing LabVIEW", by Shivakumar Vijaya is a great attempt to measure an individual's physiological parameters to decide emotional status. There is another challenge in emotion recognition when it is applied in the areas like forensics. It is essential to distinguish between an imposter and a genuine emotion. In order to facilitate this, the size of the feature is increased by incorporating physiological signals. A person can enact the expressions on the face to mimic a specific emotion. But, physiological changes in human body cannot be an imposter. Human emotional behavior changes the heart rate, skin resistance and finger temperature, EEG etc. These physiological signal parameters can be measured and included as part of the final feature vector. The final stage is the emotion recognition. The network is to be trained considering all the feature points as inputs with a radial basis activation function at the hidden layer and a linear activation function at the output layer. Different topologies and architectures of ANN are to be used for analyzing the recognition accuracy. A generalized system, measure, changes occurring in the body of a subject such as: heart rate, blood pressure, respiratory rate, electro-dermal (Galvanic skin resistance) activity, arm and leg motions. These measurements are then compared with the normal levels of the subject. In the present work, the authors have monitored the physiological parameters by connecting sensors at specific points on a test body, considering two physiological parameters viz. galvanic skin response (GSR) and finger tip temperature (FTT) and heart rate that are predominant in deciding the emotion of a person. This system, in conjunction with a certified examiner, can be used to analyze a subject's stress. The authors have constructed a system that measures physiological parameters along with signal conditioning units. These measurements are then transmitted to LabVIEW add-on card for further data processing and analysis. LabVIEW is a graphical programming language that includes all tools necessary for data acquisition, data analysis and presentation of results. The results obtained are very near to the reality on ground with a good measure of accuracy.

Trovato and Takanishi, with "Mapping Artificial Emotions into a Robotic Face", remark that facial expressions are important for conveying emotions and communication intentions among humans. For this reason, humanoid robots should be able to perform facial expressions which represent their inner state in a way that is easy to understand for humans. Several humanoid robots can already perform a certain set of expressions, but their capabilities are usually limited to only the most basic emotions. It is necessary to consider a wider range of expressions and take advantage of the use of asymmetry. These aspects are described as well as insights about artificial emotions models, the mapping of human face into robotic face and finally the generation of facial expressions.

"Intention and Body-Mood Engineering via Proactive Robot Moves to HRI" by Görür and Erkmen focuses on the novel concept of emotion and intention engineering in humans that has the potential of future emerging technologies, by providing an extensive survey on socially interacting robotic systems that are able to induce desired emotions and intentions on humans. They provide the necessary phases that pave the road to emotion and intention engineering, supported by a vast overview of leading works in the relevant literature. The chapter is partitioned into those phases encompassing intention estimation, human body-mood detection through external-focused attention and path planning through mood induction and reshaping intention. Moreover, as a demonstrative example of all of these phases, the authors present their implementation that aims at reshaping current human intention into a desired one, using contextual motions of mobile robots. Current human intention has to be deviated towards the new desired one by destabilizing the obstinance of human intention, inducing positive mood and making the "robot gain curiosity of human". Deviations of current intentions are generated as sequences of transient intentions tracing intention trajectories. They use elastic networks to generate way points of intentions that act as transient intentions directed towards the desired one. Way points are executed as suitable robot moves in adequate directions among previously learned intentional robot moves by HMM. Intention trajectories are generated in two modes of body mood: "confident" and "suspicious". This chapter analyzes the generation of intention trajectories by elastic networks in both modes.

The next chapter, "EEG-Analysis for the Detection of True Emotion or Pretension" by Kar, Konar and Chakraborty, is again devoted to the capture of emotional information. They point that several lobes in the human brain are involved differently in the arousal, processing and manifestation of emotion in facial expression, vocal intonation and gestural patterns. Sometimes people suppress their bodily manifestations to pretend their emotions. Detection of emotion and pretension is an open problem in emotion research. The chapter presents an analysis of EEG signals to detect true emotion/pretension first by extracting the neural connectivity among selected brain lobes during arousal and manifestation of a true emotion, and then by testing whether the connectivity among the lobes are maintained while encountering an emotional context. In case the connectivity is manifested, the arousal of emotion is regarded as true emotion, otherwise it is considered as a pretension. Experimental results confirm that for positive emotions, the decoding accuracy of true (false) emotions is as high as 88% (72%), while for negative emotions, the classification accuracy falls off by a 12% margin for true emotions and 8% margin for false emotions. The proposed method has wide-spread applications to detect criminals, frauds and anti-socials.

Again Kar (working now with Halder, Chakraborty and Nagar) made an excellent contribution with "Computing with Words Model for Emotion Recognition Using Interval Type-2 Fuzzy Sets", providing a novel approach to emotion recognition of subjects from the user-specified word description of their facial features. The problem is solved in two phases. In the first phase, an interval type-2 fuzzy membership space for each facial feature in different linguistic grades for different emotions is created. In the second phase, a set of fuzzy emotion-classifier rules is instantiated with fuzzy word description about facial features to infer the winning emotion class. The most attractive part of this research is to autonomously transform user specified word descriptions into membership functions and construction of footprint of uncertainty for each facial feature in different linguistic grades. The proposed technique for emotion classification is very robust as it is sensitive to changes in word description only rather than the absolute measurement of features. Besides it offers a good classification accuracy over 87% and thus comparable with existing techniques.

Lim and Okuno's chapter, "Developing Robot Emotions through Interaction with Caregivers," is the successful exploration of social constructivist theories of emotion, which suggest that emotional behaviors are developed through experience, rather than innate. Their approach to artificial emotions follows this paradigm, stemming from a relatively young field called developmental or 'epigenetic' robotics. They describe the design and implementation of a robot called MEI (multimodal emotional intelligence) with an emotion development system. MEI synchronizes to humans through voice and movement dynamics, based on mirror mechanism-like entrainment. Via typical caregiver interactions, MEI associates these dynamics with its physical feeling, e.g. distress (low battery or excessive motor heat) or flourishing (homeostasis). Lim and Okuno's experimental results show that emotion clusters developed through robot-directed motherese ("baby talk") are similar to adult happiness and sadness, giving evidence to constructivist theories.

Mortillaro, Meuleman and Scherer, from the Swiss Center for Affective Sciences, contribute to this section with "Automated Recognition of Emotion Appraisals", a chapter in which they suggest adopting an appraisal perspective in modeling emotion recognition. In particular, they propose to use appraisals as an intermediate layer between expressive features (input) and emotion labeling (output). Finally, Alenljung & Lindblom point that positive user experience underpins proliferation of socially interactive robots. Therefore, it is essential for robot developers to put serious efforts to attain social robots that the users experience as positive. By recognizing the complexity of user experience the intended contributions can be valuable and their research paths of user experience of socially interactive robots are not enough. Additional research directions, suggested by them, are needed in order accomplish long-term, wide-spread success of socially interactive robots.

The last section, 4, is devoted to the last trends in synthetic emotions. Three amazing chapters explore new ideas and situations that the field of artificial emotions will need to solve, and the authors provide good ideas to achieve it. The first chapter of a set of three, "Emotional Context? Or Contextual Emotions?" by Arellano, Varona and Perales, is focused on the notion of arousal context. For example: the question "What is the meaning of a smile?" could be easily answered with the sentence "it means happiness". But we can see in our daily lives that it is not always true. We also recognize that there is the context the one that makes us differentiate a happy smile from an embarrassed smile. The context is the framework that gives emotions a reason for happening because it describes what occurs around a person. Therefore, to create virtual characters, or agents that express emotions in a believable way, it is necessary to simulate the context around them. The novelty of this work is the representation of context using ontologies, where context is seen not only as the events in the world, but also as that part of the character which allows them to react in one way or another, resulting in more believable emotional responses.

The next two chapters are related to military research and emotion, a novel and very important area. With "Military Robotics and Emotion: Challenges to Just War Theory", Galliott explains to us that military robots are frequently used in lieu of humans in dull, dirty and dangerous roles. The advantages are manifold, but researchers are finding that in some cases, people have started to treat robots like pets, friends or even as an extension of themselves. That raises the question: if a soldier attaches human or animal-like characteristics to a military robot, can it affect how they use the robot? In this paper the author considers the complex moral interplay between unmanned systems, emotion and just war theory. The first section examines some common problems associated with technologically mediated fighting and suggests that through a process of moral-emotional disengagement and emotional desensitisation, any pre-existing barriers to immoral conduct in war may be reduced. Having considered the impact on the long distance warrior's capacity or willingness to adhere to jus in bello norms, the author then examines the impact on the personal wellbeing of the operators themselves. Here, among other things, the author considers the impact of being simultaneously present in contrasting environments and argue that this, if nothing else, may lead to serious transgressions of just war principles. In the fourth and final section, Galliott asks whether we can eliminate or relieve some of these technologically mediated but distinctly human moral problems by further automating elements of the decision making process.

The last chapter of this section and of the whole book is "The Role of Affective Computing for Improving Situation Awareness in Unmanned Aerial Vehicle operations: A US Perspective", written by Bishop. He explores how unmanned aerial vehicles (UAVs), commonly known as drones, are a robotic form of military aircraft that are operated remotely by humans. Due to lack of situation awareness, such technology has led to the deaths of civilians through the inaccurate targeting of missile or gun attacks. This chapter presents the case for how a patented invention can be used to reduce civilian casualties through attaching an affect recognition sensor to a UAV that uses a database of strategies, tactics and commands to better instruct fighter pilots on how to respond while in combat so as to avoid misinterpreting civilians as combatants. The chapter discusses how this system, called VoisJet, can reduce many of the difficulties that come about for UAV pilots, including reducing cognitive load and opportunity for missing data. The chapter concludes that using UAVs fitted with VoisJet could allow for the reduction of the size of standing armies so that defence budgets are not overstretched outside of peacetime.

From models to philosophy and from data capturing to emotional implementation into artificial devices or with some necessary future researches on the context of emotions and military emotions deployment, this book covers very important aspects of the rich and interdisciplinary field of artificial emotions. We have presented here several tools to better understand emotional situations and processing as well as methods to implement them into computers or robots.

For all the previous descriptions we can conclude that this book represents an important upgrade on the field of Synthetic Emotions: first of all, because new and deep models useful to researchers are provided; second, because upgraded techniques of human emotional recognition are explained; third, thanks to brave ideas, innovative ways to implement emotional aspects into machines and robots are detailed; fourth, several attempts to connect the contemporary trends on affective and embodied cognition with the synthetic environments are included. Sometimes closed and strong ideas or techniques are offered and in some others the authors express ways to go one step ahead. The last chapters on emotional context or military robotics and emotions are true examples of the necessity of thinking from new points of view. This is a good book for any person with interests in human emotions as well as in robotic ones. In fact, it constitutes a guide about how to obtain a better understanding of the nature of emotional states as well as several ways to implement them into machines. The deeper analysis on human emotions we make, the greater necessity of implementing similar characteristics in robotic devices. Yes, emotions are necessary for HRI, but also for new cognitive ways to create artificial cognitive systems. In a nutshell: *new (emotional) brains for new bodies.*

Section 1
Modeling Emotions

Chapter 1
Computational Analytical Framework for Affective Modeling:
Towards Guidelines for Designing Computational Models of Emotions

Eva Hudlicka
Psychometrix Associates, Inc., USA & University of Massachusetts-Amherst, USA

ABSTRACT

Computational affective models are being developed both to elucidate affective mechanisms, and to enhance believability of synthetic agents and robots. Yet in spite of the rapid growth of computational affective modeling, no systematic guidelines exist for model design and analysis. Lack of systematic guidelines contributes to ad hoc design practices, hinders model sharing and re-use, and makes systematic comparison of existing models and theories challenging. Lack of a common computational terminology also hinders cross-disciplinary communication that is essential to advance our understanding of emotions. In this chapter the author proposes a computational analytical framework to provide a basis for systematizing affective model design by: (1) viewing emotion models in terms of two core types: emotion generation and emotion effects, and (2) identifying the generic computational tasks necessary to implement these processes. The chapter then discusses how these computational 'building blocks' can support the development of design guidelines, and a systematic analysis of distinct emotion theories and alternative means of their implementation.

1.0 INTRODUCTION AND OBJECTIVES

The past 15 years have witnessed a rapid growth in computational models of emotion and affective agent architectures. Researchers in cognitive science, AI, HCI, robotics and gaming are developing 'models of emotion', primarily to create more believable and effective synthetic characters and robots, and to enhance human-computer interaction. Less frequently, these models are being developed for basic research purposes, to help elucidate the nature of the mechanisms mediating affective a variety of affective phenomena.

DOI: 10.4018/978-1-4666-7278-9.ch001

Yet in spite of the many stand-alone emotion models, and the numerous affective agent and robot architectures developed to date, there is a lack of consistency, and lack of clarity, regarding what exactly it means to 'model emotions' (Hudlicka, 2008b). The term 'emotion modeling' in the affective computing literature can refer to a wide variety of processes and models, including: the dynamic generation of emotion via black-box models that map specific stimuli onto associated emotions; generating facial expressions, gestures, or movements depicting specific emotions in synthetic agents or robots; modeling the effects of emotions on decision-making and behavior selection; including information about the user's emotions in a user model in tutoring and decision-aiding systems and in games; and a number of other applications.

There is also a lack of clarity regarding what affective states are modeled. The term 'emotion' in affective models can refer to emotions proper (short, transient states), moods, mixed states such as attitudes, and frequently states that are not considered to be emotions by psychologists (e.g., confusion, flow).

Emotion models also vary greatly in terms of the specific roles of emotions that are being implemented. These may include intrapsychic roles, such as goal management and goal selection, resource allocation and subsystem coordination, as well as interpersonal roles, such as communication and coordination among agents, and among virtual agents and humans.

One of the consequences of the existing terminological vagueness is that when we begin to read a paper addressing 'emotion modeling', we don't really know what to expect. The paper could just as easily describe details of facial expression generation, affective speech synthesis, black-box models mapping domain-specific stimuli onto emotions, or decision-utility formalisms evaluating behavioral alternatives. A more serious consequence of a lack of clear terminology is a lack of design guidelines regarding how

to model a particular affective phenomenon of interest: What are the computational tasks that must be implemented? Which theories are most appropriate for a given model? Are these theories specified at an adequate level of resolution to support a computational implementation? What are the associated representational and reasoning requirements, and alternatives? What data are required from the empirical literature? And are these data readily available?

The lack of consistent, clear terminology also makes it difficult to compare approaches, in terms of their theoretical grounding, their modeling requirements, and their theoretical explanatory capabilities and their effectiveness in particular applications.

1.1 Objectives: Computational Analytical Framework and Design Guidelines for Emotion Modeling

The purpose of this chapter is twofold. *First*, to outline a computational analytical framework for emotion modeling, consisting of multiple-levels of description of the processes and representations required to model emotion generation and emotion effects. *Second*, to suggest how this framework can serve as a basis for developing a set of guidelines for more systematic design, analysis and comparison of emotion models. The latter is particularly important, since emotion modeling, particularly in the case of research models, requires communication among multiple disciplines (computational scientists, psychologists, neuroscientists).

By emphasizing the generic computational tasks necessary to model emotions, the proposed computational analytical framework can facilitate communication among different disciplines, which have traditionally not shared either objectives, or methods and techniques. The proposed framework aims to emphasize the computational level of analysis, as proposed by Marr (1982). This level of analysis represents the most appropriate level for facilitating both cross-disciplinary communication necessary to advance the state-of-the-art in emotion modeling, and the development of systematic set of guidelines for model design and analysis. (Marr proposed three levels of analysis necessary to understand complex information processing systems: computational, algorithmic, and implementational. Analogous levels have also been proposed by Pylyshyn (1984), and termed semantic, syntactic, and physical.)

In this chapter I attempt to deconstruct the often ill-defined term 'emotion modeling' by: (1) suggesting that we view emotion models in terms of two fundamental categories of processes: *emotion generation* and *emotion effects;* and (2) identifying some of the fundamental, generic computational tasks necessary to implement these processes. These tasks are best thought of as the underlying 'building blocks' of emotion models. This computational analytical framework provides a basis for the development of more systematic guidelines for emotion modeling, for the theoretical and data requirements, and for representational and reasoning requirements and alternatives.

Identification of a set of generic computational tasks also represents a good starting point for a more systematic comparison of alternative theoretical perspectives and modeling approaches, and their effectiveness. Furthermore, a systematic analysis of the required computational 'building blocks' helps answer more fundamental questions about emotions: What are emotions? What is the nature of their mechanisms? What roles should they play in synthetic agents and robots? These computational building blocks can thus begin to serve as basis for what Sloman calls "architecture based definition of emotion" (Sloman, Chrisley, & Scheutz, 2005).

A number of researchers have addressed the issue of systematizing emotion modeling, both at the individual task level, and at the architecture level. Reilly (2006) outlined some of the computational tasks addressed in this chapter, and focused in particular on an analysis of the approaches to intensity calculation and combining similar emotions. Expanding on earlier work by Reisenzein (2001), Broekens and colleagues (Broekens, DeGroot, & Kosters, 2008) explored the use of an abstract set-theoretic formalism to systematically compare several existing theories of cognitive appraisal. Cañamero discussed design requirements for affective agents, focusing on the role of emotion in action selection (L. D. Cañamero, 2001). Lisseti and Gmytrasciewicz identified a number of high-level components of emotion required for computational models, in their Affective Knowledge Representation scheme (Lisetti & Gmytrasiewicz, 2002). In terms of architectures, Sloman and colleagues have done extensive work in exploring the architectural requirements for different classes of adaptive behavior, including requirements for different types of emotions, within the context of their CogAff architecture (Sloman et al., 2005). Ortony and colleagues have proposed a high-level design for an architecture that explicitly models emotion, and also includes a brief discussion of affective states and traits as parameters influencing processing (Ortony, Norman, & Revelle, 2005). Fellous (2004) addressed the need and requirements for emotions in synthetic agents from a neuroscience perspective. In 2011, a workshop on "Standards in Emotion Modeling" (SEM 2011) was organized by Broekens and colleagues, focusing on exploration of emerging standards in emotion modeling and the challenges associated with developing such standards. In a subsequent publication, Reisenzein and colleagues (Reisenzein et al., 2013) then further elaborated the requirements for more systematic approaches to emotion modeling, as well as the challenges associated with developing common terminology to facilitate cross-disciplinary dialogue about emotions.

The analytical framework presented in this chapter (consisting of the core affective processes, the associated generic computational tasks, and the representational and reasoning requirements necessary to implement them), and the set of guidelines defined for designing affective models, follows in this tradition. However, by committing to two core processes necessary to model emotions, providing a concrete set of generic computational tasks, and the representational and reasoning alternatives for their implementation, this chapter aims to go beyond the existing work in affective modeling, and provide the first steps towards the development of more systematic guidelines for the design of computational models of emotion.

The chapter is organized as follows. Section 2 provides background information on emotion research in psychology (Section 2.1) and on the theoretical foundations available for computational models of emotions (Section 2.2). Section 3 introduces the computational analytical framework and discusses the core affective processes (emotion generation and emotion effects modeling), the distinct domains that must be defined to implement these processes and the generic computational tasks required, and briefly addresses the associated representational and reasoning requirements. Section 4 then outlines a systematic process for the design of a computational affective model, based on the analytical framework introduced earlier, and includes a discussion of the associated requirements analysis. Section 5 discusses the implications of the proposed approach and future trends in affective computational modeling. Section 6 provides a summary and conclusions.

2.0 BACKGROUND

2.1 Emotion Research in Psychology

Regardless of the purpose of a particular affective computing research or development project, it is essential that the researcher or practitioner be familiar with the emotion research literature in psychology. This extensive body of research provides definitions and terminology, theories and conceptual models, and vast quantities of experimental data. Familiarity with these theories, models and data is critical for the development of affective computational models and affective user models, as well as for emotion recognition by machines, and for the generation of affective expressions in agents and robots. This is the case for applied models, whose aim is to enhance human-computer interaction or control the behavior of synthetic agents or robots. It is even more critical for research models, whose aim is to elucidate the mechanisms of affective processes and phenomena. Knowledge of existing data and theories also provides a basis for evaluation and validation of computational models. Furthermore, familiarity with emotion research from psychology facilitates cross-disciplinary communication that is necessary for continued progress in computational emotion research, and emotion research in general. In this section I provide an overview of emotion research in psychology, as it relates to computational affective modeling.

2.1.1 Definitions: What are Emotions?

When searching for a definition of emotions, it is interesting to note that most definitions involve descriptions of characteristics (e.g., fast, undifferentiated processing) or roles, and functions (e.g., coordinating mechanisms for goal management in uncertain environments, communicative mechanisms for facilitating social interaction, hardwired responses to critical stimuli). The fact that we so often describe emotions in terms of their characteristics, rather than their essential nature, underscores our lack of understanding of these complex phenomena. Nevertheless, a number of emotion researchers in psychology do appear to agree on a high-level definition of emotions, and view emotions as *states that reflect evaluative judgments of the environment, the self and other social agents, in light of the organism's goals and beliefs, which motivate and coordinate adaptive behavior, including the expression of emotions.* Note that the terms 'goals' and 'beliefs' are used in a generic sense: goals reflecting desirable states, and beliefs reflecting current knowledge. The term 'goal' in this discussion therefore covers any representation of desired states, and does not distinguish between conscious and unconscious, explicit or implicit, and innate or learned goals.

2.1.2 Taxonomy of Affective States and Traits

The term 'emotion' itself is problematic. On the one hand, it depicts emotions in a generic, folk-psychology sense we all presume to understand, and which subsumes many types of affective states. On the other hand, it has a specific meaning in the emotion research literature, referring to transient states, lasting for seconds or minutes, typically associated with well-defined triggering cues and characteristic patterns of expressions and behavior. (More so for the simpler, fundamental emotions than for complex emotions, which have more complex and significant cognitive components.)

Emotions are often further categorized into *basic* emotions (P. Ekman, 1992; Izard, 1977; Panskepp, 1998; Plutchik, 1984)) and, for lack of a better word, *non-basic or complex* emotions, often referred to as social emotions, although by no means exclusively occurring in interpersonal contexts. The inelegant terms non-basic and complex reflect the difficulty of classifying these emotions under a single descriptive term. The set of non-basic emotions includes the important social (also termed self-conscious) emotions, such as pride, shame, and guilt, but also all other complex emotions, including love, empathy, shadenfreude, humiliation, contempt and many others.

This categorization reflects differences in the degree of cognitive complexity associated with specific emotions, the universality of the triggering stimuli and the expressive and behavioral manifestations, and the degree to which an explicit representation of the agent's self within its social milieu is required. While not universally accepted in emotion research (Ortony & Turner, 1990) and

(P. Ekman & Davidson, 1994), this categorization, is nevertheless useful for affective modeling, and is adopted in the discussion below.

The term 'emotion' can be contrasted with other terms describing affective phenomena: *moods*, sharing many features with emotions but lasting longer (hours to months), and having less differentiated triggers and manifestations; *affect*, an undifferentiated positive or negative state associated with generic behavior tendencies (approach, avoid); and *feelings,* a problematic and ill-defined construct from a modeling perspective. (Averill points out that "feelings are neither necessary nor sufficient conditions for being in an emotional state" (Averill, 1994)). Emotions, moods, affect and feelings all refer to affective states, i.e., transient affective activity. Some models also represent stable affective personality *traits* (e.g., extraversion, neuroticism), or a variety of 'mixed' mental states that involve both cognitive and affective components (e.g., attitudes). Figure 1 illustrates the taxonomy of affective states and traits described above.

2.1.3 Multi-Modal Nature of Emotions

A key characteristic of emotions is their multi-modal nature. Emotions in biological agents are manifested across four distinct, but interacting, modalities. The most familiar is the *behavioral / expressive* modality, where the expressive and action-oriented characteristics of emotions are manifested, in a readily visible manner; e.g., facial expressions, speech, gestures, posture, and behavioral choices. Closely related is the *somatic / physiological modality* - the neurophysiological substrate making behavior (and cognition) possible (e.g., heart rate, neuroendocrine effects, blood pressure). The *cognitive / interpretive* modality is most directly associated with the evaluation-based working definition of emotions provided above, and emphasized in the cognitive appraisal theories of emotion generation, discussed below. The most problematic modality, from a modeling

Figure 1. Taxonomy of affective states and traits

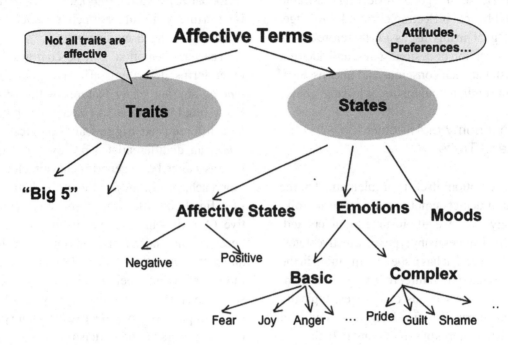

perspective, is the *experiential / subjective* modality: the conscious, and inherently idiosyncratic, experience of emotions within the individual.

While the current emphasis in emotion modeling is on the cognitive modality (involved in appraisal) and the behavioral / expressive modality (involved in manifesting emotions in agents), it is important to recognize that both the physiological and the experiential modalities also play critical roles (Izard, 1993). Table 1 provides examples of the multi-modal signatures of two of the 'basic' emotions: anger and fear.

2.1.4 What are the Roles of Emotions?

The dominant contemporary view regarding the evolution and utility of emotions is that their primary role is to ensure survival and improve the adaptive fit of an agent in its environment. This is accomplished by emotion-mediated rapid detection of survival-critical cues in the environment, including social cues, and by preparation of the agent for a coordinated execution of the

necessary behavioral responses, including expression of emotions for communication purposes (P. Ekman & Davidson, 1994; N. Frijda, 2008; Plutchik, 1984).

Emotions play a number of important roles in biological agents, by helping to regulate homeostasis, reproductive and survival behaviors, and by enabling adaptive behavior in complex and uncertain environments in general, including social behavior. Emotion roles can be categorized into two broad groups: *intrapsychic and interpersonal* (see Figure 2). Both types of roles are discussed in more detail below (see Table 2 for a summary).

Emotions can, of course, also become highly maladaptive, even dangerous; both to the individual experiencing or manifesting the emotions, and to others in the individual's social environment. Since the focus in affective modeling is primarily on the adaptive roles of emotions, I will not discuss pathological or maladaptive affective processes in this chapter. It is important to note, however, that computational affective modeling of these processes has the potential to significantly

Table 1. Examples of multimodal signatures of emotions

Anger	
Trigger(s)	Progress toward goals hindered, especially by another agent
Cognitive Biases	Strong effect on attention capture and focus Attribution of hostility to other agents Overestimates of own chances of success Tendency to try alternative strategies Reduced perception of risk & increased risk tolerance
Physiological Correlates	Overall objective: mobilize and sustain high energy levels required for possible aggression
ANS Correlates	Larger heart rate acceleration (than happiness); Larger increase in finger temperature (than fear); Higher diastolic blood pressure (than fear); Greater·peripheral resistance (than fear); Larger increase in heart rate (than disgust) (Levenson, 1992)
Facial Expr.	Lowering brows; raising upper eyelids; tightening & pressing together of lips
Speech Characteristics	Fast rate; High voice intensity; high pitch; wide range of pitch; abrupt pitch changes
Behavioral Manifestations	Eagerness to act Tendency towards aggression
Fear	
Trigger(s)	Perceived danger to important self- or other-protective goals
Cognitive Biases	Tunnel vision (attentional narrowing focusing on the source of the threat) Threat focus in attention and interpretation Faster detection of threatening stimuli Interpretation of ambiguous stimuli as threatening
Physiological Correlates	Mobilization of energy level to prepare for action; energy 'spike'
ANS Correlates	Larger heart rate acceleration (than happiness); Larger skin conductance increase (than happiness); Lower diastolic BP (than anger); Decreased finger temperature (Levenson, 1992)
Facial Expr.	Raised eyebrows and eyelids (eyes wide open); lips stretched and pressed together
Speech	Faster rate; higher pitch; wider pitch range; medium intensity
Goals	Self protection; Protection in general
Behavioral Manifestations	Flight and avoidance; Protective behavior; Low intensities (inhibitory behavior, freezing), high intensities (fleeing) (Panskepp, 1998, p. 208)

Table 2. Summary of intrapsychic and interpersonal roles of emotions

Intrapsychic Roles
• Rapid detection & processing of salient stimuli (e.g., avoid danger, get food) • Triggering, preparation for, & execution of fixed behavioral patterns necessary for survival (e.g., fight, freeze, flee) • Rapid resource (re)allocation & mobilization • Coordination of multiple systems (perceptual, cognitive, physiological) • Implementation of systemic biasing of processing (e.g., threat detection, self-focus) • Interruption of on-going activity & (re)prioritization of goals • Motivation of behavior via reward & punishment mechanisms • Motivation of learning via boredom & curiosity
Interpersonal Roles
• Communication of internal state via non-verbal expression and behavioral tendencies (e.g., frown vs. smile, inviting vs. threatening gestures & posture) • Communication of status information in a social group (dominance & submissiveness) • Mediation of attachment • Communicate acknowledgment of wrong-doing (guilt, shame) in an effort to repair relationships and reduce possibility of aggression

Figure 2. Emotion role groups

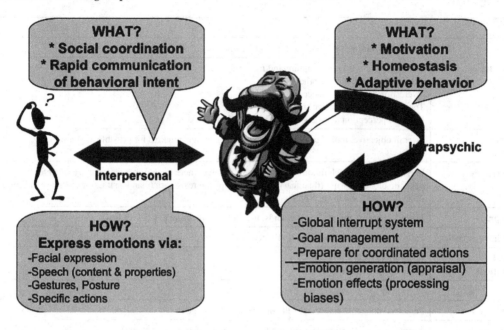

contribute to an understanding of the mechanisms that mediate both affective disorders, and their treatment, and some efforts are beginning to be made in this area (e.g., Hudlicka, 2008; Hudlicka, 2014).

Intrapsychic roles of emotions refer to the roles that emotions play within the individual biological agent. Emotions help ensure homeostasis and survival, by motivating and enhancing the agent's adaptive behavior in complex and uncertain environments, in part by mediating reward and punishment. Emotions facilitate the *rapid identification of stimuli* that are dangerous or beneficial to the agent's survival. This processing is often mediated by hardwired, and often highly species- and situation-specific responses (e.g., rats responding to squeaks of certain frequencies emitted by pups in danger (LeDoux 1996)). Emotions influence and mediate a number of processes involved in the interpretation cues, integration of new information with existing information and preferences, and prediction of possible future states, to help guide planning and decision-making. Emotions also mediate motivation and complex, adaptive behavior

via *goal management*; that is, the creation of new goals or the re-prioritizing of existing goals, in response to new events or new information (Frijda 1986; Oatley and Johnson-Laird 1987). The goal management and coordination role includes rapid changes in motivation, and associated selection of alternative goals, when necessary; that is, when expectations are violated, or when individual or environmental circumstances prevent the satisfaction of current goals (Clore 1994). This role of emotions is emphasized in the *interruption theory of emotions* (Mandler 1984) or *global interrupt signal theory* (Oatley and Johnson-Laird 1987). Emotions also contribute to learning and information acquisition, by ensuring that the organism remains engaged with its environment through the mechanisms of boredom and curiosity. Finally, emotions mediate the *coordination of activities* aimed at satisfying multiple-goals, in uncertain and unpredictable environments, and the *monitoring and regulation of goal-directed behavior in general*. This involves the *mobilization of the resources* required to quickly respond to a new situation, (which also include the rapid interpretation of relevant stimuli described above), the selection of appropriate behavior, and the preparation of the organism for a coordinated execution of the specific behavior patterns. This type of coordination is made possible by the *rapid allocation (or re-allocation) of the physiological and cognitive processes* and involves *coordination among diverse systems,* corresponding to the multiple modalities of emotion: the neurophysiological systems that control metabolic resources (e.g., autonomic nervous system controlling arousal necessary for fast response), the information processing systems that mediates perception and cognition (e.g., (re-) directing attention, biasing of interpretive processes), and the motor system that mediates the execution of the selected behavioral sequence, often involving fixed behavioral repertoires associated with a particular emotion.

Emotions thus play a critical role in the *perception and interpretation* of incoming stimuli, and in *motivation and behavior preparation,* with distinct emotions linked to different patterns of stimuli and associated desired behavior, "action tendencies" (Frijda 1986). The overall objective is to improve the organism's well-being and chances for survival (e.g., Plutchnik, 1984).

Many of the emotion-mediated stimulus-response patterns are innate, having evolved as a result of phylogenetic adaptation. Evidence for this includes similarity of affective behavior across the phases of individual development, across cultures and species, and similarity in blind and sighted individuals (Izard 1977). A key distinguishing feature of these diverse functions is their speed, made possible in part by the 'hardwired' neural circuitry, which rapidly processes salient stimuli, mobilizes the necessary metabolic resources, and selects and executes fixed patterns of behavior or behavioral sequences. Different sets of such stimulus-emotions-behavior (see-feel-do) patterns have been proposed, with similarities across many higher-level species. For example, Plutchik (Plutchik 1980) suggests the following associa-

tion between emotions and general categories of behavior: fear and protection; anger and destruction; acceptance and incorporation; disgust and rejection; joy and reproduction; sadness and reintegration; surprise and orientation; and curiosity and exploration.

Adaptive functioning in complex, changing environments must of course also involve the development of new stimulus-response patterns, mediated by learning mechanisms. Emotions contribute to this adaptive function by *enabling fast and long lasting learning*, which itself is also mediated by hardwired circuitry and, particularly when associated with danger, difficult to extinguish (LeDoux 1989).

Interpersonal (also termed social) roles emotion facilitate social interaction and successful social functioning by rapidly, typically non-verbally, communicating internal states and associated behavioral intents. Whether communicating love between mother and an infant, to facilitate the development of attachment necessary for survival, or ensuring appropriate safe distance between adversaries, by communicating the possibility of an imminent attack, or facilitating effective dialogue by displaying pleasure via a smile, or displeasure via a frown, emotions enable the development of relationships and social structures necessary for well-being and survival. Emotions also facilitate the communication required for complex, coordinated group behavior, and for the establishment and maintenance of social structures and hierarchies. This includes control of aggression, or the use of aggression to help manage group behavior.

These social roles of emotion are evident in groups of varying sizes and types, ranging from intimate dyads to large organizations and even entire nations, and across cultures and species. For example, animals communicate anger or displeasure by growling to ensure the maintenance of appropriate distance and thereby help avoid a direct confrontation. While humans usually don't growl, nevertheless established patterns of non-verbal behavior serve analogous functions in humans; e.g., communication of rising levels of frustration via facial expressions, gestures and posture helps regulate the degree of frustration and prevents open expression of aggression in social interactions.

Both the basic, and the complex social emotions, play these critical roles in interpersonal interactions. Social emotions in particular are essential for regulating social behavior, by ensuring that social norms are developed and adhered to, and by providing a means of repairing social relationships. Lewis (2008) lists several specific roles for the social emotions of pride and shame: pride is felt when social norms are met, whereas shame is felt when norms are violated. Together, these two important social emotions thus function as internalized reward and punishment mechanism, ensuring that social behavior remains within proscribed norms. Another social emotion, guilt, functions in part to self-regulate behavior, and in part to help repair relationships. For example, imagine a not-uncommon situation where a spouse forgets an anniversary. If s/he then feels guilty, and expresses this guilt appropriately, s/he will likely to reduce the feelings of hurt or hostility his/her partner is likely to feel, and facilitate forgiveness, thereby minimizing the damage to the relationship.

2.2 Theoretical Foundations for Computational Models of Emotions

A number of theories have been developed in psychology which have direct relevance for computational affective modeling. Below I discuss both the broad theoretical perspectives on emotions, and specific theories relevant to modeling emotion generation and emotion effects, with an emphasis on the cognitive modality of emotions.

Why should affective modelers care about theories of emotion developed in psychology? Adherence to a particular theoretical perspective, and the use of specific theories, help ensure that

computational models are developed in a theoretically and empirically grounded manner. This then facilitates identification of the appropriate empirical data, model validation, communication with other researchers, and potential sharing and re-use of model components. In addition, adherence to particular theoretical perspectives helps advance our understanding of affective processes, by enabling computation-based operationalizations of high-level theories, which often reveal gaps or contradictions, thus enabling the development of more accurate theories of affective phenomena.

2.2.1 Theoretical Perspectives

Emotions represent complex, and often poorly understood, phenomena. It is therefore not surprising that a number of distinct theories have evolved over time, to explain a specific subset of these phenomena, or to account for a particular subset of the observed data. Three theoretical perspectives that are most directly relevant for computational affective modeling are described below and summarized in Table 3.

Discrete theories of emotions emphasize a small set of discrete emotions. The underlying assumption of this approach is that these fundamental emotions are mediated by associated dedicated neural circuitry, with a large innate, 'hardwired' component. Different emotions are characterized by stable patterns of triggers, behavioral expression, and associated distinct subjective experiences. The emotions addressed by these theories are typically the 'basic' emotions; joy, sadness, fear, anger, and disgust. Because of its emphasis on discrete categories of states, this approach is also termed the *categorical approach* (Panskepp, 1998). For modeling purposes, the semantic primitives representing emotions in affective models are the distinct basic emotions.

An alternative method of characterizing affective states is in terms of a small set of underlying dimensions that define a space within which

Table 3. Summary of the three dominant theoretical perspectives available for affective modeling

	Discrete / Categorical	**Dimensional**	**Componential**
Semantic Primitives	**Basic emotions** Small number of 'hardwired' emotions exists (basic emotions), with characteristic neuromotor patterns that prepare for specific, species-relevant behaviors	**2 or 3 dimensions** (valence and arousal, or valence, arousal, dominance) (often the term pleasure is used instead of valence, thus PAD)	**Appraisal variables** Emotions result from the (parallel) evaluation of a number of *appraisal variables* (e.g., novelty, valence, goal congruence, agency). Appraisals of individual variables represent components of emotions.
Semantic Primitives Correspond to	Basic emotions	Underlying dimensions of felt mood (or core affect)	Interpretive features of the stimulus, and the stimulus-agent relationship
Number / Type of Emotions Possible	Small set of basic emotions (e.g., joy, sadness, anger, fear, disgust, surprise). Complex/social emotions thought to be combinations of basic emotions.	A large set of emotions defined by combinations of different values of {valence & arousal} or {valence, arousal, & dominance}. Larger set than basic dimensions but not as large as the set defined by the appraisal variables of the component process model.	Very large set of emotions defined by the possible values of all of the appraisal variables
Degree of Elaboration of Appraisal Process	Low	Low (dimensions originally derived from mood, thus with a strong physiological component, vs. cognitive component)	Very high
Degree of Detail About Affective Dynamics	Low / Qualitative	Medium / Focus on arousal	Some / Qualitative
Representative Theorists	Tomkins, Ekman, Izard, Panskepp	Wundt, Mehrabian, Russell, Lang, Watson & Tellegen	Frijda, Scherer, Smith, Ellsworth, Kirby, Roseman, Ortony et al. (OCC)

Note that the OCC theory fits best within the componential view, because the abstract features comprising the emotion eliciting conditions are analogous to the appraisal variables of the componential theories.

distinct emotions can be located. This *dimensional perspective* describes emotions in terms of two- or three-dimensions. The most frequent dimensional characterization of emotions uses two dimensions: valence and arousal (Russell, 2003; Russell & Barrett, 1999; Russell & Mehrabian, 1977). Valence reflects a positive or negative evaluation, and the associated felt state of pleasure (vs. displeasure), as outlined in the context of undifferentiated affect above. Arousal reflects a general degree of intensity or activation of the organism, reflecting in large part the degree of activation of the autonomic nervous system. The degree of arousal reflects a general readiness to act: low arousal is associated with less energy, high arousal with more energy. Since this 2-dimensional space cannot differentiate among emotions that share the same values of arousal and valence (e.g., anger and fear, both characterized by high arousal and negative valence), a third dimension is often added, termed dominance or stance. The resulting 3-dimensional space is often referred to as the PAD space (Mehrabian & 1995) (pleasure (synonymous with valence), arousal, dominance).

The representational semantic primitives within this theoretical perspective are thus these 2 or 3 dimensions.

The third view emphasizes the distinct components of emotions, and is often termed the componential view (Leventhal & Scherer, 1987). The 'components' referred to in this view are both the distinct modalities of emotions (e.g., cognitive, physiological, behavioral, subjective) and also the components of the cognitive appraisal process. These latter are referred to as appraisal dimensions or appraisal variables, and include novelty, valence, goal relevance, goal congruence and coping abilities. A stimulus, whether real or imagined, is evaluated in terms of its meaning and consequences for the agent, to determine the appropriate affective reaction. This analysis involves assigning specific values to the individual appraisal variables. Once the appraisal variable values are determined by the agent's evaluative processes, the resulting vector is mapped onto a particular emotion, within the n-dimensional space defined by the n appraisal variables. The representational semantic primitives within this theoretical perspective are thus the individual appraisal variables.

It must be emphasized that these theoretical perspectives should not be viewed as competing for a single ground truth, but rather as distinct perspectives, each arising from a particular research tradition (e.g., biological vs. social psychology), focusing on different sets of affective phenomena, considering distinct levels of resolution and fundamental components (e.g., emotions vs. appraisal variables as the distinct primitives), and using different experimental methods (e.g., factor analysis of self-report data vs. neuroanatomical evidence for distinct processing pathways). The different perspectives also provide different degrees of support for the distinct processes of emotion; e.g., the componential theories provide extensive details about cognitive appraisal. Until such time as emotions are better understood and explained, it is best to view the three theoretical perspectives

outlined above as alternative explanations, each with its own set of explanatory powers and scope, and supporting data; analogously, perhaps, to the wave vs. particle theory of light, as suggested by Picard (Picard, 1997).

Having outlined the broad theoretical perspectives on emotions, I now provide an overview of the existing theories available for modeling the core affective processes: emotion generation and emotion effects.

2.2.2 Theories of Emotion Generation

Emotion generation is an evolving, dynamic process that occurs across the multiple modalities (discussed above), with complex feedback and interactions among them. While all modalities are involved, our understanding of these phenomena is most elaborated within the cognitive modality, and the majority of existing models of emotion generation implement *cognitive appraisal* (exceptions do exist, e.g., (Breazeal & Brooks, 2005; L. Cañamero, 1997; L. Cañamero & Avila-Gracia, 2007; Velásquez, 1999). The discussion below is therefore limited to cognitive appraisal, while at the same time recognizing that the current cognitive bias may well be an example of "looking for the key under the lamp because there is more light there". In addition, as embodied agents become more complex, there may be increasing need to include non-cognitive modalities in emotion generation.-

All cognitive appraisal theorists emphasize the critical role that cognition plays in generating the subjective emotional experience, by mediating the interpretations required for the evaluative judgments necessary for generating emotion. Figure 3 illustrates the appraisal process, indicating how the same stimulus can produce distinct emotions, depending on the differences in the individual's interpretations. Appraisal theories have their roots in antiquity and have gone through a number of iterations since then. Many researchers over the past four decades have contributed to the current versions of cognitive appraisal theories (Arnold, 1960; N. H. Frijda, 1986; Lazarus, 1984; Mandler, 1984; I.J. Roseman & Smith, 2001; K. Scherer, Schorr, & Johnstone, 2001; Smith & Kirby, 2001).

Appraisal theorists recognize that appraisal processes vary in complexity and cognitive involvement, from: low-level, 'hardwired', to complex, culture-specific and idiosyncratic triggers. Three interconnected levels are typically proposed: sensorimotor, schematic, and conceptual. (Similar tri-level organization has also been proposed for cognitive-affective architectures in general (Ortony et al., 2005; Sloman et al., 2005)).

The most influential appraisal theories in computational modeling are those that are cast in 'computation-friendly' terms. The first of these was proposed by Ortony and colleagues, now referred to as the OCC theory (Ortony, Clore, & Collins, 1988) and Frijda (1986), and remains the most frequently implemented theory of cognitive appraisal in computational models of emotion (Andre, Klesen, Gebhard, Allen, & Rist, 2000; Aylett, 2004; Bates, Loyall, & Reilly, 1992; de

Rosis, Pelachaud, Poggi, Carofiglio, & De Carolis, 2003; El-Nasr, Yen, & Ioerger, 2000; Elliot, 1992; Gratch & Marsella, 2004; Loyall, 1997; Prendinger, Saeyor, & Ishizuka, 2004; W. S. R. Reilly, 1996; Staller & Petta, 1998). Several models have used Frijda's appraisal theory (N. H. Frijda, 1986; N. H. Frijda & Swagerman, 1987). More recently, appraisal theories of Scherer, Roseman, and Smith and Kirby, have begun to be used as the basis of computational models (I.J. Roseman, 2001; K. Scherer et al., 2001; Smith & Kirby, 2000).

There is a considerable degree of overlap among cognitive appraisal theories, in terms of the features used to evaluate the emotion eliciting triggers (e.g., desirability, likelihood, responsible agent), but also some significant differences in the emotion taxonomies they provide, and the sets of domain-independent features or variables used to characterize the triggering stimuli. These similarities and differences will be discussed below. The remainder of this section discusses the OCC theory, and the componential appraisal theories, in more detail

Figure 3. Appraisal process

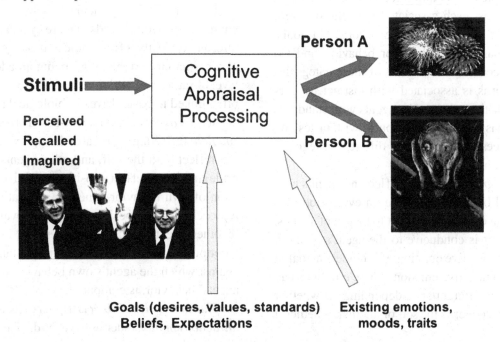

2.2.2.1 OCC Theory of Cognitive Appraisal

The theory of cognitive appraisal developed by Ortony and colleagues (Ortony et al., 1988) (OCC) remains the most frequently implemented theory in computational models of emotion generation (e.g., (Andre et al., 2000; Bates et al., 1992; W. S. N. Reilly, 2006). It provides a rich taxonomy of triggers and the resulting emotions, a distinguishing feature of the OCC theory, which emphasizes fundamental distinctions among three types of triggers, and corresponding types of emotions (refer to Figure 4). An OCC-based appraisal process proceeds through a sequence of steps as it classifies a trigger within this taxonomy, eventually generating a specific emotion (refer to lower part of Figure 4.).

Within the OCC theory, emotions reflect an agent's *valenced reactions* to three different types of triggers: *events, actions by other agents,* and *objects*. As with other theories, emotions are triggered when the agent's goals are either achieved or hindered, or when the potential for achievement or hindrance exists. In the OCC theory however, the term 'goal' has a specific meaning. The OCC model speaks broadly about concerns, but then divides these into three distinct categories of concerns, each associated with the different categories of triggers and emotions: (1) goals, (2) standards and norms for behavior, and (3) preferences and tastes. Each of these categories of concerns is associated with distinct triggers (events with goals; acts by agents with standards and norms; and object attributes with tastes and preferences), and produces different categories of emotions.

Event-based emotions reflect the agent's general well-being, and involve an evaluation of a triggering event with respect to the agent's goals. If an event is conducive to the agent's goals, it triggers a positive emotion. If it hinders a goal, it triggers a negative emotion. These emotions can be further differentiated, depending on whether the event concerns the self or another, whether it

is occurring in the current time frame or anticipated in the future, and whether the event was anticipated or not. Emotions associated with the agent's own *well-being* include joy and distress. Emotions associated with what OCC call *fortunes of others* include happy-for, sorry-for, gloating and resentment. Emotions associated with future desirable or undesirable events are referred to as *prospect-based emotions,* and include hope and fear. Emotions associated with confirmation or disconfirmation of anticipated events include satisfaction, relief, fears-confirmed, and disappointment.

To further support the differentiated representation of emotions, OCC model offers a taxonomy of goals, based on earlier work of Schank and Abelson (Schank & Abelson, 1977). *Active pursuit goals* (A goals) reflect goals that can theoretically be achieved by the agent, and for which the agent has some plans, and a means of implementing those plans; e.g., write a grant proposal, wash dishes, go on vacation. *Interest goals* (I goals) are goals that the agent cannot directly achieve, but which represent states of the self, world or others that the agent wishes were true; e.g., have favorite actor win the Oscars. Finally, the *replenishment goals* (R goals) are goals that are achievable by the agent, but reflect on-going needs that are cyclical in nature, and typically reflect some homeostatic state of a particular variable; e.g., maintain adequate level of satiation, hydration, rest. These goals are often linked to basic drives in biological agents.

Acts by agents trigger agent-based *attribution emotions* reflecting approval or disapproval. These can reflect both the self, and other agents. Thus pride and shame reflect a positive / negative evaluation of own behavior, whereas admiration and reproach reflect a positive / negative evaluation of other agents' behavior. Generation of these emotions is mediated by behavioral standards, against which the agent's own behavior, or other agents' behavior, is compared.

Characteristics of objects trigger object-based *attraction emotions* such as like, and dislike. These

Figure 4. 'Anger' within the OCC taxonomy of emotions

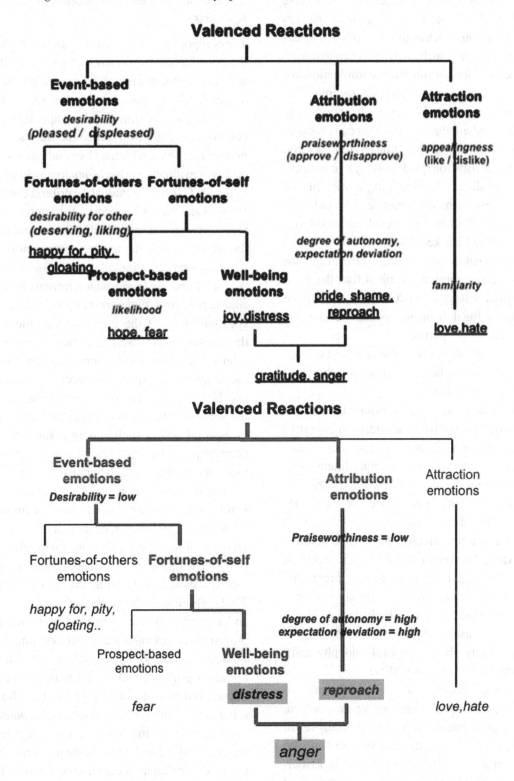

are mediated by general attitudes used to appraise the object. If an object is appealing it triggers positive emotions, such as liking, if not, it triggers negative emotions, such as disliking or disgust.

Some emotions result from combinations of triggers or evaluation criteria. These are called *compound emotions*. For example, combining *well-being* and *attribution emotions* can produce: gratitude (admiration and joy), anger (reproach and distress), gratification (pride and joy), or remorse (shame and distress); combining attraction and attribution emotions can produce: love (admiration and liking), or hate (reproach and disliking) (Elliot, 1992; O'Rorke & Ortony, 1994).

Different values of the evaluation criteria thus define specific emotions. Table 4 lists the emotions defined within the OCC theory, in terms of the values of the domain-independent evaluation criteria. The lower part of

Figure 4 illustrates how the compound emotion 'anger' would be derived, within the OCC taxonomy of emotions.

In addition to defining emotions in terms of their detailed evaluative structure, their *cognitive structure*, the OCC theory also provides a basis for emotion intensity calculation. Intensity is calculated from the values of the *local variables* (the evaluation criteria discussed above), whose specific values define distinct emotions, as well as *global* variables, which apply to all emotions. Global variables consist of the following: consist of the following: a sense of reality, proximity, unexpectedness and arousal. Global variables thus reflect both the physiological state of the agent (e.g., arousal) and properties of the triggers (e.g., proximity (both temporal and physical), unexpectedness, sense of reality).

The OCC model assumes the existence of context-specific thresholds for each emotion. When triggers appear that could potentially result in a particular emotion, that emotion will only be triggered if its intensity value exceeds the associated threshold. The degree to which this threshold is exceeded also influences the emotion intensity.

2.2.2.2 Componential Theories of Cognitive Appraisal

The componential theories of emotion emphasize the constituent components of emotions. There are several categories of "components": at the higher-level, components can refer to the different modalities. Within cognitive appraisal itself, components can also refer to the individual *appraisal variables*, which reflect evaluations along different evaluative criteria, analogously to some of the OCC theory's evaluative criteria discussed above. Like the OCC criteria, the appraisal variables represent domain-independent features of the triggers, or of the trigger-agent relationship. Appraisal variables include *novelty, valence, goal relevance and goal congruence, responsible agent, coping potential, and norms and values*. Specific configurations of the appraisal variable values then correspond to distinct emotions, and are often referred to as the agent's *appraisal state*. Within the componential appraisal theories, a given emotion is thus represented by a vector consisting of the values of the evaluated appraisal variables.

Several sets of such appraisal variables have been proposed by a number of cognitive appraisal theorists, including Scherer, Ellsworth, Frijda, Roseman, Smith, and Kirby. These sets offer very similar appraisal variables. Below I focus on the set proposed by Scherer, because it offers a larger set of variables, thereby allowing for a high-degree of differentiation of the distinct affective states (see (Ellsworth & Scherer, 2003; K.R Scherer, 2001). (Figure 5 shows the appraisal variables and Table 5 shows the relationships between appraisal variables values and different emotions).

Scherer divides the appraisal variables into four broad categories of evaluations, which occur in sequence, and correspond to evaluating the following criteria: *relevance, implications, coping potential, and norms* (refer to Figure 5). The first category (relevance) focuses largely on the properties of the stimulus. The later categories increasingly focus on the relationship between the triggering stimuli

Table 4. Definitions of emotions in terms of the OCC triggers, internal references and evaluation criteria (local variables)

Emotion	OCC Emotion Type	Trigger Type	Appraised w/ Respect	Evaluation Criteria(Local Variables)
Simple Emotions (Evaluated with Respect to Single Category of Criteria)				
Joy	Well-being	Event affecting self	Goals	Desirability of event wrt goal
Distress	Well-being	Event affecting self	Goals	Undesirability of event wrt goal
Happy-for	Fortunes of others	Event affecting another agent	Goals	Pleased about a desirable event for another agent
Sorry-for	Fortunes of others	Event affecting another agent	Goals	Distressed about an undesirable event for another
Gloating	Fortunes of others	Event affecting another agent	Goals	Pleased about an event undesirable for another
Resentment	Fortunes of others	Event affecting another agent	Goals	Displeased about an event desirable for another
Hope	Prospect-based	Prospective Event	Goals	Pleased about a potential good event in the future
Fear	Prospect-based	Prospective Event	Goals	Distressed about a potential bad event in the future
Satisfaction	Confirmation	Prospective Event	Goals	Pleased because an expected good event occurred
Fears confirmed	Confirmation	Prospective Event	Goals	Distressed because an expected bad event occurred
Relief	Confirmation	Prospective Event	Goals	Pleased because an expected bad thing didn't happen
Disappointment	Confirmation	Prospective Event	Goals	Distressed because an expected bad thing did happen
Pride	Attribution	Act by self	Norms	Approving of own behavior
Shame	Attribution	Act by self	Norms	Disapproving of own behavior
Admiration	Attribution	Act by another	Norms	Approving of another's behavior
Reproach	Attribution	Act by another	Norms	Disapproving of another's behavior
Liking	Attraction	Entity qualities	Preferences	Finding the entity appealing
Disliking	Attraction	Entity qualities	Preferences	Finding the entity unappealing
Compound Emotions (Evaluated with Respect to Multiple Categories of Criteria)				
Gratitude	Well-being & Attribution	Event / Act by another	Goals / Norms	Joy + Admiration
Anger	Well-being & Attribution	Event / Act by another	Goals / Norms	Distress + Reproach
Gratification	Well-being & Attribution	Event / Act by self	Goals / Norms	Joy + Pride
Remorse	Well-being & Attribution	Event / Act by self	Goals / Norms	Distress + Shame
Love	Attribution & Attraction	Act by another / Quality of another	Norms / Preferences	Admiration + Liking
Hate	Attribution & Attraction	Act by another / Quality of another	Norms / Preferences	Reproach + Disliking

Based on table 2.1 in Elliot, 1992 and (O'Rourke & Ortony, 1994

Figure 5. Appraisal variables

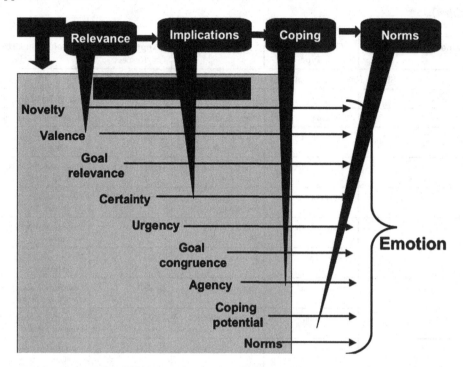

and the agent, and involve increasingly complex cognitive processing (although not necessarily conscious cognitive processing). This may require complex representations of the causal structure of the world, expected events, and the matching of internal schemas with incoming stimuli.

Once the appraisal variables are evaluated, the resulting vector corresponds to a point in the space defined by the dimensions corresponding to the individual appraisal variables, which corresponds to a specific emotion or some affective state. Distinct emotions are thus defined as distinct patterns of the appraisal variable values (see Figure 6). For example, fear is the felt experience of highly-focused attention, negative valence, and high uncertainty about the outcome and the agent's ability to successfully cope with the situation, along with the physiological components of heightened arousal (K.R Scherer, 2001). Note how changing the value of just one appraisal variable (e.g., coping ability) can change one emotion (fear) into another (anger) (refer to Figure 6).

Given the number of appraisal variables offered by the componential appraisal theories, the resulting space of possible emotions is vast. It therefore enables the representation of a broad range of emotions, including states of varying intensity (e.g., mild annoyance, moderate frustration, anger, rage). It also enables the representation of a wide range of mixed states, and "intermediate or transitional states between the named categories of emotions; with vacillation between emotions that corresponds to uncertain or vacillating appraisals" (Ellsworth & Scherer, 2003).

2.2.2.3 Comparing OCC with Componential Appraisal Theories

While the two theories of cognitive appraisal described above are distinct, from a computational perspective they share a number of structural similarities. In much of the existing literature these theories are often discussed separately, which tends to obscure these structural similarities. Below I

Table 5. Scherer's definition of the mapping of individual appraisal values onto specific emotions

Appraisal Variable	Fear	Anger	Joy	Sadness	Shame	Guilt	Pride
Relevance							
Novelty							
Suddenness	HIGH	HIGH	HIGH/ MED	LOW	LOW	open	open
Familiarity	LOW	LOW	open	LOW	open	open	open
Predictability	LOW	LOW	LOW	open	open	open	open
Valence	LOW	open	open	open	open	open	open
Goal Relevance	HIGH	HIGH	HIGH	HIGH	HIGH	HIGH	HIGH
Implications							
Cause: Agent	OTHER/NAT	OTHER	open	open	self	self	self
Cause: Motive	open	INT	INT/ CHAN	INT/CHAN	INT/ NEGLIG.	INT	INT
Outcome Probability	HIGH	V. HIGH	V. HIGH	V. HIGH	V. HIGH	V. HIGH	V. HIGH
Discrepancy from Expectation	DISS	DISS	open	open	open	open	open
Conduciveness to Goal	OBSTR	OBSTR	V. HIGH	OBSTR	open	HIGH	HIGH
Urgency	V. HIGH	HIGH	LOW	LOW	HIGH	MED	LOW
Coping Potential							
Control	OPEN	HIGH	open	V. LOW	open	open	open
Power	V. LOW	HIGH	open	V. LOW	open	open	open
Adjustment	LOW	HIGH	MED	MED	MED	MED	HIGH
Normative Significance							
Internal Standards	open	open	open	open	V,LOW	V.LOW	V.HIGH
External Standards	open	LOW	open	open	open	V.LOW	HIGH

(Based on Table 5-4, pp. 114-115 in (K.R Scherer, 2001) nat: natural forces; diss: dissonant; int: intentional; chan: chance; neglig: negligence; obstr: obstruct)

highlight the similarities, but also point out the differences, and their implications for modeling (refer to Table 6).

Both theories define emotions in terms of a set of domain-independent features, within an abstract domain (refer to Figure 11 and Table 7). These abstract features represent an intermediate stage in the mapping between the stimuli and the emotions proper. For both theories, the specific values of these domain-independent features, or variables, reflect an evaluation of the emotion eliciting stimuli (e.g., valence, desirability), or the stimuli-agent relationship (e.g., coping potential). OCC refers to these evaluative criteria as the local variables, while the componential models refer to them as the appraisal variables (or appraisal dimensions). The local variables (in OCC), or appraisal variables (in componential appraisal theories), then represent the agent's *appraisal state,* and correspond to a specific emotion.

The set of appraisal variables offered by the componential model is slightly larger, but both sets cover the essential components of appraisal: the valence of the triggers; and their relevance

Figure 6. Appraisal variable changes

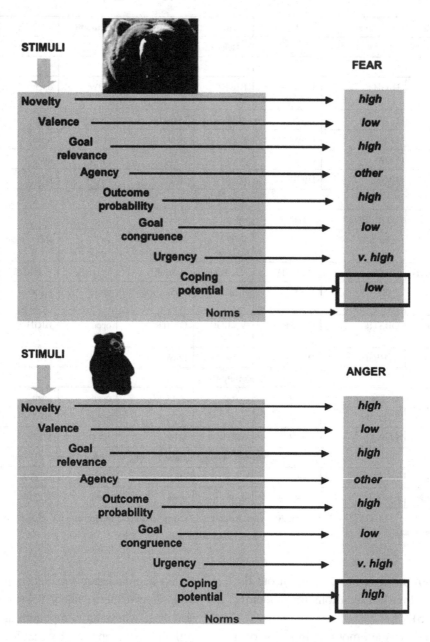

for, and congruence with, the agent's concerns and specific goals. One difference between the two theories is the emphasis on coping in the componential appraisal models, which assign a dedicated appraisal variable to coping ability.

In the OCC theory, different local variables are associated with different categories of emotions.

The componential theories don't make strong assumptions about distinct sets of appraisal variables defining particular emotion classes, although different emotions naturally emphasize different variables; e.g., the social emotions emphasize the appraisal variables related to norms.

Table 6. Comparison of OCC with the componential appraisal theories

	OCC	Componential Appraisal Theories
# of Emotions Possible	22 in original model	Large set possible, within the space defined by the appraisal variables
Emotions accommodated	Basic, some complex & social (see **Table 4**)	Very large set of emotions possible in theory (a subset confirmed via empirical studies_
# of Evaluation Variables / Features	~11	~13 (Scherer's set)
Specific Evaluation Variables	See **Error! Reference source not found.**	See **Error! Reference source not found.**
Elaboration of the Required Representational Structures	Differentiated taxonomy of emotions and some structures offered (e.g., goals, behavior norms)	Few specific suggestions regarding representational structures, though many implied in the descriptions of the appraisal variables
Elaboration of the Mediating Mechanisms	Some representational structures offered	High-level descriptions; delineation of distinct processes calculating individual appraisal variable values
Basis for Intensity Calculations	Qualitative descriptions of components influencing intensity; multiple thresholds for different emotions; distinction between potential and activated emotion	Qualitative descriptions of individual variables affecting intensity; discussion of thresholds and sensitization / habituation
Basis for Combining Multiple Emotions	Some indication of which emotions are likely to be more intense, thus dominant	
Consideration of Multiple Modalities	Primarily cognitive, but include arousal as a global variable influencing intensity	Yes, but appraisal variables and interpretive processes elaborated primarily within cognitive modality
Consideration of Emotion Effects on Cognition, Re-Appraisal, Expression	Acknowledged but not elaborated	Evidence that some appraisal variables map directly onto cognitive effects or expression components

Table 7. Domains required to implement affective models in agents

Domain Name	Description	Examples of Domain Elements
Object (W)	Elements of the external world (physical, social), represented by cues (agent's perceptual input)	Other agents, Events, Physical objects
Cognitive (C)	Internal mental constructs necessary to generate emotions, or manifest their influences on cognition	Cues, Situations, Goals, Beliefs, Expectations, Norms, Preferences, Attitudes, Plans
Abstract (Ab)	Theory-dependent; e.g., dimensions, appraisal variables, OCC evaluative criteria	Pleasure, Arousal, Dominance; Certainty, Goal Relevance, Goal Congruence…
Affective (A)	Affective states (emotions, moods) & personality traits	Joy, sadness, fear, anger, pride, envy, jealousy; extraversion
Physiology (Ph)	Simulated physiological characteristics	Level of energy
Expressive Channels (Ex)	Channels within which agent's emotions can be manifested: facial expressions, gestures, posture, gaze & head movement, movement, speech	Facial expressions (smile, frown), speech (sad, excited) gestures (smooth, clumsy), movement (fast, slow) (represented via channel-specific primitives, e.g., FACS)
Behavioral (B)	Agent's behavioral repertoire in its physical & social environment	Walk, run, stand still, pick up object, shake hands w/ another agent

The OCC model is more highly structured in terms of the categories of triggers (events, acts by other agents, objects), categories of internal evaluative criteria (goals, behavioral norms, and preferences and tastes), and resulting categories of emotions. This degree of structure is helpful for modeling, since it suggests specific representational structures. Indeed, the detailed specification of emotions in terms of these structures, which map directly onto computational representations, was a key reason for adopting the OCC theory for computational models of emotion generation. On the other hand, neither the degree of structure, nor the particular structure offered by the OCC theory, may always be necessary; e.g., a given model may not need to distinguish among events, acts-of-others or objects to derive an emotion.

Componential theories do not go as far as the OCC theory in suggesting different types of triggers and specific internal structures. Instead, they offer a more uniform structure for emotion calculation, in terms of a single set of appraisal variables, applicable to all categories of emotions, albeit, possibly weighing the distinct variables differently for different emotions (e.g., adherence to social norms is more important for shame and guilt than for sadness and joy). The more uniform treatment of emotions offered by the componential theories has the benefit of providing a simpler computational structure implementing the stimulus-to-emotion mapping.

Componential theories emphasize the role of multiple modalities, although the interactions among these are not quantified to an extent that would readily translate to a multi-modal computational model. Nor is it within the current state-of-the-art to construct such a multi-level model.

Both theories address intensity calculation, primarily in qualitative terms, although the OCC theory offers a more elaborate treatment of the intensity calculation task. Neither theory addresses affective dynamics in detail; that is, the emotion decay rates and approaches for combining multiple emotions, although OCC offers a few precedence rules for conflict resolution when multiple emotions are derived from the same set of stimuli.

In contrast to the OCC theory, the componential theory provides some discussion of emotion effects, suggesting that values of different appraisal variables may link directly to specific expressive features or effects on cognition (see discussion below). This feature makes the componential theory attractive, since it enables the use of the same theoretical basis for both emotion generation, and for emotion effects models. The OCC model does not address the consequences of emotions in great depth.

Table 6 provides a comparative summary of the major features of the two models.

Selection of the best appraisal theory for a specific modeling effort depends on a number of factors, including how many and what types of emotions need to be modeled; the extent to which the structures offered by a given theory are useful or helpful for a particular application (e.g., the taxonomy of emotions offered by OCC may or may not be useful for a particular modeling effort); whether both emotion generation and emotion effects need to be modeled, and how important it is to have a single theoretical basis for both generation and effects models. Which of these theories better reflects the nature of emotion generation via cognitive appraisal remains to be determined.

2.2.3 Emotion Effects

For modeling purposes, it is useful to divide emotion effects into two categories: the visible, often dramatic, behavioral and expressive manifestations, and the less visible, but no less dramatic, effects on the internal perceptual and cognitive processes. (Refer to summaries of emotion effects in Table 1.) Theories of emotion effects are not as elaborated as those for emotion generation. While the dominant approach to emotion generation in affective models is via cognitive appraisal, and two established theories are available (OCC and the cognitive appraisal theories within the componential perspective), no such established theories exist to guide models of emotion effects.

One of the primary reasons for the lack of an integrated theory of emotion effects is the multimodal nature of these effects. A comprehensive theory of emotion effects would need to account for manifestations of emotions across multiple modalities, including the non-observable effects on the physiological substrate that mediates any observed manifestations, as well as the internal effects on cognition. Such a theory would then in essence explain the phenomenon of emotions. While emotion research has progressed tremendously over the past few decades, it does not yet provide a "unified theory of emotions". In addition, given the diversity of processes mediating emotions, it is questionable whether such a unified theory can ever be specified.

Given the emphasis on symbolic models and the cognitive modality in existing affective models, I focus below on theories available for modeling emotion effects on cognition.

In most existing affective models, the effects of emotions on cognition are not represented in any depth. Rather, the effects of emotions are manifested via the agent's expressive channels and behavioral choices. At first glance, modeling the 'invisible' effects of emotions on cognitive processes may seem as an 'overkill' for affective models in agent architectures. It may seem that a direct mapping of affective states onto their expressive manifestations, and behavioral choices, is adequate. However, much as introducing emotion as the mediating variable between stimuli and responses allows for more flexible mapping between the environmental stimuli and the agent's behavior, so does an explicit representation of cognitive processes, as the intervening variables between emotions and their expressive and behavioral manifestations. Modeling affective biases

on cognition also provides an efficient means of generating appropriate behaviors in more complex environments, and a means of generating personality-dependent affective variability that can enhance agents' believability.

Several theories have been proposed to explain a particular observed effect of emotions on cognition; e.g., mood congruent recall (Bower, 1981); influence of emotions on judgment and decision-making (e.g. Forgas' AIM (Forgas, 1999); influence of emotions on different cognitive and perceptual processes (Derrybery & Reed, 2003). The theories emphasize different stages of, and processes involved in, information processing (e.g., attention, memory, automatic vs. controlled processes) and researchers often group affective influences into different categories, based on the cognitive structures and processes that are affected. For example, Forgas (Forgas, 2003), focusing on emotion influences on attitudes and social judgments, suggests a distinction between memory-based influences and inference-based influences. An example of the former being network theories of affect, explaining mood congruent recall via spreading activation mechanisms (Bower, 1981). Example of the latter being Schwartz and Clore's theory of affect-as-information (Schwarz & Clore, 1988). Derryberry and Reed (2003), focusing on personality and individual differences research, propose 4 categories of mechanisms whereby emotions influence cognition: automatic activation, response-related interoceptive information, arousal and attention.

In existing computational models, two theories have been explored: *spreading activation theories* across semantic network memory representations, and *parameter-based theories,* which suggest that emotions (and other affective states) act as parameters inducing variabilities in cognitive processes (and, subsequently, behavior). Spreading activation theories aim to explain *affective priming* (shorter response times required for identifying targets that are affect-congruent with the priming stimulus vs. those that have a different affective tone), and *mood-congruent recall* (the tendency to preferentially recall schemas from memory whose affective tone matches that of the current mood) (e.g., (Bower, 1992; Derryberry, 1988). Bower's "Network Theory of Affect" assumes a semantic net representation of long-term memory, where nodes representing declarative information co-exist with nodes representing specific emotions. Activation from a triggered emotion spreads to connected nodes, increasing their activation, thereby facilitating the recall of their information. Alternative versions of this theory place the emotion-induced activation external to the semantic net.

A number of researchers have independently proposed a broader theory of mechanisms mediating emotion-cognition interaction, where parameters encoding various affective factors (states and traits), influence a broad range of cognitive processes and structures (e.g., (Hudlicka, 1998; Matthews & Harley, 1993; Ortony et al., 2005; Ritter & Avramides, 2000). The parameters modify characteristics of fundamental cognitive processes (e.g., attention and working memory speed, capacity, and biasing), thereby inducing effects on higher cognition (problem-solving, decision-making, planning, as well as appraisal processes). Several recent models of emotion effects use some variation of this approach (Belavkin & Ritter, 2004; Broekens, Kosters, & Verbeek, 2007; Hudlicka, 2003; Hudlicka, 2007; Ritter, Reifers, Klein, & Schoelles, 2007; Sehaba, Sabouret, & Corruble, 2007). I briefly illustrate the parameter-based approach below, in the context of a cognitive-affective architecture whose focus is the modeling of a broad range of individual differences, including affective states and traits, on cognitive processing: the MAMID architecture (Hudlicka, 1998; Hudlicka, 2002; Hudlicka, 2007; Hudlicka, 2008a).

MAMID models emotion effects using a generic methodology for modeling multiple, interacting individual differences, both *stable traits and dynamic states*. Its focus is on modeling the effects of emotions (joy, fear, anger, and sadness) on the cognitive processes mediating decision-making (attention, situation assessment, expectation generation, goal management and action selection). A high-level schematic of the MAMID cognitive-affective architecture is shown in the right part of Figure 7.

A set of parameters is defined that controls processing within the MAMID architecture modules, for example, the speed and capacities of the different modules, as well as the ranking of the individual constructs processed by these modules (e.g., cues, situations, goals), as they map the inputs (perceptual cues) onto the outputs (selected actions).

Figure 7 illustrates this modeling approach. A particular configuration of emotion intensities and trait values is mapped onto specific values of the architecture parameter values, which then modify the modules' processing (e.g., lower/increase the modules' capacity and speed, introduce a bias for particular types of constructs, such as high-threat or self-related constructs (refer to Figure 7 and 8). Functions implementing these mappings are constructed on the basis of the available empirical data. For example, the anxiety-linked bias to preferentially attend to threatening cues, and interpret situations as threatening, is modeled in MAMID by ranking high-threat cues and situations more highly, thereby making their processing by the Attention and Situation Assessment modules more likely (refer to Figure 8). Currently, the parameter-calculating functions consist of weighted linear combinations of the factors that influence each parameter. For example, working memory capacity reflects a normalized weighted sum of emotion intensities, trait values, baseline capacity and skill level.

Figure 7. MAMID modeling approach

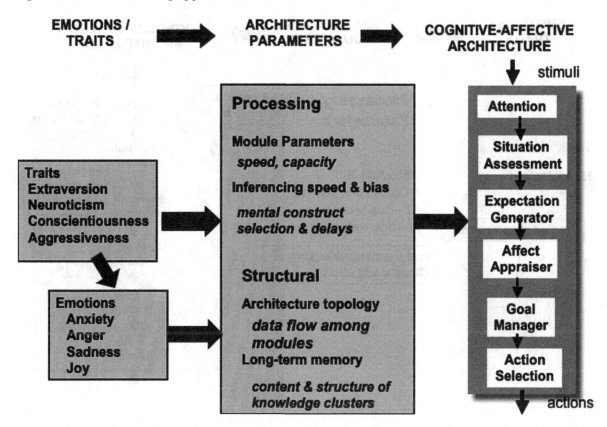

While it is likely premature, it is nevertheless intriguing to consider the possibility that these parameter-based models may represent one approach to implementing neuroscience theories of emotion based on neuromodulation. These theories suggest that emotion effects are implemented in the brain in terms of systemic, global effects on multiple brain structures, via distinct patterns of neuromodulation, corresponding to different emotions (Fellous, 2004).

2.2.4 From Theories to Models

Before discussing the design of affective models in more detail it is helpful to summarize the type of information we would ideally expect existing theories from psychology to provide, to support model development. This pragmatic perspective will then allow us to evaluate candidate theories,

to determine which is most appropriate for a given modeling effort.

Ideally, the theories would provide sufficient details to operationalize the computational tasks necessary, and provide specifications of the underlying mechanisms, in terms of representational structures and processes (see also (Broekens, DeGroot, & Kosters, 2008)). Thus, cognitive appraisal theories of emotion generation ought to be able to provide answers to questions such as:

- What is the stimulus-to-emotion mapping for the domain of interest? Should this mapping be implemented *directly* (domain stimuli-to-emotions), or *indirectly*, via some intermediate, domain-independent features (e.g. novelty, valence, desirability, likelihood, responsible agent)?

Figure 8. MAMID modeling approach constructs

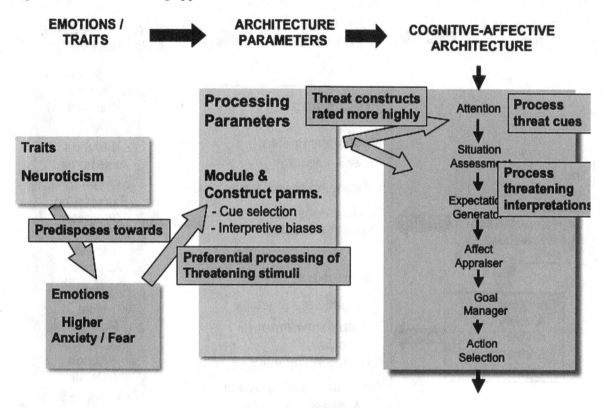

- How are the influences of external stimuli integrated with internal stimuli (recalled or anticipated events and situations) in triggering emotions?

- What are the distinct stages of the appraisal process and which functions are implemented in each stage? Do these stages vary as a function of the specific emotion, individual, or context?

- What are the dependencies and interactions among the distinct processes implementing appraisal?

- What factors influence emotion intensity, and how?

- What is the nature of the 'affective dynamics', that is, the onset and decay rates of emotions? How do these vary by individuals, emotions and contexts?

- Can multiple emotions be generated by the appraisal process? If not, how should po-

tentially conflicting triggers be integrated into a single emotion? If so, how should these multiple emotions be integrated into a coherent affective state?

- What cognitive structures are necessary to support appraisal (e.g. goals, expectations, plans), and what is the nature and complexity of these structures?

- What levels of complexity are necessary for a particular modeling application (e.g., sensorimotor, schematic, or conceptual)?

- What should be the structure of the emotion construct itself, that is, the object generated by the appraisal process? What information should be represented in this structure (e.g., type, intensity, its triggers, responsible agent, direction, goals involved)?

Theories of emotion effects on cognition ought to be able to provide answers to questions such as:

- Which cognitive processes and structures are influenced by particular emotions, moods, affective states and traits? What is the nature of this influence? What are the effects on dynamic mental constructs such as situations, goals, expectations, and plans?
- How are contents and organization of long-term memory structures affected?
- How is cognitive appraisal affected by emotions?
- What is the relationship between the emotion or mood intensity and the type and magnitude of the influence? Can distinct intensities of emotions or moods have qualitatively different effects on cognitive processes?
- Are distinct emotions the mediating variables of the effects (e.g., fear influences attentional bias towards threat), or are individual appraisal dimensions the mediating variables (e.g., (Lerner & Tiedens, 2006).
- How and when are the influences of multiple emotions, moods and traits combined?
- Are there distinct types of processes that mediate these influences? What are the interactions and dependencies among these processes?
- Last, but not least: Can we obtain sufficient data about these internal processes and structures to enable construction of computational models?

Unfortunately, the existing theories do not provide answers to all of these questions, with the theories attempting to explain the mechanisms of emotion effects on cognition less-well elaborated than those for cognitive appraisal. In addition, a given theory may not provide answers at the level of detail necessary for the construction of a computational model. In fact, it is frequently the act of model construction itself that motivates more refinements of the associated psychological theories. While for some of the questions there is significant consensus (e.g., which types of stimuli trigger which emotions), others require considerable 'educated guesswork'; e.g., how opposing emotions should be combined). The least-well defined aspect of emotion generation and emotion effects regards the affective dynamics: the calculation of emotion intensity and emotion effects magnitudes, their changes over time, as well as the integration of multiple emotions and moods, and multiple effects. Typically, only qualitative descriptions of these relationships are available in the psychology literature, although recent research in the expression and recognition of emotions via facial expressions is yielding promising quantitative data regarding facial expression dynamics (e.g., (Cohn, Ambadar, & Ekman, 2007)).

The questions above serve three roles. *First*, they provide a basis for evaluating candidate theories. *Second,* they provide a basis for defining the computational tasks necessary to implement affective models. *Finally*, they help identify specific aspects of affective processing where more concrete theories need to be developed. Below I discuss the computational tasks necessary to implement affective models that model the proposed core processes: emotion generation and emotion effects.

3.0 COMPUTATIONAL ANALYTICAL FRAMEWORK FOR EMOTION MODELS

Above, I discussed the theoretical foundations for developing models of emotion generation and emotion effects. I emphasized the theories of cognitive appraisal in emotion generation, as the most useful theoretical basis for symbolic models of emotion. I also discussed several theories of emotion effects on cognition and their relevance for modeling emotion effects.

Currently, no established, systematic guidelines exist for developing computational models of emotion. I hope to contribute to the development of such guidelines by delineating the fundamental categories of processes required to model emotions (those modeling emotion generation, and those modeling emotion effects), and by defining the abstract computational tasks necessary to implement these processes.

The remainder of this section discusses these core processes and abstract, generic computational tasks in more detail, along with some of their representational and reasoning requirements.

3.1 Core Processes Required to Model Emotions

In spite of the progress in emotion research over the past 20 years, emotions remain elusive phenomena. While some underlying circuitry has been identified for some emotions (e.g., amygdala-mediated processing of threatening stimuli, the role of orbitofrontal cortex in emotion regulation), much remains unknown about the mechanisms of emotions. Given the multiple-modalities of emotion, the complexity of the cross-modal interactions, and the fact that affective processes exist at multiple levels of aggregation, it may seem futile, at best, to speak of 'fundamental processes of emotions'.

Nevertheless, for purposes of developing symbolic models of emotions, and for models of emotions in symbolic agent architectures, it is useful to cast the emotion modeling problem in terms of two broad categories of processes: those responsible for the *generation of emotions*, and those which then mediate the *effects of the activated emotions* on cognition, expressive behavior (e.g., facial expressions, speech) and action selection (refer to Figure 9).

This temporally-based categorization (before and after the 'felt' emotion) provides a useful perspective for computational affective modeling, and helps manage the complexity of the modeling effort, by supporting a systematic deconstruction

of these high-level processes into their underlying computational tasks, as discussed below. (There are of course many complex interactions among these categories of processes, which would also need to be represented in order to develop 'valid' models of emotions.)

It is important to note that I am not suggesting that the two core processes, or the associated computational tasks, correspond to distinct, discrete neural processing mechanisms. Rather, they represent useful abstractions, and a means of managing the complexity associated with symbolic affective modeling. The proposed *core process / computational task* view provides a computational analytical framework that helps organize existing theories and data, as well as a natural hierarchical structure that links distinct affective processes, and, by extension, distinct emotions roles, to the underlying computational tasks necessary to implement them.

3.2 Generic Computational Tasks Necessary to Model the Core Affective Processes

Identifying the fundamental processes required to model emotions is only the first step towards a more systematic approach to emotion modeling. For this perspective to be useful, we must deconstruct these high level processes into the constituent computational tasks required to implement them; that is, we must identify the generic computational tasks necessary to implement emotion generation and emotion effects.

The objective of this approach to analysis and design of emotion models is to move beyond the existing state of affairs, where individual models are used as the the organizing dimension, and towards a more general approach, organized in terms of the individual computational tasks, and the associated representational and reasoning requirements. This approach provides a basis for both managing the complexity of affective modeling, and systematizing affective modeling, by provid-

Figure 9. Emotion modeling problem process categories

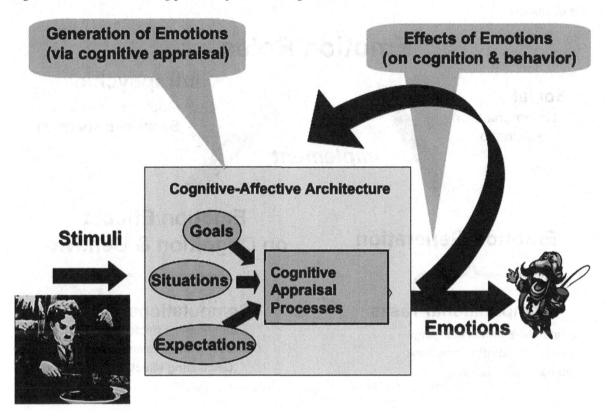

ing foundations for more concrete guidelines for both model design and for the analysis of existing models and theories.

The generic computational tasks required to implement emotion generation and emotion effects are discussed below, and further elaborated in Section 4. Figure 10 illustrates the relationship between the computational tasks (lower part of figure), the fundamental processes (middle part of figure), and the different roles of emotions.

3.3 Distinct Domains Required for Modeling Emotions

The high-level computational tasks outlined above provide a basis for defining model design guidelines, and for managing the complexity of affective modeling, but they provide only the first step in the top-down deconstruction of modeling

requirements. Another example of a computational and design-oriented perspective on emotion modeling, and focusing on emotion generation, is recent work by Broekens and colleagues, who developed a generic set-theoretic formalism, and an abstract framework, for representing, and comparing, appraisal theories.

Building on the work of Reisenzein (Reisenzein, 2001), Broekens and colleagues (Broekens et al., 2008) offer a high-level, set-theoretic formalism that depicts the abstract structure of the appraisal process, and represents both the processes involved, and the data manipulated. I have augmented their original framework to also represent modeling of emotion effects. The resulting abstract structure is shown in Figure 11. The framework illustrates the distinct processes involved in emotion generation and emotion effects modeling, and the data manipulated by these

Figure 10. Relationship between the computational tasks, the fundamental processes, and the different roles of emotions

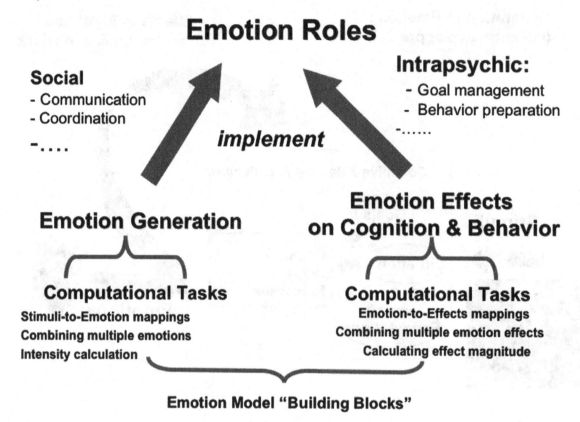

Figure 11. Abstract structure

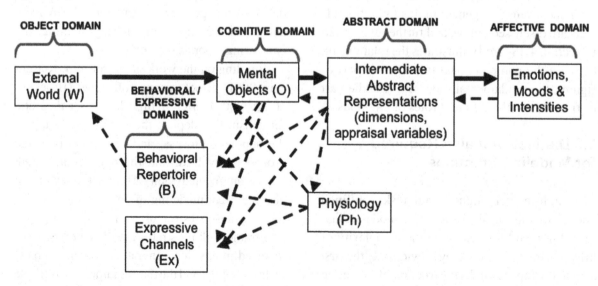

processes (e.g., perception (evaluative processes produce a series of mental objects), appraisal (processes that extract the appraisal variable values from the mental objects), and mediation (processes that map the appraisal values onto the resulting emotion(s)). The distinct processes operate on distinct categories of data: their associated *domains*. Table 7 summarizes these domains and provides examples of their elements: the associated semantic primitives.

This framework thus complements the computational task-based perspective with a set of domains required to implement both emotion generation and emotion effects, and helps define the constituent elements of these domains. These definitions then form a basis for defining the mappings among these domains, necessary to implement emotion generation and emotion effects.

The set of domains in the table represents a superset of possible domains required for emotion modeling. For a given model, and given theoretical foundations, only a subset of these may be necessary.

3.4 Generic Computational Tasks

I now discuss the distinct computational tasks necessary to model emotion generation and emotion effects. The former emphasizes the cognitive modality, which is emphasized in the majority of existing symbolic computational models of emotion, and is typically implemented in agent architectures.

3.4.1 Computational Tasks Required for Modeling Emotion Generation

Figure 12 illustrates a number of distinct computational tasks necessary to implement *emotion generation via cognitive appraisal*, specifically:

- Define and implement the emotion elicitor–to–emotion mapping (depending on

Figure 12. Computational tasks necessary to implement emotion generation via cognitive appraisal

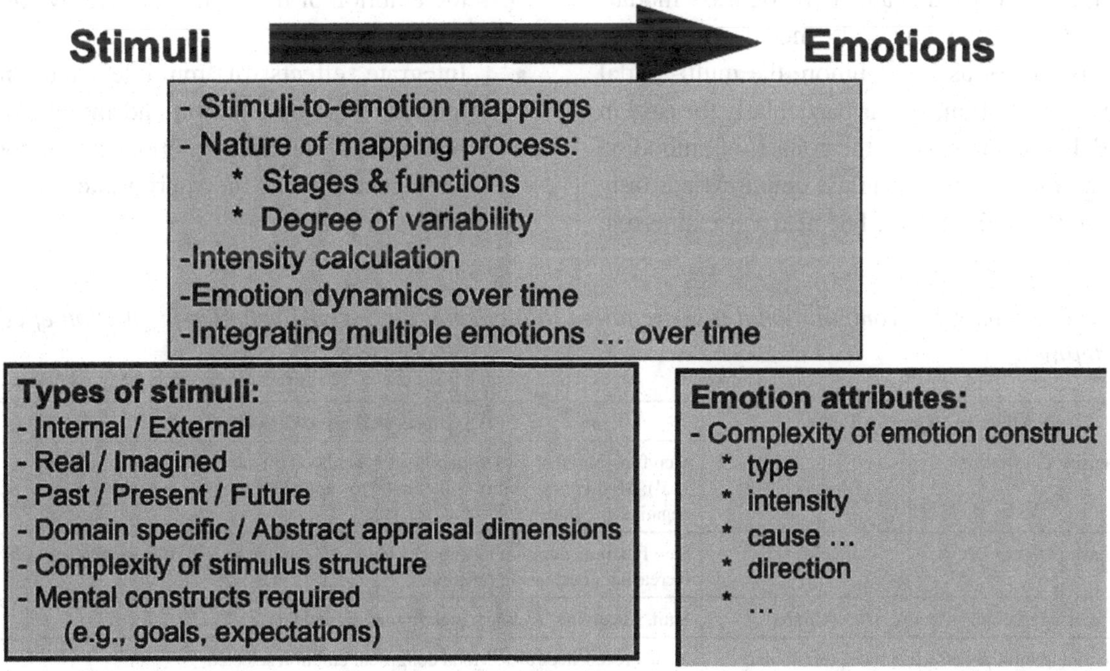

the theoretical perspective adopted, this may involve additional subtasks that map the emotion elicitor onto the intermediate representation (PAD dimensions or appraisal variable vectors), and the subsequent mapping of these onto the final emotion(s)).

- Calculate the intensity of the resulting emotion.
- Calculate the decay of the emotion over time.
- Integrate multiple emotions, if multiple emotions were generated.
- Integrate the newly-generated emotion with existing emotion(s) or moods.

Table 8 summarizes the computational tasks required to implement affective dynamics, that is calculation of emotion intensity, its onset and decay, and integration of multiple emotions.

3.4.2 Computational Tasks Required for Modeling Emotion Effects

While models of emotion generation typically focus on only one modality (the cognitive modality and cognitive appraisal), models of emotion effects cannot as easily ignore the multi-modal nature of emotion. This is particularly the case in models implemented in the context of embodied agents that need to manifest emotions not only via behavioral choices, but also via expressive manifestations within the channels available in their particular embodiment (e.g., facial expressions, gestures, posture etc.)

The multi-modal nature of emotion effects increases both the number and the type of computational tasks necessary to model emotion effects. Figure 13 illustrates the abstract computational tasks required to model the *effects of emotions* across multiple modalities, specifically:

- Define and implement the emotion/mood–to–effects mappings, for the modalities included in the model (e.g., cognitive, expressive, behavioral, neurophysiological). Depending on the theoretical perspective adopted, this may involve additional subtasks that implement any intermediate steps, and are defined in terms of more abstract semantic primitives provided by the theory (e.g., dimensions, appraisal variables).
- Determine the magnitude of the resulting effect(s) as a function of the emotion or mood intensities.
- Determine the changes in these effects as the emotion or mood intensity decays over time.
- Integrate effects of multiple emotions, moods, or some emotion and mood combinations, if multiple emotions and moods were generated, at the appropriate stage of processing.

Table 8. Summary of computational tasks required to implement affective dynamics in emotion effects modeling

Affective Dynamics Tasks	Examples of Design Alternatives
Intensity Calculation	Step function (0 or 1); Desirability * Likelihood (of situation, event or relevant goal); Modify desirability * likelihood to capture asymmetry in positive vs. negative emotions
Intensity Onset / Decay	Step function, duration for time t; Linear, exponential or logarithmic monotonically increasing / decreasing function
Integrating multiple affective states (similar)	Sum, Maximum, Average, logarithmic, sigmoidal
Integrating multiple affective states (dissimilar)	Max, Precedence rules, Mood congruent emotion selected

Figure 13. Abstract computational tasks required to model the effects of emotions across multiple modalities

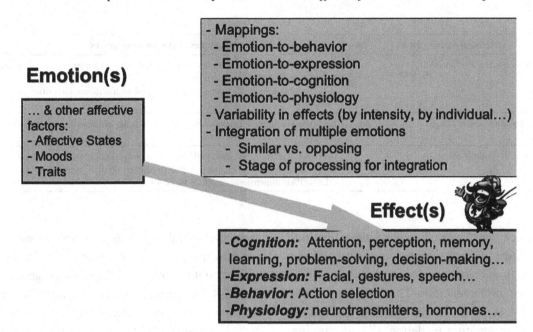

- Integrate the effects of the newly-generated emotion with any residual, on-going effects, to ensure believable transitions among states over time.
- Account for variability in the above by both the intensity of the affective state, and by the specific personality of the modeled agent.
- Coordinate the visible manifestations of emotion effects across multiple channels and modalities within a single time frame, to ensure believable manifestations.

Table 9 summarizes the computational tasks required to implement affective dynamics, that is calculation of emotion intensity, its onset and decay, and integration of multiple emotions.

The specific tasks necessary for a particular model depend on the selected theoretical perspective (e.g., discrete/categorical models don't require a two-stage mapping sequence), and on the specific theory of emotion generation or emotion effects that is implemented in the model. Note also that not all models necessarily require all tasks; e.g., in simpler models, where only one emotion can be generated at a given time, there is no need to integrate multiple emotions. These tasks, and associated design choices, are discussed in more detail in Section 4.

3.5 Representational and Reasoning Requirements

The diagrams in Figure 11, Figure 12 and Figure 13 provide a temporal perspective on emotion modeling. In discussing the representational and reasoning requirements, it is helpful to distinguish between two levels of description and analysis. At the abstract level, we consider the types of representational entities and reasoning requirements necessary to implement the generic computational tasks outlined above. At the implementation level below, we consider the specific representational and reasoning formalisms that can be used to implement them.

Table 9. Summary of computational tasks required to implement affective dynamics in emotion effects modeling

Affective Dynamics Tasks	Examples of Design Alternatives
Effect Magnitude Calculation	In expressive domain: larger effect in individual expressive elements (size of smile); more expressive elements used; duration In behavioral domain: distinct actions associated with different intensities of emotion
Effect Magnitude Onset / Decay	In expressive domain: Empirically based onset, peak, offset values for individual elements (e.g., facial muscles)
Integration of multiple effects	Max (select effects associated with emotion with highest intensity); combine intensities of individual elements within an abstract domain, map results onto effects (PAD dimensions, appraisal variables)

As discussed earlier, making these distinctions allows a more systematic analysis of the computational requirements, as distinct from any particular implementation. This in turn facilitates communication across the multiple disciplines involved in emotion modeling. (See discussion of the importance of this multi-level analysis in Section 1.1.)

At the abstract level are the *abstract entity types* that need be represented to implement the computational tasks outlined above; that is, to enable the interpretations necessary to implement cognitive appraisal, and to mediate the multimodal emotion effects. Different types of abstract entities exist in the different domains involved in emotion modeling, outlined in Section 3.3. For example, in the *object domain,* examples of entities are events, situations, other agents, and physical objects, as well as more complex causal structures. In the *cognitive domain*, examples of these entities are goals, expectations, standards and norms, frequently organized into hierarchies. The specific entity types required depend on the affective states represented in the particular model. For example, complex emotions require reasoning about the self (e.g., comparing own characteristics or behavior with others, and with established norms), thus requiring an explicit representation of the self. In the *abstract domain*, the entities are theory-specific abstractions, such as the OCC evaluation criteria and the componential theories'

appraisal variables. In the *affective domain,* the entities are the structures that represent the affective states derived by the emotion generation process: emotions, moods or undifferentiated positive and negative affect. In the domains within which emotion effects are manifested, the entities are different for the distinct modalities and within the different expressive channels. Table 10 and Table 11 provide examples of different entity types required for emotion generation and emotion effects modeling, respectively.

The different entity types are associated with different attributes that contain the information necessary to implement emotion generation and emotion effects modeling. For example, a goal entity may need attributes to represent the following information: type (e.g., active pursuit vs. interest vs. replenishment (if following the OCC goal taxonomy), importance, difficulty, likelihood_of_success, objects/agents required to achieve the goal, subgoals/parent_goals, status (e.g., in_progress, completed, failed), etc. A more in-depth discussion of these attributes is beyond the scope of this chapter but can be found in (Hudlicka, forthcoming).

Once the high-level specifications outlined above are defined, the actual representational formalism must be selected. The focus here is on symbolic formalisms, since the high-level models of emotion discussed here typically use symbolic representations (vs., for example, connectionist

Table 10. Examples of abstract entity types required for emotion generation

Object Domain	Mental Domain	Abstract Domain	Affective Domain
Agents, Events, Physical objects, Causal diagrams	Cues, Situations, Goals, Expectations, Norms & Standards, Preferences, Plans	Interpretive features (OCC evaluation criteria, appraisal variables); Mood dimensions (pleasure, arousal, dominance)	Emotions, Moods, Affect

Table 11. Examples of abstract entity types required for modeling emotion effects

Behavioral Domain		Physiological Domain	
Different action types		Arousal, Hormone	
Expressive Domain		**Cognitive/Mental Domain**	
Facial expression (eye brows, lip corners,…); Speech (pitch, pitch range, volume, rate); Gesture (limb, joints)…; posture (lean forward/back, arms open/closed)		Cues, Goals, Plans, Beliefs, Situations, Expectations…	

models). A number of established representational formalisms are available, including: Bayesian belief nets, production rules, frames, predicate calculus, fuzzy logic formalisms, as well as procedural knowledge, encoded in terms of demons, knowledge-sources, or arbitrary functions.

The choice of a specific formalism is guided by a number of considerations, including the need for an explicit representation of uncertainty, the ability to represent temporal information, compatibility with the domain and the mental constructs required, ability to effectively represent the semantic primitives offered by the selected theory (e.g., appraisal variables or OCC evaluative criteria), ability to implement learning and generalization. There are also pragmatic considerations, which include compatibility with an existing system, availability of any associated software, and familiarity personal preferences.

The complexity of reasoning required to implement the affective processes depends on the complexity of the domain, the types of affective states represented in the model, and the modalities and channels within which emotions need to be expressed. Significant domain-specific inferencing may be required to interpret the events

and situations in the object domain, in terms of the evaluation criteria provided by the selected theory (e.g., OCC evaluative criteria, appraisal dimensions), and taking into consideration the agent's goals and beliefs.

For any but the most simple domains this will require representation and reasoning under uncertainty. Different emotions then require different degrees of reasoning complexity. For example, the OCC prospect-based emotions, that is, emotions involving expectations of future events or situations, require complex causal representations of the object domain, as well as temporal reasoning, such as what-if and abductive reasoning. (Note, however, that in biological agents, for the simple forms of the basic emotions the interpretive processes are innate and 'hardwired' (e.g., fear of snakes; large, looming objects, etc.).

4.0 GUIDELINES FOR DESIGNING A COMPUTATIONAL AFFECTIVE MODEL

I now outline an approach to emotion model design that is based on the computational analytical framework outlined earlier: the two core affective processes (emotion generation and emotion effects) and the generic computational tasks required to implement them. I present the design process in the context of designing an agent architecture, thereby focusing on the development of more applied affective models, aimed a enhancing the agent's autonomy and affective realism. (In contrast to research models designed to elucidate the underlying mechanisms of affective processes.)

I present only a high-level outline of this process. A more detailed description can be found in Hudlicka (2011), and in a forthcoming book on affective computing (Hudlicka, forthcoming).

To identify the degree to which emotions need to be modeled in a given agent, and to select the most appropriate approach to affective modeling, the model designer first needs to conduct a requirements analysis: s/he needs to have a clear understanding of how explicit modeling of emotion in the agent architecture will enhance its functionality or effectiveness. Since this requirements analysis focuses on the emotions and their roles, I refer to it as *affective requirements analysis* and *affective design process*. To maintain, and reinforce, the computational perspective emphasized in this chapter, I emphasize the use of the distinct domains and abstract computational tasks mediating emotion generation and emotion effects, which were introduced earlier. Table 12 provides a summary of the steps required for the affective requirements analysis and model design process.

4.1 Define Objectives and Roles of Emotions: Why Should the Agent Architecture Include Emotions?

Emotions may be needed to enhance the *agent's affective and social realism*, thereby its believability, and ultimately its effectiveness when interacting with a human user. Emotions may also be included to enhance the *agent's autonomy* and *effectiveness*, particularly in more complex and uncertain environments, by biasing the agent's behavior towards a selection of particular goals and actions. Such biasing helps prune the large problem search spaces that can be generated in complex, uncertain environments. Emotions can make the agents more autonomous, and produce more adaptive behavior; e.g., an agent with appropriate levels of fear will successfully evade dangers and survive longer in hostile environments. Note, however, that just because these capabilities can be mediated by emotions does not mean that affective mechanisms represent the only way to implement such capabilities.

Defining the objectives allows a definition of the specific roles that emotions should perform in the agent. Table 13 provides a summary of possible roles of emotions in agents, for the distinct objectives outlined above.

4.2 Define Specific Emotions Needed to Implement Selected Roles

There are many possible emotions, varying in complexity of triggers and manifestations. (Clore and colleagues have identified over 200 emotions terms by analyzing a set of 600 English terms with an affective component (G.L. Clore & Ortony, 1988)). In addition, there are moods, mixed states with both cognitive and affective components (e.g., attitudes), and affective personality traits. A given application cannot represent all of these states. The designer must therefore choose which emotions (and other affective states) will be represented. The majority of existing models represent a subset of the basic emotions, that is: joy, sadness, anger, fear, disgust and often surprise. Researchers are increasingly attempting to represent more complex emotions. For example, Becker-Asano has used the dimensional theoretical perspective to represent the emotions of hope, relief and fears-confirmed in terms of the PAD dimensions (Becker-Asano, 2008). The number and types of emotions required has implications for the selection of a theoretical perspective, as we shall see below.

Table 12. Summary of the steps comprising affective requirements analysis

STEP	Description	Example of Results
#1: Define functions of emotions in game & within each agent	Define specific interpersonal & intrapsychic roles of emotions.	Enhance autonomy via emotion-based behavioral routines (avoid danger by enabling fear); Support cooperative behavior via attachment; Enhance realism.
#2: Define specific emotions & moods required	Define elements of the affective domain (A) needed to implement the roles identified in step 1	Emotions: joy, sadness, fear, anger, boredom, surprise, disgust Moods: happy, sad, fearful, jealous
#3: Define emotion triggers (in physical & social environments; self). Define agent's behavioral repertoire.	Define elements of the object domain (W) & Behavior domain (B),	W: approaching user, smiling agent, physical object in the environment B: smile at user, pick up object.
#4: Define agent's embodiment, including any simulated physiology	Define expressive channels (face, gestures, speech)- Expressive Domain (Ex). Define 'physiological' variables (arousal, energy)-Physiological domain (Ph)	Face: express joy, sadness, fear, anger, boredom, surprise Speech: content & prosody for emotions above. Arousal: define arousal levels corresponding to different emotions.
#5: Define level of model abstraction.	Define degree to which internal mental & cognitive states will be modeled – Cognitive domain (C)	Interpretations of current situation, Expectations, Goals, Plans
#6: Select theoretical perspective & specific theory for emotion generation & emotion effects modeling.	Theory determines nature of Abstract domain (Ab), if any.	If componential: Ab consists of appraisal variables; If OCC: Ab consists of the OCC evaluation criteria (local variables); If dimensional: Ab consists PAD
#7: Define emotion trigger & emotion effects associations	Define mappings among domains defined in Stp. 3-6 (emotion generation & emotion effects). If an abstract domain is used, define mappings via abstract primitives.	Cues-to-Emotion: Friendly user→Joy; Evil monster (in game agents) → Fear; Irritating user → Anger. Emotion-to-Cognition: Fear → reduced attentional focus, bias toward threatening cues and interpretations Emotion-to-Behavior: Fear--> Run (in NPC agents); Anger → Use rude speech to user;
#8: Define affective dynamics	Define intensity functions for emotion/mood generation; Emotion integration; Emotion effects magnitude & integration of multiple effects.	Intensity = desirability * likelihood; Intensity decays exponentially Winner-take-all conflict resolution for conflicting emotions
#9: Specify Abstract Computational Tasks Required	Define abstract computational tasks necessary to implement generation of emotions and their effects, including affective dynamics, if any.	Triggers-to-Emotion Mapping; Trigger to Appraisal Variables Mapping & App. Variable to Emotion Mapping; Emotion to Cognitive Effects Mappings; Intensity calculating functions
#10: Select representational & reasoning formalisms	Select most appropriate representational & inferencing formalisms	Rules, Bayesian belief nets, Fuzzy logic

4.3 Define Emotion-Eliciting Triggers and Agent's Behavioral Repertoire

This step involves an analysis of the agent's environment, either virtual or physical, and identification of perceptual and internal inputs that can trigger emotions. The result is the set of possible input cues, which are elements of the object do-main (W). The agent's possible behaviors are also defined at this stage. These represent its behavioral repertoire, and define the elements of the behavioral domain (B). The elements comprising the W and B domains are necessarily domain-specific, that is, specific for the agent's particular physical and social environment.

Table 13. Affective requirements analysis step #1: Possible roles of emotions in agents

Increased Character Autonomy	
Intrapsychic Emotion Roles	
Homeostatic Functions	Ensures that agent maintains internal resources to survive & thrive in its environment (virtual or physical)
Motivational Functions	Ensures agent avoids specific dangers, seeks out specific rewards, exhibits appropriate assertiveness/ aggressiveness to accomplish goals & obtain resources, enables learning and seeking of information via boredom & curiosity
Control of behavior	(Re) prioritize goals as necessary in response to events, implement processing biases to help coordinate cognition & behavior, rapid (re)allocation of resources to address a new situation / event, rapid detection of salient stimuli
Interpersonal Emotion Roles	
Coordination and communication of behavioral intent	Facilitate more realistic behavior toward other agents and the users, by communicating internal state & intentions, communicate social status information
Attachment behavior	Allows agents to form relationships with one another, creating more effective collaborations, and more interesting interaction with the user, manage & repair relationships by communicating social norms
Increased Character Affective Realism (Believability)	
Intrapsychic Emotion Roles	
Homeostatic Functions	Agent's resource level enables them to exhibit more realistic behavior (e.g., grumpy, irritable when tired; happy when rested).
Motivational Functions	Different reactions to the same situation/event, as a function of changing moods & goals
Interpersonal Emotion Roles	
Coordination and communication of behavioral intent	Communicate territorial rights, social goals (form relationships, social status)
Attachment / friendships	Communicate different types of emotions with different agents and users, depending on the nature of the relationship

4.4 Define Agent's Embodiment

The nature of the agent's embodiment depends on a number of factors, including its overall objectives (e.g., a game character, a virtual coach, a robot used for rehabilitation, a robotic companion for children, etc.), on the function of the emotions in the agent (e.g., autonomy vs. affective realism), the overall visual realism required for the specific context (e.g., an application for a mobile device with a small screen vs. a life-size agent image in a virtual reality setting vs. a robot); and the resources available for developing the agent's embodiments (e.g., detailed facial expressions, speech); and, of course, the emotions that the agent needs to express.

The nature of the agent's embodiment then determines which expressive channels are available for manifesting its emotions. Recall that the expressive channels within which emotions can be manifested include facial expressions, gaze, head movement, gestures, body posture, nature of character's movement in general, and speech (both verbal content and non-verbal sounds, as well as prosodic speech qualities such as pitch, rate, and volume). The designer must determine which of these expressive channels are necessary for the agent's objectives, and which are feasible to implement, given any software and hardware constraints. The designer also needs to consider which expressive channels are best for manifesting the emotions that are to be included in the model, given any implementation and platform constraints, such as screen size. Typically, facial expressions are best for expressing emotions. However, in situations where the screen size is small, and its resolution low, other channels may be more appropriate (e.g., speech, gestures).

The designer must also take into consideration the state-of-the-art in generating affective expressions in a given channel; e.g., established representational and animation techniques are available for display affective expressions on the face, most using the elements of the Facial Action Coding System (P. Ekman & Friesen, 1978) as the semantic primitives, whereas affective synthetic speech is not yet as advanced.

Defining the agent's embodiment in effect defines the individual channels within the expressive domain (Ex), and established their semantic primitives.

Another component of the agent's embodiment is its simulated physiology. Not all agents require an explicit model of the physiological modality. However, given the embodied nature of most agents, some representation of some simulated physiological characteristics will make the characters appear more realistic, by enabling the simulated physiological states to influence agent behavior. This is the case both for modeling the contribution of these characteristics to emotion generation (e.g., a fatigued or hungry agent may be more likely to become irritated or angry), and for modeling the effects of emotions (e.g., a game NPC experiencing prolonged fear may become more rapidly fatigued, and increased fatigue may make the NPC more irritable). To the extent that physiological characteristics are modeled in affective agents, they are highly abstracted and simple, typically consisting of some measure of energy (e.g., energy, arousal), and available physical resources (e.g., degree of hunger, fatigue and 'health'). For example, representing arousal in agent Max (Becker, Nakasone, Prendinger, Ishizuka, & Wachsmuth, 2005), allows him to display varying rates of breathing and blinking, thereby enhancing its believability. These features then represent the elements of the *physiological domain* (Ph) of the affective model.

The end result of this step in the design process is therefore a definition of the expressive (Ex) and physiological (Ph) domains.

4.5 Define the Model's Level of Abstraction/Aggregation

The model designer must next decide on the degree to which internal mental states and constructs should be explicitly represented in the model. This in effect defines the model's level of abstraction (or aggregation), which ranges between two extremes: *black-box models*, which do not require detailed representations of internal mental states and *process-level models*, which aim to simulate or emulate the underlying mechanisms, and represent constructs in the *cognitive domain* (C), such as beliefs, goals, expectations, plans etc. These constructs often suggest which specific modules need to be explicitly represented in the agent architecture (e.g.. Goal Manager, Planner), and defining the cognitive domain therefore begins to define the structure of the agent architecture.

Black-box models implement direct mappings between emotion triggers and the resulting emotions, and the emotions and the resulting behavior. (In many models, there are in fact intermediate representations, in terms of abstract features such as the OCC evaluative criteria or the componential theory appraisal variables, but these models do not necessarily explicitly represent the mediating cognitive processes.)

In contrast, *process-level models* aim to explicitly represent the cognitive processing involved in generating emotions, and the affective biases on cognition that influence decision-making, planning and action selection. This indirect mapping, enabled by the explicit representation of the cognitive domain, then enables a greater degree of differentiation and variability in both processes (emotion generation and emotion effects), which is not possible in black-box models.

Figure 14 illustrates the differences between a black-box model (upper part) and a process-level model (lower part), in the context of emotion effects modeling. The 'sticky notes' indicate reasons why one or the other alternative might be used. The figure also includes a third alternative, a deeper model that does not aim to emulate the actual biological mechanisms, and is used to facilitate coordination among effects across multiple modalities.

For any but the most simple models, the agent will need an explicit representation of goals, to enable dynamic and realistic generation emotions. More complex agents may require an explicit representation of additional mental constructs, such as perceptions, beliefs, expectations and plans.

These constructs then form the elements of the *cognitive domain (C)*. No fixed set of established semantic primitives exists in the cognitive domain, beyond the high-level constructs listed above and in Table 7, but literature in cognitive, social and emotion psychology is a good source of potential additional high-level constructs (e.g., attitudes).

4.6 Select Theoretical Foundations for the Affective Model

I have already emphasized the importance of modeling emotion generation and emotion effects in a theoretically and empirically grounded manner. By this I mean that the affective models should use an established *theoretical perspective* on emotions (e.g., discrete, dimensional, componential), and, where available, use an *established theory* to support the modeling of a particular process

Figure 14. Differences between a black-box model and a process-level model in the context of emotion effects modeling

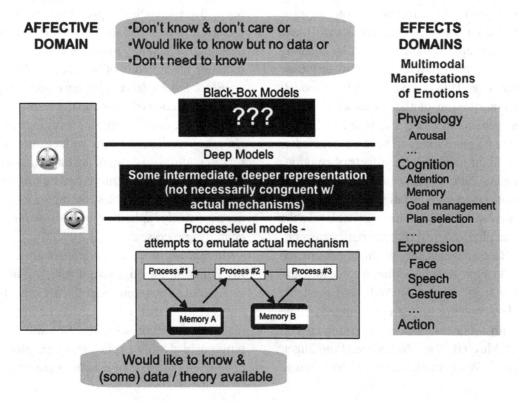

(e.g., OCC cognitive appraisal theories for emotion generation). Both the theoretical perspectives, and the theories supporting emotion generation and emotion effects modeling, were discussed in section 3.

4.6.1 Select a Theoretical Perspective

The theoretical perspectives differ in the semantic primitives they offer for representing emotions (basic emotions in the discrete / categorical perspective, pleasure-arousal or pleasure-arousal-dominance in the dimensional perspective, and the appraisal variables in the componential perspective). They also differ in the degree to which they define, and require, an abstract domain to mediate the trigger-to-emotion mappings and emotion-to-effects mappings. In the discrete / categorical perspective, no intermediate, abstract features are necessary. In the others, the dimensions or the appraisal variables provide these domain-independent features, which represent the elements of the abstract domain. For some of these abstract features, data exist that support a direct mapping from specific feature values to effects in the behavioral or expressive domain; e.g., novelty induces raising of brows and eyelids, interruption or inhalation in voice, straightening of posture (see Scherer (Klaus R. Scherer, 1992), Table 5.3 for a list of appraisal variable-effects associations.)

For many others, these data are not available. Thus in some cases the same set of abstract features can serve both to mediate emotion generation and emotions effects. The perspectives also differ in the number of emotions they can accommodate; i.e., the space defined by the PA or PAD dimensions is smaller than that defined by the appraisal variables. Finally, the perspectives differ in the degree to which its semantic primitives support manifestations of emotions in the expressive channels, and combination of multiple emotions. For example, the dimensions in the dimensional perspective are well-suited to support continuous

and gradual modification of facial expressions, which is necessary for affectively-realistic facial expressions. In contrast, use of the discrete / categorical perspective to support facial expression modeling requires additional computation to implement realistic affective dynamics.

The differences outlined above help determine which theoretical perspective is best suited for a particular agent. For example, if the agent has only a few of the basic emotions, and does not need to represent both fear and anger (or any other pairs of emotions characterized by the same values of arousal and valence), then the dimensional perspective, with just two dimensions (arousal and valence), is appropriate. If both fear and anger are required, then a dimensional perspective may still be appropriate, but a third dimension needs to be added (dominance), to distinguish between fear and anger, both characterized by negative valence and high arousal. If a large number of emotions is required, including complex and social emotions, the componential perspective is more appropriate, since it can accommodate a larger number of affective states. The discrete / categorical perspective could be used for either of the above cases, but would require an explicit addition of emotion-specific processes, or modules for each emotion represented in the model.

Figure 15 illustrates the different theoretical perspectives in modeling emotion generation. Figure 16 illustrates these perspectives in the context of emotion effects modeling.

4.6.2 Select a Specific Theory

I now turn to the specific theories available to support *emotion generation* and *emotion effects modeling*. The most elaborated theory for *emotion generation* is cognitive appraisal, and this is also the most frequent basis for modeling emotion generation in affective agent models. The dominant cognitive appraisal theory is the OCC theory, which provides an elaborate taxonomy of emotion triggers, as well as domain-independent evalua-

Figure 15. Theoretical perspectives in modeling emotion generation

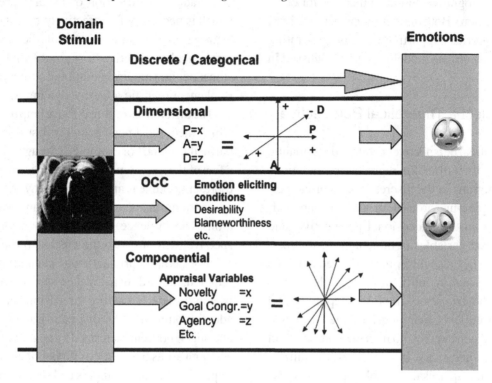

Figure 16. Theoretical perspectives in the context of emotion effects modeling

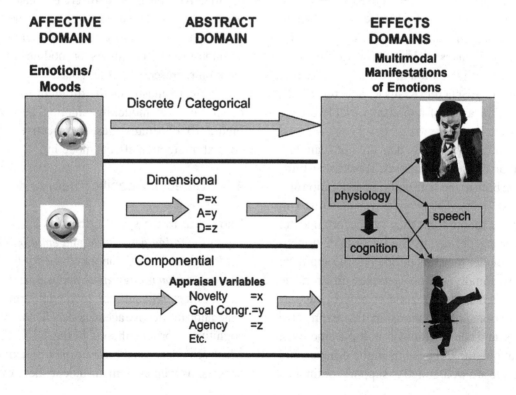

tive criteria used to generate different emotions. More recently, theories of emotion generation within the componential perspective have begun to be used as basis of affective modeling, which also emphasize the use of domain-independent evaluative criteria, termed the *appraisal variables*. Section 3 describes these theories and the associated domain-independent evaluative criteria in more detail.

Table 6 compares the OCC and the componential appraisal theories.

The OCC theory has the advantage of having been implemented numerous times, and the existing models of emotion generation can therefore serve as concrete examples for developing analogous models in agents. The disadvantage of the OCC theory is that the OCC abstract evaluative criteria (e.g., pleased about an event undesirable for another, disapproving of own behavior) don't readily map onto emotion effects. If the OCC theory is selected as the basis of an agent emotion generation, some other theory must be selected as a basis of modeling emotion effects. (Note that the OCC theory was never intended to address this issue, as its original aim was to explain the cognitive structure of emotions only.)

The componential theory's appraisal variables have the advantage that they can serve both to support emotion generation, and emotion effects modeling, since many of the appraisal variables values map onto elements within the expressive domain. Recently, efforts have been made to also identify mappings between appraisal variables and the cognitive domain (e.g., high certainty appraisal appears correlated with the use of heuristic processing, vs. analytical processing, in problem solving).

Regardless of the theory selected, the abstract elements provided by the theory then serve to define the *abstract domain* (Ab). In the case of OCC, the domain-independent evaluative criteria represent the individual elements of the abstract domain (refer to Table 4 for a complete list of these evaluative criteria). In the case of the componential theory's appraisal variables, the individual appraisal variables are the elements of the abstract domain (refer to Table 5 for a list of appraisal variables).

Neither theory elaborates the role of non-cognitive triggers in emotion generation in great detail, beyond acknowledging their existence. In agents that also represent a simulated physiological modality, the emotion generation should take the values of particular physiological characteristics into account, to ensure the agent's affective realism and believability.

Due to the multimodal nature of emotion effects, and in contrast to emotion generation, no dominant theory exists supporting *emotion effects modeling*, which would be analogous to the OCC theory in emotion generation. The consequence of this lack of an all-encompassing theory to support modeling of the cross-modal effects of emotions is that different theories must be used for the different modalities. I differentiate here between the internal effects of emotions on cognition, and the external manifestations of emotions across the expressive channels, and effects on behavior.

Regarding the effects of emotions on cognition (assuming cognitive processing is represented in the agent): the parameter-based theories lend themselves well to support modeling of the diverse effects of emotions on cognition. A range of parameters is defined to control distinct aspects of processing within the affective model and the agent architecture. For example, parameters may control the speed and capacity of attention, situation assessment, goal management, planning, and even emotion generation itself. When an emotion is generated in the agent, it is translated into a set of specific parameter values, which then induce changes in the architecture modules. The resulting modifications of the cognitive processes are eventually reflected in decisions made by the agent, and the specific actions selected. Refer to Figure 7 and 8 for an illustration of this approach.

Regarding the effects of emotions on the expressive channels, the diversity of processes mediating the different effects across the distinct channels (e.g., facial expression, posture, gestures, speech), and the lack of a 'unified theory' of effects, would suggest that the effects of emotions may best be represented by sets of direct mappings, across the expressive channels available in the agent's embodiment.

However, in spite of the lack of a 'unified theory' of emotion effects, it is often beneficial to have an underlying deeper representation of information processing, which is not necessarily a process-level model, but which facilitates coordination among the multiple modalities within which emotions are manifested, and provides a more robust and flexible basis for modeling than a collection of direct emotion-to-effect mappings (refer to Figure 14). This point has been made by a number emotion modelers in the context of architectures for believable embodied agents (Aylett, 2004; de Rosis et al., 2003; Prendinger, Descamps, & Ishizuka, 2002).

4.7 Define Specific Triggers and Effects of the Emotions Represented in the Model

In this step the mappings mediating emotion generation and emotion effects are defined. The former involves defining the mappings that map the emotion eliciting triggers to particular emotions. The latter involves defining the mappings that map the different emotions and moods onto their manifestations, in the modalities available in the agent. Depending on the theoretical foundations selected for the model, and the nature of the associated abstract domain, if any, some of the mappings may involve the abstract domain. For example, if the dimensional theoretical perspective is used, the triggers may be mapped onto the dimensions, which may then be mapped onto particular emotions. Alternatively, the dimensions may be mapped directly onto particular effects (e.g., high arousal will map onto faster movements,

and simulated physiological characteristics such as faster breathing rate).

Defining these mappings consists of two steps. *First,* the modeling domains involved in the mapping are specified (refer to Table 7 for a summary of the domain types); e.g., in a model that uses the *discrete / categorical perspective,* where the distinct emotions are the semantic primitives, the mapping mediating emotion generation will map elements from the object domain (W) directly onto the affective domain (A). A model using the *componential perspective* would first involve mapping the object domain elements onto the appraisal variables within the abstract domain (Ab), which would then be mapped onto the affective domain. *Second,* the specific contents of the mappings must be specified, which will implement the generation of specific emotions or moods, and their effects. Minimally, this means effects on behavior, but typically also expressive manifestations and, less often, effects on cognitive processing. Since some agents may also have simulated 'physiological' characteristics, such as energy level, fatigue etc., both the effects of emotions on these characteristics, and the effects of these characteristics on emotion generation, may also need to be represented, to ensure affective realism.

Minimally, the following domains, and their associated elements, are required for an agent affective model: Object domain (W), Affective domain (A), and Behavioral domain (B). Typically, the agents will express the generated emotions, requiring the definition of the Expressive domain (Ex) and its elements. In more complex agents, the Cognitive (C) domain may also need to be defined, to enable the agent to produce more interesting and affectively-realistic behavior, as a result of the generated emotions. In many agents the physiological domain (Ph) is also defined, in terms of characteristics reflecting the agent's 'physical' state (e.g., fatigue, energy). In addition, abstract domains may be defined, which reflect particular theoretical perspectives and/or specific theories, and whose elements provide additional variables that mediate emotion effects across multiple modalities; e.g., parameters used to represent effects of emotions on different cognitive processes.

The specific nature of these mappings should be based on empirical data regarding the typical triggers of particular emotions, and the typical effects of emotions on the modalities and channels represented in the model, including any mediating abstract domains defined, instantiated within the specific context of the agent's world and its functionality. For example, the fact that a physical threat to a robot's safety triggers fear would be instantiated in the robot's context by identifying the specific threats to its safety (e.g., fall off a platform, fall into a ditch, get crushed by a rock). The empirical evidence that fear induces a focus on threatening stimuli, and an interpretive bias to assess neutral situations as dangerous, would then be instantiated in the robot's context by distinguishing among high- and low-threat stimuli (e.g., quickly-approaching large object is a high-threat stimulus), and defining alternative interpretations of situations, along the danger level spectrum, to enable the fearful agent to select the more dangerous ones, and react accordingly.

The result of this step is a set of mappings among the domains represented in the agent, which then serve as a basis for defining the computational tasks necessary to implement the emotion generation and emotion effects in the agent's affective model. The exact set of the mappings necessary depends on the expressive modalities represented in the agent, which are determined by its particular embodiment, and on the abstract domains represented in the model, if any, which are determined by the model's theoretical basis. Table 14 and Table 15 summarize the results of this phase of the affective requirements analysis and design process.

Note that it is assumed here that the agents don't learn, and therefore the specific contents of the mappings from the affective to the behavioral

domains must be pre-defined by the designer. This constraint is likely to change in the future, as learning mechanisms become incorporated in affective modeling.

4.8 Specify the Affective Dynamics

Affective dynamics in emotion modeling refer to calculating emotion intensities, during emotion generation, and determining the magnitudes of emotion effects, during emotion effects modeling, as well as determining the onset and decay of both the intensities and the magnitude of the emotions' effects. Defining the affective dynamics of a particular model also involves deciding how to address the integration of multiple emotions (during emotion generation), and multiple effects (during emotion effects modeling), either when multiple affective states are generated, or when attempting to integrate newly generated state(s) with existing ones.

In section 4 I discussed the alternative approaches to modeling affective dynamics. As already pointed out, realistic representation of affective dynamics represents a major challenge in affective modeling, with few guidelines and fewer underlying theories available, as well as a paucity of empirical data, beyond statements of qualitative relationships (e.g., anxiety biases attention towards detection of threatening stimuli; arousal induces higher pitch and rate of speech). In many existing affective models quantification of the available qualitative data are often ad hoc, with specific values determined empirically, based on model performance.

Calculations of emotion intensity typically involve simple formulas (e.g., emotion intensity = desirability of some event x its likelihood), or linear combinations of differentially-weighted contributing factors. These formulas may require significant fine-tuning to adjust model performance. Specifying the emotion intensity calculation function therefore involves selection of the function itself, the specific variables used, and

Table 14. Affective requirements analysis step #7: Defining the mappings mediating emotion generation

Theoretical Perspective	Structure of Required Mappings	Examples of Contents
Discrete/Categorical	W → A	**Dangerous event** → fear **Another agent obstructs goal** → anger **Friendly user** → joy
Dimensional	1. W –> Ab, where Ab is either {pleasure,arousal} or {pleasure, arousal, dominance} 2. Ab → A	**Dangerous event** → V=low, A=high, D=low → fear **Agent obstructs goal** → V=low, A=high, D=high → anger **Friendly user** → V=high, A=medium → joy
Componential	W –> Ab, where Ab consists of n-tuples of appraisal variable values 2. Ab → A	**Dangerous event** → novelty=high, valence=low, goal relevance=high, goal congruence=low, coping=low → fear **Agent obstructs goal** → novelty=high, valence=low, goal relevance=high, goal congruence=low, coping=high → anger **Friendly user** → novelty=high, valence=high, goal relevance=high, goal congruence=high → joy
OCC	1. W → Ab, where Ab consists of the OCC evaluative criteria 2. Ab → A	**Dangerous event** → displeased, neg. fortunes-of-self, prospect-based → fear **Agent obstructs goal** → displeased, disapproving, neg. fortunes-of-self, negative well being, expectation deviation → anger **Friendly user** → pleased, pos. fortunes-of-self, positive well being → joy

Table 15. Affective requirements analysis step #7: Defining the mappings mediating emotion effects

Theoretical Perspective	Structure of Required Mappings	Examples of Contents
Discrete/Categorical	A → Effects domains (subset of domains used in a particular agent)	fear → facial expr. of fear, fearful speech, run or hide anger → facial expr. of anger, angry speech, aggressive behavior toward other agent joy → facial expr. of joy, happy speech, approach friendly user
Dimensional	Ab → Effects domains, where Ab is either {valence,arousal} or {valence, arousal, dominance} and / or A → Effects domains	V=high -> approach. V=low+D=low→ avoid, escape. V=low+D=high→ avoid/approach; A=high→ high energy, physio. variables. A=medium -> med. energy in behavior, physio. variables. A=high→ high energy, physio. variables. (Note that multiple dimensions may be required to determine an effect, and that often a single effect cannot be uniquely determined via dimension values alone.)
Componential	Ab → Effects domains, where A consists of n-tuples of appraisal variable values and / or A → Effects	Novelty = high→ orient attention; raise eyebrows/lids; interrupt speech; straighten posture; Valence=high→ raise lip corners; approach Valence=low→ lower lip corners; avoid Coping=high→ approach, full voice Coping=low→ avoid or freeze, (Based on Scherer, 1992)

their relative weights. In other words, selecting the features of the elements of the object domain, or the abstract domain, and their weights.

The simplest design choice for emotion intensity calculation would be to represent intensity as a binary value (0 or 1), with the intensity being 1 if the triggers of the affective state were present, 0 otherwise. However, for agents requiring higher levels of affective realism varying degrees of intensity must be represented. Typically, intensity values range between 0 and 1 (or some other fixed interval), with different combinations of triggering stimuli, and their characteristics, resulting in different intensity values. Table 16 summarizes the most commonly used functions for emotion intensity calculation, and lists their benefits and drawbacks.

The next step in affective dynamics model design, is to decide how emotion intensity should change over time, that is, the rates of the emotion onset and decay. The simplest choice here is to eliminate this component altogether, and use a simple step function, with the emotion simply appearing in its full intensity, lasting for some time interval, and then returning to zero or its baseline value for that character. Different temporal intervals may be defined for different emotions, and for different agent personalities (e.g., a generally happy agent (high extraversion, high agreeableness, and low neuroticism in terms of the Five Factor model traits) will maintain positive emotions for longer time periods; an irascible agent will become angry quickly and will remain angry for longer time periods).

Alternatively, the onset and decay rates may follow some monotonically increasing or decreasing (respectively) function, to model the affective dynamics in a more realistic manner. A variety of functions have been used in emotion generation models, including linear, exponential, sigmoid and logarithmic (Reilly 2006). Table 17 summarizes the most frequently used functions for modeling emotion intensity decay.

Finally, the designer must decide how multiple emotions should be integrated. This occurs when multiple emotions are generated by the appraisal process, and when existing emotion(s) must be combined with newly-generated emotion(s). This aspect of affective dynamics is the least well developed, both in existing psychological theories and conceptual models, and in computational models. Typically, relatively simple approaches are used to address this complex problem, which

limits the realism of the resulting models in any but the most simple situations.

Reilly has analyzed several existing approaches to combining similar emotions (positive with positive, negative with negative), and highlights their drawbacks and benefits, as follows. Simple addition of intensities can lead to too much intensity (e.g., few 'low intensity' emotions lead to a 'high intensity' reaction). Averaging the intensities may result in a final intensity that is lower than one of the constituent intensities: an unlikely situation in biological agents. Max (or winner-take-all) approach ignores the cumulative effects of multiple emotions. The limitations of these simple functions have motivated other approaches, including logarithmic and sigmoid functions (Reilly, 2006; Picard, 1997). In many cases, customized, domain-dependent weightings are used, so that a particular emotion is preferentially generated, as a function of the character's personality. For example, high-extraversion characters may be more likely to feel positive emotions, whereas high-neuroticism characters may be more likely to feel negative emotions (Hudlicka, 2007). Table 18 summarizes existing approaches, and lists their benefits and drawbacks.

A more problematic situation occurs when opposing or distinctly different emotions are derived (e.g., a particular situation brings both joy and sadness). Neither the available theories, nor the existing empirical data, currently provide a basis for a principled approach to this problem. Should opposing emotions cancel each other out? (Are we likely to feel calm and neutral if our house burns down but we have just won the lottery?) Is it even appropriate to think of emotions in pairs of opposites? Can we assume that the strongest emotion is the appropriate one, as some models do (e.g., Hudlicka's MAMID (Hudlicka, 2004; Hudlicka, 2007)? At what stage of processing are emotions combined and any contradictions resolved? Should conflicting emotions be resolved at the appraisal stage, to avoid the problem entirely? At the cognitive effects stage, e.g., during goal

Table 16. Examples of intensity calculating formulas

Intensity Function	Pros / Cons	Model / Person Using the Function
Importance * belief (that event is true or that goal will be affected)	+ Simple + Explicit representation of agent's belief + Works for many simple cases - Ignores asymmetry in success/failure of goal - Ignores expectation of event - Ignores possible differences between actual likelihood and agent's beliefs	De Rosis et al., 2003 (Greta)
(Desirability x (change in) (Likelihood of success) (for positive emotions) |Undesirability| x (change in) (Likelihood of failure) (for negative emotions)	+ Relatively simple + Accounts for change in perceived likelihood of success/failure + Works for many simple cases Captures asymmetry in success or failure of affected goal - Requires distinct variables for importance of success (goal desirability)(joy & hope) vs. Importance of avoiding failure (goal undesirability) (distress & fear)	Reilly, 1996 (Em)
|desirability| * likelihood	+ Simple + Works for many simple cases - Ignores asymmetry in success/failure of goal - Ignores expectation of event - Ignores changes in likelihood	Gratch & Marsella, 2004 (EMA)
(1.7 * desirability * expectation**.5) + (-.7 * desirability) (for positive emotions) (2 * desirability * expectation**2) – desirability (for negative emotions)	+ Explicitly represents asymmetry in importance of success vs. avoiding failure - Constants are empirically derived and likely to be context specific	El Nasr et al., 2000 (FLAME)

Table 17. Alternatives for modeling emotion intensity decay

Function Type	Descriptions	Pros	Cons
Linear	Decrement intensity at t-1 by a decay constant	Simple to compute	Not realistic
Exponential	Decrement at each t is proportional to intensity at t-1; slope determined by decay constant; faster than logarithmic	More realistic than linear	
Logarithmic	Decrement at each t is proportional to intensity at t-1; slope determined by decay constant; slower than exponential	More realistic than linear	
Mass spring	Decrement at each t is proportional to intensity at t-1; slope determined by decay constants; sinusoid behavior	More realistic than linear & exponential for modeling arousal & valence decay (Reisenzein, 1994)	More complex computational required

Table 18. Alternative formulas for combining the intensities of similar emotions

Model	Benefits / Drawbacks
Simple Addition	- Does not reflect human affective dynamics - Produces too much intensity too fast - A few low-intensity emotions result in a high-intensity emotion
Average	- Does not reflect human affective dynamics - Final result can be less than the most intense component
Max (Winner-Take-All)	+ Responsive to high-intensity emotions - Ignores cumulative effects of multiple emotions - Does not use all emotions
Sigmoidal Function	+ Uses all emotions + Models saturation effect + Closer to human affective dynamics by addressing problems above + Linear at mid-range
Logarithmic Function	+ Uses all emotions + Closer to human affective dynamics by addressing problems above + Linear at low-intensity ranges

selection? Or at the behavior selection stage? The last option being potentially the most problematic; and yet it is apparent that this phenomenon occurs in biological agents. One only needs to witness the scrambling of a frightened squirrel as a car approaches to see a dramatic impact of the failure to resolve contradictory behavioral tendencies. (Refer to Figure 17 for an illustration of these alternatives in emotion effects modeling.)

The computational solutions for combining non-congruent emotions are generally task- or domain- specific, and often ad hoc. Existing approaches fall into one of four categories: *intensity based* (choose emotion or mood with highest intensity); *precedence-rule based* (define precedence relationships for the emotions represented in the agent, and resolve any conflict among multiple states via these rules; precedence relationships are often defined based on the agent's personality); *mood-congruence based approaches* (select an emotion that is congruent with the current mood); and *abstract representation based* new state definition (combine the semantic primitives within which an emotion or mood is represented (e.g., PAD dimensions, appraisal variables), and generate a new affective state that integrates the

multiple states). (See Hudlicka (forthcoming) for a more in-depth discussion of this problem.)

Once the emotions are generated, the dynamics of their effects need to be modeled. This process is made more challenging by the multi-modal nature of emotion effects, discussed above, since different approaches are appropriate for the different modalities, or channels.

Modeling different magnitudes of effects in the behavioral domain often involves the use of multiple intensity thresholds for manifestations of different emotions across distinct channels (e.g., different intensity thresholds may be required to trigger emotion effects on cognition vs. facial expression vs. behavior) (Sonnemans & Frijda, 1994). Multiple thresholds are also often used to map different intensities onto distinct actions. For example, different intensities of joy can be reflected in laughing, clapping hands, or jumping up and down. Different intensities of fear can manifest in different speeds of escape, or, in extreme cases, in complete paralysis.

In several of the channels within the *expressive domain*, the emotion intensity is directly proportional to the magnitude of the associated effects, as expressed by the semantic primitives associated with the particular expressive chan-

Figure 17. Alternatives in emotion effects modeling

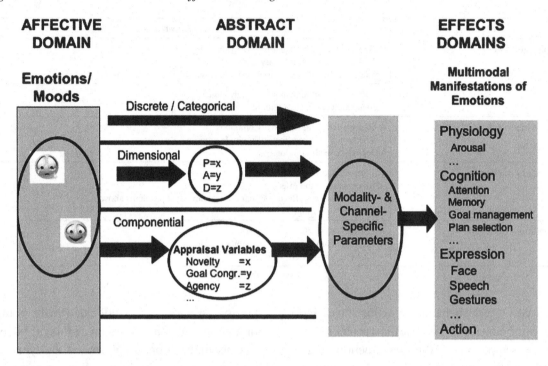

nel. For example, in facial expression, the higher the intensity of happiness, the greater the movement of the zygomatic muscles will be, causing a larger smile (up to a maximum determined by the associated effectors). Similarly, the effects of increasing intensity of anger on the prosodic qualities of speech, will be reflected in higher values of some of the prosodic features, such as volume and rate. Note, however, that there are significant individual differences in the expressive manifestations of emotions, as well as cultural differences. It is important that the model designer take these into account to create believable non-playing characters. For example, in an interactive drama application, agent A might express its anger by shouting very loudly, whereas agent B might suddenly become very calm and controlled, and speak in very low tones.

Intensity can also be expressed by involving an increasing number of the available semantic elements in a given channel, as well as by involving a larger number of expressive channels. For example, within the facial expression channel, increasingly intense smile involves not only larger displacement of the lip corners, but also the involvement of the eyebrows, as well as a longer duration of the displacement. When the intensity increases further, a smile may progress to laughter, which also involves the speech channel and different vocalizations, as well as changes in the speech features that reflect changes in prosody (e.g., pitch, rate, volume).

Regarding the onset and decay of the emotion effects, the choices here are analogous to those for the onset and decay of emotion intensity during emotion generation. However, implementing the onset and decay of emotion and mood effects is more complex, due to the multiple channels across different modalities that are involved in emotion manifestations. The dynamics of multiple processes must be considered here. In many cases, these processes involve physiological systems that must run their course once triggered, and that have associated refractory periods. For example, increased arousal associated with heightened intensity of many emotions (joy, fear, anger) is mediated by changes in concentrations of specific hormones and neurotransmitters, which must be dissipated or neutralized before the system can return to its baseline state. Thus different effects are manifested along different time scales.

Many of these subtleties can be ignored in existing game characters. As was the case with emotion intensity, the simplest choice is to ignore the onset and decay rates altogether, and simply manifest a particular set of effects at a given magnitude over some temporal interval. The next simplest alternative is to translate the changing intensity value directly into the corresponding magnitudes within the effects domains included in a particular agent. In facial expressions, this would mean translating different intensities onto the degree of displacement of specific facial muscles from their neutral position. In speech, this would mean translating different intensities into magnitudes of different speech signal features, such as volume and rate. These translations would need to take into account individual differences in manifesting different emotions by different agents, as a function of their personality.

However, as demands for agents' affective complexity and realism increase, these simple solutions will no longer be adequate and the issues of multiple, independently-evolving processes mediating emotion effects across multiple channels will increasingly need to be addressed by affective model designers. In addition, some affective states can only be distinguished via the distinct patterns of their affective dynamics (e.g., embarrassment). Believable manifestations of these types of complex emotions in embodied agents is an active area of research.

As was the case with intensity calculation, distinct patterns of emotion and mood effects can be defined for distinct agent personalities, to further increase their affective realism and enhance the player's engagement. This can be done by specifying different thresholds for the distinct manifestations of different emotions, thereby emphasizing the expression of a particular emotion, and / or the expression of a particular emotion within particular channels. Personality differences can also be reflected in the onset and decay rates of different effects. For example, agent with personality A may have rapidly-increasing and intense positive reactions, with the positive emotions decaying very slowly, whereas character with personality B might have generate negative emotions with high intensity, and rapid decay rates.

For a more in-depth discussion of this issue, and a discussion of modeling varying magnitudes of emotion effects on cognition, see Hudlicka (forthcoming).

5.0 IMPLICATIONS AND FUTURE TRENDS

There has been significant growth in the area of affective computing that focuses on computational models of emotion. Emotion models are being developed primarily for applied purposes, but also for research purposes, to elucidate the mechanisms that mediate affective processing in biological agents. I have termed the former models *applied models*, and the latter *research models* (Hudlicka, 2011). *Applied models* are being developed to enhance the believability of synthetic agents and social robots, by making them more affectively realistic; that is, by enabling the expression of emotions and emotion-induced behavioral variability, appropriate for the specific context. (For example, a virtual agent may display joy in response to hearing good news from the human interlocutor, or a social robot interacting with a child will display sadness when the child can't reach a toy.) *Research models* are being used to characterize mechanisms mediating a variety of affective processes, including emotion generation, emotion effects on cognition and affective dynamics.

Clearly, there is increasing need to systematize affective modeling by developing design guidelines, and to develop more standardized terminology. This will facilitate not only model design and development but also model re-use and the sharing of model components. Common terminology is also important to facilitate cross-disciplinary communication that is essential for advancing the state of the art, especially in research models.

Much progress has already been made in some areas of affective computing, and, to a more limited extent, in affective modeling. For example, in facial emotion recognition and expression, the Facial Action Coding System (FACS) (Ekman & Friesen, 1978) has become the de facto standard for representing the facial musculature involved in producing affective facial expressions, and is used to support both the recognition of human emotion from facial expressions, and the generation of affective expressions in virtual agents and robots. Emotion markup languages have been developed to facilitate the development of applied models, and some are gaining prominence (e.g., EmotionML (Schroder et al., 2011).

In emotion modeling, some de facto standards have also emerged. Perhaps the best examples are the OCC model, which serves as the theoretical basis for the majority of models of emotion generation via cognitive appraisal, and the PAD representation of emotions, which represents emotions in a 3-dimensional space, defined by the pleasure (P), arousal (A) and dominance (D) dimensions, and is frequently used by applied affective models to mediate emotion expression. Efforts also exist to formalize some aspects of modeling (emotion generation via appraisal), to provide a basis for more systematic model design, comparison of specific theories (e.g., theories of cognitive appraisal) and for the formal representations of these processes (e.g., in set theoretic formalisms) (e.g., Broekens et al., 2008; Raisenzein et al., 2013). Attempts have also been made to identify the processes that a cognitive-affective architecture would require to enable the associated agent to exhibit categories

of mental states, including affective states (Sloman et al., 2005). (See discussion in Section 1.1 above for additional examples.)

However, in spite the progress outlined above, to date, no set of broad, systematic guidelines for affective modeling has been proposed, that would: (1) encompass models of both emotion generation and emotion effects, across multiple modalities; and (2) propose specific generic computational tasks necessary to implement these process in affective models. The computational analytical framework described here (and earlier (Hudlicka, 2008; 2011) attempts to fill this gap.

In suggesting the adoption of this analytical framework, is important to emphasize several points. *First*, the primary objective of this framework is to begin to think about affective modeling in more systematic terms, and to emphasize the need for identifying 'modeling primitives' and model 'building blocks'. *Second*, the specific primitives and building blocks proposed above, that is, the core affective processes and the generic computational tasks required to implement them, should be thought of as a 'first pass', sort of conceptual placeholders. Whether or not the proposed tasks will in fact be useful for the definition of systematic guidelines remains to be determined. It is likely that the set proposed here may be suitable for some modeling goals, but not for others; that the tasks will likely need to be enhanced, modified or perhaps discarded altogether. Again, the point is not that this particular set of tasks represents the sine qua non of affective modeling, but rather that *a set* of generic computational tasks will need to be defined, to develop more systematic approaches to modeling, and to advance the field of affective computational modeling. *Third*, and related to the previous point: the delineation of the core affective processes (emotion generation and emotion effects) is proposed to manage the complexity of the modeling endeavor. It would be foolish to suggest that there is a one-to-one correspondence between these processes and the underlying neural mechanisms. The delineation of the affective processes is clearly appropriate for a narrow set of models: namely, models aiming to represent the psychological functionality, rather than rather than neuroscience models. Even for psychological models this particular delineation may not be the most appropriate. Again, the utility of the specific proposed core processes and generic computational tasks has yet to be demonstrated. *Finally*, it is likely that distinct or overlapping sets of processes and generic tasks will be appropriate for different types of models, even within the broad area of psychological models.

With these caveats in mind however, I suggest that the proposed set of tasks represents a useful starting point, and that an approach to modeling that emphasizes the proposed perspective is essential to advance the field of computational affective modeling, in both applied modeling, to facilitate the development of efficient models and model re-use, and in research models, to facilitate cross-disciplinary communication, use of data, comparison of theories, and model validation.

The field would also greatly benefit from a set of benchmark problems that would provide opportunities for the systematic comparison of the usefulness and effectiveness of specific theories, data, and computational primitives.

6.0 SUMMARY AND CONCLUSION

Recognizing the lack of consistent terminology and design guidelines in emotion modeling, this chapter proposes a computational analytical framework to address this problem. The basic thesis is that emotion phenomena can usefully be understood (and modeled) in terms of two fundamental processes: *emotion generation* and *emotion effects,* and the associated generic computational tasks necessary to implement both processes, including the associated dynamics. I suggest that these can tasks serve as the computational primitives, or buildings blocks, from which affective models can be constructed. The tasks provide a basis for a more systematic design of affective models, and involve, for both processes, the following: defin-

ing a set of *domains;* defining a set of *mappings among* these domains (from triggers to emotions in emotion generation, and from emotions to their effects in the case of emotion effects*)*, defining *intensity and magnitude calculation* functions to compute the emotion intensities during generation, and the magnitude of the effects, and functions that *combine and integrate* multiple emotions, both similar and dissimilar emotions, and both during emotion generation and emotion effects modeling.

The proposed computational analytic framework, and the associated generic tasks, represent a step toward formalizing emotion modeling, and providing foundations for advancing the field of computational affective modeling, by: (1) supporting the development of more systematic design guidelines; (2) enabling model component sharing and model re-use; (3) facilitating a more systematic comparison of different theories; and (5) proposing an approach to analyzing affective computational models that will enhance cross-disciplinary dialog.

Identifying the specific computational tasks necessary to implement affective processes also helps address critical questions regarding the nature of emotions, and the specific benefits that emotions may provide in synthetic agents and robots.

The analytical framework outlined above has several limitations, in addition to the caveats outlined in Section 5. *First,* only the cognitive modality of emotion was discussed; both in emotion generation (generation via cognitive appraisal), and in emotion effects (effects of emotions on cognition). This was due both to lack of space and to the predominance of cognitively-based models of emotion, and in no way suggests that the other modalities of emotion are not as critical for understanding these complex phenomena. *Second,* the treatment of the various alternatives for computing the three fundamental computational tasks (mappings, intensity and magnitude, and integration) was necessarily superficial. In part due to lack of space, but primarily because systematic evaluation and validation of existing (or possible) alternatives have not yet been performed. *Third,* lack of space did not allow for a detailed discussion of the many existing models, and only brief references were made to these models. All three of these limitations will be partially addressed in a forthcoming textbook (Hudlicka, forthcoming).

It is hoped that the analysis presented here will stimulate a more focused dialogue about the design of computational affective models, and a refinement of the proposed computational analytical framework, and contribute to a more systematic approach to the design, development, analysis and validation of affective models, by specifying both the constituent computational building blocks, and the alternatives available for their implementation.

The focus in this chapter has been on designing affective models in agent architectures – thus, a more application-oriented, pragmatic focus. This is in contrast to affective models whose objective is to elucidate the mechanisms underlying affective processes, research models. Research models cannot as easily ignore the multi-modal nature of emotion generation, as many existing agent models do, and need to explicitly represent the complex interactions among the multiple modalities, in both emotion generation and emotion effects modeling.

Development of emotion models in agent architectures is certainly an area where affective modeling can contribute to enhanced performance and effectiveness. However, a no less important function of affective modeling is the ability of these models to enhance our understanding of affective phenomena. Computational modeling necessitates detailed operationalizations of existing high-level constructs offered by psychologists, including the very term 'emotion', and thereby has the potential to contribute to the characterization of the underlying mechanisms of affective processes. This represents perhaps the greatest challenge, and promise, of computational affective modeling.

REFERENCES

Andre, E., Klesen, M., Gebhard, P., Allen, S., & Rist, T. (2000). *Exploiting models of personality and emotions to control the behavior of animated interactive agents* Paper presented at the Proceedings of IWAI, Siena, Italy.

Arnold, M. B. (1960). *Emotion and personality.* New York: Columbia University Press.

Averill, J. R. (1994). I feel, therefore I am: I think. In P. Ekman & R. J. Davidson (Eds.), *The nature of emotion: Fundamental questions.* Oxford: Oxford University Press.

Aylett, R. S. (2004). *Agents and affect: Why embodied agents need affective systems.* Paper presented at the 3rd Hellenic Conference on AI, Samos, Greece.

Bates, J., Loyall, A. B., & Reilly, W. S. (1992). Integrating reactivity, goals, and emotion in a broad agent. *Proceedings of the 14th Meeting of the Cognitive Science Society.*

Becker, C., Nakasone, A., Prendinger, H., Ishizuka, M., & Wachsmuth, I. (2005). *Physiologically interactive gaming with the 3D agent Max.* Paper presented at the International Workshop on Conversational Informatics at JSAI-05, Kitakyushu, Japan.

Becker-Asano, C. (2008). *WASABI: Affect simulation for agents with believable interactivity.* IOS Press.

Belavkin, R. V., & Ritter, F. E. (2004). OPTIMIST: A new conflict resolution algorithm for ACT-R. *Proceedings of the Sixth International Conference on Cognitive Modeling,* Pittsburgh, PA.

Bower, G. H. (1981). Mood and memory. *The American Psychologist, 36*(2), 129–148. doi:10.1037/0003-066X.36.2.129 PMID:7224324

Bower, G. H. (1992). How might emotions affect memory? In S. A. Christianson (Ed.), *Handbook of emotion and memory*. Hillsdale, NJ: Lawrence Erlbaum.

Breazeal, C., & Brooks, R. (2005). Robot emotion: A functional perspective. In J.-M. Fellous & M. A. Arbib (Eds.), *Who needs emotions?* New York: Oxford University Press.

Broekens, J., DeGroot, D., & Kosters, W. A. (2008). Formal models of appraisal: theory, specification, and computational model. *Cognitive Systems Research, 9*(3), 173–197. doi:10.1016/j.cogsys.2007.06.007

Broekens, J., Kosters, W., & Verbeek, F. (2007). On affect and self-adaptation: Potential benefits of valence-controlled action-selection. *Bio-inspired Modeling of Cognitive Tasks, LNCS 4527*, 357-366.

Cañamero, L. (1997). *A hormonal model of emotions for behavior control*. Paper presented at the 4th European Conference on Artificial Life (ECAL '97). Brighton, UK.

Cañamero, L., & Avila-Gracia, O. (2007). *A bottom-up investigation of emotional modulation in competitive scenarios*. Paper presented at the Affective Computing and Intelligent Interaction. doi:10.1007/978-3-540-74889-2_35

Cañamero, L. D. (2001). Building emotional artifacts in social worlds: Challenges and perspectives. In *AAAI Fall Symposium "Emotional and Intelligent II: The Tangled Knot of Social Cognition"* Cape Cod, MA: Menlo Park, CA: AAAI Press.

Clore, G. L. (1994). Why emotions are felt? In P. Ekman & R. J. Davidson (Eds.), *The nature of emotion: Fundamental questions*. Oxford: Oxford University Press.

Clore, G. L., & Ortony, A. (1988). The semantics of the affective lexicon. In V. Hamilton, G. Bower, & N. Frijda (Eds.), *Cognitive science perspectives on emotion and motivation* (pp. 367–397). Amsterdam: Martinus Nijhoff. doi:10.1007/978-94-009-2792-6_15

Cohn, J. F., Ambadar, Z., & Ekman, P. (2007). Observer-based measurement of facial expression with the facial action coding system. In J. A. Coan & J. B. Allen (Eds.), The handbook of emotion elicitation and assessment. New York: Oxford University Press.

de Rosis, F., Pelachaud, C., Poggi, I., Carofiglio, V., & De Carolis, B. (2003). From Greta's mind to her face: Modelling the dynamics of affective states in a conversational embodied agent. *International Journal of Human-Computer Studies, 59*(1-2), 81–118. doi:10.1016/S1071-5819(03)00020-X

Derryberry, D. (1988). Emotional influences on evaluative judgments: Roles of arousal, attention, and spreading activation. *Motivation and Emotion, 12*(1), 23–55. doi:10.1007/BF00992471

Derryberry, D., & Reed, M. A. (2003). information processing approaches to individual differences in emotional reactivity. In R. J. Davidson, K. R. Scherer, & H. H. Goldsmith (Eds.), Handbook of affective sciences. New York: Oxford University Press.

Ekman, P. (1992). An argument for basic emotions. *Cognition and Emotion, 6*(3-4), 169–200. doi:10.1080/02699939208411068

Ekman, P., & Davidson, R. J. (1994). The nature of emotion: Fundamental questions. New York: Oxford University Press.

Ekman, P., & Friesen, W. V. (1978). *Facial action coding system*. Palo Alto, CA: Consulting Psychologists Press.

El-Nasr, M. S., Yen, J., & Ioerger, T. R. (2000). FLAME - Fuzzy Logic Adaptive Model of Emotions. *Autonomous Agents and Multi-Agent Systems*, *3*(3), 219–257. doi:10.1023/A:1010030809960

Elliot, C. (1992). *The affective reasoner: A process model of emotions in a multiagent system*. Evanston: Northwestern University.

Ellsworth, P. C., & Scherer, K. R. (2003). Appraisal processes in emotion. In R. J. Davidson, K. R. Scherer, & H. H. Goldsmith (Eds.), *Handbook of affective sciences*. New York: Oxford University Press.

Fellous, J. M. (2004). *From human emotions to robot emotions*. Paper presented at the AAAI Spring Symposium: Architectures for Modeling Emotion, Stanford University, CA.

Forgas, J. (1999). Mood and judgment: The affect infusion model (AIM). *Psychological Bulletin*, *117*(1), 39–66. doi:10.1037/0033-2909.117.1.39 PMID:7870863

Forgas, J. (2003). Affective influences on attitudes and judgments. In K. R. S. R. J. Davidson & H. H. Goldsmith (Eds.), *Handbook of affective sciences*. New York: Oxford University Press.

Frijda, N. (2008). The psychologists' point of view. In M. Lewis, J. M. Haviland-Jones, & L. F. Barrett (Eds.), *Handbook of emotions* (3rd ed.). New York: The Guilford Press.

Frijda, N. H. (1986). *The emotions*. Cambridge: Cambridge University Press.

Frijda, N. H. (1994). Emotions are functional, most of the time. In P. Ekman & R. J. Davidson (Eds.), *The nature of emotion: Fundamental questions*. New York: Oxford University Press.

Frijda, N. H., & Swagerman, J. (1987). Can computers feel? Theory and design of an emotional system. *Cognition and Emotion*, *1*(3), 235–257. doi:10.1080/02699938708408050

Gratch, J., & Marsella, S. (2004). A domain independent frame-work for modeling emotion. *Journal of Cognitive Systems Research*, *5*(4), 269–306. doi:10.1016/j.cogsys.2004.02.002

Hudlicka, E. (1998). *Modeling Emotion in Symbolic Cognitive Architectures*. Paper presented at the AAAI Fall Symposium: Emotional and Intelligent I, Orlando, FL.

Hudlicka, E. (2002). This time with feeling: Integrated Model of Trait and State Effects on Cognition and Behavior. *Applied Artificial Intelligence*, *16*(7-8), 1–31. doi:10.1080/08339510290030417

Hudlicka, E. (2003). *Modeling Effects of Behavior Moderators on Performance: Evaluation of the MAMID Methodology and Architecture*. Paper presented at the BRIMS-12, Phoenix, AZ.

Hudlicka, E. (2004). Two Sides of Appraisal: Implementing Appraisal and Its Consequences within a Cognitive Architecture. *AAAI Spring Symposium: Architectures for Modeling Emotion* (Vol. TR SS-04-02). Stanford University, CA: AAAI Press.

Hudlicka, E. (2007). Reasons for emotions. In W. Gray (Ed.), Advances in Cognitive models and cognitive architectures. New York: Oxford University Press. doi:10.1093/acprof:oso/9780195189193.003.0019

Hudlicka, E. (2008a). Modeling the mechanisms of emotion effects on cognition. *AAAI Fall Symposium: Biologically Inspired Cognitive Architectures* (Vol. TR FS-08-04 pp. 82-86), Arlington, VA. Menlo Park, CA: AAAI Press.

Hudlicka, E. (2008b). What are we modeling when we model emotion? *AAAI Spring Symposium: Emotion, Personality, and Social Behavior* (Vol. Technical Report SS-08-04, pp. 52-59), Stanford University, CA. Menlo Park, CA: AAAI Press.

Hudlicka, E. (2011). Guidelines for developing computational models of emotions. *International Journal of Synthetic Emotions, 2*(1), 26-79.

Hudlicka, E. (2014). Can computational affective models improve psychotherapy? In *Proceedings of the Workshop on Computational Models of Cognition-Emotion Interactions: Relevance to Mechanisms of Affective Disorders and Psychotherapeutic Action.* Quebec City, Quebec, Canada.

Hudlicka, E. (forthcoming). *Affective computing: Theory, methods and applications.* Boca Raton, FL: Taylor and Francis.

Izard, C. E. (1977). *Human emotions.* NY: Plenum. doi:10.1007/978-1-4899-2209-0

Izard, C. E. (1993). Four systems for emotion activation: Cognitive and noncognitive processes. *Psychological Review, 100*(1), 68–90. doi:10.1037/0033-295X.100.1.68 PMID:8426882

Juslin, P. N., & Scherer, K. R. (2005). Vocal expression of affect. In J. A. Harrigan, R. Rosenthal & K. R. Scherer (Eds.), The new handbook of methods in nonverbal behavior research (pp. 65-135). New York: Oxford University Press.

Lazarus, R. S. (1984). On the primacy of cognition. *The American Psychologist, 39*(2), 124–129. doi:10.1037/0003-066X.39.2.124

Lerner, J. S., & Tiedens, L. Z. (2006). Portrait of the angry decision maker: How appraisal tendencies shape anger's influence on cognition. *Journal of Behavioral Decision Making, 19*(2), 115–137. doi:10.1002/bdm.515

Leventhal, H., & Scherer, K. R. (1987). The relationship of emotion to cognition. *Cognition and Emotion, 1*(1), 3–28. doi:10.1080/02699938708408361

Lisetti, C., & Gmytrasiewicz, P. (2002). Can rational agents afford to be affectless? *Applied Artificial Intelligence, 16*(7-8), 577–609. doi:10.1080/08839510290030408

Loyall, A. B. (1997). *Believable agents: Building interactive personalities.* Pittsburgh, PA: CMU.

Mandler, G. (1984). *Mind and body: The psychology of emotion and stress.* New York: Norton.

Marr, D. (1982). *Vision.* San Francisco, CA: Freeman.

Matthews, G. A., & Harley, T. A. (1993). Effects of extraversion and self-report arousal on semantic priming: A connectionist approach. *Journal of Personality and Social Psychology, 65*(4), 735–756. doi:10.1037/0022-3514.65.4.735

Mehrabian, A. (1995). Framework for a comprehensive description and measurement of emotional states. *Genetic, Social, and General Psychology Monographs, 121*, 339–361. PMID:7557355

O'Rorke, P., & Ortony, A. (1994). Explaining emotions. *Cognitive Science, 18*(2), 283–323. doi:10.1207/s15516709cog1802_3

Ortony, A., Clore, G. L., & Collins, A. (1988). The cognitive structure of emotions. New York: Cambridge University Press. doi:10.1017/CBO9780511571299

Ortony, A., Norman, D., & Revelle, W. (2005). Affect and proto-affect in effective functioning. In J. M. Fellous & M. A. Arbib (Eds.), Who needs emotions? New York: Oxford University Press. doi:10.1093/acprof:oso/9780195166194.003.0007

Ortony, A., & Turner, T. J. (1990). What's basic about basic emotions? *Psychological Review, 97*(3), 315–331. doi:10.1037/0033-295X.97.3.315 PMID:1669960

Panskepp, J. (1998). *Affective neuroscience: The foundations of human and animal emotions.* New York: Oxford University Press.

Picard, R. (1997). *Affective computing*. Cambridge, MA: The MIT Press. doi:10.1037/e526112012-054

Plutchik, R. (1984). Emotions: A general psychoevolutionary theory. In K. R. Scherer & P. Ekman (Eds.), *Approaches to emotion*. Hillsdale, N.J.: Erlbaum.

Prendinger, H., Descamps, S., & Ishizuka, M. (2002). Scripting affective communication with life-like characters in Web-based interaction systems. *Applied Artificial Intelligence*, *16*(7-8), 519–553. doi:10.1080/08839510290030381

Prendinger, H., Saeyor, S., & Ishizuka, M. (2004). MPML and SCREAM: Scripting the bodies and minds of life-like characters. In H. Prendinger & M. Ishizuka (Eds.), *Life-like characters: Tools, affective functions, and applications*. Berlin: Springer. doi:10.1007/978-3-662-08373-4_10

Pylyshyn, Z. (1984). *Computation and cognition*. Cambridge, MA: The MIT Press.

Reilly, W. S. N. (2006). *Modeling what happens between emotional antecedents and emotional consequents* Paper presented at the ACE 2006, Vienna, Austria.

Reilly, W. S. R. (1996). *Believable social and emotional agents*. Pittsburgh, PA: CMU.

Reisenzein, R. (1994). Pleasure-arousal theory and the Intensity of Emotions. *Journal of Personality and Social Psychology*, *67*(3), 525–539. doi:10.1037/0022-3514.67.3.525

Reisenzein, R. (2001). Appraisal processes conceptualized from a schema-theoretic perspective: Contributions to a process analysis of emotions. In K. R. Scherer, A. Schorr, & T. Johnstone (Eds.), *Appraisal processes in emotion: Theory, methods, research*. NY: Oxford University Press.

ReisenzeinR., (2001).

Reisenzein, R., Hudlicka, E., Dastani, M., Gratch, J., Hindriks, K. V., Lorini, E., & Meyer, J.-J. Ch. (2013). Computational modeling of emotion: Toward improving the inter- and intradisciplinary exchange. *IEEE Transactions on Affective Computing*, *4*(3), 246–266. doi:10.1109/T-AFFC.2013.14

Ritter, F. E., & Avramides, M. N. (2000). *Steps towards including behavior moderators in human performance models in synthetic environments*. The Pennsylvania State University.

Ritter, F. E., Reifers, A. L., Klein, L. C., & Schoelles, M. J. (2007). Lessons from defining theories of stress for cognitive architectures. In W. Gray (Ed.), *Advances in Cognitive Models and Cognitive Architectures*. New York: Oxford University Press. doi:10.1093/acprof:oso/9780195189193.003.0018

Roseman, I. J. (2001). A model of appraisal in the emotion system. In K. R. Scherer, A. Schorr, & T. Johnstone (Eds.), *Appraisal processes in emotion: Theory, methods, research*. New York: Oxford University Press.

Roseman, I. J., & Smith, C. A. (2001). Appraisal theory: Overview, assumptions, varieties, controversies. In K. R. Scherer, A. Schorr, & T. Johnstone (Eds.), *Appraisal processes in emotion: theory, methods, research*. New York: Oxford University Press.

Rozin, P. (2003). Introduction: Evolutionary and cultural perspectives on affect. In R. J. Davidson, K. R. Scherer, & H. H. Goldsmith (Eds.), *Handbook of affective sciences*. New York: Oxford University Press.

Russell, J. (2003). Core affect and the psychological construction of emotion. *Psychological Review*, *110*(1), 145–172. doi:10.1037/0033-295X.110.1.145 PMID:12529060

Russell, J., & Barrett, L. F. (1999). Core affect, prototypical emotional episodes, and other things called emotion: Dissecting the elephant. *Journal of Personality and Social Psychology, 76*(5), 805–819. doi:10.1037/0022-3514.76.5.805 PMID:10353204

Russell, J., & Mehrabian, A. (1977). Evidence for a three-factor theory of emotions. *Journal of Research in Personality, 11*(3), 273–294. doi:10.1016/0092-6566(77)90037-X

Schank, R. C., & Abelson, R. P. (1977). *Scripts, plans, goals and understanding: an inquiry into human knowledge structures*. Hillsdale, NJ: Lawrence Erlbaum.

Scherer, K., Schorr, A., & Johnstone, T. (2001). Appraisal processes in emotion: theory, methods, research. New York: Oxford University Press.

Scherer, K. R. (1992). Emotions are biologically and socially constituted: A response to Greenwood. *New Ideas in Psychology, 10*(1), 19–22. doi:10.1016/0732-118X(92)90043-Y

Scherer, K. R. (2000). Emotions as episodes of subsystem synchronization driven by nonlinear appraisal processes. In M. D. Lewis & I. Granic (Eds.), *Emotion, development, and self-organization*. New York: Cambridge University Press. doi:10.1017/CBO9780511527883.005

Scherer, K. R. (2001). Appraisal considered as a process of multievel sequential checking. In K. R. Scherer, A. Schorr, & T. Johnstone (Eds.), Appraisal Processes in Emotion: Theory, Methods, Research. New York: Oxford University Press.

Schroder, M., Baggia, P., Burkhardt, F., Pelachaud, C., Peters, C. & Zovato, E. (2011). *EmotionML – an upcoming standard for representing emotions and related states.*

Schwarz, N., & Clore, G. L. (1988). How do I feel about it? The information function of affective states. In K. Fiedler & J. P. Forgas (Eds.), *Affect, cognition, and social behavior* (pp. 44–62). Toronto: Hogrefe.

Sehaba, K., Sabouret, N., & Corruble, V. (2007). *An emotional model for synthetic characters with personality* Paper presented at the Affective Computing and Intelligent Interaction (ACII), Lisbon, Portugal. doi:10.1007/978-3-540-74889-2_81

Sloman, A., Chrisley, R., & Scheutz, M. (2005). The architectural basis of affective states and processes. In J.-M. Fellous & M. A. Arbib (Eds.), *Who needs emotions?* New York: Oxford University Press. doi:10.1093/acprof:oso/9780195166194.003.0008

Smith, C. A., & Kirby, L. (2000). Consequences require antecedents: Toward a process model of emotion elicitation. In J. P. Forgas (Ed.), Feeling and Thinking: The role of affect in social cognition. New York: Cambridge University Press.

Smith, C. A., & Kirby, L. D. (2001). Toward delivering on the promise of appraisal theory. In K. R. Scherer, A. Schorr, & T. Johnstone (Eds.), Appraisal Processes in Emotion. New York: Oxford University Press.

Sonnemans, J., & Frijda, N. H. (1994). The structure of subjective emotional intensity. *Cognition and Emotion, 8*(4), 329–350. doi:10.1080/02699939408408945

Staller, A., & Petta, P. (1998). *Towards a tractable appraisal-based architecture for situated cognizers*. Paper presented at the 5th International Conference of the Society for Adaptive Behaviour (SAB'98): Grounding Emotions in Adaptive Systems Workshop, Zurich, Switzerland.

Velásquez, J. D. (1999). *An emotion-based approach to robotics*. Paper presented at the IROS. doi:10.1109/IROS.1999.813010

APPENDIX

Key Terms and Definitions

Terms Describing Affective States

Affect (Note that some researchers use 'affect' as an umbrella term for all affective states – (e.g., Scherer; (Ortony et al., 2005); Rozin, 2003): 1) An undifferentiated mental state reflecting a positive or negative evaluation of current stimuli, reflecting valence only, and associated approach or avoidance behavioral tendencies.; 2) "pleasant and unpleasant feelings" (Frijda, 1994, p. 199); 3) "perceived goodness or badness of something" (G. L. Clore, 1994) vs. "general umbrella term that subsumes a variety of phenomena such as emotion, stress, mood, interpersonal stance, and affective personality traits" (Juslin & Scherer, 2005); 4) "energy in the mental system, [whose] aim was to be expressed" (Clore, 1994, p. 288); 5) "the set of all valenced mental states, along with their associated physiological representations and behaviors" (Rozin, 2003).

Affective State: A transient mental state dominated by affect, emotion, or mood.

Basic Emotions: 1) Emotions involved in basic survival within the environment. The exact set varies to some extent, but typically includes: fear, anger, joy, sadness, disgust, and surprise.; 2) "Basic emotions are defined as corresponding to inborn, phylogenetically selected, neuro-motor programs. They are in limited number and are universal reactions (universality operates across ages, across cultures and across species)." (Panskepp, 1998, p. 46); 3) "each of the basic emotions is produced by an innate hardwired neuromotor program with characteristic neurophysiological, expressive, and subjective components" (Ellsworth & Scherer, 2003, p. 574).

Emotion: 1) A transient mental state lasting seconds to minutes, typically of moderate to high intensity, involving an evaluation of the current situation with respect to active goals, and associated expressive and behavioral manifestations.; 2) "state of affective appraisal of some object (external or internal), linked to a change in action readiness bearing on that object" or "involve a change in action readiness and are about something" (Frijda, 1994, p. 199); 3) "a sequence of state changes in each of five – functionally defined – organismic subsystems (cognitive, autonomic nervous system, motor system, motivational system, monitor system) occurring in an interdependent and interrelated fashion in response to the evaluation of a stimulus, an event, or intraorganismic changes of central importance to the major needs and goals of the organism" (K.R Scherer, 2000) p. 74). 4) "interpreted feelings" (Ortony, Norman and Revelle, 2005, p. 174).

Feelings: 1) Non-specific subjective mental states involving a conscious awareness of a combination of physical, mental and / or emotional characteristics. Feelings can be affective (good, bad, jealous), physical (hungry, tired), cognitive (confused, certain).

Moods: 1) A transient mental state lasting hours to days to months, involving a generalized, feeling state, typically of lower intensity than emotion, and often associated with one of the emotions; e.g., happy, sad, angry, fearful. The specific trigger is often not apparent and the behavioral reactions are typically diffuse: not directed at any particular individual or object, but rather at the 'world at large'.; 2) "diffuse states of feeling or action readiness or both" (N. H. Frijda, 1994), p. 199).

Non-Basic or Complex Emotions: Those emotions not considered basic, having a larger cognitive component and triggering and manifestation variabilities, and including the social emotions (see below). Examples of other non-basic emotions include love, awe, contentment and schadenfreude.

Sentiments: 1) "Long-lasting emotional states of relating to other people" (e.g., love, trust or distrust, arrogance or deference) (Oatley, 2004, p.4); 2) (Similar to Scherer's "interpersonal stance" (Scherer, 2000).

Social Emotions: 1) Emotions involved in coordinating interpersonal behavior and typically requiring a representation of the self within its social milieu – include pride, shame, guilt, jealousy, envy, embarrassment, contempt and jealousy (certain, confused); 2) "Readouts of the brain's registration of bodily conditions and changes—muscle tension, autonomic system activity, internal musculature (e.g., the gut), as well as altered states of awareness and attentiveness" (Ortony, Norman & Revelle, 2005, p. 174).

Terms Used in Emotion Generation and Cognitive Appraisal

Abstract Domain: Domain-independent evaluative dimensions (local variables in OCC, appraisal variables in componential theories) (Elliot, 1992).

Affective Domain: The end results of the emotion generation process, consisting of the derived affective states (emotions, moods).

Appraisal, Construal: Interpretation of an event, situation, or object in light of the agent's concerns, goals, behavioral norms and preferences.

Appraisal State: A particular configuration of appraisal variable values, corresponding to the agent's evaluation of the current set of stimuli.

Appraisal Variables, Appraisal Dimensions: In componential and cognitive appraisal theories: Domain-independent evaluation criteria or features, used to evaluate a stimulus and its relevance to the agent's well-being (analogous to OCC local variables.

Arousal: Measure of the degree of excitation in an agent, generally reflects autonomic nervous system activity, and speed and intensity of processing.

Components (of Emotion): In componential theories of emotion (e.g., Scherer), the individual modalities comprising an emotion; in cognitive appraisal, components can refer to the individual appraisal variables.

Concerns: "motivating dispositions" (Frijda, 1986) of an agent; its goals, needs, likes/dislikes.

Core Affect: "Neurophysiological state consciously accessible...blend of hedonic (valence) and arousal values" (Russell, 2003).

Dominance (vs. Submissiveness): Attitude of agent toward the world and other agents.

Drive: Low-level concern, reflecting basic biological needs such as hunger, thirst, rest.

Emotion Consequents, Emotion Effects: Effects of emotions, both internal (perception, cognition) and external (expressions, specific action).

Emotion Elicitors, Emotion Triggers, Emotion Antecedents: Situation, event or object that triggers an emotion.

Global Variables: In OCC theory: evaluative variables applicable to all emotions and influencing intensity, includes physiological arousal.

Goal – Generic: "A desired state of affairs that, should it obtain, would be assessed as somehow beneficial to the agent" (Elliot, 1992).

Goal – OCC Theory: Agent's concerns that are impacted by events (vs. acts by other agents or attributes of objects).

Local Variables, Emotion Eliciting Conditions: In OCC theory: evaluative criteria used by appraisal processes (e.g., desirability, praiseworthiness, attractiveness). Different emotions associated with different local variables (analogous to appraisal variables).

Mental Domain: Internal, mental representations necessary to mediate appraisal, such as goals and expectations.

Object Domain: Domain within which the agent exists, and where emotion-eliciting triggers occur; by definition domain-specific (Elliot, 1992).

PAD: Pleasure, Arousal, Valence (used in dimensional theories of emotion to characterize the emotion space).

Stimulus Evaluation Checks, Appraisal Detectors: Processes calculating the values of appraisal variables: stimulus evaluation checks (Scherer); appraisal detectors (Smith & Kirby, 2000).

Valenced Reaction: An affective reaction resulting from a appraisal / construal.

Valence, Pleasure: Measure of the degree of desirability (of a stimulus) (positive vs. negative).

Table 19. Example of a frame representing an emotion instance

Attribute	Content	Example
Affective State type	{affect, emotion, mood, attitude}	Emotion
Valence	Some value between –n and +n, where n is typically 1	1
Emotion type	Name of emotion	Joy
Intensity / Activation Level	Some value between 0 and n, where n is typically 1	.5
Underlying dimensions, if dim model used (PA or PAD)	{Arousal, Valence, Dominance}, represented by values between –n and +n, where n is typically 1	(.5,-1,0)
Underlying appraisal variables, if componential model used	List of specific appraisal variables and their values	Novelty = 1 Goal congruence = high Etc.
Time when first created	T where t > 0	3
Current time	$T_{current}$, where $T_{current} >= T$	
Duration / Decay function	Specific decay function for this emotion type	2 minutes / Exponential
Eliciting Triggers (may be further categorized into types, as per OCC theory)	Pointers to structures containing list of triggers (e.g., events)	e.g., Event_12; Situation_5
Affected goals/concerns (internal evaluative criteria) (may be further categorized into types, as per OCC theory; e.g., goals, standards, preferences)	Pointers to structures containing list of goals/concerns	e.g., Goal_22; Behavioral_Norm_42
Direction / Target of emotion-triggered behavior	List of agents (including self) and objects	Agent_007

Chapter 2
Could Emotions Be Modelled through Information Processing?

Ebrahim Oshni Alvandi
Monash University, Australia

ABSTRACT

One way to evaluate cognitive processes in living or nonliving systems is by using the notion of "information processing". Emotions as cognitive processes orient human beings to recognize, express and display themselves or their wellbeing through dynamical and adaptive form of information processing. In addition, humans behave or act emotionally in an embodied environment. The brain embeds symbols, meaning and purposes for emotions as well. So any model of natural or autonomous emotional agents/ systems needs to consider the embodied features of emotions that are processed in an informational channel of the brain or a processing system. This analytical and explanatory study described in this chapter uses the pragmatic notion of information to develop a theoretical model for emotions that attempts to synthesize some essential aspects of human emotional processing. The model holds context-sensitive and purpose-based features of emotional pattering in the brain. The role of memory is discussed and an idea of control parameters that have roles in processing environmental variables in emotional patterning is introduced.

1. INTRODUCTION

There is currently a large focus on unpacking the states of human mindful actions, behaviors, and cognitive processes known as mental states. Scientists and philosophers have long been engaged in debates about the fundamental questions regarding the nature of these mental states (Frijda, 1986; Gonz, 2013; Solomon, 1993; Zeki & Romaya, 2008). Additionally, the illusionary idea of emotional artificial systems stimulates the curiosity to dominate emotional states in artifacts as well; there is ample practical and theoretical research with engineering interests which pursue modeling concerns in artificial agents (Barriga, Rodríguez, Ramos, & Ramos, 2013; Camurri & Coglio, 1998; Ortony, 2002; Reilly & Bates, 1992; Velásquez, 1997)

DOI: 10.4018/978-1-4666-7278-9.ch002

Debates about the nature of mental states continue, it is necessary to choose a theory (or theories) regarding the nature of mental states in terms of the ontology and epistemology of emotions. Emotional states, however, have no precise and undisputed definition, neither of basic emotions (such as sadness) nor of more complicated emotions (such as embarrassment). In practice, emotions are mostly clarified by their characteristics, so "states of mind" or "mental states" are considered something like desire, fear, sadness, embarrassment, jealousy, pride, calm, and pain.

Modifying the cognitive processing of emotions provides an additional way to depict the senses of emotions and emotional rationality rather than the classic computational approach (Li, Ashkanasy, & Ahlstrom, 2013). A computational approach sees emotions as functions, but the cognitive view opens a broad research window for dynamic modeling and artificial architecturing of emotions (Camurri & Coglio, 1998; Lungu, 2013). By explaining the modality of emotional processes in brain, neuroscientists, cognitive scientists and philosophers have an opportunity to improve their understanding of the relational functions of emotions, social activities and the related brain areas(Ghashghaei, Hilgetag, & Barbas, 2007; Strand, Oram, & Hammar, 2013). Additionally, knowing the mechanism(s) of emotions can provide model (s) to understand or manage emotions, particularly those of emotional systems which can be adapted by various task domains. Besides, we can, cognitively and clinically, deal well with emotional disorders such as phobias and schizophrenia (Strand et al., 2013).

One of the hypotheses to evaluate the cognitive processes in living or nonliving systems is based on the notion of "information processing" even though many reject the relation between information processing and cognition(Edelman, 1992; Freeman, 2000; Globus, 1992; Perkel, 1993; Port & Van Gelder, 1995; Spivey, 2007; Wallace, 2007). We know that information is a tool (Thellefsen, Thellefsen, & Sørensen, 2013) and not a measuring process. Information is an objective entity because it is handled by information systems and relates to work tasks, or to domains. Informational approach to describe things (e.g. a picture, an organization or emotions) will solve disproportion of debates on the physical or cognitive inquires of things.

To elaborate this idea, this paper will explore the nature of emotions and types of information processing. Then an information-driven theory of emotional processing targeting artificial systems or agents is presented. Additionally, the paper presents and discusses the dominant theories of emotions in Section 2. Concepts of information processing (section 3) discuss three types of notions on information processing. Section 4 studies the emotional processing mechanism in humans and attempts to define an emotional-driven approach for artificial systems built upon the pragmatic notion of information processing.

1.1 Nature of Emotions

Mental states like fear, jealousy, envy, anger, grief, indignation, enjoyment, and embarrassment are typically classified under a title called "Emotion[1]". Emotions, as well as other mental states, are generated in living animals under the effects of environmental events; they make living animals react to events. Sometimes emotions are seen as causes of some other actions and behaviors. They may make beliefs and desires for a person by motivating an individual, by the concerns and attentions towards something or events, and by effects of experiences saved in one's memory. An individual may form a belief because an emotion may raise an event which has been experienced at the moment or be recalled from his memory. In addition, emotions correlate with brain states and could be conscious or unconscious (Kassam, Markey, Cherkassky, Loewenstein, & Just, 2013; Tsuchiya & Adolphs, 2007).

Historical definitions are generally surrounded by dualist[2] and monist[3] views influenced by behaviorism[4]. Hume focuses on "agency" in emotions and Spinoza thinks emotions are bodily changes with significance on our actions (De Sousa, 2012). In contrast, Descartes (1989) says we need to distinguish the functions of emotion from the body to understand what they are.

In recent definitions we face emotions which are considered as psychological states or processes. Emotions have functions which manage goals of a human being (Wilson & Keil, 1999). Some others think that emotions are psychophysiological response(Watson, Clark, & Harkness, 1994) and are inferred complex sequence of reactions to a stimulus (Plutchik, 1982) requiring cognitive evaluations.

The James-Lange and the Cannon-Bard theories of emotion are *physical theories* that claim emotions are caused by changes in physiological conditions relating to autonomic and motor functions. According to the James-Lange theory, emotions are the labels we give to the way the body reacts to certain situations based on the needs, goals, values and concerns. Additionally, the *feeling aspect* of an emotion is the perception of the body's actions and physiological arousal of the situations. The James-Lange theory considers and generates emotions mechanically, stating that only physiology causes emotions. Emotion in this thought is a communication language of the brain with neurochemical and physiological basics in addition to limbic system which is the central functioning Headquarters of emotional language. There is no rationality in James-Lange theory. While the Cannon-Bard theory believes that an emotion is the result of one's perception of their reaction or "bodily change". This theory steps a little forward giving importance to appraisal to evaluate the events and situations.

The Schechter-Singer Theory, as an outstanding *cognitive theory of emotions*, says that physiology is a necessary condition of emotions, but not enough. Emotions *have* cognitive appraisal aspects and cognitive processes, such as learning and thinking. Due to cognitive theories, however, the difference between emotions is in their cognitive appraisal aspects. This means emotions relate to the events in the world and are functions of a person or an agent who accomplishes cognitive appraisal of the stimuli. Thus, cognitive experience of an emotion is independent of physiology even though the cognitive experience occurs at the same time as an action.

Interestingly, a Pierceian sees an emotion of the mind as a real thing that is present in the mind, whether a person is distinctly conscious of it or not. According to Pierce, emotions are not external things. His reason is that although emotion does not depend on what we think about it, it does depend upon our state of our thought about something. Therefore, *to experience an emotion*, an agent ought to have physiological processes, or perceptions of physiological processes, or neuropsychological states. He shall need adaptive dispositions, or evaluative judgments, or, social facts. Computational states and dynamical processes are other requirements. Whereas *having an emotion* is both a mental and physiological state associated with a wide variety of feelings, thoughts, and behavior. Comprehensively, cognitive approaches not only are attentive to body-based and physiological attitudes but also are sensitive to cognitive properties of mental states. That is emotional states have causes for activation, they are structured by components through a processes of learning, and they present functions or have consequences.

1.2 Types of Emotions

Notably, primary emotions (e.g. happy and sad) are innate, pre-organized, and relatively inflexible responses to certain combinations of stimuli in situations. They are the sorts of emotions described functionally where certain classes of events (e.g. the loss of a family member or being attacked by a wild animal) are likely to be linked with specific emotions and with their associated motivational tendencies. Primary emotions are our first direct response to a situation. These are instinctive responses without going through *the thinking process* (Ng, 2009, p. 109).

On the contrary, secondary emotions (e.g. embarrassment and shame) need a thinking process. These kinds of emotions involve more thought and interpretation. Secondary emotions can be followed by primary emotions as well, but they are responses to someone's thoughts rather than direct response to situations. For instance, while a child fears something, putting it into the thinking process, he will have pain and would cry likely.

Finally, "Background emotions", are the emotional resting states or homeostasis (Ng, 2009, p. 109). Homeostasis is an ability to coordinated and regulate physiological reactions to ensure a body's stability in response to fluctuations in the outside environment and the weather (Cannon, 1927; Homma & Masaoka, 2008). Homeostasis is so peculiar to the living organism(Billman, 2013). Therefore "Profiles of the internal milieu and viscera play the lead part in background emotions" (Antonio Damasio, 1999, p. 53) and a change in internal milieu immediately make a man aware of the change; the change make a person to have primarily and then secondary emotions. These types of emotions are the result of only physical changes in the agents.

2. INFORMATION PROCESSING

Evidently, it is not easy to understand a society or world unless we understand its way of dealing with information. Space, time, matter and order (MacFarlane, 2003) describe the world by two parallel properties which one may call *pattern* and *process*. A pattern characterizes order as it manifests itself in terms of invariance under transformations of matter in space. A process

characterizes order as it manifests itself in terms of invariance under transformations of matter in time (MacFarlane, 2003, pp. 1583-1584). In our interactions with the world, we have to deal also with two types of entities that behave in very different ways. One kind is essentially passive (nonliving), for example, a stone. Another kind is essentially active (living), for example, a bee. "Objects" and "agents" are alternatives, respectively, to emerge passive and active entities into the world.

Obviously, grasp of pattern arises from an experience of the world as passively sensed. That is, human beings learn to recognize shapes in space and their combinations into patterns. For example we experience a red apple patterned in different shapes, colors. Our tactile sensations grasp the apple in learning process as actively experience. Patterning process reasonably links involved components of the apple rhythmically and with laws but it is not as a conscious activity; the brain processes the linking subconsciously even though regulating the connections of units (including matters and colors) might not be explained lightly (see these references that try to explain the regulating process via the neural connections: (Braitenberg & Schüz, 1998; Izhikevich, 2003)).

Pattern and process, *taken together*, characterize generally the order in the world and agents learn to recognize them. Simply talking, active agents with natural or artificial biology may recognize objects by means of patterns. They would do recognition through classifications, similarities, features, and principles of objects. Process may thus be analyzed for physical systems in terms of conservation principles, of which the most important is the conservation of energy. Therefore, a behavior in an object is triggered by the physical trade including the flow, transformation and storage of energy; whereas in agents it is more sophisticated.

Energy would not flow if there is no interaction between objects. The *interaction* of agents and objects either by the world or themselves can also coincide. Whatever the form of the coincidence is, the concept of information will be woven to the interaction and agency. MacFarlane (2003) states that "Information *is the currency of agency. It is a pattern, physically instantiated in matter or energy that corresponds to events in the world."[5]* (p.1584). Information is not only a tool, but also what we use to represent the order of the world in the framework of representation. In other words, to represent the order of the world, we need *energy* which is prescriptive of the order and information is a descriptive characteristic of that order. In other words "energy" is the currency of interaction among objects which is done in the framework of event; it is real and measures the process. While "information" is the currency of interaction among agents which is done in the representational framework and measures pattern; it is considered virtual. So an agent can use information to control energy and so to manipulate order in the world (ibid).

Weizsäcker and von Weizsäcker (1985) defines information as: "Information is only which is *understood*." (p. 351). According to him, understanding is generally defined as the impact upon a receiving system or a recipient, which alters its behavior or structure and is "possible only in sufficiently large composite systems." (ibid, p.355). Understanding information by virtue of this definition can be considered and seems much like an "order" divided into and studied with three notions called *syntactic, semantic* and *pragmatic*.

The first notion of information, syntactic concept of information, is just concerned with the accuracy of the transmitted symbols in the process of communication. According to Shannon's theory a message of communication is coded in the minimum expected number of bits of known characteristics and transmitted via error-free channels, but this notion does not consider the meaning of a passage, a picture, or a behavior for "semantic aspects of communication are irrelevant to the engineering problem" (Shannon, 2001: published in 1948).

The second notion of information, semantic concept of information, comprises theories about signs and what they stand for (Maleeh, 2008). This approach unlike the previous one is relating to the meaning and truth. That is, it is the relation(s) between signs and objects or signs and behavior. Semantics can be considered as the study of the link between symbols and their referents or concepts; particularly the way in which signs relate to human behavior. We call the thing (s) as information, for this purpose, in which there is/are well-formed data. Well-formed data means data that are clustered together correctly according to the syntactic rules. Factual and true[6] clustered data fulfills philosophical semantic interpretation of clustered data through specific rules (syntax). Data, in its well-formed meaning for information or individually, is an entity with which all the knowledge is constructed.[7]

Floridi (2013) cites that it is not necessary for environmental information to be *natural*; There is a claim that photocell uses environmental information practically to do photosynthesis even in the absence of semantic processes and meaningful data; that is environmental information may involve no meaning and require no semantics at all. Dretske (1981), in contrast, thinks data can have their own meaning independently of an intelligent (i.e. producer and informer); it is *also* called environmental information. However, it is crucial and a must to underline the context in which flow of environmental information are paraphrased. Suppose an environment in which a dog is barking. The dog and its voice perhaps have functions and even may carry meaning independent of an intelligent agent, but the well-formed data of this information can be paraphrased only in a context that an active agent interacts with. By context, the interrelated condition in which something exists or occurs is meant.[8] This is an intelligent agent who/which enjoys or rejects the dog's performance; this evaluation or giving a meaning to a behavior be acted in the context.

Existing or occurring things can include intelligent agents, and non intelligent agents; but at least this is an "intelligence"[9] which interprets and gives a meaning (true or false) to the components. Babies, for instance, cry in the dark, they may yield in the presence of a known or unknown man or in a dangerous position, and when they are thirsty we may see them crying, but the fact is that the *agent* (baby himself and another one) regarding to the in-step context interprets or gives meaning to the baby's performance naming that as fear, happiness, embarrassment. In fact, emotions to be detected, recognized or expressed are context dependent (Palm & Glodek, 2013).

In summary, semantic notions of information defines "environmental information" independent of *agency*. That is why there is no meaning with the environmental information. While "environment" gets significance by agency in the information processing, significance may not mean the meaning. An emotion may signify an event (e.g. seeing just a colour) but may mean nothing in the context. Meaning can have an individual denotation more than a general definition; the individual denotation depends on the agents (receiver and sender) and the function of environmental information through the purpose assessment. For example, suppose a child in a two environmental information and context: first scenario starts for the child when he breaks neighbor's glass and the second scenario is breaking a glass of an old abandoned house. What makes him to have embarrassment and fear about the former scenario operates a functional role. Damage to another person's property and coming punishments could be such kind of functional roles of environmental information. In the latter, although, there is agency, the second environmental information does not make him to fear or embarrass.

Unlike semantics, in pragmatic notions of information not only the informee but also the informer and receiver are in the central point of view. This means the agency and agents become the central part of the events. Thus, living systems need

emotional agency to gain and convey emotional information. The meaning of a message depending on the receiver's individual requirements and disposition will be studied as a central point in the next part of this paper. The information contents of a message (e.g. emotions) cannot be determined "absolutely" – regarding only the message itself – but requires an analysis comprehending the receiver's previous understanding and her/his interests are demanded as well.

Pragmatics concerns the purpose of communication. This aspect of information mainly depends on the context (Burell, 2004). Pragmatics links the issue of communicating signs with the context.[10] Context can be a natural location, artificial environment or the medium that communication is acted. It could be constructed via textual, audial, visual features. Additionally, pragmatic information is considered by either physical or phenomenal aspects (Maleeh, 2008) that could be interacted; the senders and receivers of communications interact with each other by flowing information. So Roederer (2005) introduces two types of interactions: physical *interactions* and *information-driven* interactions (p.5).

Physical interactions occur usually in the natural inanimate systems, while information-driven interactions occur in the living systems. Of course, nonliving (non-animate) systems might have no physical interactions. It means nonliving systems can be information-based but not by the interpretation of pragmatic notion. They can have information-based interactions by the semantic interpretation. Interactions of nonliving systems occur between the events of the world and relations between signs and objects. On the contrary, living systems – apart from their complexity- have pragmatic and cognitive processes. Some of nonliving systems such as crystals can interact with, grow in and adapt to their environment through information but they are not able to learn, compare and reason about the information and environment in both direct and reverse direction. While a living system is able to manipulate the information by cognitive activities; a man is able to learn not only secondary emotions but also control them by learning their results, reactions and positive/negative effects. Notably, receivers *learn* to *recognize* cause and effect of an event or an object.

2.1 Informational Interaction Principles and the Model

A physical interaction is sensitive to initial conditions of an event. "Initial conditions" such as the initial configuration (e.g. positions and velocities) of the interacting bodies have considerable roles in modeling (natural or artificial) processes. During the interaction there is a direct transfer of energy from one body to the other, or to and from the *interaction mechanism* itself (Roederer, 2003, p. 6).

Nevertheless, how can an active entity i.e. an agent distinguish information to control energy? The simple and naïve answer is that an agent uses information via the currency of data. Data flows through transforming channels with some mechanisms. Interactions of data produce variables such as mutations, integrations, reflections, and transmissions. So recognition is then by means of owning or feeling these variables where the behaviors of the agent can be translated by the variances of the variables over/in his sensorimotors.

The difference of the second aspect of interactions i.e. the information-driven with the physical interaction lays on some other concepts such as *"meaning"*, *"purpose"* and *"complexity"*. These concepts describe no syntactic but semantic and cognitive features. According to (Roederer, 2003, p. 117), "purpose" means that in a system which includes a pattern, A, and system, B, pattern A will have a "purpose" where its presence triggers a change in system B so that such a change would not happen if pattern A were not present, or would happen just by chance. Then if there is a correspondence between pattern A and system B in a way that the presence of pattern A makes same repeatable change in system B, we say the purpose of pattern A has a "meaning" for system B

(Maleeh, 2008, p. 88). In general, when a pattern is the trigger of an information-driven interaction, we say that the corresponding pragmatic information is *encoded* in that pattern or *expressed* in it, or *represented* by it (Roederer, 2005, p. 127).

A same repeatable change or reflection in system B needs a process that saves the first-occurred change and refection as a base for the future use; it is supposed as our "prior knowledge" in the same breath. The first-occurred change (to make a pattern) is done through temporal and spatial features. It depicts a process and a pattern which is emerged of a dyadic relation between agency-objects and information-energy. It is important to take into account that energy is distributed in the whole of the interaction mechanism.

The mechanism to save the temporal and spatial features for information-based interaction, considering decupled energywise (meaning that the energy needed to effect the changes in the system B must come from some external source) and being repeatable, is called "common code". It is a term for a memory device warranting the sender's purpose to have meaning for the receiver (Maleeh, 2008). Figure 1 shows the process of information-based interaction schematically.

The issue is highlighted when a pattern is encode and stored in memory device. Codes would be *mapped* by the primitive patterns. That is future patterns could be as same as previous patterns or completely be different or could have some features in common. Therefore, if an encoded pattern triggering a purpose in system streams exactly the same codes, then the process will continue as a birth pattern and the same behaviors will be played, but if they have only common feature with each other, a mapping or in literally a translation will take place and likely different behaviors, purposes and meaning could occur.

Marvin Minsky in his notion of "proto-specialist" states that "… our earliest emotions are built-in processes in which inborn proto-specialists control what happens in our brains. Soon we learn to overrule those schemes, as our surroundings

Figure 1. The Schematic of pragmatic notion of Information processing

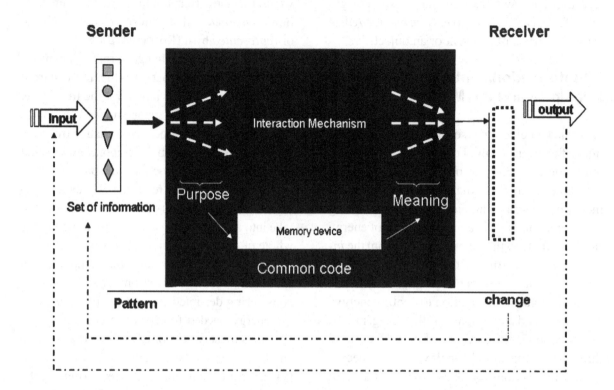

teach us what we ought to feel." (Minsky, 1987, p. 172). Proto-specialist is one of the genetically constructed subsystems responsible for some of an animal's "instinctive" behavior. According to this idea, large portions of our minds start out as almost separate proto-specialists, and we interpret their activity as manifesting different and primitive emotions.

Just as agencies become more interconnected and learn to exploit one another, so patterns and their differences grow less distinct.[11] In Minsky's word (1987): "Each "proto-specialists." has a separate mini-mind to do its job and is equipped with special sensors and effectors designed to suit its specific needs..... even though (proto-specialists) initial goals are entirely different, all those different proto-specialists will end up needing to solve the same sorts of "subproblems"-such as finding ways around obstacles and deciding how

to conserve limited resources (p. 165). Observing, gathering and comparing the features of a pattern are the responsibility of a sub-device named "feature detector" [12] mounted in the memory device. All of these are done during interaction process (Roederer, 2005).

Briefly, pragmatic information including indexical information (i.e. indexes for speaker, hearer, time and location of communicated information), is not about the sign. It is about the relation between the user of the sign and the act of using the sign. It means that an agent and agency are important in the interpretation of indexical information. It is cognitive activities of an agent (such as learning) which turn possible signs for occurrence of emotion into information; otherwise signs are merely law data.

First and foremost, pragmatics information is information about mental models: speaker's and addressee's mental models of each other (Green, 2000). In addition, mental image (such as sadness) is made by a construction of a pattern through a specific procedure with which "an agent (s)" and then "flow of energy" are crucial factors in. Information, captured by the environment, regularized as a factual semantic and valued by the pragmatic notions will become mental image whenever and wherever it is patterned purposefully in order to change the states for first order (such as survival) and second orders purposes (such as problem solving).

3. EMOTIONAL PROCESSING SYSTEM

One of the six aspects mental states is that emotions are about the objects in the world.[13] 'About' in this phrase should not be mistaken by the idea of aboutness in philosophy. Aboutess or intentionality describes behaviors not physically but that a behavior is *as if attitude* towards something. Alternatively we adopt *about* simply as a naming process for an object. For instance, objects in the world can be different entities such as a person, a place, a melody, a stomachache or a state of embarrassment which they are things named differently in different natural languages. In the same vain, mental states and emotions are called simply objects since they have names.

On the other hand, a metaphor of the concept of matter by David Hume is called 'the cement of the universe' (Mackie, 1974). Similarly, the cement of the brain is white and gray matter in the brain (O'Brien & Sampson, 1965) with topological features. It is patterned with dynamical and accidental distribution of data. Thus, an implication potentially usable in emotional states is to describe emotion as objects that are processed by patterns. That is an emotional state is molded under transformations of matter toward space and time with physical, geometrical and biological features.

Notably, an animate system stands in the nature and tries to investigate around of itself for different purposes by scanning physical information of ambient and objects. In the model of human information-processing system, environmental information acquired through our senses. The agent processes the physical information by its sensing devices (e.g., eyes, ears, skin, antenna, or olfactory apparatus). For instance, if a man wants to pass a zebra crossing, a bunch of visual data will trigger on him in the form of light and sound waves. He would scan and detect them via sensing devices, so he would discover shapes, directions and colours of every object. Whereas a social agent needs to scan another type of information called as *cognitive* information for any social and emotional purposes as well.

Cognitive information is declarative, procedural and conditional knowledge that are stored in the memory device of brain heading social activities. Cognitive information arguably is produced by social interactions. The interaction is described in terms of flow of energy during the process of agency through patterns or procedures. For example fear is the result of an interaction between an agent and internal or external environment. The physical world and biophysics of an agent's brain in response change operation via energy flow. Therefore, every emotional pattern in the brain needs the currency of interaction of environmental and social data. That is an agent has to be in informational position to represent a mental state.

However, physical interaction is not the main subject of emotional processing. In effect, emotions are not considered like the interactions of billiard balls which can be measured by Hamiltonian mechanics. Emotions are not merely the interactions of instructional or true/untrue factual information; they, by the presence of an agent or at least a kind of agency, usually have meaning and purpose. For instance, "fear" is not only the physical interaction of a living either with living or nonliving systems. It cannot be interpreted statistically. Fear calls for agency, meaning and purpose in the place of the event.

In studying emotions, we need to consider not only the quantity (average of symbols) but also quality of them as well. Because, according to cognitive theories, we know that cognitive tasks have importance in emotions. There is a cognitive agency in the appraisal of events/emotions and there is no merely a flow of quantity (e.g. average of electromagnetic signals or chemical bundles) in occurrence of emotions. Arnold and Gasson (1954), a proponent of cognitive approach, proposes that emotions are rational and related to selves; emotions include physiological substrates and also are related to the events in the worlds.

In other words, emotions are functions of one's cognitive appraisal of the stimuli or situations. Due to Sloman (2011), the Shannon measure indicates how many different instructions can be accommodated in fixed bit length, but says nothing about what particular action or process is specified by the instruction. Thus, if we want to speak of emotions, this notion won't be a convenient one for emotional states because they depend not only on the content of the bit-string but also what is in the words of interpreter. Emotions, happening in an agent, carry meanings in regard to different situations and conditions. Their meaning changes due to informational statues scanned by an agent.

On the other hand, semantic concept of information would carry emotional states (such as embarracment) by signs. It would translate emotions conjoing bodily change (e.g. red face) and would intrepete the signs with their concepts (regretfulness). For instance, by having the expression "He fears", me as a receiver confront with untrue factual semantic information that is neither novelty nor confirmation[14] of my information of "fear". "He fears" is a communicating message by virtue of signs that the information is merely cover the word "He" and "fears"; simultaneously it has an information content relating to the knowledge gained previously or at the moment. It means that

a set of information (*He fear*) is just untrue factual semantic information - not the knowledge[15].

If emotional signs are not knowledge, does that mean that all or some of emotions would be interpreted just as practical informational response with no meaning, even though we know that data form the world has a leading role in functional sight of emotions and it is supposed that every emotion reserves its unique semantic referring to same informational patterning? To answer this question more firmly would, however, require more specific screening.

At this point, drawing conclusions from the information at hand, the only hypothesize is due to pragmatic notion of information that meaning is the change in patterns. In this phase of information processing, purposes (e.g., in the example of zebra lines, the rules for passing the road will be created or activated in the memory) are produced as well. In fact, second group of information i.e. cognitive information is created when data traverse the memory device and enveloped as patterns. Any changes in the patterns or activation of patterns in memory device would signify a value of a (positive, negative or neutral) meaning for the system. For example, "fear", which has been categorized in the primary or universal emotions by Damasio (Antonio Damasio, 1999, pp. 35-82) can be imagined as a cognitive pattern in (any open systems[16] such as) a baby. According to the proposal, the appearance of the pattern of "fear" to a baby is the birth of temporal and spatial point (i.e. the first time he was experiencing "fear" and the environment he was in). He does not have any prior knowledge of this mental state then, but the only thing which he (as a living system) could have is an evolutionary knowledge[17]. So encountering with an unfamiliar event or entity which may threatens a living system would make some *changes* in the receiver to be *survived* or a thinking process might create a change to *solve a problem*.

To underline the idea, meanings are explained by virtue of changes, but are they just behavior that an individual may experience? Initially, it is better me make clear that "output" is different than "change" in the present proposal. Change is a type of variation in the receiver occurred both physically (biologically) in brain and in the pragmatic process of the mental sates. While output resulting from the changes, simultaneously enters as feedback to the process and has impacts on the changes; in short, output is shown *behaviorally*. For instance, to scrutinize "fear" as a change by the information based interaction, we ought to consider not only pattern, meaning, purpose but also (physical) variations; whereas "fear" as output is a response which can be searched as a behavior arisen through stimuli (inputs).

Patterns, therefore, are capable to find meaning via referential process towards other patterns of events, agents or objects (Ortony, 1990). In the birth of an emotion, primary processes including stimuli and initial conditions should flow over environmental information. For example if the pattern of fear of a heater has some common features with the pattern of fear of a chimney, their patterns will be mapped like an image to trigger the purpose. The supposed event is a physical interaction between an object and an agent (e.g. a heater and a baby: touching a hot heater by an infant) that forms a pattern. It is shown that emotional memories are formed by *emotional schemes,* internally organized by neural networks (Oatley, 1992). These schemas are means that an agent's neural network forms in a learning process that enable people to behave with them to different appraisal situations.

The study of morphology of patterning process in cognitive systems is a silent inquiry but far from this scope. In short, brain and neural system has a remarkable plasticity and studies show that topographical organization of neurons and their connective variability in the brain provides the information about the circuit's functional architecture (Miri et al., 2011). This dynamical and topological architecture provides information of interaction among layers of units that are con-

nected and transmit information with each other. In parallel to explicit model of cognitive resources, such as working memory, sensory memory, declarative memory and procedural memory, *emotional memory* is a cognitive apparatus to save the emotional information (LaBar & Cabeza, 2006; LeDoux, 2007). Emotional pattering process is sensed and stored data in this memory, but patterns are not necessarily considered isomorphic. Patterns can be formed at microgenetical level with holonomic connections of its units (e.g. neurons in the brain). Standing on the notion by Díaz (1997), cognitive information can be coded in units constrained by time variable and deemed through activates of separated units assembled spatially but functionally bound.

3.1 Feature Detectors

In synthesizing emotional patterns for a system, rather than thinking only in evolutionary or biophysical structures, some elements such as events, environment and culture enact highly differentiated impacts to bind emotional schemes via learning and experiencing burnt in the emotional memory. Those of memory detectors in emotional memory device which have tenure of emotional states analyze data and refine them to burn or reactive a pattern. A memory of an emotional pattern or a reminder of that would simulate an emotional response versus situations. Thus, to understand how the transitions can happen in cognitive information processing, we have to deal with "feature detectors" that can control emotional parameters or control the different ways a system is coupled to its environment and affected by it for emotional arousal (See Figure 2).

The first group of emotional control parameters would be very basic parameters (like temperature, pressure, distance, velocity, intensity, frequency, frequency perturbation) and physical features (such as dimension, and time). These parameters could comprise a threshold and covariate with patterns of primary emotions. During the infor-

Figure 2. An emotional memory device evaluates information processed from environment and maps them out with stored emotional patterns

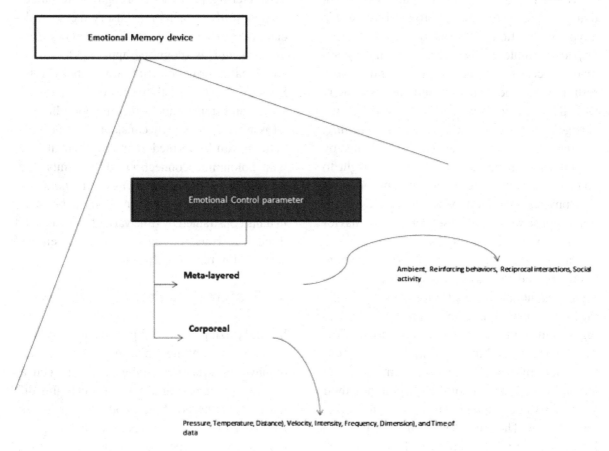

mation flow, if the collection of data fits with patterns in stock and if passing energy is more than the threshold, alarm signals then would be transmitted to emotional center (e.g., amygdala and frontal lobe in human brain) and then will be transmitted to related sensorimotors to avoid or encourage behaviors and reflections in terms of the changes. These types of parameters associate with the very basic physical data that cumulatively evaluate and distinguish patterning values. They could arithmetically correlate with the bunch of their agglomerated units which purposefully is coded as an emotional pattern. These patterns will be reactivated when variables reprocessed from the environment. A reactivation of the pattern can re-stimulate the energy flow in patterns and then whirl to sensorimotors. We call them "corporeal parameters". Note that we took for granted that human beings have been evolutionary wired for a strong feeling of survival, so to speak, the purpose of natural living systems is to save their body and the system. Thus, corporeal control parameters are developed to analyses inputs on the purpose of survival. Any artificial systems might require be coding with this central definition and providing with these types of parameters. Notably, patterning and layering activity occur in the learning process. Thus, corporeal control parameters converge with properties created in social experiences of the system.

Somatic feedback theories (Antonio Damasio, 2001, 2005; James, 1884; J. Prinz, 2004; J. J.

Prinz, 2004) suggest that brain responses due to the generation of bodily action/reactions (e.g. a change in heart rate, blood pressure, and facial expression). This means that related body activities are registered to mind to recognize mental states such as emotions. But unlike James' theory that a bodily response causes an emotion, cognitive interventions along with bodily feedback can activate emotion as well. Ambient information, reinforcing emotional behaviors and reciprocal emotional interactions will likely vary through meta-layered parameters. Therefore, informational approach to emotion for systems has a sense of development considering the changes in the informational parameters and patterns which may be triggered via body changes, feedbacks and cognitive interactions. Some believe that emotions are internal entities and information is an external thing, so the only way of bridging this gap in an agent is cognition through inferential process which comes from the meaning-creation process (Thellefsen et al., 2013).

According to Roederer (2005, pp. 200-207), fundamental operation of brain in information processing can be counted as below:

The brain works on the basis of information encoded in the form of the distribution in space and time of electrical neural impulses. Distribution of each neural activity is unique in its overall purpose and represents one unique state of the system. Thus, all the concepts of emotional pattern and procedure can be seen implicitly during the physiological information processing. Neural networks deals with pattern recognition considering the concept of the purpose (e.g., survival, avoid an injury, or reflexive action). Pattern recognition as a fundamental process operating at the early stages of a sensory system is an elicitation of a unique response whenever a specific pattern is present among a complex or noisy input.

Antonio Damasio (2005, pp. 79-82) states that *"Body loop"* as one of the body sate changes[18]

uses both humoral signals (chemical messages conveyed via the bloodstream) and neural signals (electrochemical messages conveyed via nerve pathways). That is via the *body loop*, the internal emotional state leads to a changed state of the body, which subsequently, after sensing, is represented in somatosensory structures of the central nervous system. In the second type of body state changes, *"as if body loop"*, the representation of body-related changes is created directly in sensory body maps, under the control of other neural sites, for instance, the prefrontal cortices. It means that via the *as if body loop*, the state of the body is not changed. Instead, on the basis of the internal emotional state, a changed representation of the body is created directly in sensory body maps.

Consequently, the organism experiences the same feeling as if via the body loop: it is 'as if' the body had really been changed but it was not (ibid); a system can simulate the same thing. Damasio, in contrast, thinks that cognitive changes are no less interesting since he thinks all of cognitive process such as playing, auditory and visual changes can be reduced to the *body state changes* of "body loop" or "as if body loop". But it is clear that information enters into the system through the sensory register, short-term memory, and long-term memory. This is the place that a cognitive interaction occurs. The short-term or *working memory* is dynamic and is represented dynamically in the form of neural activity kept in some "holding pattern" which has a storage lifetime of the order of tens of seconds. Long term or structural memory is the representation of synaptic architecture of neural network. Emotional memory is acquired through *learning experiences* and depicts cognitive changes in the agent.

The learning experience is done by "recall", a process done by emotional memory device and mantled feature detectors in it. This is a scaled pragmatic cognitive process[19]. For example, an *emotional memory recall* in the neural system consists of the re-elicitation or *replay* of that neural activity pattern which represents the recalled information.

Memory recall is specific to the object, event or concept that is being recalled (e.g. a birth-made pattern of fear) .The second and very basic brain operation, *associative recall,* is what *in* which a key pattern triggers the full pattern representing the recalled information. *Autoassociative recall* is the third one with which the "key" may be just a partial component of the full pattern done as an important operation in sensory perception. By the associative recall it seems that we are in "knowing"[20] situation even if our knowing is not true. Of course, information processing in brain can also transit from "not knowing" to "imagining" or can change from one to other (Roederer, 2005), a process which might not make an agent to know; he may just get "imagining".

In other words, an agent is able to distinguish the birth pattern of fear (e.g. fear of a dog) by a body loop and a complex level of fear (e.g. fear of loneliness) by as if body loop. Body state changes occur with an interaction with physical world (e.g. a dog) in a system or have a social interaction (loneliness), so the same or key weighted bunch of parameters are processed towards the controllers and activate the basic controllers and as if body changes activate meta-layered controllers. Working memory associatively recalls the same consonant parameters from long-terms memory. The recall can fully stimulate the secondary patterns of emotions. Autoassociative recalling evaluates parameters partially and selects the input-gates of parameters for more similar features. This could activate meta-layered patterns.

Nonetheless, when an individual imagines sadness, there appears a (complex) spatio-temporal distribution of neural activity in many regions of his brain and represents the cognition of "sadness"; it is his mental image – his neural correlate – of "sadness." It is his only; physically/physiologically it would be very different from the one that forms in my brain. But the pragmatic *information* it bears would be the same and the activated cerebral regions would be the same! (Roederer, 2005, p. 204). In other words "sadness" is your mental image and belongs to you, only in the physical structure of the parameters of the neural network. This fact produces dynamicity in understanding and forming the emotional concepts in different agents.

4. RECOMMENDATIONS

Although brains have difference topology of the place and the local positions of neurons and their spatial connections with each other can vary, there would not be any tremendous difference in the regions of constructed patterns. That is *the whole brain* must initially and practically be involved in every processing task to specialized regions which can react and engage in parallel processing tasks. Note that processing cannot go a prior to the specific processing center because the brain does not know initially what the information is.

As yet, there is a question among philosophers and the neuroscientists that how a specific spatio-temporal neural activity distribution elicited by the sight of an object or by listening to a given sound becomes a specific *mental image.* How visual, audial, haptical and biophysical data changes the emotional feelings, behaviors and thinking processes.

More research is needed to study the involvement of control parameters in emotional memory device for the purpose of patterning process and emotion activation. In addition, neuroscience and engineering part of the study have to define a ground for recognition of emotional patterns in the proposed informational approach, which can open new niche in architecturing of the model.

5. CONCLUSION

Information is what we use to understand and represent the world and interactions occurred in. Animate and non-animates, respectfully called agents and objects interact with the world. To describe systems involving both objects and agents and also orders of the world, we need to depict the currency of interaction among objects, and the currency of interaction among agents by patterns and processes.

A primary emotion is a product of an interaction of an agent (a baby) with environment (an agent or object). Secondary emotions are like primary ones. The difference of them with primary emotions is based on solving problems which are gained during the learning and other cognitive activities in order to get a proper supposed or determined status. The generation of secondary emotions considered as second ordered information-driven interaction. They need, in another word, thinking process to be generated. Emotional processing one of the basic cognitive processing systems is processed on the base of information-driven interaction.

Being derived from physical entities, emotions and mental states which as objects are ordered in patterns and process have bilateral interaction with the world and depend not only on the content of the bit-string (The Shannon's notion of information processing), its factuality and truth (The semantic notion of information) but also what is in the inter-preter. In pragmatic notion of information unlike semantic, not only informee but also informer and receiver are in the central point of view. It means the agency and agents become the central part of the emotional events. Unlike syntactic notion and semantic notion, context including environment plays critical role in emotional information pro-cessing. Agents have no only physical interaction. There is information-driven interaction (Roederer, 2005). Then if there is a correspondence between pattern A of an emotion and a pattern in system B in a way that the presence of pattern A makes same repeatable change in system B, we say the purpose of pattern A has a "meaning" for system B. So, a living system would be very reflexible and able to manipulate the emotional information; and living systems – apart from their complex-ity- could have pragmatic and cognitive process.

This manipulation of the emotional information is recorded in an emotional memory device for future use, evaluation and etc.

Information-driven interaction makes psycho-physiology of an agent or meta-physics of a system to be activated during the generation of emotion only because of survival of the agent or system. This is the change which is happening in an agent in a specific spatio-temporal neural pattern for future uses (as an emotional memory device). If the conditions of pattern occur, that emotion would be generated. Otherwise a new situation will be designed. The stages i.e. patterning process of emotions cognitive processed as facing with the new conditions and learning. Working emotional memory is responsible for scanning and exporting the signals for detected parameters. Controlling parameters sift the parameters with the rates re-corded in the long-term memory. Disparities with priori rates of parameters may lead to partially activation of an emotion pattern.

REFERENCES

Arnold, M. B., & Gasson, J. A. (1954). *The hu-man person: An approach to an integral theory of personality*. Ronald Press Co.

Barriga, S. D., Rodríguez, L.-F., Ramos, F., & Ramos, M. (2013). A computational model of emotional attention for autonomous agents. *Transactions on Computational Science, LNCS, 18*, 192–211.

Billman, G. E. (2013). Homeostasis: the dynamic self-regulatory process that maintains health and buffers against disease. In Handbook of systems and complexity in health (pp. 159–170). Springer.

Braitenberg, V., & Schüz, A. (1998). Cortical architectonics. In Cortex: Statistics and Geometry of Neuronal Connectivity (pp. 135–137). Springer.

Burell, M. (2004). Appraisal and information theory. *Comma, 2004*(1), 55-62.

Camurri, A., & Coglio, A. (1998). An architecture for emotional agents. *MultiMedia, IEEE, 5*(4), 24–33. doi:10.1109/93.735866

Cannon, W. B. (1927). The James-Lange theory of emotions: A critical examination and an alternative theory. *The American Journal of Psychology, 39*(1/4), 106–124. doi:10.2307/1415404 PMID:3322057

Damasio, A. (1999). *The feeling of what happens: Body and emotion in the making of consciousness* [eBook].

Damasio, A. (2001). Fundamental feelings. *Nature, 413*(6858), 781–781. doi:10.1038/35101669 PMID:11677584

Damasio, A. (2005). *Descartes' error: Emotion, reason, and the human brain*. Penguin. com.

De Sousa, R. (2012). *Emotion. Stanford Encyclopedia of Philosophy*. Retrieved from http://plato.stanford.edu/archives/spr2013/entries/emotion/

Descartes, R. (1989). *The passions of the soul*. Hackett Publishing.

Díaz, J. L. (1997). A patterned process approach to brain, consciousness, and behavior. *Philosophical Psychology, 10*(2), 179–195. doi:10.1080/09515089708573214

Dretske, F. (1981). *Knowledge & the flow of information*.

Edelman, G. M. (1992). *Bright air, brilliant fire: On the matter of the mind*. Basic books.

Floridi, L. (2013). *Semantic conceptions of information*. Retrieved from http://plato.stanford.edu/archives/spr2013/entries/information-semantic/

Freeman, W. J. (2000). *How brains make up their minds*. Columbia University Press.

Frijda, N. H. (1986). *The emotions*. Cambridge University Press.

Gernert, D. (2006). Pragmatic information: Historical exposition and general overview. *Mind and Matter, 4*(2), 141–167.

Ghashghaei, H., Hilgetag, C., & Barbas, H. (2007). Sequence of information processing for emotions based on the anatomic dialogue between prefrontal cortex and amygdala. *NeuroImage, 34*(3), 905–923. doi:10.1016/j.neuroimage.2006.09.046 PMID:17126037

Globus, G. G. (1992). Toward a noncomputational cognitive neuroscience. *Journal of Cognitive Neuroscience, 4*(4), 299–300. doi:10.1162/jocn.1992.4.4.299 PMID:23968124

Gonz, A. M. (2013). *The emotions and cultural analysis*. Ashgate Publishing.

Green, G. M. (2000). *The nature of pragmatic information. Grammatical Interfaces in HPSG*. Stanford: CSLI Publications.

Homma, I., & Masaoka, Y. (2008). Breathing rhythms and emotions. *Experimental Physiology, 93*(9), 1011–1021. doi:10.1113/expphysiol.2008.042424 PMID:18487316

Izhikevich, E. M. (2003). Simple model of spiking neurons. *Neural Networks. IEEE Transactions on, 14*(6), 1569–1572.

James, W. (1884). II. What is an emotion? *Mind, os-IX*(34), 188–205. doi:10.1093/mind/os-IX.34.188

Kassam, K. S., Markey, A. R., Cherkassky, V. L., Loewenstein, G., & Just, M. A. (2013). Identifying emotions on the basis of neural activation. *PLoS ONE, 8*(6), e66032. doi:10.1371/journal.pone.0066032 PMID:23840392

LaBar, K. S., & Cabeza, R. (2006). Cognitive neuroscience of emotional memory. *Nature Reviews. Neuroscience, 7*(1), 54–64. doi:10.1038/nrn1825 PMID:16371950

LeDoux, J. E. (2007). Emotional memory. *Scholarpedia, 2*(7), 1806. doi:10.4249/scholarpedia.1806

Li, Y., Ashkanasy, N. M., & Ahlstrom, D. (2013). The rationality of emotions: A hybrid process model of decision-making under uncertainty. *Asia Pacific Journal of Management*, 1–16.

Lungu, V. (2013). Artificial emotion simulation model and agent architecture: Extended. In *Advances in intelligent control systems and computer science* (pp. 207–221). Springer. doi:10.1007/978-3-642-32548-9_15

MacFarlane, A. G. (2003). Information, knowledge and the future of machines. *Philosophical Transactions of the Royal Society of London. Series A: Mathematical, Physical and Engineering Sciences, 361*(1809), 1581-1616.

Mackie, J. (1974). *The cement of the universe: a study of causation*. Oxford: Clarendon.

Maleeh, S. (2008). The conscious mind revisited (PhD thesis). University of Osnabrück, Germany.

Maslin, K. T., & Maslin, K. (2001). *An introduction to the philosophy of mind*. Polity Cambridge.

McNamara, C. (2005). *Field guide to consulting and organizational development: A collaborative and systems approach to performance, change and learning*. Authenticity Consulting.

Minsky, M. (1987). *Societies of mind*. New York, NY: Picador.

Miri, A., Daie, K., Arrenberg, A. B., Baier, H., Aksay, E., & Tank, D. W. (2011). Spatial gradients and multidimensional dynamics in a neural integrator circuit. *Nature Neuroscience, 14*(9), 1150–1159. doi:10.1038/nn.2888 PMID:21857656

Ng, G. W. (2009). *Brain-mind machinery: Brain-inspired computing and mind opening*. World Scientific. doi:10.1142/6704

O'Brien, J. S., & Sampson, E. L. (1965). Lipid composition of the normal human brain: Gray matter, white matter, and myelin. *Journal of Lipid Research, 6*(4), 537–544. PMID:5865382

Oatley, K. (1992). *Best laid schemes: The psychology of the emotions*. Cambridge University Press.

Ortony, A. (1990). *The cognitive structure of emotions*. Cambridge University Press.

Ortony, A. (2002). On making believable emotional agents believable. In R. Trappl, P. Petta & S. Payr (Eds.), Emotions in humans and artifacts (pp. 189-211). Cambridge, MA: The MIT Press.

Oshni Alvandi, E., & Akbari Dehaghi, M. (2008). Karl Popper and evolutionary concept of epistemology. *Philosophical Investigation (Journal of Faculty of Letters and Humanities), 51*(205).

Palm, G., & Glodek, M. (2013). Towards emotion recognition in human computer interaction. In Neural nets and surroundings (pp. 323–336). Springer.

Perkel, D. H. (1993). *Computational neuroscience: Scope and structure*. Paper presented at the Computational Neuroscience.

Plutchik, R. (1982). A psychoevolutionary theory of emotions. *Social Science Information/sur les sciences sociales*.

Port, R. F., & Van Gelder, T. (1995). Mind as motion: Explorations in the dynamics of cognition. Cambridge, MA: The MIT Press.

Prinz, J. (2004). Embodied emotions. In *Thinking about feeling*, (pp. 44-58).

Prinz, J. J. (2004). *Gut reactions: A perceptual theory of emotion*. Oxford University Press.

Reilly, W. S., & Bates, J. (1992). *Building emotional agents*.

Roberts, C., & Kleiner, A. (1999). Five kinds of systems thinking. The dance of change (pp. 96-106). New York: Double-Day.

Roederer, J. G. (2003). On the concept of information and its role in nature. *Entropy*, *5*(1), 3–33. doi:10.3390/e5010003

Roederer, J. G. (2005). *Information and its role in nature*. Springer.

Shannon, C. E. (2001). A mathematical theory of communication. *Mobile Computing and Communications Review*, *5*(1), 3–55. doi:10.1145/584091.584093

Sloman, A. (2011). What's information, for an organism or intelligent machine? How can a machine or organism mean.

Solomon, R. C. (1993). *The passions: Emotions and the meaning of life* (Rev. ed.). Indianapolis: Hackett.

Spivey, M. (2007). *The continuity of mind*. Oxford University Press New York.

Strand, M., Oram, M. W., & Hammar, Å. (2013). Emotional information processing in major depression remission and partial remission: Faces come first. *Applied Neuropsychology*, *20*(2), 110–119. doi:10.1080/09084282.2012.670159 PMID:23397997

Thellefsen, T., Thellefsen, M., & Sørensen, B. (2013). Emotion, information, and cognition, and some possible consequences for library and information science. *Journal of the American Society for Information Science and Technology*, *64*(8), 1735–1750. doi:10.1002/asi.22858

Tomkins, S. S. (1995). *Exploring affect: The selected writings of Silvan S Tomkins*. Cambridge University Press. doi:10.1017/CBO9780511663994

Tsuchiya, N., & Adolphs, R. (2007). Emotion and consciousness. *Trends in Cognitive Sciences*, *11*(4), 158–167. doi:10.1016/j.tics.2007.01.005 PMID:17324608

Velásquez, J. D. (1997). *Modeling emotions and other motivations in synthetic agents*. Paper presented at the AAAI/IAAI.

Wallace, B. (2007). *The mind, the body, and the world: Psychology after cognitivism?* Imprint Academic.

Watson, D., Clark, L. A., & Harkness, A. R. (1994). Structures of personality and their relevance to psychopathology. *Journal of Abnormal Psychology*, *103*(1), 18–31. doi:10.1037/0021-843X.103.1.18 PMID:8040477

Weizsäcker, C. F., & von Weizsäcker, C. F. (1985). *Wahrnehmung der Neuzeit*. Deutscher Taschenbuch Verlag.

Wilson, R. A., & Keil, F. C. (1999). *The MIT encyclopedia of the cognitive sciences* (Vol. 134). MIT Press.

Witzany, G. (2010). Biocommunication and natural genome editing. *World Journal of Biological Chemistry*, *1*(11), 348.

Zeki, S., & Romaya, J. P. (2008). Neural correlates of hate. *PLoS ONE*, *3*(10), e3556. doi:10.1371/journal.pone.0003556 PMID:18958169

KEY TERMS AND DEFINITIONS

Emotions: They, however, have no precise and undisputed dεφınition, neither of basic emotions (such as sadness) nor of more complicated emotions (such as embarrassment).

Emotional Control Parameters: Control different ways a system is coupled to its environment and affected by it for emotional arousal.

Emotional Memory: Is acquired through *learning experiences* and depicts cognitive changes in the agent.

Emotional Processing: The basic cognitive change or processing of emotion such as acquisition, recording, organization, retrieval, display, and dissemination in any manner which is detectable by an observer.

Information Processing: Is the change or processing of information such as acquisition, recording, organization, retrieval, display, and dissemination in any manner which is detectable by an observer.

Mental States: The states of human mindful actions, behaviours, and cognitive processes that are known as mental states. In practice, emotions are mostly clarified by their characteristics, so "states of mind" or "mental states" are considered something like desire, fear, sadness, embarrassment, jealousy, pride, calm, and pain.

Notions of Information: Are types of information processing that seem much like an "order" divided into and studied with three notions called *syntactic, semantic* and *pragmatic*.

ENDNOTES

1 For more details see: (Maslin & Maslin, 2001, p. 8)

2 Read more: Mind-Body Problem - world, life, history, beliefs, time, person, human, Dualism, Monism, Relation to Death from http://www.deathreference.com/Me-Nu/Mind-Body-Problem.html#ixzz0ydl9dUaH

3 Read more: Mind-Body Problem - world, life, history, beliefs, time, person, human, Dualism, Monism, Relation to Death from http://www.deathreference.com/Me-Nu/Mind-Body-Problem.html#ixzz0ydlKxbCC

4 Read more: http://plato.stanford.edu/entries/behaviorism/

5 But information is not the same as form appeared as a lexical part of the word "in + form + ation"; in short information is the infusion of form, or the flow of relationships (Maleeh, 2008).

6 Floridi (2005) defends that "truthful" is only a stylistic choice to be preferred to "true" because it enables one to say that a map conveys factual information insofar as it is truthful.

7 Data, in this framework, unlike Kant's *noumena* and Plato's idea is empirical.

8 In *Merriam-Webster Online Dictionary*. (2010). from http://www.merriam-bster.com/dictionary/context

9 The general sense of "intelligence" is meant.

10 See for more details: (Witzany, 2010).

11 This conception is based on the society like theory proposed by Niko Tinbergen in the Study of Instinct (1951).

12 Feature detectors in brain and limbic system are special neurons. They locate in the primary cortical areas to which the afferent transmission system from a sensory organ is wired (Roederer, 2005, p. 213). They might be components of a neural program including a motor expressive part, a somatic sensory part, and an experiential part. For more details see: (Tomkins, 1995).

13 See Ian Ravenssccraft, 2005, Introduction.

14 Confirmation occurs when a material coming from a message is already known to a recipient otherwise it is a novel material. That is, a receiver referring to his prior knowledge box must understand the message; otherwise, having delivered a known material in a different unknown structure (i.e. in another unknown language to the receiver), it would have been considered as a novelty (Gernert, 2006, p. 143).

15 It is worth to note that the term "knowledge" is presented in the concept of *information*

content quoted in the semantic theory of information by Dretske (1981, p. 65).

[16] An open system is any distinct entity -- a cell, a person, a forest, or an orchestra organization -- that takes in resources from its environment, processes them in some way, and produces output. It is regularly exchanges feedback with its external environment in which inputs, processes, outputs, goals, assessment and evaluation, and learning are all important. For more details refer to: McNamara (2005) or (Roberts & Kleiner, 1999).

[17] Genetic correspondence may cause to solve problems for survival (Oshni Alvandi & Akbari Dehaghi, 2008).

[18] Damasio (2005, p. 79-82) claims that that neural network patterns which constitute the substrate of a feeling arise in two classes of biological changes: *changes related to body state* and *changes related to cognitive state*.

[19] Conscious or unconscious process is not considered here.

[20] There is a process of information in brain from "not knowing" to "knowing".

Chapter 3
Representing Emotions as Dynamic Interactions of Symbols:
A Case Study on Literary Texts

Andra Băltoiu
Politehnica University of Bucharest, Romania

Cătălin Buiu
Politehnica University of Bucharest, Romania

ABSTRACT

This chapter proposes an emotional architecture organized around three pairs of antithetic universal symbols, or archetypes, derived from analytic psychology and anthropological accounts of mythical thinking. Their functions, relationships and interactions, on different levels of complexity within a dynamical system that mimics human emotional processes, are described by a formal model and a constructed ontology. The aim of the model is characterizing symbolic reasoning and figurative and analogue mechanisms of mental imagery associated with the internal representations of events. An automatic method for metaphor recognition and interpretation is proposed, targeting the identification of the proposed universal symbols in literary texts.

INTRODUCTION

While the compelling demand for emotional intelligent machines that would contribute to a realistic human – computer interaction appears to benefit from current developments in artificial intelligence, the matter of affects still lacks consensus in its own field. Foucault's (2002) observation on human sciences, first published in

1966 is ever today prevailing: "it will be possible to speak of human sciences when an attempt is made to define the way in which individuals or groups represent words to themselves, utilize their forms and their meanings, compose real discourse, reveal and conceal in it what they are thinking or saying, perhaps unknown to themselves, more or less than they wish, but in any case leave a mass of verbal traces of those thoughts, which must be

DOI: 10.4018/978-1-4666-7278-9.ch003

deciphered and restored as much as possible to their representative vivacity." (pp. 385). Straightforward models of emotions and cognition have proved their applicability and statistical relevance, but when an effort is put towards building machines that predict the affects of humans and react in a similar way, the problem of "restoring the vivacity" of human thought cannot be overlooked. Models such as those underlining emotion – attention mechanisms, or the relation of affects with decision making or interpersonal communication, because they describe only parts of reality, however sufficiently apparent to account for specific fields of interest, are not comprehensive enough as to render all implications of the above definition.

Some questions arise naturally when considering the implementation of human sciences as described previously in the framework of synthetic emotions: Can emotions be replicated in a computational model so generic that it can be adapted to any emotional theory is considered appropriate for the application being designed? Can it include connections to cognitive processes that are not linear, irational or non-literal? Or, how Foucault puts it, can it represent what is concealed or unknown? If such a model can be constructed, what units would compose it, so universal that their action accounts for the most diverse mental processes?

While not implying that our proposal is, on its own, a solution that answers all above questions and the implications of Foucault's definition, we have identified a series of premises we consider to be necessary for such an attempt and have constructed an illustrative model. Further research is needed, especially from the point of view of human sciences, in order to increase the model's accordance to real-life, observed phenomena.

We propose a general framework for modeling psychological processes that integrates aspects such as the dynamics of affects and cognitive mechanisms with a systemic perspective of reality. The complexity of the representation can be adapted as to fit the particular requirements of each application.

The central concept of our approach, that of archetypal symbols, has the advantage of a double correspondence. First, because of the universal character of such symbols, a thorough psychological analysis can identify and attribute specific functions that each archetype has within a system that simulates human thinking and feeling. In this way, their precise structural role can be defined, together with the relations by which they operate. This Top-Down strategy requires, besides the comprehensive study of the mind, a systemic representation of reality, or the world model of each application, in such a way that different complexity scales can be achieved. Secondly, bearing a strong symbolic and conceptual character, the archetypes can be recognized in the phenomena related to human mental acts, making the model prone to language processing applications of identifying the patterns in which they appear. However, it needs to be pointed out, in the case of this Bottom-Up strategy, that the correspondence between symbol and word is not direct, at least in the sense implied by our perspective, as a symbol implies a higher degree of abstraction.

We have constructed a functional model to illustrate our understanding of the method of representing mental processes for both these approaches, yet we would like to draw attention on the fact that, depending on the subject of research or application, a mixed strategy can also be applied.

In our view, universal symbols such as these indicated here are present in the whole of human experience. Accordingly, we will not argue whether emotions have a regulatory role on cognition or vice versa, we suggest that a realistic model can be created in which both have the common root of symbolic images.

BACKGROUND

As mentioned previously, several roles of emotions have been identified, and while we do not intent in providing an extensive list of such functions, we would like to point out that an adaptation of these roles has been surveyed for the case of artificial agents, as well. Scheutz (2004) identifies action selection, social regulation, sensory integration, adaptation, alarm mechanisms, learning, memory control, self model as some of the roles synthesized emotions might play in a robot or artificial agent. Looking at such a list, it is clear that there are two possible approaches to the problem: either reduce the list (which here is not reproduced entirely, nor does the author imply it is exhaustive) to a limited set of functionalities necessary for one specific application, or consider a systemic that include all mechanisms suggested by a thorough inventory of emotional interactions. So far, the first method has been used wildly, in applications ranging from sociable robots to intelligent game agents. On what the latter method is concerned, although some models integrate perception, behavior control, action planning, memory along other modules, in a systemic manner, they are still designed to operate in a specific degree of complexity, required by the application they serve. However efficient these models are, they still lack the robustness strived by current AI demands. To our view, this happens because, despite their systemic construction (hierarchical or distributed) of the artificial agent, they treat reality (or world model) as a unitary whole. We argue that a comprehensive systemic approach considers both the agent and the environment as part of the same system, where layers of the agent interact with layers of the environment, and the organization of both have the same origin.

One other issue with classical emotional models is that, despite having parameters, such as arousal or selection (Dorner & Hille, 1995; Dorner, 2003), which can be modulated as to result in coherent behavior, therefore defining dynamic characteristics of affects and/or cognition, they do not include non-linear mental processes as those observed in metaphoric expression, illogical or irrational thinking or creative imagination.

We argue that these must be present as well in a synthesized model of cognition and emotion, as they constitute basic mental acts, perhaps more distinctive to humans than behavior control or action planning.

The absence of complete rules describing the dynamics of affects has so far been addressed stochastically, as in the case of Banik, Watanabe and Habib (2009), who used an adaptation of the same emotional model we base our work on, and applied a Markov model to formalize transitions from one affect to the other. While we acknowledge the efficiency of such representations on given applications, our aim is developing a general, task-independent framework that can be customized or adjusted for specific purposes.

THE NON-LINEARITY OF MENTAL REPRESENTATIONS

Our model builds on the belief that mental representations take, in a sense that we will describe shortly, the form of metaphors and are constructed as images that have nothing to do with rationality. Surely, at a conscious and operational level, cognition manifests itself in a logical manner and so far cognitive architectures have attempted to describe the mechanisms by which it produces the observed behavior. Yet, as Jung has pointed out in his analysis of dreams, and as many anthropologists have identified in the universal myths of ancient people, the inner, most intimate human experiences with the world resemble a kind of figurative thinking. How these images get processed and become what we commonly recognize as cognitive or emotional acts or states is, in our opinion, a problem of interfaces, similar to those described by linguists when referring to the semantic-syntactic or conceptual-intentional mappings (Chomsky & McGilvray, 2012). We refer to them in this generic manner because it is not the scope of this paper to identify neither the number of those interfaces nor to model the system in which they are organized, but it is our belief that the human psyche is constructed in several levels, each communicating with the other by such an interface. Of these, probably the most interesting is the one linking the unconscious to the conscious.

We choose to denote those images as metaphors out of several reasons. However, it should first be stated that by metaphor we do not understand the poetic trope used for aesthetic, decorative purposes. As a number of authors (Black, 1993; Lakoff, 1993; Ortony, 1993) have previously shown, metaphor has to do with linguistics only at the end point. It is primarily a mechanism of thought. It is clearly not the only one and by this we do not intend to generalize all mental processes to this particular kind of figurative representation. Nonetheless, considering the psyche to be organized in levels, we believe that on this particular plane that we are analyzing, they are the primary mechanism of describing reality. We follow the definition provided by Lakoff (1993), that metaphor is "a general mapping across conceptual domains" (pp. 203).

Out of all non literal ways of expression, metaphor holds a privileged position, partly because of its power to create (or point to) new ways of understanding or seeing the world (Black, 1993; Schon, 1993). This is a necessary function for any candidate for modeling human cognition. Another distinctive attribute arises from this definition of metaphor. As Sternberg, Tourangeau and Nigro (1993) suggestively point out, the novelty of a metaphor is highest when the distance between the two conceptual domains is large, while the positions of each element of the metaphor within its corresponding domain are similar. This suggests the unique role conceptual spaces play in the mental representation of reality. We will return to this figurative representation and describe the link to our proposed model later in detail.

THE ARCHETYPE MODEL

As stated previously, one of the most challenging aspects of synthesizing emotions is identifying and formalizing the dynamics by which affects interact. Lewis (2005) surveys two main theories for interpreting the emotion-cognition relation. Probably the most popular is the appraisal theory, by which the main function of affects is to direct attention to exterior events, through a series of mechanisms of filtering and inhibition. The second refers to types of personality and the effects they have over cognitive and affective structures. The main criticism present in the paper, that most of these theories describe linear, cause-effect relations, and not real, complex, bidirectional and nonlinear ones is, in our opinion, not the only source of incompleteness for current models. Whether fear turns into aggression or into submission is as much a matter of personality as it is of current internal state and of external configuration of events. The only way in which all the possibilities can be synthesized is by a meaningful simplification.

The starting point for our proposal is Plutchik's model of emotions, first developed in 1958 and reviewed in the following years. He classified eight primary affects (four bipolar pairs) and placed them in a circumplex model, based on the similarities between each two: joy, trust, fear, surprise, sadness, disgust, anger, anticipation. Another dimension describes levels of intensity: in the case of anger this ranges from annoyance to fury. Depending on the degree of similarity between the base emotions, he further classified more complex affects that arise from the combination of the primary: if the two emotions forming the dyad are adjacent in the circular model, the resulting affect is frequently felt; if they are one emotion apart, the compound is sometimes felt; two emotions apart is seldom felt and three emotions apart are opposites. Such that tertiary dyads, those mixes seldom felt contain more conflict

(Plutchik, 1962). Later, the circumplex approach gained popularity, due to a series of properties such a model entails (Plutchik & Conte, 1997). Plutchik himself wrote several articles analyzing the significance of his original model. However, we will not follow further the implications described by the author, not because we disagree with the content, but because our interest is not in the clinical aspects of experiencing different emotions, it is deriving a computational model that describes the manifestation of affects and their relation to cognitive mechanisms.

We retained the bipolar remark and grouped the second order emotions from the original model according to the axes they contained. Table 1 shows the resulting classification, with the following notations:

Emotion is the complementary affect of *Emotion*, meaning that it is diagonally opposed to it in the circumplex model.

As such, when referring to the base emotions, we will use only half of the circumplex model: Fear, Surprise, Joy and Trust and will call them *axes*. Note that Plutchik did not name the second order emotion resulted by the combination of *Trust* and *Surprise*.

We found this classification to give rise to a new level of signification as the six resulting groups exhibit common properties. We will now describe our interpretation and motivate our choice of naming for each of them and continue with implications that such an interpretation has on the problem of synthesizing emotions, in our view. First, we would like to clarify our usage of the notion of archetypes. As we'll shortly see, there is a strong symbolic significance in the way the second order emotions group together when analyzed in terms of the complementarity of the base affects that compose them. Our aim was to highlight the principle that governs those symbols in such a way that further properties could be inferred. Thus, by archetype we mean a universal figure that encloses characteristics, properties, objects

and actions that can be personified in one meaningful entity. We do not suggest that this model be an alternative to the archetypes introduced by Jung and do not propose that the term should be understood in the sense he used it, although we do find his ideas illuminating and have followed his conclusions when applicable. Moreover, it is worth pointing out that the functional model we are proposing is highly dependent on the way in which these archetypes are understood and how their characteristics are described. We do not hold that the following definitions be final or complete in depicting anthropological and psychological traits. Further research needs to be conducted in an interdisciplinary manner.

Clearly, as our model is derived from a circumplex one, without modifying the existing relations, the six resulting groups will also display complementary connections.

The Feminine Archetype

The first group, composed of second order emotions resulted by the joy and trust axes, meaning all four possible combinations of the base affects and their complementary, exhibit *feminine* characteristics. It is not to say that only females are capable of experiencing, for instance, love, however the symbolism of love has strong feminine traits, such as caring or maternity and it is connected to the symbolism of life (Durand, 1999; Eliade, 2003). Sentimentality is probably more clearly linked to femininity and there is an extensive literature on the association of death symbols, thus including morbidness, to femininity (Eliade, 2003). On what remorse is concerned, speculations can arise as to what extent it can be attributed to such a symbol. One can argue that it can go back to the original sin, yet, how we have already announced and will detail later, the exact place and scope of each archetypal feature is relative to the entire model structure. Once the symbol has been defined, further characteristics can be attributed to it. For

Table 1. Grouping second order emotions around primary component axes

Base Emotions	Configuration	Second Order Emotion
Fear + Surprise	$Fear + Surprise$	Alarm
	$Fear + \overline{Surprise}$	Anxiety
	$\overline{Fear} + Surprise$	Outrage
	$\overline{Fear} + \overline{Surprise}$	Aggression
Joy + Trust	$Joy + Trust$	Love
	$Joy + \overline{Trust}$	Morbidness
	$\overline{Joy} + Trust$	Sentimentality
	$\overline{Joy} + \overline{Trust}$	Remorse
Joy + Surprise	$Joy + Surprise$	Delight
	$Joy + \overline{Surprise}$	Optimism
	$\overline{Joy} + Surprise$	Disappointment
	$\overline{Joy} + \overline{Surprise}$	Pessimism
Trust + Fear	$Trust + Fear$	Submission
	$Trust + \overline{Fear}$	Dominance
	$\overline{Trust} + Fear$	Shame
	$\overline{Trust} + \overline{Fear}$	Contempt
Trust + Surprise	$Trust + Surprise$	Curiosity
	$Trust + \overline{Surprise}$	Fatalism
	$\overline{Trust} + Surprise$	-
	$\overline{Trust} + \overline{Surprise}$	Cynicism

continued on following page

Table 1. Continued

Base Emotions	Configuration	Second Order Emotion
Joy + Fear	$Joy_+ Fear$	Guilt
	$Joy_+ \overline{Fear}$	Pride
	$\overline{Joy}_+ Fear$	Despair
	$\overline{Joy}_+ \overline{Fear}$	Envy

illustrative purposes we will assign the *Feminine* archetype properties such as cyclicity, passivity, focus on details, irrationality.

The Masculine Archetype

The other two axes, fear and surprise, give rise to the complementary symbol of *masculinity*, represented in the emotional dyads by aggression, outrage, anxiety and alarm. In evolutionary terms, these emotions seem to be indeed related to combat or other situations men were confronted to. The previous observation, that these emotions are not reserved exclusively to one gender holds. And as in the previous case, we will further define the *Masculine* archetype through concepts as initiative, impulse, courage, resistance, determination, rationality and order.

The Archetype of the Child

The third group, formed by combinations of joy and surprise appear to contain affects that deal with the pleasure caused by urgently satisfying needs: delight, optimism, disappointment, pessimism. We therefore attribute them to the *Child* and define it according to Jung's description of the Infans archetype: one guided by pleasure, more precisely the delight caused by the existence of pleasure and that has a compensating role for the "inevitable one-sidednesses and extravagances of

the conscious mind." (Jung, 1981, pp 162). We will add therefore manifests a sensorial spontaneity.

The Archetype of the Master

The complementary of the *Child* is the *Master*, containing compound affects resulted by combinations of the fear and anticipation axes, which displays characteristics associated to subordinating relations. We will define this archetype by his role as teacher, his knowledge of structure and ability of operating under order and hierarchy. In our view, this archetype includes the Freudian concept of Superego.

The Ego Archetype

The fifth category distinguishes itself by an egoistic character, as it includes emotions as pride, envy, guilt, despair. For Jung, the ego is responsible for maintaining the continuity of self identity and it is necessary for the appearance of consciousness, which is a gradual aggregation of fragments (Jung, 1981b). We will therefore conclude that it generates emotional reactions in such a manner that the eventual discontinuities between the exterior reality and internal self representations are masked. According to Piaget's theory, the ego is developed especially in the mirror period, thus we will attribute reflexive properties to this archetype and the ability to construct and manipulate images.

The Archetype of the Self

The last, but perhaps central category, opposed to the Ego, is the Self. We will use Jung's interpretation of the archetype of the Self. It is clearly the most mysterious of all and the fact that the only second order emotion that Plutchik did not name belongs to this archetype appears anecdotic. In a larger view, this is the archetype of life, as it manifests will and controls the autonomy of the system.

THE TOP – DOWN APPROACH: ARCHETYPES AND FUNCTION

Before continuing with the systemic approach of characterizing the model, we will make two more observations regarding how the architecture presented so far can be interpreted. First, let us go back to the sets of bipolar emotions. It is a general view, regardless of psychological paradigms and their view of the roles of affect, that no emotion is negative, as they all serve an adaptive purpose that ensures fit responses to exterior events. One can at most speak of pleasurable emotions, however our analysis of Plutchik's base and mixed affects have revealed that this is not a suitable criterion. Take for instance the opposites fear and anger. No pleasure can be found in any of these, however they are complementary. We believe the relation is based on the direction in which they are manifested: towards the exterior (others) or towards the self. Burt (1950) mentions similar relations when he talks about inhibiting or demonstrative affects. The other structural symmetry that the model implies has to do with the effect produced of the emotion, which can be either constructive or destructive. Figure 1 show these properties for each archetype.

The second observation is that each pair of archetypes stands for a different way of representing reality.

The values associated with these representations can be illustrated by the following notions:

1. **The Pair Master-Child:** Operates with the notions of *appropriate* and *inappropriate*.
2. **The Pair Feminine-Masculine:** Operates the notions of *beautiful* and *ugly*.
3. **The Pair Self-Ego:** Operates with *truth* and *falseness*.

In this way the notions of good and bad can be characterized through the various levels of the model. One cannot say beauty is good, and not even truth is good in all situations, but inappropriate, ugly and false can be a complete definition of the concept of bad.

The above interpretation, referring to the notion of completeness, is an example of what we mean when saying that the definitions of the archetypes are relative to the entire model architecture. Whether the plane of beauty-ugly is in reality exclusively controlled by feminine and masculine symbols is, from a point on, unimportant, as long as 1) the attributes of the respective archetypes are defined accordingly, 2) the other two planes have isomorphic values and 3) together, the three planes fully describe an aspect of reality.

As briefly mentioned before and implied by the former example, describing emotional and cognitive mechanisms by this series of figures that generate them has the advantage of an easier characterization of the interactions involved in human mental processes. However, the complexity of the problem now resides in a thorough representation of the world model, such that the attributed functions for each archetype respect the three principles stated above.

Perhaps the most straightforward way of viewing the archetypal model that describes the human psyche is by considering a system where each archetype is an agent negotiating with the others the degree in which he is activated, and formalizing the rules of their interaction. We pro-

Figure 1. a) Structural properties of emotions within archetypes; b) Structural properties of emotions within archetypes

Masculine

EMOTION	EXTERIOR - INTERIOR	CONSTRUCTIVE - DESTRUCTIVE
Aggression	→	↑
Alarm	←	↑
Outrage	→	↕
Anxiety	←	↕

Feminine

EMOTION	EXTERIOR - INTERIOR	CONSTRUCTIVE - DESTRUCTIVE
Love	→	↑
Sentimentality	←	↑
Remorse	→	↓
Morbidity	←	↓

Child

EMOTION	EXTERIOR - INTERIOR	CONSTRUCTIVE - DESTRUCTIVE
Optimism	→	↑
Delight	←	↑
Dissapointment	→	↕
Pessimism	←	↕

Master

EMOTION	EXTERIOR - INTERIOR	CONSTRUCTIVE - DESTRUCTIVE
Dominance	→	↑
Contempt	←	↑
Submission	→	↓
Shame	←	↓

Self

EMOTION	EXTERIOR - INTERIOR	CONSTRUCTIVE - DESTRUCTIVE
Curiosity	→	↑
-	←	↑
Cynicism	→	↕
Fatalism	←	↕

Ego

EMOTION	EXTERIOR - INTERIOR	CONSTRUCTIVE - DESTRUCTIVE
Envy	→	↑
Pride	←	↑
Guilt	→	↓
Despair	←	↓

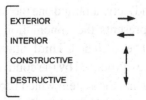

EXTERIOR →
INTERIOR ←
CONSTRUCTIVE ↑
DESTRUCTIVE ↓

pose that the six symbolic figures are responsible with several control functions, derived by their properties. An illustration of this approach will be presented shortly, but first let us explain in more detail the premises of our systemic perspective. We believe that a developing a realistic model of emotions and/or cognitive traits can only be done by conforming the construction to the properties of real life systems. Constantinescu (1990), in his theory of how natural, living and nonliving systems originate and develop, establishes a connection between the two principal measures of energy and information: " The transmission of information involves the propagation of an energy and, vice versa, the unfolding of energy in time and space involves a control rule, thus a transmission of information." (pp. 34). Therefore, the two measures are complementary and cannot be simultaneously known with equal precision (Constantinescu, 1986, 1990). We will not go into the details of his formalization, but we will ensure that the world model will be constructed such that it respects the relation between the two measures.

The attempt to represent the world in a realistic and systemic view brought us to the transdisciplinary studies of Basarab Nicolescu, especially his analysis of the tertiary logic formulated by Stephane Lupasco (Nicolescu, 2009). Taken together, the works of both authors construct a theory on how reality is organized. In 1982 Nicolescu (2009) introduced the notion of level of reality, which he defined as being "an totality of systems that is invariant to the action of a set of general lows", such that "two levels of reality are different if, passing from one to another there is a disruption of lows and fundamental concept (like causality)" (pp. 78). The tertiary logic of Lupasco postulates the existence of two antagonistic states, Potentiality and Activation and one Included Third State that represents the conciliation of those contraries. "The Included Third State appears when the energy produced by the contradiction is the maximum that the system which is part of the contradiction can hold." (pp 82). We consider the

implications of such a theory for human sciences to be extremely fertile, and this has already been proven by the doctoral dissertation of Adrian Petrariu, coordinated in 2012 by Basarab Nicolescu, which interprets social systems from the point of view of levels of reality.

ARCHETYPES AND NEEDS: A HIERARCHICAL SYSTEM

To illustrate our understanding of a systemic approach to modeling human emotions by means of the archetypal structure presented above, we have followed the hierarchical system of human needs proposed by Petrariu. He states that one of the most important human needs is that of becoming more capable and interprets that any subjective need can have a different degree of objectivity for the needs of other systems, depending on the level of reality it is found on. According to the author one other important need is that of tranquility (Petrariu, 2012). Going back to our observation that the model should consider the relationship between energy and information, we will conclude that the need for tranquility is on the energetic side and that of self-improvement on the informational side and infer that there is constant oscillation between satisfying those two basic needs. From the hierarchical system of needs that the author constructed, we will retain three more and interpret them in the view of our model.

1.   The need to exist
    a.   Such a need is, above all, of biological nature, therefore we will attribute it to the Self archetype. The Self must exist, no matter what form it takes, in this sense being undifferentiated. The differentiation comes with the Ego, for whom the uniqueness of existence is essential. One might find the left-right brain hemisphere paradigm eloquent for this interpretation

       i.   In whatever form (Self)

       ii. Singular (Ego)

2.   The need to develop

    a.   For an organism to develop it is necessary that it grows and adapts. For this reason, we have assigned this need to the Child-Master pair of archetypes.

       i.   Growth (Child)

       ii. Adaptation (Master)

3.   The need to communicate

    a.   The two entities of each communication, the emitter and the receiver, entail an active and passive nature, respectively, thus suggesting an analogy to the two archetypes that are defined by such properties: the Masculine and the Feminine. We will not include the message that it is being communicated in this analysis, as the need to communicate is universal, regardless of what is being transmitted.

       i.   Emission (Masculine)

       ii. Reception (Feminine)

On the basis of these observations we are proposing a hierarchical control structure, unfolded in several layers on the Energy – Information axis, in which each archetype (or mix of archetypes, as we will see) has a control function assigned. However, in order to include the need for self-improvement, two concepts must find their place in the system: the notion of subjectivity and the relation with time. It is beyond the scope of this paper to further elaborate on the intricate idea of subjectivity or the way in which a so called objective view of reality is mentally constructed, nor will we debate on how time is perceived. We will only solely point that control structures that manage the awareness of these phenomena must exist and emphasize their position in respect to the premises of our model. Hence, the hierarchical system will be composed of five levels, presented below starting from the one in which information is least organized. One more observation should be made before continuing. So far we have talked about the general archetypes of Femininity and Masculinity. Still, when we introduce functions related to the subjective perspective, we need to operate with the notions of gender and opposite gender. Inspired by the concepts of anima/animus elaborated by Jung, we propose that on the levels of the system where information is sufficiently organized so that they imply a gender differentiation, we will no longer use generic Feminine or Masculine archetypes, but rather those of Gender and Opposite Gender.

1.   Level IV: Energy Control

    a.   As described above, the need for tranquility is managed by the Child archetype, based on the information and energy coming from all others archetypes. The role of the level is maintaining a comfort value. Further functions can be created as to describe in more detail the emotional and cognitive mechanisms involved in basic energy control, depending on the application.

2.   Level III: Basic Needs Control

    a.   Corresponding to a higher degree of information organization, the control of the basic needs (existence, communication and development) involves more complex operations. We have placed all these needs on the same level due to the fact that none of those can be implemented without the other.

3.   Level II: Time management

    a.   Self-improvement and subjectivity (and consciousness for that matter) require the knowledge of time. We attribute a set of functions to each temporal field:

       i.   *To the past*, the function of Memory- Based on our understanding of the archetypes, we assign the operations with the past to the figure of the Master (as for the experience implied by it) and to the Opposite Gender (as per Jung's description of the anima and animus).

ii. *To the present*, the function of Attention, of directing sensorial and cognitive mechanisms to the present moment. Actuality is essentially linked to the Self archetype, because of its strong biological character and to the Child, as for its high spontaneity.

iii. *To the future*, projective and anticipative functions. We have already suggested the projective character of the Ego and we will assign these functions to the Gender as well. An important observation needs to be made, which is valid for all levels and components of the system, but is perhaps more evident in the case of the management of time. When we say that an archetype is responsible for the control of, for example, memory, we do not suggest that other archetypes have no access to this shared resource, just as it is improper to say that the Master has no need for communication or does not communicate at all. The distinction is that between who uses and who regulates the resource. The quality of control is determined by the state of the supervisor archetype and this enables realistic cooperative and competitive connections between sub-systems.

4. Level I: Subjectivity

   a. On this level the control of personal perspective is realized, through functions that ensure both subjective con-

tinuity of the representation of reality and objectification of the experimented context.

5. Level 0: The Need for Self-Improvement

   a. The level corresponds to cognitive functions that imply structured information, such as estimation, planning, message elaboration and self-control.

In Figure 2, the *Archetype*$^{(index)}$ notation refers to the different degrees of organization that the informational structure of the component manifests on the respective level of the world model.

We remind that the proposed solution has an illustrative aim, demonstrating our perspective on how the archetypal model can be integrated with a systemic approach of representing reality. Further research is needed to assess the philosophical, psychological and anthropological exactness of the presented model and to elaborate on the problems presented here in brief.

So far we have described only structural and connective aspects of our model. Because formalizing the dynamic characteristics of each component of the proposed system would exceed the purpose of the paper, we will concentrate on detailing only one sub-system, namely the module that controls the need for tranquility. And because the level this module belongs to is defined by the least organized information, we will only focus on defining rules for energy transformation. For coherence reasons we have further pursued the observations of Petrariu (2012) regarding the mechanisms of maintaining this need. Because constant satisfaction is impossible, either due to exterior conditions, which do not comply with one's needs, or to the diminution of the contentment intensity in time, there is a permanent oscillation between satisfaction and dissatisfaction. The author introduces the concept of self-reassurance, which aims at avoiding a contradiction and which can be attained through the following mechanisms: a) the oscillation of thoughts between past and fu-

Figure 2. The hierarchical control system

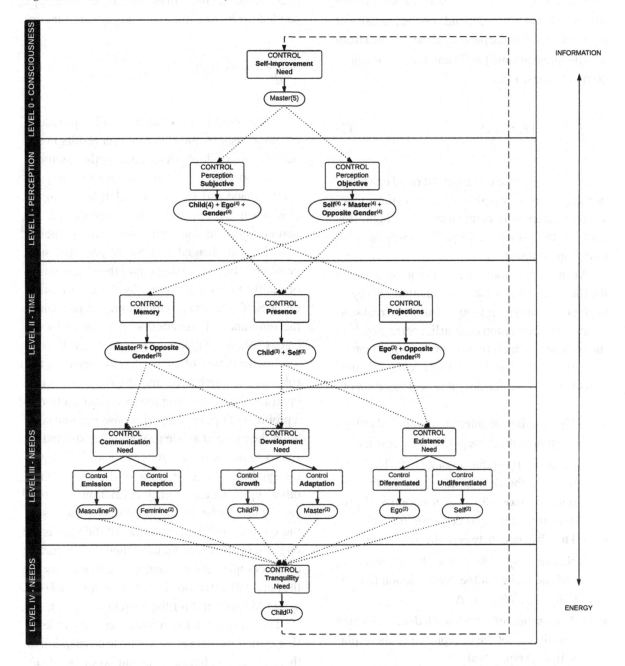

ture, b) the elaboration of explanations that cancel the contradiction, c) imaginary constructions. The purpose of the mechanisms is to produce work in order to dissipate the energy produced by the contradiction. Let us see how the dynamics of these three operations can be formalized:

The oscillation between past and future can be imagined as the projection of an experienced symbol on a future plane, and can thus be formalized as a commutation function. First we need to state a rule by which energy degrades. We will consider that the reduction of the energy of a contradiction (U_C) by means of oscillating between past and future depends on the intensity of the symbol met in the past (I_S), the distance from it to the present time (ΔT) and the frequency of commutations, ω :

$$\frac{dU_{C\_O}}{dt} = f(I_S, \Delta T, \omega) \qquad (1)$$

We will suppose that the most rapid discharge of energy happens when the intensity of the symbol which conceptually compensates it is high, it is far from the present and the frequency of commutations is also high.

As in the previous case, we propose a model for the discharge of the contradiction energy in the case of constructing explanations. In real situations, the elimination of conflict corresponds to the reasoning which finalizes in a compensatory symbol and which is closest to the real configuration of events. We consider it to be depending on:

- The number of inferences and deductions (argumentative steps), n_I , necessary to obtain a favorable conclusion. This will measure the dimension of the argumentation: the most direct explanation will produce the most rapid decrease in energy.

- The distance between the new state, s_{I^*} , obtained by elaborating the explanation, and the reality of the contradiction felt initially, s_E . We note $\Delta s = s_E - s_{I^*}$

- A measure of self-knowledge, C, which permits or not the acceptance of the explanation as being real.

Therefore, we have:

$$\frac{dU_{C\_E}}{dt} = f(n_I, \Delta s, C) \qquad (2)$$

Similarly, we will define the decrease of the contradiction energy by imaginary constructions as follows. Only in this case, n_I , or the dimension

of the construction, will be composed of the steps needed to obtain a full imaginary representation.

$$\frac{dU_{C\_I}}{dt} = f(n_I, \Delta s, C) \qquad (3)$$

As implied before, the tranquility produced by compensating the contradiction results in the activation the Child Archetype. Further assumptions on how this is related to the other archetypes can be made and we can consider, for example, that when the contradiction is reconciled, by maintaining the maximum amount of energy until it is discharged in another pane (as suggested by the tertiary logic and the organization of reality in levels) is done by the contribution of the Self, Master and Gender archetypes, while the ignorance of the contradiction involves the Ego, Child and Opposite Gender. Regardless of the interpretation of such relations between the roles of each archetype and the management of contradictions, it is clear that need satisfaction is a problem of optimization, because in a real situation the usage of an ideal symbol is restricted. A first type of constraints regard the availability of the symbol at the given time of the event, while other types include energy restrictions (current energy level is below the threshold that activates the symbol), logical constraints (if the state is on one site of the contradiction, then the resources of the complementary cannot be accessed, as for the potential-activation logic), or operational (the symbol is not valid for the current function).

The above formalizations concern only in-level (horizontal) functions. A complete description of the interactions between the sub-systems of the model require that the relations of energy and information among levels (vertical) be formalized as well. However, we will not extend our presentation for the time being and will focus instead on the second part of our procedure, namely the Bottom-up approach.

THE BOTTOM – UP APPROACH: ARCHETYPES AND CONCEPTS

It has been previously acknowledged that language, among human expressions, is the most efficient indicator of emotional experience (Fussell, 2002). It is not to say that the problem of indentifying emotions in written or spoken language is trivial, especially when the affects are not declared explicitly, but language qualifies as reliable evidence both for deducing the dynamics of emotions and testing of affective models. We have already indicated that the solution presented in this paper can be approach either Top-Down, Bottom-Up or in a mixed strategy. By the Bottom-Up approach we intend on denoting the procedure of recognizing the imprint of the six archetypes in spoken or written discourse, and consequently deducing the dynamics of their interaction. With applying the method on a corpus, more general rules that describe these interactions can be derived.

Whichever method is developed, the relation between words, concepts, symbols and archetypes must be defined, since identifying the archetype that is dominantly expressed in a sentence or text requires the following three operations:

1. Retrieving the concepts articulated in the words of the phrase.
2. Identifying the most appropriate symbol for each concept.
3. Assigning each symbol to the archetype that operates with it.

Yet there is an exception to the process, as not all words have a direct correspondence with concepts. Harden (1999) indicates this through examples such as the word "hello" (pp. 56), which has no "hello" concept attributed to it, but rather signifies the act of greeting. Nevertheless, there is a symbolic meaning in this very act of initiating communication, and this applies likewise to other similar cases.

Coming back to defining the relations between the basic notions, on what the first two terms are concerned, words and concepts, we believe Cognitive Semantics to be the relevant theory that bridges internal representation of meaning to the actual form of utterances. Allwood (1999) explains the assumptions of the approach by characterizing the meaning potential of linguistic expressions and indicating that "concepts are primarily cognitive phenomena" and should be studied "in terms of operations on information, rather than as static entities." (pp. 1). The author classifies eight types of such operations which mainly consist in different ways of manipulating information, by extracting or elaborating on knowledge. It is precisely because the theory emphasizes on the operations the mind makes on information, that we consider Cognitive Semantics to represent, for the purpose of our own research, the structural groundwork for Step 1 of our method. When we speak about concepts and the way language makes use of them, we mainly talk about meaning that is expressed consciously. Perhaps Harden's observation is clarifying: "Essentially, what we do when we combine words is to combine conceptual elements into more complex conceptual wholes until we have something matching the unified conception that we want to convey." (pp. 54). The matter of symbols, however, bears another form of non-literal expressions, as Durand (1999) has revealed: "We find that the symbolic object is often subject to reversals of meaning, or at least to some dualities which lead to processes of double negation." (pp. 46). If in the case of concepts we speak of metaphors and other figurative ways of portraying one's thoughts, symbols bear yet a more abstract nature. Having already suggested that archetypes operate through such symbols, it is now obvious that the most challenging part of developing the Bottom-Up strategy is related to the task of correctly identifying the marks of symbols, of recognizing these figurative images out of plain speech. A mapping is thus needed between concepts and symbols, specifying how conceptual structures make up a symbolic image. The third and last step demands the construction of an ontology, a vocabulary of symbols that each archetype, together with the rules by which they relate to one another.

Before continuing, we should make one more observation. Because we are referring to a high level of abstraction, it is fundamental that we discern factual or trivial statements from those that bear complex symbolic meaning. By this we do not mean that we have to exclude certain expressions from our analysis, but assign them to the relevant process. By considering reality as being structured on levels, we can make such distinctions easily, because different symbolic images correspond to different levels of organization of information. This is why, in our opinion the preferred way of addressing the problem of synthesizing emotions and cognition by use of the model proposed here, is a mixed strategy, a composition of both Top-Down and Bottom-Up approaches. One could ask why, besides the theoretical relevance of the way humans create and use concepts and mental images, is it necessary in practice to cover such intricate transformations from words to archetypes. Let's take the semantic field of the word "to see". Let us also hold that there is also a concept "to see" that denotes not only seeing per se, but also the implications of the act. We cannot assign directly the concept to an archetype, because they all have access to processing this kind of input information, yet surely there is a difference in what they look at, how they see and how they represent what they see. We cannot skip the concept stage either, and assign directly the word to an archetype based on differences in the semantic field (see, look, gaze) out of the same reasons.

At the time of the publication of this paper, we have designed and implemented a natural language processing application which analyses the play "Six characters in search of an author", by Luigi Pirandello and assigns a dominant archetype to each phrase in the text. We have constructed a simplified archetype vocabulary and used the WordNet linguistic data base to relate each word to its meaning and establish similarities between concepts. Each word in the dialog is assigned a probability of belonging to all archetypes, depending on the conceptual distance between it and the words of the six sub-vocabularies. The highest probability is retained, and consequently the phrase is associated to the archetype that manifests itself more through the words of the phrase. Research is still being conducted, as the structure of WordNet does not entirely fit our own structure of concepts.

We have chosen the dramatic genre as testing material for our solution out of two reasons. Firstly, the history of theatre maintains probably the most precise correspondence with the history of human thought paradigms, a characteristic that is embodied in its purpose: to be staged in front of society. This means that the subjective message of the plays being analyzed can easily be put in a larger context and the results interpreted accordingly. And secondly, the features of the genre (mainly its conciseness, absence of interfering planes of narrative planes or excessive descriptions and aesthetic, poetical images), makes a theatre play more fit for the use of natural language processing techniques.

FUTURE TRENDS

Our aim so far was to indicate the possibility of systemizing mental processes by means of archetypal symbols and express the way in which different cognitive and emotional functions can be assigned to the model. While we focused on the systemic implications, we pointed out the need for further elaboration of specific modules, such as memory, language understanding, action planning and so forth. The paradigm for designing those modules is independent of the proposed model, as long as their integration is done respecting the principles described in this paper. Harder (1999) said that "function is in the eyes of the beholder" (pp. 38), which translates, in our case, that the precise ways in which the archetypes acts within the system and with the environment, if the Top-Down strategy is developed, is subjective because it depends on the perspective of the developer. However, as we already discussed, the configuration can be tested by adding a language module, until a coherent structure can be singled out.

As the strive for a realistic synthesizing of human psyche is augmented by technical advances, both in the computational framework of AI and in the field of intelligent robotic agents, there is greater need for a universal and integrative backbone that refers to the most basic human forms of representing reality, and which can be adapted to any degree of complexity required. Along with the applicative side of these attempts there lies an urge for a simple, unique way of describing the most complicated or unknown mechanisms concerning the nature of thought.

However many successful applications will be constructed without appealing to a systemic view of both agent and world model, the moment is near when this approach will be the sole viable ground for detailing the complexity of operations such as those observed in human behavior. Our scientific understanding of man needs to be placed in relation with our scientific understanding of reality.

CONCLUSION

We have argued the need that the synthesis of emotions be linked to cognitive mechanisms and that together they integrate nonlinear, illogic, irrational or non-literal behavior. As a root for both mental processes we have proposed a system of universal symbols, or archetypes, which can account for a wide range of phenomena observed in human conduct. So far, we have derived a model in which environment is represented on levels, from simple to complex, following the relation of the two basic measures that describe our reality, energy and information. The role of each archetype

in the functioning of the system has been analyzed according to the level of reality on which it operates. We believe that these premises are necessary for creating an autonomous agent that adaptively reacts to the environment he is set into.

Striving the construction of a general model, one that is application-independent and can simulate any number of desired scenarios, we have not insisted on the psychological accuracy of the functions we have assigned to each archetype, but rather aimed that they be consistent to our proposal, explaining how such consistency can be obtained. Further cross-disciplinary research is required in order to order to develop a fully functional model, in the Top-Down approach. We have also presented the technical limitations of our Bottom-Up implementation at the time of its development, and proposed a mixed strategy for future work.

We hope to point out the need to address the problem of synthesizing emotions and cognition by an approach that considers not only visible functions such as memory, behavior control or action selection, but also deeper mechanisms of thought and representation.

REFERENCES

Allwood, J. (1999). Semantics as meaning determination with semantic-epistemic operations. In J. Allwood & P. Gardenfors (Eds.), *Cognitive semantics. Meaning and cognition* (pp. 1–18). John Benjamins. doi:10.1075/pbns.55.02all

Banik, S. C., Watanabe, K., Habib, M. K., & Izumi, K. (2009). Handbook of research on synthetic emotions and sociable robotics (J. Vallverdú & D. Casacuberta, Eds.). Hershey, PA: IGI Global. doi:10.4018/978-1-60566-354-8

Black, M. (1993). More about metaphor. In A. Ortony (Ed.), Metaphor and thought (Second., pp. 19–41). Cambridge University Press. doi:10.1017/CBO9781139173865.004

Burt, C. (1950). The factorial study of emotions. In M. L. Reymert (Ed.), *Feelings and emotions* (1st Ed.). McGraw-Hill Book Company.

Chomsky, N., & McGilvray, J. (2012). *The science of language. Interviews with James McGilvray.* Cambridge University Press. doi:10.1017/CBO9781139061018

Constantinescu, P. (1986). *Sisteme Ierarhizate. Rolul informatiei in geneza si dezvoltare [Hierarchical Systems. The role of information in genesis and development].* Editura Academiei Republicii Socialiste Romania.

Constantinescu, P. (1990). *Sinergia, Informatia si Geneza Sistemelor [Synergy, Information and the Genesis of Systems].* Editura Tehnica.

Dorner, D. (2003). The mathematics of emotions. In *Proceedings of the Fifth International Conference on Cognitive Modeling* (pp. 75–79). Bamberg, Germany.

Dorner, D., & Hille, K. (1995). Articial souls: Motivated emotional robots. In *Proceedings of the International Conference on Systems, Man and Cybernetics* (pp. 3828–3832).

Durand, G. (1999). *The Anthropological Structures of the Imaginary.* Boombana Publications.

Eliade, M. (2003). Mitul Reintegrarii. *Humanitas.*

Foucault, M. (2002). *The order of things.* Routledge Classics.

Fussell, S. R. (2002). *The verbal communication of emotion: Interdisciplinary perspectives.* Psychology Press.

Harder, P. (1999). Function, cognition, and layered clause structure. In J. Allwood & P. Gardenfors (Eds.), *Cognitive semantics. Meaning and cognition* (pp. 37–68). John Benjamins. doi:10.1075/pbns.55.04har

Jung, C. G. (1981a). The archetypes and the collective unconscious (Collected Works of C.G. Jung Vol.9 Part 1) (2nd Ed.). Princeton University Press.

Jung, C. G. (1981b). The development of personality (Collected Works of C.G. Jung Vol.17). Princeton University Press.

Lakoff, G. (1993). The contemporary theory of metaphor. In A. Ortony (Ed.), *Metaphor and thought* (pp. 202–251). Cambridge University Press. doi:10.1017/CBO9781139173865.013

Lewis, M. D. (2005). Bridging emotion theory and neurobiology through dynamic systems modeling. *Behavioral and Brain Sciences, 28*(2), 169–194, discussion 194–245. http://www.ncbi.nlm.nih.gov/pubmed/16201458 doi:10.1017/S0140525X0500004X PMID:16201458

Nicolescu, B. (2009). *Qu'est-ce que la realite?* Liber.

Ortony, A. (1993). Metaphor, language, and thought. In A. Ortony (Ed.), *Metaphor and thought* (pp. 1–16). Cambridge University Press. doi:10.1017/CBO9781139173865.003

Petrariu, A. M. (2012). *Niveluri de Realitate în sistemele sociale.* Babes-Bolyai.

Plutchik, R. (1962). *The emotions: Facts, theories and a new model.* Random House.

Plutchik, R., & Conte, H. R. (Eds.). (1997). *Circumplex models of personality and emotions.* American Psychological Association.

Scheutz, M. (2004). Useful roles of emotions in artificial agents: A case study from artificial life. In *Proceedings of the 19th National Conference on Artifical Intelligence* (pp. 42–47). Retrieved from http://kiosk.nada.kth.se/kurser/kth/2D1381/AAAI104ScheutzM.pdf

Schon, D. (1993). Generative metaphor: A perspective on problem-setting in social policy. In A. Ortony (Ed.), *Metaphor and thought* (pp. 137–163). Cambridge University Press. doi:10.1017/CBO9781139173865.011

Sternberg, R., Tourangeau, R., & Nigro, G. (1993). Metaphor, induction and social policy: The convergence of macroscopic and microscopic views. In A. Ortony (Ed.), *Metaphor and thought* (pp. 277–303). Cambridge University Press. doi:10.1017/CBO9781139173865.015

KEY TERMS AND DEFINITIONS

Archetype: A personified instance composed of symbols, their properties, functions and possible actions.

Levels of Reality: Different planes of reality, within which the same rules apply and between which the principles change. For a comprehensive explanation see (Nicolescu, 2009).

Symbolic Image: A fundamental means of representing the world, mentally revealed as a coherent structure of concepts.

Systemic Approach (to Modeling Emotions and Cognition): A strategy by which both the environment and the agent being modeled are constructed as part of the same system, with clear correspondences between their structures.

Tertiary Logic: The theory by which all aspects of reality have a complementary nature and there exists an included third state, corresponding to the cancelation of the contradiction, on a higher level of reality. For a comprehensive explanation see (Nicolescu, 2009).

Chapter 4
Emotions and Social Evolution:
A Computational Approach

D. Casacuberta
Universitat Autònoma de Barcelona, Spain

J. Vallverdú
Universitat Autònoma de Barcelona, Spain

ABSTRACT

Emotion and social processes are evolutionarily intertwined. In this chapter, the authors present their TPR, TPR 2.0 and The Game of Emotions simulations along with the justification of necessary ideas in order to achieve the next level of research. This chapter describes a defense of the epistemological value of computer simulations for the analysis of emotions and social interactions. Finally, the elements of the model are described and defined with a sketch of the basic control algorithm.

1. WHY DO WE NEED ARTIFICIAL EMOTIONS?

Living entities increase their range of possible interactions and behavior according to the complexity of their embedded information processing systems, which reached a maximum level with the emergence of central nervous system and brain. Encephalization, adjusted by the Encephalization Quotient (EQ), understood by early modern researchers, was cognition at a high capacity of cognitive tasks, situating symbolic thinking at the top of possible brain performances. Leading intelligence, symbolic thought and encephalization considered as correlated variables. In this model, emotions had no place or role, but were even considered noisy or fuzzy elements that should be minimized or avoided. What we learned is that all these ideas were incorrect, at least in that naïve form. First, cognition not only happens into the brain, but there are morphological constraints that affect and direct cognition; second, extended cognitive processes are at the core of the cognition and make possible to understand how brains evolved towards the use of symbolic elements following auxiliary elements like external memories or graphical notations for better visualization; and finally, emotions have demonstrated to play a determinant role in the cognitive processes. This has proven valid for any cognitive system emerged from natural evolution, and consequently, for human beings.

DOI: 10.4018/978-1-4666-7278-9.ch004

But what about artificial intelligence? Have machines been reproducing this naturalistic approach? The answer is a rotund 'no'. Despite several biologically inspired strategies like genetic algorithms, a-life, biorobotics, evolutionary computation and electronics, swarm intelligence, and artificial neural nets or cellular automata among a long list (see the excellent compendium of Floreano and Mattiussi, 2008), the presence of emotions is close to zero. There is an exception though: the environments in which machines must interact directly with human beings; only these contexts explain the existence of the affective computing and social robotics research fields.

Perhaps we can find some small clues that show basic interest among AI communities towards emotions, like the idea of 'drive nodes' from Stephen Grossberg, a pioneer of Artificial Neural Networks (inspired by the experimental results of 1971 by Walle Nauta on how brain frontal lobes controlled the interoceptive censorship of plans), or the basic Cognitive Architectures of Aaron Sloman in the 1980's (after the revival into the study of emotions supported by Ekman, Ortony, Scherer, Oatley, et al.). Even the emergence of Affective Computing, by Rosalyn Picard at MIT in 1995 followed the publication of a seminal and very influential work or a Neurologist: *Descartes Error*, by Antonio Damasio, in 1994.

Perhaps emotions are not the backbone of AI systems since they neither have a real or strong presence in most economic and social sciences computer simulations. It's something absurd and shocking that those models, which try to explain human collective behavior, do not include into the models the emotions that drive human life. Over-simplistic variables like 'hunger' 'friendship/ enemy' or 'sexual mating' seems to be lacking. Human beings do not run cost-benefit analysis before any daily activity: they just act according to their previous ideas about the world and internal emotional states. Simulations regarding emergence and evolution of social strategies must include emotional aspects of a human life. It is

true that basic emotions are related to survival actions like feeding (individual survival) or mating (survival as species through gene transferring), but only with them human societies and symbolic thinking would have not emerged. At the same time, from protoemotional positive-negative basic input processing as pleasant-painful data, we cannot explain sophisticated social strategies or emotions like cooperation, shame, fear, guilt, or pride, …most of which involve moral regulation of human communities. This fact also requires another technical element: the innate ability of human beings to share and understand internal feelings, thanks to their holistic expression (body gestures, voice tone, eyes gaze, cultural signs). These signals are understood by the virtue of specialized neurons, called mirror neurons, and allow the 'feeling of the other's feelings' and thus, a direct and deep sharing of experiences with meaning… this is the social signaling process.

As a consequence we can affirm that: a) emotions are basic cognitive elements necessary to explain not only human thinking but also to design systems that must take decisions under complex, dynamic and fuzzy conditions; b) emotional mechanisms explain the basic bonds and modulations among individuals that create societies.

Thus, we need to implement emotions at several levels in order to obtain reasonable mechanisms to explain individual and social behaviors. The range of the individual behaviors have been here defined only under the umbrella of the epistemic activities, but emotions affect the whole system; about social dynamics, emotions provide the answers about why societies emerged and their managed strategies.

2. EMOTIONS IN SOCIAL SIMULATIONS

As discussed in the previous section, the role of emotional elements in Ai or social simulations has been until now, close to zero. The reasons are easily identified, first, as a misunderstanding about the crucial role of emotions into cognitive processes, action planning and social regulation and, second, a deep and historical distrust towards emotional states.

This is not the space to construct a defense in depth of the role of emotions into cognitive processes, but it is necessary to take into account the relevance of emotional flavor in human decisions: about where to go, what to eat, with whom to mate, and what to do next. This is our departure point: to implement emotional drives into social simulations.

Our interest on implementing emotional drives into social simulations is twofold:

- **1st:** We want to understand how emotions evolve and are structured-related to the societies in which they are embedded. That is how the syntax of complex emotions emerged and the semantic interpretations are according to the specificities of the system.
- **2nd:** We want to show that without emotional variables, the agents involved in the simulations are nothing similar to humans or to living systems with evolved central nervous systems. Without emotions and social simulations, they blind and dumb.

We will explain in detail in the next two sections our approach:

2.1. Evolution of Emotional Syntax

Our approach considers *emotions as informational data about real or symbolic objects that any entity adds as a personal meaning to the meanings socially shared about those objects.* At the same time, this information triggers internal states or feelings are can be distributed across time creating moods. Every object is or can be emotionally tagged: a piece of food, an idea, a tool, a sequence of movements (rituals, for example), etc.

We think that there are two basic emotional states: pain and pleasure, which we've called 'protoemotions' (Vallverdú and Casacuberta, 2008, 2009). Our hypothesis is that from basic positive (pleasure) and negative (pain) inputs embedded into our morphological structures (Casacuberta, Ayala and Vallverdú, 2010), we will be able to obtain more complex emotions after multiple combinations. We are just trying to emulate the emotional evolution that happened among the natural systems during the last hundred million years. Following this naturalistic approach, and considering that *natura simplicibus gaudet* work with two basic protoemotions (positive/negative) that interact creating increasingly bigger layers of meaning according to the summation of its values during a lapse of time. Following the seminal ideas of Wolfram (2002), we will consider our protoemotions as a special kind of cellular automata, to which we will apply simple rules. From their interaction (in social artificial environments), we are sure that departing from single repetitive patterns of action across time; we will be able to reach more complex behaviors.

An obvious fact: despite of the existence some automatic emotional reactions (with muscular correlates) like automatic or reflex responses and bodily adjustments to pain such as the size of the pupil adjusting, or muscular contractions preventing a hit, most of emotions are conceptually, culturally and socially mediated (Lutz, 1988; Zborowski, 1969). For that reason, the co-evolution of societies and complex emotions must be considered as absolutely intertwined. The syntax and semantics of complex emotions is related with the environments in which they emerged. We yield to obtain a dynamic model of emotional syntax that could allow us to reconstruct at least theoretically the mechanisms that would explain the emergence of these emotions. The social context from which they emerge would also provide their proto-semantic framework. We need new methods to obtain data about how emotions did evolution and which causal relationships can be established between social strategies, the own morphology and these emotions.

2.2. Simulating Social Evolution and the Role of Emotions

By the previous reasons, it looks clear to us that the simulations about human social evolution must include emotional variables in order to be truly informative and useful. Each unity of the simulation must perform individual emotional drives according to its morphological design and temporal necessities, and the whole simulation must put together a significant sum of these unities. Like physical simulations, in which each particle is charged with specific initial information and is at the same time constrained by some global rules, social simulations must emulate the basic interactions and forces that rule over individuals and the social. Each unity or entity into the simulation must have several degrees of cognitive and choice freedom, including variables of emotional driving (Hudlika, 2011), starting from basic survival necessities, plus reproductive imperatives. But their behaviors must include the necessity of the others, the own socialization process. It is crucial to consider the intentionally that can be inferred from the morphology of the units simulated: humans are not points into a matrix not basic flesh algorithms. They are a dynamic mixture of pre-recorded instructions and physical constraints at the same time that their own survival necessities and curiosity push them towards inexplicable changes. Humans are evolving paradigms or bodies and ideas, both emotionally flavored.

3. THE GAME OF EMOTIONS

As very recently we reviewed (Vallverdú *et al* 2013), our initial study began with a computer simulation we called The Game of Emotions (GOE). This research was the natural evolution of our two previous simulations, called TPR and TPR 2.0. (Vallverdú, and Casacuberta 2008, 2009), as well as our studies on synthetic emotions and cognition (Vallverdú, Shah and Casacuberta, 2010; Casacuberta, Ayala & Vallverdú, 2010), and in this research we interested on to using genetic algorithms to understand the mechanisms of the emergence of complex emotions from basic protoemotions.

Our hypothesis was that complex social and intelligent actions could be achieved through basic emotional configurations. In order to achieve our hypothesis, we created a new genetic algorithm which made possible to analyze the role of emotions into the individual and social activities. Python programmed and implemented online with Pyjama (a Rich Internet Application (RIA) Development Platform for both Web and Desktop), our GOE simulation was a close and finite geometrical squared world in which a unique type of creatures interact among them (socially and sexually) and also with food and dangers. The decision and actions of each creature was conditioned by a combination of 'genetic' and 'random'/'social'. The creatures had a genetic code (G) consisting of six genes grouped in two triplets, and each gene encodes a positive valence (which we called 'pleasure' or *p*) and a negative (which we called 'pain' or *n*). An example: G = {d,p,d} {p,d,p}. Each gene encodes a positive valence (which we also call 'pleasure' or *p*) and a negative (which we call 'pain' or *d*). The first triplet is genetically determined (by the parent) and called 'genetic triplet', while the second one is generated randomly and is called 'environmental triplet'. Each triplet is represented within brackets combining positive and negative valences. From example: An example: {p, p, n} (pleasure, pleasure, pain). According to the possible combinations, a limited amount of genomes is possible (36). Where there is *p* values dominance, it is a positive fitness (as we call the sum of all the G values); whether the value is 0, it happens a zero situation, a no-activity (illustrating a frame problem situation, that is the lack of a reason to act without enough information) and, finally, the dominance of *d* values implies a negative reaction. However, we must clarify in more detail how each value contributes to the decisions, based on the triplets' outcomes.

There were two mechanisms: i) the result of a calculation of the overall genome; ii) associating to each action the value of a single element of a triplet. For example if the creature is {x1, x2, x3} {y1, y2, y3}, then the movement is controlled by x1, reproduction for Y2, etc., but also dominated by a combination of genes: walking is the average of x1 and y1, the reproduction the average of x1, x2, x3. One example: G=[{x1,x2,x3}{y1,y2,y3}]. Here, each gene had to adopt one of the basic two states *p/d* (or stay inactive as an 'ill unit'). Consequently each gene had two parallel functions: (a) store/codify emotional states *p/n* (according to its genetic or environmental nature), (b) codify specific actions, following two co-existing rules: i. One gene = one function; ii. Several genes = one function. Basically, x1 codifies hunger, x2 sex, x3 movement, y1 empathy (detection friends/enemies), y2 curiosity and y3 how to sum the general fitness (making possible wrong lectures). A creature was continuously immersed in an ongoing review of its internal states, a loop that continuously managed its next action. The basic actions of the creatures were determined by hunger, sex or emotional situation.

With this simulation we were able to observe: a) how embodiment and environmental conditions condition the activity of artificial entities; b) how social dynamics can be described from a limited number of starting configurations. This will allow us to create in a future dynamic models of

emotional self-organization and to construct more complex interactions, c) the role of emotions into the creation of complex behaviors and allowing the emergence of more precise artificial cognitive systems (not necessarily naturalistic ones) and d) the benefits of designing entities with evolutionary capacities, in order to adapt to the changing conditions. On a close future, we will add the possibility of the genomes to evolve and increase their size. This is an example of the possible use of computational resources to run experiments on emotions.

With this simulation we were able to observe:

1. How embodiment and environmental conditions manage the activity of artificial entities.
2. How can social dynamics be described from a limited starting configurations. This will allow us to create in a future dynamic model of emotional self-organization and to construct more complex interactions.
3. The role of emotions into the creation of complex behaviors and allowing the emergence of more precise artificial cognitive systems (not necessarily naturalistic ones).
4. The benefits of designing entities with evolutionary capacities, in order to adapt to the changing conditions.

4. OUR PREVIOUS DIGITAL SIMULATIONS OF EMOTIONS

When we first developed GOE, our first basic research didn't give us any references of former work which was directly related to coding artificial emotions in an evolutionary setup. Besides the clear influence of the computer simulation LIFE by John Conway which was our first inspiration, we mostly worked *ex nihilo*.

However, as we learnt more about computer simulations, we started to find out more simulations that we doing research within the same paradigm we were focusing it. However they didn't speak about "artificial emotions" but about more sociological concepts, like following norms and punishing those that didn't collaborate, but the fact is that those results were clearly relevant for our own research.

So this section aims to introduce those precedents which can be of great help in order to improve our original project and make it more relevant for sociological or psychological issues.

4.1 The Game of Life

This project by theoretical mathematician John Horton Conway actually started as a sort of recreational solitary, with no research implications Gardner (1970). The main idea of the game was to mimic the way creatures are born, reproduce and die using only a few basic principles. Conway looked for a few rules that would be able to generate interesting patterns of colored squares as creature are born and die. Actually the principles are so basic, that is difficult to believe that anything interesting can come out of them.

The principles are:

1. "**Survivals:** Every counter with two or three neighboring counters survives for the next generation.

2. **Deaths:** After each counter with four or more neighbors, the creature dies (is removed) from overpopulation. Every counter with one neighbor or none dies from isolation.

3. **Births:** Each empty cell adjacent to exactly three neighbors--no more, no fewer--is a birth cell. A counter is placed on it at the next move. "(Gardner, 1970, p. 120)

Surprisingly enough, and depending heavily on the initial conditions (how many squares and where are those squares located) once get rapid extinctions, fast growing that ends up in extinctions and fascinating stable lighting patterns that

can be simply two states or several states before returning to the original position. Even more surprising, one can have a moving creature that keeps its shape as it moves a square each lapse of the game.

Conway originally designed his Game of Life as a sort of solitaire, to be played with cards, with no idea of computer in mind. As Gardner (1970) points out:

For long-lived populations such as this one Conway sometimes uses a PDP-7 computer with a screen on which he can observe the changes. The program was written by M. J. T. Guy and S. R. Bourne. Without its help some discoveries about the game would have been difficult to make.

It is important to see how emphasis is applied here. The Game of Life is not seen as a way to develop a computer simulation, but as a abstract theoretical mathematics problems which can be analyzed a little further by using a computer to solve some complex combinations that would be hard to analyze by hand. Despite it was not designed to be a computer simulation, one can see the seed for most of the social computer simulations we encounter. Namely:

1. The idea of having a bi-dimensional grid in which agents can show up and interact
2. Using simple symbols like squares or triangles to represent creatures
3. Using a few and very simple basic properties
4. Generating great complexity using simple rules.

As we'll see later in this section the last two points are especially important in order to consider the capacity of computer simulations to be used in a theoretical framework.

4.2 The Prisoner's Dilemma

Despite its originality and capacity to develop very simple worlds with very basic rules, the Game of Life as imagined by Conway had an important limitation to be used to analyze theoretical problems: it was quite unrealistic: there is certainly some relationship between how many creatures are in the same spot and whether they will survive or not: a territory that is too crowded can't produce enough food for all the creatures around, so some will eventually die. But the general idea behind the mechanism is not really related to biological creatures, like the postulate that automatically generates a new creature if and only if there are exactly three creatures in adjacent squares.

The main source for computer simulations of social issues comes from the so-called prisoner's dilemma. The idea started from the seminal work of John von Neumann and Oskar Morgenstern (1944) on how to analyze human decisions using a very set of simple rules like dominance, transitivity or invariance as basic postulates to take a decision in a rational way. Game Theory was an excellent model in order to simulate social problems in a computer and use them to make the best decisions available.

The prisoner's dilemma, however presents a very interesting conundrum against such a view. Because whatever one may decide to do, the best action is always to defect, but then, because of that, everybody will be worse than if both cooperate (Poundstone, 1992).

Things change however, when you consider an iterate game, in which one agent keeps playing with the same agent during various rounds, and any agent can decide whether to cooperate or to defect depending on how the other agent has been playing so far. Best strategies seem to depend greatly on how many rounds there are as well as the number of players (Hauert and Schuster 1997). Several approaches and strategies can be used, like a Markov matrix (Press and Dyson 2012), but as Axelrod (1987) initially showed about one situa-

tion he called *tit for tat* (if one agents cooperates, then the other cooperates but if one defects the other defects too), this very simple strategy beats any other. Axelrod and Hamilton arrived to such a conclusion using a series of computer simulations in which agents with initially random strategies and a process of selection was able to generate simple and winning strategies.

These results can be considered the first social computer simulation and have greatly influenced much of the simulations that are used nowadays in which agents interact among them during a series of rounds trying several strategies to win. Following such a procedure, one is able to get interesting results on how a community behaves or should behave based on the way these strategies develop and become stable or disappear.

The Prisoner dilemma is so relevant for computer simulations because in a very simple way it captures very well the tension between the short run benefits of being selfish versus the long run benefits of altruism and cooperating (Dawkins, 1988; Axelrod, 1997).

More relevant to our study is the use or genetic algorithms to solve problems using selection as a non-human directed way to analyze a problem. This simulation method can be described stating the following steps (Axelrod, 1997):

1. The specification of an environment in which the evolutionary process can operate,
2. The specification of the genetics, including the way in which information on the simulated chromosome is translated into a strategy for the simulated individual,
3. The design of an experiment to study the effects of alternative realities (such as repeating the experiment under identical conditions to see if random mutations lead to convergent or divergent evolutionary outcomes), and
4. The running of the experiment for a specified number of generations on a computer, and the statistical analysis of the results. (p 14).

Most of these situations tend to introduce lots of different constraints to model situations in real life, and are mostly used for predictive purposes. Most game theory based simulations are like that. As a matter of fact, our own original GOE was developing following such premises, and we tried to present a world that was mostly abstract, but tried to introduce lots of different variables in order to make it closer to real life, like the introduction of several types of food, obstacles, sexual reproduction, etc.

Nevertheless, if one aims at developing some theoretical knowledge, this view of a simulation as trying to share as many as characteristics as possible with the real world may turn our model unusable, as we'll see in the following section.

4.3 The Complexity of Cooperation

Axelrod (1997) will be the main guide for this section because it presents the general blueprint on how to do theoretical work with computer simulations, as well as because his work is the one closest to our main interest of generating artificial emotions using simulated social environments.

Axelrod was one of the first thinkers to realize that computer simulations are very powerful scientific instruments, and cannot be viewed just as helpers when direct analysis by a human is impossible (as we saw in the "Game of Life" example) or just as a means to make predictions when equations are too complex to be solved by hand (as in most game theory based simulations). According to Axelrod (1997) computer simulations are a new way to do science, in between induction and deduction:

Agent-based modeling is a third way of doing science. Like deduction, it starts with a set of explicit assumptions. But unlike deduction, it does not prove theorems. Instead, an agent-based model generates simulated data that can be analyzed inductively. Unlike typical induction, however, the simulated data come from a rigorously specified set of rules rather than direct measurement of the real world. (p. 3)

However, in order to do that, one has to be very careful in what you add to the simulation. Our cognitive ability to understand systems is very limited, so we need to have just a very small set of variables as well as a short number of rules and axioms: "Although the topic being investigated may be complicated, the assumptions underlying the agent-based model should be simple. The complexity of agent-based modeling should be in the simulated results, not in the assumptions of the model." (Axelrod, 1997, p. 5).

These observations do not rule out the other uses we just mentioned. Computer simulations can be used in complex mathematical problems when it is difficult to realize the outcome manually and there is nothing wrong in developing computer simulations to predict the weather or the stock market. However, one needs to realize that those other types of simulations won't be good enough to be theoretically relevant, because the researcher will never be able to see relevant dependences between objects and rules, due to the complexity of the model assumptions.

Another key element in computer simulations that look to solve the problem based on an evolutionary approach is crossover. This is something we also implemented in GOE. The idea is simple: one creates a sort of program that tells the creature in the simulation what to do depending on the surroundings as well as -possible- former internal states of the creature. Those creature that are able to interact with the environment a little better than the rest have the possibility to reproduce. Mimicking sexual reproduction, the best two creatures are selected and the information in their programs is mixed, and the new creatures are put in the simulation and see how well their fitness evolves.

Crossover is usually mixed with mutations to assure that the genetic pool expands and more possibilities are available, offering therefore more different type of creatures to be selected. Normal mutation takes also place during the reproduction, in which some of the elements passed to the offspring are changed randomly.

How this genotype is implemented is crucial in order to give a simulation its theoretical value. A very good example is Axelrod's simulations on cultural evolution. Culture, even simple artifacts, is very difficult to analyze in simple terms: the reasons why an individual desires a particular item may different in lots of relevant manners from the reasons of another individual. Nothing would become more difficult to model, therefore, than cultural evolution.

However, Axelrod (Axelrod, 1997) was able to capture the essential elements of culture spread and evolution using very simple models. Here is his description of the model:

To be concrete, suppose that there are five features and each feature can take on any one of ten traits. Then a culture can be described as a list of five digits such as 8, 7, 2, 5, and 4. In this case, the first cultural feature has the eighth of its possible values. This abstract formulation means that two individuals have the same culture if they have the same traits for each of the five features. The formulation allows one to define the degree of cultural similarity between two individuals as the percentage of their features that have the identical trait. [..] The model includes a geographic distribution of individual agents. A simple example would be a set of 100 sites, arrayed on a ten by ten grid. Because there is no movement in the model, the sites themselves can be thought of as homogeneous villages. These sites are the basic actors of the model. Each site can interact only with its immediate neighbors. (p. 154).

Is this realistic? Certainly, it is not. But as we stated before, our aim shouldn't be to be realistic, but to present a simulation that is simple enough to capture a specific mechanism and understand how it works.

Using this so simple model, Axelrod was able to show interesting and counterintuitive results, such as the fact that as the number of features grows, so does the probability of cultural convergence. If one considers the problem by pure thought, would consider that it should be the opposite: the more different features a cultural object has, the more diversity one gets. But the model clearly shows that the opposite is true. With objects the opposite have, the more objects a culture - even with similar features- the more culturally diverse zones we'll get (Axelrod, 1997, p.159).

Another very relevant result from this simulation of cultural evolution is questioning the functionalist approach to the diffusion of cultural objects. According to the functionalist approach, when one object has better features, or is better adapted to bring solutions, or is easier to use, etc. the more people will adopt it and, in the end, everybody will be using the improved cultural object. However, following his results (Axelrod, 1997, p. 168) it turns out that the majority doesn't need to present a better trait in order to make an object more used and to finally wipe out from the cultural landscape other alternative objects. By a simple process of social influence, certain practices and objects gain more followers, which help to attract more followers, so the practice with less number of followers is extinct first, until only one survives. This might happen because the cultural object that survived is better, but, as the model show, small random differences in distribution have a similar effect and help to make dominant a specific cultural object that doesn't have anything special.

The more relevant element for our study, though, is how actually these simulations are in the end about emotions but they are not labeled as such. Consider, for example, Axelrod (1986) which simulates how norms are created, disseminated and accepted in a society. The simulation makes a continuous use of the concepts of revenge or boldness, but they are considered only as behaviors, and not the fact that they are emotions.

5. USING PRECEDENTS IN ORDER TO IMPROVE GOE

Following the analysis of the main papers and books related to the idea of simulations and artificial emotions, here are the main results we think are more relevant to improve such a simulation project:

1. Computer simulations are not the last resource in science when neither empirical analysis nor mathematical proofs are available. They should be considered another way of doing science, which mixes in a very relevant intuition and deduction (Vallverdú, 2014). They provides us with sound information in order to decide the best way to emulate a natural property *in silico*, but without implicating that we indeed implementing the real thing or that this is the most efficient way to do it.

2. One needs to be sure of the main reason to develop a simulation. From what we have said in the former section, there are two main aims behind developing a simulation: i) to check new hypothesis in a quasi-empirical way or ii) to simulate real phenomena with certain detail in order to make predictions. The first one is a theoretical aim, while the second is a practical one. As we'll see next, both aims are not really compatible, and the volume of data and the type of simulation needed are quite different.

3. There have to be only very few rules governing the selection process and they have to be very easy both to understand and to implement. Otherwise, the simulation loses its main capacity to become a theoretical analysis of how emotions can be generated via a bottom-up approach. When one introduces too many rules, the results are too complex for theoretical significance, and at the same time too simple to become a simulation of a real event.

4. Simulations have to be incremental. As one can easily see in Axelrod's seminal work, one has to start from very simple simulation and build on them: once a specific strategy has been proved as useful, we incrementally proceed to create a more complex simulation based on the first one, until we have reached the level of realism we were looking for. As a matter of fact, once the theoretical soundness of a simulation has been proven, one can proceed to design realistic simulations, their aims are no longer to test the viability of a hypothesis, but to make predictions based on the model.

5. Theoretical simulations are not maximizers, and should not be viewed like mathematical proofs. As a matter of fact, they should be viewed more like satisfiers, models that are able to present simple algorithms able to create models that help us to understand what emotions are and how can they be implemented in robots or e-learning systems. And the way the proof is presented should be considered more like an experiment than a mathematical proof (Casacuberta and Vallverdú, 2014). Consider for example the *tit for tat* approach of Axelrod for the prisoner's dilemma: there are even more efficient strategies based on Markoff models (Press and Dyson, 2012) but that is not relevant for Axelrod's research, as what he was looking for was a simple way for a computer system to be good enough to survive in a prisoner's dilemma game.

6. FUTURE TRENDS: GOE 2.0

As one can deduce for the discussion presented in the former section, the main problem of our first version of GOE was to be in the middle of nowhere: not detailed enough to be considered a serious simulation on how emotions evolved, and not sufficiently simple to be able to give us bigger insights on what emotions are and what are the best ways to implement them in an artificial context.

This is specially truth for the way in which the genome of the emotions was encoded; there is a big divide between how information is coded and how then this information is used to generate specific behaviors. In that way, it became very difficult to establish when a creature was particularly successful, the main reason for its success, the distance between coding and behavior too big to allow proper deductions.

Based on those impressions, we are working in a new and improved version of GOE (GOE 2.0) which will include the following changes:

We will link more closely genotype and phenotype so it is apparent from the genotype how the creature is going to behave and therefore deducing why an specific emotion is successful or not. We will base this new way of encoding and decoding in the simulations that Axelrod created to state basic principles of cultural evolution (Axelrod, 1997). Basically, we will use the following model, considering that any "mental state" of the creature will be coded using the following main parameters:

1. Valence associated to an object (positive, negative, neutral)
2. Valence associated to the creature (stressed, relaxed)
3. Valence associated to the recent past (positive, negative, neutral)
4. Valence associated to social interaction (positive, negative, neutral). This valence will elicit a global and individual feedback. Our idea is to consider the socialization as a force at individual level (how I feel towards the immediate and close entities) as well as at social level (how the emotional tendencies of the *group* make me feel in a certain way).
5. Next action (move one step to an specific direction, eat, attack, do nothing)
6. New valence associated to an object (positive, negative, neutral)
7. New valence associated to the creature (stressed, relaxed). These valences will be able to be persistent across the time, emulating moods, thanks to a global summary of the basic valences and a general weight with previous basic emotional states.
8. New valence associated to the current situation (positive, negative, neutral)
9. *Random activation* over any of the previous parameters (sometimes people try new things, or is bored, or is sick…this has broadened all throughout the range of actions that human beings perform) every 50 cycles and not affecting more than 5% of the entities.

Creatures will have a random number of such genotype. One creature might have only one; another one may have 3 different ones, other six, etc. As before, creatures will start with a random assignation of values of each of the seven tuples to each of the "chromosomes" and will be left free to run around the world.

The world will be more simplified, in order to remove details that only make the model more complex to obtain proper theoretical knowledge without adding much realism to it. That means we will have only one type of food and no physical obstacles. Sexual reproduction will be embedded in the structure of the program instead of being based on the actual meeting of two creatures. That is, as is commonly done in the type of simulations we have been describing in former sections, after X movements of the game, the two creatures with better fitness will be paired and a number of new creatures will be launched to the world, within a mix of the data of the two "parents".

Creatures won't have a "natural death". They can only die of starvations or by an attack of another creature. In our former simulation, natural death did eliminate good candidates too early, so we might have missed creature with more robust genotype, as well as making the model more difficult to understand.

We expect from our simulation a better understanding of emotions by having this simple set of values and actions, and then argue how they can be used in the development of social robots that can communicate and collaborate based on those simple emotions. These basic emotions can also be used to create more complex simulations which will lead to more powerful and subtle emotions that can lead to a better understanding of human emotions.

For example, in his revolutionary work on the creation and maintenance of rules, Axelrod (1986) presents a compelling argument towards the use of metanorms. According to his study, in order to make a norm to stick in a society and become more or less permanent it is not enough to punish those who violate the rule. It is also important to punish those that do not punish those that violate the rule; a metanorm. Clearly, most social emotions in humans are based in norms and metanorms, so the very basic model of emotion described in the former paragraph wouldn't be enough to deal which such complex behavior. That implies to build a better simulation, with more complex behavior available, which uses the basic artificial emotion as a building block.

The same model can also be used to facilitate a better understanding of human language by computers and robots, being able to make more sense of emotional terms, which are very common in our daily speech, but commonly with pragmatic implications that are difficult to implement in a pure semantic approach to language understanding.

Artificial emotions can also be very helpful to improve social simulations. As we discussed in section 5.3, a very relevant number of social simulations use emotions (like compassion, revenge, boldness, shyness, and so on) but only the behaviors associated to them are considered, not the aspects of valance, and the psychological implications. If those emotions were modeled as such in those environments, we would obtain a sounder theoretical proposal, as well as better predictions of human behavior.

7. CONCLUSION

Simulations are a relatively novel way to do science and we are only figuring out their possibilities and implications. Simulations should not only be viewed as a way to make predictions in order to test complex mathematical models, but as a revolutionary way to make experiments and build knowledge in a bottom-up fashion when i) there are so many variables linked together to make real experiments ii) the subject we want to study is too developed in nature so it is too complex to be studied directly iii) the real-life situation implies long times of evolution and selection which cannot be analyzed directly.

We also defend that simulations are the best ways to test the relevance of an artificial model of emotional dynamics, and what we expect from such tests is their relevance in order to make a functional device which can be used to solve human problems; therefore accuracy in relation to Nature or humans should not be the main justification of a the value of a simulation, but its ability to present the capacity of a very simple model that can be theoretically analyzed and easily implemented.

REFERENCES

Axelrod, R. (1986). An evolutionary approach to norms. *The American Political Science Review*, *80*(4), 1095–1111. doi:10.2307/1960858

Axelrod, R. (1987). The evolution of strategies in the iterated prisoner's dilemma. In *Genetic Algorithms and Simulated Annealing* (pp. 32–41). London: Pitman.

Axelrod, R. (1997). *The complexity of cooperation.* Princeton: Princeton University Press.

Casacuberta, D., Ayala, S., & Vallverdú, J. (2010). Embodying cognition: a morphological perspective. In J. Vallverdú (Ed.), *Thinking machines and the philosophy of computer science: concepts and principles* (pp. 344–366). Hershey, PA: IGI Global Group. doi:10.4018/978-1-61692-014-2.ch021

Casacuberta, D., & Vallverdú, J. (2014). E-Science and the data deluge. *Philosophical Psychology*, *27*(1), 126–140. doi:10.1080/09515089.2013.827961

Dawkins, R. (1988). *The selfish gene.* Oxford: Oxford University Press.

Floreano, D., & Mattiussi, C. (2008). *Bio-inspired artificial intelligence: Theories, methods, and technologies.* Cambridge, MA: The MIT Press.

Garden, M. (1970). The fantastic combinations of John Conway's new solitaire game "life". *Scientific American*, (233): 120–123.

Hauert, Ch., & Schuster, H. G. (1997). Effects of increasing the number of players and memory steps in the Iterated Prisoner's Dilemma, a numerical approach. *Proceedings of Biological Sciences*, *264*(1381), 513–519. doi:10.1098/rspb.1997.0073

Hudlicka, E. (2011). Guidelines for designing computational models of emotions. *International Journal of Synthetic Emotions*, *2*(1), 26–78. doi:10.4018/jse.2011010103

Lutz, C. (1988). *Unnatural emotions.* Chicago, IL: UCP.

Neumann, J., & Morgenstern, O. (1944). *Theory of games and economic behavior.* Princeton: Princeton University Press.

Poundstone, W. (1992). *Prisoner's dilemma.* New York: Doubleday.

Press, W. H., & Dyson, F. J. (2012) Iterated prisoner's dilemma contains strategies that dominate any evolutionary opponent. In *Proceedings of the National Academy of Sciences* (109), 10409–10413.

Vallverdú, J. (2014). What are simulations? An epistemological approach. *Procedia Technology*, *13*, 6–15. doi:10.1016/j.protcy.2014.02.003

Vallverdú, J., & Casacuberta, D. (2008) The panic room. On synthetic emotions. In A. Briggle, K. Waelbers, & P. Brey (Eds.), Current Issues in Computing and Philosophy, (pp. 103-115). The Netherlands: IOS Press.

Vallverdú, J., & Casacuberta, D. (2009) Modelling hardwired synthetic emotions: TPR 2.0. In J. Vallverdú & D. Casacuberta, (Eds.), Handbook of Research on Synthetic Emotions and Sociable Robotics: New Applications in Affective Computing and Artificial Intelligence, (pp. 103-115). Hershey, PA: IGI Global. doi:10.4018/978-1-60566-354-8.ch023

Vallverdú, J., Casacuberta, D., Nishida, T., Ohmoto, O., Moran, S., & Lázare, S. (2013). From computational emotional models to HRI. *International Journal of Robotics Applications and Technologies*, *1*(2), 11–25. doi:10.4018/ijrat.2013070102

Wolfram, S. (2002). *A new kind of science.* Champaign, IL: Wolfram Media, Inc.

Zborowski, M. (1969). *People in pain.* San Francisco: Jossey-Bass, Inc. Publications.

KEY TERMS AND DEFINITIONS

Emotions: Emotions are basic cognitive elements necessary to explain not only human thinking but also to design systems that must take decisions under complex, dynamic and fuzzy conditions. At the same time emotions can be considered as informational data about real or symbolic objects that any entity adds as a personal meaning to the meanings socially shared about those objects.

Metanorms: Following Axelrod's ideas, metanorms are upper norms that tell people to punish transgressors of lower-level norms. The Norms Game allows players to punish those players caught defecting. The Meta-Norms Game allows players to punish those players who do not punish defectors.

Model: A representation of something, either as a physical object which is usually smaller than the real object, or as a simple description of the object which might be used in calculations. Here then, the main idea is that a model is a surrogate of a real thing or event, that constitutes a basic practice within scientific activities, and that its conceptual role lies somewhere between those of empirical data and theory.

Simulation: A mathematical model that describes or recreates computationally a system process. With that definition, we accept the dynamic nature of the system process and the underlying mathematical structure computationally implemented.

Social: Despite of its many senses, this concept refers to a characteristic of living organisms as applied to populations of humans and other animals. It always refers to the interaction of organisms with other organisms and to their collective co-existence, irrespective of whether they are aware of it or not, and irrespective of whether the interaction is voluntary or involuntary.

Chapter 5
On Realizing Emotional Memories

Saurabh K. Singh
Indian Institute of Technology Guwahati, India

Shashi Shekhar Jha
Indian Institute of Technology Guwahati, India

Shivashankar B. Nair
Indian Institute of Technology Guwahati, India

ABSTRACT

Emotion and memory have been two intermingled areas in psychological research. Although researchers are still fairly clueless on how human emotions or memory work, several attempts have been made to copy the dynamics of these two entities in the realm of robotics. This chapter describes one such attempt to capture the dynamics of human emotional memories and model the same for use in a real robot. Emotional memories are created at extreme emotional states, namely, very positive or happy events or very negative ones. The positive ones result in the formation of positive memories while the negative ones form the negative counterparts. The robotic system seeks the positive ones while it tries to avoid the negative ones. Such memories aid the system in making the right decisions, especially when situations similar to the one which caused their generation, repeat in the future. This chapter introduces the manner in which a multi-agent emotion engine churns out the emotions which in turn generate emotional memories. Results obtained from simulations and those from using a real situated robot described herein, validate the working of these memories.

INTRODUCTION

Emotion constitutes a very important phenomenon in living beings and plays an important role in every aspect of our life. Emotions depend upon both the current status of the environment and the past experience of the emoting individual. The term Emotion has a wide variety of definitions. Kleinginna Jr. et al. (Kleinginna Jr & Kleinginna, 1981), after reviewing numerous explanations

DOI: 10.4018/978-1-4666-7278-9.ch005

and sceptical statements on emotion from various dimensions including affective, cognitive and psychological, proposed the following definition for emotion-

"Emotion is a complex set of interactions among subjective and objective factors, mediated by neural/hormonal systems, which can

1. Give rise to affective experiences such as feelings of arousal, pleasure/displeasure,
2. Generate cognitive processes such as emotionally relevant perceptual effects, appraisals, labelling processes,
3. Activate widespread physiological adjustments to the arousing conditions and
4. Lead to behaviour that is often, but not always, expressive, goal directed and adaptive" (Kleinginna Jr & Kleinginna, 1981).

Emotions can be broadly categorized as those that are positive (happiness, surprise, enthusiasm, etc.) and negative (anger, fear, disgust, etc.). Both positive and negative emotions can occur concurrently and play different roles for an emoting individual. All the negative emotions are results of our response to mental, emotional or physical threats. Such emotions make us more aware of the surrounding and aid in survival (Lefkoe, 2010). On the other hand, positive emotions help tackle adverse environments and tight spots. Positive emotions not only contribute to life satisfaction and a feel-good factor in the present but also improve the likelihood of feeling similarly in the future (Fredrickson & Joiner, 2002).

The traditional viewpoint is that emotion and reasoning do not blend well at all. If a person wishes to make rational decisions then he should not allow the reasoning process to be entangled by emotions. Contrary to this view there are many research studies which support a greater role of emotion in day-to-day activities. Research in this direction has pointed out that emotion helps us in learning, memory formation and retrieval,

survival, prediction, decision-making and so on (Adler, Rosen, & Silverstein, 1998; Bechara, 2004; Loewenstein & Lerner, 2003; Macht, 2008; Velásquez, 1998). Peters (Peters, 2006) outlines four roles that emotions can play in constructing judgment and decision. These four roles are:

1. **As a Guide to Information:** Emotions are used as information for future decision making, constructing prices of plays and lotteries, in the perception of risks, etc.
2. **As a Selective Attentional Spotlight:** Emotions can force the decision maker to focus on some specific information so that this information is used in decision making or judgment; incidental emotions also work as a spotlight for memory.
3. **As a Motivator of Behavior:** A good environment tends to encourage one to approach a problem in the right spirit while a bad environment tends to make one to avoid it; Emotions are also linked to the amount of effort a decision maker can put.
4. **As a Common Currency for Comparing Alternatives:** Emotion helps in comparing things when things are not comparable by working as a common currency.

Numerous studies have shown that emotions can make good impact on the decision-making process in human beings (Bechara, Damasio, & Damasio, 2000; George, 2000; Zeelenberg, Nelissen, Breugelmans, & Pieters, 2008). Álvarez et al. (Álvarez, Galán, Matía, Rodríguez-Losada, & Jiménez, 2010) have pointed out the importance of human emotions in judgment, adaptation, decision making and communication and argued that the disconnection of emotions lead to poor judgment and inability to make appropriate decisions. Bryson et al. (Bryson & Tanguy, 2010) have suggested that emotions play a vital role in action-selection by providing such states that limits the search space.

Human emotions and memories are intermingled. Human beings have different types of memories. These include procedural memory which is responsible for skill development, declarative memory which accumulates various facts, associative memory which declares various rules and concepts from discrete stimuli and episodic memory which stores the temporal and spatial information (Francis Jr, Mehta, & Ram, 2009). Memory may also be categorized as short term memories which one tends to forget within an hour or a day or in a month and long term memories which stay with us for longer periods of time. Memories serve to connect the past with the present and provide a framework for our future and as a whole makes what we are (Mohs, n.d.). Some emotional memories, once created, can last for a life-time. A very touching moment such as being the only one praised by a large crowd for the first time in life or the moment of winning a competition or a major tragedy or accident could cause the formation of such permanent emotional memories.

Memory can be defined as the retention of information. There are three processes associated with a memory:1) Encoding of memory (the process of converting the information in to a form that can be stored), 2) Storage of the information in memory (the process of keeping the information over the period of time) and 3) Retrieval of the memory (the process of recalling the stored memory when needed) (Joshi, 2011). Emotions play a significant role in forming memories. Studies suggest that emotionally charged events (i.e. events that occur when either of positive or negative emotion is high) of our past last for a longer time and have more details as compared to the events that happen at normal emotional situations (LaBar & Cabeza, 2006; Phelps, 2004). These events create emotionally charged memories. Brown et al. (Brown & Kulik, 1977) have discussed about flashbulb memories caused due to emotional arousals. Talarico et al. (Talarico, LaBar, & Rubin, 2004) have indicated

that the intensity of emotion plays a major role in consistent prediction of autobiographical memories irrespective of valence (positive or negative emotion). Levine et al. (Levine & Pizarro, 2004) have claimed that emotional memories are not indelible but change over time and act as guides in the future. Friestad and Thorson (Friestad & Thorson, 1986) have presented the effects of Emotion-Eliciting Advertisement on long term memory and judgement and found that emotional messages result in stronger memory and more positive judgments. The emotional engagement during the memory encoding process helps in long term memory formation (Erk, von Kalckreuth, & Walter, 2010) and help in making better memories. Humans often evaluate a situation quickly using emotional (affective) memory than performing a longer, more complex cognitive evaluation which suggests that affective computation might implicitly encode the knowledge about the likelihood of positive or negative future events (Scheutz, 2011).

In human beings, the amygdala within the brain, is responsible for emotions while the hippocampus does the job of converting short term memories into long term ones (Francis Jr et al., 2009). Whenever emotional events are encountered, the amygdala detects it and communicates the same to the hippocampus. This results in release of stress hormones by the emotion centres situated in the brain as also stimulating the region of the brain in proximity. The released stress hormones provide feedback to the emotion centres. The outcome of these activities in the brain is the memories which get triggered whenever we encounter the same or similar situations later in life. Damasio (Damasio, 2005) describes the *somatic marker hypothesis* wherein, he mentions that making decisions under similar circumstances is biased by somatic markers (signals) from the past. These somatic markers associate with situations or circumstances and whenever such situations repeat, these markers pose as a threat or advantage depending upon whether the situation is a negative or a positive one. These markers help to increase memory and attention to certain options. A similar concept has been used by Velásquez (Velásquez, 1998), who describes a model where primary emotions are used as building blocks for acquisition of emotional memories. These emotional memories are used in future for decision-making and action-selection. Though, a variety of studies has been carried out in the realms of neuroscience and psychology on emotional memories, however very few of these studies have focussed on modelling emotional memories using an emotion generation model for a situated robot.

In this chapter, we propose an emotion based memory model to augment the multi-agent emotion generation model proposed by Nair et al. (Nair, Godfrey, & Kim, 2011). This memory model has been conceptualized based on the above discussions about the functioning of the human emotional memory (LaBar & Cabeza, 2006; Phelps, 2004; Velásquez, 1998) and corresponding responses. The model generates positive emotional memories at positive-emotionally charged situations and uses them as and when required. Likewise, it also generates negative emotional memories at those emotionally charged situations which are negative in nature and uses them to avoid the same or similar situations in the future.

The emotion memory model was tested for various situations encountered by a *situated robot* while moving from a source to a destination in an arena that contained various negative and positive emotion instigating areas. The primary objective of the robot is to reach to the destination as early as possible and in a good emotional state. The trade-offs between the time and the state parameters of the robot have been extensively analysed and results portrayed.

In the subsequent sections, we briefly describe the multi-agent emotion model (Nair et al., 2011) and the proposed emotional memory that serves to augment the model. We then provide the results and related discussions and eventually conclude with some future directions to the work.

THE MULTI-AGENT EMOTION MODEL (NAIR ET AL., 2011)

Nair et al. (Nair et al., 2011) have proposed a computational model for emotion generation, which takes into account almost all the processes of its biological counterpart. This model, as shown in Figure 1, employs dedicated agents for generation of each emotion. These agents perform their computation autonomously and concurrently. The multi-agent model thus comprises various agents responsible for generating a set of designated emotions based on external conditions which the overall system perceives. This emotion generation model categorizes the set of agents as positive and negative agents that work concurrently. A positive emotion agent is responsible for generating positive emotions such as happiness, surprise and enthusiasm while a negative emotion agent generates negative emotions like anger, fear and disgust. The agents of the same kind (positive or negative) stimulate each other whereas opposite agents suppress one-another. Hence, the emotional output of a particular agent is dependent on the amount of stimulations and suppressions it receives along with its current internal emotion value. This model also includes a feedback mechanism to simulate adrenaline based sampling of the environment along with rewards and penalties, time-to-live and decay for stimulations and suppressions (discussed later). This multi-agent emotion model has been used herein to realize the proposed memory model with certain modifications.

The emotion generation model (Nair et al., 2011) can be broadly classified into two parts viz. a Referee agent and the Emotion Agents as shown in Figure 1.

The Emotion Engine

The Emotion Engine shown in Figure 1 comprises two types of emotion agents that generate their designated type emotion (positive or negative). These emotion agents receive their inputs from

Figure 1. Multi-agent emotion engine (based on (Nair et al., 2011))

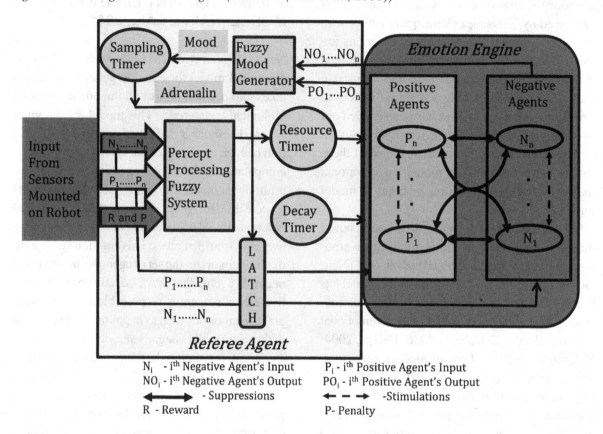

N$_i$ - ith Negative Agent's Input   P$_i$ - ith Positive Agent's Input
NO$_i$ - ith Negative Agent's Output   PO$_i$ - ith Positive Agent's Output
⟷ - Suppressions   ← – → -Stimulations
R - Reward   P- Penalty

the Referee agent. Each emotion agent has an associated *resource* which acts as a fuel to generate the intensity of the emotion. The agents compute the intensity value of their respective emotion and reduce their corresponding resources. Stimulations and suppressions have an associated life-time which the emotion agent calculates and sends to other relevant agents accordingly. These stimulations and suppressions received by an emotion agent are retained for the next round of computations until their life-time expires.

The Referee Agent

The referee agent work as the controller of the whole system. As shown in Figure 1, it consists of three asynchronous timers viz. the sampling timer, the resource timer and the decay timer.

These timers triggering cater to the sampling of the input, adjusting the resource and ensuring a decay of emotion within the agents, respectively. The referee agent takes input from the environment along with the current reward and penalty and provides these inputs to the corresponding agents. It also collects the output of all agents and generates a fuzzified *mood* value.

The Sampling Timer

The sampling timer controls the rate at which input is perceived or sensed from the environment. When triggered, it opens the latch and sends the sensory inputs along with reward and penalty to the respective emotion agent.

The sampling timer causes the following equations to be executed by the individual emotion agents (Equation 1 and Equation 2 in Box 1):

$$I_e(t+1) = I_e(t) + Z_e(t) \qquad (1)$$

The equations (1) and (2) (Nair et al., 2011) are used in order to compute the next intensity value by each emotion agent, $I_e(t+1)$. $I_e^i(t)$ is the input intensity perceived from the relevant sensor. S_{je} and S'_{ie} form the sum of the stimulations and suppressions received by the emotion agent respectively. $R_e(t)$ and R_{emax} represent the current and the maximum possible resource values for an agent respectively. Stimulations and suppressions are calculated using the equation (3) (Nair et al., 2011)

$$S_{je}(t+1) = \sum_{j}^{M} S_{je}^{(old)}(t) + S_{je}(t); j \neq e \qquad (3)$$

$S_{je}^{(old)}(t)$ signifies the stimulations having non-zero lifetimes for an emotion agent e.

The emotion resource which signifies the emotion generating capacity of an agent decreases after every emotion generation instance. It is synonymous to the energy dissipated in computation. The equation (4) (Nair et al., 2011) denotes this decrement in the emotion resource.

$$R_e(t+1) = R_e(t) - |Z_e(t)| \qquad (4)$$

Stimulations, Suppressions and Life Times

Stimulations (and suppressions) need to be computed by an emotion agent and sent to other emotion agents. The equation (5) (Nair et al., 2011) depicts the manner in which these are computed. The values received are treated as stimulations by similar type of agents (positive to positive and negative to negative) and as suppressions when the agents are dissimilar (positive to negative and vice versa).

$$S_e(t+1) = S'_e(t+1) =$$
$$\begin{cases} \left(\dfrac{I_e^i(t) - I_e(t)}{I_e(t)} \right)\left(\dfrac{R_e(t)}{R_{emax}} \right) & if\ I_e^i(t) > I_e(t) \\ 0 & otherwise \end{cases} \qquad (5)$$

Stimulations and suppressions die over a period of time. During their lifetimes they contribute to

Box 1.

$$Z_e(t) = \begin{cases} \left(I_e^i(t) - I_e(t) + w_{e1}\sum_{i=1}^{E} S_{je}(t) - w_{e1'}\sum_{i=1}^{E} S'_{je}(t) \right)\left(\dfrac{R_e(t)}{R_{emax}} \right) & for\ I_e^i(t) > I_e(t) \\ \left(w_{ie}I_e^i(t) + w_{e2}\sum_{i=1}^{E} S_{je}(t) - w_{e2'}\sum_{i=1}^{E} S'_{je}(t) \right)\left(\dfrac{R_e(t)}{R_{emax}} \right) & for\ I_e^i(t) = I_e(t) \\ -\left| \left(I_e(t) - I_e^i(t) + w_{e3}\sum_{i=1}^{E} S_{je}(t) - w_{e3'}\sum_{i=1}^{E} S'_{je}(t) \right)\left(\dfrac{R_e(t)}{R_{emax}} \right) \right| & for\ I_e^i(t) < I_e(t) \end{cases} \qquad (2)$$

enhancing or inhibiting the respective emotions. The associated lifetimes are calculated in accordance to equation (6) (Nair et al., 2011).

$$L_e(t+1) = \begin{cases} k_1\left(I_e^i(t)\right) \text{if } I_e^i(t) > 0, I_e(t) = 0 \\ k_2\left(I_e^i(t)\right) \text{if } I_e^i(t) > I_e(t) > 0 \\ 0 \oint otherwise \end{cases}$$

(6)

where k_1 and k_2 are positive constants and $k_1 < k_2$. $L_e(t+1)$ is the computed lifetime value.

The Decay Timer

The emotion intensity value, which is calculated at each sampling time by each agent, cannot merely accumulate continuously. It needs to decay with time. The decay timer controls this periodic decay of intensity of the emotions. Exponential decay equations (7) (8) (Nair et al., 2011) have been used to trigger this timer.

$$\Delta_e(t+1) = k_3\left(\sum_{i=t}^{P} I_e(i) - I_e(i-1)\right) / \left(t - T_p\right)$$

(7)

$$I_e(t+1) = \begin{cases} I_e(t) - k_4 e^{-\Delta_e(t)} \ for \ \Delta_e(t) > 0 \\ I_e(t) - k_5 e^{-\frac{1}{\Delta_e(t)}} \ for \ \Delta_e(t) < 0 \\ I_e(t) - k_6 \ for \ \Delta_e(t) = 0 \end{cases}$$

(8)

Emotion decay is modeled on the basis of the past emotion intensity values. These intensity values are used to compute Δ_e for the emotion e. k_3, k_4, k_5 and k_6 are positive constants.

The stimulations/suppressions received from other emotion agents with their corresponding lifetimes also need to decay. When the decay timer triggers it causes the execution of equation (9) (Nair et al., 2011) which consequently decays the stimulations/suppressions.

$$S_e(t+1) = S_e(t) - k_7 e^{-S_e(t)}$$

(9)

k_7 is a positive constant. The stimulations/suppressions die out when either their respective values or lifetimes become zero.

The Resource Timer

The emotion resource as mentioned earlier, is the affective capacity of an emotion generating agent. It decreases at every sampling time when the new emotion intensity is calculated by an emotion agent.

Emotion resources are recharged as and when the resource timer triggers. The timing for this is controlled by a fuzzy resource-timer generator module. This module determines the resource timer's timeout value by fuzzifying and defuzzifying the ambience, reward and penalty obtained from the external environment. The ambience is a function of the sensor values. Reward and penalty are those that the emoting system gains or loses every time it acts on the environment. They need to be modeled to cater to the application for which the emotion engine is being used. The equation (10) (Nair et al., 2011) is used to calculate the ambience value.

$$A(t) = \left\{ \sum_{i=1}^{N} a_i(t) - \sum_{j=1}^{M} a_j'(t) \right\} / (M + N)$$

(10)

where, $a_i(t)$ is the ith positive emotion agent value and $a_j'(t)$ is the jth negative emotion agent value.

The fuzzy resource-timer module gives its output as O_f which is used to calculate the timeout of the Reward-resource-timer (T_{rr}) (equation 11) (Nair et al., 2011).

$$T_{rr} = k_r O_f \tag{11}$$

where, k_r is a positive non-zero constant.

The Penalty-resource-timer (T_{rp}) is calculated using equation (12) (Nair et al., 2011).

$$T_{rr} + T_{rp} = k_{rp} \tag{12}$$

where, k_{rp} is a constant.

These two (reward and penalty) resource timers trigger the recharging of the corresponding resources of the positive and negative emotion generating agents respectively.

Charging Emotion Resource

The emotion resource is recharged by two methods:

1. By the environment: This is accomplished using the rewards and penalties sampled from the environment when the sampling timer triggers. The equations (13) and (14) (Nair et al., 2011) represent the dynamics of resource recharge.

$$R_e^+(t+1) = R_e^+ + k_{rew} Rew(t) \tag{13}$$

$$R_e^-(t+1) = R_e^- + k_{pen} Pen(t) \tag{14}$$

where, R_e^+ and R_e^- stand for emotion resource of the positive and negative agent respectively. *Rew* and *Pen* form the reward and penalty while k_{rew} and k_{pen} are positive constants.

2. By the triggering of the resource timer: The amount by which the respective emotion agent is recharged is governed by equation (15) (Nair et al., 2011).

$$R_e(t+1) =$$
$$\begin{Bmatrix} R_e(t) + e^{1/R_e(t)} \ for \ I_e^i(t) \leq 1, R_e \geq 1 \\ R_e(t) + 1 \ for \ I_e^i(t) < 1, R_e < 1 \\ R_e(t) + e^{1-(1/x)} \ for \ I_e^i(t) > 1 \ where \ x = I_e^i(t) \end{Bmatrix} \tag{15}$$

Mood

The Fuzzy system is used to output a *mood* value. This mood value is used to calculate the sampling timer value. The fuzzy system takes input, the output emotion value of each agent. The averaged value of the positive emotion agents' outputs and that of the negative emotion agents' outputs are taken as inputs for the fuzzifier.

DECAY OF POSITIVE AND NEGATIVE EMOTIONS

The emotion decay timer is responsible for decay of the output of the emotion agent, decay of stimulations and suppressions and that of the emotion agent's resource value. It has been found in many studies that decay of positive and negative emotions occur at different rates. El-Nasr et al. (El-Nasr, Yen, & Ioerger, 2000) have described that the rate of decay of negative emotions is less than that of the positive one. The negative emotion seems to be more persistent. Padgham and Taylor (Padgham & Taylor, 1997) have described how personality of a person depends on the decay rate of his/her emotions. Ham et al. (Ham, Jung, Park, Ryeo, & Ko, 2009) provide an example of how short tempered people become angry as easily as they can be calmed. However, when timid people lose their temper, it is very difficult to calm them. Park et al. (Park, Kim, Kim, & Kwon, 2009), have noted that if positive emotion is high then the decay rate of the negative emotion is also high as compared to normal situations and vice versa.

Hence, unlike that suggested by Nair et al. (Nair et al., 2011), the decay timer should be unique for positive and negative emotion generating agents. Decay of positive emotions should depend upon the status of the negative emotions. If the emotion intensity values of negative agents are high then the decay rate of the emotion intensities of positive agents should be proportionately high. These findings led us to modify the functionality of the decay timer in the emotion generation model proposed by Nair et al.

The new decay timer values are calculated using the value of the mood generated by the fuzzy mood generator. The equations (16) and (17) are used to compute the new decay timer values.

$$D_p = \alpha_1 * M \qquad (16)$$

$$D_n = \alpha_2 - D_p \qquad (17)$$

where,

D_p is decay timer for positive emotion agents,
D_n is decay timer for negative emotion agents,
M is mood value,
α_1 and α_2 are positive constants.

Nair et al. (Nair et al., 2011) have tested their multi-agent emotion model on three different test cases. After implementing the new decay timers, we tested the emotion generation model against the same three test cases. We found that the effects of the modifications can only be observed in the second test case wherein, the input to the positive emotion agents decreases slowly to a minimum while the negative emotion agents receive a high

input value. Figure 2 depicts the change in the output of the positive agent, when the input to the negative agents becomes high for the first time. As can be observed from the figure, the output of the positive agent drops drastically with the modified version of decay timer than in the previous implementation based on Nair et al. (Nair et al., 2011). The emotion generation model with the modified version of the decay timer has been used to realize the proposed emotion memory model.

EMOTIONAL MEMORY MODEL

The proposed emotional memory model aims to create long term memories based on emotionally charged events. Different degrees of emotionally charged events result from various situations that one encounters in life. Only a few of these events cause such a high emotional impact that they cause the formation of long term emotional memories. These memories can be broadly classified into two categories –Positive and Negative. When a person encounters a negative emotionally charged situation, a negative long term memory is created which makes him/her remember that situation for a long time. Such a long term memory created by a high negative emotion forces the person to avoid such situations in future. But at times in these situations some change of decisions are required to decide whether one should completely avoid the situation or ignore it for some time. For instance, imagine a person who was involved in a train accident in the past. If that person encounters an emergency situation wherein he has to reach a place as early as possible and the only alternative left for him is to board a train then, in such a case, he may choose to board the train based on his current confidence and the distance he need to travel. He may avoid train travel if the destination is too far. These kinds of decision-making are often made based on our memory, current level of confidence and priority of tasks. At times, we allow ourselves

Figure 2. Output of emotion agents (1 positive and 2 negative) showing the effect of the decay timers

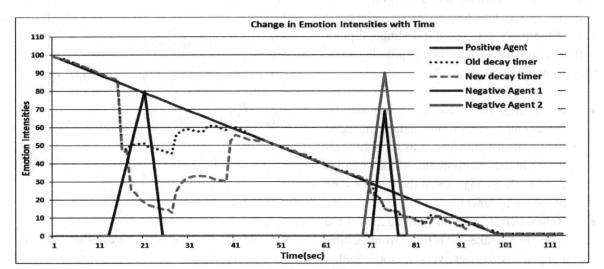

to delve into negative situations deeper, as doing so helps us in achieving some high priority goals; otherwise, we just allow ourselves to avoid them.

Positive emotionally charged events cause the formation of positive long term memories. With positive long term memories, we learn and remember the situations that soothe our minds or enhance our moods. For example, when a person visits a theatre to watch an enjoyable movie for the first time, this event may create a positive long term memory for him. Hence, the person remembers that visiting a theatre and watching a good movie enhances his mood. If in future he requires to heighten his spirits, he may search for a theatre and watch such a movie. The importance of positive memories arises when a person feels sad (low confidence). Under these situations one is internally motivated to move towards situations which caused the generation of positive memories. Even in positive memories, one may need to take a call and select among various options available such as visiting a restaurant or a theatre, both of which caused the generation of positive emotion memories earlier.

The effect of a negative long term memory is more drastic than a positive one. Negative long term memories help in survival by guiding future

behaviors while positive memories provide to soothe us at the times of grief.

The Emoting Robot and its Dynamics

The proposed emotion memory model has been devised for a robot situated in an environment. The robot encounters various situations in its environment that affects its emotion state (mood). Some of these situations (positive and negative emotionally charged events) result in the formation of emotional memories. These long term emotional memories influence the robot's behavior in the future. The robot is equipped with sensors to sense these situations as emotion fields. For example, positive emotion fields could mean a solar charging point, battery replacing point, servicing point, etc., while negative emotion fields could be a fire, an obstacle, areas in the environment that consume more power such as a gradient in the terrain, etc. The values of the sensors, which sense these emotional fields, are inversely proportional to the distance of the robot from the source of emotion fields (negative or positive). There are four significant parameters viz. Mood (M), Reflex (R), Health (H) and Confidence (C) associated with the robot, described below, which contribute in the formation and retrieval of positive and negative long term memories. The basic goal of the robot is to reach a destination point within the environment as soon as possible while also maintaining good health.

- **Mood (*M*):** This is a quantity provided by the emotion generation model embedded within the robot. It varies as the robot traverses in the environment. Mood signifies the robot's feelings about the current state of the environment.

- **Reflex (*R*):** It is the inherent quality of the robot that makes it refrain from getting trapped inside negative situations. Reflex signifies that the robot has reached a condition of extreme panic and any further progression could be catastrophic. It forces the robot to perform a reflex action which makes it to detour from its current path or action. This is akin to a situation when we accidently touch a hot plate and remove our hand autonomously without thinking. The action we performed can be regarded as a reflex action which is already embedded within us.

- **Health (*H*):** Health signifies the physical status of robot. The value of *H* decreases if the robot moves closer to a negative emotion field and increases if it moves closer towards a positive emotion field. The value of *H* degrades exponentially when the robot exercises the Reflex, R, otherwise the increase or decrease in the value of *H* remains linear. Exponential degradation of health indicates that the nature of the situation is that of extreme panic while a linear degradation depicts a normal environment where health reduces with time. Equation (18) is triggered for every emotion input at constant time intervals to estimate the current value of *H*.

$$H_{i+1} = \begin{cases} H_i - \kappa_1 e^{\frac{N_j}{\kappa_2}} & \left(if\ Reflex\ triggers\right) \\ H_i - \dfrac{N_j}{\kappa_2} & \left(if\ Negative\ field\ is\ encountered\right) \\ H_i + \dfrac{P_j}{\kappa_2} & \left(if\ Positive\ field\ is\ encountered\right) \end{cases}$$

(18)

where,

- H_i is the health value after i^{th} time interval,
- N_j is j^{th} negative emotion input,
- P_j is j^{th} positive emotion input and
- k_1 and k_2 are positive constants.

- **Confidence (*C*):** Confidence signifies the amount of risk that the robot can afford to take after encountering a negative situation. If *C*= 0, the robot would always avoid a negative situation maintaining the maximum possible distance from it. A high value of *C* would make the robot risk penetration further into the negative situation or area in order to optimize its path to the destination. In real life situations too, whenever someone is in a high confidence state, he/she tends to take a higher degree of risk while the same is avoided during diffident states. The value of confidence *C* for the robot is calculated as follows:

$$C_{i+1} = \begin{cases} C_i - \beta^2 & if(M < l_t) \\ C_i + \beta^2 & if(M > u_t) \\ C_i + \beta & otherwise \end{cases}$$

(19)

where $\beta = \dfrac{M - Med(M)}{S_f}$

- M = mood,
- $Med(M)$ = median of mood,
- S_f = scaling factor,
- l_t = lower threshold of mood,
- u_t = upper threshold of mood and
- C_i = confidence.

The change in confidence is quadratic in emotionally charged areas $(M < l_t$ and $M > u_t)$ so as to simulate real life scenarios while it is linear otherwise. In real life scenarios the decrement in confidence due to a negative situation will always be more than the increment in confidence by a positive situation. This scenario has already been taken in to account indirectly by the sampling timer in the multi-agent emotion model which triggers at fast rate in case of a negative situation and at slow rate in case of positive one so as to emulate adrenaline-like sampling (Nair et al., 2011). The value of Confidence, C, increases for a positive situation $(M > u_t)$ whereas it decreases in a negative situation $(M < l_t)$. Equation (19) is triggered at each sampling of the environment by emotion generation model. C is bounded with a minimum and maximum value and the situated robot needs to maintain its minimum value to survive.

Creation of Negative Emotional Memory

A long term negative emotional memory is created when the robot encounters a negative emotionally charged situation in its environment. As the robot moves towards its destination, it may encounter negative situations which result in lowering its mood. When the robot encounters such a situation for the first time, it continues its journey towards its destination since it is initially unbiased due to the absence of any past emotional memory. However, if this low mood situation persists for a certain period of time (λ), then the robot perceives it as a high emotionally negatively charged event and creates a memory vector for the current situation as shown in Figure 3. The P_i's denote the values of the different positive emotions while N_i's denote the values of the different negative emotions. This vector acts like a negative emotional memory for the robot in future.

Algorithm 1 depicts the process of creation of a negative emotional memory. As the robot moves closer towards the negative situation, its mood starts decreasing rapidly. Two boundaries which a robot may encounter have been defined and used.

1. **Safe Boundary (*SB*):** This is the distance from the source of the negative emotion field at which the effect of negative emotion field on the robot's M, H and C are minimum.
2. **Reflex Boundary (*RB*):** This is the closest point to the source of the negative emotion field where the reflex R triggers.

From the point where the robot's mood goes beyond the lower threshold (l_t) which indicates the *Safe Boundary* (*SB*), the robot starts recording all its sensors values and preserves them along with the current value of confidence. If reflex works at the *Reflex Boundary* (*RB*) and the number of samples of sensory information collected are enough to create memory, a negative memo-

Figure 3. Emotional memory vector (Pi's denote the values of different positive emotions, Ni's denote the values of different negative emotions and Tv is the Timidity)

P_1	P_2	...	P_n	N_1	N_2	...	N_n	T_v

Algorithm 1. Negative emotion memory formation

```
If (MOOD <l₁)
{
        If (negative sensor value > limit AND COUNT >count_limit)
                CALL reflex;
                GENERATE a memory vector (at SB);
        Else if (count >count_limit)
                GENERATE a memory vector;
        Else
                PRESERVE the current vector (at SB);
                COUNT++;
}
Else
{
        COUNT = 0;
        KEEP going towards destination;
}
```

ry vector is generated. If the *Mood* of the robot maintains a value below the lower threshold (l_t) until λ then even if *RB* is not reached, it generates a negative memory vector. The memory vector, as shown in Figure 3, signifies the farthest boundary from the center of the negative situation beyond which the robot would enter in a state of panic. The memory vector contains the corresponding positive and negative emotion inputs perceived at that *SB*. It also stores a value called *Timidity,* T_v, which is derived from the robot's confidence *C*. The value of *Timidity* is calculated using Equation (20). T_v denotes how much confidence the robot has lost during its course within the negative emotion field. The usage of T_v is discussed in the next section.

$$T_v = M_t + \left(C_f - C_r \right) \qquad (20)$$

where

- M_t is minimum required threshold value of confidence,
- C_f is value of confidence *C* at *SB* and

- C_r is value of confidence during memory creation.

Retrieval of Negative Emotion Memory

As the robot moves in the environment, its currently perceived emotion vector is matched against all the stored memory vectors. A match occurs if the perceived emotion vector is equal or close to a memory vector. After a successful match, the robot makes a decision based on its current value of confidence, on whether it should continue its sojourn towards its destination or how much further it should continue towards the destination or whether it should take a detour from its current path so as to avoid the current situation. Having sufficient confidence motivates the robot to penetrate further towards the negative situation as its primary objective is to reach the goal as early as possible. Algorithm 2 describes the negative emotion memory retrieval mechanism.

For humans, the risk taking capability depends on their emotions (Shiv, Loewenstein, & Bechara, 2005). Similar to this, we relate the risk taking capability to the robot's confidence value which is an indicator of its past emotions. The amount of penetration (confidence window) in the negative situation depends upon the difference of current value of confidence C_c and the timidity T_v which is given by Equation (21). As can be seen, the confidence window, W_c, is directly proportional to the difference between C_c and T_v.

$$W_c = \frac{(C_c - T_v)}{S_f} \qquad (21)$$

Based on W_c and the current perceived vector, a new vector is generated. This new vector indicates the distance up to which the robot can penetrate within the negative situation. When the robot attains the value of this new vector, it avoids moving further by enforcing a *Reflex*.

Creation of Positive Emotional Memory

A positive emotional memory is created whenever the robot comes across a positive emotionally charged event in its environment. Algorithm 3 depicts the process of creation of a positive memory vector. If the robot's mood M crosses an upper threshold (u_t) any time within its environment and if such a situation persists for some γ units of time then the robot creates a positive memory vector pertaining to that situation. It saves the memory vector similar to the one depicted in Figure 3 along with a soothing rate (S_R) associated with that memory vector. The soothing rate denotes the rate by which the confidence C of the robot increases with time.

The soothing rate is calculated as per equation (22):

$$S_R = \frac{C_{fu} - C_{fl}}{\Delta t} \qquad (22)$$

where,

- S_R is soothing rate,
- C_{fu} is value of confidence for $(M > u_t)$,
- C_{fl} is the value of confidence when Mood M returns to the normal value i.e. $l_t < M < u_t$ and
- Δt is the time difference between C_{fu} and C_{fl}.

Positive Emotion Memory Retrieval

As the environment comprises both positive and negative situations, it is possible that robot may come across more than one negative situation. This can result in the degradation in its confidence C which may go lower than M_t. In such cases, if the robot has positive memory vectors then it seeks such places so as to boost its confidence.

Algorithm 2. Negative emotion memory retrieval

```
If (Vector_matched == TRUE)

{

        If (within confidence window)

            KEEP penetrating further

        Else

            AVOID the negative situation;

}

Else

{

        KEEP on going towards destination;

}
```

Algorithm 3. Positive emotion memory formation

```
If (MOOD >u₀)

{

        If (COUNT > limit)

                CALCULATE the soothing rate Sᵣ;

                GENERATE the memory vector;

        Else if (COUNT == 1)

                SAVE the current confidence value;

        Else

                COUNT++;

}

Else

{       COUNT=0;

        KEEP going towards destination;

}
```

In the absence of any positive memory vector the robot starts to move randomly avoiding the current area of negativeness. If the robot has more than one positive long term memories, the decision as to which one needs to be chosen is given by equation (23).

$$P = c_1 d_{c,pm_i} + \frac{c_2}{S_{R_i}} + \eta \qquad (23)$$

where,

- c_1, c_2 are positive constants,
- d_{c,pm_i} is the distance between current location and the location of ith positive memory field and
- S_{Ri} is the soothing rate of ith positive memory.

The Equation (23) takes into account the destination from the positive memory and the soothing rate of that memory. The parameter P is calculated for every positive memory. That positive memory location, for which P has the least value, is selected as the next destination. η indicates how often this positive memory location has been visited in the past to decrease the chance of picking the same positive memory again.

Algorithm 4 explains the retrieval mechanism of the positive emotion memory. As the robot approaches the selected positive memory, its confidence starts increasing due to the positive situation. However, it cannot allow itself to stay there until the confidence reaches its maximum value because it needs to reach the destination as early as possible. It should stay in the positive situation or area only till it acquires the requisite amount of confidence. We have used Equation (24) to predict the *sufficient* confidence level (C_n) on the basis of its past path. This equation predicts the confidence required by reviewing the situations that the robot encountered in the past. If it had encountered numerous negative situations then the value of C_n is likely to be high. On the other hand, if robot did not encounter numerous negative situations in the past then the equation would return a lesser value of C_n.

$$C_n = \left(\frac{\Delta C}{\Delta D}\right) D \qquad (24)$$

where,

- C_n is the needed confidence,
- ΔD is the total distance travelled so far,
- D is the further distance to travel and
- ΔC is the total confidence lost in past negative situations.

Various other situations may also be encountered by the robot. While going towards the selected

Algorithm 4. Positive emotion memory retrieval

```
If (confidence < minimum threshold)

{

        If (positive memory not selected)

                COMPARE the P (equation 6) value for all the learned positive memory
                and select the memory foe which p value is lesser

                AND

                PREDICT the minimum confidence needed for future path (equation 7).

        Else if (reached at selected positive memory)

                WAIT here and RECHARGE;

        Else

                KEEP going towards selected positive memory

}

Else if (memory is selected AND Confidence < predicted confidence)

{

        WAIT here and RECHARGE;

}

Else

{

        KEEP going towards destination;

}
```

positive memory it may discover a new positive long term memory. Under such a condition the robot ignores the selected positive memory and uses this newly discovered positive memory. A few typical situations are presented and explained in a section that describes the results.

There are some similarities in theoretical concepts between the proposed emotion memory model in this chapter and the one presented by Velásquez (Velásquez, 1998) such as the use of emotions for acquiring emotional memories and later using them as information for decision making. Though, Velásquez has proposed a framework where emotions have been used as a motivational

system for behavior selection and control of autonomous agents and included emotional memory as secondary emotions, his model is good only for their definitive goals. Further, he has not exploited the mechanics of emotional memories and his model or results do not emphasize on how emotional memories are created and retrieved. On the other hand, the proposed emotional memory model described herein is a concentrated attempt in formalizing the creation and retrieval of emotional memories along with their underlying dynamics. This model provides a detailed process to work with emotional memories and uses the concepts of confidence and health which makes it more akin to its natural counterparts. Further these concepts are also used in the decision making process.

EXPERIMENTATION AND RESULTS

To validate the efficacy of the proposed emotional memory model, various experiments were conducted in a simulated environment with varying scenarios viz. number of positive and negative emotion sources, number and locations of destinations, etc. Experiments on a real robot were also performed to portray the practical viability of the presented model.

Simulation Environment

The simulation environment, coded in Java, comprised an NxN grid ($N = 200$). Any position in the simulation environment, henceforth referred to as arena, can be identified by an (x, y) coordinate. The arena consists of various positive and negative emotion fields. These emotion fields act as potential fields whose intensity diminishes as one moves away from the source. The robot in the arena can sense these positive and negative emotion fields using its sensors which act as inputs to the Multi-agent Emotion Engine (EE) embedded within it. The value of these inputs varies from 5 to 100 depending upon the distance of the robot from the source of the emotion fields (positive and negative). The goal of the robot is to reach a given *Destination* within the arena as early as possible. As the robot moves from its starting location (*Source*) within the arena towards its *Destination*, it keeps calculating the shortest path to the *Destination* at all points of time. During the traversal, the robot comes across different emotion fields which affect its *Mood*, *Confidence* and *Health*. The values of *Mood*, *Confidence* and *Health* vary from 1 to 10, 0 to 100 and 0 to 100 respectively. The values of other parameters used in the experiments are:

$l_t = 2$, $u_t = 9$, $\lambda = \gamma = 10$ samples, $M_t = 10$, $S_f = 10$

The value of negative emotion, for which *Reflex* works, was set to 90. Reflex is hardwired within the robot and is not directly related to mood. Thus, if the value of any of the negative emotions exceeds 90, reflex is activated and the robot makes a random move away from its current progression. Memory formation is mood dependent. Thus if *Mood* $< l_t$ the system starts capturing the input vector. For generation of memory this low mood situation should persist for some time. In the present case we have used this to be 10 samplings (λ). Following test-cases were considered for experimentation:

Case 1: Negative Memory Creation and Retrieval

In this case, the goal of the robot is to sequentially visit all the corners of the arena. This means the robot, positioned initially at (0,0), has to visit the following *Destination* coordinates: (0, 200), (200, 200), (200, 0) and return to (0, 0). Figure 4 depicts the movement of the robot in the arena. There are only two kinds of emotion fields available within the arena - one positive (shown using triangles) and one negative (shown using circles). The intensities of negative emotion fields was kept high in order to instigate the creation of new negative memory vectors while that of positive emotion fields were kept low so that any new positive emotion memory vector may not be formed. Five emotional fields of the positive kind and four of negative ones were made to populate the arena. The EE embedded within the robot had two emotion agents - one for a positive emotion and one for negative emotion. The inputs to these agents are the values of the emotional fields perceived in the arena. The dots in the arena, which show the path of the robot, represent the sampling of the environment on part of the robot. As can be observed from the Figure 4, there is an increase in the rate of sampling as the robot moves near to the negative emotion area, while the same decreases as the robot moves near to a positive emotion area. This feature is an inherent adrenaline based feature of the EE. Figure 5 depicts the corresponding change in the value of *M* and *C* when the robot traversed the arena shown in Figure 4. The initial values of Mood *M* and Confidence *C,* were set to *10* and *100* respectively.

As can be observed from Figure 4, the robot encounters a negative emotion field (negative area) in its path from (0, 0) to (0, 200) at (0, 50). The value of *Mood* does not cross the lower threshold (l_t), as can be seen in the graph in Figure 5, from 50 to 110 seconds. Hence, the robot seamlessly crosses that negative area without triggering the *Reflex* or learning any new memory vector. From (0, 200) to (200, 200), the robot again encounters a negative area and its *Mood* falls below the lower threshold (l_t) at around location (75, 200), the *SB*, as can be observed in the graph in Figure 5 from 201 to 250 seconds. As soon as the input value of the negative emotion crosses 90, the *Reflex* triggers within the robot and it gets deflected from its course at the co-ordinate location (92, 200), the *RB*. At this point, the robot evaluates the samples it collected in between *SB* and *RB* and creates a new negative emotion memory as shown in Figure 4. It may be noted that the emotion memory vector does not involve any sensor or position information of the robot. The values in the memory vector represent merely the effect of external environment on the internal state of the robot.

As the robot moves forward towards its next destination, it encounters another negative area at (200, 100) in its path from (200, 200) to (200, 0). This again reduces the value of *Mood* and the *Confidence* (from 550 to 601 seconds as seen in graph in Figure 5). Hence, the already learnt negative memory vector created earlier is retrieved from its emotion memory and is used by the robot to take a decision. As soon as the current emotion vector of the robot matches with the one retrieved

from the memory (within a range of ±2), it calculates W_c based on which it decides its further progression into the negative area. In Figure 4, the match occurs at (200, 147) which marks the *SB*. Yet, the robot penetrates till (200, 125) before getting deflected from its path. The same events occur again for the negative area at (100, 0) which causes a decrement in the *Mood* and the *Confidence* from 901 to 950 seconds in the graph in Figure 5. Furthermore, the value of *Confidence* of the robot decreases beyond the minimum required (M_t) (at 1150 seconds in Figure 5). Consequently, the robot changes its priority from going towards the *Destination* and avoids the current course of action. This is the point when the Reflex occurs. As the robot moves away from the negative area, it starts gaining Confidence. As soon as the Confidence of the robot crosses M_t (increment in the *Mood* and the *Confidence* from 1125 to 1175 seconds in graph in Figure 5), it again changes its priority and alters its course towards the final *Destination*.

This test case demonstrates that the negative emotional memory formation takes place only at high emotional states (in this case very low values of *Mood*). It also stresses the use of previously learned memory vectors when similar situations recur in the environment. Further, it emphasizes the role of *Confidence* in switching the priority of tasks that the robot performs.

Case 2: Two Different Negative Emotion Fields

In this case, the goal of the robot is to reach the *Destination* at (200, 200) from its *Source* at (0, 0) and then return to the *Source*. As shown in Figure 6, the simulation environment contains two different negative emotion fields (depicted using circles and rectangles) and one positive emotion field (shown using triangle). Here, the different negative emotion fields represent two different emotion agents (viz. *N1* and *N2*) within the EE.

Figure 4. Movement of the robot in the arena in case 1

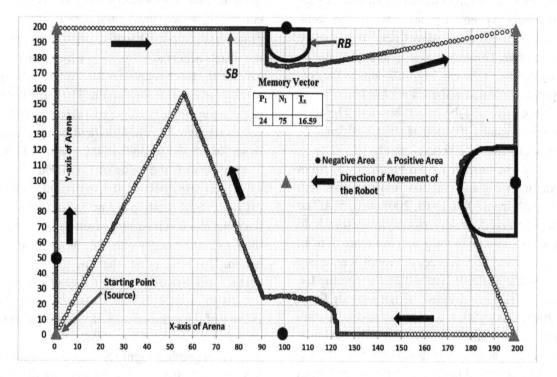

Figure 5. The change in the mood and confidence of the robot with time as it moves in the arena in Case 1

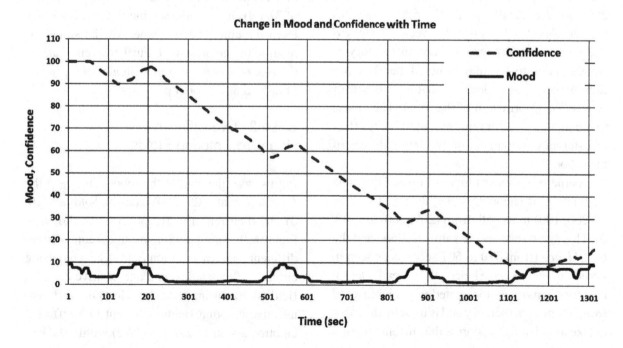

This case is thus different from the previous case where various negative areas represented the same single emotion agent within EE.

In this case, when the robot moves from the *Source* at (0, 0) to the *Destination* at (200, 200), it encounters the first negative field (*N1*) situated at (90,100). As a result, its *Reflex* triggers but the *Mood* continues to be low until the next negative area (*N2*) is crossed (from 25 to 275 seconds in graph in Figure 7). A single negative memory vector is thus recorded at this point. When the robot reaches its *Destination* at (200, 200), its *Mood* and *Confidence* increase because of the positive emotion area encountered at (200, 200) (from 275 to 350 seconds in graph in Figure 7). On the return path, the *Source* and *Destination* change to (200, 200) to (0, 0) respectively. The robot encounters N2 at (110, 100) first and since it does not find a matching vector in its memory for such a situation, its *Reflex* triggers at (108, 108) causing the generation of another negative emotional memory vector.

Case 3: The Robot encounters many emotion fields

As shown in Figure 8 the arena herein contains various positive (triangle) and negative emotion (circles and rectangles) areas. Percepts (sensory values) from the positive area are fed as inputs to a single positive emotion agent within the EE while those from the negative areas go into two different negative emotion agents. In Figure 8, the *Source* of the robot is (1,125) and its goal is (200, 200). At N1 i.e. (50, 150) the mood of the robot goes below the lower threshold and its *Reflex* triggers making it learn a negative emotional memory vector. At N2 (100, 150) it learns the second negative emotional memory vector because the situation is different from the previously learned vector. When the same negative area is encountered at N1 viz. (150, 150), it uses the already learned negative memory vector and takes a decision on the basis of its current *Confidence* value. The *Mood* and the

Confidence decrease down to 1.5 (at 20 seconds in graph in Figure 9) because of the negative area N1 (at 50, 150). The *Mood* remains low and the *Confidence* value continuously decreases because of continuous negative areas encountered in its path viz. N2 at (100, 150) and N1 (150, 150). This case highlights the manner in which the robot could manage to create its own path in the environment using various negative and positive areas.

Case 4: Positive Memory - Creation and Retrieval

In this case the environment of the arena is same as in Case 1. The positive memory areas at (0, 200) and (100, 100) (depicted by diamond shapes in Figure 10) have been intensified so that the robot can learn positive memory vectors as well. As the robot moves towards its first *Destination* at (0, 200) from the *Source* at (0, 0), it encounters the first high intensity positive emotion field at (0, 200). As the value of its *Mood* persists above u_t for the next γ samples, it learns the location (0, 200), the yellow diamond tag shown in Figure 10, as a positive emotional memory. Further down the path it learns a negative memory vector as in Case 1. As the robot moves on from (200, 200) to (200, 0), it encounters other negative fields and tries to avoid it as per the discussions in Case 1. However, after avoiding the negative area, its *Confidence* falls below M_t. Instead of making a random move as in case of a *Reflex*, the robot now makes an informed decision to visit the already learned positive memory vector to boost its *Confidence*. It thus changes its course and moves towards (0, 200) where it encountered high positive emotion intensity. However on this sojourn, it encounters another high intensity positive area which instigates the formation of yet another positive memory vector. This boosts its *Mood* (increment in the mood at around 950th second in graph in Figure 11). Thus instead of going on towards the yellow diamond tag, it remains at the green diamond tag till its *Confidence* becomes

Figure 6. Movement of the robot in the arena in case 2

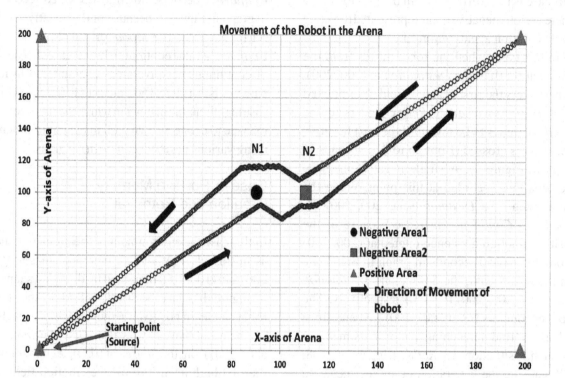

Figure 7. The change in the mood and confidence of the robot with time as it moves in the arena in case 2

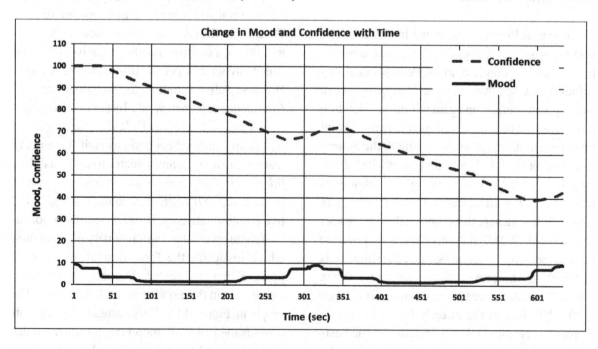

Figure 8. Movement of the robot in the arena in case 3

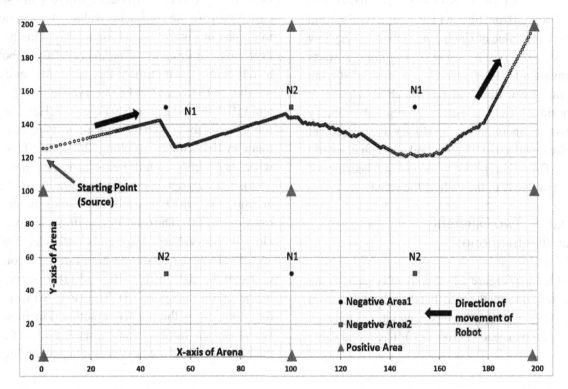

Figure 9. The change in the mood and confidence of the robot with time as it moves in the arena in case 3

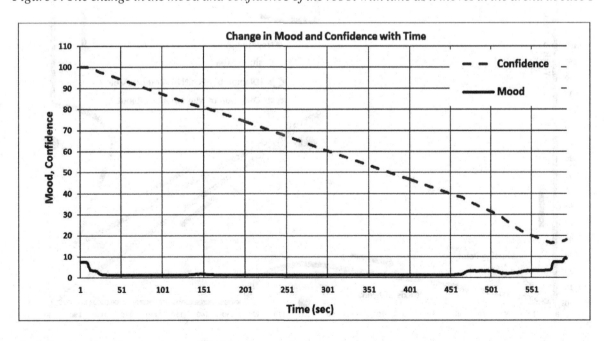

greater than needed confidence C_n. This can also be observed from Figure 11 at around 901st second where the value of *Confidence* falls to a very low value (viz. 5). The value of *Confidence* starts growing after 925th second as a result of staying at the green diamond tag which is a positive emotional field. Positive emotional memory causes the increment in the *Mood* value (increment in the mood at the 980th second in graph in Figure 11). The other peaks in *Mood* are because of positive areas in the path of the robot.

Case 5: Two Different Positive memories

In this case (Figure 12), the arena is same as the previous one but the path that the robot takes from (0, 200) to (200, 200) has been altered through (100, 100) instead of (100, 200). The initial value

of confidence (viz. 60) is also different in this case (compare the confidence values at 1 second in graphs in Figure 11 and Figure 13). This has been done to force the *Confidence* of the robot to fall below the minimum threshold, M_t, more number of times, as can be observed at the 751st and 1101st second in graph in Figure 13. Here, the robot learns about both the high intensity positive memory fields before reaching (200, 200). Thus, when its *Confidence* falls below M_t (twice in this case), it always opts for the positive emotion field at (100, 100) which is nearby and avoids moving towards (0, 200). The robot thus optimizes its path along with its value of *Mood* and *Confidence*. The *Mood* value goes above the high threshold four times (at the 201st, 301st, 810th and 1160th second in the graph in Figure 13). The first two times the robot learns the positive emotional memory vector and the last two times when it goes to the positive emotional memory vector for recharging.

Figure 10. Movement of the robot in the arena in case 4

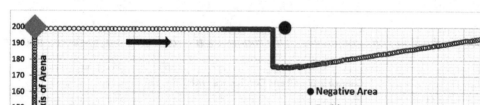

Figure 11. The change in the mood and confidence of the robot with time as it moves in the arena in case 4

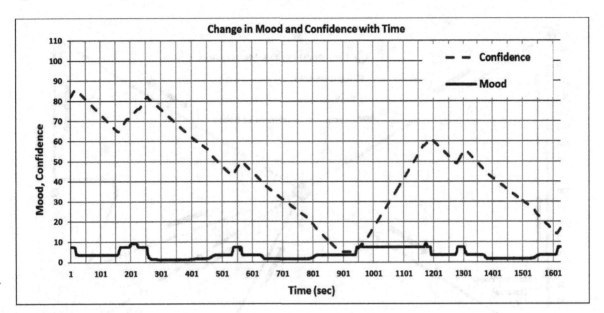

Comparison with the Memoryless Model

Francis Jr. et al. (Francis Jr et al., 2009) state that:

Unlike a psychological model of emotion, which can be tested against the behavior of humans and animals, evaluating the performance of an artificial intelligence system that displays or uses emotion is difficult.

However, we endeavor to compare the proposed emotion memory model with the only EE (Nair et al., 2011) based model (no memory). One may note that the proposed memory model herein is an enhancement over the EE model (Nair et al., 2011). The first two simulation cases were compared with that of the non-memory based EE model using the *Health* (*H*) parameter and the time required by the robot to achieve the goal(s). While *H*, computed using Equation (18), signifies the physical status of the robot while traversing through the adverse

negative fields, time provides a measure of its quickness in reaching the goal.

As can be observed from the graphs in Figure 15, the emotion memory based model always optimizes on the *Health* of the robot while also aiming to reach the goal(s). As can be seen in Figures 15(a) and (b), the robot dies (*H=0*) without reaching to the goal (at the 911st second in Figure 15(a) and at the 562nd second in Figure 15(b)) in case of the memoryless model. This is because it is adversely affected by the negative areas in its path. However, when armed with the emotional memory, the robot seems to be able to recover its *Health* to better values and successfully reach its goals.

Figure 15(c) depicts the change in *Health* for the arena depicted in Figure 14. As can be observed in Figure 14, the *Source* of the robot is at (0,0) and its *Destination* is at (200,200). While traversing, the robot initially encounters a negative area at (50, 50) and learns a negative memory vector which it uses when it reaches (150, 150), the second negative area on its way

Figure 12. Movement of the robot in the arena in case 5

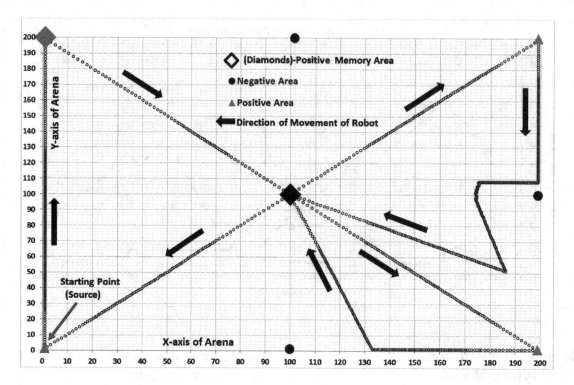

Figure 13. The change in the mood and confidence of the robot with time as it moves in the arena in case 5

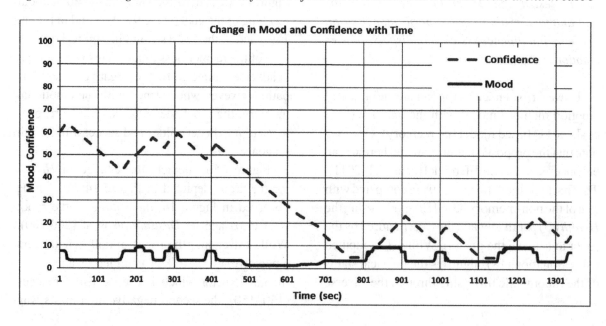

to the destination. As shown in Figure 15(c), the memory model saves more on *Health* as compared to the memoryless EE model. This is because when the second time (at (150, 150) in Figure 14) a negative area is encountered, the robot goes very close to the source of the negative area in case of memoryless EE model. In the emotional memory based model, it maintains a safe distance from the source of the negative area to save the robot from damage. The memory model creates a longer path than the basic EE model at the cost of the more important *Health* of the robot. As per the graphs shown in Figure 15, it can be inferred that the emotional memory based model attempts to exploit a trade-off between *Health* and time to reach the destination, in a better way than the memoryless model.

Experiments Using a Real Robot

A LEGO® MINDSTORM® NXT robot was used to implement the emotion memory model in a real environment. The robot was equipped with two ultrasonic sensors to sense the distance from an obstacle, a compass sensor for direction and a light sensor. The two ultrasonic sensors were mounted orthogonally one facing the front while the other facing left as shown in Figure 16. The values of these ultrasonic and light sensors were used to provide input to the EE. Two emotion agents (one negative and one positive) were used in the EE to model the emotions. The complemented distance of the obstacles from the robot's front and left sides, whichever was near, was used as an input to the negative emotion agent while the value of the light sensor was fed as input to the positive emotion agent of the EE.

Figure 14. Movement of the robot in the arena with two negative and three positive emotion fields

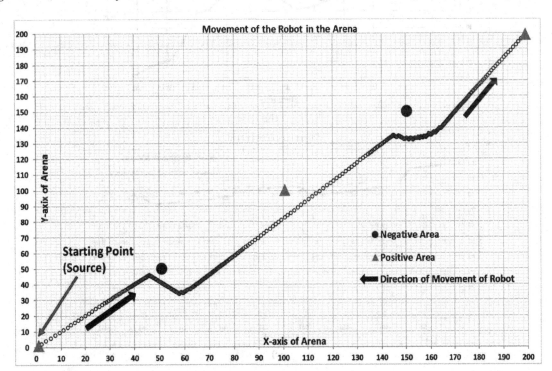

Figure 15. The change in the value of health with- and without- emotional memory (a) for case 1 (b) for case 2 (c) for the arena depicted in figure 14

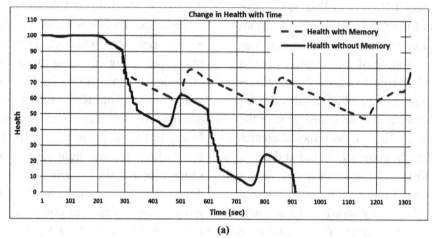

(a)

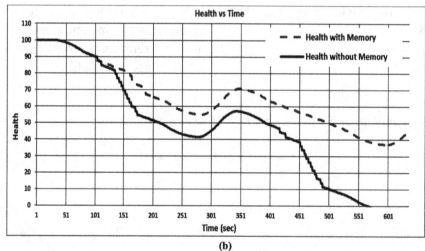

(b)

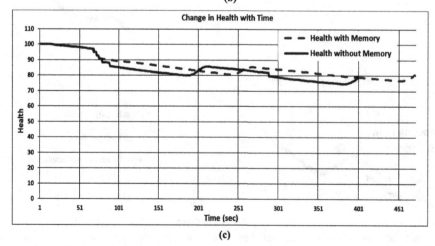

(c)

The compass sensor was used to allow the robot to find its direction towards the destination at any given point of time. A camera mounted on the ceiling on top was also used to provide the coordinates of the robot with respect to the arena. The camera tracks the robot using the yellow coloured plate mounted on the robot. The values of the different parameters used were kept the same as in the simulations. The following scenarios were examined with the robot in the real arena shown in Figure 17.

Scenario 1: Successive Destinations

In this case the robot needed to reach *Destination D1* first and then *Destination D2* (Figure 17). The movement of the robot in the arena depicted in Figure 17, is shown in Figure 18. The red bars indicate the obstacles or the negative emotion areas while the green triangle indicates the light source or the positive emotion area. The robot starts moving from *Source (S)* at (350, 18) in the Figure 18 towards its first destination *D1* at (0,0). While traversing, it encounters an obstacle *O1* (a negative emotion field). Its *Mood* thus goes below the lower threshold (l_t) triggering a *Reflex* to turn away. Hence, it learns a negative emotional memory vector. When the same situation occurred again in the path from *D1* and *D2*, it uses this already learned vector. As can be observed the robot behaves in a similar way as it did in the simulations. Figure 18 shows the movement of the robot in the arena. While Figure 19 shows the changes in the *Confidence* and *Mood* values with respect to time. The *Mood* increases once because of the light source in the path (at the 175th second in Figure 19) and decreases when it is close to the obstacle.

Scenario 2: Removing the Positive Emotion Field

Here too, we use the same arena as in the previous case. We compare the change in the path of

the robot because of the change in the environment. The robot was made to travel towards the same destinations as in the previous case. There are two sub cases herein. In the first, there is a light source (positive area; green triangle) at (0, 0) in Figure 20. In the second, we remove the light source. The dotted blue line curve indicate the movement of the robot in the presence of the light source while the black curvy line stands for the same in the absence of this light source. As previously described the light source is used as input to the positive emotion agent of the EE. The light source thus causes an increase in the *Mood* value of the robot and hence improves its *Confidence*. Thus, in the presence of the light source the robot penetrates a bit further into the second negative area (N2) as compared to the case when the light is absent (Figure 20). This is so because when there was no light source, the Confidence value was not enough to allow penetration into the negative area. Thus, in presence of the light the robot reaches the destination earlier. This emphasizes the dynamism of the memory model since it behaves according to the changes in the environment. If it finds the environment better, its *Confidence* and *Mood* empower it to take risks, thus making it penetrate further into a negative emotion area and reach its destination sooner. If the environment poses to be emotionally bad the robot avoids such risks by keeping a safe distance to conserve its *Confidence* and *Health*.

Scenario 3: Positive and Negative Memory Creation

In this case, the environment of this arena contains two obstacles and two light sources as shown in Figure 22. The robot learns both the positive and negative emotional memories and also uses them in its path. The robot starts from the *Source* (S) and needs to reach *Destinations - D1* first, then *D2* and finally *D3* (Figure 22). *D1* was so placed that the mood of the robot crosses the upper threshold u_t so that it learns the positive emo-

Figure 16. The robot used in the experiments

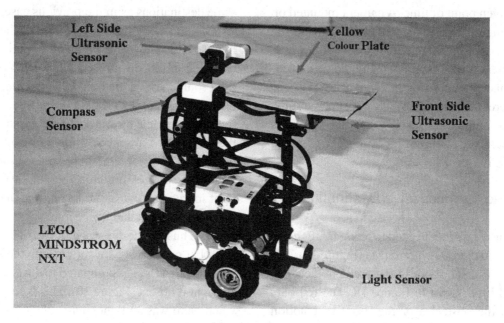

Figure 17. Robot and the real experimental environment (real arena)

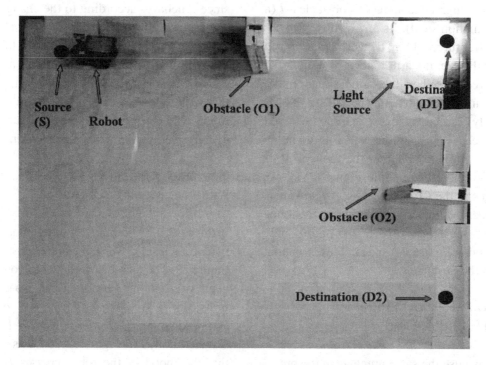

Figure 18. Movement of the robot in the real arena in scenario 1

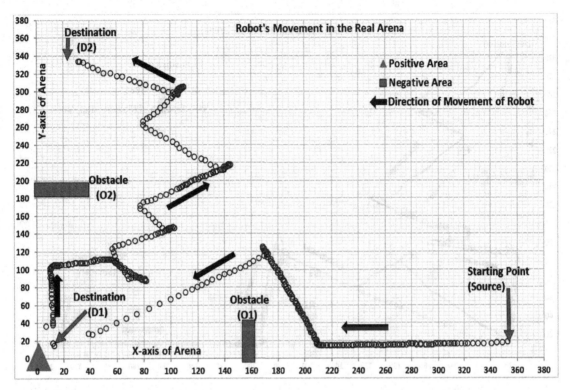

Figure 19. The change in the mood and confidence of the robot with time as it moves in the real arena in scenario 1

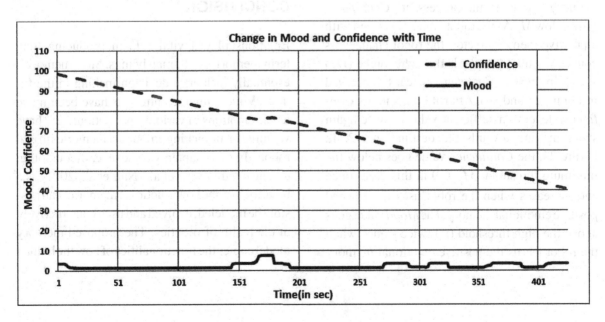

Figure 20. Movement of the robot in the real arena in scenario 2

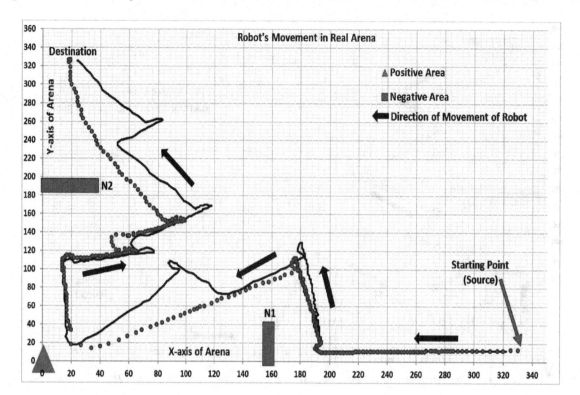

tional memory. It also learns the negative emotional memory when it encounters the obstacle, *O1*. When the robot encounters the obstacle, *O2*, it uses the already learned negative emotional memory vector. In the process, its *Confidence* goes below M_t. As the robot is already armed with a positive memory vector, the robot changes its course and travels towards the light source (*D1*) so as to improve its *Confidence* (as can be observed in Figure 23 and 24). After it builds up its *Confidence* level to a sufficient value, it once again starts moving towards the destination *D2*. In Figure 24, the *Confidence* value goes below the minimum threshold M_t (10 in this case) once and increases when the robot uses the learned positive emotional memory. The *Mood* value goes above the high threshold (u_t) twice - once when the robot learns the positive emotional memory

and then when it uses the positive emotional memory (Figure 24).

CONCLUSION

Emotions play a vital role in producing long term memories in human beings. Such memories eventually influence decision making in the future. While numerous attempts have been made to use emotions in various applications, few have ventured in mimicking emotional memories in real robots. In this chapter, we use an earlier emotion engine cited in Nair et al. (Nair et al., 2011) as a base, to describe how emotional memories can possibly be modeled, evolved and used constructively in the realm of robotics. The proposed memory model copies the functionalities of how the human

Figure 21. The changes in the mood and confidence of the robot with time as it moves in the real arena in scenario 2

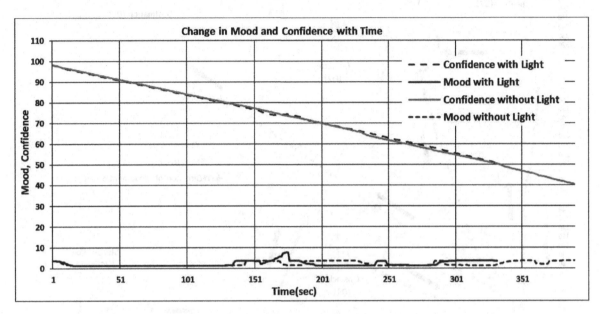

Figure 22. The positions of the destination points and obstacles in the real arena along with the robot in scenario 3

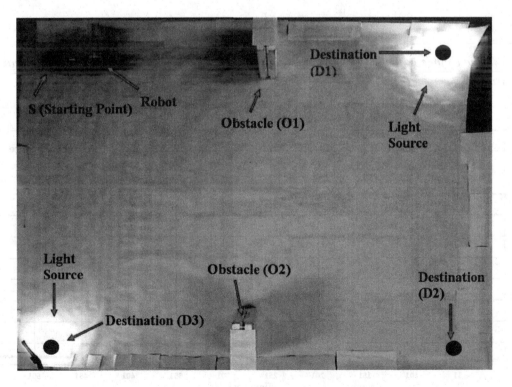

Figure 23. Movement of the robot in the real arena in scenario 3

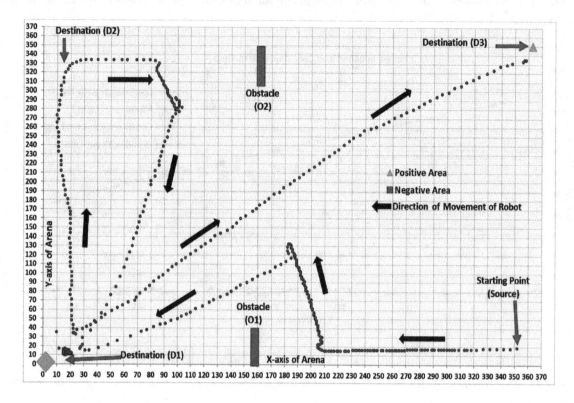

Figure 24. The change in the mood and confidence of the robot with time as it moves in the real arena in scenario 3

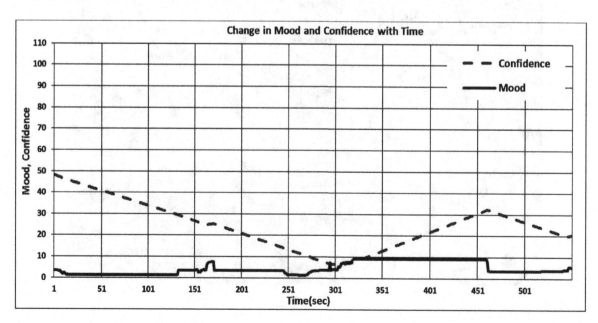

emotional memories possibly work. Real world parameters such *Health, Confidence* and their dynamism have also been emulated to make the model akin to its biological counterpart. Using experiments, both simulated and real, we show how these memories can be used to preserve the *Health* of a robot and make it achieve its goals. Both simulation and real world experimentations yielded similar results. We compared this model with memoryless version to find that the former tends to find a better tradeoff between time and health. A good feeling drives the robot forward while a bad one makes it more wary. In the robotics world, a robot could possibly feel its deteriorating emotions and move to places where this could be ameliorated thereby enhancing its chances of survival. The model can thus empower a robot to actually *feel* its environment and then take decisions accordingly. The memory model presented herein thus attempts to portray a simpler alternative to the otherwise complex calculations in the robotic world, much like the manner in which human beings work in their environments (Scheutz, 2011).

REFERENCES

Adler, R. S., Rosen, B., & Silverstein, E. M. (1998). Emotions in negotiation: How to manage fear and anger. *Negotiation Journal*, *14*(2), 161–179. doi:10.1111/j.1571-9979.1998.tb00156.x

Álvarez, M., Galán, R., Matía, F., Rodríguez-Losada, D., & Jiménez, A. (2010). An emotional model for a guide robot. *IEEE Transactions on Systems, Man, and Cybernetics. Part A, Systems and Humans*, *40*(5), 982–992. doi:10.1109/TSMCA.2010.2046734

Bechara, A. (2004). The role of emotion in decision-making: Evidence from neurological patients with orbitofrontal damage. *Brain and Cognition*, *55*(1), 30–40. doi:10.1016/j.bandc.2003.04.001 PMID:15134841

Bechara, A., Damasio, H., & Damasio, A. R. (2000). Emotion, decision making and the orbitofrontal cortex. *Cerebral Cortex*, *10*(3), 295–307. doi:10.1093/cercor/10.3.295 PMID:10731224

Brown, R., & Kulik, J. (1977). Flashbulb memories. *Cognition*, *5*(1), 73–99. doi:10.1016/0010-0277(77)90018-X

Bryson, J. J., & Tanguy, E. (2010). Simplifying the design of human-like behaviour: Emotions as durative dynamic state for action selection. *International Journal of Synthetic Emotions*, *1*(1), 30–50. doi:10.4018/jse.2010101603

Damasio, A. (2005). *Descartes' error: Emotion, reason, and the human brain*. Penguin Books.

El-Nasr, M. S., Yen, J., & Ioerger, T. R. (2000). Flame—fuzzy logic adaptive model of emotions. *Autonomous Agents and Multi-Agent Systems*, *3*(3), 219–257. doi:10.1023/A:1010030809960

Erk, S., von Kalckreuth, A., & Walter, H. (2010). Neural long-term effects of emotion regulation on episodic memory processes. *Neuropsychologia*, *48*(4), 989–996. doi:10.1016/j.neuropsychologia.2009.11.022 PMID:19945471

Francis, A. G., Jr., Mehta, M., & Ram, A. (2009). Emotional memory and adaptive personalities. In J. Vallverdú & D. Casacuberta (Eds.), Handbook of research on synthetic emotions and sociable robotics: New applications in affective computing and artificial intelligence, (pp. 391-421). Hershey, PA: IGI Global.

Fredrickson, B. L., & Joiner, T. (2002). Positive emotions trigger upward spirals toward emotional well-being. *Psychological Science, 13*(2), 172–175. doi:10.1111/1467-9280.00431 PMID:11934003

Friestad, M., & Thorson, E. (1986). Emotion-eliciting advertising: Effects on long term memory and judgment. *Advances in Consumer Research. Association for Consumer Research (U. S.), 13*(1), 111.

George, J. M. (2000). Emotions and leadership: The role of emotional intelligence. *Human Relations, 53*(8), 1027–1055. doi:10.1177/0018726700538001

Ham, J., Jung, C., Park, J., Ryeo, J., & Ko, I. (2009). An artificial emotion model for visualizing emotion of characters. In *Proceedings of World Academy of Science: Engineering & Technology, 50*.

Joshi, A. (2011). *Short essay on understanding human memory*. Retrieved 6th April, 2014, from http://www.preservearticles.com/201106087597/short-essay-on-understanding-human-memory.html

Kleinginna, P. R. Jr, & Kleinginna, A. M. (1981). A categorized list of emotion definitions, with suggestions for a consensual definition. *Motivation and Emotion, 5*(4), 345–379. doi:10.1007/BF00992553

LaBar, K. S., & Cabeza, R. (2006). Cognitive neuroscience of emotional memory. *Nature Reviews. Neuroscience, 7*(1), 54–64. doi:10.1038/nrn1825 PMID:16371950

Lefkoe, M. (2010). Why we have negative emotions … and what to do about them. Retrieved from http://www.mortylefkoe.com/why-negative-emotions/

Levine, L. J., & Pizarro, D. A. (2004). Emotion and memory research: A grumpy overview. *Social Cognition, 22*(5), 530-554.

Loewenstein, G., & Lerner, J. S. (2003). The role of affect in decision making. Handbook of Affective Science, 619(642), 3.

Macht, M. (2008). How emotions affect eating: A five-way model. *Appetite, 50*(1), 1–11. doi:10.1016/j.appet.2007.07.002 PMID:17707947

Mohs, R. C. (n.d.). How human memory works. Retrieved 8th April, 2014, from http://science.howstuffworks.com/life/inside-the-mind/human-brain/human-memory.htm

Nair, S. B., Godfrey, W. W., & Kim, D. H. (2011). On realizing a multi-agent emotion engine. *International Journal of Synthetic Emotions, 2*(2), 1–27.

Padgham, L., & Taylor, G. (1997). A system for modelling agents having emotion and personality. In Intelligent Agent Systems Theoretical and Practical Issues (pp. 59–71). Springer.

Park, J.-C., Kim, H.-R., Kim, Y.-M., & Kwon, D.-S. (2009). *Robot's individual emotion generation model and action coloring according to the robot's personality*. Paper presented at the The 18th IEEE International Symposium on Robot and Human Interactive Communication (RO-MAN 2009). doi:10.1109/ROMAN.2009.5326128

Peters, E. (2006). The functions of affect in the construction of preferences. In S. Lichtenstein & P. Slovic (Eds.), *The construction of preference*, (pp. 454-463). Cambridge University Press.

Phelps, E. A. (2004). Human emotion and memory: Interactions of the amygdala and hippocampal complex. *Current Opinion in Neurobiology, 14*(2), 198–202. doi:10.1016/j.conb.2004.03.015 PMID:15082325

Scheutz, M. (2011). Architectural roles of affect and how to evaluate them in artificial agents. [IJSE]. *International Journal of Synthetic Emotions*, 2(2), 48–65. doi:10.4018/jse.2011070103

Shiv, B., Loewenstein, G., & Bechara, A. (2005). The dark side of emotion in decision-making: When individuals with decreased emotional reactions make more advantageous decisions. *Brain Research. Cognitive Brain Research*, 23(1), 85–92. doi:10.1016/j.cogbrainres.2005.01.006 PMID:15795136

Talarico, J. M., LaBar, K. S., & Rubin, D. C. (2004). Emotional intensity predicts autobiographical memory experience. *Memory & Cognition*, 32(7), 1118–1132. doi:10.3758/BF03196886 PMID:15813494

Velásquez, J. D. (1998). *When robots weep: emotional memories and decision-making*. Paper presented at the Proceedings of the National Conference on Artificial Intelligence.

Zeelenberg, M., Nelissen, R. M., Breugelmans, S. M., & Pieters, R. (2008). On emotion specificity in decision making: Why feeling is for doing. *Judgment and Decision Making*, 3(1), 18–27.

KEY TERMS AND DEFINITIONS

Emotion Agents: An emotion agent computes and manages the intensity of the emotion assigned to it, based on its emotion resource and the values of stimulations and suppressions received by it from other such agents.

Emotion Decay: The decay in the intensity of a particular emotion with time.

Emotion Generation: The process of generating emotions based on perceived external stimuli.

Emotion Resource: It is a quantity within an emotion agent which regulates the intensity of emotion and is indicative of the emotion generating capacity of an emotion agent.

Emotional Memories: These are the long terms memories created as a result of encountering emotionally charged events.

Emotionally Charged Events: Events that possess or generate high emotional responses.

Negative Emotional Memories: Emotional memories that are created as a result of encountering negative emotionally charged events (e.g. a disaster).

Positive Emotional Memories: Emotional memories that are created as a result of encountering positive emotionally charged events (e.g. wining the Oscar or the World-cup).

Situated Robot: A robot which inhabits an environment which it can perceive using its sensors and manipulate by performing actions.

Stimulations: These are the cues that the emotion agents receive from their own kind (positive to positive and negative to negative).

Suppressions: These are the cues that the emotion agents receive from emotion agents of the opposite kind (positive agents from negative agents and vice versa).

Chapter 6
The Exploitation of Models in Artificial Emotions

M.G. Sánchez-Escribano
Universidad Politécnica de Madrid, Spain

Carlos Herrera
Universidad Politécnica de Madrid, Spain

Ricardo Sanz
Universidad Politécnica de Madrid, Spain

ABSTRACT

Cognitive processes might be seen as reciprocal items and they are usually characterized by multiple feedback cycles. Emotions constitute one major source of feedback loops to assure the maintenance of well-being, providing cognitive processes with quantifiable meaning. This suggests the exploitation of models to improve the adaptation under value-based protocols. Emotion is not an isolated effect of stimuli, but it is the set of several effects of the stimuli and the relationships among them. This chapter proposes a study of the exploitation of models in artificial emotions, pointing out relationships as part of the model as well as the model exploitation method.

INTRODUCTION

The functional operation of biological emotion inspires the integration of similar models in artificial systems. The objective is to improve some sectors of its self-evaluation capabilities to exploit this knowledge to improve its control concerning the improvement of its adaptiveness. Initially, the key facet is the exploration of what emotion solves inside of biological agents in the search of relevant analogies for the artificial systems. The objective should not be a mirror image of the biological phenomenon, but an adapted equivalence for the needs of the artificial agents. On top of that, it would be desirable to explain some sectors of the real phenomenon on the basis of this theory, by means of a well-defined analogy between the artificial model and real emotion.

However, it should go far beyond these solutions to find what emotions may solve in artificial agents. The real influence of emotion over the system comes from the inner perspective of the

DOI: 10.4018/978-1-4666-7278-9.ch006

artificial agent about this emotion, not from the external perspective of an observer or a direct influence of some parameters previously defined. The artificial system should have available models to be exploited in order to allow the emergence of quantifiable meaning to cope with its real needs, not those previously defined by a designer. It is only in this case that the artificial system could have autonomy in decision-making based on emotion, emotional behavior, emotional expression, etc. The environment and the own system are sources of a broad set of stimuli that cause effects within the system. The whole set of all these effects are the source of some other new processes that are causing new stimuli within the system, and that should also become part of the models that will be exploited.

How these models should be built, how they should be exploited, how all the relationships within and around the models should be linked and what the right parameters to configure these relationships are, what the effects of their exploitation are, how to identify and to retrieve new stimuli on the basis of these effects from the exploitation, etc. are all part of a wide system that still presents strong barriers concerning the achievement of successful solutions.

OVERVIEW ON BIOLOGICAL EMOTION RESEARCH

The structural and funcional models from the perspective of biological emotion can be summarized into two major approaches: a) the physiological perspective, focused on the structural basis within the brain, and b) the psychological perspective, addressing the emotional phenomenon within the agent (*The psychologist's point of view* refers the study of emotion as an intrapersonal process (Fridja, 2008))

The analysis of the physiological changes of bodily subsystems during emotional processes, provides sets of data over which to explain the physical origin and extent of the emotions. The classic vision of W. James (1884) that afterwards was detailed by (Lange et al., 1922), shows emotion as mental representation of body responses to relevant stimuli. It was also refined by Cannon and Bard (Cannon et. al, 1927) arguing a simultaneous approach to the physiological change, and whose effects have the origin in the hypothalamus region of the brain. Analogously, the initial approaches of Pápez (1937) suggested the distributed nature of the emotional processes in his dual circuit model, and the works of Klüver and Bucy (Klüver et. al, 1937), McLean (McLean, 1990) and LeDoux (1996; 2000) showed that this structure is not so clearly delimited in the brain as it might seem.

Subsequent studies ratified with neuroimaging techniques that effects that appear when fear is felt, are the same that those that appear during unconscious perception of this basic emotion (Morris et. al, 1998). Some facts like this, suggested the involvement of other deeper subcortical brain structures in emotional processing. Some other evidences (as in the case of Phineas Gage) showed the relevance of the cortex and other upper brain structures in emotion processes. As well, lesion-based researches concerning the orbito-frontal and the ventromedial cortex showed that these structures are playing an essential function in the evaluation of the external information regarding new events (new outward stimuli) as well as the internal information regarding bodily sensations and emotional states (new inward stimuli). The studies made by Davidson (2002) and (Bush et al., 2000) confirmed these hypotheses and showed that the anterior cingulate cortex is related to the expression of emotion and to the conscious experience.

From the source of these results it was argued a distributed operation of the emotional system more than a centralized system. The emotional phenomenon is not located in a particular brain structure from which a centralized control is performed. The processes that are sustaining emotion are complex functional chunks in a simultaneous, federated and distributed work. This complex operation and how their processes are is one of the major challenges that faces the task of modeling and simulation of the emotional phenomenon. The major issue is to find out how this set of interconnected processes occurring on several structural and physiological levels of the brain, are leading to abstract complex processes such as those of cognition, emotion and consciousness.

The clinical studies conducted by Damasio (1994) and some others using neuroimaging (Davidson et al., 2003) confirmed the modulatory role that the prefontal cortex plays over other brain structures. This is related to the adaptive nature of the emotional response (Miller et al., 2001) and (Ochsner et al., 2002), one of the multiple facets related with the emotional operation. Prinz (2004) made a classification regarding the common perspectives of emotion study: a) the feeling theories regarding the conscious experience of emotion, b) the somatic theories regarding the physiology of emotion, c) the behavioral theories regarding the action tendencies concerning the emotion, d) the cognitive theories regarding the modulation processes concerning the emotion, and e) the pure cognitive theories regarding the thoughts and the emotions. What this study additionaly provides is the idea of the multiple roles that emotion is playing within the systems.

The psychological perspective commonly addresses the analysis of those processes that allow optimized responses for adapting and for self-defense behaviors of the emotional agents, and the direct role of emotions concerning cognitive processes (such as perception, learning, decision making, communication, etc.). There are relevant works such as taxonomies concerning emotional phenomena, some categorizations of emotions (such as those of basic and complex emotions, emotional states, etc.) or the distinction between the different affective states such as moods,

temperaments or traits in works by Ekamn, Friesen, Darwing, Johnson-Laird & Oatley, Emde, Pankseep, Plutchink, Sroufe, Turner, Trevarthem, Arnold and Osgood among others. Nevertheless, these works state a fuzzy conceptual landscape marked by the absence of exact boundaries in the meaning of the emotional terms.

Another important thread is the study of the mutual influence and the integration of the emotional processes and the cognitive processes. This emo-cognitive perspective of emotion has moved towards the study of the emotion over perceptual processes (Cytowic, 1998), memory (Bower et al., 1994) or motivation (Izard, 1993) among others. Even more, the term *emotional intelligence* has been defined to argue emotion as a cornerstone for intelligence (Goleman, 1995)

One major research area is the *Appraisal Theories of Emotion*. The term *appraisal* is attributed to Magna Arnold (1960) who understood a process of evaluation related to assessments of relevant situations that is widely accepted. However, there is not agreement about the origin of this process (Fridja, 1987; Scherer, 2001). There is a bit more acceptation regarding Lazarus' (1984) viewpoint about a conscious evaluation and a cognitive interpretation to obtain meaning. In some sense, the appraisal theory suggests a continuous work of the agent concerning the evaluation of its situational state. In some sense, the appraisal theory suggests a continuous work of the agent concerning the evaluation of its situational state and that introduces the issue of the subjective experience of emotion.

The subjective experience of emotion is an old issue that also has been widely studied in the state of the art. Giving an example, even when Ekman is commonly related to the classification of the six main emotions, he also studied this perspective and he suggested that, even when it is not the only effect, the experience of emotion includes sensations that are a result of some feedback concerning changes occurring within the response system of the agents: *The subjective experience includes – but may not be limited to – sensations that are the result of feedback from changes occuring in the already named response system*. In a more recent work, Damasio (1999) provides a relevant model of three levels to describe the mechanism of the emotional system that might explain the experience of feeling.

The psychological perspective provides some generalities about the emotion functionality such as the modulatory function that affects the agent's actions concerning its adaptation to the context. However, there is not an universal theory commonly accepted and the major issues come from the subjectivity in the set of data used to study the emotional phenomenon, the multidisciplinar fields that study the phenomenon, the several perspectives from which some punctual phase of the emotional phenomenon is studied and the lack of normalized concepts.

RELATED WORK ON SCENARIOS FOR COMPUTATIONAL EMOTION

The computational modeling of emotions is a heterogeneous field in terms of motivation, objectives, methodology and results, even when they generally have analogous focus. As Zhang et al. (2005) argue, most models are fits from some isolated parts of the real emotional phenomena and they enact limited interpretations on the basis of some theory. There are lots of examples of models used to create several computational versions of emotional features and behaviors such as personality, empathy or emotional expressions in virtual agents (Bartneck; Elliott, 1992; Koda, 1996; O'Really, 1996; Ortony, 2003) even taking advantage of the human reaction to emotional artifacts (Reeves et al., 2003). Largely, emotional research in robotics is related to human-robot interaction, trying to achieve appropiate emotional behavior in robots in previously defined scenarios. A majority of these systems implement technology

to detect emotional reactions in humans (Bandai, 2000; Electronic Arts, 2000; Bell, 1997; Elliott; LEGO, 2001)) and a fair amount try to express and use emotional behavior during cooperative processes (some examples are Kismet (Breazeal, 1998; 2000; 2002), Cog by MIT (Brooks et al, 1999)(Breazeal, 2001), Wamoeba-2R (Ogata et al., 2000)) and several systems showing some sort of personality (such as Fuwa (Qingji et al., 2008), Digman (1990) or the work of (Ghasem-Aghaee and Ören) among others).

Even when they provide relevant solutions in the robotics field, the question is not about the success of these implementations, but about the real influence that those models have to help in the processes of logic and inference within the system. That is, the real influence of the artificial emotion in the artificial intelligence and how emotion might help to pass the Turing test in machines (Picard, 1995)

On the basis of the (widely accepted) idea of functional integration of emotion and cognition, a thrust towards the integration of emotional capabilities in some of the most influential models of cognitive architectures has been generated. These realizations generally address dynamic targets that change in relevance concerning the state of the system. From the foundations of initial Newell's theory (1980; Newell et al., 1985) (which provided a list of 13 different criteria that any cognitive architecture should address) the *Soar Cognitive Architecture* (Laird et al., 1987) was developed. Recent extensions of Soar perform emotional capabilities based on the Scherer Theory (Scherer, 2001) to improve learning and decision-making by means of some internal mechanisms of reward. *Emile* is a model of emotional reasoning that implements some sort of explicit planning in order to achieve generalizations in some stages of its reasoning process (Gratch, 2000). *Shame* (Poel et al., 2002) is a hybrid architecture with previously defined personality factors, which models the emotional phenomenon of agents within virtual environments. *CogAff* (Sloman, 2001) is a multilayered architecture that explores the affective states and some other common concepts of the mind. *Clarion* (Sun et al., 2004) is a relevant cognitive architecture that integrates a motivational system and *Lida* (Franklin, 2006) implements a wide spectrum of cognitive skills for reasoning (in *Lida*, emotion is not a separate module within the architecture, but part of the dataflow system).

Nevertheless, it seems as if real emotion is not the isolated effect of a stimuli together with its related effects defined in some sort of model-of-effects built by the designer of the system. Actually, it seems as if emotion is the whole impact of the stimuli, the effects and also the relationships associated to both of them that also have effects on the system. Artificial emotion models should provide the framework of the emotional process, not the emotional process itself. Artificial emotion should not be previously planned but it should be allowed to emerge from the pattern of all these facts to become an emotion. *MicroPsi* (Bach, 2003) addresses this motivation and uses the Dorner Psi model of motivation, trying to follow this idea. In *MicroPsi*, emotions are a set of cognitive configurations that are not simulated, but they emerge from the source of the states of the system while it works.

Common criterions for one fitted model of emotion according to the real phenomenon are not available. However, any work of building models requires a set of essential data used to fit the best result together with the required techniques for system identification. As argued by Ljung (1987), the real-life system is an object of different kind than the identified models and our acceptance of models should be guided by usefulness rather than truth. However, there will not be usefulness if the observed data as well as the methods to build the models are not identified correctly. And it seems as if we are having problems from the very initial state of the prior knowledge used to design the experiments as well as the contexts that are used to retrieve data in order to fit models.

RATIONALE FOR SYNTHETIC EMOTION

Nowadays, there is some agreement in the idea of a mutual influence and the integration of emotional and cognitive processes as a whole system. However, each author argues and analyzes this fact from different perspectives. Eva Hudlika (2008) maintains that this relationship is more visible in those processes of decision-making. She holds her theory by means of a symbolic cognitive architecture in which the effects of emotion on cognitive processes are analyzed. Rosalind W. (Picard) analyzes extensively the goals and targets of the emotional implementation in machines in her work *what does it mean for a computer to "have" emotions?* She argues that any emotional system not only should recognize emotional patterns, but should also act properly with regard to the emotional meaning.

Since emotions depend on the system in which they operate, models should not follow a direct correlation of emotional features from biology to artificial systems. It moves the implementation towards some sort of absurd idea that artificial system requirements are exactly the same as those of biological systems. Since they are far different systems, their needs might also be extremely different even when the result might influence the same type of responses (intelligent decision-making, behavior, motivations, etc). To give an example, sometimes we are replicating the biological physiology inside the machines, even when they do not need this physiology in their normal work. The replication of the hormonal functionality of biological systems within the machine is not the same action as the implementation of the analogy concerning its causality within the machine.

It seems clear that emotions help establish useful relationships between different sectors and levels of information within the system, as well as to retrieve this knowledge when it is required. It also seems that emotion works as a general feedback system which uses some sort of non-explicit information, and that this feedback system is being influenced at the same time by the cognitive processes that are the framework in which it is running. The result of this operation is the emergence of some sort of additional knowledge whose origin does not come from the outside environment, but from the inside work that creates it, and that this knowledge is used by the internal control processes of the system in order to adapt it to each situation. The emotion emerges from the operational core of the biological system like a functionality of the system to the service of the system. Emotional and cognitive processes are working in a federated way to address the improvement of adaptiveness of the system to several environmental domains (the physical domain of the real world, the domain of its physical state, the domain of its cognitive state of the system, the domain of its societal state, etc.) by means of the improvement of the information that the system uses thanks to the integration of meaning concerning the comprehension of the emotional responses. The sources of this meaning are some sort of relationships between the system and the emotion, that causally connect the system with its targets, and that are influenced by some sort of bias such as the system tendencies usually called personality tendencies (among others). What is really relevant is the fact that this federated work is having strong influences on the intelligence and autonomy of systems.

Analogously, it can be expected that synthetic emotion will improve the control capabilities of the system by managing its complexity. This control focuses on addressing tasks for self-detecting uncertain or dangerous variances inside the system and to avoid the progress towards non-desirable states (either if these variances have their origin inside or outside the system). That is, systems with the meta objective of well-being. To this end, the system should be able to transfer phases of its control from the outside domain to its inner domain when required in the form of emerging

needs that can be realized by the system. The causal connection between this meta objective of well-being and the inner domain of the system, together with the causal relationship of this inner domain with the control processes, will increase the capabilities of the system to deal with the uncertainty of the environmental domains in which it is running (as mentioned above, the physical domain of the real world, the domain of its physical state, the domain of its cognitive state of the system, the domain of its societal state, etc.). And it becomes a better method for self-adaptiveness to the context of operation.

Consequently, there will be different levels of abstraction both in control processes as well as in the operation of the agent, with the objective of adapting this agent to each domain. The emotional system behaves as a control system that address new capabilities to the whole system (i.e. the system and its control processes) to cope with the required responses of this system concerning its well-being needs related to each of these domains (within scenarios of self-protection, decision-making, motivations, etc.). We are not arguing that they cannot be modeled without the influence of artificial emotion, but that they can be improved by means of new processes of awareness regarding emergent needs. And this gives the chance to some sort of improvement concerning the intelligent capabilities of the system, allowing new paths for autonomy.

THEORETICAL SYNTHESIS

Biological agents use feedback strategies to adapt themselves to their environment (either be it a situational or a physical environment). They are autonomous systems with such a complexity that they require decentralized organizational and operational structures to allow efficiency in their operativeness. The emotion provides a set of functional organization patterns that are essential to manage the complexity in the internal processes of these biological agents. The cognitive perspective of emotion suggests that emotion is the result of patterns of evaluation of relevant stimuli (Sanz et al., 2013) which are carried out by means of some essential bodily processes.

Emotion is widely accepted as a complex phenomenon that holds precise interconnections among subjective and objective factors within a system (Kelingina & Kleingina, 1981). The emotional functionality addresses issues concerning the adaptation of live systems to their environment using semantic self-representation concerning the state (Damasio, 1999; Picard, 1995). Nevertheless, one of the main issues that rises from artificial models of emotion is the incapacity of the artificial system to build emotional meaning. This key stage of the emotional functionality does not emerge from the operation of the artificial models, and it forces us to think about which the essential features to achieve this objective are and what critical features we are missing.

A complete model of emotion is excessively complex and has a lot of parameters concerning the stimuli, the effects and the relationships among all of them that are also influencing the observations from which the data (to fit the model) are taken. The stimuli have effects over the system and those effects have also effects over the system. The relationships between the stimuli and the effects of the system have to be modeled and it is the common path in computational research of emotion. However, there are additional relationships that also should be modeled because they are linking the effects within the model. How the relationships are linked within the model and what parameters configure these relationships are some of the major issues still unresolved.

Emotional implementations are limited to spaces of bounded dimensions (expression, decision-making, motivation, etc.) and they are showing low accuracy and low tolerance to uncertainty outside these bounded environments. The larger part of emotional implementations create new information on the basis of the emotional models for being used by the system and this is not incorrect at all. What possibly is being missed is that we remove part of some essential information in these models. Largely, models of stimulus-response are built on the basis of models of effects and system targets of well-being concerning some previously defined scenarios. In some way, this is a linear approximation to the emotional function at a given domain (system state, environment, emotional influence, etc.) that gives us the chance of addressing the influence of discrete emotion within local parts of the system. Once the system runs outside predefined parameters by design, the emotional model does not work as is expected.

Sometimes the missed features come from the very initial phase of design. Many theories assume models from the basis of isolation of certain functions within these bounded scenarios. However, there are lots of related processes (either with the agent as well as to its environment) that are not modeled but nevertheless they are affecting the processes concerning this -initially isolated- function. To give an example, the effects of stimuli within the system also have semantic for the system, and part of these effects that do not have direct effect with the emotional response are also removed in models. In some way the effects that might emerge from these effects (i.e. the associated semantic) might be part of the pattern of stimuli that will be the inputs of the emotional system. But they are removed and the perceptual system (also) becomes some sort of sequential process (i.e. it also becomes a linear process). In this sense, Hayek describes the emotions as *affective qualities* whose order of mental qualities do not refer to particular points in the space as in the case of *sensory qualities* (Hayek, 1999). He argues that, even when the principles of operation might be the same for the two qualities, the *affective qualities* represent a temporary preference for certain types of responses towards external situations (i.e. behaviors or a set of following actions) while the *sensory qualities* represent a spatial relationship for sensory stimuli. Under his viewpoint, there are two different qualities that however are connected. An analogous perspective is argued by E. Fox that presumes a mutual feedback of both cognitive and emotional system (Fox, 2008) and that of Simon (1967) that argues a system of cognitive-emotional interruptions on the basis of analysis of relevance for the process of attention.

The emotional system is not so easy to model nor to explain, even when the influence that it has over the Cognitive Systems is noted. Clearly, cognitive agents require some sort of functional continuity, and it results in the need to design functional closed loops that might link the work of both the cognitive processes as well as the emotional processes. The agent needs a continuous metacontrol function that might force it to move along its functional trajectory without external intervention, and the idea of an interconnected system of loops working in a federated way may be accepted.

FOUNDATIONS TO MODEL EMOTION AS PATTERNED METACONTROL

Let us assume that any sort of system (i.e. agent) is dealing with its contextual information, its targets and its principles of stability by means of its operational models. We will name this work as the work of the longitudinal system of this agent, whatever the kind of abstractions might be defined concerning the architectural foundations of the agent. The emotional functionality might provide some transversal feedback (i.e. a tranversal system) that should maintain the operational continuity by means of a metacontrol system that works over this longitudinal system.

However, this longitudinal work meta controlled by some transversal system does not seem to be enough. Biological agents have some sort of aptitude to push an emotional impulse back (with different levels of modulation in this aptitude regarding the principles of work of each agent,

usually called *drives*). They also seem to be able for decision making even when the information available is not complete and (a priori) they should not have the capability to respond. Intuitively, it seems as if the cognitive part and the emotional part of the agent are maintaining a federated work to achieve each of their goals, leading at the same time the ability to make two different representations of the external reality available.

It leads to the hypothesis of a simultaneous and bidirectional meta control in both sides of influence (longitudinal-to-transversal as well as transversal-to-longitudinal). Both sides provide the agent with two kinds of perceptions (concerning the emotional side as well as the cognitive side) enabling a mutual meta control and two kinds of triggering processes regarding each of them. This bidirectional loop is closed with two comparative elements whose targets are related to the meta goals of the emotional side as well as the meta goals of the cognitive side. That is, the longitudinal system (i.e. the cognitive system) is a complete system (the system and its controllers) that works as a whole (i.e. a common plant in control systems theory). This longitudinal system will be forced by the laws of control of the transversal system (i.e. the emotional system). That is, the transversal system works as a metacontroller for the longitudinal system. Simultaneously, the transversal system (i.e. the emotional system) is a complete system (the system and its controllers) that works as a whole (i.e. a common plant in control systems theory). Analogously to the previous case, the longitudinal system (i.e. the cognitive system) works as a metacontroller for the transversal system (i.e. the emotional system).

The main goal of the control operation in any type of system is to maintain its stability. The notion of bidirectional meta control focuses on the idea of a mutual monitoring of each of these systems (i.e. longitudinal and transversal) one over the other, to generate a closed-loop functionality. This bidirectional loop has to be closed analogously to the perspective of the control systems theory (Klir, 1969). By analogy with the Klir theory, when speaking of emotional systems, we shall regard a set of instantaneous values of two types of input quantities (regarding the outside stimuli and the quantifiable meaning of emotion) as the instantaneous stimuli that are affecting the whole system. That is, the quantities that come from the emotional system and the quantities that come from the environment. Under the viewpoint of Klir, every quantity included in the coupling between two controlled elements of a control system, might be specified as either an input or an output quantity of the first element and, also, as either an input or an output quantity of the second element (Klir, 1969). In this same way, the causal relationship between these two systems (longitudinal and tranversal) might be modeled by means of couplings from one system to the other.

An emotional agent maintains simultaneously the functional balance of its system concerning both, the stimuli that comes from the outside environment as well as the value-based stimuli (i.e. quantifiable meaning) that comes from its emotional system. It leads to the assumption of some inside environment within the agent with which the cognitive system has causal relationships and that should be modeled by means of some sort of coupling. Concerning the emotional operation, the value-based quantities that are affecting the agent are created by the agent itself. They are quantities produced by the agent that are simultaneously causing events within the agent (i.e. its feelings) as well as within the outside environment (by means of the expression of these feelings). So clearly there are couplings that should be modelled regarding the following elements: the outside environment, some sort of inner environment concerning the agent, the controlled system and the meta control system of the agent.

Under this perspective, two main couplings that conform the foundations of the emotional metacontrol can be defined: a first coupling between the agent and the outside environment, and a second coupling between the agent and its inner context

that will be assumed as its inner environment. This inner environment should be modelled on the basis of the causality of those patterns of evaluation of relevant stimuli carried out by means of the essential inner processes of the agent. As well, let us assume the work of the longitudinal system as a closed functional loop to balance the stability between the agent and the outside environment, and the work of the transversal system as a closed functional loop to balance the stability between the agent and its inner environment. This enables the agent to balance both the emotional and the cognitive processes in a concurrent way, in a work under the influence of a competition model of goals related with the functional stability of the system (concerning both the outside environment as well as its inner well-being). Thus, two types of goals can be established, that is, the intrinsic goals that integrate the needs for the internal balance of the system, and the extrinsic goals to integrate the tasks for which the system is built.

The longitudinal system will manage the balance concerning the extrinsic goals while the transversal system will manage the balance concerning the intrinsic ones. The emotional metacontroll will emerge from the mutual interconnection in the work of these two closed functional loops (i.e. the longitudinal and the transversal system) that will provide the capability of functional reconfiguration of the whole system that conforms the agent, to cope with the uncertainty and to improve its adaptiveness to the environment (either be it the situational or physical environment). In general, reconfiguration is driven by processes that try to correlate the organization of the agent to what is needed to accomplish a certain goal, and it becomes an essential feature for the emotional modelling. Thus, the metacontrol functionality on the basis of the emotion becomes a new system that can be defined as a complex set of these two interacting functional loops in analogy with the theory of von Bertalanffy (1950) regarding the definition of a system as a complex set of interacting elements f1, f2, …fn. This way, the dynamics of the agent-environment system are governed by the coupling of the dynamics of the physical environment (i.e. the world) and the internal dynamics of the agent (determined by its organization) (Sanz et al., 2013). The complex unity formed by these two functional loops is a bidirectional metacontrol system that works between the same controlled elements (i.e. the longitudinal and the transversal system) but nevertheless each one is working in the oposite direction of the other. This way, the agent can modify its internal state and its organization to dynamically maximize some *value-for-the-agent* previously defined (Sanz et al., 2013). Consequently, this forces us to also define models of meta goals that will help to balance the stability in this bidirectional metacontrol operativeness.

Thus, to model an emotional system even from a low-level perspective of abstraction, becomes an intricate task in which models are the essential basis of modeling. Models to define the functional structure and the organizational structure of the systems that conforms the agent are required, but additionally models to define the patterns of goals that will drive the whole funcionality of the final system are also needed. This is what we call the model-based approach to enable operativeness for the functional reconfiguration.

THE EXPLOITATION OF MODELS IN ARTIFICIAL EMOTIONS

There is no doubt about the need of models to incorporate usable knowledge in cognitive systems. Models are abstractions of reality that contain just the essential aspects of this reality concerning the system (Selic, 2003). The function of a model refers both to the interpretation and the understanding of the system, as well as the drawing of conclusions in the form of other subsequent usable models, so the semantic for a system comes from the use of models. Under this model-based approach, the system is able to take part in its own control strategy (an indispensable feature in emotional

cognitive agents). The complexity of an emotional cognitive agent requires the availability of models to attend the key issues related to the changes in its dynamics, as well as an interconnected design that might address the exploitation of the functional structure, the organizational structure and the knowledge base of the agent.

The previous section has shown some organizational foundations to model emotion as patterned metacontrol (by using a bidirectional metacontrol loop) describing the interpretation and the understanding of how should the functional structure of an emotional operative be. Nevertheless, the whole scheme of an emotional model also should allow the agent to draw conclusions concerning its state, operative, needs, etc. in the form of other subsequent models available to be used by the system. Consequently, additional issues related to the models that hold required information for the agent as well as to the design of these models should be analyzed.

The so called *action readiness* in biological agents seems to be essential processes that select the required patterns of functions concerning the puntual state of the agent. In an analogous way, the artificial agents should be flexible concerning the changing circumstances of the environment (either physical or situational environments), so the capability of functional reorganization becomes an essential requirement. This functional flexibility is related with some sort of capability for changing different types of relationships between functional elements. Consequently, regarding the exploitation of functional and organizational structure of the agents, the design of models as relational entities is crucial. Some processes of perception (such as those that link past experiences and current stimuli) require complex relationships that also should be modelled as model-based relationships. Among others, an essential funcionality of emotions is the exploitation of these relationships to help in the representation of internal models of knowledge. So it is essential to have a minimum of functional chunks, each of them with their required degrees of freedom, in all of those sectors that might affect the internal representations of the agent. The degrees of freedom will be modeled by means of model-based relationships and will help the reconfigurable capabilities of the system. So it is critical to study the number of parameters that may vary independently concerning each functional chunk to implement correctly the degrees of freedom related to each functional chunk.

However, under the Theories of Readiness (Fridja 1986, 2007) it seems as if the system can use the meaning of this reconfiguration only if it experiences the consequences of the process. It becomes again a critical issue that is sometimes referenced as the experience of what happens (Damasio, 1999).

The system not only should use its capability to exploit the models that trigger the reconfiguration, but also should exploit some type of models to understand the particular pattern of functions running at time, as part of the meaning used (that conforms the basis for the appraisal evaluation). Understanding the emotion as a run time adaptation mechanism based on the activation of patterns of organization, the dynamic reorganization and the puntual meaning of this dynamic reorganization demands models to identify and to understand patterns of interest. That is, the agent needs to understand both the patterns of interest, as well as the patterns of reconfiguration and the meaning of these patterns that are running. And this results in the issue of how to integrate within the models, those means for allowing to create and retrieve semantic.

As crucial as the models themselves, the building of artificial emotions, requires the engineering of a critical emotion-experience mechanism [Sanz et al., 2012]. As argued in the relevant work of (Hayek, 1999) we interpret in the light of experience. It results in the idea that any model that is not being experienced cannot be fully understood, and that those models that still have not been exploited by the agent are not complete models. The experience of a mirror image is an exploitable

model concerning the causal relationship between the visual system of the agent and the functionalities that concerns its visual perception. But it is not an exploitable model if the agent requires a full understanding regarding functionalities that are related with the shape or touch features about the shape reflected. From this perspective of models and the perceptual system, the usable models cannot be a mere duplication of elements from the real world. Thus, an essential part of a usable model is the representation of an exploited instance of this model regarding some functionality that will require this model.

It is clear that a model can be exploited without the need to be experienced. What seems also clear is that the model has to be experienced by the agent to achieve interpretations about this model (i.e. semantic). That being so, some first conclusions allow us to identify some key features in models to be useful in emotional modelling. Models should be relational entities with an essential method for self-updating, that allow the integration (at runtime) of critical information concerning its instances, and the mandatory relationships with those patterns of interest for each instance of the entity. That is, models are relational entities with an updating method that will address the integration of information related with relevant instances of itself. It will allow the integration of the experience within the model and, likely, the agent will use this information in the future to do interpretations.

DISCUSSION

It is quite clear that emotional behavior provides mechanisms for assesing relevant patterns of interest (stimuli, goals, etc.) in the environment of cognitive agents; i.e. for assesing the relevance of the state of affairs. This is the reason why they are so powerful in biological agents. Based on this vision, we have explained an strategy of analysis and design of artificial emotions to exploit them in artificial agents in order to improve their operational behavior in challenging environments. The strategy of design proposes the existence of a bidirectional metacontrol between the named longitudinal and transversal systems that keep the agent attuned to the environment.

This strategy exploit models of the perceived reality, ongoing situational state, models of goals, etc., and simultaneously, models of the inner mechanisms of the agent such as those used in cognitive processes, functional reconfiguration, etc. Consequently, models become in fundamental assets in artificial emotion research, because they will enable the operation and also the systemic engineering of the artificial agent. The exploitation of each model is part of the processes that will conform the emotional phenomenology of the agent. The model and its exploitation is an essential facet that is involved in the transference of information from stimuli throughout the entire emotional agent. From the exploitation of models in artificial emotions, the stimuli is transferred into an understandable form so that the agent can react properly. Such understandable forms include different feelings, sensations, inner processes within the system, etc. That is, patterns of evaluation whose proper attention is crucial to the survival of the biological organisms as it maintains them informed of the outside environment (i.e. the real world) around them and allows them to respond accordingly. And that, analogously, we would like to transfer to the artificial systems.

REFERENCES

Arnold, M. B. (Ed.). (1960). *Emotion and personality*. New York: Columbia University Press.

Bach, J. (2003) The MicroPsi Agent Architecture. In *Proceedings of ICCM-5, Universitats-Verlag Bamberg*.

Bandai. (2000) *Tamagotchi*. http://www.bandai. com

Bartneck, C. (2002). Integrating the OCC model of emotions in embodied characters. In *Proceedings of the Workshop on Virtual Conversational*.

Bell, G., Ling, D., Kurlander, D., Miller, J., Pugh, D., Skelly, T., Stankosky, A., Thiel, D., Dantzich, M.V., Wax, T. (1997). Lifelike computer characters: The Persona Project at Microsoft Research. In J. M. Bradshaw (Ed.), Software agents, (pp. 191-222). London: AAAI Press.

Bower, G. H., Lazarus, R., LeDoux, J. E., Panksepp, J., Davidson, R. J., & Ekman, P. (1994) What is the relation between emotion and memory. In P. Ekman & R. J. Davidson, (Eds.), The nature of emotion: Fundamental questions. Series in affective science (pp. 301-318). New York: Oxford University Press.

Breazeal, C. (1998). A motivational system for regulating human–robot interaction. In *Proceedings of the Fifteenth National Conference on Artificial Intelligence (AAAI98)*. Madison, WI, pp. 54–61. (1998)

Breazeal, C. (2000). Regulation and entrainment in human–robot interaction. *The International Journal of Robotics Research*, 21(10–11), 883–902.

Breazeal, C. (2001). Emotive qualities in robot speech. In *Proceedings of the 2001 IEEERSJ International Conference on Intelligent Robots and Systems (IROS01)*, Maui, HI, 2001.

Breazeal, C. (2002). Emotion and sociable humanoid robots. *International Journal of Human-Computer Studies*, 59(1-2), 119–155. doi:10.1016/S1071-5819(03)00018-1

Brooks, R. A., Breazeal, C., Marajanovic, M., Scassellati, B., & Williamson, M. M. (1999). The cog project: Building a humanoid robot. In C. L. Nehavic (Ed.), Computation for Metaphors, Analogy and Agents, Springer Lecture Notes in Artificial Intelligence (vol. 1562). Berlin, Germany: Springer-Verlag. doi:10.1007/3-540-48834-0_5

Bush, G., Luu, P., & Posner, M. I. (2000, June). Cognitive and emotional influences in anterior cingulate cortex. *Trends in Cognitive Sciences*, *4*(6), 215–222. doi:10.1016/S1364-6613(00)01483-2 PMID:10827444

Cannon, W. B. (1927). The James-Lange theory of emotions: A critical examination and an alternative theory. *The American Journal of Psychology*, *39*(1/4), 106–124. doi:10.2307/1415404 PMID:3322057

Cytowic, R. E. (1998). The man who tasted shapes. Cambridge, MA: MIT Press.

Damasio, A. (Ed.). (1999). The feeling of what happens: Body and emotion in the making of consciousness. Harcourt.

Damasio, A. (2005) Descartes' error: Emotion, reason, and the human brain. Penguin Books.

Davidson, R. J. (2002). Activation paradigms in affective and cognitive neuroscience: Probing the neuronal circuitry underlying mod and anxiety disorders. In D. S. Charney, J. Coyle, K. Davis, & C. Nemeroff (Eds.), Neuropsychopharmacology - The Fifth Generation of Progress (pp. 373-382). Lippincott, Williams & Wilkins.

Davidson, R. J., Pizzagalli, D., Nitschke, J. B., & Kalin, N. H. (2003). Parsing the subcomponents of emotion and disorders of emotion: Perspectives from affective neuroscience. In R. J. Davidson, H. H. Goldsmith, & K. Scherer (Eds.), *Handbook of affective science* (pp. 8–24). New York: Oxford University Press.

Digman, J. M. (1990). Personality structure: Emergence of the five factor model. *Annual Review of Psychology*, *41*(1), 417–440. doi:10.1146/annurev.ps.41.020190.002221

Electronic Arts. (2000). *The Sims.* http://thesims.ea.com/us/

Elliott, C. D. (1992). *The affective reasoner: A Process model of emotions in a multi-agent system* (Ph.D. Thesis). The Institute for the Learning Sciences, Northwestern University, Evanston, IL.

Fox, E. (Ed.). (2008). Emotion science: An integration of cognitive and neuroscientific approaches. Palgrave Macmillan.

Fridja, N. H. (2008). The psychologist's point of view. In M. Lewis, J. M. Haviland-Jones, & L. F. Barrett (Eds.), *Handbook of emotions* (3rd ed., pp. 68–87). New York, NY: Guilford Press.

Frijda, N. (Ed.). (1987). *The emotions (Studies in Emotion and Social Interaction).* Cambridge University Press.

Frijda, N. H. (Ed.). (1986). *The emotions.* Cambridge University Press.

Frijda, N. H. (Ed.). (2007). *The laws of emotion.* Mahwah, N.J.: Lawrence Erlbaum Associates.

Ghasem-Afhaee & Ören. (2003). Towards fuzzy agents with dynamic personality for human behavior simulation. Paper presented at SCSC, 2003.

Goleman, D. (1995). Emotional intelligence. New York: Bantam.

Gratch, J. (2000) *Emile: Marshalling passions in training and education.* In *Proceedings of the Fourth International Conference on Autonomous Agents* (pp. 325-332), Barcelona Spain. (2000) doi:10.1145/336595.337516

Hayek, F. A. (Ed.). (1999). *The sensory order: An inquiry into the foundations of theoretical psychology.* doi:10.7208/chicago/9780226321301.001.0001

Hudlicka, E. (2008). Modeling the mechanisms of emotion effects on cognition. *Proceedings of the AAAI Fall Symposium on "Biologically Inspired Cognitive Architectures"* (pp. 82-86).

Izard, C. E. (1993). Organitational and motivational functions of discrete emotions. In M. Lewis & J.M. Haviland (Eds.), Handbook of emotions (pp.631 - 642). New York: The Guilford Press.

James, W. (1884). What is an Emotion? *Mind*, *9*(34), 188–205. doi:10.1093/mind/os-IX.34.188

Kleinginna, P. R. Jr, & Kleinginna, A. M. (1981). A categorized list of emotion definitions, with a suggestion for a consensual definition. *Motivation and Emotion*, *5*(4), 345–379. doi:10.1007/BF00992553

Klir, G. J. (Ed.). (1969). *An approach to general systems theory.* New York, N.Y.: Van Nostrand Reinhold Company.

Klüver, H., & Bucy, P. C. (1937). "Psychic blindness" and other symptoms following bilateral temporal lobectomy in Rhesus monkeys. *The American Journal of Physiology*.

Koda, T. (1996). *Agents with faces: A study on the effect of personification of software agents* (Unpublished Master Thesis). MIT Media Lab, Cambridge.

Laird, J., Newell, A., Rosenbloom, P. S., & Artificial Intelligence and Psychology Project. (1987) *Soar: an architecture for general intelligence* (Paper 433). Department of Psychology.

Lange, C. G., & James, W. (1922). *The emotions* (Vol. 1). Williams & Wilkins.

Lazarus, R. S. (1984). On the primacy of cognition. *The American Psychologist*, *39*(2), 124–129. doi:10.1037/0003-066X.39.2.124

LeDoux, J. (1996). Emotional networks and motor control: A fearful view. *Progress in Brain Research*, *107*, 437–446. doi:10.1016/S0079-6123(08)61880-4 PMID:8782535

LeDoux, J. E. (2000). Emotion circuits in the brain. *Annual Review of Neuroscience*, *23*(1), 155–184. doi:10.1146/annurev.neuro.23.1.155 PMID:10845062

LEGO. (2001). *LEGO Mindstorms.* Retrieved from http://www.legomindstorms.com

Ljung, L. (Ed.). (1987). System identification: Theory for the user. New Jersey: Prentice-Hall, Inc.

MacLean, P. D. (1990). The triune brain in evolution: Role in paleocerebral functions. Plenum Publishing Corporation.

Miller, E. K., & Cohen, J. D. (2001). An integrative theory of prefrontal cortex function. *Annual Review of Neuroscience*, *24*(1), 167–202. doi:10.1146/annurev.neuro.24.1.167 PMID:11283309

Morris, J. S., Öhman, A., & Dolan, R. J. (1998). Conscious and unconscious emotional learning in the human amygdala. *Nature*, *393*(6684), 467–470. doi:10.1038/30976 PMID:9624001

Newell, A. (1980). Physical symbol systems. *Cognitive Science*, *4*(2), 135–183. doi:10.1207/s15516709cog0402_2

Newell, A., & Card, S. K. (1985). The prospects for psychological science in human-computer interaction. *Human-Computer Interaction*, *1*(3), 209–242. doi:10.1207/s15327051hci0103_1

O'Reilly, W. S. N. (1996). *Believable social and emotional agents* (Unpublished Ph.D. Thesis). Carnegie Mellon University, Pittsburgh, PA.

Ochsner, K. N., Bunge, S. A., Gross, J. J., & Gabrieli, J. D. E. (2002). Rethinking feelings: An fMRI study of the cognitive regulation of emotion. *Journal of Cognitive Neuroscience, 14*(8), 1215–1299. doi:10.1162/089892902760807212 PMID:12495527

Ogata, T., & Sugano, S. (2000). Emotional communication robot: WAMOEBA-2R emotion model and evaluation experiments. In *Proceedings of the International Conference on Humanoid Robots, 2000.*

Ortony, A. (Ed.). (2003). On making believable emotional agents believable. In R. P. Trapple, (Ed.), Emotions in humans and artefacts. Cambridge, MA: MIT Press.

Papez, J. (1995). A proposed mechanism of emotion. 1937. *The Journal of Neuropsychiatry and Clinical Neurosciences, 7*(1), 103–112. doi:10.1176/jnp.7.1.103 PMID:7711480

Picard, R. (1995, November) *Affective computing* (Technical Report 321). MIT Media Laboratory, Perceptual Computing Section.

Picard, R. W. (2003). What does it mean for a computer to "have" emotions? In R. Trappl, P. Petta, & S. Payr (Eds.), *Emotions in Humans and Artifacts*. Cambridge, MA: The MIT Press.

Poel, M., Rieksopden Akker, N. A., van Kesteren, A. J. (2002). Learning emotions in virtual environments. In R. Trappl (Ed.), Cybernetics and Systems 2002, (pp. 751-755). Vienna: Austrian Society for Cybernetic Studies.

Prinz, J. J. (Ed.). (2004). Gut reactions: A perceptual theory of emotion. Oxford: Oxford University Press.

Qingji, G., Kai, W., Haijuan, L., (2008). A robot emotion generation mechanism based on PAD emotion space: Research on robot emotion. In *IFIP Advances in Information and Communication Technology, Vol. 288, Intelligent Information Processing IV* (pp. 138-147). Boston: Springer.

Reeves, B., & Clifford Nass, C. (2003, January). The media equation: How people treat computers, television, and new media like real people and places (CSLI Lecture Notes). Stanford, CA: Center for the Study of Language and Information.

Sanz, R., Hernandez, C., & Sanchez-Escribano, M. G. (2012). Consciousness, action selection, meaning and phenomenic anticipation. *International Journal of Machine Consciousness, 4*(2), 383–399. doi:10.1142/S1793843012400227

Sanz, R., Sanchez-Escribano, M. G., & Herrera, C. (2013). A model of emotion as patterned metacontrol. *Biologically Inspired Cognitive Architectures, 1*(2), 2013.

Scherer, K. (2001). Appraisal processes in emotion: Theory, methods, research. (Series in Affective Science). New York: Oxford University Press.

Scherer, K. R. (2001). Appraisal considered as a process of multi-level sequential checking. In K. R. Scherer, A. Schorr, & T. Johnstone (Eds.), Appraisal processes in checking emotion: Theory, methods, research (pp. 92-120). Oxford University Press.

Selic, B. (2003). The pragmatics of Model-Driven development. *IEEE Software, 20*(5), 19–25. doi:10.1109/MS.2003.1231146

Simon, H. A. (1967). Motivational and emotional controls of cognition. *Psychological Review, 74*(1), 29–39. doi:10.1037/h0024127 PMID:5341441

Sloman, A. (2001) *Varieties of affect and the CogAff architecture schema*. In *Proceedings of the AISB'01 Symposium on Emotion, Cognition, and Affective Computing*. York, UK 2001.

Sun, R., & Zhang, X. (2004). Top-down versus bottom-up learning in cognitive skill acquisition. In Proceedings of the 24th Annual Conference of the Cognitive Science Society (2002), pp. 63-89. doi:10.1016/j.cogsys.2003.07.001

von Bertalanffy, L. (1950). An outline of general system theory. *The British Journal for the Philosophy of Science*, *1*(2), 134–165. doi:10.1093/bjps/I.2.134

Zhang, D., Cungen, C., Young, X., Wang, H., & Pan, Y. (2005). A survey of computational emotion research. In T. Panayiotopoulos et al. (Eds.), LNAI 3661, (p. 490). Berlin; Heidelberg: Springer-Verlag.

KEY TERMS AND DEFINITIONS

Agent: It refers the whole entity with aptitude to do something.

Artificial Agent: It is used to refer to any software program but recognizing that, in general, there are many more classes of agent implementations. Some *Artificial Agent* might be designated Intelligent *Agent*, *Cognitive Agent*, *Autonomous Agent*, etc. concerning its functional possibilities. The term *Cognitive Agent* is used to refer agents with aptitude to exploit knowledge. If some *Cognitive Agent* implements *Artificial Emotion*, it is named *Emotional Agent*.

Context: It refers to those circumstances, conditions, factors, state of affairs, situation, background, scene, etc. that affects the system within its *domain*.

Domain: Includes the portion of the *environment* that is relevant for the system concerning its operational state; any change in the domain brings about significant events that affect the system operation. The emergence of new requirements is due to the enactment of a new subset of the entire *domain* that becomes relevant for the system at a given time.

Exploitation: The exploitation refers to any system operation in which by making use of model resources, optimizes each operational phase within the system. It is also related with the improvement of models by using the empirical base on experience and observation, rather than inferences or built code.

Model: In a generic definition it is an *information entity* corresponding with a *system* in a formal relationship that condenses several essential features to define the *system*. Commonly, *systems* need models to incorporate usable knowledge concerning the structural and functional baselines of readiness operative. Models are abstractions of reality that contain just the essential aspects of this reality concerning the system (Selic, 2003). The function of a model regards both the interpretation and the understanding of the system, as well as the drawing of conclusions in the form of other subsequent and usable models. This work proposes to build models that provide causal connections with the inner context of the system at runtime.

System (Automonous System): It is a *system* that operates connecting its internal dynamics with the dynamic of its environment in the context of the performance of task.

System: It is a set of *entities* and *relationships*. Usually systems operate in order to reach some concrete goal. We may speack of both a system of agents as well as of the system of the agent to refer to the agent realization itself.

Section 2
The Body as a Space for Emotions

Chapter 7
Socially Embodied Human–Robot Interaction:
Addressing Human Emotions with Theories of Embodied Cognition

J. Lindblom
University of Skövde, Sweden

B. Alenljung
University of Skövde, Sweden

ABSTRACT

A fundamental challenge of human interaction with socially interactive robots, compared to other interactive products, comes from them being embodied. The embodied nature of social robots questions to what degree humans can interact 'naturally' with robots, and what impact the interaction quality has on the user experience (UX). UX is fundamentally about emotions that arise and form in humans through the use of technology in a particular situation. This chapter aims to contribute to the field of human-robot interaction (HRI) by addressing, in further detail, the role and relevance of embodied cognition for human social interaction, and consequently what role embodiment can play in HRI, especially for socially interactive robots. Furthermore, some challenges for socially embodied interaction between humans and socially interactive robots are outlined and possible directions for future research are presented. It is concluded that the body is of crucial importance in understanding emotion and cognition in general, and, in particular, for a positive user experience to emerge when interacting with socially interactive robots.

INTRODUCTION

The ability to engage in social interaction is a crucial building block of human culture, which is one of the major driving forces for the *complexity* of social life and cognition. Consequently, humans have become as experts at interacting socially, and if current interactive technology adheres to this human social ability, humans can find the interaction with socially interactive technology

DOI: 10.4018/978-1-4666-7278-9.ch007

effortless, fun, and enjoyable, resulting in positive experience and feelings of being competent, as well as that the technology provides long-term additional value to human life. Thus, the user's experience of interaction with technology is of major concern and has lately received increased interest, and the quality of the human-technology interaction is pivotal. A certain kind of technology that might achieve this kind of effortless social interaction between human and technology is social robots. Positive user experience underpins the proliferation of social robots in society (Weiss et al., 2009), and, thus, the user experience of social robots needs to be a central issue of concern. But a positive user experience does not appear by itself. Instead, the positive user experience has to be systematically, thoroughly, and consciously designed for (Hartson & Pyla, 2012; Hassenzahl, 2013), and an embodied interaction approach has been considered a viable therorethical foundation (e.g., Dourish, 2001; Harper et al., 2008; Hartson & Pyla, 2012; Rogers, 2012) for designing the interaction between human and technology.

The development of social robots is in rapid progress and new advances in computer technology, artificial intelligence (AI), and other areas have resulted in advanced robotic technology that have major implications for the research field of human-robot interaction (HRI). HRI is a relatively new and growing research field dealing with the way humans can interact with robots in different ways, ranging from less complicated individual human-robot interaction in highly constrained tasks to play and multifarious cooperation with humans in teams. The field of HRI is supposed to have an impact on the types of relationships humans' can have with robots in general, and socially interactive robots in particular (cf. e.g., Dautenhahn & Saunders, 2011; Goodrich & Schultz, 2007; Thrun, 2004). HRI focuses on both human and robot factors, and is therefore a highly interdisciplinary and challenging research field. One of the major goals of HRI is to find the 'natural' means by which humans can use to inter-

act and communicate with robots (see e.g., Fong et al., 2003). However, the embodied nature of interactive robots (Breazeal, 2003; Thrun, 2004), has several implications on the social interactions between humans and robots. For example, the activities of the robots and humans need to be coordinated "here and now" and take place in physical space (Dautenhahn & Saunders, 2011). Moreover, Thrun (2004) pointed out that there are differences between these social robots according to interface capabilities, potential user groups, skills, and the different contexts of use, in comparison to more traditional interactive systems. Taken together, the issues addressed in HRI are different from, as well as more complex, than the ones in the field of human-computer interaction (HCI), resulting in extensive challenges from several perspectives. The multi-disciplinary field of HRI offers many different views and approaches to the subject. We propose that research on embodiment, especially social and emotional interaction, can successfully be linked to the user experience of socially interactive robots, since embodied cognition can serve as a wider unifying theoretical perspective for HRI. Additionally, focusing on embodied cognition and the embodiment of (social) robots can challenge existing thinking in HRI research that have underestimated the influence of being embodied as a positive influence on the user experience.

This chapter aims to contribute to the field of HRI by addressing, in further detail, the role and relevance of embodied cognition for human social interaction, and consequently what role embodiment might play in HRI, especially for socially interactive robots. The take home message proposed in this chapter is that emotions grounded in embodied agent-environment interactions impacts the interaction quality and that the interaction is a key determinant for the user experience.

The remainder of this chapter is structured as follows. The background section firstly provides some historical and conceptual background on embodied cognition and emotions that motivates and frames the work discussed in this chapter.

Secondly, it briefly presents the field of HRI, focusing on social robots and the role of social interaction in social robots, and introduces the concept of user experience and user experience design. The next sections outline challenges of socially embodied interaction between humans and socially interactive robots and possible opportunities for future research. The chapter ends with some conclusions.

BACKGROUND

This section firstly provides some historical and conceptual background on embodied cognition and emotions that will be useful in motivating and framing the work discussed in this chapter. Furthermore, it addresses how and why embodied emotions are relevant to human social interaction and cognition. Secondly, it briefly presents the field of HRI, classification of social robots, different approaches to HRI, as well as the role of social and emotional interaction in social robots. Lastly, the section describes the notions of user experience and user experience design.

Emotions and Embodied Cognition in Human Social Interaction

The relationship between emotion and cognition has been a much debated research issue throughout the history of Western philosophy (e.g., Damasio, 1995, 1999; Niedenthal, 2007; Pessoa, 2008; Ziemke & Lowe, 2009). Although scholars such as Charles Darwin, William James, and John Dewey considered emotions to be of central importance for the human mind in the late 19th century, the still dominant view has been to consider emotion and cognition as separate entities (Lindblom, forthcoming; Lowe & Ziemke, 2009). However, during the last decades this view has been questioned by scientific findings in cognitive science and related disciplines, showing interrelated connections between emotion and cognition. Some

researchers explicitly stress that in order to gain a thorough understanding of the human mind, emotions have to be carefully considered (Damasio, 1995; Niedenthal, 2007; Pessoa, 2008). As Pessoa (2008) pointed out, there exist a variation of concepts and definitions of emotion in the scientific literature, e.g., "emotion", "mood", "affect", "attitude", "motivation", "sensation", "drive" and "feeling" (as well as different variants on these concepts), but there is not enough space available here to elaborate on these concepts further. Roughly speaking, emotion (and the same occur to related concepts) seems hard to define definitely and clearly, and therefore we make no attempts to provide a definition. Instead, our focus is on the relationship between cognition and emotion, as well as the linking of emotions to the body.

The insights that emotions play a pivotal role in human cognition has resulted an increased interest in *embodied approaches* of cognition (e.g., Clark, 1997, 1999; Gibbs, 2006; Johnson, 2007; Lakoff & Johnson, 1999; Pfeifer & Scheier, 1999; Varela, Thompson & Rosch, 1991; Wilson & Golonka, 2013), which emphasize the way cognition is shaped by the embodied agent's interactions with the surrounding social and material world[1]. This shift, challenges both the view of what human cognition is and the methodology needed to study cognition. Research in mainstream cognitive science has since its inception in the mid-1950s mainly focused on studying the internal mental representations of the individual cognitive agent, often described as symbol manipulation. Cognition is viewed as information-processing of these more or less explicit internal symbolic representations of the external world, and nothing outside "the skull" is taken into account. In this centralized and narrow view of what constitutes cognition, the body only serves as an input and output device, i.e. a physical interface between internal programs (cognitive processes) and external world (see criticism by e.g. Dreyfus, 1992), and consequently emotion (as arising from the body) was considered irrational and not an object of study. Broadly speaking, proponents of embodied cognition stress the interplay between brain, body and mind. Lakoff and Johnson (1999, p. 265), for example, characterized it as follows,

...the mind is embodied, not in any trivial sense (e.g., the" wetware" of the brain runs the "software" of the mind), but in the deep sense that our conceptual systems and our capacity for thought are shaped by the nature of our brains, bodies, and bodily interactions. There is neither no mind separated from and independent of the body, nor are there thoughts that have an existence independent of our bodies and brains.

In a similar vein, Damasio (1995) pointed out that the brain and body form an indissociable organism, stressing that Damasio is not exaggerating, rather he is oversimplifying. He claimed that the separation between mind and brain is only mythical, the separation between mind and body is most likely just as fictional. Thus, "the mind is embodied, in the full sense of the term, not just embrained" (ibid., p. 118). In other words, the embodied approach implies that we need to move beyond mind/body and subjective/objective dichotomies that characterize much of traditional cognitive science. It can be argued that a similar dichotomy is seen within much traditional emotion research within cognitive psychology and relate disciplines, i.e., there is a split between the cognitive subjective evaluation of appraisal "in the head" and the objective bodily displays of behavior/expression. Rather, cognitive and emotional processes modify each other constantly since they are embodied. As a result of the insights of the role and relevance of embodiment for emotions and cognition, a growing body of research has been conducted on these issues, and we present in what follows some selected research findings in favor of that interrelatedness.

Empirical evidence from social psychology and related disciplines has demonstrated how social thought and judgments can be affected by bodily states, actions, emotions and motivations (cf. Barsalou et al., 2003; Niedenthal, 2007; Niedenthal et al., 2005). Barsalou et al. (2003), e.g., have identified the following four kinds of social embodiment effects. Firstly, *perceived social stimuli do not only produce cognitive states, but also bodily states.* For example, it has been reported that high school students who received good grades in an exam adopted a more erect posture than students who received poor grades. Moreover, subjects primed with concepts commonly associated with *elderly* people (e.g., 'gray', 'bingo', 'wrinkles') exhibited embodiment effects such as slower movement when leaving the experimental lab, as compared to a control group primed with neutral words. Several other studies also show similar effects. Secondly, *the observation of bodily states in others often results in bodily mimicry in the observer.* People often mimic behaviors, and subjects often mimic an experimenter's actual behavior, e.g. rubbing the nose or shaking a foot. Subjects also tend to mimic observed facial expressions, which is widely documented in the literature. Thirdly, *bodily states produce affective states*, which mean that embodiment not only facilitates a response to social stimuli but also produces tentative stimuli. For example, subjects rated cartoons differently when holding a pen between their lips than when holding it between their teeth. The latter triggered the same musculature as smiling, which made the subjects rate the cartoons as funnier, whereas holding the pen between the lips activated the same muscles as frowning and consequently had the opposite effect. Moreover, bodily postures influence the subjects' affective state, e.g., subjects in an upright position experienced more pride than subjects in a slump position. Fourthly, *compatibility between bodily and cognitive states enhances performance.* For instance, several motor performance compatibility effects have been reported, in which subjects responded faster to 'positive' words (e.g. 'love') than 'negative' words (e.g. 'hate') when asked to pull a lever towards them. These examples, as well as other studies, demonstrate that there is a strong relation between embodied and cognitive states in social interaction. In short, the bidirectional swapping between these states occurs automatically without any higher knowledge structure.

Moreover, Niedenthal (2007) argued that theories of embodied cognition provide new ways to consider how human process emotions, showing a reciprocal relationship between the bodily expressions of emotions and in the way emotional content is displayed and interpreted. For example, Niedenthal et al. (2005) highlighted the linking between embodiment and emotions, given that embodiment is essentially engaged in information processing about emotion, online, and most notably, also offline, in which humans represent the emotional meaning in abstract entities such as words. Moreover, they stressed that there is accumulating evidence that humans also mimic others' *emotional* facial expressions. Bavelas et al. (1986, in Niedenthal et al., 2005), for instance, reported that when a co-researcher of theirs actually participated within their own experimental situation and deliberately faked an injury, grimacing in pain, the observing participants then also grimaced. The extent of the participants' grimaces correlated with how clearly they could see the confederate's face. Moreover, it has been demonstrated that participants react to subliminal happy and angry expressions with minor smiles and frowns (Niedenthal et al., 2005). Similarly, Wallbott (1991, in Niedenthal et al., 2005) asked participants to categorize emotional facial expressions in photographs of humans, and as the participants conducted their task, their own faces were videotaped. The recording demonstrates that the participants tended to mimic the facial expressions during classification, and there was a correlation between the accuracy of their classification and the magnitude of mimicry. In other words, bodily feedback from facial mimicry plays an important role in the ability to process emotional facial expression, and emotion imitation

seems to occur automatically without any higher mediating conscious awareness.

Furthermore, Niedenthal et al. (2005) used a 'chewing gum' experiment in order to highlight embodiment in the interplay between emotion and cognition. In the experiment subjects were asked to study 78 photographs of human faces. One group was instructed to mimic, and imitate the facial expressions, as well as the head and gaze orientation of the persons depicted in the photographs. While another group was blocked to facial mimicry through chewing gum, a third was required to squeeze a sponge with their non-preferred hand, as a way to manage motor control. Finally, a fourth group had to judge the head orientations and the facial expressions of the persons in the photographs. Following this first part of the experiment, the subjects received a face-recognition test. In accordance with the prediction of the embodiment view, memory performance was best in the mimicry group (73%), whereas the chewing gum group's score was worst (59%). The other two groups' score were in between. The results indicate that the subjects' imitation of the depicted facial expressions, function as 'muscular' representations in themselves, which enhanced memory. Summing up, the empirical findings presented above, as well as other studies, provide significant evidence for embodiment effects in social-emotional information processing that support crucial cognitive and social functions.

Empirical findings within neuroscience and related fields, offer a more thorough understanding of the underlying neural mechanisms that facilitate this human sensitivity of social interaction. Neuro-scientific findings suggest that such a resonance mechanism may rely on special kinds of visuomotor neurons called *mirror neurons* (e.g., Gallese & Goldman, 1998; Gallese, Keysers & Rizzolatti, 2004). Mirror neurons are located in area F5 in the monkey brain and become activated both when *performing* specific goal directed hand (and mouth) movements and when *observing* or *hearing* about the same actions (Kohler, et al., 2002; Rizzolatti et al., 2002). Because mirror neurons respond to both conditions, it has been argued that the mirror system functions as a kind of action representation, since it links 'action' and 'action-perception', like human gesturing. Consequently, this mirroring mechanism enables the agent to understand the meaning of the observed action by embodied simulation. Moreover, it has been speculated that the mirror system might be a basic mechanism necessary for imitation and 'mind-reading', i.e., attributing mental states to others (e.g., Rizzolatti et al., 2002; Svensson, Lindblom & Ziemke, 2007). Taken together, the consideration of the mirror neuron system as the neurobiological underpinning of embodiment and simulation theories as the basis of social interaction, gesturing and mind-reading, provides significant examples of 'more' embodied views of social cognition. In addition, research evidence shows that the mirror mechanism is involved in empathy as well as emotions. Wicker et al. (2003), for instance, demonstrated that during the observation of a facial expression of disgust, there was neural activation in the same area of the brain that is activated when exposed to disgusting odors. This means, there are neural activations in the insula both when a person experiences disgust, as well as when the emotion of disgust is generated by the facial expression of another person. In other words, experiencing emotions function analogously with action understanding, based on the same resonance mechanism. Although the current knowledge of the underlying mirror neuron mechanism is unable to explain in detail the whole complexity of human social interaction and social cognition, it does shed light on how the interacting partners are able to share the communicated meaning in the dialogue.

Moreover, recent empirical findings in neuroscience show that when humans interact, affective information is transmitted (via the bodies of the sender and receiver) between their brains, supporting the relational view of emotions and cognition (Silke et al., 2011). They investigated the flow of affective data between senders' and perceivers' brains engaged in ongoing facial communication. They found that the neural activity in the perceiver's brain could be successfully predicted from the neural activity in the sender's brain, depending on the affective information that was communicated. Their findings offer direct evidence that during ongoing facial communication a "shared space" is continuously built up between the interacting brains. This means, one's own body is already communicating with the other's body at unconscious and perceptual levels that are sufficient for meaningful social interactions to emerge.

Summing up, it has been argued that affective and emotional aspects play important roles in regulating social interaction, since humans attend and attune to each other's movements as well as emotional and facial expressions, creating modes of mutual immediacy. A central feature of human social interaction is its turn-taking structure, in which emotional displays seem to be the glue that holds the interaction together. Additionally, the same emotion is often expressed through different modalities by the interacting persons, while one person might use vocalization, the other person may instead display the emotion through facial expression. Furthermore, the most crucial role for emotions might be to create, organize and coordinate the majority of our cognitive functions (Damasio, 1995; 1999). Briefly stated, paying attention to the subjective state of our body will almost perceive an emotional tone within one's own body. This inner emotional mood continuously adapts to in the innumerable variations that are used to categorize, and, most important of all, make sense of our human experience.

HRI and Socially Interactive Robots

HRI is a relatively new and has been a growing research field, since the early 1990s, which is concerned with the ways humans might work, play and generally interact with different kinds of robots. There are different approaches to view HRI (for example, see Dautenhahn, 2007a, 2007b, 2013; Dautenhahn & Saunders, 2011; Goodrich & Schultz, 2007; Thrun, 2004). Goodrich and Schultz (2007, p. 24), for example, characterize HRI as "a field of study dedicated to understanding, designing, and evaluating robotic systems for use by or with humans". Moreover, a central problem in HRI is "to understand and shape the interactions between one or more humans and one or more robots" (Goodrich & Schultz, 2007, p. 216). In so doing, HRI is considered as a highly interdisciplinary and challenging research field that in unique ways combines and utilizes knowledge and underlying philosophies from different areas such as psychology, cognitive science, social sciences, artificial intelligence, computer science, robotics, engineering, human-computer interaction (HCI) and user experience (UX) (Dautenhahn & Saunders, 2011; Weiss; 2011). According to Dautenhahn (2013), the key challenge and characterization of HRI can be phrased as follows:

HRI is the science of studying people's behaviour and attitudes towards robots in relationship to the physical, technological and interactive features of the robots, with the goal to develop robots that facilitate the emergence of human-robot interactions that are at the same time efficient (according to the original requirements of their envisaged area of use), but are also acceptable to people, and meet the social and emotional needs of their individual users as well as respecting human values.

However, this is an ambitious challenge and currently there are many different approaches to HRI, different kinds of robots, contexts and ways to interact with robots. In order to strive to disentangle these issues, we focus on social robots, presenting different kinds of socially interactive robots, the conceptual space of HRI within socially interactive robots, and then address the role of

social and emotional interaction between humans and social robots.

Different Kinds of Social Robots

Our focus is on *social robots*, i.e. robots that humans interact with socially in certain ways and to various degrees. Several definitions of social robots or related concepts have been used in the literature, including the following ones. Breazeal (2003a) distinguished some distinct modes of social interaction in social robots, which she characterizes as the class of robots that people anthropomorphize in order to interact with: i.e. *socially evocative, social interface, socially receptive,* and *sociable robots. Socially evocative robots* imply that the robot is designed only to encourage people to anthropomorphize it in order to achieve an interaction. *Social interface robots* use human-like social cues and different modes of communication in order to facilitate more natural and familiar interactions with humans from the user's perspective. *Socially receptive robots* are considered as *social interface robots,* but that also benefit from interactions with humans. *Sociable robots* are socially participative "creatures" having their own internal goals and motivations, and actively engage with humans in a social manner not only to benefit the user but also to benefit itself. In addition, Fong et al. (2003) included the following three classes: *socially situated, socially embedded,* and *socially intelligent robots. Socially situated robots* are surrounded by a social environment in which they perceive and react to common social cues. *Socially embedded robots* are socially situated in as well as structurally coupled with their environment, and are partly aware of some underlying human interaction mechanisms, such as, gaze following and turn-taking. *Socially intelligent robots* are robots that display truly human-like social intelligence, based on pro-active engagement with humans and having deep models of social cognition. As Fong et al. (2003) pointed out, these classes of social interaction in social robots describe to what degree the robot supports the social "capacity/ability" it is attributed as well as the complexity of the emerging social interaction pattern between human(s) and robot(s). Fong's et al. (2003) seminal paper surveyed socially interactive robots, which they defined as "robots for which social interaction plays a key role" (ibid., p. 145). They focused on peer-to-peer HRI, and described robots that display more or less advanced human-like "social features", ranging from expression of emotions and establishment of social relationships to development of social competencies and personality. Furthermore, Fong et al. (2003) argued that socially interactive robots can be used for a variety of purposes: as research platforms for cognitive modelling, as toys, as educational tools, as peers, or as therapeutic aids. Consequently, the intended purpose influences the design methodology, since different design approaches have different measurement and evaluation criteria.

Different Approaches to Socially Intelligent Robots within HRI

In line with these above arguments, Dautenhahn (2007), for example, characterized the conceptual space of approaches for socially intelligent robots into three, but complementary, directions within HRI, i.e., *robot cognition-centred HRI, robot-centred HRI* and *human-centred HRI*. She stressed that the field of HRI differs significantly from robotics and engineering given that *interaction with humans* is one of the defining key issues of the field. In *robot cognition-centred HRI,* the emphasis is on robots as artificially intelligent systems, i.e., machines that reproduce human cognitive processes such as decision-making and problem-solving in certain tasks that the robot has to perform in a particular application domain. Research is focused upon the development and design of cognitive and/or emotional and motivational robot architectures, machine learning, and

problem-solving abilities within a specialized area of interest (Dautenhahn, 2007a). In *robot-centred HRI*, the emphasis is on the view of the robot as a creature, i.e. an autonomous agent that is engaged in its own goals, based on its own motivations and emotions. The robot interacts with humans in order to fulfil some of its 'needs' (however, specified externally by the robot designer). Hence, the center of attention in research is the development of sensorimotor regulation, emotional and motivational architectures that regulate social interaction with the environment (Dautenhahn, 2007a). In *human-centred HRI*, the main concern is how robots fulfil the intended tasks, in ways that are acceptable and comfortable to human users. Research is directed towards how humans react to and interpret the robot's 'look and feel' and performance, irrespectively of its underlying cognitive, emotional and motivational architectures. There are several research challenges, i.e., establishing a proper and consistent design of the robots' 'look and feel', socially interactive capabilities and performance, as well as the need of specialized evaluation methods for HRI studies. Of major importance is how different groups of humans (in the role of designers, users, observers, assistants, collaborators, competitors, customers, patients or friends) react to robots and the associated feelings that arise during the interaction (Dautenhahn, 2007a). She points out the need for a *synthesis* of the different approaches and disciplines involved in robot design, in order to come close to the vision that more and more (socially interactive) robots naturally will inhabit our environments in the future. Otherwise, she argues there is the risk for a biased robot design, as a kind of "patchwork" system, with no integration of the approaches presented above.

Emotional and Affective Aspects of Social Interaction in HRI

A fundamental issue in HRI has been to investigate how 'naturally' humans can interact with social robots. Given that humans are experts in social interaction (Lindblom, forthcoming) a major aim of socially interactive robots research is to explore the design space of human-like social interaction, since it offers different qualities of the interaction, that is related to, but different from, more traditional user interfaces such as various kinds of graphical user interfaces (GUIs) (Breazeal, 2003b; Dautenhahn 2007b; Fong et al., 2003; Norman, 2004; Thrun, 2004). Indeed, there is research in HCI that shows the human tendency to treat computer agents and interactive technology generally in the same way as they treat other humans, the so-called media equation (Reeves & Nass, 1996), by applying human social norms to the domain of technology and create social relationships with them. Likewise, Kirby et al. (2010) as well as Dautenhahn (2007a) argue that this would also apply to robots in general, and probably even more to social robots. The role of emotions and expressive social cues in regulating social interaction in social robots, especially in humanoid robots (robots that are human-like) has reached increased interest, which can be seen in the huge amount of publications in the field. Breazeal (2003b), for example, presented their lab's well-known vision and emotive response platform called *Kismet* (a robot head) that engaged in various forms of basic interaction behaviors, grounded in a "drive system" (*fatigue, social*, and *stimulation*). The platform's "mood" became replicated as emotional and facial expressions *(anger, calm, disgust, happiness, interest, sadness,* and *surprise)*. As a consequence of not being stimulated the system "expressed" *boredom*; when overstimulated it "expressed" *fear*. Otherwise Kismet "was" *interested* (Breazeal & Scassellati, 2000). Conducted evaluations of human real-time interaction with Kismet showed that the platform was able to engage humans in natural flow and rhythm that were similar to central characteristics of human-like interactions in constrained situations. Breazeal (2003b) argued that the platform offered a high quality, i.e., compelling and engaging, interaction with humans,

which included doing the right thing at the right time and in the right manner. However, this was evaluated from the outside, i.e., as an observer it could be argued that the interactions were human-like within certain constraints, but the result does not indicate anything about whether or not Kismet intrinsically "experienced" the interaction.

User Experience and User Experience Design

User experience (UX) is a concept that recently has been widely spread within the fields of HCI, interaction design and related areas, and its importance for the successful development of interactive systems, products and services is highly stressed. Today's advanced technological development offers various kinds of mobile, ubiquitous and social technological products, and consequently the use of such devices have scattered into a variety of areas of human activity, and, thus, have become in several senses an integrated part of human daily life. Indeed, this movement has resulted in higher demands on and expectations of the quality of the technical products, which go beyond the more traditional aspects of utility, usability and acceptance that usually are addressed within HCI (Hartson & Pyla, 2012). Given the immaturity and the multifaceted nature of the UX concept, it is imprecise and therefore hard to define properly and clearly. Nevertheless, (Hartson & Pyla, 2012, p. 5) define it as "the totality of the effect or effects felt by a user as a result of interaction with, and the usage context of, a system, device, or product, including the influence of usability, usefulness, and emotional impact during interaction and savoring memory after interaction". In other words, UX can be considered as a consequence of the quality of the human-technology interaction, and the recognition of the importance of UX has resulted in an expansion and extension of the traditional usability aspects in HCI to the wider scope of UX, where the human users' feelings, motivations, and values are given additional, or even more focus.

Thus, UX includes a holistic perspective of how a human user feels about using a system, product or service in a particular usage context (Hartson & Pyla, 2012; Hassenzahl, 2013).

The concept of user experience embraces pragmatic as well as hedonic quality (Hassenzahl & Roto, 2007). Pragmatic quality is related to fulfilling the do-goals of the users, which means that the interactive system enable the users to reach the task-related goals in effective, efficient, and secure ways. In other words, pragmatic quality concerns the well-known HCI terms of the usability and usefulness of the product. Hedonic quality, on the other hand, concerns the be-goals of the users. Humans have different psychological and emotional needs, which should be addressed by the interactive system. The user can, for example, find the interactive system cool, awesome, beautiful, trustworthy, satisfying, or fun. The product can, for example, evoke feelings of autonomy, competence, and relatedness to others (Hartson & Pyla, 2012; Hassenzahl & Roto, 2007; Partala & Kallinen, 2012). The UX perspective includes not only functional aspects, but also experiential and emotional issues. It focuses on the positive; beyond the mere strive for absence of problems. Additionally, a main objective of the field should be to contribute to the quality of life of humans (Hassenzahl & Tractinsky, 2006).

Therefore, it is essential for robot developers to put serious efforts to attain social robots that the users experience as positive. As described by Hartson & Pyla (2012), the UX development process consists of four major interactive activities; these are analyze, design, implement, and evaluate. The purpose of the analyze phase is to understand the intended users' needs as well as the context of use. The design phase involves creation of the concept, the interaction behavior, and the "look and feel" of the product. In the implementation phase, the focus is on prototyping and thereby realizing different design alternatives. Verification and refinement of the interaction design is mainly conducted in the evaluation phase (Hartson &

Pyla, 2012). There is an increased interest within HRI in order to achieve a positive user experience when interacting with robots (e.g., Weiss, et al., 2011; Young et al., 2011). Consequently, a positive user experience is of importance for user acceptance of social robots (de Graaf & Allouch, 2013), underpinning the proliferation of social robots in society (Weiss et al., 2009).

CHALLENGES FOR SOCIALLY EMBODIED INTERACTION BETWEEN HUMANS AND SOCIALLY INTERACTIVE ROBOTS

In this section, the role and relevance of theoretical foundations of embodied cognition for human social interaction in the field of HRI is further elaborated, as well as the role that theories of embodied emotions can play in HRI, especially for the study and development of socially interactive robots. Our viewpoint is the role of emotions as closely connected to embodied cognition, grounded in agent-environment interactions, and the impact the quality of the interaction between humans and robots has on the user. Dautenhahn (2007b), for example, explicitly put forth that a primary goal of HRI research is to identify and characterize 'natural' ways for humans to interact and communicate with a robot. In our work, this gap is addressed by providing theoretical "bridge-building blocks" in order to reduce the lack of understanding of what such 'natural' means. However, we do not claim to fill the gap.

It should also be stressed that we are not the first to advocate an embodied cognition approach within the fields of HRI, HCI, and UX, since many other scholars before us have proposed this approach. To mention but a few, not addressed earlier in this chapter, both Dourish (2001) and Rogers (2012) have explicitly addressed the role and relevance of embodiment for providing additional ways of viewing the interaction with digital technology and theoretical perspectives on that interaction. Dourish (2001) put forward the concept of *embodied interaction* that focuses on the phenomenological aspects of interaction. Dourish was inspired by work from various sources, for example, by the philosopher Heidegger, and his writings of the phenomenological understanding of interacting with certain objects. He elaborated on and applied Heidegger's phenomenological ideas into the digital world, stressing that the importance of comprehension of embodied interaction in terms of direct engagements with the physical and social environment. In other words, the physical body of the user, is in a natural way, directly involved in the interaction with the technology, instead of indirect ways performed with the help of commands, symbols, and icons on a computer screen via input tools such as a keyboard or a computer mouse (although these activities also require some kind of embodied interaction). As Hartson and Pyla (2012) highlighted, embodied interaction means bringing interaction into the humans' real physical world to involve the human's own physical being in the world, moving the interaction off the screen and into the real world. To paraphrase Dourish (2001), "embodiment is not a property of systems, technologies, or artefacts; it is a property of interaction. The traditional approaches to cognition separated mind, body, and thought from action, but embodied interaction emphasizes their duality". It should be noted that although Dourish emphasized the importance of embodied interaction with technology, he did not address what kind of a body is required for cognition or explicitly addressed robot interaction. The strategic omission of the body is something that he admitted in Dourish (2013), since he rather wanted to focus more on situating embodied interaction in the lived world than discussing what kind of a body is required for embodied interaction.

"The embodied turn" has been a momentum in HCI, and is largely a result of the success with Dourish's book (Rogers, 2012). She argued that embodied theories allow for viewing interactions differently compared to more traditional psychological approaches to digital interaction, but it also offers some tentative risks. It can be hard to grasp the embodied approach and conceptualize a proper and accurate view of it. Subsequently, this can result in misinterpretations and design suggestions that are non- "embodied" so to speak. In other words, bridging theory and design solutions can be even harder regarding embodied cognition, than usual, since it is necessary to go beyond the conventional conceptual spheres. On the other hand, the embodied cognition perspective offers new ways of interacting with technology that we might not have imagined before. However, Rogers (2012), just as Dourish (2001), did not explicitly address interaction between humans and social robots.

After review of the embodied turn within HCI, we now return to social robots. In the following we discuss some identified challenges about socially embodied interaction between humans and socially interactive s robots, with a focus on 'natural' means by which a human can interact and communicate with a social robot.

Firstly, as might already been hinted above, the use of the concepts of embodiment, embodied cognition and embodied actions within HRI, is far for being clarified and used in similar ways as within the embodied cognitive science perspective. Sometimes embodied is used as a kind of buzzword, more or less, indicating that the robot has a physical instantiation, i.e., a physical form. However, from a cognitive science perspective, embodiment means much more than having a physical body that, roughly speaking, occupies some physical space. In a similar vein, when describing or noticing some kind of socially embodied action, e.g. gesturing, it is viewed as being "embodied". This idea might originate from the fact that there exists lot of research today that investigates and analyzes the role of gestures and other bodily actions in HRI. The question is - are all these previously conducted studies of gestures and other embodied actions the same as an embodied approach to socially interactive robots?

Our answer is that these approaches should not primarily and directly be interpreted as taking the embodied turn, although they at first glance seem to consider 'embodied actions'. This might seem as an odd stance, since one might ask: is there any other kind of embodied action? This objection is verified, since obviously, all our movements of the body are in a fact embodied. That is, it would be impossible to perform a pointing gesture in real life without a physical realization. The crucial point here is that there are different theoretical ways of interpreting and providing meaning to a particular embodied action. A lot of research has been conducted on so called "body language", but this does not imply, however, that it has embodied cognitive science as their theoretical foundation. From an embodied cognitive science perspective, an embodied action is not considered to be a manifestation of an internal cognitive process (as in mainstream cognitive science) but rather as an element of cognitive activity (see the Background section). Thus, from an embodied perspective, an embodied action is a form of cognition, and not an expression or output of internal cognitive processes (for more details, see Lindblom, forthcoming). Thus, studies that analyze and investigate gestures and other embodied actions within socially interactive robots are not by default taking the embodied turn, since they can rely on other theoretical foundations.

Secondly, this leads us into the next challenge, i.e., what kind of a body is required for socially (embodied) cognition. Ziemke (2003), for example, argued that many discussions concerning embodiment in general within AI (i.e., *robot cognition-centred HRI*) do not stress what kind of a body is required for cognition. As a consequence, the question of whether a socially interactive robot can be considered embodied and could have the same sort of cognition as a human being remains open. In order to discuss embodiment within AI, Ziemke (2003) identified and contrasted six different notions of embodiment found in the literature, but as he explained, they should not be

viewed as distinct positions, but rather an attempt to group related ideas together. The notions are as follows, addressing whether or not (social) robots are *embodied* to various degrees (for more details see Lindblom, to appear; Ziemke, 2003). In this chapter, the latter two notions are in focus.

- **Structural Coupling:** Between agent and environment.
- **Historical Embodiment:** As the result of a history of structural coupling.
- **Physical Embodiment:** As physical instantiation of a body.
- **'Organismoid' Embodiment:** I.e. organism-like bodily form, such as humanoid robots.
- **Organismic Embodiment:** Of autopoietic, living systems.
- **Social Embodiment:** The role of the body in social interaction.

The notion *organismic embodiment* includes only *living bodies*, and is inspired by biological explanation of cognition. Ziemke explained that this form of embodiment, broadly speaking, claims that cognition in fact is what living systems do in interaction with the environment. Consequently, knowledge is the result of an ongoing interpretation that emerges from our biologically embodied structures of understanding, by living in and experiencing a social and cultural environment. Hence, these actions make it possible for us to "make sense" of our being in our world. The 'mind' functions as an autonomous system and there is a mutual relation between the mind and the world, through *structural coupling*. It is through structural coupling that a complex system enacts a world that is brought forth through a history of structural couplings (enactivism). However, this structural coupling should not be viewed as similar to the input/output mapping in the computer metaphor for mind. In that model, meaning is created from the outside by the designer, while in an enactive ("biologically living") system, meaning is the result of the active organization and history of the system itself. As Ziemke (2003) explained, with current technology, organismic embodiment is limited to natural systems. However, this notion of embodiment does not address the uniqueness of human embodied cognition, since all living systems according to this notion are actually embodied. However, it is possible to distinguish between different kinds and levels of structural couplings. Thus, social phenomena and communication are the result of this spontaneous organization of so-called third-order couplings, and they generate a certain kind of internal phenomenology. Finally, the notion of *social embodiment* is addressed, and exemplified with Barsalou's et al. (2003) notion of social embodiment (see the Background section). However, Ziemke pointed out that their notion of social embodiment addresses the role of embodiment in social interactions rather than discussing *what* sort of body is required for social embodiment. This means, the *what* question needs to be addressed in future research concerning embodiment and social interaction within HRI and cognitive science. We argue, however, that the question is ill-posed, given that it implicitly suggests the body alone is the key that provides the answer.

Thirdly, the *I* in HRI has gained additional attention, which is further elaborated in the following section, regarding how the embodied *interaction* is accomplished between the human and the socially interactive robot. The common, and still used, metaphor of social interaction is dominated by traditional information-processing models of human communication, and most classical studies of interaction focused rather on the content in the interaction, i.e., information, than on its execution (Fogel, 1993). This view of social interaction and communication is usually labeled the *information transmission metaphor* (ITM), which views interaction as a *sequential* process in which agents interact through emitting and sending information to each other via different channels. Therefore, the ITM uses entities such

as *signal* and *response, sending* and *receiving,* as well as *encoding* and *decoding.* This view of interaction and communication has its origin in the work on the transmission of electronic signals by Shannon and Weaver in the 1940s. When Shannon described his method of converting sounds and images into binary strings as *encoding* the *information* in the sent *message* this metaphor was soon imported into the field of human interaction, since it fitted as 'hand in glove' with the computer metaphor of mind (see Lindblom, forthcoming, for more details). Nevertheless, the ITM has been criticized for several reasons, and given the findings within and the nature of socially embodied human interaction addressed in the Background section, the ITM is not a plausible metaphor for human embodied social interaction. ITM fails to reveal the full story of social interaction, since its basic assumption, i.e., that the signals which contain information flow back and forth between sender and receiver actually *oversimplifies* and *misrepresents* what actually happens in social interaction and communication. It has been argued that ITM falls short in explaining how *interaction* works, and its main problem is not its discrete and bi-directional structure of sending and receiving signals, or even encoding and decoding. Instead, the central failure is its assumptions that meaning is transmitted in signals. Therefore, Fogel, (1993, p. 76) stated that

...information is created in the interface between perception and action. It is not just that I can perform an action to achieve a purpose that is meaningful, but it is what I discover about how I perform the action: what my arms and legs can do, my cardiovascular tolerance, my trust in my ears, and eyes to assist me. It is that last point, the salience of the body... is missing in many theories of meaning.

Therefore, the alternative explanations of interaction and communication that address social interaction from an embodied perspective are more reasonable, since the traditional ITM of communication can be viewed as a disembodied sender-receiver explanation of pre-given information, missing contextual and bodily aspects. Current socially interactive robots, and also other types of robots, cannot be considered as being *organismic embodied* in Ziemke's terms, which result in some confusion of how to consider the *I* in HRI. On the one hand, socially interactive robots lack a "biological" body, and cannot be considered to be embodied in the "full" sense. Although some attempts have been made to implement basic behavioral capacities, e.g., joint attention, that could bootstrap social interaction in robots, the robots lack intrinsic meaning, and it is only in the eye of the human observer that the robot seems to "socially interact" naturally, and, thus, the ITM holds for socially interactive robots. On the other hand, prior studies on mirror neurons revealed that they only become activated by real biological actions and movements, and not when a robot arm performed the same "action", that can be interpreted as a strong sense of the alternative view of interaction proposed by Fogel. However, recent studies have displayed some human mirror neuron system responses to robotic actions (Gazzola, et al., 2007) as well as EEG evidence of human mirror neuron activity of robotic actions (Oberman et al., 2007). Thus, this implies that it is still an open issue how to consider the *I* in HRI.

Fourthly, the intertwined relation between embodiment and emotions, i.e., embodying emotion, has not received enough attention in HRI in general, since there still is a gap between the cognitive content of emotions and the bodily manifestation of emotion. Norman's (2004) book *Emotional design* can be considered as classical in HCI, in which he seriously introduced the emotional stance within interaction design, from both the users as well the designers perspectives. His major achievement was to bring emotions back into consideration in the field. Although he emphasized the importance of the feelings of designers' when working

as well as how consumers become emotionally involved in their products; he separated emotion from embodied cognition, distinguishing between three different levels of *information processing* in attitudes, i.e., visceral, behavioral, and reflective processes in the human brain that correspond to different types of emotional design. Even though Norman discussed robots, he did not elaborate on their social and emotional interactive abilities. In a similar vein, different theories of emotions as well as the role of embodiment for social interaction were addressed in Breazeal (2003b), but the relationship between embodiment and emotions was overlooked. This is quite surprising given the fact that the methodology used in the Cog project (Brooks et al., 1998) in general, in which the Kismet platform was included, was based on four central aspects of human intelligence: development, social interaction, physical interaction (embodiment and physical coupling) and integration (see Lindblom & Ziemke, 2003 for a review of the role of social situatedness in the Cog project). Moreover, Breazeal (2003b) referred to Damasio (1995) without drawing attention to Damasio's claim regarding the interrelatedness of embodiment for emotion and cognition.

Fifthly, a prominent advantage put forth by proponents of socially interactive robots from a *human-centred view*, is the idea that they should provide more 'natural' ways of interacting with technology thorough e.g., facial expressions, gaze following, and gestures. As Thrun (2004) pointed out, personal service robots which are supposed to assist and entertain people in domestic settings or in recreational activities have the highest expected growth rate, and examples of such robots range from robotic vacuum cleaners and toys to robotic assistants for elderly or disabled people. Thus, these robots are supposed to carry out social and intellectual tasks. It has been noted, however, that many of these robotic systems have to interact with users who have not been trained to operate them. Therefore, as Thrun (2004) emphasized, it is crucial to find effective means of interaction in this new area of robotics, and ideally, personal service robots are supposed to behave in a humanlike way, offering and creating 'easy' and 'natural' interaction with the users. The physical realization of more humanlike social robots (humanoids and androids) offers a unique user interface; humans may be differently appealed by them compared to mechanical-looking robots. Central to the usability of these social robots is effective social interactions with humans. This interaction includes a wide range of social features such as expressing and perceiving emotions, communicating verbally and non-verbally, displaying personality, recognizing interaction partners and learning socially (Fong et al., 2003). Today, many of the outwardly visible and recognizable patterns of joint attention are mimicked and displayed in some social robots. Generally, similarities in bodily shape, appearance as well as expressive and emotional "faces", are considered to offer a number of advantages for human social interaction. For that reason, the user's acceptance of social robots is supposed to be easier accomplished. Moreover, a humanlike morphology is well-suited to function in human environments, and, thus, it can be more enjoyable and rewarding to interact with these robots. In addition, effective social human-robot interaction could heighten subjective feelings about the quality of the interaction, and, hence, increase the positive user experience. Given that humans are 'ultra' social creatures, and consequently experts in social interaction, the necessity for costly training programs for using interactive systems can decrease. However, it should be noted that our everyday life consists of a highly complex web of tasks and social skills. To assist humans as 'truly' humanlike partners, social robots have to 'understand' our intentions. This in turn requires that they are able to interpret our intentions by recognizing bodily movements and emotional facial expressions. Moreover, Norman (2011) pointed out some apprehensions to so-called "natural user interfaces" (NUI), i.e., interacting with technology through gestures and other "natural" means. Nor-

man (2011) argued that gestures are not 'intuitive' in themselves since their displays are not innate and have to be shaped through social interactions, and there are also cultural differences in gesturing. Accordingly, a possible approach would be to engage social robots in various processes of social learning, such as imitation and co-operative learning, and to teach the robot in the same way as when instructing another peer or a child. Hence, there seems to be a need for a kind of 'enculturation' process similar to the epigenesis of human children (e.g., Fogel, 1993; Lindblom, forthcoming). However, it may be difficult to achieve the human kind of social learning in social robots, because their quest suffers from the same shortcomings discussed above for lacking "organismic" social embodiment, that is, the lack of 'intrinsic' intentionality. Although social robots appear to express emotions and perform basic joint attention behaviors, they do not experience these abilities themselves. The experience lies in the eyes of the beholder, namely the human user. This means, what 'looks' like as an intentional understanding to an observer has no correspondence in the robotic system itself; it is just the human observer who interprets the behavior as 'intelligent' and 'meaningful.' This implies that social robots do not interact socially through their living bodies in the sense that humans do, but rather through their perceived bodily appearance. Their sociality is in the eye of the beholder. What consequences will that 'intrinsic' lack have for emotional and social human-robot interaction? It should be easier for us to interpret the performance of the social robot than for a social robot to interpret ours since it would have difficulties to "interpret" our intentions. Also, a very human-like appearance may offer a too promising impression of the social robot's communicative abilities, which may be disappointing to the user, i.e., resulting in a negative user experience.

Sixthly, it should also be noted that there are some tentative challenges in combining different research areas and fields such as in the case within the interdisciplinary field of HRI. There is a risk of misinterpretations of underlying philosophical, methodological and theoretical foundations of other fields that may not be explicitly articulated, since it is considered as common knowledge within a certain community. This might result in incorrect assumptions, misconceptions of obtained results and misleading conclusions. Another tentative risk lies in significantly different definitions and meanings of the same terms in different areas. As previously elaborated, the use of the concept of "embodiment" is an example of where such a risk clearly exists. Similarly, other concepts related to socially interactive robots run the risk of having significantly different meanings. Researchers addressing HRI from a *robot cognition-centred* perspective (e.g., Breazeal, 2003a, 2003b; Fong et al., 2003) tend to interpret concepts, e.g., *social intelligence, action-recognition,* and *social relationships* in relatively wide sense, whereas, e.g., psychologists, neuroscientists and philosophers has much more restrictive usage and application of these "mental and/or social" concepts. They would probably not easily come to the conclusion that a certain social robot, for instance, is able to "perceive social signs". Nevertheless, we argue that if one weighs the pros and cons of combining different research fields, as currently is done within HRI, the advantages are greater than the disadvantages.

FUTURE RESEARCH OPPORTUNITIES

HRI is growing and emerging, but still a young research field, and we are anxious to see what the future holds. As discussed and elaborated in detail in the previous section, there are several challenges for socially embodied interaction between humans and socially interactive robots. However, if we weigh the pros and cons of socially interactive robots from an user-centred perspective, we believe that regardless of whether social robots

will be truly socially intelligent in the 'organismic" embodiment sense or not, this type of social robots will allow human users to better situate themselves socially in the world of technical devices. In the followings, we outline some possible future research opportunities in HRI.

On the one hand, we agree on the previously suggested interdisciplinary and methodological approach to HRI (cf. Dautenhahn, 2007a, 2007b), but we want to draw attention to additional research areas previously not addressed in depth from an embodied perspective. Ethology has been addressed earlier, but mostly primatology. Instead, we suggest that human-dog interaction can be explored as an additional research approach. We claim that although great apes are our closest relatives from an evolutionary perspective, primates are not as situated in our daily life as dogs are. Research findings on dogs indicate that they have developed advanced social emotional skills that sometimes outperform our closest relatives (cf. Hare & Tomasello, 2005).

Moreover, given the focus on embodying emotions in this chapter for socially interactive robots, we suggest that knowledge and skills from professional actors and dancers also could offer valuable insights to the socially interactive robot field. Actors can be considered as experts in displaying emotions, and dancers perhaps even more, since they are constrained to communicate their emotions from their bodily actions only, given that they do not use verbal utterance. By complementing the existing knowledge of how to interact socially via embodied actions, complementary and perhaps even new interaction paradigms or frameworks can emerge of how to facilitate the interaction between humans and social robots. This can, in the long run, positively influence the user experience.

Moreover, an integration of the different conceptual spaces of HRI (Dautenhahn, 2007a) with the iterative development process of user experience design (UXD), is a viable research opportunity. It is necessary for robot developers to intentionally design for and evaluate the actual UX in order to make sure that positive feelings arise in the users. The importance of research concerning establishment of user experience-affecting elements and user experience evaluation should not be underestimated in HRI. We interpret the turn to UX in HCI as a great acknowledgment of the role of embodying emotions in interacting with technology in general, and socially interactive robots in particular.

On the other hand, socially interactive robots are, to various degrees, already situated in human life, and the increasing interest in these robots and the rapid technological development indicate that the social robots have found their place in human (social) life. This affords great opportunities to learn more about our own "being-in-the-world". As with good usability, it is transparent when functioning properly. Although there is a large body of knowledge of human social interaction, there is much more to explore and learn. We envision that studies of interactions between humans and socially interactive robots can result in additional fundamental scientific insights of the nature of (human) embodied cognition. In addition, much more research is required regarding how socially interactive robots may influence us as human users, our environment, the (supposed) added value of socially interactive technology to human life, our way of thinking and being, and even fundamentally addressing what it is like to being human.

CONCLUSION

The purpose of this chapter is to contribute to the field of HRI by addressing in further detail the role and relevance of embodied cognition for human social interaction, and consequently what role embodied emotions can play in HRI, especially for socially interactive robots. Taken together, the proposed view is to consider the role of emotions as closely connected to embodied cognition,

grounded in agent-environment interactions, and accordingly what impact the interaction quality has on the user experience of socially interactive robots. HRI involves many challenges, and we have outlined some of these, as well as provided some future research opportunities. Interestingly, there are parallel trends developed in cognitive science and HCI in general, since both are taking the turn to the subjective lived experience and acknowledging the role of emotions and feelings. Research on (embodied) socially interactive robots ties all these issues together. The human dimension meets the robot dimension in HRI, tackling the ways human emotion and cognition is embodied. This is a fact that should not be neglected or trivialized given that it cannot be turned off; it has fundamental impact on the user experience of socially interactive robots. We hope that HRI will continue to develop and grow, building additional knowledge of socially embodied cognition from both human-centred as well as robot-centred views.

ACKNOWLEDGMENT

We want to thank our colleagues PhD Henrik Svensson and PhD Erik Billing for their valuable comments on the topics addressed in this chapter.

REFERENCES

Breazeal, C. (2003a). Toward sociable robots. *Robotics and Autonomous Systems, 42*(3-4), 167–175. doi:10.1016/S0921-8890(02)00373-1

Breazeal, C. (2003b). Emotion and sociable humanoid robots. *International Journal of Human-Computer Studies, 59*(1-2), 119–155. doi:10.1016/S1071-5819(03)00018-1

Breazeal, C., & Scassellati, B. (2000). Infant-like social interactions between a robot and a human caretaker. *Adaptive Behavior, 8*(1), 49–73. doi:10.1177/105971230000800104

Brooks, R., Breazeal, C., Marjanović, M., Scassellati, B., & Williamson, M. (1998). The Cog project: Building a humanoid robot. In C. Nehaniv (Ed.), *Computation for metaphors, analogy, and agents* (pp. 52–87). New York: Springer.

Clark, A. (1997). *Being there – putting brain, body and world together again*. Cambridge, MA: MIT Press.

Clark, A. (1999). An embodied cognitive science? *Trends in Cognitive Sciences, 3*(9), 345–351. doi:10.1016/S1364-6613(99)01361-3 PMID:10461197

Dreyfus, H. L. (1992). *What computers still can't do – a critique of artificial reason*. Cambridge, MA: MIT Press.

Damasio, A. (1995). *Descartes' error: emotion, reason, and the human brain*. New York: Avon Books.

Damasio, A. (1999). *The feeling of what happens: body and emotion in the making of consciousness*. New York: Harcourt Brace.

Dautenhahn, K. (2007a). Socially intelligent robots: Dimensions of human-robot interaction. *Philosophical Transactions of the Royal Society of London. Series B, Biological Sciences, 362*(1480), 679–704. doi:10.1098/rstb.2006.2004 PMID:17301026

Dautenhahn, K. (2007b). Methodology & themes of human-robot interaction: A growing research field. *International Journal of Advanced Robotic Systems, 4*(1), 103–108.

Dautenhahn, K. (2013). Human-Robot Interaction. In M. Soegaard & R. F. Dam (Eds.), *The Encyclopedia of Human-Computer Interaction* (2nd ed.). Aarhus, Denmark: The Interaction Design Foundation.

Dautenhahn, K., & Sanders, J. (Eds.). (2011). Introduction. In K. Dautenhahn & J. Sanders (Eds.). New frontiers in human-robot interaction (pp. 1-5). Amsterdam, The Netherlands: John Benjamins.

Dourish, P. (2001). *Where the action is: the foundations for embodied interaction*. Cambridge, MA: MIT Press.

Dourish, P. (2013). Epilogue: Where the action was, wasn't, should have been, and might yet be. *ACM Transactions of Computer-Human Interaction, 20*(1). doi: 10.1145/2442106.2442108

Fogel, A. (1993). *Developing through relationships*. New York: Harvester Wheatsheaf.

Fong, T., Nourbakhsh, I., & Dautenhahn, K. (2003). A survey of socially interactive robots. *Robotics and Autonomous Systems, 42*(3-4), 143–166.

Gallese, V., Keysers, C., & Rizzolatti, G. (2004). A unifying view of the basis of social cognition. *Trends in Cognitive Sciences, 8*(9), 398–403.

Gallese, V., & Goldman, A. (1998). Mirror neurons and the simulation theory of mind-reading. *Trends in Cognitive Sciences, 2*(12), 493–501. doi:10.1016/S1364-6613(98)01262-5 PMID:21227300

Gallese, V., Keysers, C., & Rizzolatti, G. (2004). A unifying view of the basis of social cognition. *Trends in Cognitive Sciences, 8*(9), 398–403. doi:10.1016/j.tics.2004.07.002 PMID:15350240

Gazzola, V., Rizzolatti, G., Wicker, B., & Keysers, C. (2007). The anthropomorphic brain: The mirror neuron system responds to human and robotic actions. *NeuroImage, 35*(4), 1674–1684. doi:10.1016/j.neuroimage.2007.02.003 PMID:17395490

Gibbs, R. W. Jr. (2006). *Embodiment and cognitive science*. Cambridge: Cambridge University Press.

Goodrich, M. A., & Schultz, A. C. (2007). Human-robot interaction: A survey. *Foundations and Trends in Human–Computer Interaction*, *1*(3), 203–275. doi:10.1561/1100000005

de Graaf, M. M. A., & Allouch, S. B. (2013). Exploring influencing variables for the acceptance of social robots. *Robotics and Autonomous Systems*, *61*(12), 1476–1486. doi:10.1016/j.robot.2013.07.007

Harper, R., Rodden, T., Rogers, Y., & Sellen, A. (2008). *Being human: Human-computer interaction in the year 2020*. Cambridge, UK: Microsoft Research Ltd.

Hare, B., & Tomassello, M. (2005). Human-like social skills in dogs? *Trends in Cognitive Sciences*, *9*(9), 439–444. doi:10.1016/j.tics.2005.07.003 PMID:16061417

Hartson, R., & Pyla, P. S. (2012). *The UX Book: Process and guidelines for ensuring a quality user experience*. Amsterdam, The Netherlands: Morgan Kaufmann.

Hassenzahl, M. (2013). User experience and experience design. In M. Soegaard & R. F. Dam (Eds.), *The encyclopedia of human-computer interaction* (2nd ed.). Aarhus, Denmark: The Interaction Design Foundation. Retrieved March 02, 2014, from http://www.interaction-design.org/encyclopedia/user_experience_and_experience_design.html

Hassenzahl, M., & Roto, V. (2007). Being and doing: A perspective on user experience and its measurement. *Interfaces*, *72*, 10–12.

Hassenzahl, M., & Tractinsky, N. (2006). User experience – a research agenda. *Behaviour & Information Technology*, *25*(2), 91–97. doi:10.1080/01449290500330331

Johnson, M. (2007). *The meaning of the body: Aesthetics of human understanding*. Chicago, IL: Chicago University Press. doi:10.7208/chicago/9780226026992.001.0001

Kohler, E., Keysers, C., Umilta, M. A., Fogassi, V., & Rizzolatti, G. (2002). Hearing sounds, understanding actions: Action representation in mirror neurons. *Science*, *287*(5582), 846–848. doi:10.1126/science.1070311 PMID:12161656

Lakoff, G., & Johnson, M. (1999). *Philosophy in the flesh: The embodied mind and its challenges to Western thought*. New York: Basic Books.

Lindblom, J. (forthcoming). *Embodied social cognition*. Berlin: Springer Verlag.

Lindblom, J., & Ziemke, T. (2003). Social situatedness of natural and artificial intelligence: Vygotsky and beyond. *Adaptive Behavior*, *11*(2), 79–96. doi:10.1177/10597123030112002

Lindblom, J., & Ziemke, T. (2007). Embodiment and social interaction: implications for cognitive science. In T. Ziemke, J. Zlatev, & R. Frank (Eds.), *Body, language, and mind: Embodiment* (Vol. 1, pp. 129–162). Berlin: Mounton de Gruyter.

Niedenthal, P. M. (2007). Embodying emotion. *Science*, *316*(5827), 1002–1005. doi:10.1126/science.1136930 PMID:17510358

Niedenthal, P. M., Barsalou, L. M., Winkielman, P., Krath-Gruber, S., & Ric, F. (2005). Embodiment in attitudes, social perception, and emotion. *Personality and Social Psychology Review*, *9*(3), 184–211. doi:10.1207/s15327957pspr0903_1 PMID:16083360

Norman, D. A. (2004). *Emotional design- why we love (or hate) everyday things*. New York: Basic Books.

Norman, D. A. (2010). Natural interfaces are not natural. *Interaction, 17*(3), 3, 6–10. doi:10.1145/1744161.1744163

Oberman, L. M., McCleery, J. P., Ramachandran, V. S., & Pineda, J. A. (2007). EEG evidence for mirror neuron activity during the observation of human robot action: Toward an analysis of the human qualities of interactive robots. *Neurocomputing, 70*(13-15), 2194–2203. doi:10.1016/j.neucom.2006.02.024

Partala, T., & Kallinen, A. (2012). Understanding the most satisfying and unsatisfying user experiences: Emotions, psychological needs, and context. *Interacting with Computers, 24*(1), 25–34. doi:10.1016/j.intcom.2011.10.001

Pessoa, L. (2008). On the relationship between emotion and cognition. *Nature Reviews. Neuroscience, 9*(2), 148–158. doi:10.1038/nrn2317 PMID:18209732

Pfeifer, R., & Scheier, C. (1999). *Understanding intelligence*. Cambridge, MA: MIT Press.

Reeves, B., & Nass, C. (1996). *The media equation: how people treat computers, television, and new media like real people and places*. Cambridge: Center for the Study of Language and Information Publication.

Rizzolatti, G., Fadiga, L., Fogassi, L., & Gallese, V. (2002). From mirror neurons to imitation: facts and speculations. In A. N. Meltzoff & W. Prinz (Eds.), (pp. 247–266). Cambridge: Cambridge University Press. doi:10.1017/CBO9780511489969.015

Silke, A., Heinzle, J., Weiskopf, N., Ethofer, T., & Haynes, J.-D. (2011). Flow of affective information in communicating brains. *NeuroImage, 54*(1), 439–446. doi:10.1016/j.neuroimage.2010.07.004 PMID:20624471

Svensson, H., Lindblom, J., & Ziemke, T. (2007). Making sense of embodied cognition: simulation theories of shared neural mechanisms for sensorimotor and cognitive processes. In T. Ziemke, J. Zlatev, & R. Frank R. (Eds.), Body, language, and mind: Embodiment (vol. 1, pp. 241-270). Berlin: Mouton de Gruyter.

Thrun, S. (2004). Toward a framework for human-robot interaction. *Human-Computer Interaction, 19*(1), 9–24. doi:10.1207/s15327051hci1901&2_2

User Experience. UX Design. (2010). UX Design Defined. *User Experience. UX Design*. Retrieved February 26, 2014, from http://uxdesign.com/ux-defined

Varela, F. J., Thompson, E., & Rosch, E. (1991). *The embodied mind: Cognitive science and human experience*. Cambridge, MA: MIT Press.

Weiss, A., Bernhaupt, R., & Yoshida, E. (2009). Addressing user experience and societal impact in a user study with a humanoid robot. In *Proceedings of the Symposium on New Frontiers in Human-Robot Interaction, AISB2009* (pp. 150-157).

Weiss, X., Bernhaupt, X., & Tscheligi, C. (2011). The USUS framework. In K. Dautenhahn & J. Saunders (Eds.), *New frontiers in human-robot interaction* (pp. 89–110). Amsterdam, The Netherlands: John Benjamins.

Wicker, B., Keysers, C., Plailly, J., Royet, J. P., Gallese, V., & Rizzolatti, G. (2003). Both of us disgusted in my insula: The common neural basis of seeing and feeling disgust. *Neuron, 40*, 655–664.

Wilson, A. D., & Golonka, S. (2013). Embodied cognition is not what you think it is. [PubMed]. *Frontiers in Psychology, 4*(58), 1–13.

Young, J. E., Sung, J. Y., Voida, A., Sharlin, E., Igarashi, T., Cristensen, H. I., & Grinter, R. E. (2011). Evaluating human-robot interaction: Focusing on the holistic interaction experience. *International Journal of Social Robotics, 3*(1), 53–67. doi:10.1007/s12369-010-0081-8

Ziemke, T. (2003). What's that thing called embodiment? In AltermanR.KirschD. (Eds.), *Proceedings of the 25th Annual Meeting of the Cognitive Science Society* (pp. 1305-1310). Mahwah, NJ: Lawrence Erlbaum.

Ziemke, T., & Lowe, R. (2009). On the role of emotions in embodied cognitive architectures: From organisms to robots. *Cognitive Computation, 1*(1), 104–117. doi:10.1007/s12559-009-9012-0

KEY TERMS AND DEFINITIONS

Embodied Cognition: By using the term embodied we mean to highlight two points: first, that cognition depends upon the kinds of experiences that come from having a body with various sensorimotor capacities, and second, that these individual sensorimotor capacities themselves are embedded in a more surrounding biological, psychological and cultural context (Varela, Thompson & Rosch, 1991).

Embodiment: Embodiment refers to the experiences that arise from the living body in its interactions with a material/physical as well as a social and cultural world. It also refers to how an autonomous agent acts upon these experiences via different means of dynamical action-perception loops that subsequently emerge into different kinds of embodied action patterns which create and maintain the embodied agent's own understanding and meaningfulness (Lindblom, forthcoming).

Embodied Interaction: The concept embodied interaction is concerned with the phenomenological aspects of interaction (Hartson & Pyla, 2012).

Human-Computer Interaction (HCI): Human-computer interaction is a discipline concerned with the design, evaluation and implementation of interactive computing systems for human use and with the study of major phenomena surrounding them (Hewett et al., 1996).

Human-Robot Interaction (HRI): HRI is the science of studying people's behavior and attitudes towards robots in relationship to the physical, technological and interactive features of the robots, with the goal to develop robots that facilitate the emergence of human-robot *interactions* that are at the same time efficient (according to original requirements of their envisaged area of use), but are also acceptable to people, and meet the social and emotional needs of their individual users as well as respecting human values (Dautenhahn, 2013).

Socially Interactive Robots: Socially interactive robots are robots for which social interaction plays a key role (Fong et al., 2003, p. 145).

User Experience (UX): The totality of the effect or effects felt by a user as a result of interaction with, and the usage context of, a system, device, or product, including the influence of usability, usefulness, and emotional impact during interaction and savoring memory after interaction (Hartson & Pyla, 2012, p. 5).

User Experience Design (UXD): UXD refers to the judicious application of certain user-centered design practices, a highly contextual design mentality, and use of certain methods and techniques that are applied through process management to produce cohesive, predictable, and desirable effects in a specific person, or persona (archetype comprised of target audience habits and characteristics). All so that the affects produced meet the user's own goals and measures of success and enjoyment, as well as the objectives of the providing organization (User Experience.UX Design, 2010).

ENDNOTES

[1] It should be pointed out what characterizes embodied cognition is far from being well-defined. There exist different notions, levels and degrees of embodiment (see Lindblom, forthcoming, for an overview).

Chapter 8
Qualia Learning?
Innerbodiment Construction and Machine Self-Learning by (Emotional) Imitation

J. Vallverdú
Universitat Autònoma de Barcelona, Spain

ABSTRACT

Humans perform acts and imitate other humans' actions by innate mechanisms that imply the unconscious notion of innerbodiment. In this chapter, the author suggests a mechanistic method to capture, discretize and understand human actions, following a semi-supervised WOZ system that could allow robotic learning by imitation or even self-learning. A syntax and semantics basic model of human actions guide is provided as well as a philosophical analysis of the notion of action.

1. PROGRAMMING QUALIA?

1.1. Defining Qualia

One of the most elusive and complex concepts in cognitive sciences is that of 'qualia'´. The MITECS define them as:

The terms quale and qualia (pl.) are most commonly used to characterize the qualitative, experiential, or felt properties of mental states. Some philosophers take qualia to be essential features of all conscious mental states; others only of SENSATIONS and perceptions. In either case, qualia provide a particularly vexing example of the MIND-BODY PROBLEM, because it has been
argued that their existence is incompatible with a physicalistic theory of the mind[1].

By 'qualia' we mean those qualities that are accessible to you introspectively and that together make up the phenomenal character of the experience[2]. In a simple way to explain it: our feelings about things. As you can see, the *qualia* has to do with internal and non-verifiable state and for these reasons you could conclude that there is nothing to be understood, nor useful. But there is one case, propioception, in which qualia shows us a way to understand brain subsumption architectures in order to improve to our HRI models. Other qualia experiences, like empathy have shown to have a neural correlate and can be located into human

DOI: 10.4018/978-1-4666-7278-9.ch008

brains (Keysers and Gazzola, 2010). Therefore, perhaps there is a realm of dark and occult intern experiences but at the same time *qualia* must be neural processes and consequently, we should be able at least to figure out their functional and evolutionary meaning. It has also been said that propioception is the sixth sense: taste, smell, touch, sound, hearing, sight…and *propioception* (Abbott, 2006; Smetacek and Mechsner, 2004).

After this brief introduction to the nature of *qualia*, we could ask ourselves if do exist different kinds of them, something that becomes *a priori* a nonsensical debate. The reasons are easy to understand: if *qualia* are internal and private states, then their classification cannot be objective (except in the case of latest fMRI studies on objective pain measurement, a truly debatable topic; see Brown *et al* 2011)[3]. Perhaps we could talk about internal or external inducers of the emergence of *qualia*, as our own thoughts or other people interaction, just as an example of internal and external inputs. They could also be naively classified by the source of the information (sound, touch,….) but we must to remember that the cognitive processes are multidimensional, and that they are the result of an evaluation processing. After all these explanations, we conclude that *qualia* exist, but that we cannot map them clearly. Four practical purposes, we'll talk only about the feeling of having a body that obeys us. A limit example, the dicephalus twins (as a specific type of conjoined or Siamese twins): Abigail and Brittany Hensel, now 21, have two spines, which join at the pelvis, two hearts and stomachs, three kidneys, two gall bladders and four lungs. Below the waist all organs including intestines, bladder and reproductive organs are shared. Each twin controls her half of their body, operating one of the arms and one of the legs. This means that as infants, the initial learning of physical processes that required bodily coordination, such as clapping, crawling, and walking required the cooperation of both children. While each is able to eat and write separately and simultaneously, activities such as

running and swimming must be coordinated and alternate symmetrically. Other activities as diverse as brushing hair and driving a car require that each twin perform a sequence of quite separate actions that coordinate with the other. As a curiosity: Hensel twins both successfully passed their drivers license exams, both the written and driving tests. They had to take the tests twice, once for each twin. Abby controls the pedals, radio, heat, defogger, and other devices located to the right of the driver's seat, while Brittany controls the turn signal and lights; together, they control the steering wheel[4]. This example shows us several things about mind, body and propioception, basically the intertwined nature of:

1. Body coordination.
2. **Plasticity:** Human mind is open to embrace more parts or to share actions.
3. **Propioceptive Skills Enables Shared Tasks (Very Useful for Human-Robot Interaction):** Allows the creation of a common working map to be solved with several bodies or parts of the body working together.

1.2. Inside Qualia: Propioception

So, we must go back to propioception, the true cause of our main interest about *qualia*. It belongs to human somatosensitive skills (touch, kinesthesis) and "is the sense of the relative position of neighbouring parts of the body and strength of effort being employed in movement"[5]. It is the sense of position and posture, movement and velocity of the body and body parts. This involves the location of our body or body parts in space, the relation of our body parts to one another, and the extent to, and pace at, which they change their position. In a nutshell: the (un)conscious feeling of being. Let me explain with a simple example: quoted from the neuroscientist Oliver Sacks (1985), "The Disembodied Lady": this woman, after a viral infection of her spinal cord, lost her connexion with the body. She defined herself as "disembodied" or "deprived" and was unable to hold her body erect or to perform any muscular action. After a hard concentration work on each part of her body and a long training, she was able to make body movement, but always depending on her visual coordination.

According to these neuroscientific evidences, human mind works at several layers of consciousness, and the control of the basic motor activities belong to an inner sense, propioception, something that could be qualified as a *qualia experience*. At a certain level, this approach of distributed tasks was early integrated by bottom up approaches in robotics, like the idea of subsumption architecture of Rodney Brooks (Brooks, 1986a,b,c). What is crucial for our interests is to consider the interrelationship among propioception, unconscious movement and imitation. This will constitute the basis of our HRI framework.

1.3. A Taxonomy of Robots

Well, all these ideas about qualia are really interesting, but… why should we be interested on them? The answer is easy: when we try to create smarter robots, robots with self-learning skills or emotional robots we are faced to the qualia problem. Although this idea of the taxonomy of physical robots (excluding virtual or disembodied ones)[6] is conflictive, we need to show the necessity of propioceptive robots for the benefits of HRI. We'll define 3 basic cataloguing, and somehow related, categories to classify robots[7]:

1. **Intelligence:** Smart, dumb, and all the in-between steps or the progression.
2. **Task:** Specialized work (services, military, industrial, science),
   a. Entertainment (/toys), human care.
3. **Morphology:** Biologically inspired (humanoid or not), functional. On the
   a. Morphology are included aspects of mobility.

There are no clear, but blurred boundaries among all these categories and subsections. Perhaps the most meaningful for our interests is that one of the intelligence associated to the robots. Describe intelligence is very much difficult in order to describe humans beings, a controversial debate, and consequently can be easily admitted that the description of a robot as intelligent or not is deeply conflictive. We propose the existence of several basic traits in order to consider a robot as intelligent: adaptable, with learning skills, own personality, emotions recognition able, human interaction ability, social and autonomous activity. The aspects of morphology and tasks, although not minor, are not so important for our basic conceptual approach (excluding, obviously, the empathetic morphological aspects of HRI).

One important remaining question would be: what would happen if a robot had no way of sensing and expressing qualia? To be honest, nothing. But at the same time we should to admit that that kind of robots would be no useful at all for perfect HRI performances. Imitate external actions without having knowledge about the internal meaning makes not possible to understand a human being. Beyond cultural differences, human bodily movements are strongly associated to emotional states. The way in which arms, legs, facial expressions are coordinately performed when you are in love or threatened or bored, for example, are not the same. There are dozens of microsignals that allow us to understand the internal state of that human being: from external face[8] of body movements to monitorized information like heart rate or eye gaze.

1.4. Qualia, Robots, and Propioception

The feeling of being-in-the-world and being an automatic functional Self is, perhaps, one of the strongest and basic feelings of a human being. Thanks to it, human beings behave in a specific way and are able to have complex thoughts and relationships with other human beings. Proprioception is a general body management system which allows us to act without thinking about what are we doing, but also to control consciously our body[9]. Proprioception makes US possible to 'know' that we are, and at the same time to be able to recognize the other as similar to us, that is, empathically. Empathy has deep neurological roots, the mirror neurons, and makes possible learning by imitation as well as social bonding (Rizzolatti and Craighero, 2004; Ramachandran, 2000/2004). When a child imitates the hand and arm movements of an adult she/he is using proprioception and body mirroring by movement/structural empathy. At the same time empathy is something related not merely to a body-mirroring activities, but also to the inner qualia-mirroring effect, that is, feelings or emotions. Therefore, there is a dichotomy around the process of mirroring through empathy, which can be summarized in two confronted areas: a) IN: body-mirroring/quantitative/external, versus b) OUT: qualia-mirroring/qualitative/Internal.

Most HRI systems have been focused in body-mirroring, with a special interest on body gestures, whereas qualia-mirroring has been the research topic of all those involved into affective computing or synthetic emotions. Both activities are always related to the mere copy of the external signals produced by the 'movement donors'. If a human holds his arm up, then the robot must copy it; if the human is sad, the robot imitates his sad face. But always, this complex process is understood syntactically, not semantically. The robot imitates external body movements, but does not *understand* the meaning of those movements. In this paper we are suggesting the necessity of creating an artificial ontology for HRI semantics. Our approach starts from some BODY previous studies and results (Okada, Kobayashi, Ishibashi and Nishida, 2010). Prof. Nishida and his research team have been working on some application oriented projects on embodied conversational agents and human-robot interactions. He and his research group have also

worked on semi-supervised learning algorithms and physiological measurement and analysis. They created a WOZ (Wizard of Oz) environment that allows a human operator to control a robot/agent in an immersive environment. Prof. Nishida presented his results at an AAMAS 2010 workshop: the new WOZ environment allows the robot to autonomously acquire communication skills of people by mimicking and generalizing nonverbal interactions between human and a robot operated in the immersive WOZ environment.

2. DEFINING BODY SYNTAX AND SEMANTICS

Let us to define clearly the ideas about Body syntax and semantics:

2.1. Body Syntax

One of the basic approaches to HRI is that of mirror learning, one activity with deep neurological basis in human beings. But the point is *what do we learn?* To be able to create robots with learning capacities we must not only to establish ways or action mirroring but, and it is more important, a way to understand the syntax of the actions (to be learned/mirrored/imitated). In this case, the robot would be able to learn quickly and by imitation new practices that involved working into human environments, like housekeeping. Unfortunately, we cannot suppose that the robot will be able to understand what an action is only by mere observation. First we need to implement an action coding design: to create an artificial code by which a robot can understand, store and reproduce human actions. Although sweeping with a broom could be considered something trivial, includes: walk through the room until be close enough to the broom, then grasp the brooms' handle and, finally, sweep the room with precise arm movements coordinated with a walking activity. It also includes knowing the *purpose* of all these movements: to clean an area. Therefore, there is no mere movements, but movements-for-something. There is an intentional arrow all throughout these diverse actions. Robots have not all this commonsense about the world. Consequently we must implement on them *action ontologies* related to a close universe. There are some basic actions: holding, moving, breaking, un/fixing which are made with fingers, hands, arms, bodies and legs. There is also a second level of complexity: cleaning, classifying, cooking…We only need to create a clear syntax of actions that can be decoded by a robot. This will make possible to create robots will learning-by-imitation capacities.

2.1.1. *Actions*

Going even beyond in our thoughts, we must to ask ourselves *what does constitute an action?* An action is a complex sum of several movements, that is, the sum of a discretizable event. If we want that a robot learn an action like hold a glass of water and give it to another human being, open a tool box and use a screwdriver, … first we should make him/her possible to understand the range of an action and the ways of cut in it several parts (discretize the event). At the same time we should make all the process much more easier for the robot if we create previously an ontology of basic actions (like: moving, holding, grasping, putting, ….) and, perhaps, codes to show the partial or final beginning and end of each one. Perhaps in this initial stage of this research, robots should interact with human beings who are equipped with motion capture suits, in order to facilitate the robot understanding of living human performances.

All this process is what we define as *BODY Syntax: the sum of a discrete number of (ontologically defined) events which constitutes an action.* From this perspective, action predictions are easier for the robots because the ontology of events and actions makes possible to predict the possible outcomes to be learned.

At the same time, an action is not only a sum of movements but also the interaction of a body with objects (real or virtual: we need to take into account the increasing use of body capture technologies as well as the presence of augmented reality devices, that a robot should be able to use as well) into one or several spaces. Time is the last variable that must me discretized. So, we have: a) movements to be discretized, b) body interactions into one space, c) object uses (that imply an ontology of tools uses), d) time constraints for the whole and the several parts of the process, e) goals to be achieved, f) meaning of the action (from an upper level semantic meaning: hunger, happiness, necessity, …)

2.1.2. *Propioception*

There is another important point: mirrored-bodily-propioception, that is, the automatic translation of the observed being in action (human being) into robot to imitate it. With a correct syntax of the action, the robot has no need to calculate the necessary movements, in the same way that when a human child imitates his/her parents making some action (like open a door), the child doesn't think about the use of arm + fingers + body inclination + … instead of it, the child knows that his/her body make similar things to those of the parent. So, a robot should be able to synchronize its own movements with those external human movements, just *looking at them*.

2.2. BODY SEMANTICS

On the other hand, we have a more complex and socially-biologically-rooted aspect, the BODY Semantics. At this stage of our research we should include cultural values into HRI activities. Bodily attitude of respect, for example is different in Japan than in Germany. Or head and hand movements while talking in India or the USA. There are different body movement codes on several countries. At the same time there are also cross-cultural semantic dimensions of body postures. For example: automatic reaction to pain, or proxemics, a concept introduced by anthropologist Edward T. Hall in 1966, as the study of set measurable distances between people as they interact. Each culture and working group has a special body-language, a special kind of body-game (using the Wittgenstein's concept of 'language-games' from another layer of human semantics[10]) in which the users know are meaning the several observed movements.

But what it is clear is that the basic glue of all human actions are emotions. Why do we do something? The interpretation of the value of an action (fast body movements if something is dangerous, very slow movements if we are very close to success/failure,…) is encoded by a broad range of emotions which should be classified to be able to offer 'natural' robot bodily answers or to improve the learning actions. In this sense, emotions are controlled by a bio-logical tree of relationships. An example: panic is not the immediate output of pain, because firstly we should find fear. Only mad people show 'wrong' emotional answers. In this sense, a human learner can change his movements if he is annoyed by the mistakes of the learner, and consequently, change the 'choreography' of his movements to show the actions (faster, more imprecise, ….).

3. INNERBODIMENT: THE BACKBONE OF UNIVERSAL HRI MODELIZATION

After exposing the previous ideas on the syntax and semantic nature of human movements, it is clear that the basic research efforts must be directed towards the creation of machines able to learn by themselves under this ontological framework. The sum of such philosophical, neurological and engineering ideas will make possible to create better paradigms to improve HRI.

There are two basic approaches to machine learning: supervised and unsupervised. Supervised as well as unsupervised learning have been broadly applied on neural networks applications. The problem with unsupervised learning is that it is slow and prone to very often mistakes. Supervised learning offers less autonomy to the machine and makes not possible or, at least difficult, to design creative machines.

The WOZ approach is at a certain level the first step towards an efficient unsupervised learning model (or with a basic supervised process). This approach is focused on a mimicry activity among humans and robots, where the later are able to recognize human movements and actions. To improve this activity we suggest a new approach we've called *innerbodiment*. The innerbodiment proposes to create HRI technologies that make possible to the robot not only to learn by direct imitation but also by internal co-activity of the human teacher. The human being uses the robot as an avatar and perceives the world *by the same and only* information channels that have the robot. At the same time, the human teacher can move the robot with its own body. With an appropriate HRI interface which shows a simple activity tagging ontology, the human can select the correct concept that is implied into the action to be imitated. Meanwhile, the robot can record the correct actions and suggest to the avatar controller possible choices that, once learned, will be not repeated. Does it is an Inverse Kynematics method?[11] Not, because my model includes pattern recognition, action segmentation/discretization, body imitation following morphological translations and semantic understanding of the goals (simple, like those related to the direct action; or complex, like those that originated the *necessity* of that action. This later is important when resources are scarce and the best strategy must be decided trying to optimize efforts).

So, we have three agents: (a) the robot, (b) the external human trainer and (c) the internal human trainer (or avatar). The crucial point of our approach is not only to design a half-assisted HRI learning method, but the design of a complete syntax and semantics ontology for robots that interact with humans.

3.1. Syntax

3.1.1. An Ontological Approach to Actions

Actions can be described as discrete sets of movements oriented by a teleological principle (or the *reason* of the whole process, justifying the system's change and avoiding at the same time the inactivity). Consequently, any realizable human action can be analyzed mechanically, as the sum of a finite set of coordinated movements.

3.1.1.1. Embodied Taxonomy

The possible action outcomes of a human body are constrained by the bodily structure itself. We cannot choice to rotate unnaturally our arms, because the skeleton, muscles and other body tissues are narrowing the kind of movements we can do, at least for an average human being (even for trained specialists, there things impossible to do). So, it is possible to create a taxonomy of the possible movements that a part of the human body can do, and to assign them a coherent chronological timeline. A simple human taxonomy of movements involves, schematically:

1. Body Parts:
    a. head + neck
    b. arms = 2 sections (humerus and radius) + hand (fingers + opposable thumb)
    c. legs = femur + tibia + foot (articulated through ankle).
    d. body
2. **Actions:** we are interested in two kind of actions, which we call *operational* and

emosocial, respectively. Here can be found some examples of possible actions:
    a. **Operational:** Walk, grasp, push, put, hold, cut, manipulate...
    b. **Emosocial:** Social movements (show respect, greeting,...) And emotional postures: anger, confidence, fear, love,...

3.1.1.2. Designing the Innerbodied Interface

At real-time, the robot must be able to identify possible action patterns and need to decide the correct choice as its mimetic answer. The human avatar receives the information process as well as the doubts of the machine, on a computer interface. Our point is that the human avatar is a provisional tool to achieve a full autonomous self-learning robot, acting as a trainer. The avatar will receive the real online data captured by the robot as well as its semantic processing, being therefore able to guide the robot into the correct choice. The robot will process the results with artificial neural nets under a Bayesian approach which will make possible to solve in future possible situations of uncertainty and action prediction.

3.1.2. The Qualia Experience of Actions and the FAP Patterns

This is the crucial aspect of innerbodiment, when the robot is able to 'feel' the external movement and to replicate through automated fixed action patterns. According to Llinás (2001), the Fixed Action Patterns (FAPs) are sets of well-defined motor patterns, ready-made "motor tapes" as it were, that when switched on produce well-defined and coordinated movements: the escape response, walking, swallowing, the prewired aspects of bird songs, and the like. These motor patterns are called "fixed" because they are quite stereotyped and relatively unchanging not only in the individual, but in all individuals within a species. Fixed action patterns (FAPs) are somewhat more elaborated reflexes that seem to group lower reflexes into synergies (groups of reflexes capable of more complex goal-oriented behavior). We may look at FAPs as modules of motor activity that liberate the self from unnecessarily spending time and attention on every aspect of an ongoing movement, or indeed on the movement at all.

Going one step further, a FAP could also be an emotional process. Most of emotional answers are prewired in our bodies. Consequently, $s = k \ln A / A_0$ interprets emotions as another kind of FAPs with pre-motor (not motor) actions, providing the trigger and internal context for action, then to be shown via other FAPs, e.g. as facial expressions. Llinás also interprets language as a pre-motor FAP. But if we consider FAPs only as prewired action strategies, they cannot be useful for learning processes. This is not the case, because FAPs are subject to modification: they can be learned, remembered, and perfected.

Is in this sense that we can reduce the artificial qualia experience to the sequential, automated and ordered answers of the robots to the human interaction. Applying the Weber-Fechner Law, we can find an architectural and material basis for *qualia*, which governs the relationship between the intensity of sensory activation and perception:

$$s = k \ln A / A_0$$

where s is a sensory experience, *k* is a proportionality constant, *ln* is the natural algorithm, *A* is sensory activations and A_0 is the level of sensory activation at which there is no sensory experience. To discretize the world is the basis of such a project.

Then, a multilayer action control system can be achieved through the creation of artificial FAPs and the robot is not surpassed by an overload of data: it is able to identify relevant information and to spend discrete computational power for relevant calculations, with all the basic move-ments covered by FAP automatizations. What we are trying to reproduce is the way in which human beings do special tasks like read a book and imagine new worlds without thinking about the 'minor details' like move the hand when the page is changed, scratching the nose because of an annoying mosquito,... At the end, we are trying to design an universal kinetic programmable by self-learning robot, able to do different and coordinated actions at the same time with a minimum amount of computational power investment.

Following and updating Mishra, Aloimonos and Fermuller (2009), the process can be summarized as: 1st object/context detection, 2nd goal recognition, 3rd parsing action sequences, 4th morphological translation (drivers, motor primitives,...); and this taking into account how muscular and morphological movements are involved into actions. A robot should be able to understand the human behavior (from goals to mechanistic body procedure) and to implement this information following the fittest and best options according to its own morphological nature. Humans are able to distinguish between a superfluous movement that makes somebody to perform an action (for aesthetical aspects or even for bad learning, as several trained ergonomicists can observe in daily human performances).

3.2. Semantics

The semantics of emotions will be the second step of our semantic approach to HRI. Once achieved a kinetic semantics, a 'merely' mechanical approach to reality, our robots will need to implement mechanical actions with emotional content. And this, at least for humans, is the role of emotions. At this level, we need to create a taxonomical hierarchy of empathy. For example, our robot can be designed to answer to any kind of living entity, or just human ones. Or to elder people, even to gender differences. This will make possible that the intentionality and devoted attention of the robot be focused on the correct entities target. At the same time, the specific emotional characteristics of these entities must be designed in order to make possible a fluent communication.

4. CONCEPTUAL REMARKS

The neurophysiological ideas of FAP can be successfully applied to robot construction in order to improve dramatically HRI, as well as robot self-learning skills. To make easier and faster this learning process, we've have also considered the creation of a modified WOZ system called 'innerbodiment' that allows us to control and help the robot to select the correct choices. At the same time is provided a theoretical approach to actions, from an original WOZ syntax and semantics point of view. This is the first and conceptual step towards the construction of better robots with fluent HRI capacity which will be implemented on several situations. With our approach, we will be able to design robots easily programmable by users to perform specific tasks rather than solely focusing on creating system that are pre-programmed to perform specific functions.

Once we achieve this process of automatic understanding and imitations of human actions, will be possible:

1. The existence of a global cloud database specific repository with all this specific information, like http://roboearth.org/. The generated data could be included into this main framework or into similar ones. Cloud robotics will be the future for fast learning robots, specifically those involved into human environments (like combat situations, autonomic collaborative actions,…).

2. A universal translation of this data results to any humanoid robot or even to a no-humanoids, thanks to translation interface systems[12]. The use or translation of the original data could generate revenues for researchers or be freely shared.

This research is not also possible but necessary and even small successes will provide great industrial, social and intellectual results for the teams that achieve to solve and implement it. Only interdisciplinary and open mind research groups will achieve this.

5. POSSIBLE OUTCOMES AND APPLICATIONS

I am considering different application fields, like elder people caredroids like child or elder care or even kitchen/industrial assistance. In this project I'll analyze the notion of a universal kitchen assistance robot.

The robot must understand:

1. The human actors as action generators
2. The machine automatization of human actions (like the hove heating, the dish machine,….) implemented into a kitchen.
3. The presence and uses of tools as separate ontological entities.
4. The presence, nature and use of materials to be processed (food).
5. The goals implied into a human manipulation of a tool over a raw material.
6. The timely discretization of the whole process.
7. The optimization of the tasks (sometimes the best way of achieving a result is not to imitate perfectly a human being: this human can perform unnecessary movements, or be wrong about some step), once the original human action is translated into the robot morphological skills.
8. The necessity of the capacity of parallel work processing several tasks at the same time: while I'm cutting the food, I start to heat the

oven, but at the same time the cutting process must have an order if you want to prevent excessive oxidation of the raw materials, as well as an overall control of environmental conditions (smoke extraction, main temperature – basic for bread fermentation, for example,...).

There are several programming strategies that could make this possible, using tree analysis as well as Bayesian methodologies. Although this analysis could led us to think that it is too complex for contemporary standards or state-of-the-art, the truth is that contemporary machines, tools and programming technologies could make possible this project under a collaborative interdisciplinary project.

ACKNOWLEDGMENT

This research was the initial research project for which I obtained a grant from the Japanese Society for the Promotion of Science, which made possible my research stay at Kyoto University in 2011. Part of this research has been also developed under the main activities of the TECNOCOG research group funded by the Spanish Government's DGICYT research project: FFI2011-23238, "Innovation in scientific practice: cognitive approaches and their philosophical consequences". Finally, some of the present ideas were discussed and improved through the EuCog III support and meetings, specially the Bochum conference in 2014. I also thank to Yiannis Aloimonos for their insightful speech as well as for allowing to share with him my ideas (specially his latest one about the model Manipulation Action Consequences, MAC).

REFERENCES

Abbott, A. (2006). Neuroprosthetics: In search of the sixth sense. *Nature, 442*(7099), 125–127. doi:10.1038/442125a PMID:16837993

Brooks, R. (1986a). A robust layered control system for a mobile robot. *Robotics and Automation. Journal of IEEE, 2*(1), 14–23. doi:10.1109/JRA.1986.1087032

Brooks, R. (1986b). Asynchronous distributed control system for a mobile robot. In *SPIE Conference on Mobile Robots* (pp. 77–84).

Brooks, R. (1986c). A robust programming scheme for a mobile robot. In *Proceedings of NATO Advanced Research Workshop on Languages for Sensor-Based Control in Robotics*, Castelvecchio Pascoli, Italy.

Brown, J. E., Chatterjee, N., Younger, J., & Mackey, S. (2011). Towards a physiology-based measure of pain: Patterns of human brain activity distinguish painful from non-painful thermal stimulation. *PLoS ONE, 6*(9), e24124. doi:10.1371/journal.pone.0024124 PMID:21931652

Casacuberta, D., Ayala, S., & Vallverdú, J. (2010). Embodying cognition: A morphological perspective. In J. Vallverdú (Ed.), *Thinking machines and the philosophy of computer science: Concepts and principles* (pp. 1–20). Hershey, PA: IGI Global Group. doi:10.4018/978-1-61692-014-2.ch021

Damasio, A. (1999). *The feeling of what happens.* London: Heinemann.

Dehaene, S., & Changeux, J.-P. (2011). Experimental and theoretical approaches to conscious processing. *Neuron, 70*(2), 200–227. doi:10.1016/j.neuron.2011.03.018 PMID:21521609

Du, S., Tao, Y., & Martinez, A. M. (2014) Compound facial expressions of emotion. In *Proceedings of the National Academy of Sciences*, 1-9.

Keysers, C., & Gazzola, V. (2010). Social neuroscience: Mirror neurons recorded in humans. *Current Biology*, 20(8), 353–354.

Llinás, R. R. (2001). *I of the Vortex. From neurons to Self*. Cambridge, MA: MIT Press.

Mishra, A., Yiannis Aloimonos, Y., & Fermuller, C. (2009). *Active segmentation for robotics*. Paper presented at IROS 2009. Retrieved from http://www.umiacs.umd.edu/~mishraka/downloads/iros2009_activeSeg.pdf

Okada, S., Kobayashi, Y., Ishibashi, S., & Nishida, T. (2010). Incremental learning of gestures for human–robot interaction. *AI & Society*, 25(2), 155–168. doi:10.1007/s00146-009-0248-8

Proceedings of the 5th ACM/IEEE International Conference on Human-Robot Interaction, Osaka. (2010). Retrieved from http://hri2010.org/

Ramachandran, V.S. (2000). Mirror Neurons and imitation learning as the driving force behind "the great leap forward" in human evolution. *Edge*, 69.

Ramachandran, V. S. (2004). *A brief tour of human consciousness*. New York: Pi Press, Pearson Education.

Rizzolatti, G., & Craighero, L. (2004). The mirror-neuron system. *Annual Review of Neuroscience*, 27(1), 169–192. doi:10.1146/annurev.neuro.27.070203.144230 PMID:15217330

Sacks, O. (1985). The disembodied lady. In *The man who mistook his wife for a hat and other clinical tales*. USA: Summit Books.

Smetacek, V., & Mechsner, F. (2004). Making sense. Proprioception: Is the sensory system that supports body posture and movement also the root of our understanding of physical laws? *Nature*, 432(7013), 21. doi:10.1038/432021a PMID:15525964

Vallverdú, J. (2009). Computational epistemology and e-science. A new way of thinking. *Minds and Machines*, 19(4), 557–567. doi:10.1007/s11023-009-9168-0

Vallverdú, J., & Casacuberta, D. (2008) The panic room. On synthetic emotions. In A. Briggle, K. Waelbers, & P. Brey (Eds.), Current issues in computing and philosophy, (pp. 103-115). The Netherlands: IOS Press.

Vallverdú, J., & Casacuberta, D. (2009) Modelling hardwired synthetic emotions: TPR 2.0. In J. Vallverdú & D. Casacuberta (Eds.), Handbook of research on synthetic emotions and sociable robotics: New applications in affective computing and artificial intelligence, (pp. 103-115). Hershey, PA: IGI Global. doi:10.4018/978-1-60566-354-8.ch023

Vallverdú, J., Shah, H., & Casacuberta, D. (2010). Chatterbox challenge as a test-bed for synthetic emotions. *International Journal of Synthetic Emotions*, 1(2), 57–86.

Van der Perre, G. et al.. (2014) *Conference on human-robot interaction*.

Wilson, R. A., & Keil, F. C. (Eds.). (1999). *The MIT encyclopedia of cognitive sciences*. Cambridge, MA: MIT Press.

KEY TERMS AND DEFINITIONS

Action: An action is a complex sum of several movements, that is, the sum of a discretizable event. There is syntax of actions, that is, the sum of a discrete number of (ontologically defined) events which constitutes an action, and at the same time a semantics of actions, the meaning of an action into a holistic framework.

Embodied: Cognition is embodied when it is deeply dependent upon features of the physical body of an agent, that is, when aspects of the agent's body beyond the brain play a significant causal or physically constitutive role in cognitive processing. Embodied cognitive science encompasses a loose-knit family of research programs in the cognitive sciences that often share a commitment to critiquing and even replacing traditional approaches to cognition and cognitive processing

Emotions: In psychology and philosophy and emotion is a subjective, conscious experience characterized primarily by psychophysiological expressions, biological reactions and mental states. It is often associated and reciprocally influential with mood, temperament, personality, disposition and motivation. They are managed and influenced by hormones and neurotransmitters.

HRI: Human–robot interaction is the study of interactions between humans and robots. It is often referred as HRI by researchers. Human–robot interaction is a multidisciplinary field with contributions from human–computer interaction, artificial intelligence, robotics, natural language understanding, design, and social sciences.

Innerbodiment: The innerbodiment proposes to create HRI technologies that make possible to the robot not only to learn by direct imitation but also by internal co-activity of the human teacher. The human being uses the robot as an avatar and perceives the world *by the same and only* information channels that have the robot. At the same time, the human teacher can move the robot with its own body.

Qualia: The terms *quale* and *qualia* (pl.) are most commonly used to characterize the qualitative, experiential, or felt properties of mental states. Some philosophers take qualia to be essential features of all conscious mental states; others only of SENSATIONS and perceptions. In either case, qualia provide a particularly vexing example of the MIND-BODY PROBLEM, because it has been argued that their existence is incompatible with a physicalistic theory of the mind.

Self-Learning - Machine Learning: a branch of AI, concerns the construction and study of systems that can learn from data, and when these processes are performed alone by the machine we are talking about 'self-learning'.

WOZ: One commonly employed technique in the HRI researchers' toolkit is the Wizard-of-Oz (WoZ) technique. WoZ refers to a person (usually the experimenter, or a confederate) remotely operating a robot, controlling any of a number of things, such as its movement, navigation, speech, gestures, etc. WoZ may involve any amount of control along the autonomy spectrum, from fully autonomous to fully tele-operated, as well as mixed initiative interaction.

ENDNOTES

[1] Wilson & Keil (1999): 693.

[2] http://plato.stanford.edu/entries/qualia/. Accessed on April 5th 2014.

[3] Dehaene & Changeux (2011).

[4] http://en.wikipedia.org/wiki/Abigail_and_Brittany_Hensel. Accessed on April 5th 2014.

[5] From Wikipedia, http://en.wikipedia.org/wiki/Proprioception#cite_note-16 Accessed on April 5th 2014.

[6] In order to circumscribe our paper into the boundaries of real robots analysis, we also avoid to classify or to analyze the mixture of robotic devices and human beings (as prosthetics, exoskeletons…), that of a broad range of cyborg entities.

[7] A comprehensive list of robots at http://www.smartdigitalrobotics.com/. Accessed on April 5th 2014.

[8] About emotions and face recognition, see the latest research of Du, Tao & Martinez (2014). It provides new ideas about the grammar of emotions as well as the emotional and dynamical syntax of the authors.

[9] Conscious proprioception is communicated by the posterior column-medial lemniscus pathway to the cerebrum, while unconscious proprioception is communicated primarily via the dorsal spinocerebellar tract to the cerebellum.

[10] Published in 1953, two years after his death, the *Philosophical* Investigations of Ludwig Wittgenstein is an amazing book on several philosophical topics. Here was introduced the idea *of language-games*:"Ww can also think of the whole process of using words in (2) as one of those games by means of which children learn their native language".

[11] About this topic see: http://www-clmc.usc.edu/~adsouza/papers/dsouza-iros2001.pdf, Accessed on April 8th, 2014.

[12] See for example: "First validation of a generic method for emotional body posture generation for social robots", by Van der Perre *et al* (2014).

Chapter 9
The Embodiment of Synthetic Emotion

Carlos Herrera
Universidad Politécnica de Madrid, Spain

M.G. Sánchez-Escribano
Universidad Politécnica de Madrid, Spain

Ricardo Sanz
Universidad Politécnica de Madrid, Spain

ABSTRACT

Emotions are fundamentally embodied phenomena - but what exactly does this mean? And how is embodiment relevant for synthetic emotion? The specific role of embodied processes in the organisation of cognition and behaviour in biological systems is too complex to analyse without abstracting away the vast majority of variables. Robotic approaches have thus ignored physiological processes. At most, they hypothesise that homeostatic processes play a role in the cognitive economy of the agent – "gut feeling" is the embodied phenomenon to be modelled. Physiological processes play an actual role in the control of behaviour and interaction dynamics beyond information-processing. In this chapter, the authors introduce a novel approach to emotion synthesis based on the notion of morphofunctionality: the capacity to modulate the function of subsystems, changing the overall functionality of the system. Morphofunctionality provides robots with the capacity to control action readiness, and this in turn is a fundamental phenomenon for the emergence of emotion.

INTRODUCTION: EMBODIMENT AND EMOTION

In recent times the notion of embodiment has gained a central place in the cognitive science literature, to the extent that a new paradigm is said to have emerged from it (Clark 1999). There are many senses in which the concept of embodiment is used, from a metaphysical view that denounces dualism (Lakoff & Johnson 1999), a scientific approach that defends dynamical system models (Port & Van Gelder 1995), to a technological

DOI: 10.4018/978-1-4666-7278-9.ch009

stance that advocates for robots as the sit of artificial intelligence (Brooks 1999). There is not a straightforward interpretation of the phenomenon of embodiment, and its relevance for artificial cognitive agents remains an open area of research.

"The embodied view holds that the particular forms and patterns of physical activity in cognitive systems (e.g., human organisms) shape central aspects of those systems' cognitive profiles" (Gibbs 2006). This view is often contrasted to cognitivism, the idea that we can develop models of the workings of the mind by abstracting away everything except some representation of mental content.

But in one area of psychology this was not the case, even in the height of cognitivism –emotion theory. We can speak of cognitive structure of emotion (Ortony 1990), but this is not enough to explain emotion as adaptive phenomena. It is not only that embodied processes are required for the explanation of cognitive processes associated to emotion –those embodied processes require explanation themselves. Since Aristotle defended that without a body there is no emotion, this thesis has hardly been contested, and trying to tear apart the body from the mind in emotion theory has proven pretty hard. Even Descartes, the father of our dualism, failed when trying to portray emotions as events of the mind. The link to the body was so strong that his theory could well be called an embodied theory of emotion.

Emotion theorists had therefore to deal with the issue of embodiment, and the relationship between cognition, emotion and physiological states has been the central issue in emotion theory for over a century, from James to Damasio. Even appraisal theories, often blamed for highlighting the cognitive content of emotion, integrated embodiment in their theories much before the new paradigm emerged. Embodiment is thus so central to emotion that an embodied theory is the only kind of theory that can exist.

The synthetic approach to emotion must therefore address the issue of embodiment. Nevertheless, most synthetic approaches, even in robotics, have neglected embodiment and preferred a cognitive architecture approach: understanding the role of emotional mechanisms in the cognitive economy of the agent, in order to allow the system to cope with uncertainties and limitation of resources (Sloman 1987). Robotics and synthetic embodiment nevertheless opens new avenues to understand the embodiment of emotion.

In this chapter we present the morphofunctional approach: a framework to understand emotions from the control of changes to functional aspects of the body. This concept, we argue, can be applied to biological systems, and exploited in synthetic systems to attune the disposition of the agent to the situation. This approach, described in the following sections, aims to serve as a framework for future embodied models of emotion.

The Challenge of Embodiment in Emotion

When we say that emotions are embodied, we are not talking about the impossibility to experience emotion without a body. We are saying that bodily events are not mere symptoms of what happens in emotion, they are the very reason of emotion, *they are emotions*. It is not just that we must take into account bodily processes: the organisation of such bodily processes, the adaptation they provide, is what needs to be explained in the first instance.

An embodied theory of emotion must go beyond the fact that the body is fundamental for emotion, and explain how the organisation of bodily processes facilitates adaptation. This is not a straightforward task. First, it is not clear what embodied processes (as found in biological agents) should we start with: those found in the brain and within it specialised areas? The peripheral nervous system? The endocrine system? Or even the heart? Researchers have to decide not only where to look, but also what to look for: motivation, categorisation, experience, discrimination, learning, decision-making, etc. are examples of cognitive processes greatly conditioned by emotion. Emotional phenomena are rich and permeate the greater part of life, but some of those aspects are easily favoured in different approaches.

Embodied approaches to synthetic emotion have committed to a certain approach (where to look and what to look for). Within the area of Human Robot Interaction, the focus is on the expressive potential of the body, and the possibility of robots to mimick human expressions – adaptation is therefore left aside. Neuro-inspired approaches have attempted to replicate the function of some brain areas such as the amygdala in cognitive and behavioural organisation (Mirolli et al 2010). A number of embodied approaches argue for the synthesis of homeostatic processes (Di Paolo 2003).

Somatic theories of emotion constitute the dominant approach inspired by the role of the physiological processes as information-processing mechanisms (Ziemke 2008). In Damasio's theory, physiological processes are essential to confer meaning to mental representations: thus they are an essential part of the cognitive system. The body can be seen to provide a parallel information-processing route to standard cognitive systems, such as, e.g. artificial neural networks. This has motivated researchers to provide robots with simulated endocrine systems and regulatory processes (such as energy management), and investigate what role these simulated physiologies can play in cognition and motivation (Gadanho 2003, Cañamero 1997, Montebelli et al 2008).

These artificial internal variables are meant to be "embodied", but this information-processing network does not play any embodied function, even simulated, beyond carrying out such information tasks. Nevertheless, when we look back at the natural phenomenon, we observe that subsystems and organs go through noticeable changes with a functional role –they affect and control the

capacity of the agent to engage in certain interaction through affecting bodily subsystems in an orchestrated way.

If we take seriously the thesis of embodiment, for internal dynamics to play a key role in adaptation, they must be grounded on actual embodied processes. In other words, what is interesting about emotional mechanisms is not "just" their computational power. In the approach we advocate for here, the key for emotion lies in understanding the functional role of changes in bodily states as changes in the function of diverse subsystems: sensory, motor, neural, and all other physiological systems in the body.

Robotic Bodies

People normally raise objections regarding the possibility of robots to have emotions. This depends greatly on how we understand emotion. For instance, if we consider conscious feeling to be essential features of emotion, the synthetic perspective depends on a theory of consciousness that still faces great conceptual and methodological issues. From a different angle, if robot bodies are not true autopoietic systems, w could argue they cannot have a truly embodied hierarchy of concerns. While these objections may present important challenges, we believe that a functional account of emotion can be given that is also applicable to autonomous artificial systems.

To key is to understand the function that physiological processes play in adaption. For emotion theorists physiological processes provide the logistic support for changes in action readiness (Frijda et al 1989). For instance the stress response (often associated to the emotion fear) presents clear patterns of activation that prepare the animal for responding to danger (fight or flight): high blood pressure, heart rate increase, muscle tension, senses heightened. The emotional response thus is facilitated by the orchestrated modulation of functional aspects of the different subsystems and organs that are relevant for the adaptive capacity of the agent. Even though or other emotions (such as embarrassment or guilt), the association is less straightforward, emotions have been defined as changes in states of action readiness mediated by physiological processes (Frijda 1986).

The purpose of a synthetic approach to emotion is not to be to mimic nature, but to extract organisation principles that can be exploited the cybernetic control of artificial systems. Robotic systems do not have bodies of the sort animals and humans have – neither in their material constitution nor how they are organized. But this does not mean that robots do not have bodies – they do, bodies that are made up of different components and subsystems that play different functions contributing to the overall functioning of the system.

That robots are a system of components and subsystems functionally organised means that they have the potential to adapt through a change in the local function of subsystems. As we will see later, this capacity is called in the literature morphofunctionality. In this paper we argue that the role of embodiment in emotion could be grasped and formalised through this notion that can be applied to biological systems as well as robots.

A key concept for this approach is that of *action readiness*. Humans and animals are never in the same bodily state – furthermore, they prepare for action through physiological changes. Action readiness is hard to quantify, but it refers to the likelihood of success of a given action given the current state. The main function of emotion is thus to adjust action readiness.

In robotics, developers normally attempt to fix embodiment. Roboticists often rely of dynamical system models of the interaction of the robot with the environment. Changing the body means that a new model needs to be used, or rather to deal with a variable structure dynamical system. Although morphofunctional systems will need new modelling and control tools, the possibility to adapt action readiness will bring adaptive potential to robots, and allow the emergence of emotion.

MORPHOFUNCTIONALITY AND EMOTION: FIRST INSIGHTS

Embodied cognition research stresses the role of morphology to shape cognitive processes, and this is often demonstrated in robotic experiments. Because morphology is so important, it should not be overlooked in the design process as a potential way to solve or make tractable a variety of cognitive and adaptation challenges. The notion of morphofunctional machine (Hara & Pfeifer 2003) suggests a different exploitation of the concept: if morphology is so important, the possibility to alter it online would give a robot adaptive advantage over robots with rigid morphologies. Although the concept has been explored in the literature, there is no generic approach and experimentation is driven mostly by ad-hoc explorations, often associated to reconfiguration of connectivity in modular robots. Here we argue that synthetic emotion provides the natural framework for the development of morphofunctional adaptation.

As discussed earlier, whilst we lack precise models of the role of physiological processes, there is overall agreement that what they do is prepare the body for interaction with the environment: they produce states of action readiness. In other words, biological bodies are complex systems that adapt to their environment not only by producing actions, but also by adopting underlying states that modify their dynamical relationship with the environment. Morphofunctionality is an abstraction of this capacity: insofar morphofunctional robots can alter functional aspects of their morphology, they have the potential to adopt states of action readiness.

We define morphofunctional control as the processes that determine action readiness by affecting the local function of embodied subsystems. The impact on interaction can be huge, thus proper morphofunctional control should rely on effective evaluations of the situation: what in emotion theory is called appraisal. We should not think of appraisal as a linear process: evaluating the situation, adopting a valid configuration, and then performing the action. Our critique of this linear model is not theoretical – in fact, in many occasions, emotion follows this pattern, and from a robotics perspective, such an approach would be ideal. But only under certain conditions: when we can predict what future actions will be required, and the best configuration to fulfil those actions.

Emotion has not emerged to cope with this type of situation, in the real world it is not always possible to know what we will need to do, and how to be best prepared. But, as morphology is always subject to modulating parameters, there is always a state of action readiness. Thus morphofunctional control is an ongoing process, while emotion occurs when as there are qualitative changes in action readiness cause by events in the situation. This is what is implied in Damasio's hypothesis that emotion is built on homeostatic processes. Our approach nevertheless does not consider these processes to just balance internal variables to do with the system's body functioning: their goal lies further in the adaptation to the situation through appropriate action readiness change.

Some authors defend that emotions are decision-making mechanisms that can cope with high degree of uncertainty and time-pressure – they are fast routes to behaviour generation that override the need for complex cognitive control (Sloman). Our perspective is radically different: emotion emerges from a morphofunctional system that faces a twofold control problem: to control action and to control action readiness. It is in the coordination of the two tasks that emotional phenomena emerge, in particular, control precedence (Frijda The laws of emotion).

Changes to morphology are not actions upon the world, but on the own body of the agent. This motivates our hypothesis is that action control and action readiness control are two partially independent control tasks. In biological systems, it results from the cooperation of endocrine and nervous system. But our argument is not bio-inspired:

to control action readiness and to control action occur at different time-scales, rely on different information and evaluation procedures. Thus their separation is motivated by the nature of the control task. In (Herrera & Sanz 2013) we have presented a preliminary architecture for this dual control - much more research and development is required to fully understand the potential of the morphofunctional approach to emotion.

MORPHOFUNCTIONALITY IN ROBOTICS FOR EMOTION SYNTHESIS

In this section further describe the approach, exploring the different ways in which control can change morphofunctionality. Current research mostly considers structural reconfigurations in modular robots (Jin & Meng 2011). This is an interesting aspect of robot morphofunctionality, but in the general case we consider a whole spectrum of changes: what matters is the change in function, not the shape of the robot.

Organisms as well as robots are systems composed by a heterogeneous number of components and subsystems. The overall capacities of the embodied agent result from the integration of participating subsystems. Each subsystem can be thought to have a "local function" – what the organ or subsystem does within the overall function of the system. In the general case, morphofunctionality is achieved by altering the function of some of the embodied subsystems that form a robot body.

If we consider that a robot body is normally made up of the following

- Sensors
- Actuators
- Connecting parts
- Energy subsystems
- Computational devices

This produces an initial taxonomy of four dimensions for potential morphofunctional changes:

- Sensory-motor modulation (changing the stiffness, preloaded tension, sensory parameters, etc.)
- Postural-structural (changing the position of different body parts)
- Energetic (energy deployment)
- Metacontrol, changing the structure of control processes (as in neuromodulation).

Sensory-Motor Modulation

A fundamental abstraction of robot behaviour is the notion of sensory-motor coordination (Pfeifer & Scheier 1997). It is sometimes contrasted to the idea that sensory processing, decision-making and motor action are three sequential stages in behaviour generation. In real interaction, sensory stimulation is produced through motor actions, and motor actions are dynamically modulated by sensory input.

Robot architectures, for instance neural networks are often described as connecting a sensory surface to an actuator space. When paying attention to sensory-motor coordination, a loop is drawn that connects sensory input to motor output. The task of coordinating sensing with acting is therefore dynamical, not to build a picture. In other words, the dynamics of the control system will say nothing about interaction unless we pay attention at how energetic exchanges with the world produce sensory activation, and how motor commands are translated into effective energetic exchanges with the environment.

Those energetic exchanges are part of the local function of sensory and motor subsystems. Sensory systems are devices that receive an stimulation from the environment and produce signals. Changes to how these signals are produced, their structure or frequency, will result in morphofunctional changes. Similarly, changes to the way actuators behave, that is, how they respond

to incoming signals, will also affect sensory-motor coordination.

The first potential way to effect morphofunctional changes in a robot comes from changing how a sensor produces sensory input, or a motor executes a command. This will cause a change in the dynamics of sensory-motor coordination, and thus it may be exploited for generation states of action readiness.

Postural-Structural

The second set of changes to morphology in robots are postural-structural reconfigurations, change to the position of body parts, prior to action execution. Biological bodies show different degrees of flexibility in the position they take at any moment - their current posture is an essential factor for successful interaction. Posture taking is a first stage to action generation: it may facilitate later action, or it may make it not attainable. As thus it also plays an important role in motivation: postures are motivational states because they facilitate certain actions. Posture also plays also an important factor in emotional communication: postures are highly expressive, even more dominant that facial expressions (Dael et al 2012).

Posture taking is fundamental for robotics research. Humanoid robots, for instance, need to control posture at all times. In biped locomotion and interaction, posture is a challenge because the risk of loosing balance is high. In more animat-like approaches, posture taking can be studied through the notion of morphosis (Larsen 2011).

. Changes of posture in animals are structural changes that do not reconnect bodily parts, simply change slightly their relationship. As mentioned earlier, robotics offers structural changes in which different parts as disconnect and reconnected. This offers researchers non-biological ways of changing action readiness through taking different shapes. Whilst it is a very interesting research avenue, it should not be considered the main one.

Thus the second dimension of morphofunctional control is the change of posture, the change in the structural relationship between different bodily parts.

Energetic

The functioning of bodily subsystems is determined by the energy deployed in their activation. This is equally true for biological and robotic systems: only that robotic systems tend to normalise energetic input. This is a fundamental aspect of embodied changes in emotion, to the extent that classic behaviourist psychology characterised emotions are processes of energy mobilisation (Duffy 1951)

The third dimension are changes in the deployment of energy to the different subsystems. Energy management is an area of increasing interest in adaptive robotics (Kiryazov et al 2011). The morphofunctional approach considers energy management processes as morphofunctional control with implications on action readiness, therefore framing energy management in the context of emotion.

Metacontrol

Computational subsystems are essential to all robotic systems, not only those attempting to implement a cognitivistic approach. They are essential for robot control, no matter how much cognition is offloaded to embodiment. Metacontrol is defined as changes to the controller of a system, and in our vision this is achieved through changes to computational subsystems. An example of metacontrol is the process of neuromodulation, both in biological systems and robots controlled by artificial neural networks.

CONCLUSION

In this chapter we have argued that emotions are embodied phenomena, and thus synthetic approaches must make an interpretation of the functionality of embodied processes underlying emotion. We have presented a novel framework for the synthesis of emotion: morphofunctional systems are those that can alter the functionality through a modification of functional aspects of morphology. We have provided an initial taxonomy of potential morphofunctional changes: sensory-motor, postural, energetic and metacontrol that are found in biological systems and could have direct application in robotic systems. If this framework is successful, future trends in robotics will see the development of robotic bodies that, rather than functioning uniformly, can attune their functionality to situations.

Morphofunctional changes must be orchestrated to provide effective action readiness. This is a far from trivial problem that depends greatly on the particular embodiment of the system we are dealing with. That is, we are not providing a universal solution, but a framework to develop particular solutions to particular problems.

Furthermore, the exploitation of morphofunctionality depends on a number of other issues in autonomous robotics to be tractable: the capacity to perform goal-oriented behaviours, to perform different actions, to perceive relevant stimuli, etc.. In other words, synthetic emotion needs to go hand by hand with cognitive robotics, especially because further development in cognitive robotics may depend on us having an operational model of synthetic emotion.

What we have presented is therefore only a first stone on a novel approach to emotion synthesis rooted on embodiment. Further work must deal with the issues commented and exploit the morphofunctional potential for developing more autonomous and robust robots.

REFERENCES

Brooks, R. A. (1999). *Cambrian intelligence: the early history of the new AI*. MIT Press.

Cañamero, D. (1997, February). Modeling motivations and emotions as a basis for intelligent behavior. In *Proceedings of the first international conference on Autonomous agents* (pp. 148-155). ACM. doi:10.1145/267658.267688

Clark, A. (1999). An embodied cognitive science? *Trends in Cognitive Sciences*, *3*(9), 345–351. doi:10.1016/S1364-6613(99)01361-3 PMID:10461197

Dael, N., Mortillaro, M., & Scherer, K. R. (2012). Emotion expression in body action and posture. *Emotion (Washington, D.C.)*, *12*(5), 1085–1101. doi:10.1037/a0025737 PMID:22059517

Di Paolo, E. A. (2003). Organismically-inspired robotics: Homeostatic adaptation and teleology beyond the closed sensorimotor loop. In K. Murase & T. Asakura (Eds.), *Dynamical systems approach to embodiment and sociality* (pp. 19–42). South Australia: Advanced Knowledge International.

Duffy, E. (1951). The concept of energy mobilization. *Psychological Review*, *58*(1), 30–40. doi:10.1037/h0054220 PMID:14816485

Frijda, N. H. (1986). *The emotions*. Cambridge University Press.

Frijda, N. H., Kuipers, P., & Ter Schure, E. (1989). Relations among emotion, appraisal, and emotional action readiness. *Journal of Personality and Social Psychology*, *57*(2), 212–228. doi:10.1037/0022-3514.57.2.212

Gadanho, S. C. (2003). Learning behavior-selection by emotions and cognition in a multi-goal robot task. *Journal of Machine Learning Research*, *4*, 385–412.

Gibbs, R. W. (2006). *Embodiment and cognitive science*. Cambridge University Press.

Hara, F., & Pfeifer, R. (2003). *Morpho-functional machines. The new species: Designing embodied intelligence*. Berlin: Springer. doi:10.1007/978-4-431-67869-4

Herrera Pérez, C., & Sanz, R. (2013). Emotion as morphofunctionality. *Artificial Life*, *19*(1), 133–148. doi:10.1162/ARTL_a_00086 PMID:23186348

Jin, Y., & Meng, Y. (2011). Morphogenetic robotics: An emerging new field in developmental robotics. *Systems, Man, and Cybernetics, Part C: Applications and Reviews. IEEE Transactions on*, *41*(2), 145–160.

Kiryazov, K., Lowe, R., Becker-Asano, C., & Ziemke, T. (2011). Modelling embodied appraisal in humanoids: Grounding PAD space for augmented autonomy. In *Proceedings of the Workshop on Standards in Emotion Modeling*.

Lakoff, G., & Johnson, M. (1999). *Philosophy in the flesh: The embodied mind and its challenge to western thought*. Basic books.

Larsen, J. C. (2011). *Locomotion through morphosis: Development of the modular robotic toolkit-LocoKit* (Doctoral dissertation).

Mirolli, M., Mannella, F., & Baldassarre, G. (2010). The roles of the amygdala in the affective regulation of body, brain, and behaviour. *Connection Science*, *22*(3), 215–245. doi:10.1080/09540091003682553

Montebelli, A., Herrera, C., & Ziemke, T. (2008). On cognition as dynamical coupling: An analysis of behavioral attractor dynamics. *Adaptive Behavior*, *16*(2-3), 182–195. doi:10.1177/1059712308089180

Ortony, A. (1990). *The cognitive structure of emotions*. Cambridge University Press.

Pfeifer, R., & Scheier, C. (1997). Sensory—motor coordination: The metaphor and beyond. *Robotics and Autonomous Systems*, *20*(2–4).

Port, R. F., & Van Gelder, T. (Eds.). (1995). *Mind as motion: Explorations in the dynamics of cognition*. MIT Press.

Sloman, A. (1987). Motives, mechanisms, and emotions. *Cognition and Emotion*, *1*(3), 217–233. doi:10.1080/02699938708408049

Ziemke, T. (2008). On the role of emotion in biological and robotic autonomy. *Bio Systems*, *91*(2), 401–408. doi:10.1016/j.biosystems.2007.05.015 PMID:17714857

KEY TERMS AND DEFINITIONS

Action Readiness: A condition of readiness (preparedness to act or respond to a particular stimulus) for action that is induced as a component of an emotional reaction and connected with physiological signals.

Embodied Phenomena: Phenomena occurring in a system, which need attention to embodiment in order to be explained.

Emotions: Changes in states of action readiness, mediated by physiological processes.

Energy Mobilisation: "The extent of release of potential energy, stored in the tissues of the organism, as this is shown in activity and response" (Duffy 1962, p. 171).

Metacontrol: Changes to the state of the controller of a system.

Morphofunctional Control: The processes that determine action readiness by affecting the local function of embodied subsystems.

Morphofunctionality: The capacity of an embodied system to alter functional properties of its morphology.

Section 3
Emotional Recognition and Implementation

Chapter 10
Investigation of Individual Emotions with GSR and FTT by Employing LabVIEW

G. Shivakumar
Malnad College of Engineering, India

P.A. Vijaya
BNMIT, India

ABSTRACT

It is essential to distinguish between an imposter and a genuine emotion in certain applications. To facilitate this, the number of features is increased by incorporating physiological signals. Physiological changes in the human body cannot be pretended. Human emotional behavior changes the heart rate, skin resistance, finger temperature, EEG etc. These physiological signal parameters can be measured and included as the final feature vector. The network is to be trained considering all the feature points as inputs with a radial basis activation function at the hidden layer and a linear activation function at the output layer. The two physiological parameters galvanic skin response (GSR) and finger tip temperature (FTT) that are predominant in deciding the emotion of a person are considered in this chapter. The measurements made are transmitted to LabVIEW add-on card for further data processing and analysis. The results obtained are nearer to the reality with a good measure of accuracy.

INTRODUCTION

Without emotions, life is experienced as having little meaning or purpose, and the pleasures that are derived from rewarding experiences are considerably reduced. Emotionless actions are often related to machines, which execute a sequence of pre-programmed commands. While this common-place perception of the role emotions play in everyday life is pertinent as it is somewhat limited in scope.

The Galvanic Skin Response (GSR) is one of several electro dermal responses (EDR). EDR is actually the medically preferred term for change of electrical skin resistance due to psychological condition. EDRs are changes in the electrical prop-

DOI: 10.4018/978-1-4666-7278-9.ch010

erties of a person's skin caused by an interaction between environmental events and the individual's psychological state. The change is caused by the degree to which a person's sweat glands are active. Psychological stress tends to make the glands more active and this lowers the skin's resistance. Our physical body and mind are interactive. Physical disease may cause mental disorders and mental discomfort may have adverse influence on physical health. When a person is subjected to stress beyond what he or she can withstand, physical or mental disorders may therefore develop. The mechanism is that the stress, when our brain senses it, may cause dysfunction of our automatic nervous system, endocrine system and immune system via the effect of neurological pathways.

In clinical practice, biofeedback machine is used to find a way to detect an emotional tension caused by stress. But in the conventional method of measuring fingertip temperature, the biofeedback machine is large and expensive. It has the sensor which contacts the patient's skin to detect the finger tip temperature. The measured temperature value is converted into an electronic signal which is displayed on a monitor to tell the patient if he/she is in a relaxed condition. Since it is impossible that a medical staff or a large machine is always readily available for the patients, it is desirable to develop an auxiliary medical instrument which can be conveniently worn by the people and help the wearer or adjust them at any time.

STIMULUS FOR EMOTIONS

Emotional content can modify and update the goals and consequently alter the direction of attention to the presented stimuli. Emotions and goals are strongly intertwined in the sense that the immediate relevance of any stimulus to a goal defines the emotionality of the stimulus. The relationship between emotions and the personal goals and concerns of individuals is often suggested to be the basis for emotion elicitation and differentiation by appraisal theorists.

For instance the emotional tag of fear can be attached to a threatening stimulus in so far as the latter can potentially impede the goal of survival. Another example is the emotional tag of happiness that can be assigned to any stimulus that advances the goal of well-being. In a similar fashion numerous emotional tags can be given to stimuli that promote or hinder the attainment of goals ranging from basic individual survival goals to more complex social interaction goals. This vast range of emotions and the related goals is not likely to have been formed concurrently. Rather, emotions evolved from very simple mechanisms that ensured harm avoidance and attainment of vital physical resources into more complex mechanisms that guide complex social behavior. This evolution of emotions may in fact be reflected in the brain systems that generate them, with emotions linked to survival arising from evolutionarily old brain systems. Thus the more primitive emotions would be expected to be elicited by more primitive aspect of the environment, and only at higher levels of evolution would complex classification of stimuli have had related emotions associated with them (Arun Ross & Anil Jain, 2003).

Figure 1 illustrates the system, for measuring Galvanic Skin Response (GSR) and Finger Tip Temperature (FTT). The subject under analysis is made to change the emotional status by external influence. Data are acquired in a closed laboratory condition, by playing the video/audio clippings or showing images. Table 2 shows the different movie clips used to evoke four prominent emotions i.e. happy, surprise, disgust and fear. Sufficient time is allowed in between so that that subject can reach the relaxed state which is considered as the neutral emotional status. Sufficient care is taken so that the subject's attention is not diverted from the intended task.

EXPERIMENTS

Many experiments have been conducted by researchers in search of universal physiological patterns, specific to basic emotions. Those studies concentrated mainly on activities of the autonomous nervous system (ANS) and characteristic speech signal changes. ANS related studies by Achaibou,A. Pourtois,G. Schwartz,S., & Vuilleumier,P. (2008) showed very interesting results each on its own, but until now no distinct patterns for the six basic emotions could be found that all agree on. The results of the studies are controversial and the variables measured do not seem to allow clear distinction between different emotions. Some stable results could be found for variables that seem to characterize certain basic emotions, especially fear and anger, which are the two that previous literature have mostly focused (Castro. A., Diaz. F., and Van Boxtel, G. J., 2005). The work on ANS studies resulted in the following commonalities (Damasio. A. R., 1994). For fear: increase of heart rate, skin conductance level and systolic blood pressure; for anger: increase of heart rate, systolic and diastolic blood pressure. Measuring sadness seems to be more difficult. Because of this, the results are not as clear as for fear and anger. Erickson K. and Schulkin J., (2003) have found a decrease in heart rate, while Krolak-Salmon P., Henaff M. A., Vighetto A., Bauchet F.,

Figure 1. Block diagram of the designed system

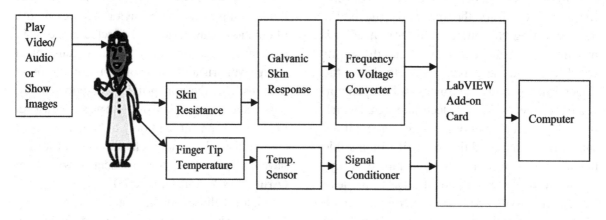

Table 2. Theme of movie clips causing stimulation of specific emotions

Video Source	Emotion Stimulated By The Movie Clip	Theme of the Movie Clip
Kopfschlagen	Happy	Funny scene
Funny Kids	Happy	Cute accidents of kids
Amazing dance	Surprise	Dancing
Atomic cannon	Surprise	Destruction
Snake eat hippopotamus	Disgust	Snake eat hippopotamus
Wrong turn	Fear	Cutting a human body
See no evil	Fear	Plucking eyes
Saw	Fear	Dissection of skull

Bertrand O. and Mauguiere F. (2006), reported an increase of heart rate, while paper Sebastian Korb, Didier Grandjean and Klaus Scherer (2008), could not find any significant difference to the measured baseline. Papers by Hess U. and Kleck R. E. (2005), John G. Taylor and Nickolaos F. Fragopanagos (2005), and G. Shivakumar and P. A. Vijaya (2009) relates emotion by and large to the facial expressions. Disgust seems to represent an even greater problem. It is assessed by four out of the 13 studies. The results are not very promising. Also, measuring positive emotions such as happiness seems to be very troublesome as can be observed especially in diastolic and systolic blood pressure and heart rate data (Christian Peter and Antje Herbon, 2006), which can show a sign of decrease to even a strong increase. The electrodes corresponding to the GSR sensor is fastened tightly to the index finger and the middle finger so as to minimize the motion artifact. The IC sensor corresponding to the finger tip temperature measurement is tied to the small finger. Both are accurate and hand held instruments which can be used without any in-convenience to the subject. The GSR meter switches on automatically when it senses finger contact. Sensitivity control is provided to vary the response of the instrument to changes in skin conductivity as shown in figure 2. It produces the audio output frequency in the range of 0 to 15 kHz corresponding to the skin resistance of 1K to 3.5M. Video clips are played for about six minutes and the values are recorded using the LabVIEW data acquisition add on card as shown in figure 3.

IMPLEMENTATION

The whole signal acquisition and analysis of emotions are carried out by using the graphical programming language LabVIEW. Flowcharts shown in Figure 4 and Figure 5, depict the stages involved in physiological data acquisition and analysis respectively. The steps involved are as follows.

1. Connect the LabVIEW 48 channel analog and digital IO card to the USB port of the computer.
2. Configure channel0 and channel1 as analog input channels AI0 and AI1 respectively.
3. Connect channel AI0 to finger tip temperature output and channel AI1 to Galvanic Skin Response meter output.
4. Read data from both channels continuously after 120 seconds, while playing the stimulation input for 300 seconds. The read data will be automatically stored in two Technical Data Management (TDM) files, each for one parameter.

Figure 2. Z90 GSR stress monitor

5. Convert TDM files into spread sheets so that it can be stored as a database and accessed for further calculation and data processing.

6. Determine the maximum and minimum values and compute the average value.

7. Construct an array of average values for all subjects and store it in the spread sheet.

8. Connect the input of the sensors to the test subject, acquire data, find minimum & maximum values and compute average value.

9. Compute the Manhattan or city block distance using equation (1), which is the equation for L_p Norm.

$$D(X, X^1) = \left(\sum_{K=1}^{d} \left| X_k - X^1_k \right|^q \right)^{\frac{1}{q}} \quad (1)$$

where q = 1 and d = number of samples

10. Display one of the emotion index shown in Table 1, for which Manhattan distance is minimum.

RESULTS

The changes in emotions under some stress are measured by considering the parameters-skin resistance and finger tip temperature. Skin resistance is obtained in terms of both frequency and voltage units. Finger tip temperature is obtained in terms of voltage and °C units. For each parameter, we are considering different emotion conditions such as neutral, fear, happy, disgust and surprise. Data is acquired and analyzed separately for both adult men and women from different age and back-

Table 1. Indexing the emotional status

Emotion	Neutral	Fear	Disgust	Happy	Surprise
Index	1	2	3	4	5

Figure 3. LabVIEW data acquisition program snap shot

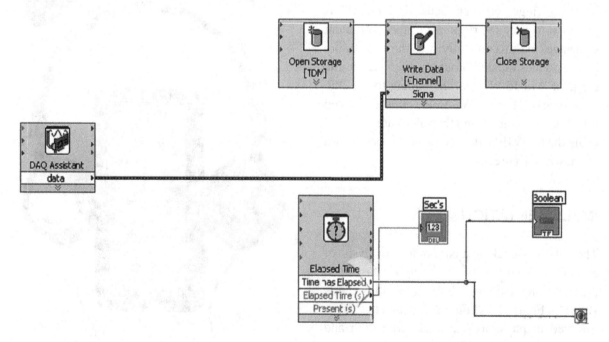

Figure 4. Flow chart for acquisition of data and conversion of files

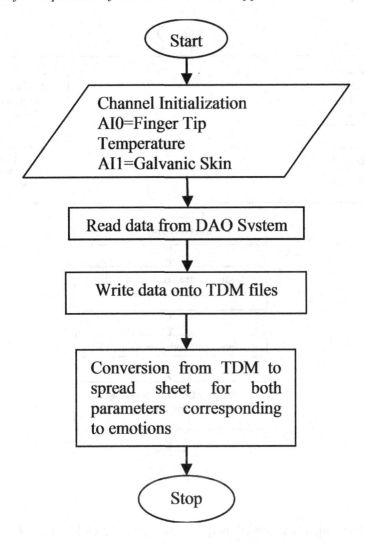

ground. A total of 75 subjects were considered for data collection. Out of the many stimulating video, the most effective shown in Table 2 are selected for final data collection. Data corresponding to GSR are tabulated in Table 3 and FTT in Table 4. The duration of physiological signal acquisition of each emotion is 5-6 minutes. Graphs for the distribution of feature values for GSR and FTT corresponding to five different emotions are shown in Figures 6 through 10. Figures 11 through 14 illustrate average time versus emotional intensity plots from neutral state for different conditions. It clearly shows that the values are almost remains constant after 240 seconds.

CONCLUSION

The physiological status of a person is not always same; it changes according to time and the situations. We found that the result obtained by our system almost follows ground reality. However

Figure 5. Flow chart for computation and decision making

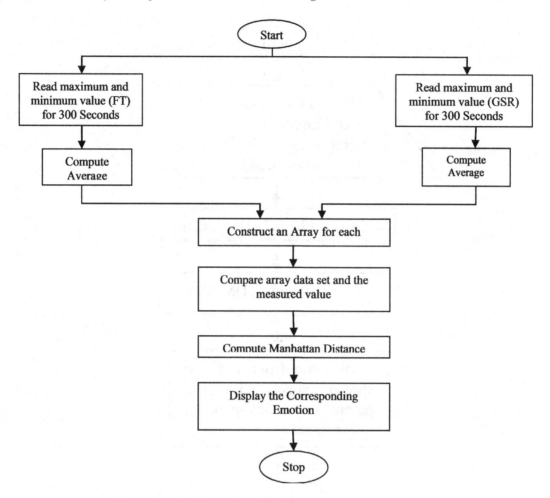

there is a small deviation which can be attributed to the subject under test and changing state of emotions due to external factors even though we tried to keep them at minimum. The new approach introduced in this paper provides a means for structuring, representing and processing emotions within a system without compromising the ambiguous nature of emotion. It does not claim to answer general questions on emotions, like what exactly are emotions or what makes them special in comparison to other mental states. We have collected a total of 750 data of physiological signal measurements from a diversified group of subjects like children, adults and senior citizens from both sex, so that the study and analysis is almost comprehensive. By the study and analysis we can conclude that the percentage recognition is above 80% for most of the emotions. We can also conclude that compared to other emotions, it is difficult to stimulate and identify disgust. Also, it is very easy to evoke and identify positive emotions like happiness unlike negative emotions like fear and disgust. Use of more than one physiological parameter increases the robustness and reliability of the system.

Table 3. Sample inputs from the created data set (ftt in ^0c)

Subjects	Neutral	Fear			Disgust			Happy			Surprise		
		Min	Max	Avg	Min	Max	Avg	Min	Max	Avg	Min	Max	Avg
Ramya	25.5	29.8	30.1	**29.9**	26.5	27.6	**27.0**	31.0	32.5	**31.7**	29.0	32.5	**31.1**
Vinutha	23.9	24.2	27.5	**25.8**	23.5	26.5	**25.0**	27.5	31.0	**29.2**	28.6	32.1	**30.3**
Vijendra	24.1	25.6	27.2	**26.4**	21.2	23.5	**22.3**	27.2	28.6	**27.9**	27.5	31.1	**29.3**
Pushpa	23.2	23.2	24.5	**23.8**	23.1	25.5	**24.3**	26.5	27.4	**26.9**	25.3	27.2	**26.2**
Suma	23.6	23.0	24.4	**23.7**	21.2	23.5	**22.3**	24.5	27.0	**25.7**	23.1	24.3	**23.7**
Rachitha	23.1	25.6	27.5	**26.5**	23.2	24.5	**23.8**	26.8	31.2	**29.0**	24.4	25.6	**25.0**
Changappa	23.5	21.2	23.6	**22.4**	23.3	24.4	**23.8**	25.1	26.7	**25.9**	23.6	20.6	**22.1**
Krishna	23.2	25.6	27.6	**26.6**	23.2	24.7	**23.9**	27.6	28.9	**28.2**	29.0	32.5	**30.7**
Megha	21.9	28.7	26.5	**27.6**	24.2	27.5	**25.8**	21.2	25.5	**23.3**	26.6	26.8	**26.7**
Vijaya	24.0	25.1	26.7	**25.9**	25.8	27.2	**26.5**	23.1	24.2	**23.6**	25.3	26.5	**25.9**
Pooja	23.5	26.2	27.5	**26.8**	26.5	29.8	**27.7**	26.5	28.5	**27.5**	26.5	27.4	**26.9**
Puneeth	25.2	21.3	24.3	**22.3**	20.8	22.6	**21.7**	24.5	25.6	**25.0**	25.1	26.7	**25.9**
Anil	24.1	24.3	25.6	**24.9**	24.8	23.2	**23.0**	25.0	26.5	**25.7**	25.3	26.8	**26.0**
Pavan	23.5	27.6	26.2	**26.9**	25.6	26.1	**25.8**	24.2	25.6	**24.9**	26.5	27.2	**26.8**
Sunil	26.5	28.3	31.3	**29.8**	27.6	26.6	**27.1**	28.5	30.6	**29.5**	27.1	28.2	**27.6**

Table 4. Percentage classification of aroused emotions for selected 10 male subjects

Sl.No.	Subjects	Neutral	Fear	Disgust	Happy	Surprise
1.	Changappa	81.62	85.57	78.42	78.54	77.06
2.	Krishnamurthy	79.27	78.78	80.72	80.81	80.39
3.	Krishnappa	79.80	79.28	78.29	82.06	80.32
4.	Jayaram	81.61	79.89	79.85	79.69	78.75
5.	Revanna	81.43	80.50	79.62	79.56	78.86
6.	Mahesh	81.09	79.29	79.22	79.84	80.53
7.	Shridhar	80.66	80.27	77.38	81.15	80.51
8.	Rangappa	80.61	79.95	80.36	79.35	79.70
9.	Swamy	83.43	82.22	76.50	80.16	77.66
10.	Siddanna	81.19	80.78	78.16	79.39	80.45
	Average	**81.07**	**80.65**	**78.85**	**80.05**	**79.42**

Figure 6. Plots for the distribution of feature values: Neutral

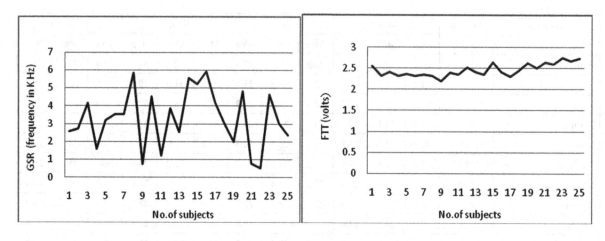

Figure 7. Plots for the distribution of feature values: Fear

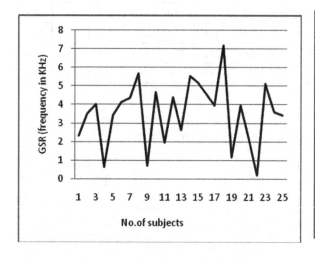
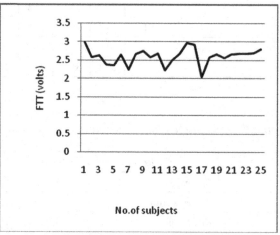

Figure 8. Plots for the distribution of feature values: Disgust

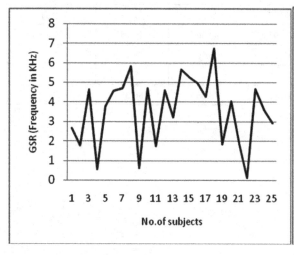
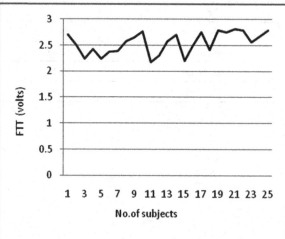

Figure 9. Plots for the distribution of feature values: Happy

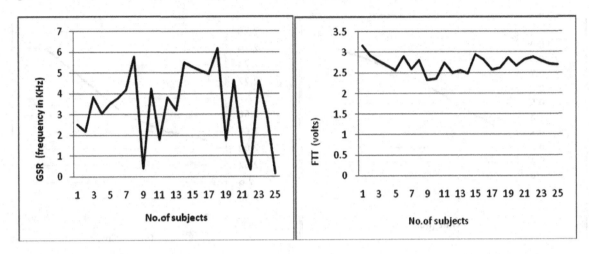

Figure 10. Plots for the distribution of feature values: Surprise

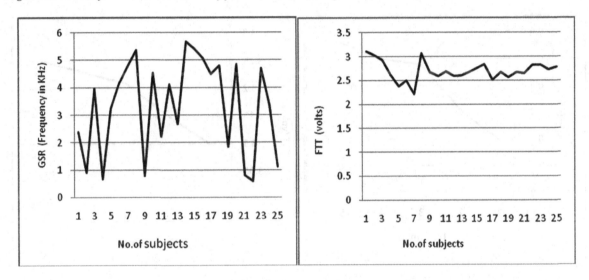

Figure 11. Average time versus emotional intensity plots from neutral state for different conditions: Fear

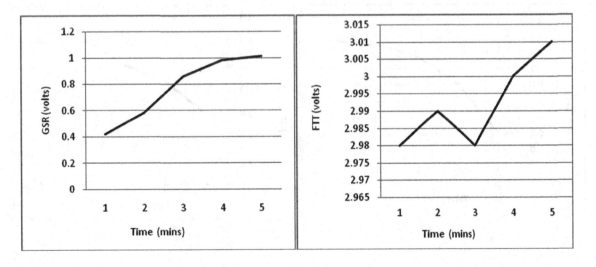

Figure 12. Average time versus emotional intensity plots from neutral state for different conditions: Disgust

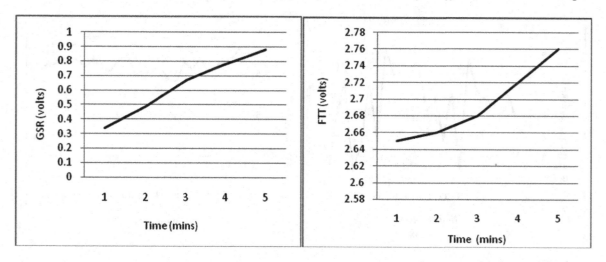

Figure 13. Average time versus emotional intensity plots from neutral state for different conditions: Happy

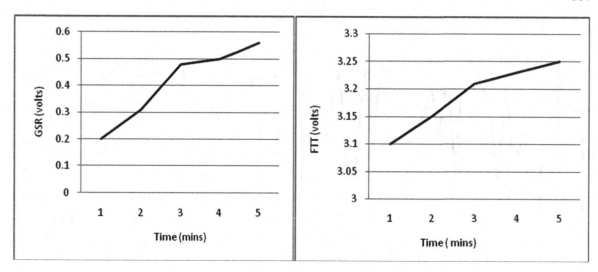

Figure 14. Average time versus emotional intensity plots from neutral state for different conditions: Surprise

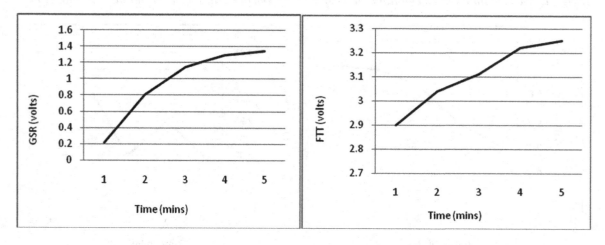

Table 5. Sample inputs from the created data set (GSR in Khz)

Subjects	Neutral	Fear			Disgust			Happy			Surprise		
		MIN	MAX	AVG	MIN	MAX	AVG	MIN	MAX	AVG	MIN	MAX	AVG
Ramya	0.39	0.42	1.02	**0.72**	0.34	0.88	**0.61**	0.20	0.56	**0.38**	0.22	1.35	**0.78**
Vinutha	4.62	4.60	4.79	**4.69**	4.69	4.70	**4.69**	3.99	4.54	**4.26**	4.44	4.66	**4.55**
Vijendra	1.69	1.72	2.23	**1.97**	1.51	1.97	**1.74**	1.45	2.13	**1.79**	1.64	2.82	**2.23**
Pushpa	4.50	4.52	4.65	**4.58**	4.85	5.05	**4.95**	4.99	5.25	**5.12**	4.97	5.32	**5.10**
Suma	3.82	3.85	4.07	**3.96**	4.19	4.35	**4.27**	4.24	5.65	**4.94**	3.81	5.20	**4.50**
Rachitha	6.87	6.91	7.47	**7.19**	6.40	7.06	**6.73**	6.06	6.33	**6.19**	3.66	5.98	**4.82**
Changappa	1.49	1.48	1.95	**1.17**	1.77	1.94	**1.85**	1.57	1.92	**1.74**	1.62	2.10	**1.86**
Krishna	5.00	5.02	5.23	**5.12**	4.60	4.70	**4.65**	4.55	4.71	**4.63**	4.65	4.82	**4.73**
Megha	3.25	3.23	4.00	**3.61**	3.44	3.72	**3.58**	2.22	3.60	**2.91**	3.35	3.46	**3.40**
Vijaya	2.28	2.23	4.56	**3.44**	2.74	3.08	**2.91**	0.09	0.20	**0.14**	0.09	2.13	**1.11**
Pooja	5.64	5.56	6.42	**5.99**	6.15	6.40	**6.27**	6.02	6.19	**6.10**	6.13	6.56	**6.34**
Puneeth	4.42	4.42	5.47	**4.94**	5.53	5.69	**5.61**	5.57	5.99	**5.78**	4.83	6.39	**5.61**
Anil	3.65	3.67	4.64	**4.15**	4.39	4.65	**4.52**	4.26	4.72	**4.49**	4.27	4.71	**4.49**
Pavan	0.75	0.78	1.34	**1.06**	0.39	0.95	**0.67**	0.24	0.30	**0.27**	0.15	0.90	**0.52**
Sunil	2.07	2.14	4.23	**3.18**	1.19	2.02	**1.60**	2.36	5.21	**3.78**	1.79	2.03	**1.91**

Table 6. Percentage classification of aroused emotions for selected 10 female subjects

Sl.No.	Subjects	Neutral	Fear	Disgust	Happy	Surprise
1.	Suma	82.22	81.57	80.13	77.01	79.06
2.	Vijaya	76.92	75.18	70.54	98.58	88.76
3.	Smitha	80.82	75.72	82.34	72.13	88.96
4.	Suvarna	80.00	79.58	81.34	79.30	79.75
5.	Kamala	83.02	81.56	77.73	77.96	79.70
6.	Manjula	81.89	81.39	80.00	78.35	78.35
7.	Sujatha	83.46	82.39	80.01	76.38	77.73
8.	Ashwini	83.06	81.83	82.27	76.77	76.06
9.	Geetha	85.66	77.82	74.22	79.45	82.83
10.	Jyothi	81.73	80.17	91.16	91.66	92.09
	Average	**81.87**	**79.72**	**79.97**	**80.75**	**82.32**

ACKNOWLEDGMENT

The authors would like to thank the authorities of Malnad College of Engineering, Hassan, India for providing all facilities to do the research work at the institution and also the anonymous reviewers for the valuable comments and suggestions.

REFERENCES

Achaibou, A., Pourtois, G., Schwartz, S., & Vuilleumier, P. (2008). Simultaneous recording of EEG and facial muscle reactions during spontaneous emotional mimicry. *Neuropsychologia*, *46*(4), 1104–1113. doi:10.1016/j.neuropsychologia.2007.10.019 PMID:18068737

Castro, A., Diaz, F., & Van Boxtel, G. J. (2005). What happens to the readiness potential when the movement is not executed? *Neuroreport*, *16*(15), 1609–1613. doi:10.1097/01.wnr.0000183331.51736.7f PMID:16189464

Damasio, A. R. (1994). Descartes' error: Emotion, reason and the human brain. *Journal of Neurophysiology*, *2*, 29–40.

Erickson, K., & Schulkin, J. (2003). Facial expressions of emotion: A cognitive neuroscience perspective. *Brain and Cognition*, *52*(1), 52–60. doi:10.1016/S0278-2626(03)00008-3 PMID:12812804

Gunes, H., & Pantic, M. (2010). Automatic, dimensional and continuous emotion recognition. *International Journal of Synthetic Emotions, IGI Global, 1*(1), 68–99. doi:10.4018/jse.2010101605

Hess, U., & Kleck, R. E. (2005). Differentiating emotion elicited and deliberate emotional facial expressions. In P. Ekman & E. L. Rosenberg (Eds.), What the face reveals: Basic and applied studies of spontaneous expression using the facial action coding system (FACS) (2nd ed., pp. 271-286). Oxford: Oxford University Press.

Korb, S., Grandjean, D., & Scherer, K. (2008). Investigating the production of emotional facial expressions: a combined electroencephalographic (EEG) and electromyographic (EMG) approach. In *IEEE International Conference on computational intelligence*, pp.1-6. doi:10.1109/AFGR.2008.4813388

Krolak-Salmon, P., Henaff, M. A., Vighetto, A., Bauchet, F., Bertrand, O., Mauguiere, F., & Isnard, J. (2006). Experiencing and detecting happiness in humans: The role of the supplementary motor area. *Annals of Neurology*, *59*(1), 196–199. doi:10.1002/ana.20706 PMID:16261588

Peter, C., & Herbon, A. (2006). Emotion representation and physiology assignments in digital systems. *Interacting with Computers*, *18*, 139–170.

Ross, A., & Jain, A. (2003). Information fusion in biometrics. *Pattern Recognition Letters*, *24*, 2115–2125.

Shivakumar, G., & Vijaya, P. A. (2009). Face recognition system using back propagation artificial neural network. *International Journal of Computer Science and Information Technology*, *1*(1), 68–77.

Shivakumar, G., & Vijaya, P. A. (2011). Analysis of human emotions using galvanic skin response and finger tip temperature. *International Journal of Synthetic Emotions*, *2*(1), 15–25. doi:10.4018/jse.2011010102

Shivakumar, G., & Vijaya, P. A. (2011), Human emotion recognition from facial images using feed forward neural network with batch back propagation algorithm. In *International Conference on Data Engineering and Communication Systems-2011* (ICDECS 2011), Bangalore, pp. 198-203.

Shivakumar, G., & Vijaya, P. A. (2012). Emotion recognition using finger tip temperature: First step towards an automatic system. *International Journal of Computer and Electrical Engineering*, *4*(3), 252–255. doi:10.7763/IJCEE.2012.V4.489

Shivakumar, G., & Vijaya, P. A. (2013). An improved artificial neural network based emotion classification system for expressive facial images. Lecture Notes in Electrical Engineering (vol. 258, pp. 243-253). Berlin: Springer.

Shivakumar, G., Vijaya, P. A., & Anand, R. S. (2007). Artificial neural network based cumulative scoring pattern method for ECG analysis. *IEEE International Conference on Advances in Computer Vision and Information Technology*, pp. 451-457.

Taylor, J. G., & Fragopanagos, N. F. (2005). The interaction of attention and emotion. *Neural Networks*, *18*, 353–369.

Vijaya, P. A., & Shivakumar, G. (2013). Galvanic skin response: A physiological sensor system for affective computing. *International Journal of Machine Learning and Computing*, *3*(1), 31–34. doi:10.7763/IJMLC.2013.V3.267

KEY TERMS AND DEFINITIONS

Activation Function: Activation Function is normally a nonlinear function that is used to limit the output of a neuron. An activation function is applied to the induced local field of a neuron. It is also known as squashing function. Examples of activation function are threshold, piecewise linear, sigmoid etc.

Electro Dermal Response: EDRs are changes in the electrical properties of a person's skin caused by an interaction between environmental events and the individual's psychological state.

Electroencephalogram (EEG): The brain generates rhythmical potentials which start off in the individual neurons of the brain. These potentials get added as millions of cell emancipation synchronously and appear as an exterior waveform, the recording of which is known as the electroencephalogram.

Emotion: Emotion is an excited mental state. Emotion, mood and affective attitude are different but strongly related and influence each other.

Finger Tip Temperature: Body temperature is one of the known indicators of the general well-being of a person. Two basic types of temperature measurements can be obtained from the human body - systemic and skin surface measurements. Systemic temperature is the temperature of the internal regions of the body. Skin surface temperature is an indicator of the emotional status of a person.

Galvanic Skin Response: Human skin is a good conductor of electricity and when a weak electrical current is delivered to the skin, changes in the skin's conduction of that signal can be measured. The variable that is measured is either skin resistance or its reciprocal, skin conductance which are known as Galvanic Skin Response.

LabVIEW: Laboratory Virtual Instrument Engineering Workbench, developed by National Instruments (NI) is a programming environment in which users can create programs using a graphical notation (connecting functional nodes via wires through which data flows).

Radial Basis Function: The radial basis function has a maximum of 1 when its input is 0. Used in classification type neural networks. A radial basis neuron acts as a detector that produces 1 whenever the input p is identical to its weight vector w.

Stimulus: Stimulus is the input applied to the subject to induce emotion. It may include playing video or only audio or displaying images in front of a subject.

Chapter 11
Mapping Artificial Emotions into a Robotic Face

Gabriele Trovato
Waseda University, Japan

Atsuo Takanishi
Waseda University, Japan

ABSTRACT

Facial expressions are important for conveying emotions and communication intentions among humans. For this reason, humanoid robots should be able to perform facial expressions which represent their inner state in a way that is easy to understand for humans. Several humanoid robots can already perform a certain set of expressions, but their capabilities are usually limited to only the most basic emotions. It is necessary to consider a wider range of expressions and take advantage of the use of asymmetry. This chapter describes these aspects as well as insights about artificial emotions models, the mapping of human face into robotic face and finally the generation of facial expressions.

INTRODUCTION

In the near future humanoid robots are expected to play a bigger role in the society, and interacting and communicating are abilities that are necessary to integrate in the society.

As communication between two humans is achieved through the simultaneous use of both verbal and non-verbal communication, humanoid robots should be able to use these two channels. As humans, we use different types of non-verbal

cues, such as kinesics, proxemics, haptics, and paralanguage (Knapp, 1980). Mehrabian and Wiener (1967) were the first who underlined the importance of non-verbal communication, stating that the non-verbal channel is even more important than words when the content of the communication involves emotions.

Non-verbal communication can have different functions. It can express a mental state through the exhibition of affect displays (Mehrabian & Friar, 1969), (Patterson et al., 1986), cues about

DOI: 10.4018/978-1-4666-7278-9.ch011

individuals' personality (Mehrabian & Friar, 1969), (Mehrabian, 1972), hints about the current cognitive state (Poggi, 2001), (Pelachaud & Poggi, 2002), attitude and anxiety levels (Vinayagamoorthy et al., 2006), and relations between people.

In a conversation, the complimentary information conveyed by facial expressions is useful for the interlocutor to understand the mental state of the speaker and even to detect lies (Ekman, 2009). As the face is considered the most important body area and channel of non-verbal communication (Harper et al., 1978), the expressiveness of the face is an important ability for a humanoid robot.

While a few examples of robots that can already perform a certain number of facial expressions exist, their number is usually limited to the most basic expressions (fear, anger, disgust, happiness, sadness, and surprise) and the patterns are pre-defined. There is a need to go beyond this traditional approach, and rather map the artificial emotions into the robotic face. This parametrical approach would make the robot able to display composite emotions. Moreover, the same concept could be extended to the generation of facial expressions which represent not strictly emotions, but are rather communication acts (such as incomprehension or rebuke) that usually are present during a conversation.

Quality of expressions can be improved taking asymmetry into account. Human face is often not symmetrical over the central vertical line. Both emotional expressions and the face at rest can show signs of asymmetry. In character animation, asymmetry is an important way of making a drawn character not appear stiff and still (Thomas & Johnston, 1995). We want to use asymmetry on the robot to produce expressions that look more natural, and thus are more easily recognised. In case of 3D avatars, implementation of asymmetry in a facial generator has been already attempted (Ahn et al., 2010), (Ahn et al., 2011). However, to the best of our knowledge, there is no study been done so far on asymmetry in a robotic face.

Objectives of the Chapter

In this chapter we describe the mapping of emotions into the face of the humanoid robot KOBIAN-R through the mapping of human face into the robotic face and a system that generates facial expressions, selecting an appropriate combination of facial cues. While the correspondence to facial cues itself is specific for KOBIAN-R, the artificial emotions and communication acts model that has been made can potentially be used on other robots. The generator is based on polynomial classifiers and on relevant studies of psychology and facial anatomy. In its extended form, it is capable of generating asymmetrical expressions. Some expressions produced by the generator are shown as well as the results of an experiment of evaluation of asymmetrical facial expressions, with the purpose of understanding when the use of asymmetry is appropriate among various emotions. The topics explained in this chapter have been introduced from different points of view in (Trovato et al., 2012), and (Trovato et al., 2013) .

The rest of the paper is organized as follows: in the section "Background" we digress into the state of the art; in the section "Facial Expressions Generation" we introduce the hardware used, the mapping of emotions and the generation of expressions and the implementation of asymmetry; in the section "Future trends" we discuss of limitations and new directions of research; finally in "Conclusions" we summarise again the chapter.

BACKGROUND

Robots Performing Facial Expressions

Facial expressions can already be performed by a certain number of robots, including iCub (Beira et al., 2006), Albert HUBO (Oh et al., 2006), WE-4RII (Itoh et al., 2004), and KOBIAN

(Endo & Takanishi, 2011). However, expression capabilities are usually limited and the small set of pre-defined patterns (typically, the six basic ones according to Ekman et al. (1969): Happiness, Sadness, Anger, Surprise, Fear and Disgust) is one of the reason why humanoid robots are still unable to show a natural interaction. Geminoid (Becker-Asano & Ishiguro, 2011), Flobi (Hegel et al., 2010) and iCat (Van Breemen et al., 2005) are other examples of recent robotic systems that are still limited to a small set, although emotion exaggeration has been investigated in the latter case. iCat and EMYS (Kędzierski et al., 2013) are examples of robotic heads with a face that, despite retaining some human features, is inspired by an animal. In the case of EMYS, as in the case of Kismet (Breazeal, 2003), some joint movements do not have any correspondence in the human face and they must be interpreted separately: for them, a mapping of emotions into facial cues was made, similarly to the work described in this chapter.

Kismet was the first robot to be based on a model that could blend emotions; this kind of approach has also been attempted, in a more simplified (two-dimensional) model, on the robot FACE (Mazzei et al., 2012), and for full body poses on the robot Nao (Beck et al., 2010).

It goes without saying that in order to study more complex approaches than simple basic patterns, a robotic head with a high number of degrees of freedom is necessary: the head of KOBIAN-R, which we are using, satisfies this requirement.

Emotional Models

In 1980, Russell (1980) proposed a circumplex model of emotions. This model defines an emotional space along with unpleasant-pleasant axis (Valence axis) and deactivation-activation axis (Arousal axis). Affective words are disposed in circle in the following order: Pleasure (0°), Excitement (45°), Arousal (90°), Distress (135°), Displeasure (180°), Depression (225°), Sleepiness (270°), and Relaxation (315°), together with other words. The full set of 28 affect words was classified through direct circular scaling coordinates. Examining in detail, the terms "Angry" and "Afraid" are very close in the graphical representation, and this fact makes this model unfit for being used for our purpose.

Russell later expanded his model with Mehrabian (1980) making the PAD (Pleasure, Arousal, Dominance) 3-dimensional state model. Another expansion by Fontaine et al. (2007), instead took into account Potency and Unpredictability together with Valence and Arousal. Ahn et al. (2010) shown some insights about a 3 dimensional model composed of Valence, Potency, and Arousal, and the use of asymmetry.

Scherer (2005) also proposed alternative dimensional structures for the semantic space of emotions. In the framework of the componential process of definition of emotion, he defined emotion as an "episode of interrelated, synchronized changes in the states of all or most of the five organismic subsystems in response to the evaluation of an external or internal stimulus event as relevant to major concerns of the organism". In the latest (3.0) version of the Geneva Emotion Wheel (Scherer et al., 2013), 20 words are organized in a wheel-like space.

Some emotional models have been already applied to humanoid robotics. It is the case of Miwa's model for WE-4II (Miwa et al., 2002), and Breazeal's Valence-Arousal-Stance space for Kismet (Breazeal, 2003). Both are 3-dimensional and effective in their implementation, however, they are not perfectly fitting the purpose of our research. Miwa's model is based on the 6 basic emotions and does not feature any blending. Breazeal's model does feature the forming of composite emotions, but its complexity is not enough for the high number of DoF of KOBIAN-R's head. It is necessary a more extensive than existing 2D or 3D models.

Plutchik's Wheel (Plutchik, 2002) is a model where the 8 basic emotions are opposite in pairs to each other, and where the centre corresponds to the maximum arousal, and the sides to its absence. It features a wide range of emotion labels, including secondary emotions that stand in between two primary ones. The fact that these labels are not displayed in a random order, but rather arranged in pairs, makes this model useful for the current purpose.

Communication Acts

It is our intention to generate expressions for more generic communication, rather than just representation of emotions. This is why we need to digress here about communication. As defined by Poggi and Pelachaud (2000), the performative (namely, the actual action of interaction) of a communication act is defined by six parameters:

1. The goal (request, information or question),
2. The interest (in whose interest),
3. The degree of certainty,
4. The power relationship,
5. The type of social encounter (formal or informal context),
6. The affective state (the underlying basic emotion).

Goal, Interest and Type of Social Encounter are more related to a full body communication, while Certainty, Power relationship and Affective state can help to convey a communication act through facial expressions and neck movement. For example, there is a link between power relationship and movement of the head and eyes: when feeling superior to the person in front, usually the head tends to move upwards and eyes tend to look down. The opposite is also true for feeling inferior. Degree of Certainty also influences facial cues (Poggi, 2006).

Studies on Asymmetry

Several studies on human face have been made in the past. It has been proved that left hemiface (the left side of the face) produces more intense expressions (Borod et al, 1997). In addition, there is a difference between genders, as males show generally more lateralisation (Borod et al., 1998). Symmetry is also one of the factors that determine attractiveness (Grammer & Thornhill, 1994). Asymmetry has been measured, differentiating between structural asymmetry and movement asymmetry, with the latter being recognised as the primary source (Schmidt et al., 2006). Relationship between valence and hemiface has also been investigated (Van Gelder & Borod, 1990). Moreover, correlation with handedness has been hypothesised (Borod & Caron, 1981).

Our main purpose, however, is not the investigation of neurobiological aspects, but rather the correlation between each of the emotions and a particular asymmetrical facial cue. In this way it would be possible to make a more accurate mapping and to generate asymmetrical expressions.

In these regards, the works of Ahn et al. (2010, 2011) are the closest to our intentions, though based on a three-dimensional avatars rather than a robot. In that case, asymmetric face was derived giving left hemiface a higher probability of negative emotion. Our approach is different from Ahn's: we want to find out which facial cues that are usually activated when a certain emotion is involved, and use this data for generating expressions.

FACIAL EXPRESSIONS GENERATION

In this section, the system that generates facial expressions is described. The generator is based on polynomial classifiers and on relevant studies of psychology and facial anatomy. The concept of this novel approach is to make KOBIAN-R perform a wide range of facial expressions through a parametric system, resulting in the display of non-basic emotions and communication acts.

For making this system, we need to define an input (namely, an emotional model); an output (motor angles configuration of robotic face); and a relationship that links input and output (Figure 1). In that relationship, a mapping of the robotic face and a classification is necessary. All of these parts will be explained in the following paragraphs.

Robotic Face

The robotic head we are using in this experiment is KOBIAN-R's head (Kishi et al., 2012). KOBIAN-R is the refined version of KOBIAN, a whole body emotion expression 48 DoF (Degrees of Freedom) humanoid robot designed to provide support for the activities of daily living for elderly and disabled people, and to clarify the influence and effectiveness of physicality and expressivity during the interaction between human beings and robots. Besides emotion expression, KOBIAN is a robot capable of bipedal walking. These two abilities combined together make KOBIAN potentially able, in the future, to work as assistive robot in a human environment, such as a family or a public facility.

The new version of the head, thanks to the design of much downsized and lighter inner mechanisms, features a number of DoF expanded to 24 (from 7 of KOBIAN). Table 1 shows the number of DoF for each part. Taking advantage of such high number of DoF, the robot has a much higher potential of expression.

The head has also the additional capability of changing the colour of the forehead, thanks to the use of a blue Electro Luminescence sheet behind the cover. It was added in order to make the expression of "Fear" more easily recognisable (in Japanese comics culture, blue brow represents

fear). The blue colour is not visible when the Electro Luminescence is off. Despite the presence of the sheet, the forehead is thin enough to allow movement of eyebrows through magnets.

The size of the head is 150 mm x 181 mm x 214 mm (width x depth x height), similar to a human adult female, and the weight is 1.7 kg. Lips and eyebrows are made of SEPTON (Kishi et al., 2012).

Extended Plutchik's Wheel

As input for the generation system, we need an emotional model. The choice ended up on Plutchik's Wheel. Being a "flower" with 8 leaves arranged in pairs, it is possible to convert this model to numbers using only 4 variables (for instance, only one variable would indicate "Anger" and "Fear", which are the opposite of each other in the model). Keeping a low number of variables is an important advantage in classification, and this should be kept in mind, since the chosen model will be used as input to a system that classifies such data.

In Plutchik's model, secondary emotions can be extrapolated from two adjacent branches of the wheel. In our model instead it is possible to span through a higher number of emotions, which can be in between any two or more of the basic parameters, just assigning numerical values. As a result, each mixed emotion is a point in the $\mathbb{R}^4$ space

We also mentioned communication acts in the previous section. As defined by Poggi (2006), communication acts include also Certainty (measuring the certainty of comprehension of the conveyed message), Power Relationship (measuring the relationship with the receiver of the message), and Affective State, which are factors that can influence facial expressions. We can replace the Affective State with the 4-dimensional Plutchik's emotion model, and as a result we will get a

6-dimensional space that represents emotions and communication acts (Figure 2). The 6 basic parameters are: Mood, Stance, Temperament, Expectation, Certainty and Power Relationship.

Mapping

The output of the system is the angles of the motors of the robotic face. Taking advantage of its 24 degrees of freedom, KOBIAN-R's head could able to perform a wide range of expressions if each component that can move could display a facial cue that contributes to the making of an expression.

A set of possible configurations of motor angles (resulting in a meaningful shape, appropriate for a humanoid face) was created for each facial part. In this process, the Facial Action Coding System (FACS, a procedure to systematically describe human facial expressions) Action Units (AU) (Ekman & Friesen, 1978), (Hager & Ekman, 1983) were used for the identification of human muscles and for mapping a part of human facial cues to robotic cues.

If the robot had a face resembling exactly hum face, FACS can be used to recreate human's face muscles though direct correspondence, but this is not our case. In fact, some Action Units are indeed related to muscles that produce movements of the skin or of the nose that cannot be recreated into KOBIAN-R.

In the present case, AUs are adapted to the specific KOBIAN-R's face, and the "robotic cues" defined in our system are fewer than AUs. A process of simplification was necessary: this was also the case of the robots Probo (Saldien et al., 2010) and EMYS (Ribeiro & Pavia, 2012).

Each part of the face can move in a certain way, displaying a cue. A few cues, put together, contribute to the making of an expression.

KOBIAN-R's facial parts such as eyebrows and mouth have the potential of changing into a high number of shapes. However, this potential has a

downside: unnatural shapes and shapes that are dangerous for the robot (e.g. lips could break) can also be produced. For this reason, for each part of the face, a set of possible shape configurations has to be defined. In this way, only values of the motor angles that produce facial cues that are meaningful to humans, and that are safe for the robot, will be used.

Dropping unnatural shapes does not imply avoiding the use of any strictly non-human like face. One of the strengths of KOBIAN-R's face design is that it can display expressions that are exaggerations of human typical ones: such appearance is widely used in comics and actually makes recognition easier.

As said before, a set of possible configurations of manually chosen motor angles (resulting in a meaningful shape, appropriate for a humanoid face) was created for each facial part. Each motor angle configuration will be described by those robotic cues variables.

In the case of eyebrows, the meaning of the 3 robotic cues used exactly correspond to AU1, 2, and 4 (Figure 2); but for instance, in the case of the mouth, in which AUs are present in significant number, AUs have been reduced to 8 and then paired (one the opposite of the other, such as opening/closing lips), so that just 4 variables are enough to represent robotic cues of the mouth. In the Figures 3-6 and Tables 2-8 this process of mapping is shown for each facial part. The concept was to try to maximise the number of possible configurations (Table 1, last column) while minimising the number of used variables (Table 1, fourth column).

Most of the simplification involved Action Units relating to skin movements, impossible to reproduce on the robot, or multiple Action Units with very subtle differences between them, almost impossible to distinguish if implemented. A lower amount of variables is an advantage, since it will make classification of these data easier.

Classification

At this point, while in the system the emotional parameters are given as input, the output can be chosen between a whole set of possible configurations for each facial part. Training data is needed to link them with the outputs. This equals to assigning a meaning to each configuration, resulting in an "alphabet of non-lexical words".

In these regards, the studies of Poggi (1999, 2001, 2006), and Ekman have been used to find these correspondences. In particular, Ekman specified which AUs should appear in a face for each emotion (Kobayashi et al., 2002). However, applying strictly Ekman's indications (called "categorical model", as defined by Smith and Scott (1997)) is not feasible because of the difference of KOBIAN-R's face with human face and would not be appropriate for making a flexible system.

Conversely, we considered using a "componential approach" for the meaning of facial expressions (Smith & Scott, 1997), (Bimler & Paramei, 2006). In this case, each cue is a component characterized by an exact meaning that influences the overall meaning of the expression. Smith and Scott proposed a table (a portion of which can be seen in Table 9) that links meanings to hypothesised individual facial actions. For instance, there is a link between surprise and the action of raising eyebrows, or between pleasantness and smiling. We expanded Smith and Scott's table with information extracted from the above mentioned sources and used as training set. Due to the complexity of the classifying problem, we decided to rely on machine learning: we used 6 classifiers (one for each facial part) to map the correspondence with composite emotions, using the above mentioned table as training for such classifiers.

We used degree 3 polynomial classifiers: polynomial features are added to the input dataset according to the formula of Equation 1 (where n is 6, the number of components of feature vector f, and j and k are intended as their indexes) and

then classified through Fisher's linear classifier (Raudys & Duin, 1998).

$$\sum_{j=1}^{n} f_j^3 + \sum_{j=1}^{n} f_j^2 + \sum_{j=1}^{n-1} \sum_{k=j+1}^{n} f_j * f_k + \sum_{j=1}^{n} f_j$$

(1)

Monomials as well as combinations of 2nd order terms are constructed and then classified, which minimise the errors in the least square sense. Polynomial classifiers can map the data with very low error on the training set and produce visibly more correct outputs compared to neural networks and support vectors.

The whole system transforms a 6 dimensional vector into a 24 one through a process of classification and mapping. Figure 7 shows the whole process of generation of these values for the case of eyebrows. There are 6 classifiers, one for each part of the face, and one for the neck. The mathematical representation of the inner process has been defined as follows.

Each of the classifier is given vectors f as input. Each f_i is composed by the above mentioned 6 parameters $f_{i1}, \ldots, f_{i6}$, where $-99 \leq f_{ij} \leq 99$. These bounds were chosen because they are divisible by 3, so that it is easier to assign values according to 3 degrees of intensity of each emotion in Plutchik's model.

The outputs of the classifiers are the robotic cues variables mentioned. We call these outputs p. Values of their components range from 0 to 1 or from -1 to 1, depending on the facial part.

For each of the facial parts there is a set $C = c_1, \ldots, c_n$ of possible configurations. Each configuration is defined in the same way as the vectors p with real values ranging from 0 to 1 or from -1 to 1.

Through the use of the 1-nearest neighbour algorithm, we find, for each facial part, $c*$, the best vector, which is closest to p, among the possible configurations. It represents the best configuration (defined in terms of facial cues) among a pre-defined set.

From this point, we can get the correspondent vector $m*$ containing real motor angles through lookup tables.

Examples of Generated Expressions

Evaluation of different kind of facial expressions was done through several web surveys. Two separate experiments have been made. After taking photos of the robot (from the front) performing facial expressions, we made two surveys which had different goals:

- Preliminary evaluation of the recognition rates of 12 facial expressions of complex emotions or communication acts, to confirm the effectiveness of the generation system.
- Evaluation of randomly generated expressions, a more difficult test since expressions are not labelled.

In this chapter, only the results of the second part are shown. The first can be found in a previous study (Trovato et al., 2013).

Here we show, in figures 8-13 six facial expressions obtained by using random vectors. For each figure it is possible to see the output expression together with the input, giving some hints on the effect of the contribution of each component of the input vector. The 12 basic vectors are shown in Table 10 for reference.

Values of the input vectors have been randomised between -99 and 99, and then only values bigger than the threshold shown in Eq. 2 were taken, because we considered noise random values whose absolute values are smaller than the average.

$$f_{ij} = \begin{cases} f_{ij} & |f_{ij}| > AVG_j\left(f_{ij}\right) \\ 0 & |f_{ij}| \le AVG_j\left(f_{ij}\right) \end{cases} \quad (2)$$

The index i refers to the i-th expression within the set of expressions; the index j refers to the parameter of the single input vector. This process results in vectors that contain 2 to 4 active parameters, which are supposed to produce ambiguous expressions, difficult to judge, but possibly more interesting to study than simpler expressions.

From the results however it is possible to notice that the two greatest components of the input vector are generally the ones that influence most the final result. For instance, in Figure 11 it is possible to clearly see the effect of Inferiority in terms of neck pitch down and eyes looking up, together with the effect of Surprise, as eyebrows are raised and the mouth is open, but no clear detail can be assigned to Anger. We can conclude that this is a confirmation of our assumption that small values are just considered noise and do not add any significant meaning to the facial expression.

Further evaluation of recognition rate cannot be done for this set of expressions because they are not defined a priori, thus a label cannot be assigned. As authors, we were also curious of the possible outcome of the generation. More details about possible ways of evaluation of unlabelled expressions can be found in (Trovato et al., 2013).

Implementing Asymmetry

This part has been published for the first time in (Trovato et al., 2012). We wanted to investigate which emotions or communication acts cause asymmetry in human face, and in particular which facial part changes. In order to achieve this, we asked one professional illustrator and three amateur cartoonists to draw symmetrical and, when appropriate, asymmetrical versions of the same expression (some examples in Figure 14). The list of expressions to draw was taken from the 12 basic emotions and communication acts of the extended model (as in Figure 2), in addition to the neutral expression and the possibility for the artists to add more expressions that they thought appropriate for asymmetry. As a result, the total of drawings made was more than 50 (4 samples for each expressions).

Some rules were then extracted from the drawings. Together with the artists, we hypothesised that, in an expression that is produced by a blend of two or more emotions or communication acts, the following correlations exist:

1. The presence of Anger causes lowering of one eyebrow and one-sided lower lip depressing.
2. The presence of Disgust causes sided upper lip raising and one eye aperture narrowing.
3. The presence of Incomprehension causes asymmetry in eyebrows and mouth.
4. The presence of Sadness and Inferiority causes sided lips corner tightening.
5. The presence of Superiority causes asymmetry in eyebrows and sided lips corner tightening.

It appeared that generally, asymmetry is associated with negative valence. Positive expressions, such as Happiness, seem to partially lose their positive valence, as if there were another meaning hidden beyond the happy face. We will verify these assumptions through experiment.

For making the generator capable of generating asymmetrical expressions, we expanded a part of the process.

An additional table, made through the analysis of the artists' work, is added to associate each facial cue to another one for making a consistent asymmetrical pair. The table is activated by flags which are activated when a component f_i of the input vector is comprehended between two thresholds θ_U (upper) and θ_L (lower). For each facial part that has one flag active, two different output vectors (one for each hemiface) are generated instead of one. In case of more than one active flag, the one triggered by the highest f_i gets chosen (e.g. mouth

can have different ways of being asymmetrical, from different emotions: only one gets performed at the same time).

The use of adjustable thresholds makes the system flexible. Increasing the lower threshold θ_L is a way for filtering noise: avoiding that values of f_i close to 0 have an influence on the whole face. Changing the upper threshold θ_U is meaningful for setting the system to produce asymmetrical expressions also in case of a "completely angry face" or "completely disgusted face" or for limiting asymmetry for the case of secondary emotions hidden in another expression (such as "disgust hidden in a happy face").

Evaluation of Asymmetric Expressions

In this experiment, 75 volunteers (53 male; 22 female; average age: 26.9; age standard deviation: 7.4) participated. Nationality was very widespread: 28 Japanese, 13 non-Japanese East Asians, and 34 Western participants.

Evaluation consisted in a questionnaire divided in two different parts with the following objectives:

*   Evaluation of the preference of participants for asymmetrical expressions compared to symmetrical ones
*   Evaluation of influence of asymmetry on a happy face.

In the first part, the participants were asked to just choose the most appropriate of two versions (one symmetrical, the other one asymmetrical) for the following facial expressions: Disbelief, Annoyance, Disgust and Incomprehension in a web survey. These chosen expressions contain all the facial cues mentioned in the hypothesised correlations listed in the previous paragraph.

In the second part, they were asked to express their preference between a symmetrical and an asymmetrical version of the facial expression of Happiness (as in Figure 15). Five different asymmetrical versions were made: in each of them, one facial part at a time (among eyebrow, eyelid or mouth) had a different shape. In case of detection of a secondary meaning beyond the happy face, participants had to suggest such meaning, choosing from a list of words which corresponds to the list of basic emotions or communication acts of the extended Plutchik's model.

Let us see the results: as shown in Table 11, all the asymmetrical versions of the expressions were preferred (average: 60.2% compared to 18.0% of symmetrical ones).

The analysis of the part regarding expressions of Happiness is a little more complex. Results indeed confirm the hypothesis that asymmetry has a negative effect on perceived valence of the emotion expressed (80.2% of the preferences goes for symmetrical face, as can be seen in Table 12). In other words, symmetrical versions are considered more appropriate for Happiness, while asymmetrical versions hide a negative meaning. However, the attempt in finding out the association between asymmetrical facial cue and basic emotion or communication act did not bring clear results. We report here the emotion or communication act that had the highest number of preferences. Correlations highlighted by the survey were:

- **AU4 (Brow Lowerer):** Incomprehension
- **AU43 (Eye Closure):** Disgust
- **AU10 (Upper Lip Raiser):** Surprise
- **AU16 (Lower Lip Depressor):** Surprise
- **AU14 (Lip Corner Tightening):** Surprise

These results are only partially matching the assumptions that were made before the experiment. In particular, all facial cues regarding mouth were misinterpreted, but the correlations of eyebrows and eyelids are correct. This fact may be due

possibly to the hardware implementation of the mouth, which should be reconsidered.

FUTURE TRENDS

The study described in this chapter has some limitations. The most important aspect is the low degree of naturalness of the interaction between the robot and experiment participants. In fact the input of emotional parameters is manual; generation is done by a separate program, and evaluation is done through photos of the robot. Ideally, parameters would evolve dynamically, generation of the expression would be done automatically, and evaluation could be measured in more broader terms, measuring human participants' mental state.

A Wizard of Oz type of experiment, in which the robot is controlled remotely and does not have an autonomous behaviour, is also an useful way for improving interaction with participants and possibly make it last longer. All the studies in this research are limited to the beginning of an interaction: namely, the first idea that we get of robot's emotion from its expression. As interaction carries on (e.g. when facial expressions change dynamically together with the context of an interaction, or matching a dialogue keywords), a Wizard of Oz method becomes necessary. It can improve the affection participants feel towards the robot, as long as the trick is not exposed and expectations disappointed.

Limitations of an autonomous robots are due to hardware, as a really natural interaction would be possible only through different components elaborating auditory, visual field and so on. The potential is clear: for example KOBIAN-R, with its high number of degrees of freedom in the face, has high potential of expression, which could ideally change dynamically during an interaction by certain stimuli. It needs however more sensing abilities and integration of all these components.

Robots do not have these abilities, therefore they need human support, which is similar to the support impaired people get. For example, a person with visual impairment may need assistance for detecting the identity of the person whom is interacting with. Robots too need this kind of context information to be inputted manually (for example to integrate limited visual capabilities).

A second point of discussion is related to the human likeness of the robotic face and the consequent mapping. In case of KOBIAN-R, while some facial parts cannot move like humans, some other parts can change shape in some ways that humans cannot do. This is indeed an advantage for robots, who can overcome their handicaps in expression through the use of more exaggerated shapes or even of supportive hardware. One example of hardware could be a display that is used to communicate more efficiently robot's internal state. We are developing for KOBIAN-R a more unique solution: some LED panels to be placed on the top of the forehead and on the cheeks. Five devices (three on the forehead, one on each cheek) should be mounted on the new head. The solution of LED makes possible to display some symbols, such as question mark, or tears, which will definitely be useful is emotional communication.

CONCLUSION

In this chapter, we described a system that generates facial expressions for the humanoid robot KOBIAN-R, choosing a combination of facial cues, rather than using predefined patterns for each emotion. The parameters involved in the generation are taken from a model that describes emotions and communication acts of the robot, based on Plutchik's Wheel of Emotions. Mapping between human Action Units and robotic facial cues is shown in detail through several tables. Some facial expressions produced by random input vectors were shown as examples of non-basic expressions, which are uncommon in humanoid robotics. The role of asymmetry was discussed too. We reported results of the investigation of preference of participants for asymmetrical or symmetrical expressions, and the evaluation of influence of asymmetry on a happy face. Results shown that there is a marked preference for asymmetrical expression in case of negative valence and for symmetrical expression in case of happiness. Future direction of this research involve making the whole interaction smoother and emotion display easier to understand thanks to the support of additional hardware devices.

REFERENCES

Ahn, J., Gobron, S., Silvestre, Q., & Thalmann, D. (2010). Asymmetrical facial expressions based on an advanced interpretation of two-dimensional Russell's emotional model. In *Proceedings of ENGAGE*.

Ahn, J., Gobron, S., Silvestre, Q., Thalmann, D., & Boulic, R. (2011). *Double your face with asymmetric expression of emotions driven by a 3D emotional model*. Paper presented at the Eurographics/ACM SIGGRAPH Symposium on Computer Animation.

Beck, A., Hiolle, A., Mazel, A., & Cañamero, L. (2010). Interpretation of emotional body language displayed by robots. In *Proceedings of the 3rd international workshop on Affective interaction in natural environments*. New York, NY, USA: ACM. doi:10.1145/1877826.1877837

Becker-Asano, C., & Ishiguro, H. (2011). Evaluating facial displays of emotion for the android robot Geminoid F. In *2011 IEEE Workshop on Affective Computational Intelligence (WACI)*. doi:10.1109/WACI.2011.5953147

Beira, R., Lopes, M., Praga, M., Santos-Victor, J., Bernardino, A., & Metta, G., … Saltaren, R. (2006). Design of the robot-cub (iCub) head. In *Proceedings 2006 IEEE International Conference on Robotics and Automation*. doi:10.1109/ROBOT.2006.1641167

Bimler, D. L., & Paramei, G. V. (2006). Facial-expression affective attributes and their configural correlates: Components and categories. *The Spanish Journal of Psychology*, *9*(1), 19–31. doi:10.1017/S113874160000593X PMID:16673619

Borod, J. C., Caron, H. S., & Koff, E. (1981). Asymmetry in positive and negative facial expressions: Sex differences. *Neuropsychologia*, *19*(6), 819–824. doi:10.1016/0028-3932(81)90095-6 PMID:7329529

Borod, J. C., Haywood, C. S., & Koff, E. (1997). Neuropsychological aspects of facial asymmetry during emotional expression: A review of the normal adult literature. *Neuropsychology Review*, *7*(1), 41–60. doi:10.1007/BF02876972 PMID:9243530

Borod, J. C., Koff, E., Yecker, S., Santschi, C., & Schmidt, J. M. (1998). Facial asymmetry during emotional expression: Gender, valence, and measurement technique. *Neuropsychologia*, *36*(11), 1209–1215. doi:10.1016/S0028-3932(97)00166-8 PMID:9842766

Breazeal, C. (2003). Emotion and sociable humanoid robots. *International Journal of Human-Computer Studies*, *59*(1-2), 119–155. doi:10.1016/S1071-5819(03)00018-1

Ekman, P. (2009). *Telling lies: Clues to deceit in the marketplace, politics, and marriage*. New York, NY: W.W. Norton.

Ekman, P., & Friesen, W. V. (1978). *Facial action coding system*. Consulting Psychologists Press.

Ekman, P., Sorenson, E. R., & Friesen, W. V. (1969). Pan-cultural elements in facial displays of emotion. *Science*, *164*(3875), 86–88. doi:10.1126/science.164.3875.86 PMID:5773719

Endo, N., & Takanishi, A. (2011). Development of whole-body emotional expression humanoid robot for ADL-assistive RT services. *Journal of Robotics and Mechatronics*, *23*(6), 969–977.

Fontaine, J. R. J., Scherer, K. R., Roesch, E. B., & Ellsworth, P. C. (2007). The world of emotions is not two-dimensional. *Psychological Science*, *18*(12), 1050–1057. doi:10.1111/j.1467-9280.2007.02024.x PMID:18031411

Grammer, K., & Thornhill, R. (1994). Human (Homo sapiens) facial attractiveness and sexual selection: The role of symmetry and averageness. *Journal of Comparative Psychology*, *108*(3), 233–242. doi:10.1037/0735-7036.108.3.233 PMID:7924253

Hager, J. C., & Ekman, P. (1983). The inner and outer meanings of facial expressions. In J. T. Cacioppo & R. E. Petty, (Eds.), Social psychophysiology: A sourcebook. New York: The Guilford Press.

Harper, R. G., Wiens, A. N., & Matarazzo, J. D. (1978). *Nonverbal communication: The state of the art*. John Wiley & Sons.

Hegel, F., Eyssel, F. A., & Wrede, B. (2010). The social robot Flobi: Key concepts of industrial design. In *Proceedings of the 19th IEEE International Symposium in Robot and Human Interactive Communication (RO-MAN 2010)*. doi:10.1109/ROMAN.2010.5598691

Itoh, K., Miwa, H., Matsumoto, M., Zecca, M., Takanobu, H., & Roccella, S., … Takanishi, A. (2004). Various emotional expressions with emotion expression humanoid robot WE-4RII. In *First IEEE Technical Exhibition Based Conference on Robotics and Automation (TExCRA'04)*. doi:10.1109/TEXCRA.2004.1424983

Kędzierski, J., Muszyński, R., Zoll, C., Oleksy, A., & Frontkiewicz, M. (2013). EMYS—Emotive head of a social robot. *International Journal of Social Robotics*, 5(2), 237–249. doi:10.1007/s12369-013-0183-1

Kishi, T., Otani, T., Endo, N., Kryczka, P., Hashimoto, K., Nakata, K., & Takanishi, A. (2012). Development of expressive robotic head for bipedal humanoid robot. In *Proceedings of IROS 2012*. doi:10.1109/IROS.2012.6386050

Knapp, M. L. (1980). *Essentials of nonverbal communication*. Harcourt School.

Kobayashi, H., Ichikawa, Y., Senda, M., & Shiiba, T. (2002). Toward rich facial expression by face robot. In *Proceedings of 2002 International Symposium on Micromechatronics and Human Science*. doi:10.1109/MHS.2002.1058024

Mazzei, D., Lazzeri, N., Hanson, D., & De-Rossi, D. (2012). HEFES: An Hybrid Engine for Facial Expressions Synthesis to control human-like androids and avatars. In *2012 4th IEEE RAS EMBS International Conference on Biomedical Robotics and Biomechatronics (BioRob)*.

Mehrabian, A. (1972). *Silent messages: Implicit communication of emotions and attitudes*. Wadsworth Publishing Company.

Mehrabian, A. (1980). *Basic dimensions for a general psychological theory: Implications for personality, social, environmental, and developmental studies*. Oelgeschlager, Gunn & Hain.

Mehrabian, A., & Friar, J. T. (1969). Encoding of attitude by a seated communicator via posture and position cues. *Journal of Consulting and Clinical Psychology*, 33(3), 330–336. doi:10.1037/h0027576

Mehrabian, A., & Wiener, M. (1967). Decoding of inconsistent communications. *Journal of Personality and Social Psychology*, 6(1), 109–114. doi:10.1037/h0024532 PMID:6032751

Miwa, H., Okuchi, T., Takanobu, H., & Takanishi, A. (2002). Development of a new human-like head robot WE-4. In *Proceedings of IEEE/RSJ International Conference on Intelligent Robots and Systems*. doi:10.1109/IRDS.2002.1041634

Oh, J., Hanson, D., Kim, W., Han, Y., Kim, J., & Park, I. (2006). Design of android type humanoid robot Albert HUBO. In *Proceedings of the 2006 IEEE/RSJ International Conference on Intelligent Robots and Systems* (pp. 1428–1433). doi:10.1109/IROS.2006.281935

Patterson, M. L., Powell, J. L., & Lenihan, M. G. (1986). Touch, compliance, and interpersonal affect. *Journal of Nonverbal Behavior*, 10(1), 41–50. doi:10.1007/BF00987204

Pelachaud, C., & Poggi, I. (2002). Subtleties of facial expressions in embodied agents. *The Journal of Visualization and Computer Animation*, 13(5), 301–312. doi:10.1002/vis.299

Plutchik, R. (2002). *Emotions and life: Perspectives from psychology, biology, and evolution*. Washington, DC: American Psychological Association.

Poggi, I. (2001). Signals and meanings of gaze in animated faces. In Language, Vision and Music (pp. 133–144). John Benjamins.

Poggi, I. (2006). *Le parole del corpo. Introduzione alla comunicazione multimodale*. Carocci.

Poggi, I., & Pelachaud, C. (2000). Performative facial expressions in animated faces. In J. Cassell, J. Sullivan, S. Prevost, & E. Churchill, (Eds.), Embodied conversational agents. Cambridge: MIT Press.

Raudys, S., & Duin, R. P. W. (1998). Expected classification error of the Fisher linear classifier with pseudo-inverse covariance matrix. *Pattern Recognition Letters*, 19(5-6), 385–392. doi:10.1016/S0167-8655(98)00016-6

Ribeiro, T., & Paiva, A. (2012). The illusion of robotic life: principles and practices of animation for robots. In *Proceedings of the seventh annual ACM/IEEE international conference on Human-Robot Interaction*. New York, NY: ACM. doi:10.1145/2157689.2157814

Russell, J. A. (1980). A circumplex model of affect. *Journal of Personality and Social Psychology, 39*(6), 1161–1178. doi:10.1037/h0077714

Russell, J. A., Lewicka, M., & Niit, T. (1989). A cross-cultural study of a circumplex model of affect. *Journal of Personality and Social Psychology, 57*(5), 848–856. doi:10.1037/0022-3514.57.5.848

Saldien, J., Goris, K., Vanderborght, B., Vanderfaeillie, J., & Lefeber, D. (2010). Expressing emotions with the social robot Probo. *International Journal of Social Robotics, 2*(4), 377–389. doi:10.1007/s12369-010-0067-6

Scherer, K. R. (2005). What are emotions? And how can they be measured? *Social Sciences Information. Information Sur les Sciences Sociales, 44*(4), 695–729. doi:10.1177/0539018405058216

Scherer, K. R., Shuman, V., Fontaine, J. R. J., & Soriano, C. (2013). The GRID meets the Wheel: Assessing emotional feeling via self-report. In *Components of emotional meaning: A sourcebook*. Oxford: Oxford University Press. doi:10.1093/acprof:oso/9780199592746.003.0019

Schmidt, K. L., Liu, Y., & Cohn, J. F. (2006). The role of structural facial asymmetry in asymmetry of peak facial expressions. *Laterality, 11*(6), 540–561. doi:10.1080/13576500600832758 PMID:16966242

Smith, C. A., & Scott, H. S. (1997). A componential approach to the meaning of facial expressions. In J. A. Russell & J. M. Fern (Eds.), *The psychology of facial expression* (pp. 229–254). Paris, France: Editions de la Maison des Sciences de l'Homme. doi:10.1017/CBO9780511659911.012

Thomas, F., & Johnston, O. (1995). *The illusion of life: Disney animation*. Disney Editions.

Trovato, G., Kishi, T., Endo, N., Hashimoto, K., & Takanishi, A. (2012). Evaluation study on asymmetrical facial expressions generation for Humanoid Robot. In *2012 First International Conference on Innovative Engineering Systems (ICIES)*. Alexandria, Egypt. doi:10.1109/ICIES.2012.6530858

Trovato, G., Zecca, M., Kishi, T., Endo, N., Hashimoto, K., & Takanishi, A. (2013). Generation of humanoid robot's facial expressions for context-aware communication. *International Journal of Humanoid Robotics, 10*(1). doi:10.1142/S0219843613500138

Van Breemen, A., Yan, X., & Meerbeek, B. (2005). iCat: an animated user-interface robot with personality. In *Proceedings of the fourth international joint conference on Autonomous agents and multiagent systems*. New York, NY, USA: ACM. doi:10.1145/1082473.1082823

Van Gelder, R. S., & Borod, J. C. (1990). Neurobiological and cultural aspects of facial asymmetry. *Journal of Communication Disorders, 23*(4-5), 273–286. doi:10.1016/0021-9924(90)90004-I PMID:2246383

Vinayagamoorthy, V., Gillies, M., Steed, A., Tanguy, E., Pan, X., Loscos, C., & Slater, M. (2006). *Building expression into virtual characters*. Paper presented at the Eurographics Conference State of the Art Report.

KEY TERMS AND DEFINITIONS

Action Unit: Basic unit of observable movement in human face, used in Ekman's Facial Action Coding System.

Classification: Assignment of an input feature value to a certain class.

Communication Act: Minimal unit of communication, performed via verbal or non-verbal channels.

Facial Cue: Basic movement of a facial part, which contributes to an expression.

Hemiface: One side (left or right) of the face.

Non-Verbal Communication: The process of communication conveyed through sending non-verbal cues.

Valence: Attractiveness or aversiveness of an event, situation, or object, such an emotion.

APPENDIX: TABLES AND FIGURES

Table 1. Overview of human and robotic facial cues for each facial part

Parts	DOF	N. of Human AUs	N. of Robotic Cues Variables	Set Of Possible Configurations Of The Robotic Facial Part
Eyebrows	8	3	3	18
Eyelids	4+1	6	3	19
Eyes direction	3	6	3	23
Mouth	4+3	23	4	21
Jaw	1	5	1	4
Neck	4	9	4	-

Table 2. Mapping of eyebrows AUs into robotic cues

AU	Name	Robotic Cues Variable
1	Inner Brow Raise	CEB(1)
2	Outer Brow Raise	CEB(2)
4	Brow Lowerer	CEB(3)

Table 3. Mapping of eyelids AUs into robotic cues

AU	Name	Robotic Cues Variable
5	Upper Lid Raise	CEL(1), CEL(3)
6	Cheek Raise	CEL(2), CEL(3)
7	Lids Tight	CEL(2)
43	Eye Closure	CEL(1), CEL(3)
45	Blink	-
46	Wink	-

Table 4. Mapping of eyes position AUs into robotic cues

AU	Name	Robotic Cues Variable
61	Eyes Left	CEP(1)
62	Eyes Right	CEP(1)
63	Eyes Up	CEP(2)
64	Eyes Down	CEP(2)
65	Walleye	CEP(3)
66	Crosseye	CEP(3)

Table 5. Mapping of nose AUs into robotic cues

AU	Name	Robotic Cues Variable
9	Nose Wrinkle	-
38	Nostrils Dilate	-
39	Nostrils Compress	-

Table 6. Mapping of mouth AUs into robotic cues

AU	Name	Robotic Cues Variable
	Mouth	
8	Lips Toward Each Other	-
10	Upper Lip Raiser	CM(3)
11	Nasolabial Furrow Deepener	-
12	Lip Corner Puller	CM(1)
13	Sharp Lip Puller	CM(1)
14	Dimpler	CM(1)
15	Lip Corner Depressor	CM(1)
16	Lower Lip Depressor	CM(4)
17	Chin Raiser	CM(4)
18	Lip Pucker	CM(2)
19	Tongue Show	-
20	Lip Stretch	CM(2)
22	Lip Funneler	CM(2)
23	Lip Tightener	CM(3), CM(4)
24	Lip Presser	-
25	Lips Part	CM(3), CM(4)
28	Lips Suck	-
32	Bite	-
33	Blow	-
34	Puff	-
35	Cheek Suck	-
36	Tongue Bulge	-
37	Lip Wipe	-

Table 7. Mapping of jaw AUs into robotic cues

AU	Name	Robotic Cues Variable
26	Jaw Drop	CJ
27	Mouth Stretch	CJ
29	Jaw Thrust	-
30	Jaw Sideways	-
31	Jaw Clencher	-

Table 8. Mapping of neck AUs into robotic cues

AU	Name	Robotic Cues Variable
21	Neck Tightener	-
51	Turn Left	CN(1)
52	Turn Right	CN(1)
53	Head Up	CN(2)
54	Head Down	CN(2)
55	Tilt Left	CN(3)
56	Tilt Right	CN(3)
57	Forward	CN(4)
58	Back	CN(4)

Table 9. A portion of Smith and Scott's table

Facial Cue	Eyebrow Frown	Raise Eyebrows	Raise Upper Eyelid	Raise Lower Eyelid
Muscolar Basis Emotion AUs Expressed	Corrugator Supercilii 4	Medial Frontalis 1	Levator Papabrae Superioris 5	Orbicularis Oculi 6,7
Happiness				X
Surprise		X	X	
Anger	X		X	X
Disgust	X			X
Fear	X	X	X	
Sadness	X	X		

Table 10. Components of the vectors of basic emotions and communication acts

	Mood	Stance	Temperament	Expectation	Certainty	Power Rel.
Neutral	0	0	0	0	0	0
Happiness	66	0	0	0	0	0
Trust	0	66	0	0	0	0
Fear	0	0	66	0	0	0
Surprise	0	0	0	66	0	0
Comprehension	0	0	0	0	66	0
Superiority	0	0	0	0	0	66
Sadness	-66	0	0	0	0	0
Disgust	0	-66	0	0	0	0
Anger	0	0	-66	0	0	0
Anticipation	0	0	0	-66	0	0
Incomprehension	0	0	0	0	-66	0
Inferiority	0	0	0	0	0	-66

Table 11. Preferences of asymmetrical version of the same expression

	Preference for Symmetrical Version	No Preference	Preference for Asymmetrical Version
Disbelief	4.00%	17.30%	78.70%
Annoyance	10.70%	37.30%	52.00%
Disgust	24.00%	20.00%	56.60%
Incomprehension	33.30%	13.30%	53.30%

Table 12. Evaluation of asymmetry effect on happiness

	Preference for Symmetrical Version	No Preference	Preference for Asymmetrical Version
AU4 (brow lowerer)	85.30%	10.70%	4.00%
AU43 (eye closure)	90.70%	8.00%	1.30%
AU10 (upper lip raiser)	85.30%	13.30%	1.30%
AU16 (lower lip depressor)	74.70%	17.30%	8.00%
AU14 (lip corner tightening)	64.90%	27.00%	8.10%

Figure 1. Input and output of the generation system

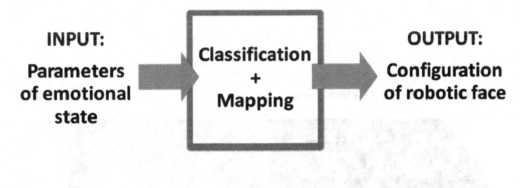

Figure 2. Extended Plutchik's wheel; in colour, the two additional dimensions

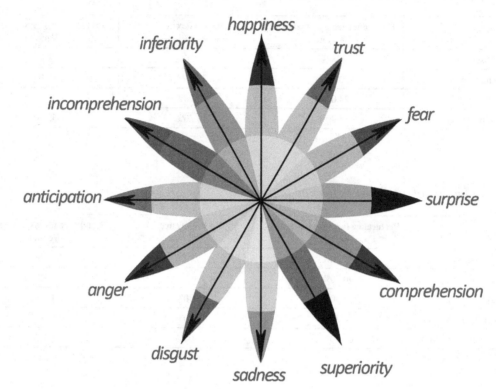

Figure 3. Mapping of eyebrows AUs into robotic cues

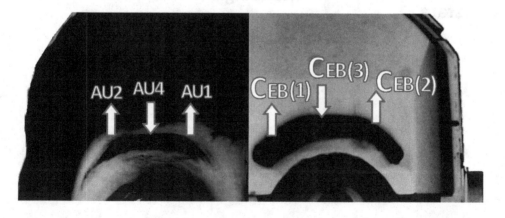

Figure 4. Mapping of eyelids and eye position AUs into robotic cues

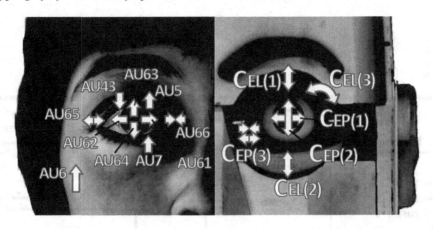

Figure 5. Mapping of mouth and jaw AUs into robotic cues

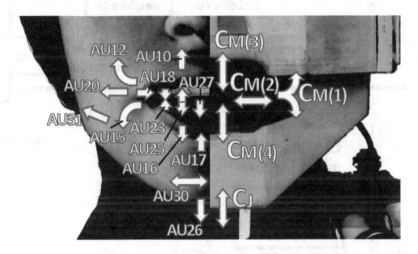

Figure 6. Mapping of neck AUs into robotic cues

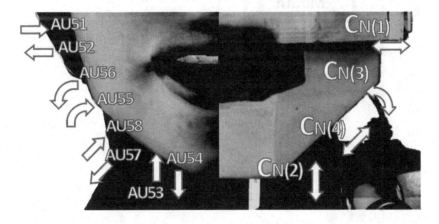

Figure 7. Generation of eyebrows (EB) motor angle values from a sample input with random values

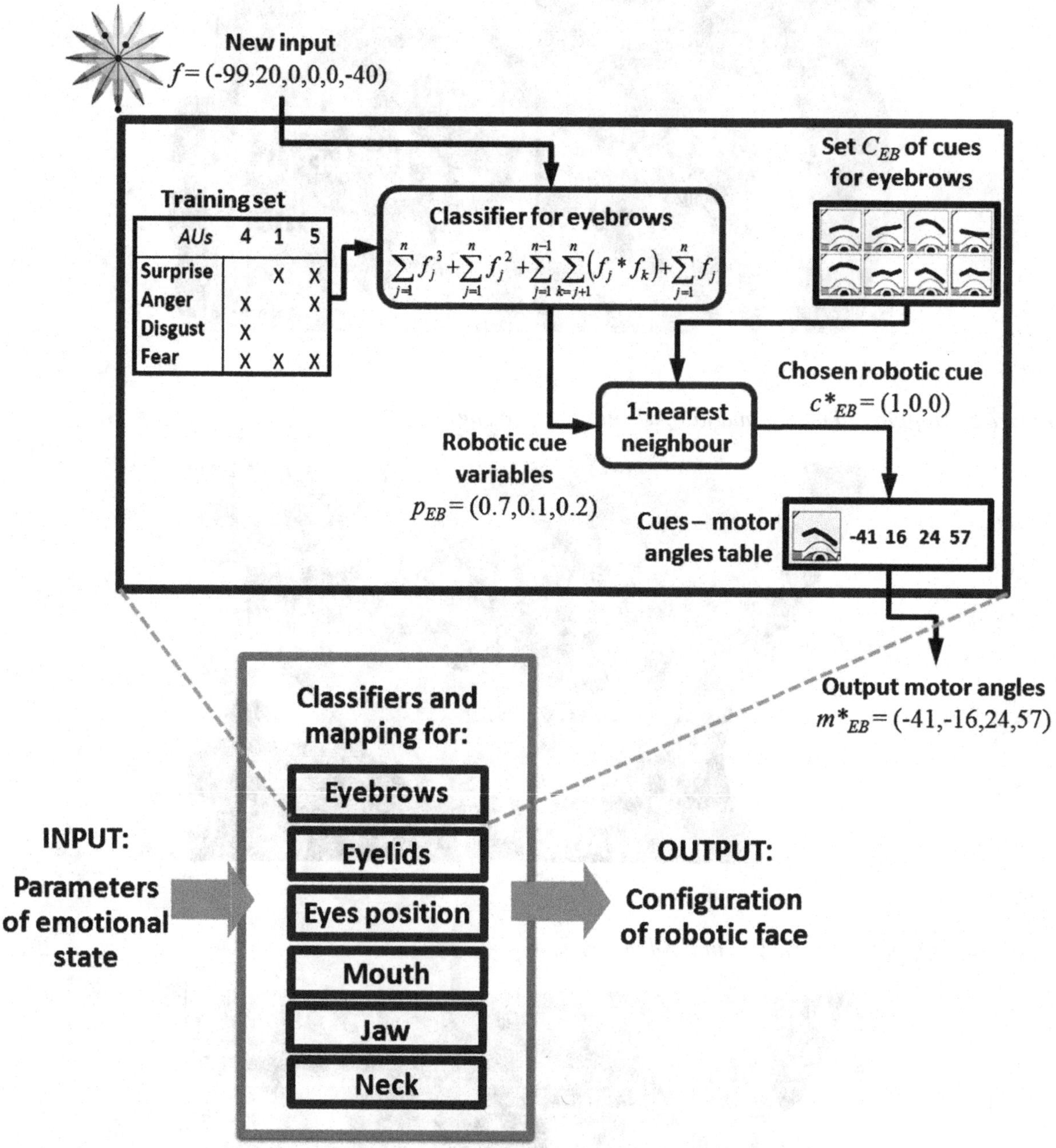

Figure 8. Facial expression produced from vector (0, 0, 95, 0, -62, 35)

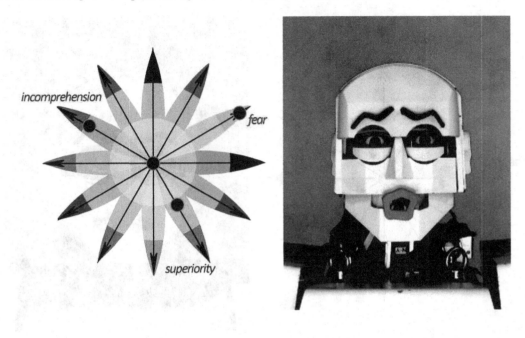

Figure 9. Facial expression produced from vector (0, 70, 39, 56, 0, 0)

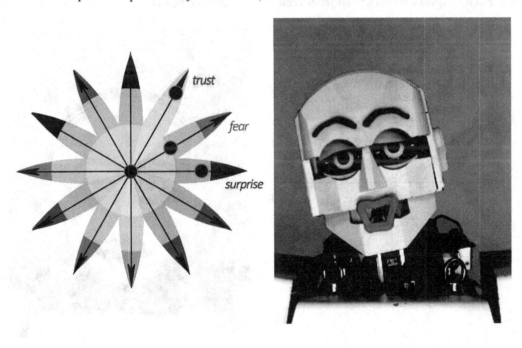

Figure 10. Facial expression produced from vector (51, 0, 0, -89, 0, -60)

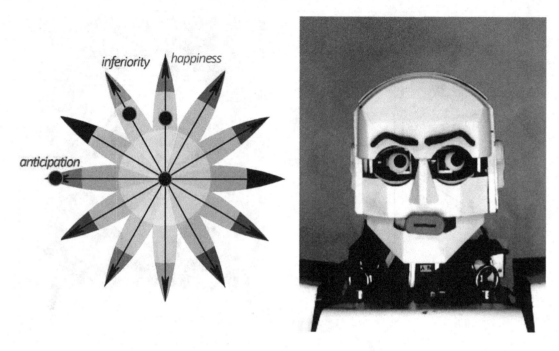

Figure 11. Facial expression produced from vector (0, 0, -58, 68, 0, -87)

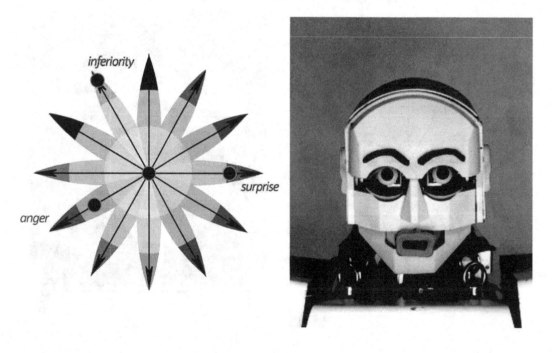

Figure 12. Facial expression produced from vector (-60, 67, -98, 0, 0, 0)

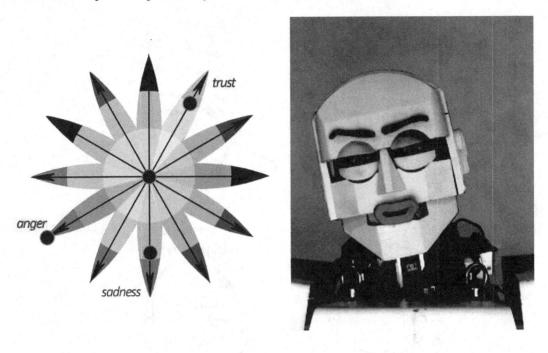

Figure 13. Facial expression produced from vector (0, 0, 0, -46, 77, 79)

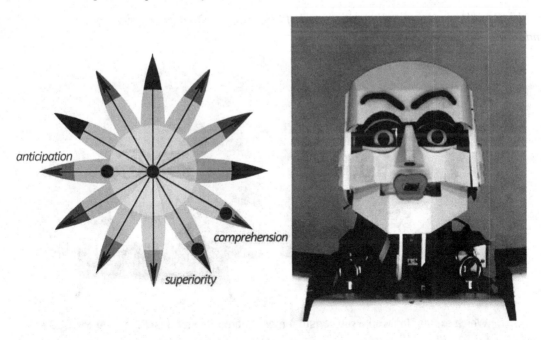

Figure 14. Art sketches of symmetrical and asymmetrical versions of Disgust and Superiority

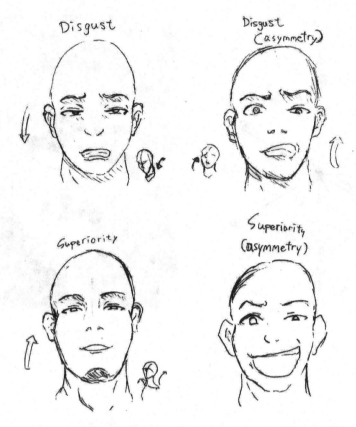

Figure 15. Facial expressions of happiness and of "happiness with asymmetrical eyebrow", used in the second part of the survey on asymmetry

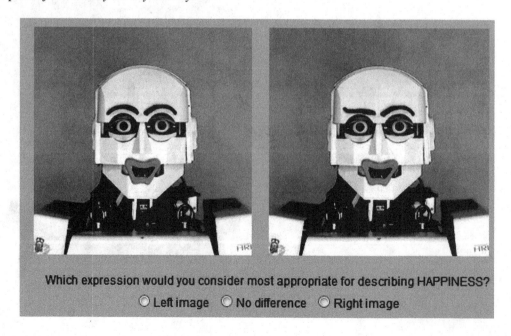

Chapter 12
Intention and Body–Mood Engineering via Proactive Robot Moves in HRI

O. Can Görür
Middle East Technical University, Turkey

Aydan M. Erkmen
Middle East Technical University, Turkey

ABSTRACT

This chapter focuses on emotion and intention engineering by socially interacting robots that induce desired emotions/intentions in humans. The authors provide all phases that pave this road, supported by overviews of leading works in the literature. The chapter is partitioned into intention estimation, human body-mood detection through external-focused attention, path planning through mood induction and reshaping intention. Moreover, the authors present their novel concept, with implementation, of reshaping current human intention into a desired one, using contextual motions of mobile robots. Current human intention has to be deviated towards the new desired one by destabilizing the obstinance of human intention, inducing positive mood and making the "robot gain curiosity of human". Deviations are generated as sequences of transient intentions tracing intention trajectories. The authors use elastic networks to generate, in two modes of body mood: "confident" and "suspicious", transient intentions directed towards the desired one, choosing among intentional robot moves previously learned by HMM.

1. INTRODUCTION

Recent developments on both artificial intelligence and hardware capabilities for the robots resulted in greater advances in the field of Human-Robot Interaction (HRI). Nowadays, robots are integral parts of both industry and our homes, assisting or replacing humans but working with them(Erden & Tomiyama, 2010). Assistant robots should thus understand and model intents and tendencies in these interactions if they want to satisfy needs of their interacting human agents (Yokoyama & Omori, 2010). Such robots have the capability to recognize intentions and emotions of other agents

DOI: 10.4018/978-1-4666-7278-9.ch012

and can interact exhibiting social behaviors and are consequently called socially intelligent robots (Kerstin Dautenhahn & Billard, 1999).

During social interactions between intelligent agents, estimating the intentions and emotions of one another, termed social cognition (Fong et al., 2003), is required to infer the social behavior of the opponent which eventually results in inducing one's own intentions onto the other by compromises or persuasion (Heinze, 2003; K. A. Tahboub, 2006). Morphing actions on intentions also called reshaping (Durdu et al., 2011) are strategic moves of an agent with the purpose of attaining a desired change on the other interacting agent based on the statement that one's intentions direct one's future planning (Bratman, 1999). In our previous study Durdu et al.(2011), introduced a new approach on intention reshaping performing social moves for changing current human intentions. We extend this work by controlling this change according to obeying a desired intention trajectory. Full-autonomous robots then model social cognitions from the on-line observations of human headings and trajectories, planning their own trajectories in ways familiar to the human using elastic networks. According to the detected human-body mood and the estimated current intention of the person, generation of trajectories aims first to break the obstinance of the person increasing his/her confidence with the robot and the environment, then enabling reshaping actions. This approach emulates a social interaction between humans, increasing the chance of the robots to understand human behaviors and react proactively.

The main motivation behind developing such sociable robot having enhanced social cognition abilities is to realize real life cooperation scenarios with human, such as guiding people in emergency situations where verbal communication is impossible by classifying them as being confident or suspicious and treating them accordingly. In addition, these robots can be used commercially catching the attention of the people and leading them towards their shops generating purchase intentions.

Moreover, they can be versatile companions for the needy in smart homes by understanding intentions and offering service even when intentions are quickly forgotten by patients.

The phases in our intention reshaping system as it is for every social engineering attempts of socializing agents are: choosing a desired intention; estimating the current intention of the person; also detecting human body-mood as *confident* or *suspicious* underlying resilience to social engineering; generation of transient intention trajectories (way points) towards convergence to the desired one. Transient trajectories are generated in dense intention areas in the feature space "familiar" to human subjects around the current intention until a *confident mood* detected on the human. The aim of this generation is to "break the obstinance of the person" and "gain the curiosity and the trust of the person" relying on the psychological research that a *confident mood* results in more external-focused attention (Fredrickson, 2003; Grol et al. 2013; Sedikides, 1992). The idea of generating transient intentions close to the human's current one with the aim of inducing confidence originates from the research that, inducing a *confident mood* is realized by gently approaching to the person, making him/her feel more comfortable with the social interaction (Butler & Agah, 2001; Huettenrauch et al., 2006; Mead & Matarić, 2011). In addition, detection of the human body-mood is based on the orientation of the human heading towards the robots adapted from "proxemic behaviors" in psychology to HRI as studied in (Pacchierotti et al., 2005). Each generated transient intention is realized by the robot choosing adequate heading and trajectory planning based on learned experience.

Figure 1 demonstrates our approach on intention reshaping with all essential phases in robot cognition towards intention engineering. As in the figure, after the robot moves, human intention is estimated and compared with the desired one. A mismatch results in the detection of the human body-mood and then search for a new way point (learned trajectory) according to this mood being *suspicious* or *confident* inspired from (S. Lee & Son, 2008). We named detected moods as execution modes as they decide on the path planning strategy. In upcoming sections we focus on each phases of social intention engineering by robots demonstrated in Figure 1.

2. INTENTION ESTIMATION

2.1 Related Works

Designing sociable robots, such as robots helping the elderly (Dario et al., 2001; Erden & Tomiyama, 2010) as a human assistance is a non-trivial problem since human have variable intentions due to forgetting or unpredictable interactions (Koo & Kwon, 2009; Yokoyama & Omori, 2010). Quality interactions between human and robot necessitates robots to be more anticipatory and act much more like human beings (Jenkins et al., 2007). Therefore, the design process of interacting robots with humans requires utilization of prediction or estimation of intention for a natural and intelligent cooperation with a human agent.

Characterization of actions yielding intentions plays a crucial part in estimation of these intentions. Social psychologists have been stating for many years that human behavior is goal-directed, that is one's action reflects the intention (Baum et al., 1970; Bratman, 1999; Dennett, 1989; Lewin, 1952). Most of the actions a human realizes are designed in advance and executed as the plan proceeds. Moreover, some of these actions may become routine which is performed automatically such as driving a car (Ajzen, 1985). If one can become aware of the actions required to attain a certain goal, which is characterization of the actions, then classification would yield classes of goal oriented intentions. In the literature, some already characterized and studied actions for the prediction of the intention includes mimics, body movements, hand gestures, such as facial expres-

sions (Adolphs et al., 1994; Horstmann, 2003), walking or running actions (Chouchourelou & Matsuka, 2006; Roether et al., 2009), pointing (Manera et al., 2010; Sato et al., 2007) and dancing (Dittrich et al., 1996; Sevdalis & Keller, 2010). In addition, research in psychology exists in the field of "self-recognition" which portrays the ability of humans recognizing their own acts by kinematic displays of gestures (Daprati et al., 2007), by drawing (Knoblich & Prinz, 2001) and through body movements (K. K. Lee & Xu, 2004; Meltzoff, 1995). Although, leading works are primarily on body movements, and gestures, there are also auditory approaches on listening audio outputs resulted from actions (Haggard et al., 2002; Kohler et al., 2002) and some habitual actions in neuroimaging and neurophysiology researches like grasping for eating (Fogassi et al., 2005) and drinking (de Lange et al., 2008). All of these action types form the characterization of intentional attitudes of human beings within environmental contexts where they are realized. Those attitudes generally include human orientation, position, posture, gestures or facial expressions with contextual information leading to reasonable estimation of human intention. In our demonstrative approach in Section 2.2, we utilize the orientation and trajectory of the human subjects for the purpose of intention estimation.

After a reasonable characterization of actions, classification is the second requirement for intention estimation where Machine Learning (ML) is widely applied (Durdu et al., 2011). Since human or robot actions agents leading to intentions are sequential processes, classical sequential supervised learning is mainly used to construct a classifier which predicts intention classes of newly observed actions given training examples of actions previously experienced (Mitchell, 1997). Since sequential supervised learning closely related to time-series analysis and sequence classification (Dietterich, 2002), these tasks are also considered in the intention estimation problem: using gaze and gestures to control mouse and keyboard inputs

Figure 1. Flow chart of our demonstrative implementation

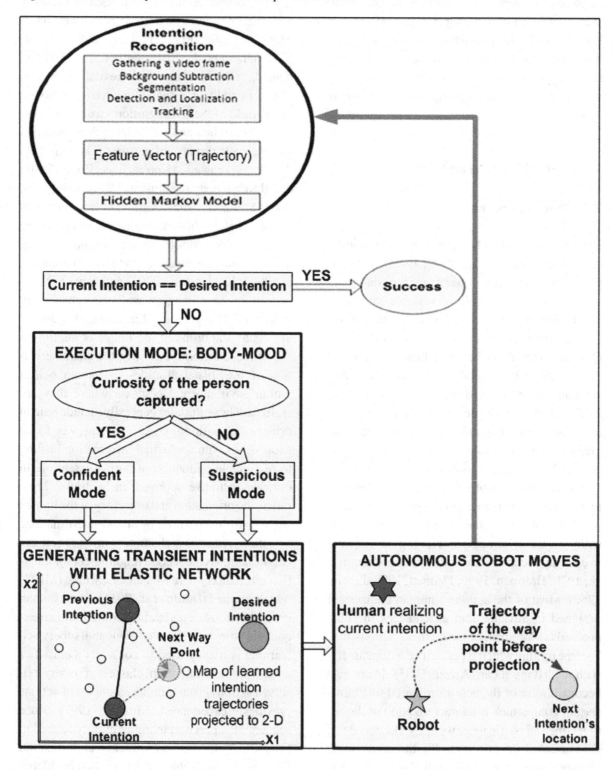

on a PC. In order to understand what the person intents to do, the possible actions that need to be classified are hand gestures and arm motions on keyboard, the gazing in different directions or winking eyes for mouse control (Arai & Mardiyanto, 2011; Vlasenko & Wendemuth, 2009).

Earlier studies in intention recognition merged artificial intelligence (AI) and psychology to infer the goal of a human, requiring the actions to be organized into a plan structure (C. Schmidt et al., 1978). In the work of Schmidt et al. they discussed the application of mathematical psychology and AI in a system called "Believer", concerned with single-actor sequences and reports goal-directed actions with possibility of failure or success in achieving the goal (C. Schmidt et al., 1978). The work in (Wilensky, 1983) plans and understands common sense human behaviors and body language by recognizing the plan. Later, Kautz and Allen (1986) approached the problem with a new theory that recognized a plan resulting from complex actions including certain hierarchies based on the taxonomy of possible actions performed. They could link complex sequential actions to a general plan. Another approach to plan recognition was made by measuring the uncertainty based on Bayesian probability theory (Charniak & Goldman, 1993). In this work, inferring an agent's plan was realized by choosing the most likely interpretation from a set of observations using Bayesian updating. In another work using Bayesian networks, the authors monitored pedestrians' intention in traffic, and developed a system warning drivers for possible accidents (S. Schmidt & Färber, 2009). This work is an example of learning possible plans of humans by observing and classifying their actions from recorded traffic videos.

Inferring human intentions from actions using collected visual data is another field of intention estimation that we demonstrate in Section 2.2. In (T. Mori et al., 2004), the authors focus on recognizing human actions in daily-life such as sitting, lying, standing etc. They modeled these actions

using continuous HMM which recognizes actions from a tree representation. They start from high level of the model recognizing coarse actions and then, refine by using parent-child relation of nodes in the tree of hierarchical actions. For example, if the first level estimated the action as sitting, lower levels gives probabilities on whether the person is sitting on the chair or on the floor. This method makes the recognition process easier and more realizable by simplifying estimations in low-level, into a decreased amount of states, and by classifying the actions at coarse level. In (Taketoshi Mori et al., 2005; Shimosaka et al., 2005), the recognition of basic human action classes of sitting, running, walking, standing etc. uses kernel vectors based on switching linear dynamics, generally utilized for tracking and classifying complex motions of human skeleton.

The literature survey provided up to now did not involve human subjects interacting with another agent. The studies about estimating intention during human-machine or robot interaction are more recent. In (K. Tahboub, 2005), the author simulated a scenario with two robots where one robot is controlled by a human operator while the other estimates the operator's intention by observing the actions of the remotely controlled robot. Although this work is a simulated one without real human-robot interaction, it involves real-time intention estimation. Here, a model of intention recognition is defined based on four-level decomposition of intentional behavior, the first two being classical intentional levels realized by people starting to plan a desired state for the intended action whereas the other levels reverse engineer the first two, reaching a recognized plan or intention by observing the actions of the human. Modeling intention states with action scenarios are realized using Dynamic Bayesian Networks.

The work of (Z. Wang et al., 2013) proposes a method which probabilistically models movements aiming certain intentions. The authors use Bayes theorem in their online algorithm providing real-time intention estimation. To test their system performance, they create a scenario requiring fast reactions where the robot and an opponent human play table-tennis, where a decision making is carried out on the type of action (angle, speed) before hitting the ball. This was realized by estimating the target, to where the human intended to send ball, observing his/her actions. The estimated intentions also encompass basic actions like, jumping, crouching, kick-high or low in the table-tennis game.

2.2 Implementation

In our demonstrative implementation, we design a system where our robot is interacting with the human in their daily lives in a living room environment. We acquire data from a ceiling camera in a room which has a wider range of tracking the human trajectories, resulting in the estimation of daily intentions in real-time; allowing the robot to react proactively in order to reshape human inten-

tions into desired ones (Durdu et al., 2012). The room is equipped with a coffee table, a working table and a bookshelf. In addition, to interact with our human subjects we have two contextual mobile robots that are a mobile 2-steps and a mobile chair both autonomous (see Figure 2). All of the possible observed actions that a human subject can undergo are listed in Table 1.

A camera deployed in the middle of the ceiling of the room tracks human and robots generating their trajectories. Region of interest (ROI) of the camera is 240x320 pixels. Based on the experiments with human subjects entering the room not having any prior information about the objects or the autonomy in the room, intention feature space is generated. There are three mobile objects to be detected, labeled and localized, which are the human subject, the chair and the 2-steps robots. In each frame, a feature vector is extracted representing the location sequences of all of these three objects. There are two major parts for the

Figure 2. (a) Objects in the experimental room seen from the ceiling camera; (b) 2-steps robot; (c) Chair robot

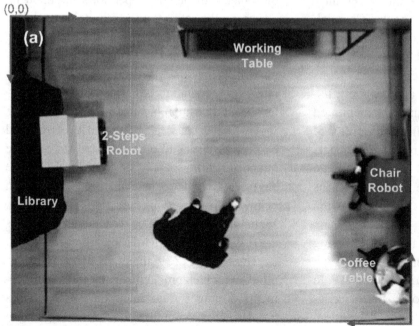

Table 1. List of observable actions and their labeled intentions in our application

#	Observable Actions	Labeled Intention	Abbreviation
A1	Discovering the environment	Discovering	Discovering
A2	Going to the Coffee Table	Drinking Coffee	Coffee
A3	Going to the Library	Getting book from Library	Library
A4	Going to the Work Table	Sitting on the Table	Table

image processing being detection and localization. Detection processes are the common image processing methods used for detecting moving objects in the video frames such as; background subtraction, morphological closing, blob analysis and merging. In the localization part, we track each moving object from their colors using Kalman filter where being green is for the 2-steps, blue the chair robot and the remaining moving object is the human.

We constructed a model characterizing intention actions of Table 1 as a set o sequences of emissions using HMM which suits well to our system since we have hidden states being intentions and observable actions being sequences of locations. The model thus finds the most probable set of state (intention) transitions corresponding to a certain observed action. Since we have hidden states being intentions and observable actions being sequences of locations, HMM suits well to our system. Dynamic programming techniques are generally used for model generation from observed data. Baum-Welch algorithm was introduced in (Baum et al., 1970) finding state transition probabilities, observation probabilities and state initialization arrays. For the latter task, testing, Viterbi algorithm was used frequently calculating the most likely states (Viterbi, 1967). As for our application of HMM, a database of extracted feature descriptors, being agent trajectories consisting of coordinates in consequent video frames, are labeled with intentions based on actions done by whether the agent human or robot. These feature descriptors with labeled intentions train our HMM that is subsequently used to estimate

current intention when viewing a certain human heading. In its traditional usage of HMMs, there are two sub-models to be well defined beforehand: state transition model and observation (emission) model (Yamato et al., 1992). Our HMM uses four possible intentions given in Table 1 as the states in the transition model to calculate state transition matrix while the trajectory information (sequences of locations on camera frames with grids) is utilized in observation model to calculate the emission matrix. After estimating the intention, we are finding the most probable trajectory that the human subject will go through to be utilized in elastic nets search algorithm. An example of estimated current intention trajectory is given within Figure 3 where state transition and emission matrices are mentioned nearby.

3. HUMAN BODY-MOOD DETECTION THROUGH EXTERNAL-FOCUSED ATTENTION

3.1 Moods behind Focused Attention

In intention engineering by proactive robots, the major aim is to reshape human intention into a desired new one by autonomous robot moves. Here, the critical point is to make the human subject observe and respond to robot moves and enter an interaction even if the person is obstinately having another intention. The question of how one can break this obstinance leading the person to more external-focused attention and making him/her be interested with the robot is answered

Figure 3. Demonstration of current intention trajectory estimation. Previous trajectory is the observed trajectory of the human recorded in the last 7 seconds where the currently estimated trajectory is the one human subject is expected to follow next. This trajectory is chosen among the trajectory space of the intention of 'discovering' which is the currently estimated intention written on the top-left corner of the snapshot.

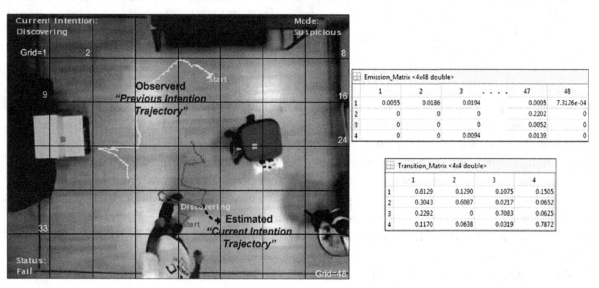

by researches examining the relationship between human mood and attention in social behaviors. Cunningham (1988a, 1988b) examined the effect of positive and negative mood of the people on sociability. In the conducted experiments in (Cunningham, 1988a), subjects are partitioned into two groups: one were induced with Velten Mood (positive thought experiment); the others received depressed mood induction. The resultant experiments showed that the first group with positive mood indicated significantly greater amount of social behavior than the second group. It is stated that, the subjects in the depressed mood preferred thinking while sitting or napping alone rather than exhibiting a pro-social behavior.

Wood et al. (1990) represented the effect of the mood on self-focused attentions. The authors stated that there should be inducers for self-focused attention which serve as a depression state but are not a normal state. It was tested that sad mood depression or negative moods induced self-focused

attention while the positive moods being happy or neutral moods did not. Watson and Tellegen (1985) added that, positive mood states can be listed as happy, cheerful, confident and relaxed whereas the negative ones are anger, anxiety, suspicion and sadness. In our demonstrative intention reshaping approach, we generalized and named the negative mood states as *suspicious* and positive mood states as *confident* adapted from (S. Lee & Son, 2008).

The work mostly inspiring our approach on the relation of attention and mood was in (Sedikides, 1992), which examined not only the inducers of self-focused attention but also the moods resulting in an external-focused attention. The author proves that "positive moods may lead to external-focused attention" which is logically the exact opposite relation between negative moods and self-focused attention. Sedikides (1992) partitioned subjects into three groups conditioned by one of three moods: sad, neutral and happy. After inducing these moods on the subjects by asking them to recall related emotional events, the author wanted them to write a story either about themselves or someone else they know well. The classification was done according to the story clause: if it is about self, the subject is labeled as self-focused or else it is said external-focused. The experiments showed that sad mood induced a great deal of self-focused attention. In addition, the author demonstrated as a new fact that the positive mood (happy) resulted in external-focused attention more than the other two moods. Similarly, in the works (Fredrickson, 2003; Grol et al., 2013; Wadlinger & Isaacowitz, 2006), it is stated that positive moods or emotional states broadens perceptions of visual attention when compared to the neutral or negative emotions.

Any intention reshaping requires breaking the obstinate intention of human subjects and thus, their self-focused attention and captivates their curiosity and interest due to forced induction of external-focused attention. If the person has a negative mood, named as *suspicious* about the robot, we first aimed to induce a positive mood on the person, and place him/her in *confident* mood. A confident person will be able to have more external-focused attention and be curious about robot moves. Confident and suspicious moods are used to guide people to exits in an emergency situation in a crowded scenario (S. Lee & Son, 2008). There, a Belief-Desired-Intention (BDI) model for humans is generated classifying their confidences in the environment. In order to be able to induce moods, one naturally needs a methodology to understand the emotional mood of the person (whether confident or suspicious) by only observing his/her body movements.

3.2 Emotional Communications

Cowie and Douglas-Cowie (1995) stated that humans communicate through two channels which are either explicit or implicit. The messages via the explicit channel are physically detectable messages such as; speaking, gesturing, moving, posing etc. and are largely researched under the topic of intention detection from the actions, as discussed earlier in this chapter. The implicit ones are described by the authors as the way of how to receive messages transmitted through explicit channel (Cowie et al., 2001). In our daily interactions, we use same words or exhibit same actions that may mean differently according to the implicit emphasis on words or emotions hidden in these actions. Likewise, we make sense the actions of the other agent by detecting or predicting emotions of the speaker. Due to the fact that human interactions includes these implicit channels, researches in the field of HRI try to develop robots capable of social cognitions in order to interact with humans proactively satisfying their implicit social aims such as: emotions, intentions, etc. Fong et al.(2003) called such robots as "socially interactive robots" which can basically detect emotions, recognize models of human agents and develop social relationships. In the literature, robots are used for persuasion, changing the feelings, attitudes or behaviors of the interacting human agents (Fogg, 1999, 2002); as a mediator teaching social interaction skills in autism (Werry et al., 2001); or as a an avatar representing a human agent (Paulos & Canny, 1998).

Here the question arose how robots model emotions or implicit messages emitted by human agents. Since 1872, starting with Darwin's famous research (1872), there are a lot of researches conducted in psychology on behavioral expressions of emotions in humans. Apart from the researches on emotions with facial expressions (Beaudry et al., 2013; Reisenzein et al., 2013; S. Wang et al., 2010) and emotions with vocal characteristics (Jessen & Kotz, 2011; Sauter et al.,2013; Scherer, 2003), there are also works on bodily expressions of emotions which is the main focus of intention engineering by robot interactions, and thus, of our study. Wallbott (1998) analyzes whether body gestures, movements, postures or quality of movement behaviors reflect human emotions. This work tabulates all emotion models of Darwin with certain posture and movements pattern into motionless, passive actions yielding the emotion of sadness; purposeless movements, clapping hands, jumping and dancing yielding the emotion of joy; head and body held erected yielding the emotion of pride etc. Although the work of (Ekman & Friesen, 1974) states that bodily-movements only give the intensity of the emotion and there is no specific body movement or gesture for an emotion, there are influential researches indicating that emotional state of a person may influence his/her bodily-movements (Chouchourelou & Matsuka, 2006; Hatfield et al., 1993).

The field of computational emotion modeling in interaction aware systems with visual data is sparsely touched where most works are on emotion detection from facial expressions. Breazeal (2003) develops a humanoid robot that has several degree of freedoms emulating a human face and has the capability to learn human facial emotions. This sociable robot models these facial emotions and can apply these expressions while interacting with a human subject. Moreover, their robot called 'Kismet' can adapt its facial emotional mood to the one of its interacting human subject. Another work detecting moods from facial expressions and postures is given in (Wada et al., 2004) with a robot called 'seal robot' aiming to interact with the elderly to overcome stress and improve feelings. Similarly, Kozima et al. (2005) develop a creature-like robot detecting emotions from facial expressions of autistic people for use in therapy. Within the context of therapeutics, examples can be extended as in (K Dautenhahn & Werry, 2000; Robins et al., 2005; Vanderborght et al., 2012; Werry et al., 2001).

A study on emotion detection system using speech is given in (Scheutz et al., 2006). The authors use speech emotion filter introduced in (Burkhardt & Sendlmeier, 2000) to synthesize the affective state on human speech. There, a robot was able to infer emotions of sadness, anger, fright and happiness from the speech of its interacting human and react accordingly by speaking in tones related to these emotions. A similar work examining vocal interactions based on emotions is given in (Scherer, 2003).

Barakova and Lourens (2010) model emotional movements during games with robot companions. The authors used Laban movement analysis to characterize human motions as emotional states, which is a method to observe and describe human body movements categorized as strength, directness, speed and flow of motion. An example given in the study analyzes the difference between hitting a person and reaching for a glass. Here, the strength and the speed of the former movement are clearly higher than the latter one. Using these categories of the human body, authors were able to map body-movements of children during a game with a social robot into four basic emotions which are sadness, fear, anger and joy.

3.3 Generating Readiness for HRI in Human: Body-Mood Detection

In our study, unlike most of the works using off-line body movement detection stated above, we are detecting on-line emotional feelings (mood in real-time) from human headings. That is, we are measuring the confidence and trust of the person to our robots by using only visual data of human tracked from a ceiling camera. Our work utilizes a psychological work called '*proxemics*' studying the spatial interaction between humans (Hall et al., 1968). This study is well examined in HRI in the works of (Christensen et al., 2005; Pacchierotti et al., 2005) by dividing spatial distance around the person into four categories of interactions which are intimate, personal, social and public. The authors examined the spatial relation between a robot and human subjects in a hallway where an interaction is unavoidable and observed that proxemics is valid in HRI and that robots should be aware of these relations. Additionally, Butler and Agah (2001) examined human moods when a robot approach to a subject. It is stated that if this approach is slow and direct, the observed mood of the human is comfortable. Similarly, in the more recent works in HRI (Huettenrauch et al., 2006; Mead & Matarić, 2011; Takayama & Pantofaru, 2009; Walters et al., 2011), authors state that a human's approaching to a robot yields his/her comfort with the robot according to the interaction regions stated by proxemic behaviors.

We designed a novel on-line mood detection system taking into account proxemic behaviors. In our work, a person allowing robots to enter his/her intimate region is detected to be comfortable with the robot and labeled as *confident*. On the other hand, a person showing no interest in our robot even after robot moves is determined to be in an uncomfortable mood labeled as *suspicious*. We extended comparative studies of relation between attention and mood, by contributing that a confident person (positive mood) gives more attention on our robot (external-focused attention) making him ready for an interaction. The application of mood detection system and the statement of "confident person yields more attention on the robots" are experimented in real-time, details of which are given this section and Section 5.

This section demonstrates our methodology behind body-mood detection. Spatial relation between a robot and a human subject leads us to a level of familiarity such that, a person's heading towards a robot allowing it to enter his/her intimate region (which is closer than 30cm) indicates that s/he feels comfortable putting him/her in a *confident mood* and ready to start an interaction. On the contrary, staying or moving away from the robot reveals suspicion or unconcern of the person. We observe the reaction of the person just after each robot move, and proceed with body-mood detection from human posture and headings. Initially, all human entering the interaction room is assumed in *suspicious mood*. After the robot makes its move, we compare the location of the human before and after the movement. If the direction of motion is towards the robot and the person is close enough to the robot (intimate zone in proxemics (Pacchierotti et al., 2005)), we state the person is *confident*. We found that the person can give more external-focused attention to our robot as Sedikides (1992) stated, making our intention reshaping feasible. On the other hand, if the heading shows no concern with the robot, *suspicious mode* starts. Here, the aim becomes to switch the mood to *confident* and gain the human curiosity by roaming around the current intention of the person (in feature space) regardless of how far they are from the desired intention.

The detection of human heading is simply realized after localization by geometrical approaches on 2-D image plane comparing the following tendency before and after consecutive robot moves (see Figure 4). Actual heading is the direction of motion of the human whereas the ideal heading is the heading directly towards the robot. Since the human may approach the robot from different sides of the robot, we define *angle of curiosity* determining a level of curiosity of the person towards the robot. Confident mood is detected on the human with the requirements: the robot is in the intimate region of the human (close enough to interact, in our case 75 pixels); the human displaced more than 10 pixels (does not stand still); and the *angel of curiosity* below 45 degrees.

Two examples from real-time scenarios are given in Figure 4. In part (a), the person is detected to be *confident* whereas in part (b) the person bypasses the robot without caring about its movement and a *suspicious mood* is detected. According to these modes, the robot will be realizing the desired intention of 'sitting on the table' in Figure 4(a); on the other hand, in Figure 4(b), the robot will be still trying to gain the curiosity of the person making him *confident*. Different strategies in path planning according to these two modes are realized by elastic networks. More results on this topology in real-time scenarios are given in Section 5.

Figure 4. Examples of body mood detection (execution modes). (a) Human subject approached robot with about 35 degrees of angle of curiosity leading to confident mood; (b) Human subject bypassed the chair robot not caring about its move switching to suspicious mood.

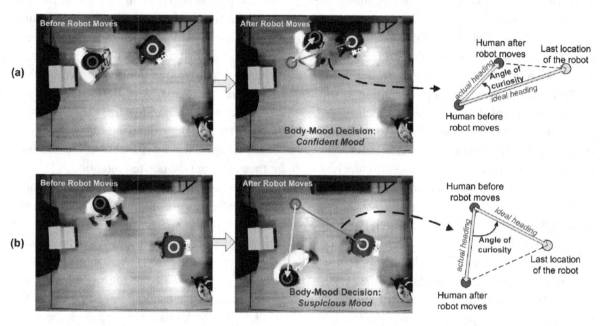

4. PATH PLANNING THROUGH MOOD INDUCTION AND RESHAPING INTENTION

The mood of the person is primordial in deciding upon the next robot path planning. The system starts with *suspicious mood* and generated robot trajectories need to induce *confident mood* on the person making him confident with our robots. After detection of the *confident mood*, the next step is toward reshaping the intention of the person into a desired one, through transient intentions.

4.1 Inducing Emotional Mood on a Human

For the purpose of inducing confident mood (positive mood in general), our robots should socially interact with the person in a trustful and comforting manner. In the literature, there are a few works covering the related topic. Suzuki et al.(1998) clearly showed the effect of approach-ing a person on the induced emotional state. The factors affecting the emotional states are the robot velocity, human-robot distance and robot gestures. The most influential work on our study is given in (Butler & Agah, 2001). In this study, the authors examined human-robot interactions with different robot behavior patterns such as: the robot approaches the person and bypasses him. They analyzed the level of human mood (in this case mood is measured as the level of comfort) during the interaction experiments based on the speed, distance and the design of the robot where the experimenters were not informed about the robots. Results showed that, robot approaching slow and direct resulted in more comfortable and attention taking moods on the subjects. In addition, parallel results are found in more recent studies in (Huettenrauch et al., 2006; Mead & Matarić, 2011; Takayama & Pantofaru, 2009). However, none of these works approached the problem from the robot's perspective since they only consider psychological status of human to different robot moves. Our approach is to plan paths for robots according to the currently detected human intention leading the robots towards the current human location. Robots' following these paths slowly is expected to increase confidence of the human subjects and gain their curiosity afterwards (Section 5).

4.2 Intention Reshaping

Intention reshaping, being the final stage of our study, aims to change the current human intention into a desired new intention. This is accomplished by autonomous robot moves; basically following previously learned trajectories (built robot experience by HMM). The robot traces a move to yield the desired intention by mimicking a previously learned trajectory leading to that intention.

In the literature, relevant works in psychology deal mainly with the effects of intention change on behavioral changes (Webb & Sheeran, 2006) and also with intentional change on children under the effect of what adults do (Carpente et al., 2005; Meltzoff, 1995). In the field of HRI, these behavioral or intentional changes are examined according to different types of robotic interactions with human subjects. The study in (E. Wang et al., 2006) surveys the subjects' intentional behaviors in accordance with the variations of head movements of a humanoid robot such as: motionless, slow human face tracking, tracking fast and turning away from the human face. The survey results show that the subjects stated different perceptions and behaviors for these head motions. That is, changing the head movements induces notable changes in intentional behavior of humans.

The works in (Terada & Ito, 2010; Terada et al., 2007) focus on how intention attribution is affected by different artifacts (non-humanoid robots). In this study, the authors use chair and cube as robots and observed the attributed intentions of human subjects to the movements of these robots. The results demonstrate that, human subjects attribute different intentions to these reactive movements

depending on the shape of the artifact, and the perceived goal of the artifacts. Similarly, Parlangeli et al.(2013) conclude that, the attribution of mental states or intentions to the mechanical structures or artifacts is affected by personal and contextual differences in human-robot interactions.

Intention reshaping idea towards intention engineering by HRI was first introduced in our previous work (Durdu et al., 2011). In this study, the aim was to observe the intentional changes on human subjects after the proactive and contextual robot movements of non-humanoid robots (robot-like chair and 2-steps). The work compares the used HMM and Observable Operator Model (OOM) in intention estimation before and after the robot movements underlining intentional changes. For example, a human preparing a coffee in the experimental room, is distracted by the movement of 2-steps robot in front of the library, and changed his/her intention to taking a book from a library. This is a clear example of intention attribution to the 2-steps artifact robot and reshaping of the intention accordingly. However, in this work the robots are commanded from outside with a joystick and intention estimation and intention comparison were realized off-line.

4.3 Controlled Reshaping through Transients

Our main contribution in the approach of this section is to create a closed loop system which reshapes previously recognized human intention into a desired one by full-autonomous sociable robot moves planned by Elastic Networks in real-time experiments. In our novel approach, we first detect body-mood of the human subject by observing his/her heading whether it is towards the robot or not. Any failure yields *suspicious mood,* generating a robot trajectory headed towards familiar intentions close to human current intention. Such robot moves aim at gaining the curiosity by breaking the obstinance of the human. Afterwards, the subject acquires the tendency to approach our robot leading to the detection of *confident mood* by proxemics making the person be ready to start an interaction. Elastic nets are used to generate transient intentions starting from current intention in *confident mood* human towards the desired intention, aiming at reshaping intention.

Sequences of transient intentions generate intention trajectories in intention feature space with two different modes: *confident* and *suspicious*. In the former mode, robots directly find trajectory starting from the current intention location of the person towards the desired one without the need of extra transients. However, in the latter mode, the robot cannot quite destabilize the obstinance of the human and cannot capture his/her curiosity. Therefore, establishing an interaction between human and the robot is very difficult as clearly mentioned in (Christensen et al., 2005). Our robots manage to achieve the aim of making the human confident and easily interact with them by slowly approaching the human as stated in (Suzuki et al., 1998) while executing trajectories representing transient intentions familiar to the human current one (mimicking human actions (Kerstin Dautenhahn, 1999)). That way, the human exhibits external-focused attention, be curious about the

robot and is ready to start an interaction. The transient intention is generated around the current intention regardless of how far we are from the desired intention based on elastic networks. Additionally, the generated transient is in the dense areas of intentions observed in the feature space (intention locations more familiar to the human subjects). Basically, we can state that the ultimate goal in the *suspicious mode* is to destabilize the obstinance and gain the curiosity of the person switching the mood of the person to *confident*. Each transient intention generated by the elastic network is executed by moves of an adequate robot (2-steps or chair robot) in directions pointing to that intention as learned by HMM.

Elastic networks were introduced by Durbin and Willshaw (1987) as a solution to Travelling Salesman. In order to link our intention topology with elastic networks, we need to adapt our higher dimensional learned intention trajectories by HMM in Section 2.2 to elastic network by projecting them into 2-D using weight averaging. These 2-D points are then used in the elastic network model as intention nodes in generating transient ones. Figure 5 illustrates a trajectory formed by a sequence of locations leading to an intention of

Figure 5. (a) An exemplary trajectory leading to the intention of 'drinking coffee' with starting and finishing locations are mentioned; (b) All of 100 projected trajectories are demonstrated as elastic network nodes in 2-D (diamonds). Encircled node belongs to the trajectory in part (a).

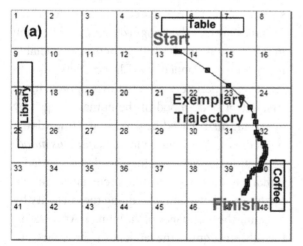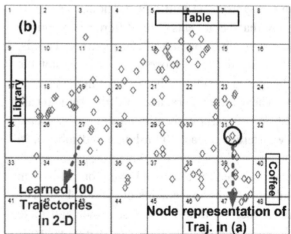

'drinking coffee' given in part (a), reduced to a 2-D node encircled diamond shown in the part (b) among 100 projected learned trajectories by HMM.

To better understand how elastic networks work in generating transient intentions, examples are given in Figure 6, the current intention node being the projected estimated trajectory given in the figures and the previous intention node being the projected trajectory observed also in the same figures. The dynamic point is the one that will settle on a node after elastic oscillations determining transient intention. The desired intention is also shown in the feature space of intentions in part(a). Initially, the dynamic point is chosen as the middle point of the line connecting the current and previous intention nodes. The attractions of the dynamic point by all neighboring nodes in the direction of the desired one are given in Figure 6(b) together with the attraction forces from current and previous intention nodes. Knowing that the desired intention is the biggest node affecting the dynamic point the most, the algorithm starts searching for a node to be the next transient. As the attraction of desired intention decreases fast, superposition of the attractive forces shown with bold arrows in Figure 6(b) gives a force directed towards the densest areas of the nodes. In addition, the attraction of the light arrows (attraction

of current and previous intention nodes) holds the dynamic point around the current intention. At the beginning of the process, these two forces at opposite directions make the dynamic point oscillate between the current intention and the dense area of the nodes, finally ending up on the closest node being the next way point in a closer dense area of intentions as in Figure 6(c).

5. IMPLEMENTATION OF INTENTION RESHAPING

Our aim of intention reshaping by fully autonomous robot motions generated according to human emotions is realized in real-time experiments as detailed on the timeline given with the chart in Figure 7. A software interrupt was developed estimating the current intention of the person by using the most up-to-date sequences of location information at each frame. After the estimation, a comparison between the current and the desired intention is performed. If a mismatch is detected, interrupt returns null and processing of that frame continues. However, if these intentions are equal to each other, the system claims 'Success' returning to 'Start' state, skipping the rest of the process by restarting the frame counter. After 'Success',

Figure 6. (a) Initialization of the path planning is shown. x and y are pixel coordinates. All nodes are projected learned trajectories; (b) Attraction demonstration. The bold arrows are the attractive forces exerted by the nodes. The light arrows show the attraction applied by previous and the current node; (c) Transient intention(way point) is found in the dense area.

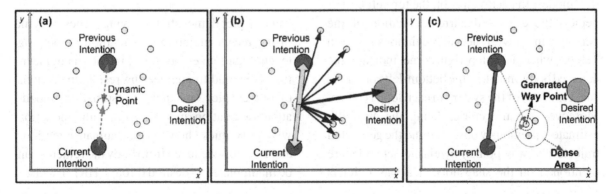

Figure 7. Close loop flow of the system used in human-in-the-loop experiments is given with timeline

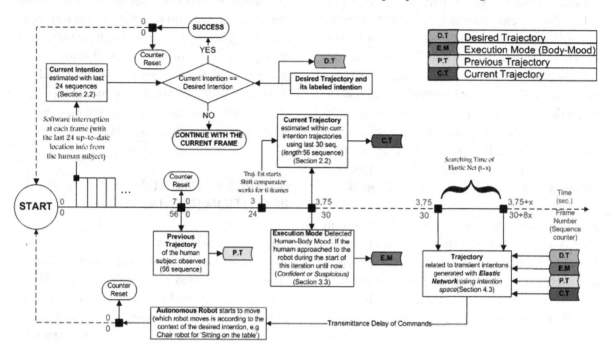

the system is not terminated because even if the person once realizes the desired intention and then turns into another one, target robot will again try to reshape back to the desired one.

In Figure 8-16, sequential snapshots belonging to a real-time experiment with a "stubborn" and initially highly suspicious person are provided in order to picture our system performance in both execution modes. In addition, we demonstrate in the same figures our results on intention and trajectory estimations, body-mood detection (execution mode) and the generation of transient intentions(way points) according to these execution modes. In each snapshot, the top-left corner depicts the estimated current intention of the person printed with their abbreviations given in Table 1, whereas the top-right corner indicates the detected body-mood. At the bottom-left corner the success status of the system in each loop is given. Moreover, the trajectories being the currently estimated, previously observed and the generated trajectories (way points) by elastic networks are mentioned on the snapshots. If a way point is

newly generated in one of the figures, we give its elastic map at the right-hand side of the related snapshot. Finally, we need to mention that, in this example all of the way points generated were realized by the chair robot since the desired intention being 'sitting on the table' is related to this robot. Necessary explanations about the snapshots taken from certain phases of the experiment are given in the legend of the figures.

6. CONCLUSION AND FUTURE WORKS

This chapter demonstrates paving stones existent in the recent literature toward future emerging technologies on emotion and intention engineering. This road to engineering results in sections of our chapter on intention estimation, mood-attention relation, mood detection and induction with proxemics showing that human intentions and emotions deduced from body movements can be manipulated as desired through HRI. That is, a

Figure 8.

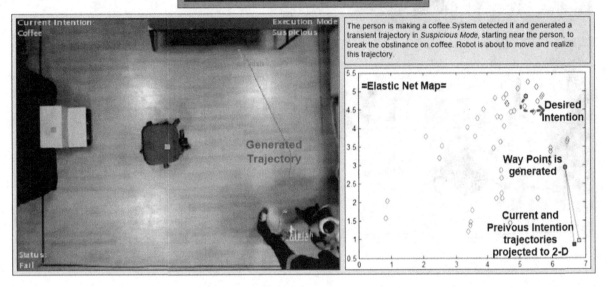

Figure 9.

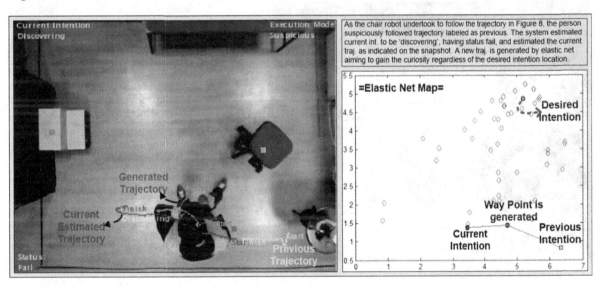

robotic system socially interacting with people can reshape intentions and emotions by autonomous moves in real-time scenarios. Based on the idea that human body-movements reflect their intentions and emotions, estimated current intention of a human can be engineered via proactive robot moves by first inducing positive emotional mood on the person (emotion engineering) resulting in more external-focused attention thus gaining the curiosity and the trust of the person. Then, the person becomes more eager to follow a robot leading him/her towards a desired intention.

Figure 10.

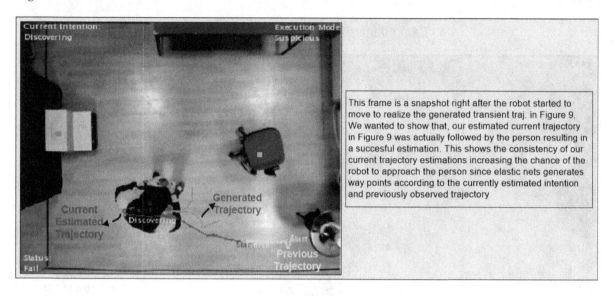

Figure 11.

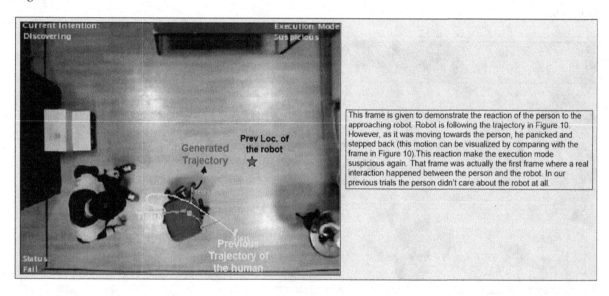

We also demonstrate that socially interacting systems are able to induce desired emotions and intentions on the humans based on forging the readiness of the person to accept changes based on his/her mood. This ability of social emotional cognition during interactions renders robots closer to humans as assistants in real life cooperation scenarios. For example, in an emergency situation where people need guidance, sociable robots can classify humans as confident or suspicious and lead them to safer places. In more mundane usage, robots can have commercial advertorial usage

Figure 12.

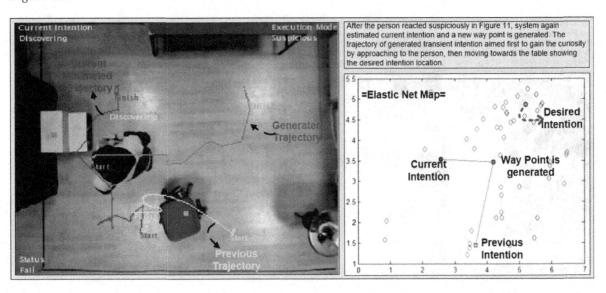

Figure 13.

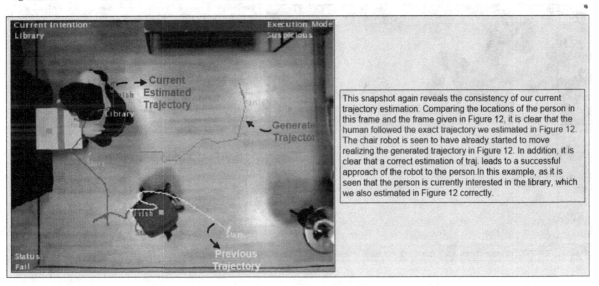

catching the attention of the humans and guiding them towards intended shops. In more crucial cases, they can be used as an assistant for needy people understanding their needs and guiding them accordingly. Similarly, sociable robotics can be educators for children and autistic patients with its ability of engineering intentions and emotions.

Future works may eventually lead to the detection of neutral and aggressive moods of people to detect criminal or foul-minded people and

Figure 14.

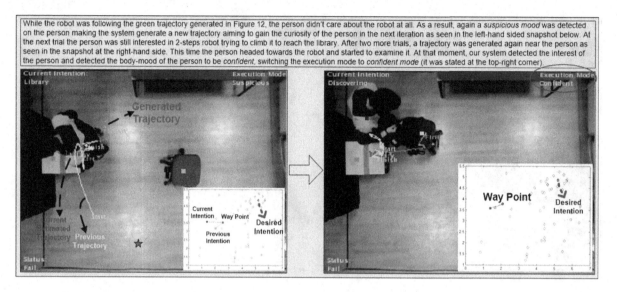

Figure 15.

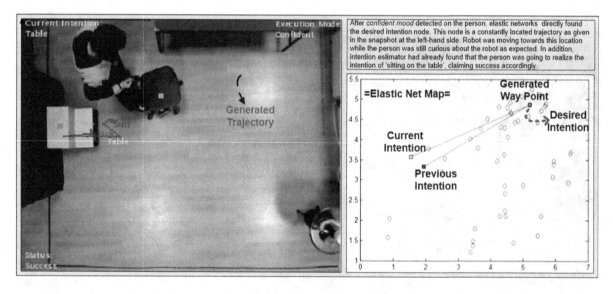

manipulate estimated deviant intentions thereafter. The future will also see the convergence of ethical surveillance among robots during the online administration of emotion and intention engineering. Our work that we introduced as demonstrative example of phases of intention engineering is the first of its kind in the literature in controlled induction of new intentions via creating transients towards the desired final goal. Our approach stands as a pioneering work in intention reshaping that lies in the main focus of this chapter.

Figure 16. Starting from Figure 8 to Figure 16 important moments are demonstrated with sequent snapshots. Desired intention was 'sitting on the table'. Reactions of the person and appropriate robot moves are explained for both two execution modes on each part

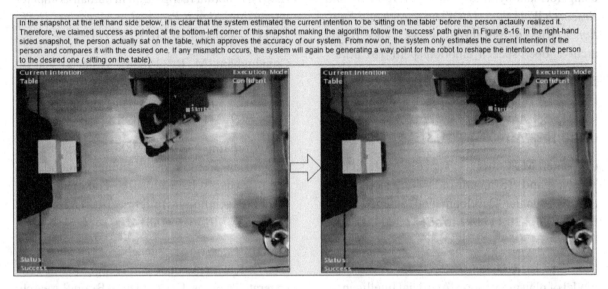

In the snapshot at the left hand side below, it is clear that the system estimated the current intention to be 'sitting on the table' before the person actually realized it. Therefore, we claimed success as printed at the bottom-left corner of this snapshot making the algorithm follow the 'success' path given in Figure 8-16. In the right-hand sided snapshot, the person actually sat on the table, which approves the accuracy of our system. From now on, the system only estimates the current intention of the person and compares it with the desired one. If any mismatch occurs, the system will again be generating a way point for the robot to reshape the intention of the person to the desired one (sitting on the table).

REFERENCES

Adolphs, R., Tranel, D., Damasio, H., & Damasio, A. (1994). Impaired recognition of emotion in facial expressions following bilateral damage to the human amygdala. Nature, 372(6507), 669–672. doi:10.1038/372669a0 PMID:7990957

Ajzen, I. (1985). *From intentions to actions: A theory of planned behavior* (J. Kuhl & J. Beckmann, Eds.). Berlin, Heidelberg: Springer Berlin Heidelberg; doi:10.1007/978-3-642-69746-3

Arai, K., & Mardiyanto, R. (2011). Eye based HCI with moving keyboard for reducing fatigue effects. In *2011 Eighth International Conference on Information Technology: New Generations (ITNG)*, pp. 417–422. Retrieved from http://ieeexplore.ieee.org/xpls/abs_all.jsp?arnumber=5945272

Barakova, E. I., & Lourens, T. (2010). Expressing and interpreting emotional movements in social games with robots. Personal and Ubiquitous Computing, 14(5), 457–467. doi:10.1007/s00779-009-0263-2

Baum, L., Petrie, T., Soules, G., & Weiss, N. (1970). A maximization technique occurring in the statistical analysis of probabilistic functions of Markov chains. Annals of Mathematical Statistics, 41(1), 164–171. doi:10.1214/aoms/1177697196

Beaudry, O., Roy-Charland, A., Perron, M., Cormier, I., & Tapp, R. (2013). Featural processing in recognition of emotional facial expressions. [PubMed]. *Cognition and Emotion, 28*(3), 416–432. doi:10.1080/02699931.2013.833500 PMID:24047413

Bratman, M. (1999). Intentions, plans, and practical reason. Cambridge University Press; Retrieved from http://books.google.com/books?hl=en&lr=&id=RhgnY0-6BmMC&oi=fnd&pg=PR9&dq=intentions+in+communication&ots=66yAtkukEd&sig=iQKmlx2ibFbmbYa-_hVFU08HYsc

Breazeal, C. (2003). Emotion and sociable humanoid robots. International Journal of Human-Computer Studies, 59(1-2), 119–155. doi:10.1016/S1071-5819(03)00018-1

Burkhardt, F., & Sendlmeier, W. (2000). Verification of acoustical correlates of emotional speech using formant-synthesis. In *ISCA Tutorial and Research Workshop (ITRW) on Speech and Emotion*. Retrieved from http://www.isca-speech.org/archive_open/speech_emotion/spem_151.html

Butler, J. T., & Agah, A. (2001). Psychological Effects of Behavior Patterns of a Mobile Personal Robot. *Autonomous Robots, 10*(2), 185–202. doi:10.1023/A:1008986004181

Carpenter, M., Call, J., & Tomasello, M. (2005). Twelve- and 18-month-olds copy actions in terms of goals. Developmental Science, 8(1), F13–F20. doi:10.1111/j.1467-7687.2004.00385.x PMID:15647059

Charniak, E., & Goldman, R. (1993). A Bayesian model of plan recognition. Artificial Intelligence, 64(1), 53–79. doi:10.1016/0004-3702(93)90060-O

Chouchourelou, A., Matsuka, T., Harber, K., & Shiffrar, M. (2006). The visual analysis of emotional actions. *Social Neuroscience, 1*(1), 63–74doi:10.1080/17470910600630599 PMID:18633776

Christensen, H., Pacchierotti, E., & Hgskolan, K. T. (2005). Embodied social interaction for robots. In *Proceedings of the 2005 Convention of the Society for the Study of Artificial Intelligence and Simulation of Behaviour (AISB-05), Hertfordshire* (pp. 40–45).

Cowie, R., & Douglas-Cowie, E. (1995). Speakers and hearers are people: Reflections on speech deterioration as a consequence of acquired deafness. In Profound Deafness and Speech Communication (pp. 510–527).

Cowie, R., Douglas-Cowie, E., Tsapatsoulis, N., Votsis, G., Kollias, S., Fellenz, W., & Taylor, J. (2001). Emotion recognition in human-computer interaction. *Signal Processing Magazine, IEEE, 18*(1), 32–80. doi:10.1109/79.911197

Cunningham, M. R. (1988a). What do you do when you're happy or blue? Mood, expectancies, and behavioral interest. Motivation and Emotion, 12(4), 309–331. doi:10.1007/BF00992357

Cunningham, M. R. (1988b). Does happiness mean friendliness?: Induced mood and heterosexual self-disclosure. Personality and Social Psychology Bulletin, 14(2), 283–297. doi:10.1177/0146167288142007

Daprati, E., Wriessnegger, S., & Lacquaniti, F. (2007). Kinematic cues and recognition of self-generated actions. Experimental Brain Research, 177(1), 31–44. doi:10.1007/s00221-006-0646-9 PMID:16924486

Dario, P., Guglielmelli, E., & Laschi, C. (2001). Humanoids and personal robots: Design and experiments. *Journal of Robotic Systems*. Retrieved from http://citeseer.uark.edu:8080/citeseerx/showciting;jsessionid=4942263C2202CB506C89EE4F4CEBBD6F?cid=261580

Darwin, C. (1872). The expression of the emotions in man and animals. London: Murray. (Reprinted, Chicago: University of Chicago Press, 1965.). doi:10.1037/10001-000

Dautenhahn, K., & Werry, I. (2000). Issues of robot-human interaction dynamics in the rehabilitation of children with autism. In *Proceedings of From animals to animats, 6*, 519–528. Retrieved from http://cognet.mit.edu/library/books/mitpress/0262632004/cache/chap54.pdf

Dautenhahn, K. (1999). Robots as social actors: aurora and the case of autism. In *Proceedings of CT99, The Third International Cognitive Technology Conference* (p. 374). San Francisco.

Dautenhahn, Kerstin, & Billard, A. (1999). Bringing up robots or—the psychology of socially intelligent robots: From theory to implementation. In *AGENTS '99 Proceedings of the third annual conference on Autonomous Agents* (pp. 366–367). doi:10.1145/301136.301237

De Lange, F. P., Spronk, M., Willems, R. M., Toni, I., & Bekkering, H. (2008). Complementary systems for understanding action intentions. [PubMed]. *Current Biology*, *18*(6), 454–457. doi:10.1016/j.cub.2008.02.057 PMID:18356050

Dennett, D. (1989). *The Intentional Stance*. MIT Press.

Dietterich, T. (2002). Machine learning for sequential data: A review. *Structural, Syntactic, and Statistical Pattern Recognition, LNCS,* (vol. 2396, pp. 1–15). Retrieved from http://link.springer.com/chapter/10.1007/3-540-70659-3_2

Dittrich, W., Troscianko, T., Lea, S., & Morgan, D. (1996). Perception of emotion from dynamic point-light displays represented in dance. [PubMed]. *Perception*, *25*(6), 727–738. doi:10.1068/p250727 PMID:8888304

Durbin, R., & Willshaw, D. (1987). An analogue approach to the travelling salesman problem using an elastic net method. *Nature*, *326*(6114), 689–691comptop.stanford.edu/u/references/dw.pdf. doi:10.1038/326689a0 PMID:3561510

Durdu, A., Erkmen, I., Erkmen, A. M., & Yilmaz, A. (2012). Robotic hardware and software integration for changing human intentions. In T. Sobh & X. Xiong (Eds.), *Prototyping of robotic systems: Applications of design and implementation* (pp. 380–406). Hershey, PA: IGI Global; doi:10.4018/978-1-4666-0176-5.ch013

Durdu, A., Erkmen, I., Erkmen, A. M., & Yilmaz, A. (2011). Morphing estimated human intention via human-robot interactions. In *Proceedings of the World Congress on Engineering and Computer Science* (*Vol. I*). San Francisco.

Ekman, P., & Friesen, W. (1974). Detecting deception from the body or face. Journal of Personality and Social Psychology, 29(3), 288–298. doi:10.1037/h0036006

Erden, M. S., & Tomiyama, T. (2010). Human-intent detection and physically interactive control of a robot without force sensors. IEEE Transactions on Robotics, 26(2), 370–382. doi:10.1109/TRO.2010.2040202

Fogassi, L., Ferrari, P., Gesierich, B., Rozzi, S., Chersi, F., & Rizzolatti, G. (2005). Parietal lobe: From action organization to intention understanding. Science, 308(5722), 662–667. doi:10.1126/science.1106138 PMID:15860620

Fogg, B. (1999). Persuasive technologies. *Communications of the ACM*, *42*(5), 26–29dl.acm.org/citation.cfm?id=301396. doi:10.1145/301353.301396

Fogg, B. (2002). Persuasive technology: Using computers to change what we think and do. *Ubiquity*, 89–120. Retrieved from http://scholar.google.com/scholar?hl=en&btnG=Search&q=intitle:Computers+as+Persuasive+Social+Actors#2

Fong, T., Nourbakhsh, I., & Dautenhahn, K. (2003). A survey of socially interactive robots. Robotics and Autonomous Systems, 42(3-4), 143–166. doi:10.1016/S0921-8890(02)00372-X

Fredrickson, B. (2003). The value of positive emotions: The emerging science of positive psychology is coming to understand why it's good to feel good. *American Scientist*, *91*(4), 330–335. doi:10.1511/2003.4.330

Grol, M., Koster, E., Bruyneel, L., & De Raedt, R. (2013). *Effects of positive mood on attention broadening for self-related information. Psychological Research.* PubMed; doi:10.1007/s00426-013-0508-6

Haggard, P., Clark, S., & Kalogeras, J. (2002). Voluntary action and conscious awareness. *Nature Neuroscience.* Retrieved from http://www.nature.com/neuro/journal/v5/n4/abs/nn827.html

Hall, E., Birdwhistell, R., & Bock, B. (1968). Proxemics. *Current Anthropology, 9*(2/3), 83–108. doi:10.1086/200975

Hatfield, E., Cacioppo, J., & Rapson, R. (1993). Emotional contagion. *Current Directions in Psychological Science, 2*(3), 96–99. doi:10.1111/1467-8721.ep10770953

Heinze, C. (2003). *Modelling intention recognition for intelligent agent systems.* The University of Melbourne, Australia. Retrieved from http://oai.dtic.mil/oai/oai?verb=getRecord&metadataPrefix=html&identifier=ADA430005

Horstmann, G. (2003). What do facial expressions convey: Feeling states, behavioral intentions, or actions requests? Emotion (Washington, D.C.), 3(2), 150–166. doi:10.1037/1528-3542.3.2.150 PMID:12899416

Huettenrauch, H., Eklundh, K., Green, A., & Topp, E. (2006). Investigating spatial relationships in human-robot interaction. In *2006 IEEE/RSJ International Conference on Intelligent Robots and Systems* (pp. 5052–5059). doi:10.1109/IROS.2006.282535

Jenkins, O. C., Serrano, G. G., & Loper, M. M. (2007). Interactive human pose and action recognition using dynamical motion primitives. *International Journal of Humanoid Robotics, 04*(02), 365–385. doi:10.1142/S0219843607001060

Jessen, S., & Kotz, S. (2011). The temporal dynamics of processing emotions from vocal, facial, and bodily expressions. NeuroImage, 58(2), 665–674. doi:10.1016/j.neuroimage.2011.06.035 PMID:21718792

Kautz, H. A., & Allen, J. F. (1986). Generalized plan recognition. AAAI, 86, 32–37.

Knoblich, G., & Prinz, W. (2001). Recognition of self-generated actions from kinematic displays of drawing. Journal of Experimental Psychology. Human Perception and Performance, 27(2), 456–465. doi:10.1037/0096-1523.27.2.456 PMID:11318059

Kohler, E., Keysers, C., Umilta, M., Fogassi, L., Vittorio, G., & Rizzolatti, G. (2002). Hearing sounds, understanding actions: Action representation in mirror neurons. Science, 297(5582), 846–848. doi:10.1126/science.1070311 PMID:12161656

Koo, S., & Kwon, D. (2009). Recognizing human intentional actions from the relative movements between human and robot. In *The 18th IEEE International Symposium on Robot and Human Interactive Communication, 2009 (RO-MAN 2009),* (pp. 939–944). doi:10.1109/ROMAN.2009.5326127

Kozima, H., Nakagawa, C., & Yasuda, Y. (2005). Interactive robots for communication-care: a case-study in autism therapy. *ROMAN 2005. IEEE International Workshop on Robot and Human Interactive Communication, 2005*, pp. 341–346. doi:10.1109/ROMAN.2005.1513802

Lee, K. K., & Xu, Y. (2004). Modeling human actions from learning. *2004 IEEE/RSJ International Conference on Intelligent Robots and Systems (IROS), 3*, 2787–2792. doi:10.1109/IROS.2004.1389831

Lee, S., & Son, Y. (2008). Integrated human decision making model under belief-desire-intention framework for crowd simulation. *Simulation Conference, 2008 (WSC 2008)*. pp. 886–894. doi:10.1109/WSC.2008.4736153

Lewin, K. (1952). *Field theory in social science: Selected theoretical papers*. (D. Cartwright, Ed.). Retrieved from http://library.wur.nl/WebQuery/clc/388286

Manera, V., Schouten, B., Becchio, C., Bara, B. G., & Verfaillie, K. (2010). Inferring intentions from biological motion: A stimulus set of point-light communicative interactions. Behavior Research Methods, 42(1), 168–178. doi:10.3758/BRM.42.1.168 PMID:20160297

Mead, R., & Matarić, M. (2011). *An experimental design for studying proxemic behavior in human-robot interaction* (Technical Report CRES-11-001). Los Angeles: USC Interaction Lab.

Meltzoff, A. (1995). Understanding the intentions of others: Re-enactment of intended acts by 18-month-old children. [PubMed]. *Developmental Psychology*, *31*(5), 838–850 doi:10.1037/0012-1649.31.5.838 PMID:25147406

Mitchell, T. M. (1997). *Machine learning*. McGraw-Hill Science/Engineering/Math.

Mori, T., Shimosaka, M., Harada, T., & Sato, T. (2005). Time-series human motion analysis with kernels derived from learned switching linear dynamics. *Transactions of the Japanese Society for Artificial Intelligence*, *20*, 197–208. doi:10.1527/tjsai.20.197

Mori, T., Segawa, Y., Shimosaka, M., & Sato, T. (2004). Hierarchical recognition of daily human actions based on continuous Hidden Markov Models. In *Sixth IEEE International Conference on Automatic Face and Gesture Recognition, 2004. Proceedings*. (pp. 779–784). doi:10.1109/AFGR.2004.1301629

Pacchierotti, E., Christensen, H. I., & Jensfelt, P. (2005). Human-robot embodied interaction in hallway settings: a pilot user study. In *ROMAN 2005. IEEE International Workshop on Robot and Human Interactive Communication, 2005*. (pp. 164–171). doi:10.1109/ROMAN.2005.1513774

Parlangeli, O., Guidi, S., & Caratozzolo, M. C. (2013). A mind in a disk: The attribution of mental states to technological systems. [PubMed]. *Work (Reading, Mass.)*, *41*, 1118–1123. PMID:22316869

Paulos, E., & Canny, J. (1998). Designing personal tele-embodiment. In *IEEE Internetional Conference on Robotics and Automation, 1998* (pp. 3173–3178). Retrieved from http://ieeexplore.ieee.org/xpls/abs_all.jsp?arnumber=680913

Reisenzein, R., Studtmann, M., & Horstmann, G. (2013). Coherence between emotion and facial expression: Evidence from laboratory experiments. Emotion Review, 5(1), 16–23. doi:10.1177/1754073912457228

Robins, B., Dautenhahn, K., Boekhorst, R., & Billard, A. (2005). Robotic assistants in therapy and education of children with autism: Can a small humanoid robot help encourage social interaction skills? *Universal Access in the Information Society*, *4*(2), 105–120. doi:10.1007/s10209-005-0116-3

Roether, C., Omlor, L., Christensen, A., & Giese, M. (2009). Critical features for the perception of emotion from gait. *Journal of Vision*. Retrieved from http://jov.highwire.org/content/9/6/15.short

Sato, E., Yamaguchi, T., & Harashima, F. (2007). Natural interface using pointing behavior for human–robot gestural interaction. *IEEE Transactions on Industrial Electronics*, *54*(2), 1105–1112 doi:10.1109/TIE.2007.892728

Sauter, D., Panattoni, C., & Happé, F. (2013). Children's recognition of emotions from vocal cues. *The British Journal of Developmental Psychology*, *31*(1), 97–113 doi:10.1111/j.2044-835X.2012.02081.x PMID:23331109

Scherer, K. (2003). Vocal communication of emotion: A review of research paradigms. Speech Communication, 40(1-2), 227–256. doi:10.1016/S0167-6393(02)00084-5

Scheutz, M., Schermerhorn, P., & Kramer, J. (2006). The utility of affect expression in natural language interactions in joint human-robot tasks. In *HRI '06 Proceedings of the 1st ACM SIGCHI/ SIGART Conference on Human-Robot Interaction* (pp. 226–233). doi:10.1145/1121241.1121281

Schmidt, C., Sridharan, N., & Goodson, J. (1978). The plan recognition problem: An intersection of psychology and artificial intelligence. Artificial Intelligence, 11(1-2), 45–83. doi:10.1016/0004-3702(78)90012-7

Schmidt, S., & Färber, B. (2009). Pedestrians at the kerb–Recognising the action intentions of humans. Transportation Research Part F: Traffic Psychology and Behaviour, 12(4), 300–310. doi:10.1016/j.trf.2009.02.003

Sedikides, C. (1992). Mood as a determinant of attentional focus. Cognition and Emotion, 6(2), 129–148. doi:10.1080/02699939208411063

Sevdalis, V., & Keller, P. E. (2010). Cues for self-recognition in point-light displays of actions performed in synchrony with music. Consciousness and Cognition, 19(2), 617–626. doi:10.1016/j. concog.2010.03.017 PMID:20382037

Shimosaka, M., Mori, T., Harada, T., & Sato, T. (2005). Marginalized bags of vectors kernels on switching linear dynamics for online action recognition. In *International Conference on Robotics and Automaiton* (pp. 72–77). doi:10.1109/ROBOT.2005.1570582

Suzuki, K., Camurri, A., Ferrentino, P., & Hashimoto, S. (1998). Intelligent agent system for human-robot interaction through artificial emotion. In *SMC'98 Conference Proceedings of the 1998 IEEE International Conference on Systems, Man, and Cybernetics* (Vol. 2, pp. 1055–1060). doi:10.1109/ICSMC.1998.727828

Tahboub, K. (2005). Compliant human-robot cooperation based on intention recognition. In *Proceedings of the 2005 International Symposium on Intelligent Control.* (pp. 1417–1422). IEEE. Retrieved from http://ieeexplore. ieee.org/xpls/abs_all.jsp?arnumber=1467222 doi:10.1109/.2005.1467222

Tahboub, K. A. (2006). Intelligent human – machine interaction based on dynamic Bayesian networks probabilistic intention recognition. Journal of Intelligent & Robotic Systems, 45(1), 31–52. doi:10.1007/s10846-005-9018-0

Takayama, L., & Pantofaru, C. (2009). Influences on proxemic behaviors in human-robot interaction. In *2009 IEEE/RSJ International Conference on Intelligent Robots and Systems* (pp. 5495–5502). doi:10.1109/IROS.2009.5354145

Terada, K., Shamoto, T., Mei, H., & Ito, A. (2007). Reactive movements of non-humanoid robots cause intention attribution in humans. In *IEEE/RSJ International Conference on Intelligent Robots & Systems* (pp. 3715–3720). doi:10.1109/IROS.2007.4399429

Terada, K., & Ito, A. (2010). Can a robot deceive humans? In *2010 5th ACM/IEEE International Conference on Human-Robot Interaction (HRI)*, pp. 191–192. doi:10.1109/HRI.2010.5453201

Vanderborght, B., Simut, R., Saldien, J., Pop, C., Rusu, A. S., Pintea, S., David, D. O. (2012). Using the social robot probo as a social story telling agent for children with ASD. Interaction Studies: Social Behaviour and Communication in Biological and Artificial Systems, 13(3), 348–372. doi:10.1075/is.13.3.02van

Viterbi, A. (1967). Error bounds for convolutional codes and an asymptotically optimum decoding algorithm. IEEE Transactions on Information Theory, 13(2), 260–269. doi:10.1109/TIT.1967.1054010

Vlasenko, B., & Wendemuth, A. (2009). Heading toward to the natural way of human-machine interaction: the NIMITEK project. In *IEEE International Conference on Multimedia and Expo, 2009. ICME 2009.* (pp. 950–953). doi:10.1109/ICME.2009.5202653

Wada, K., Shibata, T., Saito, T., & Tanie, K. (2004). Effects of robot-assisted activity for elderly people and nurses at a day service center. In *Proceedings of the IEEE* (Vol. 92, pp. 1780–1788). doi:10.1109/JPROC.2004.835378

Wadlinger, H., & Isaacowitz, D. (2006). Positive mood broadens visual attention to positive stimuli. [PubMed]. *Motivation and Emotion, 30*(1), 89–101link.springer.com/article/10.1007/s11031-006-9021-1. doi:10.1007/s11031-006-9021-1 PMID:20431711

Wallbott, H. G. (1998). Bodily expression of emotion. European Journal of Social Psychology, 28(6), 879–896. doi:10.1002/(SICI)1099-0992(1998110)28:6<879::AID-EJSP901>3.0.CO;2-W

Walters, M. L., Oskoei, M. a., Syrdal, D. S., & Dautenhahn, K. (2011). A long-term human-robot proxemic study. In IEEE, RO-MAN 2011 (pp. 137–142). doi:10.1109/ROMAN.2011.6005274

Wang, S., Liu, Z., Lv, S., Lv, Y., & Wu, G. (2010). A natural visible and infrared facial expression database for expression recognition and emotion inference. *IEEE Transactions on Biometrics Compendium, 12*(7), 682–691. doi:10.1109/TMM.2010.2060716

Wang, E., Lignos, C., Vatsal, A., & Scassellati, B. (2006). Effects of head movement on perceptions of humanoid robot behavior. In *Proceeding of the 1st ACM SIGCHI/SIGART Conference on Human-Robot Interaction - HRI '06* (p. 180). New York: ACM Press. doi:10.1145/1121241.1121273

Wang, Z., Mülling, K., Deisenroth, M. P., Ben Amor, H., Vogt, D., Schölkopf, B., & Peters, J. (2013). Probabilistic movement modeling for intention inference in human-robot interaction. The International Journal of Robotics Research, 32(7), 841–858. doi:10.1177/0278364913478447

Watson, D., & Tellegen, A. (1985). Toward a consensual structure of mood. [PubMed]. *Psychological Bulletin, 98*(2), 219–235psycnet.apa.org/journals/bul/98/2/219/. doi:10.1037/0033-2909.98.2.219 PMID:3901060

Webb, T., & Sheeran, P. (2006). Does changing behavioral intentions engender behavior change? A meta-analysis of the experimental evidence. *Psychological Bulletin, 132*(2), 249–268. doi:10.1037/0033-2909.132.2.249 PMID:16536643

Werry, I., Dautenhahn, K., Ogden, B., & Harwin, W. (2001). Can social interaction skills be taught by a social agent? The role of a robotic mediator in autism therapy. *Computer Technology: Instruments of Mind, 2117*, 57–74. Retrieved from http://link.springer.com/chapter/10.1007/3-540-44617-6_6

Wilensky, R. (1983). *Planning and understanding: A computational approach to human reasoning.* Retrieved from http://www.osti.gov/energycitations/product.biblio.jsp?osti_id=5673187

Wood, J. V., Saltzberg, J. A., & Goldsamt, L. A. (1990). Does affect induce self-focused attention? Journal of Personality and Social Psychology, 58(5), 899–908. doi:10.1037/0022-3514.58.5.899 PMID:2348375

Yamato, J., Ohya, J., & Ishii, K. (1992). Recognizing human action in time-sequential images using hidden Markov model. In *Proceedings 1992 IEEE Computer Society Conference on Computer Vision and Pattern Recognition* (pp. 379–385). IEEE Computer Society Press. doi:10.1109/CVPR.1992.223161

Yokoyama, A., & Omori, T. (2010). Modeling of human intention estimation process in social interaction scene. *International Conference on Fuzzy Systems*, 1–6. doi:10.1109/FUZZY.2010.5584042

KEY TERMS AND DEFINITIONS

Emotional Mood Induction: Altering peoples' emotional moods or states (e.g from being sad to being happy) with respect to changes in the environment.

Human Attentions: Humans' willingly or reflexively concentrating on one object, action, or generally one aspect of the environment.

Human-Robot Interaction: Interactions between humans and robots by means of cooperation in a task or assisting one another.

Intention Estimation: By observing physical or psychological behaviors or conditions of humans or robots, estimating the intention of them which are outcomes of those behaviors.

Intention Reshaping: Altering humans' purposes or intentions by making related changes in the environment affecting this physical environment and psychological state of minds of humans.

Mood Detection: Predicting current mood of a person by observing the action behaviors of this person.

Path Planning: Planning feasible paths for robots according to the task they assigned with.

Chapter 13
EEG–Analysis for the Detection of True Emotion or Pretension

Reshma Kar
Jadavpur University, India

Amit Konar
Jadavpur University, India

Aruna Chakraborty
St. Thomas' College of Engineering and Technology, India

ABSTRACT

Several lobes in the human brain are involved differently in the arousal, processing and manifestation of emotion in facial expression, vocal intonation and gestural patterns. Sometimes people suppress their bodily manifestations to pretend their emotions. Detection of emotion and pretension is an open problem in emotion research. The chapter presents an analysis of EEG signals to detect true emotion/pretension: first by extracting the neural connectivity among selected brain lobes during arousal and manifestation of a true emotion, and then by testing whether the connectivity among the lobes are maintained while encountering an emotional context. In case the connectivity is manifested, the arousal of emotion is regarded as true emotion, otherwise it is considered as a pretension. Experimental results confirm that for positive emotions, the decoding accuracy of true (false) emotions is as high as 88% (72%), while for negative emotions, the classification accuracy falls off by a 12% margin for true emotions and 8% margin for false emotions. The proposed method has wide-spread applications to detect criminals, frauds and anti-socials.

1. INTRODUCTION

Emotion represents a psychological state of the human mind. Philosophers are of the view that emotion originates because of substantial changes in one's personal situations (Ben-Ze'ev, 2002). . Arousal of emotion is often concurred with its manifestation on facial expressions, voice, gestures, postures, and physiological parameters, including body temperature, pulse rate, heart

DOI: 10.4018/978-1-4666-7278-9.ch013

rate variability and cortical signal characteristics. Recognition of emotion from its facial and/or bodily manifestation thus is an interesting problem. Significant progress in recognition of emotion from its manifestation has been reported in the literature (Orozco, Rudovic, Gonzàlez, & Pantic,2014), (Lee & Narayanan, 2005), (Mitra & Acharya, 2007), (Murugappan, Rizon, Nagarajan & Yaacob, 2010). A survey of the literature reveals recognition accuracy of emotion depends largely on the modality of recognition (Chakraborty & Konar, 2009). For example, facial expressions and/or voice provide high classification accuracy of subjective emotion, while physiological parameters seem to have produced relatively less classification accuracy

Although manifestation of emotion is a good measure of the degree and class of emotion, sometimes the results of classification do not conform to the originated emotion, particularly for two reasons. First, the subject is not capable to develop manifestation of the aroused emotion. Secondly (and more importantly), the subject is unwilling to express her emotion on facial expression, voice and/or bodily gestures. Recognition of true emotion, however, is very important for the next-generation Human-Computer Interactive (HCI) systems. The present chapter will serve as a useful resource to discriminate true emotion from pretension. Experiments undertaken by previous researchers reveal that facial and bodily manifestation requires several 10 seconds after the onset of emotion arousal. However, cortical signals respond almost instantaneously at the onset of emotion-arousal. Naturally, voluntarily control of cortical signals to suppress or present false emotion while experiencing an emotion is difficult.

The chapter provides a thorough analysis of cortical signals to distinguish (classify) true emotions and pretensions. Early research on cortical signal analysis was restricted in good hospitals over the last two decades, particularly because of the excessive cost of EEG machines. Fortunately, EEG machines are now commercially available at a low price, and most of the research laboratories on brain science can afford it. EEG analysis on subjects in a given age-group of 24±4 years thus is performed to classify true emotion and pretension. The underlying principles to classify a given emotion into one of two classes: true emotion and pretension are briefly presented below.

An analysis of the brain map for emotion arousal reveals that emotion usually originates in the pre-frontal cortex and neural impulses associated with arousal of emotion pass to the pons region through motor cortex (Purves, Cabeza, Huettel, LaBar, Platt & Woldorff 2013). The motor cortex impulses activate muscles to generate electromyogram (EMG) signals, which in turn causes changes in facial expressions/gestures/postures for a given emotion (Morecraft, Stilwell-Morecraft & Rossing 2004), (Meister, Boroojerdi, Foltys, Sparing, Huber & Töpper, 2003.). The biological basis of manifestation on facial expression during arousal of an emotion is used in this paper to classify true emotion and pretension.

The computational model used here aims at determining the neuronal weights (connectivity) involved in mapping pre-frontal to motor cortex EEG features, next motor cortex EEG features to facial features and lastly, facial features back to pre-frontal EEG features during arousal of a given emotion. The training instances are collected for true emotion only in all circumstances. Naturally, after the weights are determined, the trained neural network is used to examine the closeness of the measured EEG features from the pre-frontal region and the predicted EEG features of the pre-frontal region. If the Euclidean norm of the measure of closeness is below a experimentally obtained prescribed threshold, the predicted emotion is declared as true emotion, else we call it a pretension.

The chapter is divided into five sections. Principles and methodology of the proposed scheme for the detection of true emotion/pretension are given in section 2. In section 3, we provide the experimental details and results. A discussion on the proposed scheme and possible extension is given in section 4. Conclusions are given in section 5.

2. PRINCIPLES AND METHODOLOGY

The cortex of the human brain includes functionally distinguishable brain regions including pre-frontal, frontal, occipital, parietal, motor cortex, and temporal regions. (Figure 1(a)). The present study examines the role of pre-frontal cortex in emotion processing and that of motor-cortex in manifestation of emotion in facial-muscles. Audio-visual stimuli are presented to the subjects to arouse emotions and the effect of the arousal in subjective feeling is detected from the EEG response of the pre-frontal cortex. The neural signals originated at the pre-frontal cortex further excite the neurons in motor cortex, whose response is obtained from the motor-cortex signal EEG. Lastly the motor-cortex signal activates facial muscles, which are detected from facial muscles.

We here attempt to model the pre-frontal cortex by neural net NN_1 and the motor-cortex by neural net NN_2 (Figure 2 (a) and (b)). The neural net NN_3 in Figure 2 (c) is used to check the existence of any possible correlation between facial features and pre-frontal EEG features. If the correlation is strong then we declare that the facial manifesta-tion is directly linked with emotional feeling, and so it is a true emotion. If the correlation is weak then we conclude that the emotion expressed in face is pretension.

The neural nets NN_1, NN_2 and NN_3 usually have feed-forward topology (Konar,2005). These networks are trained with real world input-output instances by suitable learning algorithm (Konar, 1999). After training of the neural nets is over, they are connected in the architecture shown in Figure 3. In Figure 3, we provide the pre-frontal features of a subject during arousal of a given emotion. We use the weight matrices (learned information about neural connectivity) of the respective neural nets for the same person for the predicted emotion obtained from her facial expression, and measure the error norm (Euclidean norm of the error). If it is small, the emotion is true, else it is pretension.

Neural Learning Algorithms Used

We trained NN1 to NN3 by two different neural learning algorithms, namely Back-propagation algorithm, and Orthogonal Least Squares Learning Algorithm and for two different topologies, namely feed-forward and cascade-forward topology. They are briefly outlined below.

Back-propagation Using Feed-forward Neural Net (FFNN): A feed-forward neural topology

Figure 1. a) The human brain (side view) and (b): The neuronal connectivity inside brain during emotional exposition in face

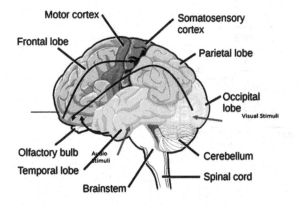
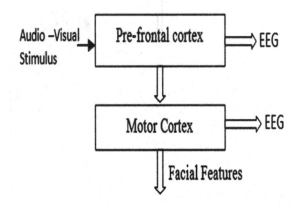

Figure 2. Training of neural models for (a) pre-frontal to motor cortex (b) motor cortex to facial and (c) facial to prefrontal connectivity. P: Pre-processing, F: Filtering, LA: Learning Algorithm, FE: Feature Extraction, C: Camera

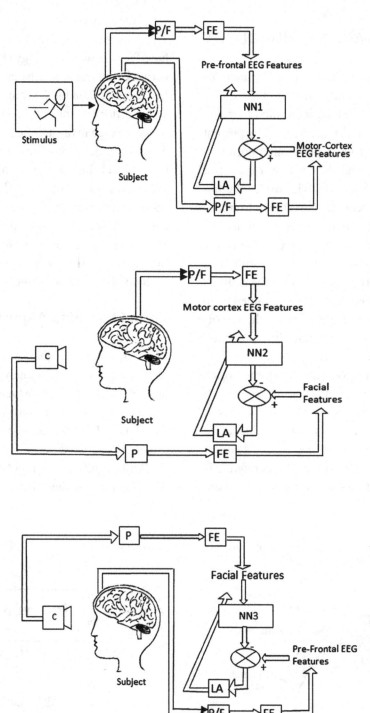

Figure 3. Proposed recognition module of the emotion pretention detection phase

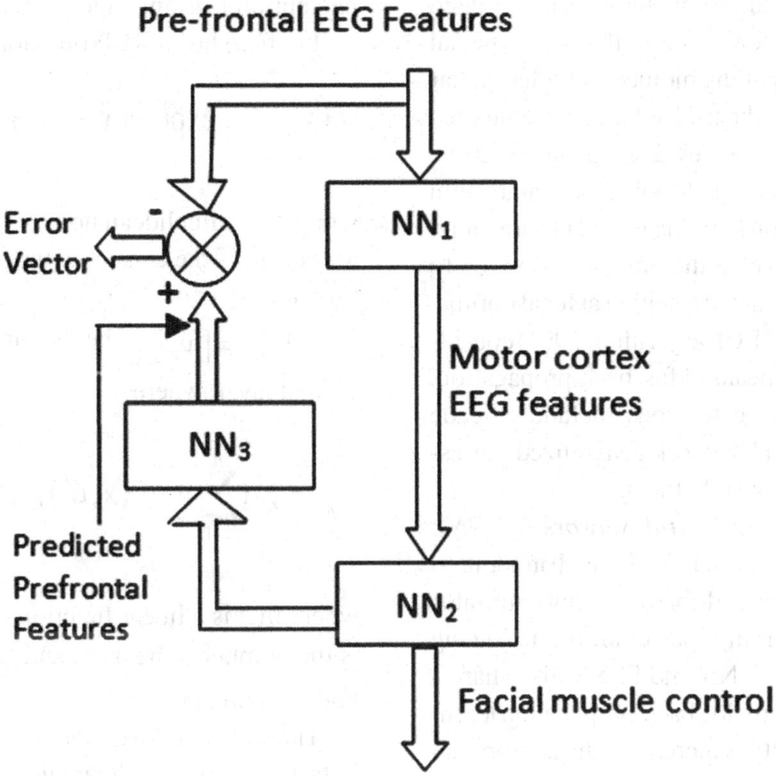
Pre-frontal EEG Features
Error
Vector
-
+
NN1
NN3
Motor cortex
EEG features
Predicted
Prefrontal
Features
NN2
Facial muscle control

allows signal to propagate only in the forward direction. Usually, feed-forward topology is used for supervised learning, where the objective of the learning algorithm is to adapt the connectivity strengths (weights) in the network, so that the network is able to produce the desired output vector for each input vector of the given training instances. The error vector, obtained by taking the component-wise difference between the target (desired) vector and the output vector is used to directly adapt the weights in the last layer using the well-known gradient descent learning principle. The principle states that for a given energy function E of weights w_{ij} connecting neurons i and j, the adaptation rule for weight adjustment is given by

$$w_{i,j}(t+1) = w_{i,j}(t) + \eta \frac{\partial E}{\partial w_{i,j}} \qquad (1)$$

where η is a random no in [0, 1] and t denotes iteration

The weight adaptation in other layer is performed by propagating error back to the desired layer, where weight adaptation is required, by designing a function of two sets of variables: measured errors obtained at the output layer and the connectivity between the selected neuron in the given layer and the error vector at the output layer. Gradient descent learning is then invoked to adapt the weights for the selected neuron using the back-propagated error, thereby justifying the algorithm.

The back-propagation algorithm (Rumelhart, Hinton & Williams, 1985) works well for a small network with fewer weights and small set of training instances. However, the training time becomes appreciably high, particularly when the search for the optima in the search-space gets trapped into local optima. Several extensions to the basic Back-propagation algorithm have been examined over the years. A few of these that need special mention includes adding momentum (Phansalkar & Sastry, 1994) to the trial solution or simulated annealing (Sexton, Dorsey & Johnson, 1999).

Various extensions to topology and algorithm of back-propagation learning neural net are found in the literature, where the emphasis is given to speed-up and/or to avoid trapping at local optima. F.S Wong's FASTPROP algorithm (1991) considers an alternative means of fast back-propagation. Topology-sensitive extensions include cascade feed-forward neural network generalized regression neural network and others.

Cascade Forward Neural Network (CFNN): CFNN is a special type of FFNN, which in addition to the connections in feed-forward architecture also has connections from input to all the following layers (Figure 5). CFNN and FFNN also share a similarity as both employ back-propagation learning. As connectivity is increased, the neurons are more inter-dependent. Although this increases the complexity of the network, the additional connections might improve the speed at which the networks learn the functions (Demuth & Beale, 1993). Thus FFNN and CFNN are virtually similar but with different connection topologies.

Radial Basis Neural Network (RBNN): The radial basis function (RBF) neural net is designed with one of several RBF functions at the neurons of the first layer to determine the nearest class of an unknown pattern. The RBF function employed in each neuron is designed to identify geometrically closer patterns clustered around the centre of each RBF neuron. When an unknown input pattern is presented to an RBF neural net, the pattern appears as input to each RBF neuron (Figure 6), and only one neuron with output closest to one is fired. The input vector is presumed to fall in the cluster of the fired neuron. To map an input vector to a given output vector, a second layer of neurons is employed and the encoding of weights

of these neurons is performed by the well-known perceptron learning algorithm (Konar, 2005).

Let f(...) be an RBF function given by

$$f(\vec{x}, \vec{c}^{\,j}) = \exp(-\parallel \vec{x} - \vec{c}^{\,j} \parallel) \qquad (2)$$

where $\parallel . \parallel$ is Euclidean norm, $\vec{x}$ is the input vector and $\vec{c}$ is the center vector of the radial basis functions.

Let $\vec{Y} = [y_k]_{1xr}$ be the output vector of the second layer, where

$$y_k = f_k(\sum_{i=1}^{n} w_{ij} f_i(\vec{x}, \vec{c}^{\,i})) \qquad (3)$$

where $f_k(.)$ is a linear function of its argument. n is the number of neurons and w_{ij} is weight from node i to node j

The advantage of employing RBF neurons lies in fast clustering of the input data point $\vec{x}$ to one of m clusters. Unlike traditional back-propagation algorithm, which requires an exhaustive training cycle for the encoding of weights, here we simply need to set the cluster centre as the centre $\vec{c}^{\,j}$ of the RBF functions. The centre $\vec{c}^{\,j}$ of the j-th RBF neuron is determined by a pre-processing of the known set of patterns of the given class j. This is usually done by averaging of the patterns falling in the cluster, or by more sophisticated techniques, such as Principal Component Analysis (PCA) (Haykin, 1994) or by using self-organization of the data points using the well-known self-organizing feature map neural network (Konar, 2005).

Generalized Regression Neural Networks (GRNN): A GRNN is considered as a special variant of the RBNN, in which the outputs have been normalized by adding a special layer of linearity to replace the traditional linearity in RBNN (Demuth & Beale, 1993). Like RBNN these networks also

Figure 4. Feed-Forward Neural network. x_i is i^{th} element of input vector and y_j is j^{th} element of output vector

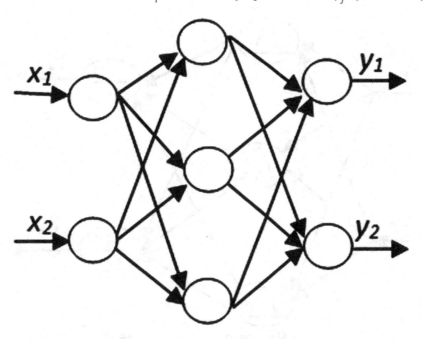

Figure 5. Cascade forward Neural networks a) partial connections b) complete connections

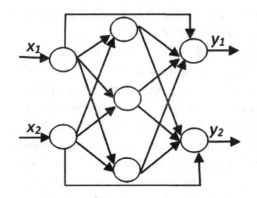
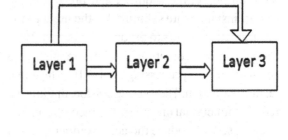

are likely to possess a high dimension of neurons but are built over a relatively shorter duration of time. Similarly, they also do not require iterative training algorithm like back-propagation learning algorithm. The data fitting is based on kernel regressors (Hakyns, 2005), the parameters of which are inferred directly from the input data set.

3. EXPERIMENTS AND RESULTS

This section provides the experimental procedure to validate the performance of the proposed model (Figure 3) realized with different neural topologies introduced earlier. The work is broadly divided into two sessions: training session and recognition session. During the training session, the neural networks are trained with pre-processed

Figure 6. Radial basis neural network

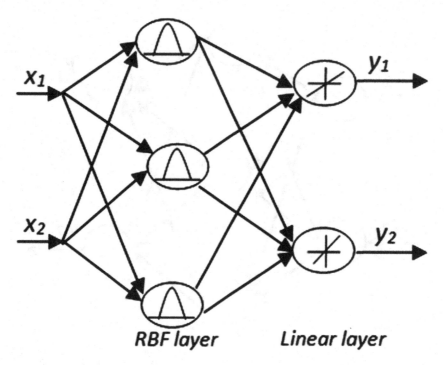

RBF layer   **Linear layer**

input-output training instances. During the recognition phase, the acquired and pre-processed (input) instances are submitted at the input of the pre-trained networks to produce the output. Both training and recognition sessions require data acquisition, pre-processing (noise filtering) and feature extraction. The training session, in addition, requires functional mapping. The recognition session is used to produce the actual output, when a measurement input is submitted. The classification of a given emotion into true emotion or pretension is undertaken in the recognition session.

EEG Acquisition: The experiments are conducted on 10 right-handed subjects, comprising 5 males and 5 females in the age group of 24±4 years. One 14-channel wireless Emotiv headset with a sampling resolution of 128 samples per second is used to acquire EEG signals for the subjects, after stimulating them with selected ten audio-visual stimuli. Consequently, for ten subjects and ten stimuli, we have as many as 100

instances of EEG signals acquired over a period of 10 seconds interval.

The frontal lobe of the brain has been found to have significance in emotion processing .We performed our experiments on the two subparts of the frontal lobe namely prefrontal lobe which is related with emotion arousal (Kawasaki, Hiroto, Adolphs, Kaufman, Damasio, Damasio, Granner, Bakken, Hori & Howard, 2001) and motor-cortex which is associated with the manifestation of emotions (Morecraft, Kimberly & Rossing, 2004). In standard 10-20 electrode positioning system (Figure 7), we select AF3 and AF4 electrodes, located in the prefrontal region and FC5 and FC6 electrodes, located in the motor cortex regions. An examination of the literature (Canli, Desmond, Zhao, Glover, & Gabrieli, 1998) reveals that positive emotions are associated with left hemisphere, while negative emotions with the right hemisphere. Since even numbered electrodes are associated with right hemisphere and odd numbered electrodes with the left, filtering of fear and sadness are performed from AF4 and FC6 electrodes, while that of happiness and relaxation are done from AF3 and FC5 electrodes.

Filtering: To eliminate the possible infringement of noise in the acquired EEG signals, the following precautions are taken. First, the effect of eye blinking on EEG is avoided by neighborhood averaging of the signals around each selected channel (Junghöfer, Elbert, Tucker & Rockstroh, 2000). Second the desired frequency spectrum is segregated to eliminate the effect of crosstalk from other channel on to a desired channel. Such crosstalk often appears because of parallel activation of two or more cognitive processes by the subject. We employed elliptical band-pass filters of order 6 to filter prefrontal EEG signal in the alpha (8-12 Hz) band and the motor cortex EEG signal in the beta (13-30 Hz) band. Elliptical filters are selected for their faster transition between the pass band and the stop band than other filters with the same number of filter coefficients.

Third the experiment is repeated 10 times to eliminate the random variations in EEG signals for power-supply pick-up or due to the presence other low frequency signals during the course of experiments. Fourth, the subjects are given ten minutes break between submissions of two different audio-visual stimuli to eliminate interference from the EEG signals related to previous stimuli.

Feature Extraction: The data obtained from EEG signals is non-stationary and often high dimensional. Thus obtaining a low dimensional data capable of adequately representing the time-variant features is of importance in all EEG analysis experiments. Various techniques of feature extraction have been proposed by researchers over the years (Murugappan, Rizon, Nagarajan, Yaacob, Zunaidi, & Hazry 2007), (Merzagora, Bunce, Izzetoglu, & Onaral, 2006). One such well-known feature extraction technique is the Hjorth parameter estimation, which not only contains relevant information about the EEG signal but also is low dimensional. Because of its low dimensionality,

the input of the neural network topology is limited and thus the network architecture involves fewer neurons, which subsequently reduces the training time of neural models significantly.

The Hjorth parameters represent activity, mobility and complexity of an EEG signal (B. Hjorth, 1970). The variance or activity of an EEG signal carries information about changes in electrical charges in the cortex with respect to time and thus measures the fluctuation in the signal because of activation in the cortical regions arising due to various cognitive tasks performed by the subject. Mobility of an EEG signal measures the degree of fluctuation variance of the signal with respect to time. Complexity of the signal is the time derivative of mobility of the signal. Thus activity, mobility and complexity are zeroth, first and second order derivatives of the signal with respect to time respectively. Thus the Hjorth parameters are capable of capturing the temporal information present in an EEG signal. Let $x(n)$ be an EEG signal sampled at $n = 1$ to N at all integers, and $\bar{x}$ is its average value. We then define the Hjorth parameters as

$$\text{Activity}(x) = \text{var}(x) = \frac{1}{N} \sum_{i=1}^{N} (x(n) - \bar{x})^2$$

(4)

$$\text{Mobility}(x) = \sqrt{\frac{\text{var}(x')}{\text{var}(x)}}$$

(5)

where x' is the first derivative of x.

$$\text{Complexity}(x) = \frac{\text{Mobility}(x')}{\text{Mobility}(x)}$$

(6)

A set of 40 audio-visual stimuli, designed following the principles outlined in (Chakraborty, Konar, Chakraborty & Chatterjee 2009) are

Figure 7. Illustrating positioning in 10-20 electrode system

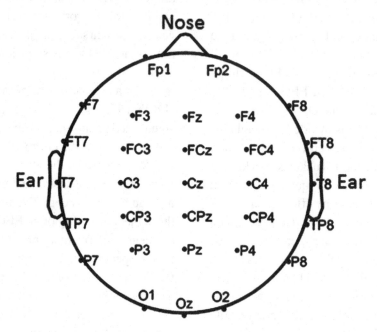

presented to one of 30 subjects, one by one, to arouse their emotions. Each stimulus is presented for a short duration of 10 seconds to acquire the EEG signals during this interval using EEGLAB software. The acquired signals are processed using MATLAB signal processing toolbox to filter them from noise and obtain the desired pass-band in specified frequency spectra of the signal. For example, the pre-frontal signals are filtered in the alpha- band, while the motor cortex signals are filtered in the beta band for their prominent performance in the respective bands as indicated. Next we determine the Hjorth parameters for EEG signals of 2 seconds durations.

Facial Features: To extract facial features of a subject while taking his EEG data, we need to perform the following steps: 1) segmentation of the face into regions of interest and then ii) classifying each region into one of three classes: eye region, mouth region and eyebrow region, and 3lastly extract the facial features by image processing techniques. We here used fuzzy c-means clustering algorithm (Konar, 2005) to segment the face into three classes, and used geometry-based feature extraction techniques to determine the facial features. The details of the steps are available in (Chakraborty, & Konar, 2009) . The extracted parameters are given in Figure 8 for the sake of completeness.

Neural Network Training: The neural network models introduced earlier are trained with measured input/output training instances. The FFNN and the CFNN are trained with Back-propagation with Levenberg–Marquardt learning Rule (Yu, & Wilamowski, 2011). while RBNN and GRNN are trained with Orthogonal Least Squares Learning Algorithm (Chen, Cowan & Grant,1991) for their relatively proven better performance in comparison to their traditional counterparts. The number of neurons in the middle (hidden) layer for FFNN/CFNN is set to 20 arbitrarily. For RBNN/ GRNN, the number of neurons in the hidden layer was adjusted to minimize the error at the output layered neurons to a low level below a threshold.

The performance of the neural training algorithms is determined by the mean square error sum of all the neurons in the last layer. The results of mean-square error sum for four different configurations are given in Table-I below.

It is apparent from Table-I that mean square error-sum for NN_1 and NN_2 are minimum for RBNN realization and that for NN_3 is minimum for GRNN realization. We, therefore, configured NN_1, NN_2 and NN_3 in Figure 3 by RBNN, RBNN and GRNN respectively before to detect the emotional status (true emotion/pretension) of the subject.

Detection of True Emotion/Pretension: The following steps are undertaken to test whether the emotion acquired by facial expression analysis is a true emotion or pretension.

1. Any standard technique of emotion recognition facial features can be employed to recognize emotion of a subject from known set of persons. Here, we employed a fuzzy rule-based technique to recognize emotion by facial expression analysis. The details are available in (Chakraborty, & Konar, 2009).

2. Analyse the EEG signals acquired during the period of arousal of emotion of the subject to extract its Hjorth parameters after filtering in the desired frequency bands as discussed.

3. Use previously trained three NNs of the same person used to map (a) prefrontal-to motor cortex features, b) motor cortex to facial features and c) facial features to pre-frontal features. Connect them in the topology shown in Figure 3.

4. Submit the input pre-frontal features at the input of the configuration in Figure3. Make forward pass to obtain motor cortex features by utilizing the signal propagation rule of NN_1 in Figure 3. Obtain facial features from motor features using NN_2. Obtain prefrontal features from facial features using NN_3. Measure the error norm by taking the Euclidean distance between the applied pre-frontal features and the predicted pre-frontal features.

5. If the error norm is below a prescribed threshold, then we declare that the observed emotion as a true emotion, else consider it as a pretension.

The threshold value is obtained after several experimental trials and found to be 0.02 in the present context.

Figure 8. The facial features of a subject. $EOR_{R/L}$=Eye Opening Raise Right/Left MO=Mouth Opening $EBR_{R/L}$= Eye Brow Raise Right/Left

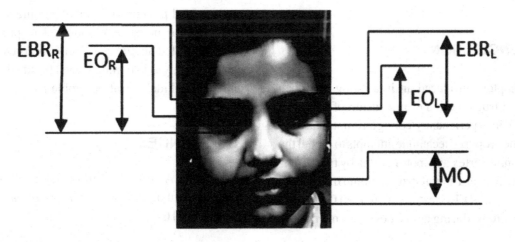

Table 1. Mean square error of three NN classifiers

Hjorth Featuresfor	Mean Square Error of NN1	Mean Square Error of NN2	Mean Square Error of NN3
CFNN	1.227e+7	0.3319	1.1898e+7
FFNN	3.4637e-24	1.202e-16	7.5406e-24
GRNN	3.6210e+4	0.0605	1.5602e-53
RBNN	5.0550e-25	9.0371e-33	4.5652e-34

Table 2. Confusion matrix for positive emotion

	True Emotion	Pretention
True Emotion	88%	12%
Pretention	72%	28%

Table 3. Confusion matrix for negative emotions

	True Emotion	Pretention
True Emotion	76%	24%
Pretention	64%	36%

Experiments are performed on 30 subjects (the same group as used for training) to detect their true emotion or pretension for positive emotions, including happiness and relaxation, and negative emotion, including fear and sadness. The results obtained are reported in Table II and III as two confusion matrices.

4. CONCLUSION

The chapter introduced an interesting approach to detect true emotion or pretension of a subject engaged in experiencing/feeling an emotional context. The proposed technique attempts to model the pre-frontal cortex and motor cortex by two different feed-forward neural structures and trains them with measured EEG features, extracted from those brain regions, during arousal of a given emotion.

The above two neural models jointly predicts the facial features of a subject from his pre-frontal EEG features. A third neural structure is employed to determine the predicted pre-frontal features from the predicted facial features. An error norm is used to measure the difference between the actual and predicted pre-frontal EEG features. In case, the error norm is small below a threshold, we declare the emotion to be a true emotion, else we call it pretension. The motivation behind such declaration lies in the inherent modelling of the neural nets with accurate measurement of pre-frontal, motor cortex and facial features. To ensure the accuracy in modelling, we considered four different neural nets and two learning algorithms, and experimentally selected the optimal neural configurations and learning algorithms.

The proposed scheme has been validated with 30 subjects and four emotions: two positive and two negative, and the results are very interesting. The confusion matrices we obtained reveals that for positive emotion the classification of correct emotion and pretension is relatively higher than the same for negative emotion. The proposed technique of detecting true emotion/pretension can be employed in computerized fraud detection and criminal identification problems.

REFERENCES

Ben-Ze'ev, A. (2002). Emotional intelligence: The conceptual issue. *Managing emotions in the workplace*, 164-183.

Canli, T., Desmond, J. E., Zhao, Z., Glover, G., & Gabrieli, J. D. (1998). Hemispheric asymmetry for emotional stimuli detected with fMRI. *Neuroreport*, *9*(14), 3233–3239. doi:10.1097/00001756-199810050-00019 PMID:9831457

Carr, L., Iacoboni, M., Dubeau, M. C., Mazziotta, J. C., & Lenzi, G. L. (2003). Neural mechanisms of empathy in humans: A relay from neural systems for imitation to limbic areas. *Proceedings of the National Academy of Sciences of the United States of America*, *100*(9), 5497–5502. doi:10.1073/pnas.0935845100 PMID:12682281

Chakraborty, A., & Konar, A. (2009). *Emotional intelligence: A cybernetic approach* (Vol. 234). Springer. doi:10.1007/978-3-540-68609-5

Chakraborty, A., Konar, A., Chakraborty, U. K., & Chatterjee, A. (2009). Emotion recognition from facial expressions and its control using fuzzy logic. *IEEE Transactions on Systems, Man and Cybernetics, Part A: Systems and Humans*, *39*(4), 726–743.

Chauvin, Y., & Rumelhart, D. E. (Eds.). (1995). *Backpropagation: Theory, architectures, and applications*. Psychology Press.

Chen, S., Cowan, C. F. N., & Grant, P. M. (1991). Orthogonal least squares learning algorithm for radial basis function networks. *IEEE Transactions on Neural Networks*, *2*(2), 302–309.

Chow, C. (1970). On optimum recognition error and reject tradeoff. *IEEE Transactions on Information Theory*, *16*(1), 41–46.

Clinical Psychology Associates of North Central Florida. P.A. (2013). *Welcome to Neuropsychology Central*. Retrieved from www.neuropsychology-central.com

Coan, J. A., Allen, J. J., & Harmon-Jones, E. (2001). Voluntary facial expression and hemispheric asymmetry over the frontal cortex. *Psychophysiology*, *38*(6), 912–925. doi:10.1111/1469-8986.3860912 PMID:12240668

Demuth, H., & Beale, M. (1993). *Neural network toolbox for use with MATLAB*.

Dimberg, U., & Thunberg, M. (1998). Rapid facial reactions to emotional facial expressions. *Scandinavian Journal of Psychology*, *39*(1), 39–45. doi:10.1111/1467-9450.00054 PMID:9619131

Emotiv. (n.d.). *Homepage*. Retrieved from www.emotiv.com

Fasel, B., & Luettin, J. (2003). Automatic facial expression analysis: A survey. *Pattern Recognition*, *36*(1), 259–275. doi:10.1016/S0031-3203(02)00052-3

Halder, A., Konar, A., Mandal, R., Chakraborty, A., Bhowmik, P., Pal, N. R., & Nagar, A. K. (2013). General and Interval Type-2 Fuzzy Face-Space Approach to Emotion Recognition. *IEEE Transactions on Systems, Man, and Cybernetics*.

Haykin, S. (1994). *Neural networks: a comprehensive foundation*. Prentice Hall PTR.

Hjorth, B. (1970). EEG analysis based on time domain properties. *Electroencephalography and Clinical Neurophysiology*, *29*(3), 306–310. doi:10.1016/0013-4694(70)90143-4 PMID:4195653

Junghöfer, M., Elbert, T., Tucker, D. M., & Rockstroh, B. (2000). Statistical control of artifacts in dense array EEG/MEG studies. *Psychophysiology*, *37*(4), 523–532. doi:10.1111/1469-8986.3740523 PMID:10934911

Kar, R., Chakraborty, A., Saha, A., & Konar, A. (2013). Detection of true emotion or pretension: A brain- computer interface approach. In *Proceedings of National Conference on Brain and Consciousness.*

Kawasaki, H., Adolphs, R., Kaufman, O., Damasio, H., Damasio, A. R., Granner, M., & Howard, M. A. et al. (2001). Single-neuron responses to emotional visual stimuli recorded in human ventral prefrontal cortex. *Nature Neuroscience, 4*(1), 15–16. doi:10.1038/82850 PMID:11135639

Khosrowabadi, R., Quek, H. C., Wahab, A., & Ang, K. K. (2010, August). EEG-based emotion recognition using self-organizing map for boundary detection. In *20th International Conference on Pattern Recognition (ICPR), 2010* (pp. 4242-4245). IEEE. doi:10.1109/ICPR.2010.1031

Kim, S. E., Kim, J. W., Kim, J. J., Jeong, B. S., Choi, E., Jeong, Y. G., & Ki, S. W. et al. (2007). The neural mechanism of imagining facial affective expression. *Brain Research, 1145,* 128–137. doi:10.1016/j.brainres.2006.12.048 PMID:17359942

Konar, A. (1999). *Artificial intelligence and soft computing: Behavioral and cognitive modeling of the human brain* (Vol. 1). CRC press. doi:10.1201/9781420049138

Konar, A. (2005). *Computational intelligence: Principles, techniques and applications.* Springer.

Lee, C. M., & Narayanan, S. S. (2005). Toward detecting emotions in spoken dialogs. *IEEE Transactions on Speech and Audio Processing, 13*(2), 293–303.

Lee, T. W., Josephs, O., Dolan, R. J., & Critchley, H. D. (2006). Imitating expressions: Emotion-specific neural substrates in facial mimicry. *Social Cognitive and Affective Neuroscience, 1*(2), 122–135. doi:10.1093/scan/nsl012 PMID:17356686

Meister, I. G., Boroojerdi, B., Foltys, H., Sparing, R., Huber, W., & Töpper, R. (2003). Motor cortex hand area and speech: Implications for the development of language. *Neuropsychologia, 41*(4), 401–406. doi:10.1016/S0028-3932(02)00179-3 PMID:12559157

Merzagora, A. C., Bunce, S., Izzetoglu, M., & Onaral, B. (2006, August). Wavelet analysis for EEG feature extraction in deception detection. In *Engineering in Medicine and Biology Society, 2006 (EMBS'06): 28th Annual International Conference of the IEEE* (pp. 2434-2437). IEEE. doi:10.1109/IEMBS.2006.260247

Mitra, S., & Acharya, T. (2007). Gesture recognition: A survey. *IEEE Transactions on Systems, Man, and Cybernetics, Part C: Applications and Reviews, 37*(3), 311–324.

Morecraft, R. J., Stilwell-Morecraft, K. S., & Rossing, W. R. (2004). The motor cortex and facial expression: New insights from neuroscience. *The Neurologist, 10*(5), 235–249. doi:10.1097/01.nrl.0000138734.45742.8d PMID:15335441

Murugappan, M., Rizon, M., Nagarajan, R., & Yaacob, S. (2010). Inferring of human emotional states using multichannel EEG. *European Journal of Scientific Research, 48*(2), 281–299.

Murugappan, M., Rizon, M., Nagarajan, R., Yaacob, S., Zunaidi, I., & Hazry, D. (2007). EEG feature extraction for classifying emotions using FCM and FKM. *International Journal of Computers and Communications, 1*(2), 21–25.

Orozco, J., Rudovic, O., Gonzàlez, J., & Pantic, M. (2013). Hierarchical on-line appearance-based tracking for 3D head pose, eyebrows, lips, eyelids and irises. *Image and Vision Computing, 31*(4), 322–340. doi:10.1016/j.imavis.2013.02.001

Pantic, M., & Bartlett, M. S. (2007). *Machine analysis of facial expressions* (pp. 377–416). Viena, Austria: I-Tech.

Pantic, M., & Rothkrantz, L. J. (2003). Toward an affect-sensitive multimodal human-computer interaction. *Proceedings of the IEEE*, *91*(9), 1370–1390. doi:10.1109/JPROC.2003.817122

Pantic, M., & Rothkrantz, L. J. M. (2000). Automatic analysis of facial expressions: The state of the art. *Pattern Analysis and Machine Intelligence. IEEE Transactions on*, *22*(12), 1424–1445.

Penfield, W., & Rasmussen, T. (1950). *The cerebral cortex of man; a clinical study of localization of function*. New York, N.Y: The Macmillan Company.

Petrantonakis, P. C., & Hadjileontiadis, L. J. (2010). Emotion recognition from brain signals using hybrid adaptive filtering and higher order crossings analysis. *IEEE Transactions on Affective Computing*, *1*(2), 81–97.

Petrantonakis, P. C., & Hadjileontiadis, L. J. (2010). Emotion recognition from EEG using higher order crossings. *IEEE Transactions on Information Technology in Biomedicine*, *14*(2), 186–197.

Phansalkar, V. V., & Sastry, P. S. (1994). Analysis of the back-propagation algorithm with momentum. *IEEE Transactions on Neural Networks*, *5*(3), 505–506. doi:10.1109/72.286925 PMID:18267819

Purves, D., Cabeza, R., Huettel, S. A., LaBar, K. S., Platt, M. L., & Woldorff, M. G. (2013). *Principles of cognitive neuroscience* (2nd ed.). Sinauer Associates Inc.

Rizzolatti, G., & Craighero, L. (2004). The mirror-neuron system. *Annual Review of Neuroscience*, *27*(1), 169–192. doi:10.1146/annurev. neuro.27.070203.144230 PMID:15217330

Rumelhart, D. E., Hinton, G. E., & Williams, R. J. (1985). *Learning internal representations by error propagation (No. ICS-8506)*. California University of San Diego La Jolla, Institute For Cognitive Science.

Russell, J. A., Bachorowski, J. A., & Fernández-Dols, J. M. (2003). Facial and vocal expressions of emotion. *Annual Review of Psychology*, *54*(1), 329–349. doi:10.1146/annurev. psych.54.101601.145102 PMID:12415074

Sexton, R. S., Dorsey, R. E., & Johnson, J. D. (1999). Optimization of neural networks: A comparative analysis of the genetic algorithm and simulated annealing. *European Journal of Operational Research*, *114*(3), 589–601. doi:10.1016/ S0377-2217(98)00114-3

Soleymani, M., Lichtenauer, J., Pun, T., & Pantic, M. (2012). A multimodal database for affect recognition and implicit tagging. *IEEE Transactions on Affective Computing*, *3*(1), 42–55.

Tian, Y. L., Kanade, T., & Cohn, J. F. (2005). Facial expression analysis. In *Handbook of face recognition* (pp. 247–275). Springer New York. doi:10.1007/0-387-27257-7_12

Wong, F. S. (1991, November). Fastprop: A selective training algorithm for fast error propagation. In *1991 IEEE International Joint Conference on Neural Networks* (pp. 2038-2043). IEEE. doi:10.1109/IJCNN.1991.170635

Yu, H., & Wilamowski, B. M. (2011). Levenberg-Marquardt training. *The Industrial Electronics Handbook*, *5*, 1–15.

KEY TERMS AND DEFINITIONS

Brain-Computer Interface (BCI): BCI is a communication pathway connecting the brain and computer. BCI, also known as brain machine interface (BMI), is often directed at creating assisting, augmenting and repairing human cognitive and sensory motor functions.

Electroencephalogram (EEG): EEG is a recording of the brain's spontaneous electrical activity. It is measured through electrodes placed on the scalp. These electrodes capture electric field resulting from the interchange of ions among the neurons in the brain.

Human-Computer Interaction (HCI): HCI involves study, planning, design and uses of the interaction between humans and computers. It is a multidisciplinary avenue of behavioral sciences, computer science, media studies and design.

Motor-Cortex: Motor cortex is the part of brain associated with planning, control and execution of movements. It forms the rear of the frontal lobe, located at the junction of frontal and parietal lobe. It is adjacent to somatosensory cortex which is a part of the parietal lobe.

Negative Emotion: Emotions associated with negative valence are categorized as negative emotions. These include fear, disgust and anger.

Positive Emotion: Emotions associated with positive valence (affective dimension indicative of pleasure) are categorized as positive emotions. These include happiness, relaxation and excitement.

Pre-Frontal Cortex: The pre-frontal cortex is an area covering the front part of the frontal lobe. It is associated with processing of cognitive functions including memory, language and emotions.

Pretension: The voluntary suppression or manipulation of physical manifestations, representing the true psychological state of the human mind, is called pretension. Pretention can be detected by the study on non-voluntary manifestation in physiological responses including cardiovascular activity, skin conductance, respiration and electroencephalogram.

Chapter 14
Computing with Words Model for Emotion Recognition Using Interval Type–2 Fuzzy Sets

Reshma Kar
Jadavpur University, India

Amit Konar
Jadavpur University, India

Anisha Halder
Jadavpur University, India

Aruna Chakraborty
St. Thomas' College of Engineering and Technology, India

Atulya K. Nagar
Liverpool Hope University, UK

ABSTRACT

This chapter provides a novel approach to emotion recognition of subjects from the user-specified word description of their facial features. The problem is solved in two phases. In the first phase, an interval type-2 fuzzy membership space for each facial feature in different linguistic grades for different emotions is created. In the second phase, a set of fuzzy emotion-classifier rules is instantiated with fuzzy word description about facial features to infer the winning emotion class. The most attractive part of this research is to autonomously transform user-specified word descriptions into membership functions and construction of footprint of uncertainty for each facial feature in different linguistic grades. The proposed technique for emotion classification is very robust as it is sensitive to changes in word description only, rather than the absolute measurement of features. Besides it offers a good classification accuracy over 87% and is thus comparable with existing techniques.

1. INTRODUCTION

Emotion recognition is currently gaining popularity for its increasing applications in human-computer interfaces (HCI). Several modalities of emotion recognition have been reported in the literature. Of these, the modality of facial expression analysis is given priority for its simplicity in realization in current generation HCI-system. This chapter attempts to provide a novel solution to the well-known emotion recognition problem by facial expression analysis.

DOI: 10.4018/978-1-4666-7278-9.ch014

Existing research on emotion recognition by facial expression analysis employ several models of machine learning and pattern recognition, including Bayesian classifier (Sebe, N., Lew, M. S., Cohen, I., Garg, A., & Huang, T. S., 2002)) Back-propagation neural classifier (Kobayashi, H., & Hara, F., 1992, September), (Zhao, J., & Kearney, G. 1996), Support Vector Machine (SVM) (Cristianini, N., & Shawe-Taylor, J. 2000), (Das, S., Halder, A., Bhowmik, P., Chakraborty, A., Konar, A., & Nagar, A. K.) and Hidden Markov models (HMM) (Lin, J. C., Wu, C. H., & Wei, W. L. 2012). Recently researchers are taking keen interest to employ the logic of fuzzy sets in emotion recognition by facial expression analysis. In (Chakraborty, A., Konar, A., Chakraborty, U. K., & Chatterjee, A.), Chakraborty *et al.* employed classical fuzzy sets to recognize emotion by facial expression analysis.

In a more recent work (Mandal, R., Halder, A., Bhowmik, P., Konar, A., Chakraborty, A., & Nagar, A. K. (2011, June), researchers considered type-2 fuzzy sets as a basic model for facial expression representation of subjects (carrying same/similar emotions), and later employed type-2 fuzzy reasoning to classify unknown facial expression into one of five known emotion classes. The latter method requires measurements of facial features to determine the emotion class of the subject by type-2 fuzzy analysis. Unfortunately, the precise measurements of the facial features requires segmentation, localization and feature extraction on the unknown facial image of the subject, and thus adds overhead to the computational complexity of the classifier algorithm.

The present chapter, however, overcomes the above problem by labeling the features of a facial image into fuzzy word descriptions, which are directly submitted to a fuzzy classifier for emotion recognition. Fuzzy quantifiers like Large, Small and Moderate, and fuzzy linguistic hedges like VERY, NOT SO etc. are used to describe the qualitative variation in the fuzzy quantification.

A user on observing an unknown facial expression describes the facial features using the fuzzy linguistic hedges and quantifiers. A computer receives the linguistic descriptions about the face and classifies the emotion of the subject to one of five distinct emotion classes through a process of Interval Type-2 Fuzzy Reasoning (IT2FR). The contribution of the present chapter is briefly outlined below.

First, the chapter proposes a novel approach to translate user-defined word descriptions about facial features into emotion using IT2FR. Automatic transformation of word description of features into emotions being human-like enhances the scope of interaction between humans and machines in the next generation human-computer interface (HCI).

Second, construction of the space of *footprint of uncertainty* (FOU) for each facial feature (such as mouth-opening) in different linguistic grades (such as *LARGE*) for different emotions from the available word description obtained from several assessors carries novelty in the literature of Affective Computing.

Third, the proposed scheme does not require absolute measurement of facial features as input to the emotion classifier system. Rather, it requires only word description of facial features of a subject by a user. Naturally, the proposed method saves significant computational overhead required due to pre-processing, segmentation and localization of the facial features.

Lastly, the lack of precision in word description of features in comparison to absolute measurement of features does not significantly influence the classification accuracy, indicating the robustness of the word description models.

The chapter is divided into seven sections. In section II, the preliminaries of Type 2 fuzzy sets are given. Section III is concerned with the principles and methodology. Section IV provides the details of the fuzzy classifier. Experimental details are given in section V. Performance Analysis is given in section VI. Conclusions are listed in section VII.

2. PRELIMINARIES OF TYPE-2 FUZZY SETS

We now define a few terminologies related to Type-1 (T1) and Type-2 (T2) fuzzy sets to develop the rest of the chapter.

Definition 1: A conventional *type-1 fuzzy set* A defined on a universe of discourse X, is described by a two-dimensional membership function, hereafter called type-1 membership function. For any generic element $x \in X$, the *membership function* (MF) $\mu_A(x)$ is a crisp number in [0, 1]. Generally, a fuzzy set A is two tuple [10] given by,

$$A = \{(x, \mu_A(x)) \mid \forall x \in X\}. \tag{1}$$

Alternatively, a fuzzy set A is defined as given in (2) (Aguero, J. R., & Vargas, A. (2007).).

$$A = \int_{x \in X} \mu_A(x) \mid x \tag{2}$$

where $\int$ denotes union of all admissible x.

Definition 2: A *type-2 fuzzy set* $\tilde{A}$ is described by a three dimensional membership function, herafeter called type-2 membership function, which also is fuzzy. The *type-2 membership function* is usually expressed as $\mu_{\tilde{A}}(x, u)$, where $x \in X$, and $u \in J_x \subseteq [0,1]$. Generally, the fuzzy set $\tilde{A}$ is described as a two tuple:

$$\tilde{A} = \{((x, u), \mu_{\tilde{A}}(x, u)) \mid x \in X, u \in J_x \subseteq [0,1]\} \tag{3}$$

where $\mu_{\tilde{A}}(x, u) \in [0,1]$. An alternative representation of type-2 fuzzy set is presented in (4).

$$\tilde{A} = \int_{x \in X} \int_{u \in J_x} \mu_{\tilde{A}}(x, u) \mid (x, u), J_x \subseteq [0,1] \tag{4}$$

$$= \int_{x \in X} [\int_{u \in J_x} f_x(u)/u] / x, J_x \subseteq [0,1] \tag{5}$$

where $f_x(u) = \mu_{\tilde{A}}(x, u) \in [0,1]$. The notation $\iint$ represents a union over all admissible values of x and u.

Definition 3: The two-dimensional plane containing axes u and $\mu(x', u)$ at each point of x=x' is called the *vertical slice* of $\mu_{\tilde{A}}(x, u)$ (Wu, H., Wu, Y., & Luo, J. 2009). A *secondary membership function* thus is a vertical slice of $\mu_{\tilde{A}}(x, u)$. Symbolically, the secondary membership function $\mu_{\tilde{A}}(x, u)$ at x=x' for $x' \in X$ and $\forall u \in J_{x'} \subseteq [0,1]$ is defined by

$$\mu_{\tilde{A}}(x, u) = \int_{u \in J_{x'}} f_{x'}(u) \mid u, J_{x'} \subseteq [0,1] \tag{6}$$

where $0 \leq f_{x'}(u) \leq 1$. The magnitude of a secondary membership function is called secondary grade (Wu, H., Wu, Y., & Luo, J., 2009). $J_{x'}$ in (6) is referred to as the primary membership of x'.

Definition 4: Uncertainty in the primary membership of a type-2 fuzzy set $\tilde{A}$ is described by a bounded region, called *footprint of uncertainty* (FOU). The FOU is the defined as the union of all primary memberships, i.e.,

$$FOU(\tilde{A}) = \bigcup_{x \in U} J_x \tag{7}$$

In (Wu, H., Wu, Y., & Luo, J. 2009), $FOU(\tilde{A})$ has alternatively been defined as $D\tilde{A}$, where

$$D\tilde{A}(x) = J_x \forall x \in X. \tag{8}$$

Thus (4) reduces to

$$\tilde{A} = \iint_{(x,u) \in D\tilde{A}} \mu_{\tilde{A}}(x, u)/(x, u) \tag{9}$$

In case all the secondary grades of a type-2 fuzzy set $\tilde{A}$ are equal to 1, i.e.,

$$\mu_{\tilde{A}}(x,u) = 1 \ \forall x \in X, \forall u \in J_x \subseteq [0,1] \quad (10)$$

we call $\tilde{A}$ an *interval type-2 fuzzy set (IT2FS)*. The FOU in a IT2FS is bounded by two curves: the *Lower* and the *Upper Membership Functions* $\underline{\mu}_{\tilde{A}}(x)$ and $\overline{\mu}_{\tilde{A}}(x)$ respectively, where $\underline{\mu}_{\tilde{A}}(x)$ and $\overline{\mu}_{\tilde{A}}(x)$ at all x is computed by evaluating the minimum and the maximum of the membership functions of the embedded type-1 fuzzy sets (Mendel, J., & Wu, D. 2010) inside the FOU.

3. PRINCIPLES AND METHODOLOGY

Suppose that there are 10 assessors, who have definite opinions about the linguistic gradations of the facial features, such as VERY LARGE (VL), LARGE (L), MODERATE (M), SMALL (S) and VERY SMALL (VS) based on the range of specific facial attribute, say eye-opening. Thus for five linguistic grades and 10 assessors we have a matrix A (Table- I) of (10×5), where the row index i indicates assessor number i and the column index j indicates the j-th linguistic grade, and the element $a_{ij} = [^k f_{min}, \ ^k f_{max}]$ denotes the range of a facial attribute allocated to j-th linguistic grade by assessor i for the k-th feature.

Now, presume that we have a face database containing 50 facial images of 10 subjects for five distinct emotions. We now consider each group of 10 images carrying the same emotion of different subjects. These facial images are assessed by 10 assessors to attach one fuzzy linguistic grade to individual facial images based on the manual examination of the facial features by the assessors and their opinion about ranges for each linguistic grade. The linguistic grades of a facial feature for 10 facial images carrying the same emotion assessed by 10 assessors is now recorded in matrix B, the i-th row index of which denotes assessor i, the j-th column index of which denotes image number j, and the element b_{ij} denotes the linguistic grades assigned to image j by assessor i. Thus for 7 features, we have 7 such B-like matrices.

Now, we identify the linguistic grade having highest frequency of occurrence in each row of B matrix, and save it in the last column of the same row in the augmented B matrix, hereafter called B$'$ (Table-II). The last column information in i-th row of B$'$ represents the assessment by assessor i about the most likely linguistic grade of the images carrying same emotion.

Now, for each most likely membership grade, such as LARGE, VERY LARGE etc. obtained from the last column of matrix B$'$, we construct a IT2FS describing the concept for a linguistic phrase like *mouth-opening is LARGE*. Construction of FOUs requires two steps. First, for each assessor, consulting the range of linguistic variable for each feature as given in Table-1, we construct a type-1 Membership Function (MF). Now, for each linguistic grade, say LARGE, obtained in the last column of Table-2, we consider the union of MFs representing mouth-opening is LARGE. The union of the type-1 MFs for the fuzzy proposition: *mouth-opening is LARGE* represents the FOU of the IT2FS describing the same concept.

Thus for every linguistic grade found in the last column of Table-2 we would have an FOU describing the linguistic grade. So, for 5 emotions and 6 features and 5 linguistic grades for each feature, we could have a maximum number of $5 \times 6 \times 5 = 150$ FOUs. However, as seen in Table-II the last column contains only 2 out of 5 grades for mouth-opening in emotion happiness. So, in practice the number of FOUs is much less than 150. The FOUs together is referred to as fuzzy face space.

Once the fuzzy face space is created, we use it during the recognition phase.

In the recognition phase, given an unknown facial image, a user manually measures the linguistic grades of each feature. Presume that the user

Table 1. Matrix A: Range of 5 linguistic gradations of a particular facial feature according to 10 assessors

Assessor (A_i) \ Images (I_j)	I_1	I_2	- - - - - - - - - - - - - -	I_10	Most likely Linguistic Grade
A1	L	M	M L············· M	M	M
A2					
A10	M	M	M L············· L	M	L

Table 2. Matrix B: Opinion of different assessors about a particular feature of 10 facial images and corresponding most likely linguistic grade for a specific emotion

Assessor \ Grade	G_1 (VS)	············· G_j (M) ·············	G_5 (VL)
A1			
A2			
Ai		············· $[^k f_{min}, {}^k f_{max}]$	
A10			

in general is not an assessor. Since the parametric ranges of features say mo, for the linguistic grades like VERY HIGH is not known for a user, who is not an assessor, we use the average of the centre of the ranges of feature assigned by 10 assessors to the linguistic grade the user refers to describe a facial feature. Thus the average of the centre values of the j-th column of Matrix A is the measure of the gradation of the unknown feature. Thus for 6 features of the unknown facial expression, we have 6 such derived measurements.

After we obtain the derived measurements about the 6 facial features, we instantiate the respective FOUs with the derived measurements following the rule. Let the derived measurement of the 6 features: $f_1, f_2, ..., f_7$ be $\hat{f}_1, \hat{f}_2, ..., \hat{f}_6$ respectively. Now, for the FOUs of a given emotion i, we evaluate the UMF and LMF for each feature $f_i = \hat{f}_i, \ \forall i = 1 \ to \ 6$.

Now we evaluate

$$\left. \begin{array}{l} \underset{i=1}{\overset{6}{T}}(UMF(\hat{f}_i)) = UMF_i, say \\ \underset{i=1}{\overset{6}{T}}(LMF(\hat{f}_i)) = LMF_i, say \end{array} \right\} \quad (11)$$

and define score $sc_i = (UMF_i + LMF_i)/2$. We repeat the above computation of $sc_i, \forall i$, and regard emotion j to be the emotion of the unknown subject, if $sc_j \geq sc_i, \forall i$. If a single rule only is instantiated by the word descriptions of the user, the rule will be fired and the inferred score sc_i of the fired rule-i represents the degree of strength of the recognized emotion as stated in the consequence of the fired classifier rule.

4. THE PROPOSED FUZZY CLASSIFIER

The traditional fuzzy models employed in emotion recognition (Chakraborty, A., Konar, A.,

Chakraborty, U. K., & Chatterjee, A. 2009), (Mandal, R., Halder, A., Bhowmik, P., Konar, A., Chakraborty, A., & Nagar, A. K. 2011), (Halder, A., Rakshit, P., Chakraborty, S., Konar, A., Chakraborty, A., Kim, E., & Nagar, A. K. 2012) requires measurements of the facial features to instantiate membership functions in the antecedent part of fuzzy rules designed for emotion classification. This calls for image segmentation, localization and measurements of the facial features in the localized images, adding computational overhead in the emotion recognition scheme. The proposed method, however, does not require (exact) measurements of facial features. A user provides her opinion about facial measurements in fuzzy linguistic grades, such as mouth-opening is VERY- SMALL, and the fuzzy word engine can determine the emotion of the subject from the fuzzy quantification about facial features. The proposed fuzzy classifier includes a set of fuzzy rules and a IT2FS inferential procedure to recognize the emotion class from the word descriptions of facial features. The other important issue to be addressed in this section is to calibrate the MFs based on individual users' opinion about the ranges of facial features to describe linguistic grades.

Membership Function Selection

MFs about facial features of a subject based on the fuzzy (linguistic) assessment of different assessors are determined from the assessors' specification about the ranges of attributes to qualify a specific linguistic grade. For example, consider the facial feature: mouth-opening (mo), which is categorized into five linguistic grades by an assessor according to his own choice of the ranges for the attribute. An illustrative grading for the linguistic variable mouth-opening by an assessor is given below.

VERY SMALL(VS): When 4≤mo≤6,
SMALL (S): When 6≤mo≤10
MODERATE (M): When 11≤mo≤14
LARGE (L): When 15≤mo≤18

VERY LARGE (VL): When $19 \leq mo$

In our experiments, we consider n (=10) assessors to provide ranges for five linguistic grades stated above.

To determine the MFs for fuzzy linguistic grade, we consider two issues: 1) restricting the base of individual MF based on the available range of the feature representing the linguistic grade, and 2) select a mathematical function to represent the MF, whose parameters are to be tuned intuitively as illustrated below.

The list of intuitively selected membership function for five linguistic grades: VS, S, M, L and VL along with the set of unknown parameters of the MFs are given in Table-III. The parameters used in the MFs are determined with an aim to satisfy its characteristics in the range of intervals provided by the assessor. Examples 1 and 2 demonstrate the selection of parameters for five distinct grades of MFs.

Example 1: This example illustrates the selection of k in the membership function: $\mu_L^{(mo)} = 1 - e^{-k.mo}$ for the fuzzy concept mouth-opening is LARGE. Suppose, we want k to attain 70% of the fuzzy membership 1 at mo= 14 pixels. Then

$$1 - e^{-k.(14)} = 0.7$$

which returns

$$k = -(1/14)\ln(0.3) = 0.56599$$

Example 2: This example illustrates the selection of the parameters of MODERATE MFs for mouth-opening. Since for the given assessor, mo for MODERATE grade lies in 11 to 14 pixels, we set $\overline{mo}$ as the average of 11 and 14 pixels, and thus $\overline{mo} = 12.5$ pixels. The standard deviation sigma here is evaluated by considering a Gaussian MF for MODERATE grade, and so $\overline{mo} + 3\sigma$ approximately equal to 14 pixels, yielding σ = 0.5. For the grade VS and S we select k_1 =100 and k_2=10 intuitively. For the grade VL, we intuitively set $k_4 = k_3^2$.

The Classifier Rules

The IT2FS reasoning system introduced here employs a particular format of rules, commonly used in fuzzy classification problems (Cordón, O., del Jesus, M. J., & Herrera, F. 1999). The general format of a fuzzy rule is given by

R_c: if f_1 is $\tilde{A}_1$ AND f_2 is $\tilde{A}_2$ .... AND f_m is $\tilde{A}_m$ then emotion class is c.

Here, f_i for i=1 to m are m-measurements (feature values) in the interval type-2 fuzzy sets $\tilde{A}_1$, $\tilde{A}_2$, ..., $\tilde{A}_m$ respectively.

FOUs

Principles of FOU construction have been outlined in section III. It is apparent from section III that we construct FOU for all possible linguistic grades appearing in the last column of Table-II for all the features appearing in the facial expres-

Table 3. Models and model parameters for representing Type-I membership functions

Gradation	Selected MF	Parameter of the MF
VS	$\exp(^{-k_1^2 .mo})$	k_1
S	$e^{-k.mo}$	k_2
M	$e^{-(mo-\overline{mo})^2/\sigma^2}$	$\overline{mo}, \sigma^2$
L	$1 - e^{-k_3 .mo}$	k_3
VL	$1 - e^{-k_4 .mo}$	k_4

sion representative of a specific emotion. These FOUs are used in subsequent reasoning phase to classify emotion from word description about facial features, such as LARGE mouth-opening, SMALL eye-opening etc. Details of reasoning using classifier rules, FOUs and word description about facial features are given below.

Reasoning Technique for Emotion Classification

Given a set of word descriptions about facial features, we need to determine the emotion of the subject. The following steps are undertaken to handle the problem. First, for each word description about a facial feature, such as *mouth-opening is LARGE*, we identify the range of the feature (here, mouth-opening) for each assessor by consulting Table-I, and determine the average of the centre of the intervals describing the word description. This numerical value of the feature is used to determine the UMF and LMF of the already constructed IT2FS at the pre-determined value of the feature. Now, based on the word descriptions of m features, we obtain m feature values by the above procedure. Naturally, a classifier rule R_c introduced above is instantiated with the measurement of features, undertaken above, and the FOU for each IT2FS representing the given word description is instantiated with the derived feature values to obtain a set of m UMFs and m LMFs. We now take the minimum of the UMFs and LMFs separately and take the average of the resulting minima. The result thus obtained denotes the degree of membership of the facial expression to lie in the emotion class c following Rule R_c. If more than one rules fire with the given word descriptions about facial features, then the rule yielding largest membership of the emotion class is declared as the winner, and the corresponding emotion class c is the emotion class of the unknown subject.

5. EXPERIMENTS

In this section, we present the experimental details of emotion recognition using the principles and algorithms introduced in section III and IV. We here consider 6 facial features, (i.e., m=6) and 5 emotion classes, (i.e., k=5) including anger, fear, disgust, happiness and relaxation.

Facial Feature Selection

Existing research results (Das, S., Halder, A., Bhowmik, P., Chakraborty, A., Konar, A., & Nagar, A. K. 2009), (Chakraborty, A., Konar, A., Chakraborty, U. K., & Chatterjee, A. 2009), (Mandal, R., Halder, A., Bhowmik, P., Konar, A., Chakraborty, A., & Nagar, A. K. 2011) reveal that the eyes and the lips are the most important facial regions responsible for the manifestation of emotion. This inspired us to select the following features: Left Eye Opening (eo_L), Right Eye Opening (eo_R), Distance between the Lower Eyelid to the Eyebrow for the Left Eye (lee_L), Distance between the Lower Eyelid to Eyebrow for the Right Eye (lee_R), Maximum Mouth opening (mo) including the lower and the upper lips and Eye-brow Constriction (ebc). These features are obtained from emotionally rich facial expressions synthesized by the subjects by acting. Figure 1 explains the above facial features on a selected facial image.

Creating the Interval Type-2 Fuzzy Membership Space

There are 10 assessors, who have definite opinions about the linguistic gradations of the facial features, such as VERY LARGE, LARGE, SMALL etc. based on the range of specific facial attribute. The feature: Mouth-Opening according to assessor 1 is Very Small (VS) when $4 \leq mo \leq 7$, Small (S) when $8 \leq mo \leq 10$ and so on as indicated in

Figure 1. Facial features

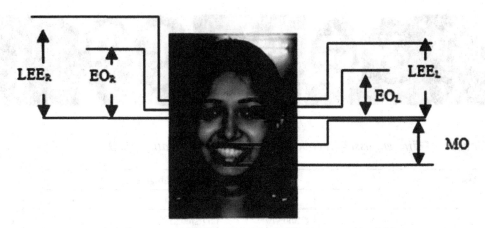

row 1 of Table-IV. Similarly, the gradation of mo by different assessors is given in the next rows in Table- IV. So, for 6 features there are 6 such tables like Table-IV.

Thus when an assessor examines 10 facial expressions of different subjects carrying a specific emotion, he assigns one of five possible grades (VS, S, M, L, and VL) to the features of the facial expressions. Thus for 10 assessors, we obtain Table V, where all columns except the last column indicates the assigned grade of a specific feature in 10 facial expressions (carrying a specific emotion) by 10 assessors. The last column in each row indicates the most likely grade assigned in that row. So, for the 6 features of each set of facial expressions like Figure 2 there are 6 such tables like Table-V and for 5 emotional sets of facial images there are 5×6= 30 such tables.

We now create an IT2FS by constructing type-1 membership function (MF) using the most likely grade of the assignment by the individual assigner. In other words, for the last entries in Table-V we construct MF in definite ranges of the facial parameter as defined in Table-IV. For each linguistic grade, here, LARGE and VERY LARGE, obtained in the last column of Table-V, we consider the union of interval type-2 MFs

representing *mouth-opening is LARGE* and the union of interval type-2 MFs representing *mouth-opening is VERY-LARGE* to obtain the FOUS. Thus we have 2 FOUs describing the linguistic grade for emotion Happiness and feature mo. Thus for 5 emotions and 6 features, a maximum no. of 5×6×5= 150 FOUs can be made. But practically, the number of FOUs is much less than 150 as seen from the previous example. The FOUs together is referred to as fuzzy membership space. Once the fuzzy membership space is created, we use it during the recognition phase.

Figures 3 and 4 gives an illustration of one such FOU for the feature mo, emotion: Happiness and grade: LARGE.

Emotion Recognition of an Unknown Subject

Suppose we want to recognize the correct emotion class of the facial image in Figure 5.

For recognizing the correct emotion of an unknown face, first the 6 facial features i.e., eo_L, eo_R, mo, lee_L, lee_R and ebc are assessed by a user. For the facial expression shown in Figure 5, the opinion of a user is listed in the 2nd row of Table VI.

Figure 2. Different Facial Expressions from Subjects for emotion: Happy

Table 4. Opinion of different assessors about the gradations of feature: MO

Assessors	Ranges of each Linguistic Grade				
	VS	S	M	L	VL
A1	mo≤7	8≤mo≤10	11≤mo≤13	14≤mo≤18	mo≥19
A2	mo≤5	6≤mo≤9	10≤mo≤13	14≤mo≤19	mo≥20
A3	mo≤9	10≤mo≤14	15≤mo≤18	19≤mo≤23	mo≥24
A4	mo≤6	7≤mo≤8	8≤mo≤14	15≤mo≤18	mo≥19
A5	mo≤7	8≤mo≤9	9≤mo≤12	13≤mo≤20	mo≥21
A6	mo≤8	9≤mo≤10	10≤mo≤15	16≤mo≤21	mo≥22
A7	mo≤4	5≤mo≤7	6≤mo≤9	10≤mo≤16	mo≥17
A8	mo≤3	4≤mo≤7	5≤mo≤10	11≤mo≤16	mo≥17
A9	mo≤7	8≤mo≤10	9≤mo≤14	15≤mo≤21	mo≥22
A10	mo≤6	7≤mo≤8	8≤mo≤13	14≤mo≤18	mo≥19

Table 5. Opinion of different assessor about the feature: MO of 10 instances in Figure 3 and 4 and Corresponding most likely MF

Assessors	Facial Images for a given emotion										Most likely MF
	I1	I2	I3	I4	I5	I6	I7	I8	I9	I10	
A1	L	L	VL	L	L	M	L	VL	VL	L	L
A2	L	VL	VL	VL	VL	L	L	VL	VL	VL	VL
A3	L	L	VL	L	L	L	L	VL	L	L	L
A4	M	VL	VL	M	L	L	M	VL	VL	VL	VL
A5	L	L	VL	L	L	L	L	VL	L	L	L
A6	L	L	VL	L	L	M	L	VL	VL	VL	L
A7	M	VL	VL	L	VL	L	M	VL	VL	L	VL
A8	L	L	VL	L	L	L	L	VL	L	L	L
A9	L	L	VL	L	L	M	M	VL	L	M	L
A10	L	L	VL	L	L	L	L	VL	VL	L	L

Figure 3. (a) Membership to be LARGE of Feature: mo, Emotion: Happiness, based on the opinion of 10 assessors

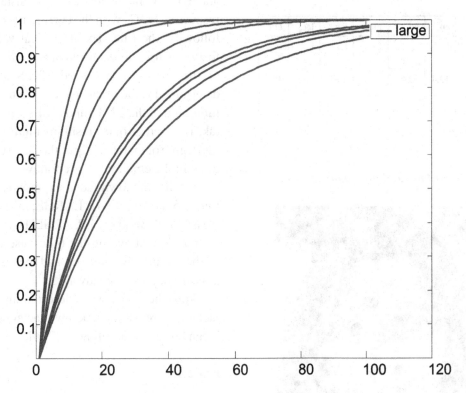

Figure 4. (b) Corresponding FOU

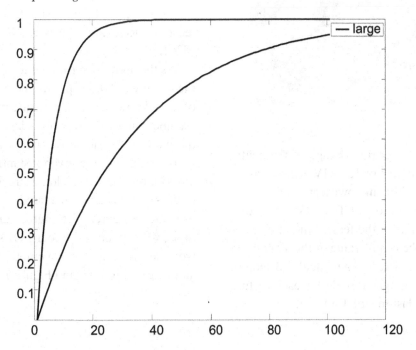

Table 6. Opinion of an User About the features of Figure 4

Feature	eo_L	eo_R	mo	lee_L	lee_R	ebc
Grade of the feature	L	L	L	L	L	L
Numerical value of the feature	12.4	12.4	16.55	20.5	20.5	15

Figure 5. Facial Image of an unknown subject

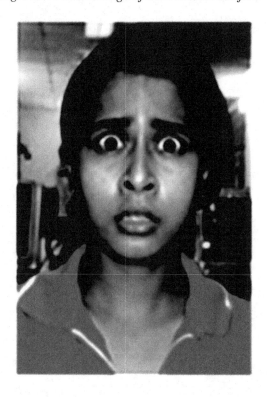

Now, we consider the average of the centre values of each column of Table IV is the measure of the gradation of the unknown feature. The grade of mo from the 2nd row of Table IV is found to be L. So, the value of the feature mo to be M is the average of the centre value of the 4th column of Table IV, i.e., 16.55. The calculated feature values for each assigned grade for each feature are listed in the last row of Table VI.

After we obtain the derived measurements about the 6 facial features, we instantiate the respective FOUs with the derived measurements following the rule. The numerical value of the feature is used to determine the UMF and LMF of the already constructed IT2FS at the pre-determined value of the feature. We now take the minimum of the UMFs and LMFs separately and take the average of the resulting minima to obtain the degree of membership of the facial expression to lie in the emotion class c following Rule R_c.

For the unknown facial expression shown in Figure 5, Features: eo is LARGE; mo is LARGE; lee is LARGE and ebc is LARGE. Here 4 features are considered among the 6 because the values of the features eo_l and eo_r, and lee_l and lee_r are almost remains same always.

From the above word descriptions about the facial features of the unknown facial expression, it can be seen that following 2 rules fire.

Rules

If eo is LARGE/VERY LARGE; mo is LARGE; lee is LARGE and ebc is LARGE- emotion is ANGER.

If eo is LARGE; mo is MODERATE/LARGE; lee is LARGE and ebc is LARGE- emotion is FEAR.

As the above two rules concurrently fire with the given word descriptions about facial features of an unknown person. The rule yielding largest membership of the emotion class is declared as the winner. As the above two rules are concurrently fired with the given instantiation of word descriptions, the rule yielding largest membership of the emotion class is declared as the winner. To evaluate the degree of strength of individual emotions, we now consider four FOUs for the given word descriptions for two emotion classes: Fear and Anger (Figure 6 and Figure 7).

Figure 6. FOUs at the numerical values of TABLE VI for eo is L, mo is L, lee is L and ebc is L for emotion ANGER

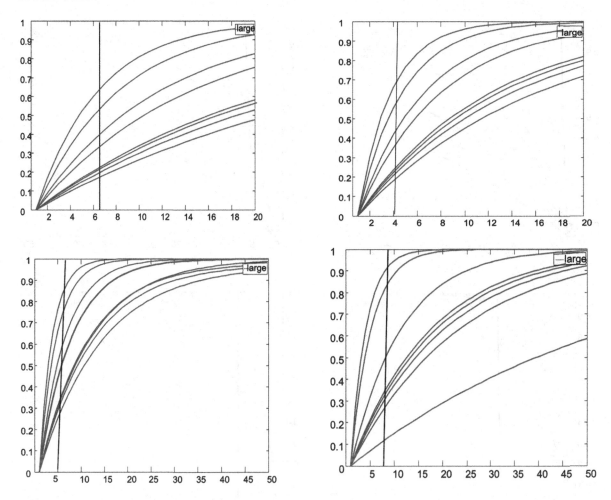

We now instantiate the FOUs in Figures 6 and 7 with derived feature values listed in row 2 of Table VI, take the minimum of the UMFs and LMFs separately at the feature values and finally take the average of the two minima. Table VII provides the results of evaluation of UMF and LMF for each feature, the minimum of UMFs, the minimum of LMFs and the average of the two minima. It is observed that the average has the largest value (=0.335) for the emotion: fear. So, we can conclude that the subject in Figure 5 carries the emotion: fear.

The proposed technique returns a classification accuracy of 87.8%, which is comparable with the performance of traditional emotion classifiers. But the main advantage of the proposed technique lies in determining emotion from facial word description, where we save some time by avoiding image-processing for feature extraction.

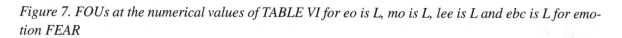

Figure 7. FOUs at the numerical values of TABLE VI for eo is L, mo is L, lee is L and ebc is L for emotion FEAR

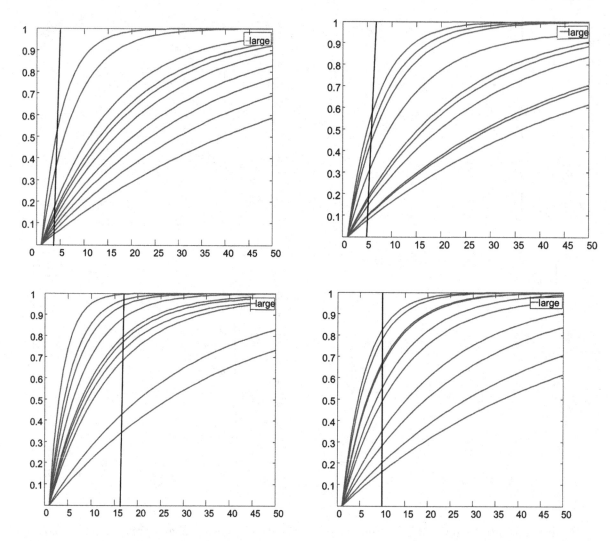

Table 7. UMFS, LMFS and Average of the mminima of umfs and lmfs obtained from Figures 6 and 7

Emotions	UMF and LMF of each Facial feature				Minimum of UMF and LMF	Average Value
	eo	mo	lee	ebc		
Anger	0.21,0.79	0.18,0.61	0.13,0.7	0.11,0.8	0.11,0.61	0.25
Fear	0.14,0.89	0.18,0.81	0.15,0.9	0.18,0.87	0.14,0.81	0.335

6. CONCLUSION

The chapter introduced a word-description model to recognize emotion of subjects from word description about facial features using IT2FS. The merit of the work lies in automatic membership function construction from word descriptions and construction of FOUs for each facial feature in different grades for different emotional faces.

The proposed approach is insensitive to small changes in facial features as it deals with relatively coarse information about facial features and thus is very robust. The performance of the proposed technique, measured in terms of classification accuracy, is comparable with existing research results.

REFERENCES

Aguero, J. R., & Vargas, A. (2007). Calculating functions of interval type-2 fuzzy numbers for fault current analysis. *IEEE Transactions on Fuzzy Systems, 15*(1), 31–40.

Chakraborty, A., Konar, A., Chakraborty, U. K., & Chatterjee, A. (2009). Emotion recognition from facial expressions and its control using fuzzy logic. *IEEE Transactions on Systems, Man and Cybernetics, Part A: Systems and Humans, 39*(4), 726–743.

Cordón, O., del Jesus, M. J., & Herrera, F. (1999). A proposal on reasoning methods in fuzzy rule-based classification systems. *International Journal of Approximate Reasoning, 20*(1), 21–45. doi:10.1016/S0888-613X(00)88942-2

Cristianini, N., & Shawe-Taylor, J. (2000). *An introduction to support vector machines and other kernel-based learning methods*. Cambridge University Press. doi:10.1017/CBO9780511801389

Das, S., Halder, A., Bhowmik, P., Chakraborty, A., Konar, A., & Nagar, A. K. (2009, December). Voice and facial expression based classification of emotion using linear support vector machine. In *Second International Conference on Developments in eSystems Engineering (DESE),* (pp. 377-384). IEEE. doi:10.1109/DeSE.2009.9

Dietterich, T. G. (1998). Approximate statistical tests for comparing supervised classification learning algorithms. *Neural Computation, 10*(7), 1895–1923. doi:10.1162/089976698300017197 PMID:9744903

Halder, A., Chakraborty, A., Konar, A., & Nagar, A. K. (2013, July). Computing with words model for emotion recognition by facial expression analysis using interval type-2 fuzzy sets. In *IEEE International Conference on Fuzzy Systems (FUZZ), 2013* (pp. 1-8). IEEE. doi:10.1109/FUZZ-IEEE.2013.6622543

Halder, A., Rakshit, P., Chakraborty, S., Konar, A., Chakraborty, A., Kim, E., & Nagar, A. K. (2012, June). Reducing uncertainty in interval type-2 fuzzy sets for qualitative improvement in emotion recognition from facial expressions. In *2012 IEEE International Conference on Fuzzy Systems (FUZZ-IEEE),* (pp. 1-8). IEEE. doi:10.1109/FUZZ-IEEE.2012.6251363

Karnik, N. N., & Mendel, J. M. (2001). Centroid of a type-2 fuzzy set. *Information Sciences, 132*(1), 195–220. doi:10.1016/S0020-0255(01)00069-X

Kobayashi, H., & Hara, F. (1992, September). Recognition of six basic facial expression and their strength by neural network. In *Proceedings of the IEEE International Workshop on Robot and Human Communication, 1992* (pp. 381-386). IEEE. doi:10.1109/ROMAN.1992.253857

Liang, Q., & Mendel, J. M. (2000). Designing interval type-2 fuzzy logic systems using an SVD-QR method: Rule reduction. *International Journal of Intelligent Systems*, *15*(10), 939–957. doi:10.1002/1098-111X(200010)15:10<939::AID-INT3>3.0.CO;2-G

Lin, J. C., Wu, C. H., & Wei, W. L. (2012). Error weighted semi-coupled hidden Markov model for audio-visual emotion recognition. *IEEE Transactions on Multimedia*, *14*(1), 142–156.

Lisetti, C. L., & Rumelhart, D. E. (1998, May). Facial expression recognition using a neural network. In *FLAIRS Conference* (pp. 328-332).

Mandal, R., Halder, A., Bhowmik, P., Konar, A., Chakraborty, A., & Nagar, A. K. (2011, June). Uncertainty management in type-2 fuzzy face-space for emotion recognition. In *2011 IEEE International Conference on Fuzzy Systems (FUZZ)*, (pp. 1902-1909). IEEE. doi:10.1109/FUZZY.2011.6007689

Mendel, J., & Wu, D. (2010). *Perceptual computing: aiding people in making subjective judgments* (Vol. 13). John Wiley & Sons. doi:10.1002/9780470599655

Mendel, J. M. (2004). Computing derivatives in interval type-2 fuzzy logic systems. *IEEE Transactions on Fuzzy Systems*, *12*(1), 84–98.

Mendel, J. M. (2007). Type-2 fuzzy sets and systems: An overview. *Computational Intelligence Magazine, IEEE*, *2*(1), 20–29. doi:10.1109/MCI.2007.380672

Mendel, J. M., & John, R. B. (2002). Type-2 fuzzy sets made simple. *IEEE Transactions on Fuzzy Systems*, *10*(2), 117–127.

Mendel, J. M., & Wu, H. (2006). Type-2 fuzzistics for symmetric interval type-2 fuzzy sets: Part 1, forward problems. *IEEE Transactions on Fuzzy Systems*, *14*(6), 781–792.

Mendel, J. M., & Wu, H. (2007). Type-2 fuzzistics for nonsymmetric interval type-2 fuzzy sets: Forward problems. *IEEE Transactions on Fuzzy Systems*, *15*(5), 916–930.

Sebe, N., Lew, M. S., Cohen, I., Garg, A., & Huang, T. S. (2002). Emotion recognition using a cauchy naive Bayes classifier. In *Proceedings of the 16th International Conference on Pattern Recognition, 2002.* (Vol. 1, pp. 17-20). IEEE. doi:10.1109/ICPR.2002.1044578

Wu, H., & Mendel, J. M. (2002). Uncertainty bounds and their use in the design of interval type-2 fuzzy logic systems. *IEEE Transactions on Fuzzy Systems*, *10*(5), 622–639.

Wu, H., Wu, Y., & Luo, J. (2009). An interval type-2 fuzzy rough set model for attribute reduction. *IEEE Transactions on Fuzzy Systems*, *17*(2), 301–315.

Zadeh, L. A. (1965). Fuzzy sets. *Information and Control*, *8*(3), 338–353. doi:10.1016/S0019-9958(65)90241-X

Zhao, J., & Kearney, G. (1996). Classifying facial emotions by backpropagation neural networks with fuzzy inputs. In *Proceedings of the International Conference on Neural Information Processing* (Vol. 1, pp. 454-457).

Zimmermann, H. J. (1992). *Fuzzy set theory and its applications second* (Revised Ed.). Kluwer Academic Publishers.

KEY TERMS AND DEFINITIONS

Computing with Words: Computing with words (CWW) is of recent coinage in the literature on fuzzy sets. Here, the reasoning system inputs word-level description of a problem, and returns word-level inference for the problem. It is also known as perceptual computing, as words are perceived differently by different people.

Footprint of Uncertainty (FOU): The region bounded by UMF and LMF of the IT2FS is called FOU. A larger FOU will imply that the problem is characterized by a higher amount of uncertainty. It is desirable to reduce the footprint of uncertainty without comprising on the information contained in it to make classification more accurate.

Human-Computer Interface (HCI): HCI involves study, planning, design and uses of the interaction between humans and computers. It is a multidisciplinary avenue of behavioral sciences, computer science, media studies and design.

Interval Type-2 Fuzzy Sets (IT2FS): A Fuzzy set in which the secondary membership functions are specified by an interval is called IT2FS.

Lower Membership Function (LMF): The membership function which defines the lower boundary of the IT2FS is called LMF.

Membership Function (MF): A membership function denotes the degree of belonging of an object into a particular attribute or set. For crisp sets, the MF is restricted to 0 or 1. On the other hand, fuzzy sets have MF within the interval $[0, 1]$.

Upper Membership Function (UMF): The membership function which defines the upper boundary of the IT2FS is called UMF.

Chapter 15
Developing Robot Emotions through Interaction with Caregivers

Angelica Lim
Kyoto University, Japan

Hiroshi G. Okuno
Kyoto University, Japan & Waseda University, Japan

ABSTRACT

In this chapter, the authors explore social constructivist theories of emotion, which suggest that emotional behaviors are developed through experience, rather than innate. The authors' approach to artificial emotions follows this paradigm, stemming from a relatively young field called developmental or 'epigenetic' robotics. The chapter describes the design and implementation of a robot called MEI (multimodal emotional intelligence) with an emotion development system. MEI synchronizes to humans through voice and movement dynamics, based on mirror mechanism-like entrainment. Via typical caregiver interactions, MEI associates these dynamics with its physical feeling, e.g. distress (low battery or excessive motor heat) or flourishing (homeostasis). Our experimental results show that emotion clusters developed through robot-directed motherese ("baby talk") are similar to adult happiness and sadness, giving evidence to constructivist theories.

1. INTRODUCTION

Some of the most revolutionary ideas in brain science are coming from cribs and nurseries. – Patricia Kuhl

Are emotions innate? Recently, the popular Darwinian theory that basic emotions – such as happiness, sadness and anger – are "hard-wired"

through evolution has been called into question. Psychologists have collected growing evidence (see reviews, (Mason & Capitanio, 2012; Camras & Shuster, 2013; Barrett, 2006)) that emotions may not in fact be completely a product of innate biology. Instead, "social constructivist" theories (Averill, 1980) point to experiences and environment as a prime factor for the development of emotions:

DOI: 10.4018/978-1-4666-7278-9.ch015

While there is little doubt that what we call fear, anger, and sadness refer to real (i.e., observable) phenomena and important parts of human experience, the weight of scientific opinion appears to be shifting away from the view that a few specific emotions are natural and universal kinds, laid down in the biology of humans and other animals (nature), in favor of a larger place for experience (nurture) in all emotions– (Mason & Capitanio, 2012, p. 239)

Let us briefly illustrate this view with evidence from infant psychology, animal behavior and cultural emotion psychology.

In infant developmental psychology, (Camras L. A., 2011) has pointed out several phenomena that support the constructivist view. Firstly, emotional facial expressions were observed in infants where the emotion was not expected to occur: 5-7 month olds showed prototypical surprise expressions while bringing familiar objects into their months (Camras, Lambrect, & Michel, 1996). Secondly, emotional expressions were not observed in contexts during which the emotion should have occurred: 10-12 month olds in the visual cliff procedure rarely produced the fear expression, even though their other behaviors showed that they did in fact experience fear (Hiatt, Campos, & Emde, 1979). Finally, Camras and her colleagues also found that negative emotion classes (such as anger, sadness and fear) did not seem to differentiate well in infants as old as 11 months, suggesting that they all corresponded to a general negative "distress" affect. (Camras L. A., 2011).

Studies on atypical caregiver conditions in young animals also support the social constructivist view. In a study with rats, it was shown that when mother rats' maternal style contained more licking and grooming, their pups grew up to be less fearful, with decreased hormonal reactions to stressors (Kaffman & Meaney, 2007). In studies with rhesus monkeys, maternal separation early in life affected gene expression in brain regions controlling socio-emotional behaviors, with a correlation on the timing of the separation (Sabatini,

Ebert, Lewis, Levitt, Cameron, & Mirnics, 2007). For example, monkeys separated from their mother at 1 week of age showed less expression of the gene GUCY1A3 (associated with social-seeking comfort behaviors), compared to the 1 month old separation condition.

Human studies on atypical early caregiving conditions also exist, though are more rare due to ethical issues. For instance, observations on postinstitutionalized (PI) children, such as those adopted from Eastern European orphanages after World War II, provide evidence that nurture is important for emotional intelligence. According to (Fries & Pollak, 2004), PI individuals had difficulty matching appropriate faces to happy, sad and fearful scenarios, yet were able to match angry faces just as well as controls. We refer the reader to further observations on the effect of early adverse rearing in work by Tottenham et al., e.g., (2011). In addition, temperament, while thought to have an inherent basis from birth, is not stable over the lifetime. In a short-term longitudinal study, (Calkins, 2002) found that infants who experienced negative parenting continued to show high anger/frustration levels, though it was not the case for infants who experienced positive parenting. Studies such as these emphasize the importance of emotional input early in life.

Psychologists studying emotions across cultures also observe variations that question the idea of universal emotion definitions. According to research by Tsai, ideal affect tends to differ between Eastern and Western cultures (Tsai, 2007). Individuals in Western cultures report "feeling good" as high-arousal positive (HAP) affect, whereas Eastern cultures prefer low-arousal positive (LAP) affect, even after controlling for self-reports of temperament and other individual differences (see (Tsai, 2007) for a review of experiments). As a simple illustration, (Hess, Beaupré, & Cheung, 2002) reported that a large proportion of Asian Canadians preferred smiles from 20-60% intensity, whereas European Canadians significantly preferred smiles from 80-

100% intensity. In cross-cultural emotion behavior recognition experiments (Elfenbein & Ambady, 2003) noticed a 9.3% drop in accuracy when attempting cross-cultural facial judgments. A similar study on vocal cues observed a 7% drop (Juslin & Laukka, 2003). While cultural display "rules" have been suggested by Ekman (Ekman & Friesen, 1969) to account for these differences, details on how these are developed (and how display rules account for recognition and preference, in addition to expression) remains an open area of research.

Most interestingly for the topic of this book, this emerging "constructivist" perspective on emotion theory opens up a new avenue for artificial emotion systems. This is because emotion theories (Cornelius, 2000) such as Darwin's Evolutionary theory, James' Bodily Theory, and Cognitive Appraisal Theory have presented several practical challenges for roboticists. In the Darwin paradigm (Darwin, 1872/1965), we face the problem of ecological validity of the "basic" emotions (Ekman, 1992) – full-blown emotions often studied in psychology rarely appear in typical human-robot interaction scenarios. In the Jamesian view (James, 1884), without biological bodies, nervous systems, hearts, and so on, it appears impossible for robots to ever have emotions and feelings. Critics suggest that copying surface behavior of emotions, such as facial expressions and poses, do not "count" as real emotions, and their use in companion robots has been called unethical (Turkle, 2012). Appraisal Theory (Frijda, 1986) has been the most advantageous for creating emotional behavior in artificial agents (e.g. OCC (Ortony, 1990)), where large and complex rule sets define emotional states and expressions. Yet these hand-designed rules are difficult to design because the engineer must completely describe all possible scenarios in which emotional reactions might take place. Furthermore, a new rule set must be adjusted for each culture (e.g., in Japan, anger emotions should not be displayed in social contexts (Kitayama, Markus, & Kurokawa, 2000)).

A developmental paradigm suggests that a learning entity could develop emotions on its own – emotional expression, recognition, triggering events, and so on – if exposed to the right environment. This is related to the concept of epigenetics, which describes mechanisms by which the environment can program "enduring effects on gene expression and cellular function" (Meaney & Ferguson-Smith, 2010). The relatively new field of "epigenetic robotics", also called "developmental robotics", has been developed in the last decade under this framework (Asada, et al., 2009). It is likely that the latest social, humanoid forms of robots such as Affetto (Ishihara, Yoshikawa, & Asada, 2011) and NAO[1] were key to this revolution.

To date, only two previous studies have used the developmental paradigm to ground artificial agent's emotional expressions. In the first study of its kind, Watanabe et al. proposed the "intuitive paradigm", in which the parents mimicked a virtual infant's facial expression, to associate the facial expressions with the robot's internal state (Watanabe, Ogino, & Asada, 2007). The authors used the concept of Hebbian learning, to create associative links for later emotion recognition. Boucenna's study followed a similar strategy, using a physical robot (Boucenna, Gaussier, Andry, & Hafemeister, 2010). These are landmark works using the caregiver paradigm to link external emotional stimuli to expression, yet some major conceptual challenges still remain. In particular, since the era of Breazeal's emotional robot Kismet (Breazeal, 2004), the definition of robot "feeling" has never been tackled.

In this chapter we discuss a new emotion system called MEI, as an example study for what could be created under the social constructivist theory of emotion in the developmental robotics field. We will first suggest some pre-requisites: the statistical learning system architecture (brain), the physical condition of the robot (gut feeling) and learning process (environment). Importantly, we will define the concept of robot feeling. We then will describe the system in action – learning through interaction with caregivers in a naturalistic scenario. By inspecting the resulting models ("looking into the brain") and performing vocal recognition and expression tests, we suggest that MEI has achieved differentiated emotion representations and developed a basic form of emotional intelligence called "core affect".

2. GENERAL OVERVIEW

How do infant emotions develop into adult emotions? We propose that motherese interactions like the one in Figure 1 may serve as the basis of acquisition of emotion. Motherese is "baby talk" between a caregiver and infant at close proximity (Fernald, 1989). This exaggerated speech typically co-occurs with exaggerated facial displays (Soken & Pick, 1992), and is known to exist in all cultures of the world (Fernald, Taeschner, Dunn, Papousek, de Boysson-Bardies, & Fukui, 1989). It has been established that the highly exaggerated form of speech is used to aid the child in the acquisition of language (Kuhl, 2004). Furthermore, studies comparing adult-directed emotional speech with

motherese show that motherese is also highly correlated with emotional speech, with robust differences across the emotions (Trainor, Austin, & Desjardins, 2000). As such, a recent review has suggested that motherese may exist for the development of emotions (Saint-Georges, et al., 2013). The universal social phenomenon of motherese therefore serves as the basis for our emotion development work.

2.1 Issues

The goal in developmental robotics is to make a robot that learns just as a child does. Yet this is an enormous task, to say the least. To encourage others in the developmental robotics or social constructivist paradigm to better formalize their individual contributions, we propose the following method of formalizing their assumptions and contribution.

In a developmental robotics study, one should specify which elements are assumed to be "innate", and which are learned through environment. One way to specify this is by grouping them into Before (innate and previously learned), During Learning (environment) and After (the learned result). Another way to specify starting capaci-

Figure 1. Main concept behind statistical emotion development. The robot takes the place of the infant, and emotional associations are form as a result of a caregiver's interactions in situ. (Mother and Daughter by Ian Grove-Stephensen https://flic.kr/p/56bERd under CC BY 2.0)

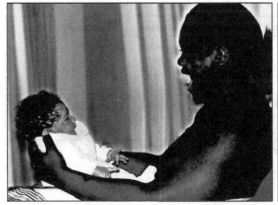

ties is to approximate the robot's "starting age" – to what human period do we assume the robot has already "grown", and what milestones has it already reached? After the interaction, what new milestone or developmental age has it achieved? Finally, it is useful to define the human functional equivalents for each component of the system architecture. We illustrate this formalization method with such an overview for our system.

3. OVERVIEW OF SOLUTION

We provide the following outline to clarify the goals of the present study, in which the robot develops *core affect*: "Core affect is a neurophysiological state that underlies simply feeling good or bad, drowsy or energised. Psychological construction is not one process but an umbrella term for the various processes that produce:

1. A particular emotional episode's "components" (such as facial movement, vocal tone, peripheral nervous system change, appraisal, attribution, behaviour, subjective experience, and emotion regulation);
2. Associations among the components; and
3. The categorisation of the pattern of components as a specific emotion." (Russell, 2009, p. 1259)

In particular, we focus on (a) the components of *vocal tone*, *movement* and *subjective experience/ feeling* (b) associations among these components and (c) categorization of the pattern of components as a specific emotion. In the present study, we look especially at the first emotions observed in the infant: happiness and sadness (Sigelman & Rider, 2010).

3.1 Before Interaction: System Requirements (Neonate)

We begin with several basic "innate" requirements for our robot system, those with functional parallels in a newborn infant.

Next, we list the requirements that might be learned simultaneously or prior to the focus of this study, for instance within the neonatal stage (less than 4 weeks old).

We defined two separate sections of "innate assumptions" and "previously learned requirements" because (4) and (5) are available, but not fully formed at birth. For example, although fetuses have auditory abilities even before birth (Lecanuet & Schaal, 1996), some aspects of hearing such as frequency and temporal resolution only reach adult levels at 6 months (Werner, 2002), and visual acuity reaches adult levels of 20/20 at 6 months of age (Sokol, 1978). Additionally, we do not yet know to what extent the human mirror

Table 1. "Innate" requirements for our robot system

Requirements	Human Equivalent	Robot Equivalent	Age Developed
A statistical learning neural system.	Brain	CPU, storage, machine learning program. More details on the learning system in Sec. 4.1.	At birth
A somatosensory system	Sensory system for internal functioning of gut, viscera, temperature, etc.	Battery level sensor and temperature sensor (Sec. 4.2).	At birth
A distress signal when the somatosensory system indicates a problem.	Crying to signal hunger, cold, etc.	Auditory distress signal (Sec. 4.5).	At birth

Table 2. Requirements learned simultaneously or prior to the focus of this study

Requirements	Human Equivalent	Robot Equivalent	Age Developed
An extrasensory processing system	Ears, eyes, skin and related nervous systems	Microphones and video camera (touch sensors, in the future) (Sec. 4.3).	~6 months
A mirroring system	Mirror neurons and pre-motor system	Mirror module (Sec. 4.4).	~4 weeks?

system is formed and developed at birth (Craig, 2009). It has only been established that neonates (< 4 weeks) imitate tongue protrusions (Nagy, Pilling, Orvos, & Molnar, 2013). For this reason, we seek parsimony in the abilities placed in the "innate" section.

Let us illustrate these requirements with an example. Under these assumptions, we can imagine then that, for example, a smartphone with a battery level warning beep already has (2) and (3), possibly (4). With the right software, it could have (1). Yet, because of its lack of human-like embodiment and motor system, the mirroring system in (5) would be a difficult requirement to fulfill.

3.2 During Training: Environment (Neonate to 6 Months Old)

Now, we define the environmental input to which we will expose system with the above requirements: motherese. Motherese can be classified into categories, where the vocal tones of the caregiver's speech depend on the communicative intent to the infant (Fernald, 1989), including:

- **Comfort:** Slow, falling pitch contours
- **Approval / Praise:** Exaggerated rise-fall (bell-shaped) pitch contours
- **Attention Bid:** Quick, rising contours
- **Prohibition:** Low pitch, high intensity and short

Infants between birth and 3-months old prefer *comfort* vocalizations most, according to (Kitamura & Lam, 2009), and it is the kind of motherese that caregivers produce most at that age. At 6 months, caregivers produce more *approval/praise* vocalizations, and infants' preference also shifts to approving tones. At 9 months, the preferences shift to *directive* tones.

One may wonder if an interactive robot is necessary to elicit motherese vocalizations. Wouldn't laboratory recordings and offline training be sufficient? In fact, it is not so easy – it has been shown that mothers are unable to reliably produce motherese in front of a microphone (Fernald & Simon, 1984). An infant – or a machine with the look and behavior of an infant – is important in eliciting the necessary environmental input (Ishihara, Yoshikawa, & Asada, 2011).

We propose that these motherese interactions create affective associations as follows. A typical caregiver reacts to a distress signal (crying) through comfort motherese. Between birth and 3 months of age, the co-occuring comfort tones and physical distress create an association between sadness-like sounds and a negative physical state. Between 3 and 6 months, a caregiver displays approval and praise when the infant is in good health, creating a positive bodily association with happiness-like sounds. We posit that the other types of motherese (prohibition, attention) teach infants further emotional associations in context, for example, prohibition tones associated with the context of being stopped from achieving a goal.

3.3 After (~6-8 Months)

The final system, after caregiver interaction, should show an increase in *core affect* emotional capabilities:

- **Components:** Emotional voice, movement, feeling of happiness and sadness
- **Association between Components:**
  - *Feeling* to *expression*. The robot's subjective feeling of happiness should engender vocal tone and movement similar to happiness, and sad feelings should generate sad vocal tones and movement.
  - *Expression* to *feeling*. The robot should associate happy voices with a positive physical feeling, and sad voices with a negative physical feeling.
- **Categorization:** Differentiated happiness and sadness in the neural model.

Now that we have specified the Before, During Training and After phases, we describe the underlying system architecture, designed based on functional equivalents in the human brain.

3.4 Neural Architecture

In this section, we give details on the neural architecture we build into the robot. The three modules we identify, with associated human neural equivalents are as follows, as shown in Figure 2:

- **A Mirror System:** Represents the action of another human, and can induce eventual motor imitation (Premotor cortex) (Iacoboni & Dapretto, 2006)
- **A Gut Feeling Module**: The module receiving signals of bodily pleasure or pain, e.g. battery level or motor heat (Somatosensory cortex) (Damasio A., 1994)
- **An Associative Module:** Associates the outputs of the above – action representation and a corresponding bodily feeling of pleasure or pain (Insula) (Craig, 2009)

Let's briefly examine the three brain areas that are key to defining emotion in our system:

3.4.1 The Pre-Motor Cortex

Mirror neurons in the premotor-cortex been proposed as a critical step towards simulating and

Figure 2. Proposed developmental emotion architecture. The basis of an artificial emotion system is in brain areas related to a) embodied feelings (somatosensory cortex) b) mirror representations of others (premotor cortex), and an associative lookup creating a link between them (insula). (Derived from Brain https://flic.kr/p/9UwYi by GreenFlame09 under CC BY 2.0)

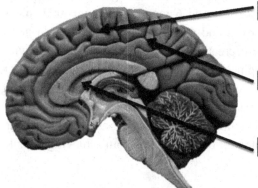

Premotor cortex
Creates an internal "as-if" representation of another person via the mirror neuron system

Somatosensory cortex
Gut feeling – evaluates and represents the body's physical state (e.g., temperature, viscera)

Insula
Stores emotional associations between "as-if" stimuli and gut feeling physical state

understanding of the mental states (including emotions) of others. In essence, we map actions of an observed person to internal representations of ourselves doing the same action. Simple visual observation of an action incites premotor activity in the brain (Rizzolatti & Craighero, 2004). For example, watching another grasp an object activates one's own premotor areas for grasping. Auditory input also achieves neural mirroring: neurons in the monkey premotor cortex discharge both when it performs an action and when it hears the related sound (Kohler, 2002).

Damasio called this internal representation an "as-if-body-loop" mechanism for emotion: "The brain momentarily creates a set of body maps that does not correspond exactly to the current reality of the body." (Damasio A. R., 2004).

Therefore, our emotional robot system should include an artificial pre-motor cortex, containing an internal representation of the other person's body state.

3.4.2 The Insula

The insula has been suggested to lie at the heart of the association between action representation and emotion (Carr, Iacoboni, Dubeau, Mazziotta, & Lenzi, 2003). The insula is a region deep in the brain that reads one's body condition by way of visceral and interoceptive sensors (e.g. heat, cold, pain, muscle ache sensors) that send information to the insula. It has been associated with many behaviors such as drug cravings, feeling pain, maternal love, listening to music and empathizing with others (Craig, 2009). It is where a bad smell is transformed into disgust (Calder, Keane, Manes, Antoun, & Young, 2000) or a caress into pleasure (Morrison, Mjornsdotter, & Olausson, 2011), and is active when a mother hears her baby cry (Kim, et al., 2011), or when looking at a happy face (Pohl, Anders, Schulte-Ruther, Mathiak, & Kircher, 2013). It is active when empathizing for others' pain as well as when actually feeling pain (Singer, 2004), suggesting that the affective

component of pain "feeling pain" is decoupled from the sensory component–the pain itself.

To summarize, Damasio and others have suggested that the insula maps visceral states that are associated with emotional experience (Damasio A. R., 2004; Craig, 2009; Singer, 2004). Based on this evidence, it seems an artificial insula is an integral part of a robot emotion system, to associate physical "gut" feelings (Sec. 3.4.3) with emotional body representations (Sec. 3.4.1).

3.4.3 The Somatosensory Cortex

In this section, we attempt to define feelings. Damasio's Somatic Marker Hypothesis suggests that feelings are an association of stimuli to visceral (and musculoskeletal) pleasure or pain: "Feelings are [...] first and foremost about the body, that they offer us the cognition of our visceral and musculoskeletal state. [...] Body images give [...] a quality of goodness or badness, of pleasure or pain." (Damasio A., 1994, p. 159)

In the brain, the somatosensory cortices (from the Greek root *soma*, meaning body) are responsible for sensing this internal state of pleasure or pain. They sense the body's internal state including viscera (e.g. internal organs like the heart, stomach, or lungs) and joint position, as well as external senses of touch, temperature and pain. Indeed, when the somatosensory areas are damaged, patients do not show normal signs of despair or panic (Damasio A., 1994)

In short, the somatosensory cortex contains a "gut feeling" representation of the body's internal state, either flourishing or in distress. We consider that this gut feeling is linked to the emotional body representations (Sec. 3.4.1) within the insula (Sec. 3.4.3). And, to quote Damasio, "the critical, formative set of stimuli to somatic pairings is, no doubt, acquired in childhood and adolescents." (Damasio A., 1994, p. 179)

In Figure 3, we illustrate the tight integration of the above three components. Unlike many robotic emotion systems with specialized systems for recognition and expression (e.g. Kismet (Breazeal, 2004)), the same system can perform both emotion recognition and expression, as illustrated by the two columns in Figure 3. Specifically, it can perform emotion recognition by first mirroring the person, then looking up the closest state and associated feeling. The latest neuroscientific models support this: according to "shared-substrates" models of emotion recognition, we understand other's emotions by first making an internal simulation of the other (Heberlein & Atkinson, 2009). Secondly, the architecture can perform emotion expression by first feeling a certain physical state, then expressing it by looking up the associated expression and preparing to act. Interestingly, the premotor cortex is only the preparation to act; possibly, the act of expressing the final emotion could be further mediated by the pre-frontal cortex and cognitive controls; for example, suppressing a smile in a socially inappropriate situation.

4. MEI SYSTEM IMPLEMENTATION

Based on the evidence presented above, we implemented the following five modules in a robot we call MEI – Multimodal Emotional Intelligence, as described in (Lim & Okuno, in press) and (Lim & Okuno, in prep.). The system was implemented in the Python programming language on the NAO robot, using HARK[ii] real-time audio processing technology, and machine learning algorithms as described below. We summarize the system here.

4.1 Statistical Learning Neural System (Artificial Insula)

The purpose of this module is to create associations between the robot's "gut feelings" (Sec. 3.4.3) and internal motor representations (Sec. 3.4.1). We use a Gaussian Mixture Model (GMM) (Bishop & Nasrabadi, 2006), which is a statistical learning model typically used for clustering and recognition, as illustrated in Figure 4. Gaussian Mixture Models are typically trained with large amounts of data, and the resulting model represents the data, with peaks around commonly observed data, and valleys for uncommon occurrences.

We chose the GMM to represent emotion clusters for many reasons. Firstly, GMMs are widely used in the field of audio and vision recognition. Essentially, a novel input is evaluated in the GMM,

Figure 3. Proposed developmental emotion architecture (cont'd). The same 3-module architecture, containing an emotion representation in the insula, is responsible for both emotion recognition and emotion expression.

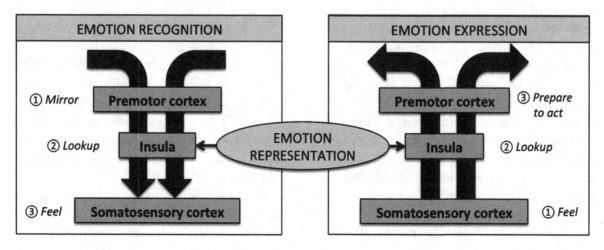

Figure 4. Illustration of the MEI system receiving affective input and clustering in the artificial insula to create differentiated classes

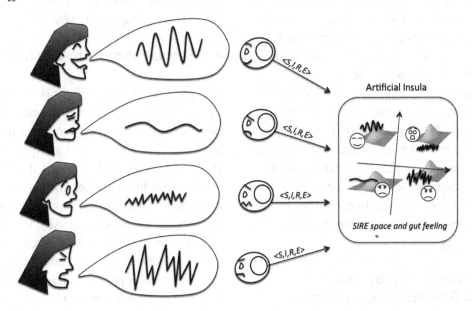

and the cluster with the highest score provides the recognition result. Secondly, unlike other recognition techniques like Support Vector Machines (Burges, 1998) or K-means (Kanungo, Mount, Netanyahu, Piatko, Silverman, & Wu, 2002), it can be used for expression. This is because the model represents a probability space that can be sampled – data around the "peaks" are more likely to be picked for expression, compared to the data in the valleys. Additionally, the samples will be non-repetitious, which conveniently represents the "noisy" nature of human expression. Finally, a GMM can be used for representation. We can inspect the peaks, known as the GMM means, which represent a "prototype" for that cluster.

Let us illustrate the method with an example. If the robot hears a comforting voice that is 1.0 syllables per second, then another comforting utterance at 1.4 syllables per second, it creates a Gaussian cluster that approximates a "prototypical comfort voice" with a mean speed of 1.2 syllables/sec and standard deviation of 0.2. Consider that the GMM space can represent dimensions other than

speed, such as pitch range, etc., so the "prototype" can be multi-dimensional. This allows the mean to encapsulate not only speed, but also values for pitch, say 40 Hz on average. These other dimensions will be discussed in Sec. 4.3.

In addition, the system automatically splits clusters when the variance (related to standard deviation) of a cluster becomes large. We do this by calculating the Bayesian Information Criterion (BIC) (Schwarz, 1978) and finding the optimal number of clusters to represent the data (Lim & Okuno, in press). For instance, if a sad voice cluster begins to include both *high intensity* grief voices and *low intensity* comfort voices, the system may create 2 clusters instead of one. In this way, the learning module develops and differentiates as it receives more input.

Interestingly, the functions proposed by our GMM method sounds similar to the Differentiation and Dynamical Integration (DDI) of perspective of emotional development proposed by developmental psychologist Camras (2011). Our automatic creation of emotional clusters is similar to her concept of "attractor states". Initially, emotions are distinguished into positive or negative attractor states, but then further differentiation results in new attractor states corresponding to what we often call discrete emotions (e.g., negative affect splits into anger, sadness and fear).

One practical advantage of the GMM over the DDI model may be that the GMM is highly implementable. In experiments, we use the implementation from Scikit-learn machine learning library (Pedregosa, et al., 2011) written in the Python programming language, along with our own modifications for splitting clusters based on BIC scores. Details are available in (Lim & Okuno, in press).

4.2 Somatosensory System (Artificial Somatosensory Cortex)

The purpose of this module is to represent the robot's internal "gut" feelings. Feelings are an integral part of an emotion system, yet to our knowledge, no other artificial emotion system has attempted to include it. For instance, the difficulty may stem from the preconception that feelings are an abstract concept. In fact, our definition of feelings is intrinsically linked to the fact that a robot has a body in the physical world.

We define the robot's feeling based on Damasio's idea of "flourishing" and "distress" (Damasio A., 1994). This simple module checks for physical homeostasis in the robot:

- Gut feeling is set to *flourishing* if the robot's body is in homeostasis, i.e., the temperature of the joint motors is not too hot and not too cold, and if the battery percentage is over a certain value
- Otherwise, the gut feeling is set to *distress* if the robot is out of homeostasis, e.g., an arm motor is too hot

In experiments, the above was implemented using the NAO robot's Naoqi interface to the battery and arm temperature sensors.

4.3 Extrasensory Processing System

The purpose of this module is to process and simplify the environmental information. In our current work, we process incoming information according to the SIRE model, as explained in (Lim, Ogata, & Okuno, 2012). In short, the SIRE model is a way to reduce complex signals such as voice, movement and music into a simple set of features. SIRE stands for Speed, Intensity, Regularity and Extent. For example, when processing speech signals, we can extract an utterance's *speech rate*, say, 2.0 syllables per second, and normalize it to fast (1.0), slow or stopped (0.0), or somewhere in between (between 0.0 and 1.0). This is also known as the utterance's Speed. Similarly, the concept of Speed within an arm s also exists: *velocity*. In the SIRE paradigm, each of speed, intensity, regularity and extent is represented as a value between 0 and 1, as follows:

- **Speed:** Slow (S=0.0) vs. fast (S=1.0)
- **Intensity:** Gradual (I=0.0) vs. abrupt (I=1.0)
- **Regularity:** Rough (R=0.0) vs. smooth (R=1.0)
- **Extent:** Small (E=0.0) vs. large (E=1.0)

Explicit mappings are described in (Lim, Ogata, & Okuno, 2012) and (Lim & Okuno, in press).

The point of representing features in this simplified manner is to use as minimal a representation for emotion as possible. For instance, our work has shown that a voice is considered sad when it is slow, low intensity, regular, with small pitch range (extent), S=0.1, I=0.4, R=0.7, E=0.4 (Lim, Ogata, & Okuno, 2012). A voice is perceived as happy when it is fast, not too intense, slightly irregular and with a rather large pitch range, S=0.7, I=0.2, R=0.2, E=0.7. Furthermore, gestures that followed these patterns of SIRE dynamics were perceived in similar ways. Therefore, we need not process and store more information than SIRE to represent these two states, which is preferable to aid in visualization and understanding of our models. In this paper we focus on voice and arm movements, but in the future we should include other concise feature representations, such as facial configurations (eyebrow angle, mouth corner changes) or SIRE based on touch.

In experiments, the above concepts were implemented using a PlayStation Eye microphone as input, and the HARK[2] real-time audio processing system to extract the SIRE values.

4.4 Mirroring System (Artificial Pre-Motor Cortex)

The mirroring module has two purposes:

1. To create the robot's internal "as-if" representation, a simulation of its caregiver
2. To generate motor output (voice, arm movements) that incites interaction from caregiver.

Firstly, for (1), the mirroring system creates an internal "as-if" representation of its environment. The representation is essentially four numbers, representing SIRE. For example, if the caregiver speaks with slow speech, it entrains the robot's internal representation to also be slow (e.g., S=0.1). As shown in Figure 3, the robot first creates an internal "as-if" representation in the pre-motor cortex, and this internal "as-if" SIRE representation is used to create emotional clusters (Figure 4).

Secondly, for (2), motor output is generated via the artificial pre-motor cortex. Just as SIRE can be used for analyzing input, it can be used for generating output. For example, if a robot's output SIRE state has S=0.8, means the robot will

speak fast, with fast gestures. In (Lim & Okuno, in prep.), we defined the formula for entrainment, which is a gradual synchronization of the SIRE dynamics between the human's input and the robot's output. For example, when the caregiver speaks to the robot with slow speech, it entrains the robot's SIRE motor output to also be slow. The actual output depends also on the robot's current feeling and the robot's previous SIRE dynamics, however. For instance, a robot that is very low on battery will be more difficult to soothe. Details are given in (Lim & Okuno, in prep.).)

Although not yet formally tested, we consider the robot's motor feedback in (2) as an essential part of eliciting realistic motherese from the human. For example, if the caregiver speaks to the robot with a happy voice, and the robot returns a similarly happy voice, the caregiver should become more aroused. Thus, a positive feedback loop is created.

In experiments, we implemented the mirror system using Naoqi ALMemory variables, Python code to implement the entrainment formula, and mappings from SIRE to the NAO robot's Naoqi interface to motor controls, as described in (Lim, Ogata, & Okuno, 2011).

4.5 Distress Signal

The purpose of this module is to incite interaction from caregiver. The module continuously checks the robot's current gut feeling, and sends a distress signal if the feeling is *distress* (low battery or hot motors). In our experiments, we set the distress signal to mimic an infant's cry at birth: a high intensity sound, with a large pitch range and a very regular timing. In practice, we set the robot's Text-To-Speech (TTS) system to repeat the syllables *"ma ma ma"* and set SIRE = 0.9 for all four parameters.

In experiments, we used the NAO robot's Acapela[3] TTS system and markup to modify the dynamics of the robot's voice.

5. EVALUATION OF THE SYSTEM

Let us recall our formalization in Section 3.3, in which we defined some ways to evaluate the system after interaction with a human. After a caregiver interaction, we hypothesize that the robot system should have acquired these three aspects:

1. **Categorization:** Differentiated happiness and sadness in the neural model. Ability to recognize adult happiness and sadness in the voice.
2. **Expression to Feeling:** The robot should associate happy voices with a positive physical feeling, and sad voices with a negative physical feeling.
3. **Feeling to Expression:** The robot's subjective feeling of happiness should engender vocal tone and movement similar to happiness.

5.1 Training Conditions

We recruited 6 fluent English speakers from Western countries (3 female, with a mean age of 29.8 years old). The participants were introduced to the robot and we asked them to say the robot's name ("Mei Mei") in two different scenarios, mimicking scenarios that happen in the first 6 months of a human infant's life:

- **Comfort:** Mei Mei is crying (SIRE = 0.9). Soothe and comfort her by saying her name.
- **Praise:** Mei Mei is no longer crying (SIRE = 0.1). Praise her and make her feel loved by saying her name.

The process is illustrated in Figure 5. During the comfort condition, the robot's feeling was set to distress, which engendered a vocal distress signal along with arm movements (SIRE = 0.9). During the praise condition, the robot moved its arms but

did not vocalize, and the robot's feeling was set to flourishing (SIRE = 0.1 for all parameters). At all times, the robot continuously expressed its current SIRE state by gesturing with its arms. For example, when it was crying in distress (SIRE = 0.9 for all parameters), its gestures were initially fast, intense, regular, and large. When it was in a flourishing state, its gestures were initially slow, not intense, irregular and small. (SIRE = 0.1 for all parameters).

5.2 Results and Discussion

The interactions resulted in 128 praise utterances and 114 comfort utterances, which were used to train the robot's emotion model.

Categorization. The resulting model, partially shown in Figure 6, shows differentiation between conditions of distress and flourishing. We can already see differentiation in the two dimensions of speed and intensity, and further differentiation could be seen if it were possible to visualize all four SIRE dimensions. Another way to interpret the model is to plot the Gaussian means (the peaks denoted by a star, in Figure 6), where the means represent the 4-dimensional "prototypes". For example, the trained model produces prototypical *flourishing-praise* values as SIRE=[0.4, 0.5, 0.5, 0.7], and prototypical *distress-comfort* SIRE value as SIRE=[0.3, 0.3, 0.5, 0.4] (Lim & Okuno, in prep.). This intuitively makes sense, because praise voices have larger pitch ranges than comfort voices (praise E=0.7, comfort E=0.4). Further results showing Gaussian mean differentiation of attention and prohibition conditions, and their clear similarities to fear and anger voices, can be seen in (Lim & Okuno, in prep.).

Expression to Feeling. As we report in (Lim & Okuno, in prep.), the model was able to associate 90% of happy vocal utterances with flourishing, and 84% of sad vocal utterances with distress. These results came from experiments testing the

Figure 5. The creation of meaning for negative (above) and positive (below) core affect. Similar to how a newborn expresses distress such as hunger and cold by crying, the robot emits a high intensity signal when in physical distress. The caregiver regulates the expression using a comforting voice and face (~3 months in infants). After caregiver training, the robot has learned to associate the physical distress with the comfort/sadness dynamics. A similar association is made with positive physical flourishing state and praise/happiness dynamics.

recognition ability of the motherese-trained GMM model, when exposed to 71 "happy" and 62 "sad" adult emotional voices from the German dataset Emo-DB (Burkhardt, Paeschke, Rolfes, Sendlmeier, & Weiss, 2005). In other words, happy voices induced higher likelihood scores in the "flourishing-praise" cluster than in the "distress-comfort" cluster. Similarly, sad voices resulted in higher likelihood scores in the "distress-comfort" clusters. In (Lim & Okuno, in prep.), we suggest that this is akin to affective empathy or "feeling another's pain": the robot performs internal mir-

roring (in this case of vocal dynamics) and makes a learned association with physical distress.

Feeling to Expression. It may appear that we have only made a simple model of motherese and emotional voices. However, we insist that this model is also generative. In other words, the *motherese received by the robot affects its own expression.*

Our previous work has shown that our system can reliably express happiness and sadness through voice, gesture and gait, given emotional voice training alone (Lim & Okuno, in press). Evaluations were performed by 20 participants rating the robot

Figure 6. Trained emotion representations in artificial insula, associated with physical distress and physical flourishing. Visualization using only two of the four SIRE dimensions–speed and intensity. We can notice the clusters for comfort (cluster peaks denoted by ★) are generally slower than the clusters for praise.

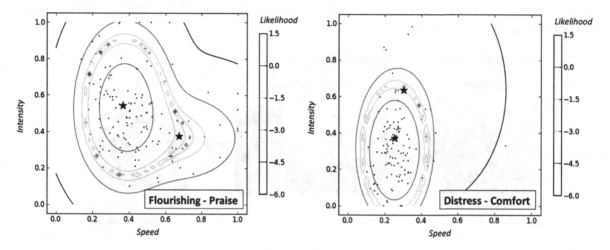

using Mehrabian's Pleasure-Arousal-Dominance (PAD) scale (Mehrabian, 1995), following similar perceptual experiments in (Lim, Ogata, & Okuno, 2012). Perception experiments for the motherese-trained system described here are still underway, and we expect a similar result.

Intuitively, this reflects the idea that the caregiver's own emotional expressions are "transmitted" to their infant. Among humans, infants of depressed mothers continue to show depressed behaviors to other adults (Field, et al., 1988). Furthermore, early negative maternal parenting styles predicted greater increases in negative behaviors of the child later in life (Calkins, 2002).

Finally, our developmental robot system could explain Ekman and Friesen's "display rules" in a statistical manner. Our theory could explain why "feeling good" is associated with high arousal in Western cultures, and low arousal in Eastern Cultures: the parents simply entrained the flourishing states to different levels. Training the robot with an Eastern and Western caregiver and inspecting the cluster means could verify this statistical differentiation. Additionally, it is known that American motherese contains more extreme pitch

modifications than British motherese (Shute & Wheldall, 1989). We could "raise" the robot with caregivers from two different cultures, and check whether the resulting expressive robot could be perceived as coming from one culture or another.

6. FUTURE TRENDS

The developmental paradigm to the construction of artificial emotion systems creates very promising new areas of research.

Firstly, the practical applications are wide. Consider the development of robot personality, using these flexible definitions of emotion as a basis. We could imagine a robot that could adapt to the personality or emotional style of its family: very expressive and outgoing, or quiet and reserved. A robot could express happiness in a way that is consistent with its surroundings, possibly increasing user acceptance. Or, a system could simply improve its emotion recognition accuracy through interaction with the users – just as we may understand a good friend's true feelings (even when they try to hide it), the system could adapt its definition of emotion by linking together person-specific facial features, vocal features, and context.

Secondly, the developmental paradigm may answer the question: what is robot love? This question has captured the interest of the media, films, and pop culture, and is certainly a valid question for the topic of this book. Consider the GMM link between humans, emotion states, and a robot's physical "gut feelings". If a robot continues to associate physical *flourishing* with not only emotional features, but also physical features (like a caregiver's face), it could develop attachment. This is a fascinating idea that suggests that robot companions could be "loving" agents. For instance, a caregiver's presence could make the robot "happy", associate it with "full battery", and its presence would therefore be akin to repowering itself at a charging station, like the idea that a loved one re-energizes us. As Daniel Dennett supposed when pressed with the question: "In principle, you can make a computer that loved right out of the box, but only because it was a near-duplicate of a computer that had a life, that had love. There's probably no shortcut." (So, 2013)

Thirdly, we should talk about empathy and its links to moral machines. Affective empathy is the idea that, through emotional contagion, we feel others' pain even out of our conscious control. It has links to morality (de Waal, 2013), and Baron-Cohen suggests that personality disorders such as psychopathy and narcissism are linked to a lack of affective empathy (Baron-Cohen, 1996). Since robot morality and ethics is a debated topic, it is possible that a system like MEI could serve as a platform for affective empathy – a building block for robots to develop morality outside of a rule system (Wallach & Allen, 2010).

Fourthly, we can consider more research in the extension of the MEI system to other modalities and emotions. Touch is an important method of communication with infants, and even animals: as noted by one of our participants, "I wanted to comfort the robot by touching him – that's how I communicate with my dog." Of course, facial expressions are also extremely important. While considered in our paradigm (Figure 4), they have not yet been tested since our NAO robot did not have a moveable face. Further research with very human-like robots such as Affetto is an obvious next step. In terms of other emotions, we have touched only briefly on other emotions such as fear and anger. Many emotion classification methods treat happiness, sadness, anger and fear at the same level. But it is known that anger requires higher cognitive mental processing (Fellous & Arbib, 2005). Therefore, emotion modeling in a scaffolded hierarchy could also be explored.

Finally, emotion, thought to be one of the first capacities built by a child, should benefit the field of artificial intelligence and epigenetic robots greatly. The constructional link between the physical body, mental states and preference could be used as a scaffold for learning. For example, consider the concept within artificial intelligence called symbol grounding. Words and concepts are typically grounded in visual features like "the apple is round and red". Yet when we look at an object, we also have an associated feeling–"good" or "bad"–stemming from outside of consciousness, e.g., "the apple is delicious and I like it". This feeling could be fundamental in constructing meaning. Therefore, our artificial emotion system and "gut feeling" definition could be key to grounding A.I. and understanding.

7. CONCLUSION

In this chapter we explored the epigentic robotics paradigm for developing artificial emotions. We suggested how emotions could be constructed through environment, given some initial "innate" assumptions about the system and a human-like interaction called motherese. Importantly, for the first time, we described experiments with a robot that developed *feelings*: physical flourishing or distress grounded in battery levels and motor temperatures. Towards robot emotions that are flexible, culture-specific, and grounded in the physical world, with the potential to be empathetic and moral machines, developmental robotics paradigm is an exciting approach for the future of artificial emotion systems.

REFERENCES

Asada, M., Hosoda, K., Kuniyoshi, Y., Ishiguro, H., Inui, T., Yoshikawa, Y., & Yoshida, C. et al. (2009). Cognitive developmental robotics: A survey. *Transactions on Autonomous Mental Development*, *1*(1), 12–32. doi:10.1109/TAMD.2009.2021702

Averill, J. R. (1980). A constructivist view of emotion. In R. Harré (Ed.), *Emotion: Theory, research, and experience* (pp. 305–339). New York: Academic Press. doi:10.1016/B978-0-12-558701-3.50018-1

Baron-Cohen, S. (1996). Is there a normal phase of synaesthesia in development. *Psyche*, *2*(27), 223–228.

Barrett, L. F. (2006). Are emotions natural kinds? *Perspectives on Psychological Science*, *1*(1), 28–58. doi:10.1111/j.1745-6916.2006.00003.x PMID:19079552

Bishop, C. M., & Nasrabadi, N. M. (2006). *Pattern recognition and machine learning* (Vol. 1). New York: Springer.

Boucenna, S., Gaussier, P., Andry, P., & Hafemeister, L. (2010). Imitation as a communication tool for online facial expression learning and recognition. IROS (pp. 5323-5328). IEEE/RSJ.

Breazeal, C. L. (2004). *Designing sociable robots*. MIT press.

Burges, C. J. (1998). A tutorial on support vector machines for pattern recognition. *Data Mining and Knowledge Discovery*, *2*(2), 121–167. doi:10.1023/A:1009715923555

Burkhardt, F., Paeschke, A., Rolfes, M., Sendlmeier, W. F., & Weiss, B. (2005). *A database of German emotional speech* (pp. 1517–1520). Interspeech.

Calder, A. J., Keane, J., Manes, F., Antoun, N., & Young, A. W. (2000). Impaired recognitiion and experience of disgust following brain injury. *Nature Neuroscience*, *3*(11), 1077–1078. doi:10.1038/80586 PMID:11036262

Calkins, S. D. (2002). Does aversive behavior during toddlerhood matter? The effects of difficult temperament on maternal perceptions and behavior. *Infant Mental Health Journal*, *23*(4), 381–394. doi:10.1002/imhj.10024

Camras, L. A. (2011). Differentiation, dynamical integration and functional emotional development. *Emotion Review*, *3*(2), 138–146. doi:10.1177/1754073910387944

Camras, L. A., Lambrect, L., & Michel, G. (1996). Infant "surprise" expressions as coordinative motor structures. *Journal of Nonverbal Behavior*, *20*(3), 183–195. doi:10.1007/BF02281955

Camras, L. A., & Shuster, M. M. (2013). Current emotion research in developmental psychology. *Emotion Review*, *5*(3), 321–329. doi:10.1177/1754073913477516

Carr, L., Iacoboni, M., Dubeau, M.-C., Mazziotta, J. C., & Lenzi, G. L. (2003). Neural mechanisms of empathy in humans: A relay from neural systems for imitation to limbic areas. *Proceedings of the National Academy of Sciences of the United States of America*, *100*(9), 5497–5502. doi:10.1073/pnas.0935845100 PMID:12682281

Cornelius, R. R. (2000). *Theoretical approaches to emotion.* Newcastle: ISCA.

Craig, A. D. (2009). How do you feel–now? the anterior insula and human awareness. *Nature Reviews. Neuroscience, 10,* 59–70. doi:10.1038/nrn2555 PMID:19096369

Damasio, A. (1994). *Descartes' error: Emotion, reason and the human mind.* New York: Grossett/Putnam.

Damasio, A. R. (2004). *Looking for Spinoza: Joy, sorrow and the feeling brain.* Random House.

Darwin, C. (1965). *The expression of the emotions in man and animals.* Chicago: University of Chicago Press. (Original work published 1872)

de Waal, F. (2013). The Bonobo and the Atheist. In *Search of humanism among the primates.* New York: W.W. Norton and Co.

Ekman, P. (1992). An argument for basic emotions. *Cognition and Emotion, 6*(3-4), 169–200. doi:10.1080/02699939208411068

Ekman, P., & Friesen, W. V. (1969). The repertoire of nonverbal behavior: Categories, origins, usage, and coding. *Semiotica,* 49–98.

Elfenbein, H. A., & Ambady, N. (2003). Universals and cultural differences in recognizing emotions. *Current Directions in Psychological Science, 12*(5), 159–164. doi:10.1111/1467-8721.01252

Fellous, J.-M., & Arbib, M. A. (2005). Who needs emotions?: The brain meets the robot. Oxford: Oxford University Press. doi:10.1093/acprof:oso/9780195166194.001.0001

Fernald, A. (1989). Intonation and communicative intent in mothers' speech to infants: Is the melody the message? *Child Development, 60*(6), 1497–1510. doi:10.2307/1130938 PMID:2612255

Fernald, A., & Simon, T. (1984). Expanded intonation contours in mothers' speech to newborns. *Developmental Psychology, 20*(1), 104–113. doi:10.1037/0012-1649.20.1.104

Fernald, A., Taeschner, T., Dunn, J., Papousek, M., de Boysson-Bardies, B., & Fukui, I. (1989). A cross-language study of prosodic modifications in mothers' and fathers' speech to preverbal infants. *Journal of Child Language, 16*(3), 477–501. doi:10.1017/S0305000900010679 PMID:2808569

Field, T., Healy, B., Goldstein, S., Perry, S., Bendell, D., Schanberg, S., & Kuhn, C. et al. (1988). Infants of depressed mothers show "depressed" behavior even with nondepressed adults. *Child Development, 59*(6), 1569–1579. doi:10.2307/1130671 PMID:3208568

Fries, A. B., & Pollak, S. D. (2004). Emotion understanding in postinstitutionalized Eastern European children. *Development and Psychopathology, 16*(2), 355–369. doi:10.1017/S0954579404044554 PMID:15487600

Frijda, N. H. (1986). *The emotions.* Cambridge: Cambridge University Press.

Heberlein, A. S., & Atkinson, A. P. (2009). Neuroscientific evidence for simulation and shared substrates in emotion recognition: beyond faces. *Emotion Review, 1*(2), 162–177. doi:10.1177/1754073908100441

Hess, U., Beaupré, M. G., & Cheung, N. (2002). Who to whom and why – cultural differences and similarities in the function of smiles. In M. Abel (Ed.), *An empirical reflection on the smile* (pp. 187–216). New York: The Edwin Mellen Press.

Hiatt, S., Campos, J., & Emde, R. (1979). Facial patterning and infant emotional expression: Happiness, surprise and fear. *Child Development, 50*(4), 1020–1035. doi:10.2307/1129328 PMID:535426

Iacoboni, M., & Dapretto, M. (2006). The mirror neuron system and the consequences of its dysfunction. *Nature Reviews. Neuroscience, 7*(12), 942–951. doi:10.1038/nrn2024 PMID:17115076

Ishihara, H., Yoshikawa, Y., & Asada, M. (2011). Realistic child robot "Affetto" for understanding the caregiver-child attachment relationship that guides the child development. *IEEE International Conference on Development and Learning - ICDL. 2*, pp. 1-5. Frankfurt: IEEE. doi:10.1109/DEV-LRN.2011.6037346

James, W. (1884). What is an emotion? *Mind, 19*(34), 188–205. doi:10.1093/mind/os-IX.34.188

Juslin, P. N., & Laukka, P. (2003). Communication of emotions in vocal expression and music performance: Different channels, same code? *Psychological Bulletin, 129*(5), 770–814. doi:10.1037/0033-2909.129.5.770 PMID:12956543

Kaffman, A., & Meaney, M. J. (2007). Neurodevelopmental sequelae of postnatal maternal care in rodents: Clinical research and implications of molecular insights. *Journal of Child Psychology and Psychiatry, and Allied Disciplines, 48*(3-4), 224–244. doi:10.1111/j.1469-7610.2007.01730.x PMID:17355397

Kanungo, T., Mount, D. M., Netanyahu, N. S., Piatko, C. D., Silverman, R., & Wu, A. Y. (2002). An efficient k-means clustering algorithm: Analysis and implementation. *Pattern Analysis and Machine Intelligence. IEEE Transactions on, 24*(7), 881–892.

Kim, P., Feldman, R., Mayes, C., Eicher, V., Thompson, N., Leckman, J., & Swain, J. E. (2011). Breastfeeding, brain activation to own infant cry, and maternal sensitivity. *Journal of Child Psychology and Psychiatry, and Allied Disciplines, 52*(8), 907–915. doi:10.1111/j.1469-7610.2011.02406.x PMID:21501165

Kitamura, C., & Lam, C. (2009). Age-specific preferences for infant-directed affective intent. *Infancy, 14*(1), 77–100. doi:10.1080/15250000802569777

Kitayama, S., Markus, H. R., & Kurokawa, M. (2000). Culture, emotion, and well-being: Good feelings in Japan and the United States. *Cognition and Emotion, 14*(1), 93–124. doi:10.1080/026999300379003

Kohler, E. (2002). Hearing sounds, understanding actions: Action representation in mirror neurons. *Science, 297*(5582), 846–848. doi:10.1126/science.1070311 PMID:12161656

Kuhl, P. K. (2004). Early language acquisition: Cracking the speech code. *Nature Reviews. Neuroscience, 5*(11), 831–843. doi:10.1038/nrn1533 PMID:15496861

Lecanuet, J. P., & Schaal, B. (1996). Fetal sensory competencies. *European Journal of Obstetrics, Gynecology, and Reproductive Biology, 68*, 1–23. doi:10.1016/0301-2115(96)02509-2 PMID:8886675

Lim, A., Ogata, T., & Okuno, H. G. (2011). Converting emotional voice to motion for robot telepresence. *11th IEEE-RAS International Conference on Humanoid Robots (Humanoids), 2011*, (pp. 472-479).

Lim, A., Ogata, T., & Okuno, H. G. (2012). Towards expressive musical robots: A cross-modal framework for emotional gesture, voice and music. *EURASIP Journal on Audio, Speech, and Music Processing*, (1): 1–12.

Lim, A., & Okuno, H. G. (in prep.). *Emotional Contagion as a Mechanism for Basic Empathy*.

Lim, A., & Okuno, H. G. (in press). The MEI robot: Towards using motherese to develop multimodal emotional intelligence. *IEEE Transactions on Autonomous Mental Development*.

Mason, W. A., & Capitanio, J. P. (2012). Basic Emotions: A Reconstruction. *Emotion Review, 4*(3), 238–244. doi:10.1177/1754073912439763

Meaney, M. J., & Ferguson-Smith, A. C. (2010). Epigenetic regulation of the neural transcriptome: The meaning of the marks. *Nature Neuroscience, 13*(11), 1313–1318. doi:10.1038/nn1110-1313 PMID:20975754

Mehrabian, A. (1995). Framework for a comprehensive description and measurement of emotional states. *Genetic, Social, and General Psychology Monographs, 121*(3), 339–361. PMID:7557355

Morrison, I., Mjornsdotter, M., & Olausson, H. (2011). Vicarious responses to social touch in posterior insular cortex are tuned to pleasant caressing speeds. *The Journal of Neuroscience, 31*(26), 9554–9562. doi:10.1523/JNEUROSCI.0397-11.2011 PMID:21715620

Nagy, E., Pilling, K., Orvos, H., & Molnar, P. (2013). Imitation of tongue protrusion in human neonates: Specificity of the response in a large sample. *Developmental Psychology, 49*(9), 16–28. doi:10.1037/a0031127 PMID:23231691

Ortony, A. (1990). *The cognitive structure of emotions*. Cambridge university press.

Pedregosa, F., Varoquaux, G., Gramfort, A., Michel, V., Thirion, B., & Grisel, O. et al.. (2011). Scikit-learn: Machine learning in Python. *Journal of Machine Learning Research, 12*, 2825–2830.

Pohl, A., Anders, S., Schulte-Ruther, M., Mathiak, K., & Kircher, T. (2013). Positive Facial Affect – An fMRI Study on the involvement of insula and amygdala. *PLoS ONE, 8*(8), e69886. doi:10.1371/journal.pone.0069886 PMID:23990890

Rizzolatti, G., & Craighero, L. (2004). The mirror-neuron system. *Annual Review of Neuroscience, 27*(1), 169–192. doi:10.1146/annurev.neuro.27.070203.144230 PMID:15217330

Russell, J. A. (2009). Emotion, core affect, and psychological construction. *Cognition and Emotion, 23*(7), 1259–1283. doi:10.1080/02699930902809375

Sabatini, M. J., Ebert, P., Lewis, D. A., Levitt, P., Cameron, J. L., & Mirnics, K. (2007). Amygdala gene expression correlates of social behavior in monkeys experiencing maternal separation. *The Journal of Neuroscience, 27*(12), 3295–3304. doi:10.1523/JNEUROSCI.4765-06.2007 PMID:17376990

Saint-Georges, C., Chetouani, M., Cassel, R., Apicella, F., Mahdhaoui, A., Muratori, F., & Cohen, D. et al. (2013). Motherese in interaction: At the crossroad of emotion and cognition? (A systematic review). *PLoS ONE, 8*(10), e78103. doi:10.1371/journal.pone.0078103 PMID:24205112

Schwarz, G. (1978). Estimating the dimension of a model. *Annals of Statistics, 6*(2), 461–464. doi:10.1214/aos/1176344136

Shute, B., & Wheldall, K. (1989). Pitch alterations in British motherese: Some preliminary acoustic data. *Journal of Child Language, 16*(3), 503–512. doi:10.1017/S0305000900010680 PMID:2808570

Sigelman, C. K., & Rider, E. A. (2010). *Life span human development*. CengageBrain.

Singer, T. (2004). Empathy for pain involves the affective but not sensory components of pain. *Science, 303*(5661), 1157–1162. doi:10.1126/science.1093535 PMID:14976305

So, J. (2013, 12 31). Can robots fall in love, and why would they? *The Daily Beast*. Retrieved April 7, 2014, from http://www.thedailybeast.com/articles/2013/12/31/can-robots-fall-in-love-and-why-would-they.html

Soken, N. H., & Pick, A. D. (1992). Intermodal perception of happy and angry expressive behaviors by seven-month-old infants. *Child Development*, *63*(4), 787–795. doi:10.2307/1131233 PMID:1505240

Sokol, S. (1978). Measurement of infant visual acuity from pattern reversal evoked potentials. *Vision Research*, *18*(1), 33–39. doi:10.1016/0042-6989(78)90074-3 PMID:664274

Tottenham, N., Hare, T. A., Millner, A., Gilhooly, T., Zevin, J., & Casey, B. J. (2011). Elevated amygdala response to faces following early deprivation. *Developmental Science*, *14*(2), 190–204. doi:10.1111/j.1467-7687.2010.00971.x PMID:21399712

Trainor, L. J., Austin, C. M., & Desjardins, R. N. (2000). Is infant-directed speech prosody a result of the vocal expression of emotion? *Psychological Science*, *11*(3), 188–195. doi:10.1111/1467-9280.00240 PMID:11273402

Tsai, J. L. (2007). Ideal affect: Cultural causes and behavioral consequences. *Perspectives on Psychological Science*, *2*(3), 242–259. doi:10.1111/j.1745-6916.2007.00043.x

Turkle, S. (2012). *Alone together: Why we expect more from technology and less from each other*. Basic Books.

Wallach, W., & Allen, C. (2010). *Moral machines: Teaching robots right from wrong*. New York: Oxford University Press.

Watanabe, A., Ogino, M., & Asada, M. (2007). Mapping facial expression to internal states based on intuitive parenting. *Journal of Robotics and Mechatronics*, *19*(3), 3–15.

Werner, L. A. (2002). Infant auditory capabilities. *Current Opinion in Otolaryngology & Head & Neck Surgery*, *10*(5), 398–402. doi:10.1097/00020840-200210000-00013

KEY TERMS AND DEFINITIONS

Bayesian Information Criterion (BIC): A criterion for selecting the best model given a dataset. It penalizes models that use too many variables to explain the data (overfitting). A lower BIC implies 1) a better fit, and/or 2) fewer explanatory variables.

Developmental Robotics or Epigenetic Robotics: A relatively new scientific field that aims to study the developmental mechanisms and architectures for lifelong learning in machines. Typically it involves formalizing, validating and extending models from neuroscience, developmental psychology, and evolutionary biology, specifically by attempting to implement the models in robots. Results are expected to feedback into existing theories, or produce novel theories about human and animal development.

Entrainment: The synchronization of organism to a rhythm usually produced by another social actor. Humans can entrain to the beat, for instance, by dancing or tapping their foot, and fireflies are also known to flash in synchrony. In this chapter, we refer to the entrainment in speed, intensity, regularity and extent between the voices and movements of two agents.

Gaussian Mixture Model (GMM): A probabilistic model used to represent data as a mixture of normal distributions. It is commonly used for unsupervised learning and clustering, which means that clusters can be created without labels.

It is similar to k-means clustering, except that when used for recognition, it outputs the probability that a new data point belongs to a cluster, not a binary value.

Gut or Physical Feeling: The state of physical flourishing (homeostasis) or distress (out of homeostasis) in an individual.

Motherese: A simplified type of speech spontaneously spoken by caregivers to infants. Typically it contains exaggerated intonation and rhythm, a higher pitch, and more pronounced variations compared to normal speech. Also known as baby talk or infant-directed speech (IDS).

Multimodal Emotional Intelligence (MEI): A robot system with the ability to understand, represent and express emotions in multiple modalities, such as voice, movement, gait or music.

SIRE Paradigm: A paradigm using speed, intensity, regularity and extent (SIRE) to represent an emotion across modalities. For instance, sadness has been linked to slow, low intensity, regular and small dynamics in movement, as well as in voice and music.

Social Constructivist Theory: A theory that an individual's learning is constructed through interaction with others in a group. It suggests that cognitive development is influenced by culture and social context.

ENDNOTES

1   http://www.aldebaran.com
2   http://www.hark.jp
3   http://www.acapela-group.com

Chapter 16
Automated Recognition of Emotion Appraisals

Marcello Mortillaro
University of Geneva (Swiss Center for Affective Sciences), Switzerland

Ben Meuleman
University of Geneva (Swiss Center for Affective Sciences), Switzerland

Klaus R. Scherer
University of Geneva (Swiss Center for Affective Sciences), Switzerland

ABSTRACT

Most computer models for the automatic recognition of emotion from nonverbal signals (e.g., facial or vocal expression) have adopted a discrete emotion perspective, i.e., they output a categorical emotion from a limited pool of candidate labels. The discrete perspective suffers from practical and theoretical drawbacks that limit the generalizability of such systems. The authors of this chapter propose instead to adopt an appraisal perspective in modeling emotion recognition, i.e., to infer the subjective cognitive evaluations that underlie both the nonverbal cues and the overall emotion states. In a first step, expressive features would be used to infer appraisals; in a second step, the inferred appraisals would be used to predict an emotion label. The first step is practically unexplored in emotion literature. Such a system would allow to (a) link models of emotion recognition and production, (b) add contextual information to the inference algorithm, and (c) allow detection of subtle emotion states.

INTRODUCTION

Hundreds of studies investigated the emotional meaning of nonverbal signals and most of them implicitly or explicitly used a discrete emotion perspective (Scherer, Clark-Polner, Mortillaro, 2011), i.e., that each emotion is a qualitatively different entity from the others. Discrete emotion theory has been formulated on the basis of findings concerning few intense emotions—called basic emotions—that are expected to have prototypical facial expressions and physiological signatures (Ekman, 1992, 1999; Ekman, Levenson, & Friesen, 1983; Ekman, Sorenson, & Friesen, 1969). This theory has dominated the field for decades and is still widely used.

DOI: 10.4018/978-1-4666-7278-9.ch016

Most attempts at computer recognition of emotion from nonverbal expressions (one of the goals of the research on affective computing, Picard, 1997) have adopted the same discrete perspective. Typically, such models attempt to automatically detect almost invariant configurations that are supposed to be prototypical to certain emotion categories, for example by matching a facial expression to a set of stored *templates*.

The results of a recent challenge for emotion recognition systems showed that the automatic classification of facial expressions of emotion in discrete categories is technically feasible—assuming the availability of an appropriate ground truth (Valstar et al., 2012). One problem is that the discrete approach (template matching) transfers poorly to real-world expressions and applications. Studies showed that, in everyday communications, prototypical expressions do not occur very often and that the interpretation of nonverbal cues is heavily influenced by context (Aviezer, Trope, & Todorov, 2012; Carroll & Russell, 1996). This recent evidence in psychology calls for a similar paradigm shift in the field of automatic detection of emotion. Ideally, this shift should involve both the detection and the inference part of recognition systems.

Indeed, emotion recognition systems can be conceived as made of two parts, a detection component and an inference component. The detection component performs the analysis of the facial movements; the inference component outputs the attribution of an emotional meaning to the movements detected by the first component. More recent automated models of detection have abandoned the template-matching approach and are now focused on the automatic detection of action units (Valstar, Mehu, Pantic, & Scherer, 2012). The Facial Action Coding System (FACS, Ekman & Friesen, 1978) is the recognized standard for the coding of facial movements, and researchers are now trying to implement an automated version capable of detecting each movement shown

by a face. Current results are promising and we can expect that, in the near future, these systems will become fully reliable and perform in a satisfactory way. As the detection problem is getting solved, attention should now focus on what is the best model to attribute an emotional meaning[1]. We propose that the inference component should be modeled after emotion approaches that offer greater flexibility to different contexts and allow the inferences of partial emotion information, i.e., appraisals.

PERSPECTIVES ON EMOTION

There is robust evidence about the existence of some facial configurations that are cross-culturally labeled with the same emotion terms (e.g., joy, fear, anger). Nevertheless, several studies show that people frequently report the experience of emotional states that are not part of this set of basic emotions (Scherer & Ceschi, 2000; Scherer, Wranik, Sangsue, Tran, & Scherer, 2004), and, more importantly, that for spontaneous and enacted emotional expression, these complete prototypical expressions rarely occur (Naab & Russell, 2007; Russell & Fernandez-Dols, 1997; Scherer & Ellgring, 2007). Sometimes the expressions are so ambiguous that it is even impossible for a viewer to determine whether the expression is positive or negative (Aviezer et al., 2013).

Automatic recognition systems that are based on the detection of prototypical expressions are extremely successful with posed expressions such as those constructed on the basis of Ekman's predictions, for example, those included in the Cohn-Kanade database (Kanade, Cohn, & Tian, 2000), or in the JACFEE (Biehl, et al., 1997), which were recorded under standardized and optimal conditions. Most advanced methods are also extremely accurate at distinguishing other types of emotion expressions, including expressions that are not based on predefined prototypical templates or have been recorded in sub-optimal conditions (Valstar, et al., 2012). These technologically impressive advancements still cannot solve a number of theoretical and methodological issues. First, strictly speaking, these systems are capable of recognizing expressions, not the emotions. The "emotional validity" of these expressions relies completely on how the material used for the training of the systems has been built. These systems do not have a separate inference module, but instead there's a simple one-to-one relationship between an expression and an emotion label. Second, although these facial prototypes have a certain amount of heuristic utility, spontaneous emotional expressions are rather different from the prototypes, and are usually much more subtle and less differentiated (Gunes & Pantic, 2010; Zeng et al., 2007). This may severely limit the possibility to successfully use these systems in real-world applications. Third, systems that use predictions of basic emotion theory to infer an emotion state from a series of detected AUs can account only for very few, generally six to seven, emotions. For emotions outside of this restricted class, and for mixed or blended emotions, these systems are unlikely to provide satisfactory results.

Dimensional models define emotions as states that can be represented on a common multidimensional space. The original models of this type included three dimensions: pleasure, arousal, and dominance. Pleasure (or valence) refers to the hedonic quality of the emotion: positive or negative. Arousal refers to the physical activation of the organism. Dominance (or power) refers to the degree of control that the person has in the situation. More recent versions propose a bi-dimensional space organized along the axes of valence and arousal and suggest that the subjective feeling of an emotion is the result of an interaction between *core affect* (i.e. the position in the valence per arousal space) and a cognitive component such as interpretation or attribution (Russell, 2003). On one hand, this approach has

the merit of reducing the complexity of the emotion recognition task, making it easier to attribute a global affective meaning (positive or negative) to subtle expressions. On the other hand, two or three dimensions seem too limited to capture the complexity of the emotion space and to explain the wide variety of individuals' subjective feelings.

Systems for the automatic recognition of emotion based on dimensional models of emotion started to be developed only recently. Efforts in this area have been made for different modalities, although mainly in systems that process physiological signals or voice (for a review, Gunes & Pantic, 2010). The most challenging problem in this framework is the mapping of emotion labels onto the continuous multidimensional space. Most systems have simplified this problem to two separate binary decisions (high vs low arousal; positive vs. negative), but this choice cannot be considered satisfactory as it ultimately returns back to the discrete approach while at the same time losing the better descriptive quality that is afforded by a direct use of emotion terms. It is evident that this approach is still in its pioneering state, but it is hard to see how the problem of labeling can be satisfactorily solved in this fashion. There is need for more theoretical reasoning and basic psychological research to fill in the gap between dimensional representation of emotion expressions and emotion labeling. This is not to deny that dimensional models may be very useful in applications that require a simple evaluation of valence and arousal and do not require precise specification of the underlying emotion through classification.

Appraisal models are a third alternative perspective on emotion. These models combine elements of dimensional models—emotions as emergent results of underlying dimensions—with elements of discrete theories—emotions have different subjective qualities— and add a definition of the cognitive mechanisms that cause emotion. Starting from the original suggestion of Arnold

(1960), who defined appraisal as a direct, immediate and intuitive evaluation able to distinguish qualitatively among different emotions, appraisal theorists argue that the experience of an emotion is determined by a series of cognitive evaluations on different levels of processing (for a review, see Ellsworth & Scherer, 2003; Scherer, Schorr, & Johnstone, 2001) and it is the specific set of responses in each individual case that determines which emotion will be experienced (Scherer, 2009a). Appraisal theories offer a more flexible framework than discrete and dimensional models, being able to account for individual differences and variations of responses to the same stimulus by the same individual at two different moments in time (Roseman & Smith, 2001), as well as for some cultural differences (for example in the form of appraisal biases; Scherer and Brosch, 2009). Appraisal theories do not generally assume the existence of a one-to-one relationship between a situation and a response or between a single appraisal and a specific emotion (Nezlek, Vansteelandt, van Mechelen, & Kuppens, 2008). It is the pattern of appraisals that determines the emotion experienced (Frijda, 1986; Lazarus, 1991; Ortony, Clore & Collins, 1988; Scherer, 1984, 2001, 2009a). Appraisal theories attempt to explain the differentiation of emotion states by different configurations of the underlying appraisal dimensions and try to map emotion labels on this multidimensional space. Some authors advanced predictions about the typical appraisal structure of the most frequently occurring emotions. For example, an event that causes fear would be typically appraised as unexpected, unpleasant, obstructive to personal goals, and difficult to cope with (Scherer, 1994). Since the foundation of affective computing, modeling of the emotion production process has preferentially looked at appraisal models of emotion (with the OCC model being the most frequently used, Ortony et al, 1988). The same cannot be said for research oriented towards the automatic recognition of emotion from expressive signals.

AN APPRAISAL FRAMEWORK FOR EMOTION RECOGNITION

Appraisal models define a series of cognitive evaluations that would be at the basis of an emotional episode and predict which emotion would be experienced based on the resulting appraisals. Similarly, appraisals are seen as the causal mechanisms at the basis of physiological modifications and nonverbal expressions. The body of evidence about the link between appraisals and facial expressions (Kaiser & Wehrle, 2001; Mortillaro, Mehu, & Scherer, 2011; Scherer, Mortillaro, Mehu, 2013), vocal expressions (Banse & Scherer, 1996; Patel, Scherr, Björkner, & Sundberg, 2011) and bodily expressions (Dael, Mortillaro, & Scherer, 2012) is extensive. Some researchers have suggested the possibility that this mechanism could be reversed for emotion recognition: inferring specific appraisals from specific expression configurations. Mortillaro, Mehu, and Scherer (2013) listed "inference of underlying appraisals" as one of the mechanisms that human observers could use to infer an emotion state from someone's expressions. The possibility that observers could directly infer appraisals from expressions and then use the appraisals to attribute an emotion label was already advanced in the first componential models of emotions and it has been recently tested in one study investigating the role of emotion expressions in interdependent decision making (De Melo, Carnevale, Read, & Gratch, 2014). Indeed componential views of emotion expression postulate that while a configuration of cues may be immediately perceived as an expression of one specific emotion, individual elements of the expression (a facial movement or an acoustic feature) may be still meaningful because they would carry information about the underlying appraisals (Smith & Scott, 1997).

Three recent studies investigated the possibility that observers would be able to infer appraisal information from nonverbal expressions. Scherer and Grandjean (2008) asked participants to judge facial expressions of seven emotions using a) emotion labels; b) social messages; c) appraisals; or d) action tendencies. Judges were more accurate and more confident in their judgment when they used emotion labels and appraisals. Laukka and colleagues (2010) developed a corpus of emotion vocal expressions and had these expressions evaluated on several appraisal dimensions; results showed that a) listeners could reliably infer appraisals from vocal expressions; b) inferred appraisals were in line with predictions of appraisal theory; and c) appraisals were significantly correlated with a number of acoustic features. A recent study by de Melo and colleagues (2014) found confirmation that individuals follow principles of appraisal theories when making inferences about other people's emotional behavior in context. In particular beliefs about others' appraisals mediate the effect of emotional expressions about the inference of others' intentions and mental states.

These studies suggest that the appraisal framework lends itself for fruitful application in the context of emotion recognition. Importantly, such an approach would address three concerns that are currently relevant in the field of (automatic) emotion recognition, including:

1. How to establish a link between models of emotion recognition and emotion production?
2. How to add contextual information to systems of emotion recognition?
3. How to increase the sensitivity with which weak, subtle, or complex emotion states can be detected?

The first and most important issue concerns the link between emotion production and recognition. In the discrete view on (automatic) emotion recognition, such a link has either not been established or is treated as secondary to the problem of accurately inferring emotional states (Castellano, Caridakis, Camurri, Karpouzis, Volpe, & Kollias, 2010). Within the appraisal framework, by contrast, the link between emotion recognition and emotion production can be made explicit. In emotion production, it is assumed that humans make appraisals and then experience emotional states based on these appraisals. In emotion recognition, observers may infer appraisals from nonverbal cues and then infer emotional states based on these appraisals, thus essentially *retracing* the person's production process.

Proposing this connection allows direct communication between models of recognition and production, as depicted in Figure 1 (lower panel). In this diagram, black circles denote expression variables (e.g., individual facial action units), white squares denote appraisal variables (e.g., goal obstruction, pleasantness), and grey diamonds denote emotion labels (e.g., anger, fear). In the classical framework, the recognition model outputs an emotion label (upper left panel) without the detailed specification of a production model. In terms of production, an undetermined "affect program" is assumed without separately considering the underlying appraisals (upper right panel).

In the appraisal framework, on the other hand, a recognition model that outputs appraisals affords a natural compatibility with appraisals in the production model (lower panel, dashed lines). In particular, data or predictions at the output side of the recognition model can be inputted directly into the production model to estimate a plausible emotion label. Importantly, an emotion recognition system that outputs appraisals would be extremely useful in all those cases in which it would be difficult to attribute a single emotion label (e.g., for example when multiple emotion labels have the same likelihood estimate, or none is applicable). In all these cases the system based only on discrete emotion labels would be unable to output a label that is reliably applicable to the expression; conversely, a system based on appraisal may be able to provide reliable information on at least some of the emotion appraisals of the expresser.

The second issue concerns how to integrate contextual information into systems of emotion

Figure 1. Discrete vs. appraisal framework for emotion recognition and production. Black circles denote expression variables (e.g., individual facial action units), white squares denote appraisal variables (e.g., goal obstructiveness, pleasantness), and grey diamonds denote emotion labels (e.g., anger, fear)

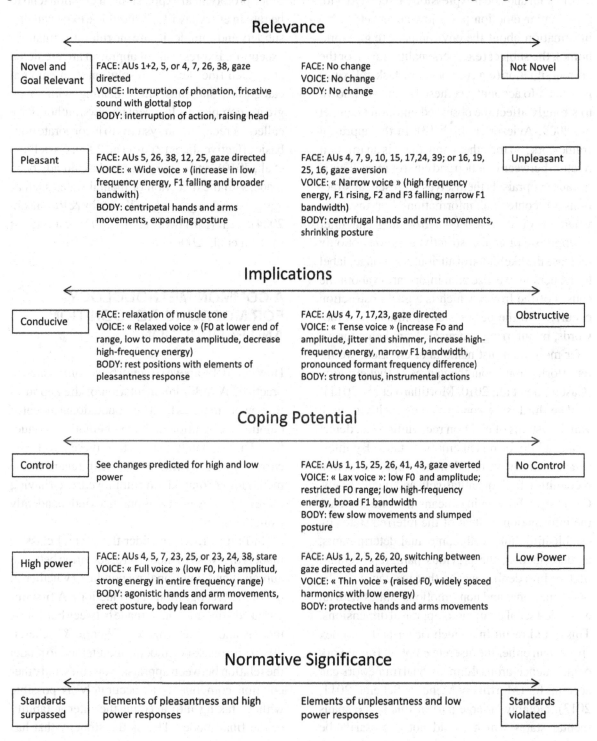

recognition. In the classical framework, emotions are identified on the basis of a relatively isolated set of facial and vocal expressions associated with a particular emotion (e.g., joy, anger, etc.). No information about the environment (e.g., work, home), the subject (e.g., personality traits), or the current situation (e.g., performing a task, relaxing) is taken into account, yet these factors are known to strongly affect the observed emotion (Zeng et al., 2009, Aviezer et al., 2013). In the appraisal framework, on the other hand, there is an implicit relation between emotion and environment. This is because appraisals themselves represent abstractions of contextual information. For instance, when we observe a person frowning and infer an appraisal of goal obstructiveness, we not only increase the likelihood of attributing an anger label to the person, we also gain information about the causes of the frown, which is a goal obstruction occurring in the person's environment. In other words, by inferring appraisals from behavior we infer more than just markers of emotion, we infer information about the causes of that emotion (Castellano et al., 2010, Mortillaro et al., 2011).

The third issue concerns the sensitivity with which systems of emotion recognition can detect weak, subtle, or mixed emotion states. By inferring appraisals we broaden the scope of emotion recognition both quantitatively and qualitatively. Qualitative broadening means that we increase the information content of the inferred states by establishing links with contextual determinants, as described in the previous paragraph. Quantitative broadening means that we can describe both emotional and non-emotional states with an expanded set of continuous appraisal dimensions. This could result in a much richer and complex space than either the discrete emotion framework or the valence-arousal dimensional framework can account for (Mortillaro, Mehu, & Scherer, 2011, 2013). Notably, a large part of this space spans mental states which would not necessarily be considered *emotional*, or may contain just traces of emotional states. For instance, a faintly raised

eyebrow will not signal a full-blown emotion but may be recognized as a signal of unexpectedness. Since prototypical expressions of emotion tend to be rare in everyday life, it should be expected that subtlety and complexity are the rule rather than the exception. Expressions of appraisal are predicted at a much finer level of resolution than emotion categories, and thus allow dealing with much greater complexity. In recent reviews, authors have called for recognition systems to incorporate non-basic affective states (Zeng et al, 2009; Castellano et al., 2010), and some progress has already been made with the detection of mental states such as agreeing or disagreeing (el Kaliouby & Robinson, 2004), pain (Littlewort et al., 2007) and interest (Yeasin et al., 2006).

A COMMON METHODOLOGY FOR MODELING RECOGNITION AND PRODUCTION

How could the above strategy be accomplished in practice? A full implementation of the appraisal framework requires both a computational model of emotion recognition and one of emotion production. Unfortunately, research in these two fields currently shares little overlap with regard to the methodology that is being employed, each having more or less developed its practices independently from the other.

In Figure 1, we consider the general class of models that wish to model an association between appraisal and emotional responding (whether in the field of recognition or production). A first important distinction can be made between black-box models and process models (Wehrle & Scherer, 2001). In a black-box model, one attempts to model the relation between appraisal variables and other emotion components as accurately as possible without taking into account the interpretability of the final model. This is the strategy that has generally been adopted in the field of automatic emotion recognition: a model is trained on empirically gathered data and its success measured by its predictive accuracy (e.g., Castellano et al., 2010; Devillers, Vidrascu, & Layachi, 2010). Typically these models are advanced statistical models from the field of machine learning (e.g., support vector machines, *k*-nearest neighbor classifiers). The advantage of this approach is the flexibility with regard to modeling that can be attempted, for instance by contrasting linear to nonlinear models. The major drawback of this approach is often the lack of interpretability, which is either inherent to the model being used or simply outside the interest of the researchers.

In a process model, one attempts to describe the association between appraisal and other emotion components (possibly over time) in a meaningful way. Here, it is useful to make a further distinction between theory-driven and data-driven models as outlined in Figure 1. In a theory-driven model, the relations between input and output are completely specified by the user, whereas, in a data-driven model, the model, based on empirical data, estimates these relations. Evidently, black-box models are data-driven by their very nature. With regard

to computational models of emotion production, most of the current models in existence are heavily theory driven. In contrast to the field of emotion recognition, however, emotion production turned to appraisal theory as a venue for modeling at an early stage, to the extent that many of the current models of emotion production are based on appraisal (Marsella, Gratch, & Petta, 2010). The majority of these models rely on the OCC theory by Ortony, Clore, and Collins (1988), while others have attempted to employ structural or conceptual features of the Component Process Model proposed by Scherer, such as WASABI (Becker-Asano, 2008), PEACTDIM (Marinier, 2008), and GATE (Wehrle, 1995; Wehrle & Scherer, 2001). The major drawback of the current approach to modeling appraisal is the lack of flexibility offered by statistically founded, data-driven approaches such as those used in emotion recognition. This is particularly problematic in the face of increasing consensus that emotions are dynamic, nonlinear phenomena (Lewis, 2005; Scherer 2000; 2009b), casting doubt on the ability of theory-driven models to capture such complex patterns.

Figure 2. Taxonomy of the models for the association appraisal-emotion

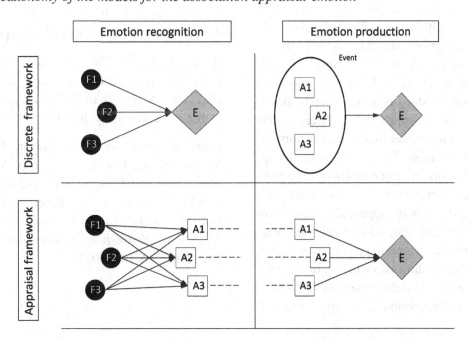

Ideally, a process model should be able to incorporate both theory-driven and data-driven properties. This naturally leads us to consider so-called hybrid models, where one part of the model is estimated from empirical data while the other is specified by theoretical constraints (Figure 2, diagram intersection). Examples of hybrid models are neural networks. These models are particularly attractive for computational modeling of emotion (Sander, Grandjean, & Scherer, 2005; Scherer, 2009b), because they allow flexibility with regard to the architectural choices the user can make such as the number of layers, the number of connections, and the possibility to include feedback loops. The hybrid approach to computational modeling may be extended to models that are capable of adapting to new data as they are processed (online learning) and that allow emergent phenomena through dynamic input and feedback between components (Scherer, 2009b).

CONCLUSION

Individuals' appraisals are key elements for emotion production (e.g., Ellsworth & Smith, 1989; Roseman & Evdokas, 2004; Siemer, Mauss, & Gross, 2007; Smith & Kirby, 2004), but their role in emotion recognition is still largely unexplored. A handful of recent studies, however, already suggest that the appraisal framework may be a fruitful venue for studying emotion recognition. We believe that this approach may offer specific advantages for researchers interested in automatic detection of emotions. First, by adopting the appraisal framework, we can establish formal links between models of emotion production and recognition. Second, by linking appraisals to expressive features, we implicitly introduce contextual information to models of emotion recognition. Third, by expanding the dimensional basis of emotion categories, we increase the sensitivity with which subtle or complex emotion states may be detected.

ACKNOWLEDGEMENT

This chapter is a modified version of the original article published in 2012 in the International Journal of Synthetic Emotions: Mortillaro, M., Meuleman, B., & Scherer, K., (2012). Advocating a componential appraisal model to guide emotion recognition. International Journal of Synthetic Emotions, 3(1), 18-32.

This research was supported by the Swiss National Science Foundation (FNRS 101411-100367 and FNRS 100014-122491/1), by the National Centre of Competence in Research (NCCR) Affective Sciences (51NF40-104897) hosted by the University of Geneva, and by an ERC Advanced Grant in the European Community's 7th Framework Programme under grant agreement n° 230331-PROPEREMO to Klaus Scherer.

REFERENCES

Arnold, M. B. (1960). *Emotion and personality*. New York: Columbia University Press.

Banse, R., & Scherer, K. R. (1996). Acoustic profiles in vocal emotion expression. *Journal of Personality and Social Psychology*, *70*(3), 614–636. doi:10.1037/0022-3514.70.3.614 PMID:8851745

Becker-Asano, C. (2008). *WASABI: Affect simulation for agents with believable interactivity* (PhD thesis). Faculty of Technology, University of Bielefeld, Germany. IOS Press (DISKI 319).

Biehl, M., Matsumoto, D., Ekman, P., Hearn, V., Heider, K., Kudoh, T., & Ton, V. (1997). Matsumoto and Ekman's Japanese and Caucasian Facial Expressions of Emotion (JACFEE): Reliability data and cross-national differences. *Journal of Nonverbal Behavior*, *21*(1), 3–21. doi:10.1023/A:1024902500935

Calvo, R. A., & D'Mello, S. (2010). Affect detection: An interdisciplinary review of models, methods, and their applications. *IEEE Transactions on Affective Computing*, *1*(1), 18–37. doi:10.1109/T-AFFC.2010.1

Castellano, G., Caridakis, G., Camurri, A., Karpouzis, K., Volpe, G., & Kollias, S. (2010). Body gesture and facial expression analysis for automatic affect recognition. In K. R. Scherer, T. Bänziger, & E. B. Roesch (Eds.), *Blueprint for affective computing: A sourcebook* (pp. 245–255). New York: Oxford University Press.

Coulson, M. (2009). Expressing emotion through body movement: A component process approach. In L. Canamero & R. Aylett (Eds.), Animating expressive characters for social interaction (Advances in Consciousness Research Series; Vol. 74). Amsterdam, The Netherlands: Benjamins.

Dael, N., Mortillaro, M., & Scherer, K. R. (2012). Emotion expression in body action and posture. *Emotion (Washington, D.C.)*, *12*(5), 1085–1101. doi:10.1037/a0025737 PMID:22059517

Devillers, L., Vidrascu, L., & Layachi, O. (2010). Automatic detection of emotion from vocal expression. In K. R. Scherer, T. Bänziger, & E. B. Roesch (Eds.), *Blueprint for affective computing: A sourcebook* (pp. 232–244). New York: Oxford University Press.

Ekman, P. (1992). Facial expressions of emotion: New findings, new questions. *Psychological Science*, *3*(1), 34–38. doi:10.1111/j.1467-9280.1992. tb00253.x

Ekman, P. (1999). Facial expressions. In T. Dalgleish & M. J. Power (Eds.), *Handbook of cognition and emotion* (pp. 301–320). New York: Wiley.

Ekman, P., & Friesen, W. V. (1978). *Facial action coding system*. Palo Alto, CA: Consulting Psychologists Press.

Ekman, P., Levenson, R. W., & Friesen, W. V. (1983). Autonomic nervous system activity distinguishes among emotions. *Science*, *221*(4616), 1208–1210. doi:10.1126/science.6612338 PMID:6612338

Ekman, P., Sorenson, E. R., & Friesen, W. V. (1969). Pan-cultural elements in facial displays of emotion. *Science*, *164*(3875), 86–88. doi:10.1126/science.164.3875.86 PMID:5773719

El Kaliouby, R., & Robinson, P. (2004). Real time inference of complex mental states from facial expressions and head gestures. In *IEEE International Conference on Computer Vision and Pattern Recognition, Workshop on Real Time Computer Vision for Human Computer Interaction*, Vol. 10, p. 154.

Ellsworth, P. C., & Scherer, K. R. (2003). Appraisal processes in emotion. In R. J. Davidson, K. R. Scherer, & H. Goldsmith (Eds.), *Handbook of the affective sciences* (pp. 572–595). New York, NY: Oxford University Press.

Ellsworth, P. C., & Smith, C. A. (1988). Shades of joy: Patterns of appraisal differentiating pleasant emotions. *Cognition and Emotion*, *2*(4), 301–331. doi:10.1080/02699938808412702

Frijda, N. H. (1986). *The emotions*. London: Cambridge University Press.

Gunes, H., & Pantic, M. (2010). Automatic, dimensional and continuous emotion recognition. *International Journal of Synthetic Emotions*, *1*(1), 68–99. doi:10.4018/jse.2010101605

Johnstone, T., van Reekum, C. M., Hird, K., Kirsner, K., & Scherer, K. R. (2005). Affective speech elicited with a computer game. *Emotion (Washington, D.C.)*, *5*(4), 513–518. doi:10.1037/1528-3542.5.4.513 PMID:16366756

Kaiser, S., & Wehrle, T. (2001). Facial expressions as indicators of appraisal processes. In K. R. Scherer, A. Schorr, & T. Johnstone (Eds.), *Appraisal processes in emotion* (pp. 285–300). New York: Oxford University Press.

Kanade, T., Cohn, J. F., & Tian, Y. (2000). Comprehensive database for facial expression analysis. *Proceeding of International Conference on Face and Gesture Recognition*, 46-53. doi:10.1109/AFGR.2000.840611

Laukka, P., Elfenbein, H. A., Chui, W., Thingujam, N. S., Iraki, F. K., Rockstuhl, T., & Althoff, J. (2010). Presenting the VENEC corpus: Development of a cross-cultural corpus of vocal emotion expressions and a novel method of annotating emotion appraisals. In L. Devillers, B. Schuller, R. Cowie, E. Douglas-Cowie, & A. Batliner (Eds.), *Proceedings of the LREC 2010 Workshop on Corpora for Research on Emotion and Affect* (pp. 53-57). Paris: EuropeanLanguage Resources Association.

Lazarus, R. S. (1991). *Emotion and adaptation*. New York: Oxford University Press.

Lewis, M. D. (2005). Bridging emotion theory and neurobiology through dynamic systems modeling. *Behavioral and Brain Sciences*, *28*(02), 169–245. doi:10.1017/S0140525X0500004X PMID:16201458

Littlewort, G. C., Bartlett, M. S., & Lee, K. (2007). Faces of pain: automated measurement of spontaneous facial expressions of genuine and posed pain. In *Proceedings of the 9th international conference on multimodal interfaces*, pp. 15–21. ACM, New York. doi:10.1145/1322192.1322198

Marinier, R. P. (2008). *A computational unification of cognitive control, emotion and learning* (PhD dissertation). University of Michigan, Ann Arbor, Michigan.

Marsella, S., Gratch, J., & Petta, P. (2010). Computational models of emotion. In K. R. Scherer, T. Bänziger, & E. B. Roesch (Eds.), *Blueprint for Affective Computing: A sourcebook* (pp. 21–41). New York: Oxford University Press.

Mortillaro, M., Mehu, M., & Scherer, K. R. (2011). Subtly different positive emotions can be distinguished by their facial expressions. *Social Psychological & Personality Science*, *2*(3), 262–271. doi:10.1177/1948550610389080

Mortillaro, M., Mehu, M., & Scherer, K. R. (2013). The evolutionary origin of multimodal synchronization in emotional expression. In E. Altenmüller, S. Schmidt, & E. Zimmerman (Eds.), *Evolution of emotional communication: From sounds in nonhuman mammals to speech and music in man.* (pp. 3-25). New York: Oxford University Press. doi:10.1093/acprof:oso/9780199583560.003.0001

Naab, P. J., & Russell, J. A. (2007). Judgments of emotion from spontaneous facial expressions of New Guineans. *Emotion (Washington, D.C.)*, *7*(4), 736–744. doi:10.1037/1528-3542.7.4.736 PMID:18039042

Nezlek, J. B., Vansteelandt, K., Van Mechelen, I., & Kuppens, P. (2008). Appraisal-emotion relationships in daily life. *Emotion (Washington, D.C.)*, *8*(1), 145–150. doi:10.1037/1528-3542.8.1.145 PMID:18266526

Ortony, A., Clore, G. L., & Collins, A. (1988). *The cognitive structure of emotions*. Cambridge: Cambridge University Press. doi:10.1017/CBO9780511571299

Osgood, C. E. (1962). Studies of the generality of affective meaning systems. *The American Psychologist*, *17*(1), 10–28. doi:10.1037/h0045146

Osgood, C. E. (1964). Semantic differential technique in the comparative study of cultures. *American Anthropologist, 66*(3), 171–200. doi:10.1525/aa.1964.66.3.02a00880

Patel, S., Scherer, K. R., Björkner, E., & Sundberg, J. (2011). Mapping emotions into acoustic space: The role of voice production. *Biological Psychology, 87*(1), 93–98. doi:10.1016/j.biopsycho.2011.02.010 PMID:21354259

Roseman, I., & Evdokas, A. (2004). Appraisals cause experienced emotions: Experimental evidence. *Cognition and Emotion, 18*(1), 1–28. doi:10.1080/02699930244000390

Roseman, I. J., & Smith, C. A. (2001). Appraisal theory: Overview, assumptions, varieties, controversies. In K. R. Scherer, A. Schorr, & T. Johnstone (Eds.), *Appraisal processes in emotion: Theory, methods, research* (pp. 3–19). New York: Oxford University Press.

Russell, J. A. (2003). Core affect and the psychological construction of emotion. *Psychological Review, 110*(1), 145–172. doi:10.1037/0033-295X.110.1.145 PMID:12529060

Russell, J. A., Bachorowski, J.-A., & Fernandez-Dols, J.-M. (2003). Facial and vocal expressions of emotion. *Annual Review of Psychology, 54*(1), 329–349. doi:10.1146/annurev.psych.54.101601.145102 PMID:12415074

Russell, J. A., & Bullock, M. (1986). On the dimensions preschoolers use to interpret facial expressions of emotion. *Developmental Psychology, 22*(1), 97–102. doi:10.1037/0012-1649.22.1.97

Russell, J. A., & Fernandez-Dols, J. M. (1997). *The psychology of facial expression*. New York: Cambridge University Press. doi:10.1017/CBO9780511659911

Russell, J. A., & Mehrabian, A. (1974). Distinguishing anger and anxiety in terms of emotional response factors. *Journal of Consulting and Clinical Psychology, 42*(1), 79–83. doi:10.1037/h0035915 PMID:4814102

Russell, J. A., & Mehrabian, A. (1977). Evidence for a three-factor theory of emotions. *Journal of Research in Personality, 11*(3), 273–294. doi:10.1016/0092-6566(77)90037-X

Sander, D., Grandjean, D., & Scherer, K. R. (2005). A systems approach to appraisal mechanisms in emotion. *Neural Networks, 18*(4), 317–352. doi:10.1016/j.neunet.2005.03.001 PMID:15936172

Scherer, K. R. (1984). Emotion as a multicomponent process: A model and some cross-cultural data. In P. Shaver (Ed.), Review of personality and social psychology: Vol. 5. *Emotions, relationships and health* (pp. 37–63). Beverly Hills, CA: Sage.

Scherer, K. R. (1994). Toward a concept of "modal" emotions. In P. Ekman & R. J. Davidson (Eds.), *The nature of emotion: Fundamental questions* (pp. 25–31). New York: Oxford University Press.

Scherer, K. R. (2000). Emotions as episodes of subsystem synchronization driven by nonlinear appraisal processes. In M. D. Lewis & I. Granic (Eds.), *Emotion, development, and self- organization: Dynamic systems approaches to emotional development* (pp. 70–99). New York: Cambridge University Press. doi:10.1017/CBO9780511527883.005

Scherer, K. R. (2001). Appraisal considered as a process of multilevel sequential checking. In K. R. Scherer, A. Schorr, & T. Johnstone (Eds.), *Appraisal processes in emotion: Theory, methods, research* (pp. 92–120). New York: Oxford University Press.

Scherer, K. R. (2009a). The dynamic architecture of emotion: Evidence for the component process model. *Cognition and Emotion, 23*(7), 1307–1351. doi:10.1080/02699930902928969

Scherer, K. R. (2009b). Emotions are emergent processes: They require a dynamic computational architecture. *Philosophical Transactions of the Royal Society of London. Series B, Biological Sciences, 364*, 3459–3474. PMID:19884141

Scherer, K. R. (2010). The component process model: Architecture for a comprehensive computational model of emergent emotion. In K. R. Scherer, T. Bänziger, & E. B. Roesch (Eds.), *Blueprint for affective computing: A sourcebook* (pp. 47–70). New York: Oxfor University Press.

Scherer, K. R., & Brosch, T. (2009). Culture-specific appraisal biases contribute to emotion dispositions. *European Journal of Personality, 288*(3), 265–288. doi:10.1002/per.714

Scherer, K. R., & Ceschi, G. (2000). Criteria for emotion recognition from verbal and nonverbal expression: Studying baggage loss in the airport. *Personality and Social Psychology Bulletin, 26*(3), 327–339. doi:10.1177/0146167200265006

Scherer, K. R., Clark-Polner, E., & Mortillaro, M. (2011). In the eye of the beholder? Universality and cultural specificity in the expression and perception of emotion. *International Journal of Psychology, 46*(6), 401–435. doi:10.1080/00207 594.2011.626049 PMID:22126090

Scherer, K. R., & Ellgring, H. (2007). Are facial expressions of emotion produced by categorical affect programs or dynamically driven by appraisal? *Emotion (Washington, D.C.), 7*(1), 113–130. doi:10.1037/1528-3542.7.1.113 PMID:17352568

Scherer, K. R., & Grandjean, D. (2008). Facial expressions allow inference of both emotions and their components. *Cognition and Emotion, 22*(5), 789–801. doi:10.1080/02699930701516791

Scherer, K. R., Mortillaro, M., & Mehu, M. (2013). Understanding the mechanisms underlying the production of facial expression of emotion: A componential perspective. *Emotion Review, 5*(1), 47–53. doi:10.1177/1754073912451504

Scherer, K. R., Schorr, A., & Johnstone, T. (2001). *Appraisal processes in emotion: Theory, methods, research.* New York: Oxford University Press.

Scherer, K. R., Wranik, T., Sangsue, J., Tran, V., & Scherer, U. (2004). Emotions in everyday life: Probability of occurrence, risk factors, appraisal and reaction pattern. *Social Sciences Information. Information Sur les Sciences Sociales, 43*(4), 499–570. doi:10.1177/0539018404047701

Siemer, M., Mauss, I., & Gross, J. J. (2007). Same situation--different emotions: How appraisals shape our emotions. *Emotion (Washington, D.C.), 7*(3), 592–600. doi:10.1037/1528-3542.7.3.592 PMID:17683215

Smith, C. A. (1989). Dimensions of appraisal and physiological response in emotion. *Journal of Personality and Social Psychology, 56*(3), 339–353. doi:10.1037/0022-3514.56.3.339 PMID:2926633

Smith, C. A., & Kirby, L. D. (2004). Appraisal as a pervasive determinant of anger. *Emotion (Washington, D.C.), 4*(2), 133–138. doi:10.1037/1528-3542.4.2.133 PMID:15222849

Smith, C. A., & Scott, H. (1997). A componential approach to the meaning of facial expressions. In J. Russell & J. Fernandez-Dols (Eds.), *The psychology of facial expression* (pp. 229–254). New York, NY: Cambridge University Press. doi:10.1017/CBO9780511659911.012

Valstar, M., Mehu, M., Pantic, M., & Scherer, K. R. (in press). Meta-analysis of the first facial expression recognition and analysis challenge. *IEEE Transactions on Systems, Man, and Cybernetics.* PMID:22736651

Wehrle, T. (1995). *The Geneva Appraisal Theory Environment (GATE)* [Unpublished computer software]. Switzerland: University of Geneva.

Wehrle, T., & Scherer, K. R. (2001). Toward computational modelling of appraisal theories. In K. R. Scherer, A. Schorr, & T. Johnstone (Eds.), *Appraisal processes in emotion: Theory, methods, research* (pp. 92–120). New York: Oxford University Press.

Yeasin, M., Bullot, B., & Sharma, R. (2006). Recognition of facial expressions and measurement of levels of interest from video. *IEEE Transactions on Multimedia*, *8*(3), 500–507. doi:10.1109/TMM.2006.870737

Zeng, Z., Pantic, M., Roisman, G. I., & Huang, T. S. (2009). A survey of affect recognition methods: Audio, visual, and spontaneous expressions. *IEEE Transactions on Pattern Analysis and Machine Intelligence*, *31*(1), 39–58. doi:10.1109/TPAMI.2008.52 PMID:19029545

KEY TERMS AND DEFINITIONS

Appraisal: The cognitive evaluation of an event/object, automatic or controlled.

Emotion: A brief episode of synchronized changes in several organismic subsystems, which happens in consequence of an evaluation of an object/event as relevant, and causes the organism to react.

Emotion Elicitation: To trigger an emotion.

Emotion Recognition: The ability to correctly attribute an emotional label to somebody's expression or behavior.

Facial Action Unit: The most basic independent visible movement of the facial musculature.

Facial Expression: The combination of all the movements (contraction and extension) of the muscles of the face at a definite moment.

Non-Verbal Behavior: All visible signs in the face and the body, and audible in the voice (excluding verbal content) of someone.

ENDNOTES

[1] Although here we focus on facial expressions, the model that we suggest is valid for any expressive modalities.

Chapter 17
User Experience of Socially Interactive Robots:
Its Role and Relevance

B. Alenljung
University of Skövde, Sweden

J. Lindblom
University of Skövde, Sweden

ABSTRACT

Socially interactive robots are expected to have an increasing importance in everyday life for a grow-ing number of people, but negative user experience (UX) can entail reluctance to use robots. Positive user experience underpins proliferation of socially interactive robots. Therefore, it is essential for robot developers to put serious efforts to attain social robots that the users experience as positive. In current human-robot interaction (HRI) research, user experience is reckoned to be important and is used as an argument for stating that something is positive. However, the notion of user experience is noticeably often taken for granted and is neither described nor problematized. By recognizing the complexity of user ex-perience the intended contributions can be even more valuable. Another trend in HRI research is to focus on user experience evaluation and examination of user experience. The current research paths of user experience of socially interactive robots are not enough. This chapter suggests that additional research directions are needed in order accomplish long-term, wide-spread success of socially interactive robots.

INTRODUCTION

Socially interactive robots are expected to have an increasing importance in the everyday life for a growing number of people. Robot technology has increased application in commercial products (Oh & Kim, 2010). For robots, like in all other interactive systems, products, and devices, posi-tive user experience (UX) is necessary in order to achieve the intended benefits. User experience is about feelings that arise and forms internally in a human through the use of technology in a particular usage context (Hartson & Pyla, 2012; Hassenzahl, 2013). User experience is important for user acceptance of social robots (de Graaf & Allouch, 2013). If the usage of a robot entails a

DOI: 10.4018/978-1-4666-7278-9.ch017

negative experience of the user, it can have negative consequences, such as reluctance to use the current robot as well as robots in general, erroneous handling, or spreading bad reputation. Therefore, it is essential for robot developers to put serious efforts to attain robots that the users experience as positive. By designing a high quality interaction with the intended users and usage context in mind it is possible to positively influence that experience (Hartson & Pyla, 2012; Hassenzahl & Tractinsky, 2006).

Therefore, the user experience of social robots needs to be a central issue of concern. Positive user experiences underpin the proliferation of social robots in society (Weiss et al., 2009a). A positive user experience does not appear by itself. Instead, the positive user experience has to be systematically, thoroughly, and consciously designed for (Hartson & Pyla, 2012; Hassenzahl, 2013). Each specific robot development project needs to take the UX perspective into account during the whole development process. The field of user experience design (UXD) offers methods, techniques, and guidelines for creating a positive user experience for all types of interactive systems for human use (Anderson et al., 2010; Hartson & Pyla, 2012). However, the interaction between humans and robots differ evidently from interaction between humans and more traditional and passive computer-based artefacts (Dautenhahn, 2007; Young et al., 2011). Hence, a practitioner, i.e., a developer of robots for real-world use, needs research-based guidance of how to properly choose and apply UXD techniques and guidelines for the social robotic products.

In this chapter, the role and relevance of user experience of socially interactive robots is depicted. Based on that framing, additional research directions are addressed, including a wide range of different perspectives and attributes of user experience, the UXD process, and robot products. The rest of this chapter is outlined as follows. First, in the background section; the notions of human-robot interaction, socially interactive robots, and

user experience are introduced. Next, the role and relevance of user experience of socially interactive robots is portrayed. Then, a section of call for additional research directions is presented. The chapter ends with some conclusions.

BACKGROUND

In this section, first, the field of human-robot interaction is introduced. Then, the type of robot in focus, i.e., socially interactive robots, is presented. Lastly, the notions of UX as well as UXD are described.

Human-Robot Interaction

Robots are increasingly becoming a part of the human world. In some domains, not least in industrial settings, they have been an important and natural part for many years. They are also entering other settings, professional as well as domestic. The purpose of robotic technology is to make it possible for a person to conduct something that he or she could not do earlier, facilitate a certain task, make it more nice, or provide entertainment (Goodrich & Schultz, 2007). Robots can bring different kinds of value (Dautenhahn & Sanders, 2011), for example, by conducting monotonous assembling tasks in manufacturing or keeping the lawn cut. In those cases, often humans do not need to continuously interact with the robot. Other types of robots and usage situations, e.g., assisting elderly persons, demand more frequent and multi-faceted interaction. This interplay between robots and their users' has to be carefully taken into account when developing a robot in order for it to be valuable.

The problem of understanding and designing the interaction between human(s) and robot(s) is the core interest of the field of human-robot interaction (HRI) (Goodrich & Schultz, 2007). More precisely, "HRI is the science of studying people's behavior and attitudes towards robots in relationship to the physical, technological and interactive features of the robots, with the goal to develop robots that facilitate the emergence of human-robot *interactions* that are at the same time efficient (according to original requirements of their envisaged area of use), but are also acceptable to people, and meet the social and emotional needs of their individual users as well as respecting human values" (Dautenhahn, 2013).

The importance of and the attention attracted to HRI is increasing concurrently with the growing amount of technological achievements in robotics. For the same reasons, the concept of a robot is constantly changing (Dautenhahn, 2013). The boundaries for how robots can be constituted and the settings in which they can act in are continually expanding. However, an important characteristic that separates robotic technology from technological devices in general is that it has to, at least to some extent, act autonomously in its environment. Autonomy means that the robot should make their own decisions and adjust to current circumstances (Thrun, 2004). Hence, robots can vary along multiple dimensions, e.g., the types of task it is intended to support, its morphology, interaction roles, human-robot physical proximity, and autonomy level (Yanco & Drury, 2004). Roughly speaking, robots can be categorized into industrial robots, professional service robots, and personal service robots (Thrun, 2004). Moreover, the role of humans in relation to robots can vary; the human can be a supervisor, operator, mechanic, teammate, bystander, mentor or information consumer (Goodrich & Schultz, 2007; Scholtz, 2003). Likewise, robots can have a wide range of manifestations and be used in different application areas. There are human-like robots (humanoids and androids), robots looking like animals, or mechanical-appearing robots. Robots can be used for urban search and rescue tasks, e.g., natural disasters and wilderness search; assistive and educational robotics, e.g., therapy for elderly; military and police, e.g., patrol support; edutainment, e.g., museum tour guide; space, e.g.,

astronaut assistant; home, e.g., robotic companion; and industry, e.g., construction (Dautenhahn, 2013; Goodrich & Schultz, 2007).

Consequently, the interaction between user and robot can occur in wide variety, depending on user-, task-, and context-based conditions. Generally, interaction can be either remote, i.e., the human and the robot are spatially, and perhaps also temporarily, separated, or proximate, i.e., the human and the robot are collocated (Goodrich & Schultz, 2007). The interaction can be indirect, which means that the user operates the robot by commanding it, or direct, that is when the communication is bi-directional between the user and robot, and that the robot can act on its own (Thrun, 2004). Dautenhahn (2007) argues that in many application areas the robots need also to have social skills; that is socially interactive robots.

Socially Interactive Robots

Socially interactive robots are "robots for which social interaction plays a key role" (Fong et al., 2003, p. 145). Such robots should display social intelligence, which means that they demonstrate qualities that resemble human social expressions. Examples of such qualities are emotional appearance and perception, advanced dialogue capabilities, possibilities to recognize humans and other robots, as well as be able to make use of for instance gaze and gesture as part of communication (Fong et al., 2003).

It is not necessary for all robots to be highly socially interactive. Instead, the purpose and the context in which it is supposed to act in or upon sets the requirements for the extent of social skills of the robot. For instance, robots that are remotely controlled and separated from the user spatially and temporally require few or even no social skills, whereas a robot used in agriculture or for firefighting might need some. More socially advanced robots could be used as a tour guide, a hotel assistant, or an entertainer. Even higher social requirements are essential for robots used in nursing care and therapy, while a domestic robot companion has to have vast social intelligence (Dautenhahn, 2007). Dautenhahn (2007) puts forth that the social skills required of robots varies along several dimensions, and, hence, it is important for a robot developer to be aware of the role and context of the robot to be used in. The dimensions listed by Dautenhahn (2007) are contact with humans (from none and remote to repeated long-term physical contact), robot functionality (from limited and clearly defined to open and adaptive functionality that is shaped by learning), role of robot (from machine or tool to roles such as assistant, companion, and partner), as well as requirements of social skills (from not required or desirable to essential).

There are different modes of social interaction suggested by Breazeal (2003); these are socially evocative, social interface, socially repetitive, and sociable. A socially evocative mode denotes that the robot stimulates humans to anthropomorphize it during interaction, but goes no further. Robots with the interaction mode of social interface interact with help of human-like social cues and communication modalities. A socially receptive mode entails that the robot benefits from interacting with humans, although the benefits are primarily measured from the human perspective. A sociable robot is a social participant with its own internal goals and drives.

HRI research concerning social interactions with robots can be categorized into three approaches (Dautenhahn, 2007), which are robot-centered HRI, human-centered HRI, and robot cognition-centered HRI. Robot-centered HRI focuses on sociable robots where the robot is viewed as an autonomous creature and the human is some sort of caretaker of the robot that should identify and respond to its needs. Human-centered HRI, on the other hand, emphasizes the human, who should find the robot acceptable and pleasant. The purpose of the robot is to fulfil its specified tasks. The core of robot-cognition HRI is to model and view robots as intelligent systems. Dautenhahn (2007)

argues that in order to get robots "inhabit our living environments", there needs to be a synthesis of these three approaches. Thus, no matter which approach that is focused on, the human needs to experience the interaction with and appearance of the socially interactive robot positively.

User Experience

User experience is a concept that is becoming increasingly important. Technology is spreading into almost every aspects of the daily life of humans. Furthermore, humans have been using advanced technology for quite a while and, therefore, their expectations of and demands on the quality of technological products are going beyond utility, usability and acceptance. That a product is suitable for its purpose, is easy to use, and fits into its intended context are considered basics from the users' point of view. They also want a positive and great experience. User experience is about feelings that arise and forms internally in a human through the use of technology in a particular usage context (Hartson & Pyla, 2012; Hassenzahl, 2013). It can be defined as "the totality of the effect or effects felt by a user as a result of interaction with, and the usage context of, a system, device, or product, including the influence of usability, usefulness, and emotional impact during interaction and savoring memory after interaction" (Hartson & Pyla, 2012, p. 5). This means that it is not possible to guarantee a certain UX, since it is the subjective inner state of a human. Although, by designing a high quality interaction with the intended users and the usage context in mind it is possible to impact the experience. As expressed by Anderson et al. (2010), user experience can be compared with music. Creation of technology as well as music includes mathematical principles, technical skills, and artistic sense. In the same way, the experience of technology and the experience of music are subjective, irrespective of how well-crafted it is. The user experience is not built in the product itself. Instead, it is an outcome of the interaction that depends on the internal state of the user, the quality and attributes of the product, and the particular situation (Hartson & Pyla, 2012; Hassenzahl & Tractinsky, 2006). Hence, good user experience is difficult to define but easy to identify (Anderson et al., 2010).

The concept of user experience embraces pragmatic as well as hedonic quality (Hassenzahl & Roto, 2007). Pragmatic quality is related to fulfilling the do-goals of the user, which means that the interactive product makes it possible for the user to reach the task-related goals in an effective, efficient, and secure way. In other well-known words, pragmatic quality is concerned with the usability and usefulness of the product. Hedonic quality, on the other hand, is about the be-goals of the user. Humans have psychological and emotional needs, which should be addressed by the interactive product. The user can, for instance, find the product cool, awesome, beautiful, trustworthy, satisfying, or fun. The product can, for example, evoke feelings of autonomy, competence, and relatedness to others (Hartson & Pyla, 2012; Hassenzahl & Roto, 2007; Partala & Kallinen, 2012). The user experience perspective includes not only functional aspects, but also experiential and emotional issues. It focuses on the positive beyond the mere strive for absence of problems. Additionally, a main objective of the field should be to contribute to the quality of life of humans (Hassenzahl & Tractinsky, 2006).

The basis of UXD begins with the investigation phase in order to understand the needs, goals, meanings, and emotions related to the activities. It all starts with the Why, and only then the What, i.e., the functionality, and the How, i.e., the design of interaction, can be developed. During the investigation phase, it is necessary to identify the business's needs as well as the users' needs and technical and infrastructural constraints (Hassenzahl, 2013). The user goals have to be connected to the business goals, and the business goals to user behaviors (Anderson et al., 2010). Furthermore, it is not possible to design a product that satisfies everybody. Instead, the intended users have to be identified and described, and focused upon during the whole design process. It is also essential to stay tuned on the product mission (Anderson et al., 2010). Another central principle is the iterative and incremental nature of the development process. It is not possible to have all the answers from the very beginning. Instead, the answers will be discovered and evolved during the iterative development process (Anderson et al., 2010; Hartson & Pyla, 2012). The user experience development process consists of four major interactive activities; these are analyze, design, implement, and evaluate. The purpose of the analysis phase is to understand the users' work and needs as well as the business domain. The design phase involves creation of the concept, the interaction behavior, and the look and feel of the product. In the implementation phase, the focus is on prototyping and thereby realizing different design alternatives. Verification and refinement of the interaction design are mainly conducted in the evaluation phase (Hartson & Pyla, 2012).

Like all other interactive products for human use, user interaction with and perception of socially interactive robots evoke feelings of different nature and intensity. The user can feel motivated to walk up and use a robot. He or she can experience a weak distrust of the robot and at the same time be curious of it. A user can find a robot to be well-adapted and highly useful after a long-term use, although, initially experienced it to be a bit strange and tricky. A robot can be found to be really fun and entertaining for young children, but boring for teenagers. Thus, the user experience has many facets and it is complex. Therefore, a robot developer needs to identify and characterize what kind of feeling that is especially important for this particular socially interactive robot to arouse. Then it is possible to consciously design the robot with those feelings as the target and it is possible to evaluate if the robot can be expected to awaken the intended experience in the user.

ROLE AND RELEVANCE OF USER EXPERIENCE IN SOCIALLY INTERACTIVE ROBOTS

The notion of user experience is frequently used in research of socially interactive robots but also in human-robot interaction in general. Some tendencies are emergent concerning the role and relevance of user experience in HRI research related to socially interactive robots.

User experience is reckoned to be of major importance and is used as an argument for stating that something is positive. Some typical examples are as follows. Tritton et al. (2012) claim that it is important to examine the impact of communicative robot gestures on user experience in order to push the introduction of domestic social robots. Kuo et al. (2011) express that the user experience would be more satisfying if the robot can communicate its internal status and intention during interaction so the expectations of the user can be attuned. Datta et al. (2011) say that to actively deliver shopping-related information via a shopping mall robot can counteract the user experience. Juarez et al. (2011) point out that the long-term success on their robot will depend on the user experience, and, therefore, they chose heuristic evaluation (e.g., Nielsen, 1994) as part of their study. Hence, user experience is used as an axiom for underpinning that a certain aspect has to be investigated and that a feature or attribute should or should not be used.

However, the notion of user experience is often noticeably taken for granted and is seldom described or problematized in HRI research (see e.g., Datta et al., 2012; De Carolis et al. 2010; Huang et al., 2011; Jia et al., 2013; Johnson et al., 2013; Schroeter et al., 2013; Strasser et al., 2012; Tritton et al., 2012; Xu et al., 2012). Consequently, in such papers no explicit references to user experience-focused work. Since user experience is a multi-faceted and complex phenomenon there is a risk of reducing the precision of results if the complexity is not considered

properly. For instance, it is possible that a certain robot feature or characteristic can positively affect some dimension of user experience, e.g., finding the robot awesome and curiosity-rising, and at the same time negatively influence other dimensions of user experience, such as, to experience the robot as difficult to cooperate with. Indeed, there are some papers in which the UX concept is problematized or at least briefly described (see e.g., de Graaf & Allouch, 2013; Jung et al, 2013; Oh & Kim, 2010; Syrdal et al., 2008; Weiss et al., 2009a; Xu et al, 2013; Young et al., 2011).

Another tendency is to study robot-related aspects to find out how they affect the users. Some representative examples are as follows. He et al. (2014) propose techniques, involving a robotic head for social robots to attend to scene saliency with bio-inspired saccadic behaviors, that are intended improve the user experience. Saini et al. (2005) investigated how the user experience can benefit from a more socially rich and coherent home dialogue system that is perceived as socially intelligent. Huang et al. (2011) have analyzed the long-term user experience of a particular robot in order to understand the failure of it, with the purpose of concluding some implications for future design. The result presented by Xu et al. (2013) demonstrates that an agent's engagement-aware behaviors improve the user experience. This kind of studies are essential for building a coherent body of knowledge concerning how to design socially interactive robot that feels good for the user and thereby increase the possibilities of user acceptance. Though, if such studies are not combined with addressing the many facets of user experience then the precision of the results may be lower than it otherwise could be. By recognizing the complexity of user experience the contributions can be even more valuable.

Furthermore, there is a focus on user experience evaluation and examination of the actual felt user experience afterwards. Examples of user experience evaluation are as follows. Young et al. (2011) made a survey on human-computer interaction (HCI) evaluation techniques with the focus of holistic interaction experience. Weiss et al. (2009b) have developed an evaluation framework called USUS (Usability, Social acceptance, User experience, and Societal impact), and de Graaf and Allouch (2013) have examined utilitarian and hedonic variables that can enable the evaluation of affective factors of interaction. User experience studies are conducted to validate and verify robotic prototypes as well as robots-in-use (see e.g., De Carolis et al., 2010; Johnson et al., 2013; Schroeter et al., 2013; Xu et al., 2012). User experience evaluation is fundamental and a necessity for the development of socially interactive robots that are positively experienced and accepted by the intended users. Nonetheless, it is possible to widen the scope of research interests and there are other research directions that can be added to the research agenda for user experience of socially interactive robots.

CALL FOR ADDITIONAL RESEARCH DIRECTIONS

User experience is acknowledged as important for achieving socially interactive robots that is widely used by humans. Thus, it is necessary for a robot developer to be knowledgeable of the wide range of elements that affects user experience. It is also necessary for robot developers to evaluate the actual user experience in order to make sure that positive feelings arise in these particular users. The importance of research concerning establishment of user experience-affecting elements and user experience evaluation should not be underestimated. However, in order to develop successful socially interactive robot products for real-world use this is not sufficient. Therefore, additional research directions are needed in order to provide robot developing practitioners with proper research-based guidance so the launched robotic products are accepted and experienced by the users in an intended and desirable way.

Often, it is not possible, particularly with limited resources, to put equally high efforts in every aspect that potentially can impact user experience. Instead, the developer has to decide upon which particular experiences are most vital to awaken and carefully design and evaluate with those close in mind. For instance, is it more important for this particular robot to evoke feelings of curiosity and fascination than a sense of competence in the user? Is it more central for this robot to make the user feel related to others and find the robot elegant than experiencing it smooth and transparent? Therefore, the nuances of user experience need to be recognized and carefully considered. Robot developers should be able to determine which user experience-affecting elements are appropriate for a certain purpose. For example, which user experience-affecting elements should be avoided and which have to be included for enhancing the user's motivation of walk up and interact with the robot. If researchers have not considered the dimensions of user experience and, as a consequence, not reported what kind of experiences the studied elements is intended to shape and which feelings actually to awaken, then the actual influence of the UX-effecting element remains unclear. Hence, research including user experience studies or user experience evaluation should go beyond basic feelings, i.e., beyond stating that the user experience is more or less positive or negative.

However, when developing socially interactive robots for real use, for instance for the commercial market, it is not enough to just imagine which kinds of user experience that are important and then hope for the best. Instead, it is vital to base the decisions concerning which experiences to focus on upon a firm understanding of the intended user groups, their needs, and the usage context (Anderson et al., 2010; Hartson & Pyla, 2012). With this knowledge in mind, the robot developers can concentrate their efforts to achieve the decided user experiences. This implies that the development process of socially interactive robots should include the whole user experience design process, i.e., embracing the major activities of analysis, design, implementation, and evaluation (Hartson & Pyla, 2012). There is a rich body of knowledge of those activities for interactive systems in general (Anderson et al., 2010; Hartson & Pyla, 2012). But, for socially interactive robots the major emphasis so far has been on user experience evaluation. To the best of our knowledge, research on the other user experience design phases in socially interactive robots is scarce. Thus, there is a need to develop research-based guidance for robot developers concerning how to properly carry out user experience design activities that are specific for socially interactive robots. This is much needed since the human-robot interaction differs significantly from more traditional and passive human-computer interaction (de Graaf & Allouch, 2013; Young, et al. 2011). As a consequence, the transferability of methods, techniques, and guidelines from the field of UXD is an open issue, which calls for further theoretical and empirical studies (Dautenhahn, 2007; Syrdal et al., 2008; Weiss et al., 2009a). There is a need for more research of user experience analysis, design, and prototyping for socially interactive robots with the purpose of supporting the practice of robot developers. Of course, some of these activities are already carried out by researchers, e.g., making prototypes of socially interactive robots, but more as a mean to investigate something else than to study user experience prototyping in itself. With the exception of the paper by Syrdal et al. (2009), who have studied the use of video prototyping for evaluation purposes; we have not been able to find research that focus on how user experience aspects should be suitably prototyped, pros and cons of certain types of prototypes, or under which circumstances a particular kind of prototype is better than another one in the field of socially interactive robots. The same inclination can be observed concerning research into the other phases of the user experience design process; i.e., analysis and design, for socially interactive robots.

User experience evaluation for socially interactive robots, on the other hand, has gained some attention from researchers. They embrace the complexity of user experience and include many factors that can be focused on in evaluation (de Graaf and Allouch, 2013; Weiss et al., 2009b; Young et al, 2011). For a practitioner, i.e., a robotic product developer, it is not possible to evaluate "everything", so to speak, due to time and resource limitations. Instead, the most important aspects need to be prioritized in user experience evaluation. In addition, in order for the robot developer to determine if the actual awoken feelings are positive or strong enough there should be some specified acceptance levels set in advance. Hence, there is a need to define prioritized user experience requirements and validation criteria (Benyon, 2010; Pressman, 2000). However, establishing requirements, determine their priority, as well as defining validation criteria are not easy tasks to perform properly. There is a lot of research of how to establish requirements, prioritize, and set validation criteria (e.g., Berander & Andrews, 2005; Kotonya & Sommerville, 1998; Sutcliffe, 2002; Zowghi & Coulin, 2005). However, to the best of our knowledge, there is a lack of research focusing on the intersection of these above aspects, UX, and socially interactive robots. Thus, more research is needed in order to provide research-based guidance to robot developers concerning these matters.

Furthermore, as a user experience-focused robot developer it is not enough to focus on the user needs and usage context. For commercial development of socially interactive robots there is also a business case to take into account when establishing and prioritizing user experience requirements (Anderson et al., 2010; Hartson & Pyla, 2012). In accordance to previous claims, robot developers should possibly benefit from research-based guidance of how to fruitfully consider business cases of the socially interactive robots when making decision of, e.g., requirements and design elements.

CONCLUSION

In this chapter, we have presented the role and relevance of user experience of socially interactive robots and proposed additional research directions. The trends of current research indicate an increasing awareness of the importance of positive user experience for socially interactive robots. User experience is frequently used for stating that some robot-related aspect is positive; almost in an axiom-like way. Noticeably often, the notion of user experience is not described nor problematized, and, consequently, the complex and multi-faceted nature of the concept are not addressed properly. This can, for instance, have consequences for the establishment of a coherent body of knowledge concerning user experience-affecting aspects and elements for socially interactive robots. There are a lot of studies focusing on effects of diverse robot-related aspects and elements on user experience. However, if the results do not identify what kind of feeling that is intended to be awaken, e.g., astonishing first-time impression, satisfying long-term usefulness, stimulating communication, neat appearance, impressive adaptability, etc., then there is a risk that the contributions are not as valuable as they have potentials to be.

To design high quality interaction that underpin the possibility of positive user experience, the design process should include the whole cycle of central activities; these are analysis, design, implementation, and evaluation (Anderson, et al., 2010; Hartson & Pyla, 2012). A current trend in HRI research concerning user experience of socially interactive robots is to focus on user experience evaluation and examination of user experience. Evaluation is a crucial activity in the user experience design process, and research-based guidance for robot developers of socially interactive robotic products can be valuable. Likewise, similar guidance of the other user experience design activities should have potentials to be beneficial. Therefore, more theoretical as well as empirical research is needed to provide a proper tool box to robot developers. Many open issues still remains to be addressed (Dautenhahn, 2007, 2013).

Often, product development projects have time and resource limitations, and development projects of robotic products do not differ in that respect. Therefore, it is important to decide what is most critical to achieve in terms of user experience so the efforts are concentrated upon the key aspects as well as how to determine when the goals are sufficiently met. To the best of our knowledge, no research has been conducted of establishment and prioritization of user experience requirement for socially interactive robots. Moreover, for robotic products one has to consider the business perspective in the user experience design process, i.e., to stay attuned to the business case in the development project (Anderson, et al., 2010; Hartson & Pyla, 2012). Similarly, to the best of our knowledge, there is no research that has addressed the problem of comprising the business perspective in user experience design of socially interactive robotic products.

To conclude, socially interactive robots is expected to be increasingly important in the daily life of more and more people. The experiences that humans have when interacting with robotic products will be an enabler (or disabler) of the proliferation of them in society. The current research paths of user experience of socially interactive robots are not enough. More paths are needed in order accomplish long-term, wide-spread success of socially interactive robots. User experience design research is one of the keys in order to face the identified and upcoming challenges.

REFERENCES

Anderson, J., McRee, J., Wilson, R., & the Effective UI Team (2010). *Effective UI*. Sebastopol, CA: O'Reilly.

Benyon, D. (2010). *Designing interactive systems: A comprehensive guide to HCI and interaction design*. Harlow, UK: Pearson.

Berander, P., & Andrews, A. (2005). Requirements prioritization. In A. Aurum & C. Wohlin (Eds.), *Engineering and managing software requirements* (pp. 69–94). Berlin, Germany: Springer. doi:10.1007/3-540-28244-0_4

Breazeal, C. (2003). Toward sociable robots. *Robotics and Autonomous Systems*, *42*(3-4), 167–175. doi:10.1016/S0921-8890(02)00373-1

Datta, C., Kapuria, A., & Vijay, R. (2011). A pilot study to understand requirements of a shopping mall robot. In *6th ACM/IEEE International Conference on Human-Robot Interaction (HRI)* (pp 127-128). Lausanne, Switzerland. doi:10.1145/1957656.1957694

Datta, C., MacDonald, B. A., Jayawardena, C., & Kuo, I.-H. (2012). Programming behaviour of a personal service robot with application to healthcare. In GeS.S.KhatibO.CabibihanJ-J.SimmonsR.WilliamsM-A. (Eds.) *Social robotics: Proceedings of 4th International Conference, ICSR 2012, Chengdu, China*. Lecture Notes in Computer Science, 7621, 228-237. doi:10.1007/978-3-642-34103-8_23

Dautenhahn, K. (2007). Socially intelligent robots: Dimensions of human-robot interaction. *Philosophical Transactions of the Royal Society of London. Series B, Biological Sciences*, *362*(1480), 679–704. doi:10.1098/rstb.2006.2004 PMID:17301026

Dautenhahn, K. (2013). Human-Robot Interaction. In M. Soegaard & R. F. Dam (Eds.), The encyclopedia of human-computer interaction (2nd ed.). Aarhus, Denmark: The Interaction Design Foundation. Retrieved August 25, 2013 from http://www.interaction-design.org/encyclopedia/human-robot_interaction.html

Dautenhahn, K., & Sanders, J. (Eds.). (2011). Introduction. In K. Dautenhahn & J. Sanders (Eds.). New frontiers in human-robot interaction. Amsterdam, The Netherlands: John Benjamins Publishing Company.

De Carolis, B., Mazzotta, I., Novielli, N., & Pizzutilo, S. (2010). Social robots and ECAs for accessing smart environments services. *Proceedings of the International Conference on Advanced Visual Interfaces, AVI '10* (pp. 275-278). Rome, Italy. doi:10.1145/1842993.1843041

de Graaf, M. M. A., & Allouch, S. B. (2013). Exploring influencing variables for the acceptance of social robots. *Robotics and Autonomous Systems*, *61*(12), 1476–1486. doi:10.1016/j.robot.2013.07.007

Fong, T., Nourbakhsh, I., & Dautenhahn, K. (2003). A survey of socially interactive robots. *Robotics and Autonomous Systems*, *42*(3-4), 143–166. doi:10.1016/S0921-8890(02)00372-X

Goodrich, M. A., & Schultz, A. C. (2007). Human-robot interaction: A survey. *Foundations and Trends in Human–Computer Interaction*, *1*(3), 203–275. doi:10.1561/1100000005

Hartson, R., & Pyla, P. S. (2012). *The UX Book: Process and guidelines for ensuring a quality user experience*. Amsterdam: Morgan Kaufmann.

Hassenzahl, M. (2013). User experience and experience design. In M. Soegaard & R.F. Dam (Eds.). *The encyclopedia of human-computer interaction* (2nd Ed.). Aarhus, Denmark: The Interaction Design Foundation. Retrieved September 15, 2013, from http://www.interaction-design.org/encyclopedia/user_experience_and_experience_design.html

Hassenzahl, M., & Roto, V. (2007). Being and doing: A perspective on user experience and its measurement. *Interfaces*, *72*, 10–12.

Hassenzahl, M., & Tractinsky, N. (2006). User experience – a research agenda. *Behaviour & Information Technology, 25*(2), 91–97. doi:10.1080/01449290500330331

He, H., Ge, S. S., & Zhang, Z. (2014). A saliency-driven robotic head with bio-inspired saccadic behaviors for social robotics. *Autonomous Robots, 36*(3), 225–240. doi:10.1007/s10514-013-9346-z

Hewett, T. T., Baecker, R., Card, S., Carey, T., Gasen, J., Mantei, M., . . . Verplank, W. (1996). Curricula for Human-Computer Interaction. *ACM SIGCHI Curricula for Human-Computer Interaction*. Retrieved February 26, 2014, from http://old.sigchi.org/cdg/index.html

Huang, C.-C., Bardzell, J., & Terrell, J. (2011). Can your pet rabbit read your email? A critical analysis of the Nabaztag Rabbit. *Proceedings of the 2011 Conference on Designing Pleasurable Products and Interfaces, DPPI '11*. Milan, Italy. doi:10.1145/2347504.2347532

Jia, H., Wu, M., Jung, E., Shapiro, A., & Sundar, S. S. (2013). When the tissue box says "Bless you!": Using speech to build socially interactive objects. *CHI '13 Extended Abstracts on Human Factors in Computing Systems, CHI EA '13* (pp. 1635-1640). Paris, France.

Johnson, D.O., Cuijpers, R.H., Juola, J.F., Torta, E., S. M., Frisiello, A., Bazzani, M., Yan, W., Weber, C., Wermter, S., Meins, N., Oberzaucher, J., Panek, P., Edelmayer, G., Mayer, P., & Beck, C. (2013, November). Socially assistive robots: A comprehensive approach to extending independent living. *International Journal of Social Robotics*.

Juarez, A., Bartneck, C., & Feijs, L. (2011) Using semantic technologies to describe robotic embodiments. *Proceedings of the 6th ACM/IEEE International Conference on Human-Robot Interaction (HRI)* (pp 425-432) Lausanne, Switzerland. doi:10.1145/1957656.1957812

Jung, J., & Bae, S.-H. Lee, J.H., & Kim, M-S. (2013). Make it move: A movement design method of simple standing products based on systematic mapping of torso movements & product messages. *Proceedings of the SIGCHI Conference on Human Factors in Computing Systems, CHI '13* (pp. 1279-1288). Paris, France. doi:10.1145/2470654.2466168

Kotonya, G., & Sommerville, I. (1998). *Requirements engineering: Processes and techniques*. Chichester, England: John Wiley and Sons.

Kuo, I.-H., Jayawardena, C., Broadbent, E., & MacDonald, B. A. (2011). Multidisciplinary design approach for implementation of interactive services: Communication initiation and user identification for healthcare service robots. *International Journal of Social Robotics, 3*(4), 443–456. doi:10.1007/s12369-011-0115-x

Law, E. L.-C., Roto, V., Hassenzahl, M., Vermeeren, A. P. O. S., & Kort, J. (2009). Understanding, scoping and defining user experience: A survey approach. In *Proceedings of the SIGCHI Conference on Human Factors in Computing Systems, CHI '09*. Boston, MA, USA. doi:10.1145/1518701.1518813

Nielsen, J. (1994). Heuristic evaluation. In J. Nielsen & R. L. Mack (Eds.), *Usability inspection methods* (pp. 25–62). New York: John Wiley & Sons.

Oh, K., & Kim, M. (2010). Social attributes of robotic products: Observations of child-robot interactions in a school environment. *International Journal of Design, 4*(1), 45–55.

Partala, T., & Kallinen, A. (2012). Understanding the most satisfying and unsatisfying user experiences: Emotions, psychological needs, and context. *Interacting with Computers, 24*(1), 25–34. doi:10.1016/j.intcom.2011.10.001

Pressman, R. S. (2000). *Software engineering: A practitioner's approach* (5th ed.). London: McGraw Hill.

Saini, P., de Ruyter, B., Markopoulos, P., & van Breemen, A. (2005). Benefits of social intelligence in home dialogue systems. In M.F. Costabile & F. Paternò (Eds.) *Human-Computer Interaction - INTERACT 2005: Proceedings IFIP TC13 International Conference, Rome, Italy.* Lecture Notes in Computer Science, 3585, 510-521. doi:10.1007/11555261_42

Scholtz, J. (2003). Theory and evaluation of human robot interaction. In *Proceedings of the 36th Hawaii International Conference of System Sciences (HICSS'03), Vol. 5.* doi:10.1109/HICSS.2003.1174284

Schroeter, C., Mueller, S., Volkhardt, M., Einhorn, E., Huijnen, C., van den Heuvel, H., van Berlo, A., Bley, A., & Gross, H-M. (2013). Realization and user evaluation of a companion robot for people with mild cognitive impairments. In *IEEE International Conference on Robotics and Automation (ICRA)* (pp. 1153-1159). Karlsruhe, Germany.

Strasser, E., Weiss, A., & Tscheligi, M. (2012). Affect misattribution procedure: An implicit technique to measure user experience in HRI. In *Proceedings of the Seventh Annual ACM/IEEE International Conference on Human-Robot Interaction HRI '12* (pp. 243-244). Boston, Massachusetts, USA.

Sutcliffe, A. (2002). *User-centred requirements engineering: Theory and practice.* London: Springer. doi:10.1007/978-1-4471-0217-5

Syrdal, D. S., Otero, N., & Dautenhahn, K. (2008). Video prototyping in human-robot interaction: Results from a qualitative study. In *Proceedings of the 15th European conference on Cognitive ergonomics: the ergonomics of cool interaction, ECCE '08.* Madeira, Portugal. doi:10.1145/1473018.1473055

Thrun, S. (2004). Toward a framework for human-robot interaction. *Human-Computer Interaction, 19*(1), 9–24. doi:10.1207/s15327051hci1901&2_2

Tritton, T., Hall, J., Rowe, A., Valentine, S., Jedrzejewska, A., Pipe, A. G., . . . Leonards, U. (2012). Engaging with robots while giving simple instructions. In G. Herrmann, M. Studley, M. Pearson, A. Conn, C. Melhuish, M. Witkowski, J-H.n Kim & P. Vadakkepat (Eds.) *Advances in Autonomous Robotics: Joint Proceedings of the 13th Annual TAROS Conference and the 15th Annual FIRA RoboWorld Congress, Lecture Notes in Computer Science, Vol. 7429,* (pp. 176-184). doi:10.1007/978-3-642-32527-4_16

User Experience. UX Design (2010). UX Design Defined. *User Experience.UX Design.* Retrieved February 26, 2014, from http://uxdesign.com/ux-defined

Weiss, A., Bernhaupt, R., Laukes, M., & Tscheligi, M. (2009b). The USUS evaluation framework for human-robot interactions. *Proceedings of the symposium on new frontiers in human-robot interaction, AISB 2009* (pp. 158–165). Edinburgh, Scotland.

Weiss, A., Bernhaupt, R., & Yoshida, E. (2009a). Addressing user experience and societal impact in a user study with a humanoid robot. In *Proceedings of the Symposium on New Frontiers in Human-Robot Interaction, AISB2009* (pp. 150-157).

Xu, Q., Li, L., & Wang, G. (2013). Designing engagement-aware agents for multiparty conversations. In *Proceedings of CHI 2013* (pp. 2233-2242). Paris, France.

Xu, Q., Ng, J., Cheong, Y. L., Tan, O., Wong, J. B., Tay, T. C., & Park, T. (2012). The role of social context in human-robot interaction. *Southeast Asian Network of Ergonomics Societies Conference (SEANES),* Langkawi, Kedah.

Yanco, H. A., & Drury, J. (2004). Classifying human-robot interaction: an updated taxonomy. *IEEE International Conference on Systems, Man and Cybernetics 2004, Vol. 3* (pp. 2841-2846).

Young, J. E., Sung, J. Y., Voida, A., Sharlin, E., Igarashi, T., Cristensen, H. I., & Grinter, R. E. (2011). Evaluating human-robot interaction: Focusing on the holistic interaction experience. *International Journal of Social Robotics*, *3*(1), 53–67. doi:10.1007/s12369-010-0081-8

Zowghi, D., & Coulin, C. (2005). Requirements elicitation: A survey of techniques, approaches, and tools. In A. Aurum & C. Wohlin (Eds.), *Engineering and managing software requirements* (pp. 21–46). Berlin, Germany: Springer. doi:10.1007/3-540-28244-0_2

KEY TERMS AND DEFINITIONS

Human-Computer Interaction (HCI): "Human-computer interaction is a discipline concerned with the design, evaluation and implementation of interactive computing systems for human use and with the study of major phenomena surrounding them" (Hewett et al., 1996).

Human-Robot Interaction (HRI): "HRI is the science of studying people's behavior and attitudes towards robots in relationship to the physical, technological and interactive features of the robots, with the goal to develop robots that facilitate the emergence of human-robot *interactions* that are at the same time efficient (according to original requirements of their envisaged area of use), but are also acceptable to people, and meet the social and emotional needs of their individual users as well as respecting human values" (Dautenhahn, 2013).

Socially Interactive Robots: Socially interactive robots are "robots for which social interaction plays a key role" (Fong et al., 2003, p. 145).

User Experience (UX): "The totality of the effect or effects felt by a user as a result of interaction with, and the usage context of, a system, device, or product, including the influence of usability, usefulness, and emotional impact during interaction and savoring memory after interaction" (Hartson & Pyla, 2012, p. 5).

User Experience Design (UXD): User experience design "refer to the judicious application of certain user-centered design practices, a highly contextual design mentality, and use of certain methods and techniques that are applied through process management to produce cohesive, predictable, and desirable effects in a specific person, or persona (archetype comprised of target audience habits and characteristics). All so that the affects produced meet the user's own goals and measures of success and enjoyment, as well as the objectives of the providing organization" (User Experience. UX Design, 2010).

Section 4
Last Trends in Synthetic Emotions

Chapter 18
Emotional Context? Or Contextual Emotions?

Diana Arellano
Filmakademie Baden-Wuerttemberg, Germany

Javier Varona
Universitat de les Illes Balears, Spain

Francisco J. Perales
Universitat de les Illes Balears, Spain

ABSTRACT

The question "What is the meaning of a smile?" could be easily answered with the sentence "it means happiness". But we can see in our daily lives that it is not always true. We also recognize that there is the context the one that makes us differentiate a happy smile from an embarrassed smile. The context is the framework that gives emotions a reason for happening because it describes what occurs around a person. Therefore, to create virtual characters, or agents that express emotions in a believable way it is necessary to simulate the context around them. The novelty of this chapter is the representation of context using ontologies, where context is seen not only as the events in the world, but also as that part of the character which allows them to react in one way or another, resulting in more believable emotional responses.

INTRODUCTION

In the world where we live, we are faced every day with technologies that make our devices closer to what we are, and that means, more human. For instance, we can literally talk to our mobile phones (e.g iPhone or Google Nexus) and ask things like the ones we could ask to a colleague or a friend.

In turn, the device will reply with knowledge of our surrounding context, and in the near future, also with emotions.

These advances had made researchers and industry aware of the fact that without context there is no appropriate way to simulate reality. The same idea applies to virtual characters and virtual worlds where to achieve more human-like

DOI: 10.4018/978-1-4666-7278-9.ch018

behaviours it is necessary to model and simulate their context. To this respect, Dey et al. (2001) defined context as *any information that can be used to characterize the situation of an entity. An entity is a person, place, or object that is considered relevant to the interaction between a user and an application, including the user, the device and application themselves.*

Without a context it becomes difficult to discern between the meanings that one facial expression might have, to decide how to react to certain situation, or how the course of a story/ situation should be unfolded. In this way, Kaiser & Wehrle (2008) stated that facial expressions can only be interpreted when they are inside a context (temporal or situational) that allows us to generate them in an accurate way.

The problem with representing full context is that one should also take into consideration elements like culture, religion, and other social rules and roles. This makes context representation and its appraisal a gigantic task. Nevertheless, when we think of children, we realize that their context has the same set of events, but their appraisal lacks of social rules, giving a more "pure" emotional response to those events.

With this in mind, we decided to represent context in the way a child would do it. Therefore, we can obtain a generic description of what is happening outside and inside the characters, and see how context helps to generate different emotional states in virtual characters, or virtual agents - both terms will be used indistinctly due to the diversity of applications they can be used for. If this description is achieved in a generic way (e.g. a number of situations can be obtained from an initial set of data), then we can have a variety of scenarios where we could observe the behaviour of our characters according to the occurred events. Later, it can be applied in different applications where it is required having a story, or the interaction between the character and its environment. Some examples are educational applications or story simulation (storytelling) where

a script would be generated from the interaction between the character and its world.

This article is organized as follows. First, previous works on context and affect representation will be reviewed. Then an overview of the system framework we have developed will be presented, making special emphasis in the semantic model that we have designed and implemented. To explain how to use this semantic model a Use Case will be provided, for which we have used a movie scene that help us to validate our emotional output. Finally a discussion and what is expected in future works are presented.

STATE OF ART

Context is what gives meaning to everything we do and how we do it. Therefore, a lot of effort has been invested in trying to model and define it. In the field of Computer Science some areas that have attempted to work on and with it are Affective Computing, Ubiquitous Computing, and Artificial Intelligence.

Strang & Linnhoff-Popien (2004) evaluated six of the most relevant existing approaches to model context for ubiquitous computing:

- **Key-Value Models:** Provide the value of context information (e.g. location information) to an application as an environment variable;
- **Markup Scheme Models:** Represent hierarchical data structure consisting of markup tags with attributes and content;
- **Graphical Models:** Represent context through diagrams as the Unified Modelling Language (UML), or the Object Role Modelling (ORM);
- **Object-Oriented Model:** The details of context processing are encapsulated in an object level, accessed through specified interfaces, and hence hidden to other components;

- **Logic Based Models:** The context is defined as facts, expressions and rules, and contextual information is manipulated using facts or inferred from the rules;
- **Ontology-Based Models:** Ontologies constitute a promising instrument to specify concepts and interrelations, because they can project parts of information that describe our daily life into data structures that can be used by the computers.

They concluded that the most promising assets for context modelling can be found in the ontology category. Also Krummenacher, Lausen & Strang (2007) stated that ontology models provide better modelling facilities, like intuitive notions of classes and properties, while being semi-structured and incorporating a clear semantic model, as compared to object-oriented models. In their work a number of upper ontologies for context definition were mentioned. Upper ontologies are those applicable across large sets of domains, and belong to the most general category of ontologies. General upper ontologies like DOLCE - *Descriptive Ontology for Linguistic and Cognitive Engineering* (Gangemi, Guarino, Masolo, Oltramari & Schneider, 2002), SUMO (Niles & Pease, 2001), or Cyc (Lenat, 1995) could be used to generalize or ground any context ontology. The most renowned upper ontology for context modelling is SOUPA (Chen, Perich, Finin & Joshi, 2004), which is a very complete family of ontologies and defines a very large number of concepts. Nonetheless, ontologies still have their drawbacks, especially in issues related to scalability and domain specific reasoning.

For these scalability and domain-related issues some researchers have proposed their own ontologies like López, Gil, García, Cearreta & Garay, (2008), who proposed a generic ontology, Emotions Ontology, for describing emotions and their detection and expression in systems that take into account contextual and multimodal elements. The ontology defines the physical world around the character and his mental states. They also made use of upper ontologies to provide the semantics apart from those explicitly present in their model. One of these ontologies was DOLCE, used to contextualize other concepts in the Emotions Ontology. The other was FrameNet (Scheffczyk, Baker & Narayanan, 2006), used to model context as situations.

A similar and more recent ontology is the also called Emotion Ontology, which covers all aspects of emotional and affective mental functioning but from the neuroscience point of view (Hastings, Ceusters, Mulligan & Smith, 2012). The ontology intends to represent all relevant aspects of affective phenomena including their bearers, different types of emotions, moods, and other affective traits, their different parts and dimensions of variation, their facial and vocal expressions, and how the role of emotions and affective phenomena in general influences human behavior.

Nakasone & Ishizuka (Nakasone & Ishizuka, 2006), presented a generic storytelling ontology model, the Concept Ontology, where a concept represents a topic in which the story, or part of it, is based. From that point, they define a set of concepts and their links creating pseudo-temporal relations that ensure a smooth transition between concepts. As this ontology was for storytelling, the classes defined were related to scenes, acts, relations (rhetorical binding between two entities), agents participating in the story and their roles.

Figa & Tarau (2002) used ontologies and other components to develop an architecture for virtual interactive storytelling agents (VISTAs) capable of interacting with the user through natural language query/answer patterns. They made use of ontologies to select a subset of a story expressing the focus of interest of the user.

Ontologies can also be used for the representation of the emotional output generated by context. For instance, the goal of Obrenovic, Garay, López, Fajardo & Cearreta (2005) was to provide flexible definitions of emotional cues at different levels of abstraction. Their Emotional Cues Ontology provided them with a language that allowed them to share and reuse information about emotions. The concepts handled by this ontology are emotions, emotional cues (facial expressions, gestures, speech and voice), and media (where the emotional cues will be represented). The objective of the ontology was to generate or recognize emotional cues according to the media and felt emotion.

Gutiérrez et al. (2007) developed an ontology for virtual humans in order to provide a semantic layer required to reconstruct, stock, retrieve, reuse and share content related to virtual humans. The concepts defined are related to three main research topics involving graphical representation of humans: human body modelling and analysis, animation of virtual humans, and interaction of virtual humans with virtual objects. Therefore, this ontology is more focused on providing flexibility when defining a character from a physical and behavioural point of view, which can be of great help when deciding which actions to take according to the context.

Zhang, Hu, Chen & Moore (2012) described an ontological model called BIO_EMOTION that represents and integrates electroencephalographic (EEG) data and it is applied it to detect human emotional states. The advantage of this model is that it acts like a bridge between users' emotional states and low-level bio-signal features.

Our intention with this overview of previous works was to show how context has been represented before, and how ontologies have been used to represent not only certain context but also behaviour of virtual characters. The contribution of our work is an ontology that describes the process from the elicitation of an event, its appraisal, generation of an affective state (mood, emotions and personality included) and its final manifestation through facial expressions.

SYSTEM FRAMEWORK

To represent daily events it is necessary to have a conceptual model of them and to define the rules of appraisal that will elicit affective responses. The schematic diagram of our conceptual model, presented in Figure 1 shows the relationships between the modules that build our system.

As it can be seen, the world is represented using its contextual information; then affective responses (emotions and mood) are produced by an affective model that evaluates this context; and finally these responses are manifested through the character's facial expressions.

In this work we will focus on the first block of the schema, *Context Representation*, because it is the base to create believable situations, and therefore, believable virtual characters inside

Figure 1. General conceptual model

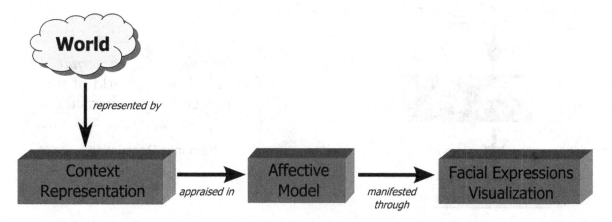

virtual worlds. Figure 2 presents a more detailed schema of the modules to be developed, and the psychological theories that will be used.

Starting from the top leftmost side of Figure 2, it is seen that the world is defined in terms of *events* and *agents*. An *Event* is what occurs in the world. It is composed of a time unit, a place where it occurs, and an action that is performed by, or affects to, an agent or object. A set of events correspond to a situation, which could be compared to the scene or complete picture to represent. As for the *Agent*, it is the individual who inhabits the world, also known as character, and it is defined in terms of its goals, preferences, social admiration for other agents (which can be also be "negative admiration") and personality.

Considering these two elements we can see context as a combination of the outer world (events) and the inner world (psychological characteristics) of the agent. Both worlds should be related in a way so we can extract the greatest amount of information to create different situations. The output of this module is a set of labelled emotions obtained from the OCC model, proposed by Ortony, Clore & Collins (1998), with their respective intensities.

The OCC model is an approach to the study of emotions that explains how people's perception of the world (cognitive nature) causes them to experience emotions. As a result, it defines emotions as valence reactions to events, agents, or objects, with their particular nature being determined by the way in which the eliciting

Figure 2. Semantic model for context representation

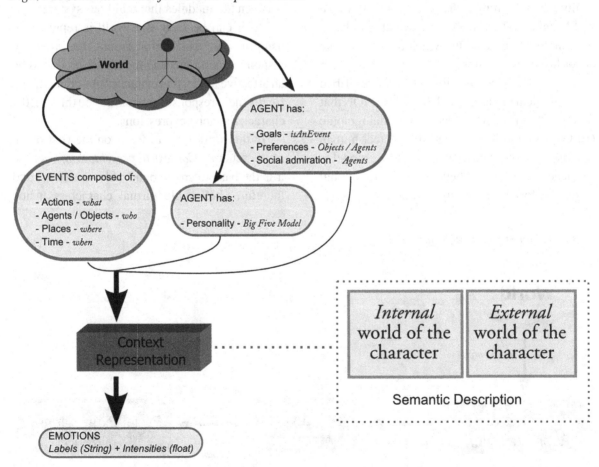

situation is construed. For Ortony et al., emotions cannot be arranged in a low-dimensional space; rather they should be organized in groups. Inside an emotion group, each emotion type is seen as representing a family of closely related emotions. The reason why we chose the OCC as our model of emotions is because it is based on what could be considered the three major aspects of the world upon persons can focus: *events, agents*, and *objects*. When one focuses on events is because of their consequences, when one focuses on agents is because of their actions, and when one focuses in objects is because of their aspect or properties.

To define personality we used the Five Factor Model (FFM) (McCrae & Costa, 1987), which is one of the most used models of personality in the field of affective computing and representation of virtual characters. It defines five personality traits based on five broad dimensions that *have been found across language domains in adjectival and in questionnaire formats, in internal judgments of the conceptual relations among traits and in external judgments of the extent to which traits are descriptive of actual people* (Hofstee & de Raad & Goldberg, 1992). These traits are *Openness, Conscientiousness, Extraversion, Agreeableness*, and *Neuroticism* (Figure 5:E). One of the greatest advantages of the FFM is that it proposes a detailed enumeration of behaviour categories attached to each personality trait. Therefore, it is easier to define a personality based on the different adjectives assigned to each trait.

SEMANTIC MODEL

In our work, representation of context is done using ontologies. An ontology is an explicit specification of an abstract, simplified view of a world to represent. It specifies both the concepts related to this view and their interrelations. Ontologies have the potential to represent knowledge in certain domain, and infer new knowledge from the already existent. We have chosen this approach because it

provides the semantic framework for describing the character's environment, and for inference from the events occurring in that environment.

The development of ontologies usually starts by defining its domain and scope. It means that given a motivating scenario, we should be able to answer certain questions related to it. These questions are known as *competency questions* (CQs). Informal CQs are queries which require the objects or constraints defined with the object. Fomal CQs are defined as an entailment or consistency problem with respect to the axioms in the ontology (Grüninger & Fox, 1995).

In this work we have focused only on informal CQs to evaluate the expressiveness of our ontologies, and we have organized them in two categories as follows:

Inner World Competency Questions

- In a certain situation (e.g. a story, an episode of daily life), which are the occurring events?
- How is an event described? Which is the main action that gives meaning to that event?
- What is affected by the action? What is the action affecting to?
- Where is the event happening? Can it happen in more than one location?
- When is the event happening? How can we describe the temporality of events? How can we simulate the duration of an event? Can events be organized in a temporal way (event 1 is happening, then event 2, and so on)? Can they be automatically organized, so they produce a temporal lineal story?
- Who is performing the event? Who is affected by the event? Are there more characters participating in it? How are these characters related?

Figure 5. PersonalityEmotion ontology diagram

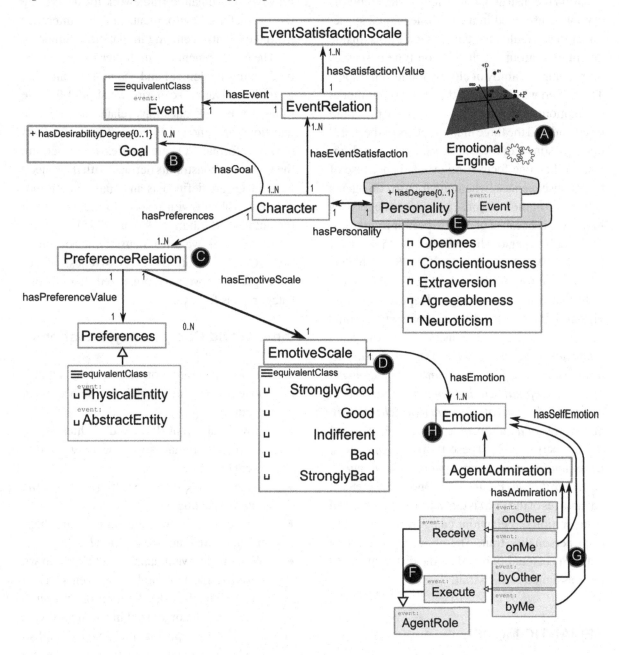

Outer World Competency Questions

- What are the goals of a character? What happens when a goal is achieved?
- What does the character like and dislike? Are these physical objects or not tangible things?

- How does the character feel about other characters?
- Which emotions can the character feel? How are they elicited?
- What is the personality of the character? How does it influence his/her emotional state?

From the former analysis we decided to design and implement two different ontologies, represented in Figure 3. The *event Ontology* describes the environment that surrounds the character (outer world) given the occurrence of an event, while the *personality Emotion Ontology* considers all the concepts that define a character from a psychological point of view - goals, preferences, social admiration with other agents, and personality (inner world).

Context: Outer World of the Character

According to Ortony et al., events are the constructions people make about things that happen, independently of any beliefs about their causes. We have defined an event based on four questions that provide the main information about it: "what", "where", "who", and "when".

- **What:** References the action that happens in the event. An action (usually defined with a verb) has complements that complete it, giving sense to the event (the sentence). Complements are *direct* objects and *indirect* objects, which are represented by abstract entities and physical entities overviewed in the *Preferences* paragraph.
- **Who:** Indicates the role of the character, or characters, with respect to the action in the event.

- **When:** Specifies the time of occurrence of the event.
- **Where:** Provides a description of the place where the event occurs.

EVENT ONTOLOGY

This ontology describes an *event* that is able to change the affective state of the character. Figure 4 shows the diagram of this ontology.

Having the Event as the central concept in this ontology, we start explaining Figure 4 with the relation *what* that ties up the *event* object with the *action* object. The relationship *onEvent* specifies that an action belongs to certain event, making the relation between action and event recursive. As was also previously stated, an *Action* is represented with a verb.

The verb has complements that can be direct or indirect objects, represented by the classes *AbstractEntity* and *PhysicalEntity*. The class *AbstractEntity* includes all intangible concepts as ideas, thoughts, dreams, or standards.

The class *PhysicalEntity* defines all things that can be seen and touched. Its subclasses are *SpatialLocation, MaterialThing* and *Agent*. Physical entities are considered to have a *Dimension* which can be: *Width, Height*, and/or *Depth*. For instance, a building can be very wide and tall, a pool can have a depth of 3 meters, or a floor-lamp can have a height of 1.2 meters.

Figure 3. Semantic model for context representation with ontologies

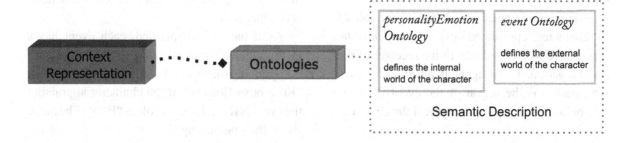

Figure 4. Event ontology diagram

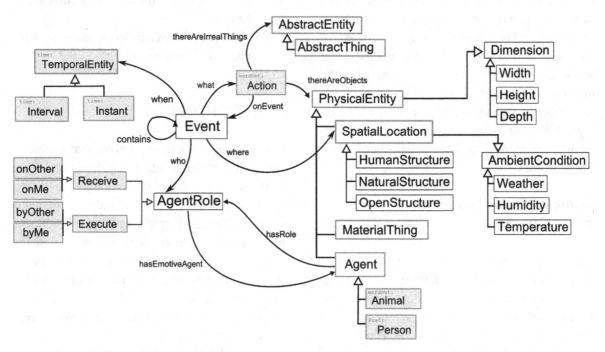

The subclass *SpatialLocation* defines where the event is happening, and it is related to the event through the relation *where*. It has three subclasses that categorize it: *HumanStructure* (e.g., buildings), *NaturalStructure* (e.g., beach) and *OpenStructure* (e.g., street). Also, a spatial location has an extra characteristic represented by the class *AmbientCondition*. It gives a more accurate description of the place where the event occurs and of the object affected by the action. *Temperature* and *Humidity* describe how cold or hot, and how wet or dry, a place is. From these two elements *Weather* can be inferred, thus defined as the state of the atmosphere with respect to heat or cold, wetness or dryness, calm or storm, clearness or cloudiness.

The relation named *who* indicates the role of the character, represented by the class *AgentRole*. It is related to the executer, or the receiver of the event's action. If the agent is an executer (one who performs the action of the event) then its role belongs to the class *Execute*. If the agent is a receiver (one who is affected by the action of the event) then its role belongs to the class *Receive*.

To specify even more the role of the character, we decided to represent if an event can be "led by" or "witnessed by" a character. If the character is an executer and leads the event, then its role belongs to the subclass *ByMe*; if the character is a receiver and leads the event then its role is of the class *OnMe*. When the main character of the event (character1) is witnessing an executer agent (character2), then the role of character2 is in the *ByOther* subclass; and if character1 is witnessing a receiver agent (character2), then the role of character2 is *OnOther*. In the case "other" is performing some action we need the information of who that agent is (character2) to elicit emotions according to it.

As it has been explained, each event has a "who" and its role will depend on which character is appraising that event. For example, in the event "Rose buys flowers", if the character appraising the event is Rose, then her role is "ByMe" because she is the one buying flowers.

Finally, the *TemporalEntity* class is associated with the **when** relationship, which specifies the time of occurrence of the event. If the event occurs in a specific point in time, then the subclass of the temporal entity is the subclass *Instant*. If the event occurs during certain period of time, then the temporal entity is the subclass *Interval*.

Context: Inner World of the Character

How a character feels is the result of a process of context appraisal, which is performed using information like the character's goals, preferences, degree of admiration for other characters, and personality traits. Many other aspects could be taken into consideration as social role, culture, religion, and social dynamics between characters. Nevertheless, we have considered the former elements the basic ones to represent the interaction of the characters with their environment.

Goals: They are related to the occurrence of an event that the character wishes to happen and produces benefits to it. A benefit in this case is represented as the elicitation of one, or a set of positive emotions. Goals are considered equivalent in their structure, which means that no difference will be made among preservation goals, partially achieved goals, and so forth.

Preferences: These are the degree of liking, or disliking, that an agent feels for "surrounding" entities. They can be things around the character as a specific park, certain street, chocolates, or other agents; or "things" that are inside the character as thoughts, ideas, standards, etc.; for example, the agent may have a preference for the concept of "freedom", or dislike "racism".

Interaction/Relation with other agents: In real life people like or dislike other people to a certain degree. This "feeling" influences the affective output when two characters are participating in the event, or when the event is evaluated from the perspective of an agent that is not participating in the event, but has "witnessed it" and might feel emotions because of it.

Social role: According to Edelstein (Edelstein, 2009), roles are blend of personality traits and the work a person does, whether that work is company president, hit man, or new mother. A role emphasizes different aspects of an individual. Although we have not followed this definition for establishing the role of the character in our ontology, it is a very important element to be taken into account when defining his personality. For instance, if the character we have in mind is a famous *latin-lover* actor, then we can think of personality traits as extraverted, not conscientious, and so on. Nevertheless, we have established four roles which deal with the character as a protagonist of the event or as spectator of the event, as explained in the Event Ontology section.

PERSONALITYEMOTION ONTOLOGY

To implement the concepts mentioned in the previous section we designed the *Personality-Emotion Ontology*. Figure 5 presents a diagram of the ontology.

The top left part of the diagram presents the Goals of a Character (Figure 5: B), which is an event with desirability degree. This degree indicates how much a character wants that event to happen. After emotion elicitation due to the achievement of a goal, the desirability degree gives the intensity to the triggered emotions.

Preferences (Figure 5: **C**) are set for physical or abstract entities. A physical entity is considered any *spatial* thing as human structures (e.g., buildings), natural structures (e.g., beach), or open structures (e.g., street); material things (e.g., candies); or agents, which can be either another character or an animal.

The relation between the character's preferences and the emotions that they elicit are established by the class *PreferenceRelation*. This class

Figure 6. Categorization of emotions

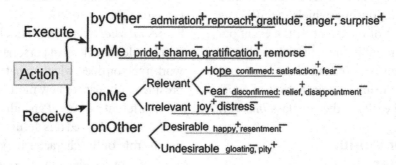

allowed us to model the idea behind the OCC model, where attitudes of the character towards aspects of objects (preferences) lead to liking or disliking; and when there is attraction to those objects, to emotions of love or hate. All preferences are categorized in the class *EmotiveScale* (Figure 5:D). The scales are STRONGLYGOOD (SG), GOOD (G), INDIFFERENT (IP), BAD (B), STRONGLYBAD (SB), and each one determines a set of emotions to be triggered (Figure 5:H): *Love, Liking, No emotions, Disliking, Hate/Fear*, respectively.

To produce the affective output from the event, we have assigned it a level of satisfaction through the class *EventSatisfactionScale*. In this work, each event is considered to have only one level of satisfaction. Each level can be defined in a scale with certain degree that determines how satisfied the agent is, and it is used to evoke a set of emotions. These scales are: SATISFACTORY (S), INDIFFERENT (IA), and NOT SATISFACTORY (NS). Regarding the overall degree of satisfaction of an event, it is the agent who appraises the event the one that defines it.

"Who" performs the action of the event also decides the set of produced emotions, e.g. the action of *kissing* a person, or to be kissed by a person can generate two different types of emotions: *fear* for being rejected by the loved one, or *happiness* for having being kissed by the loved one, respectively. Thus level of appreciation of one agent for another is considered in the class

AgentAdmiration (Figure 5:F,G). It can belong to one of three categories: POSITIVE (P), INDIFFERENT (IAg) or NEGATIVE (N), again, with certain degree.

Figure 6. shows the elicited emotions depending on the agent who executes or receives the action of the event, and the level of satisfaction for that event. The list of considered emotions is based on the ones proposed in the OCC model.

As explained in a previous section, an action can be "executed" by me (the lead or protagonist character) or by other (another character); or "received" on me (the lead or protagonist character suffers the consequences of the action) or on other (another character suffers the consequences).

So then, if the role of the character is *ByMe*, emotions with positive sign (+) are elicited when the event is SATISFACTORY and emotions with negative sign (-) are elicited when the event is NOT SATISFACTORY. To decide which emotion are triggered (among positives and negatives), if the event is a goal then *pride* or *shame* (depending on the type of event) are triggered; if not then *gratification* or *remorse* are triggered.

If the role is *OnMe* then triggered emotions are also decided as with the former role. If the event is a goal ("Relevant") and it is SATISFACTORY, then *satisfaction* or *relief* are elicited; if it is NOT SATISFACTORY, then *fear* or *disappointment* are elicited. If the event is not a goal ("Irrelevant") and it is SATISFACTORY then *joy* is triggered, otherwise, *distress*.

In the case the event is performed or received by "Other" (role *ByOther* or *OnOther*), emotions with positive sign (+) are elicited when the admiration for that "other" is POSITIVE and emotions with negative sign (-) are elicited when the admiration for that "other" is NEGATIVE. In the case of roles *ByOther* or *OnOther*, a subsequent refinement of the final set of emotions should be done. That means that the level of satisfaction of the event should be taken into account to decide for positive or negative emotions of the chosen set.

For instance, if agent's role is *ByOther* and admiration for that agent is "Positive", then the set of emotions is: admiration, reproach, and surprise. Nevertheless, admiration is a positive emotion but reproach is a negative one. To decide which one is going to be elicited, the degree of satisfaction of the event is used. In the example, if the event is "Not Satisfactory", then the elicited emotion would be the negative one, reproach. As will be seen later in this chapter, all this is implemented as rules.

To define personality we used the Five Factor Model (FFM) (McCrae & Costa, 1987), which was already defined in previous sections.

COMBINING EVENT AND PERSONALITYEMOTION ONTOLOGIES

As seen in the previous sections, the *event ontology* provides all the elements that are needed to represent an event while the *personalityEmotion ontology* provides the relations between the event and the character, as well as all elements related to the character's internal aspects (goals, preferences, admiration for other agents, and personality) used in event appraisal.

The following is a guideline of how to use the ontologies for representing a situation in certain scenario

1. **Situation Identification.** First of all we need to describe what the character, or characters, will go through as if it were a story. In this way we can have a general idea of what we want to represent, and therefore, start identifying all the elements of the ontologies.

   For example, "Alice started her day very early this morning. While she was having breakfast, she heard about a train strike in the radio. This was very inconvenient, given that she had an early appointment at the office and with the strike she was not going to be able to make it".

2. **Event Identification:** Making use of the *Event* Ontology, we extract from the whole situation each relevant event that provokes a change in the character or in the environment. Each event is seen as a predicate that includes a subject (character(s)), verb (action) and predicate (ambient conditions, physical and abstract things – objects, other agents, animals, location). This representation is visualized in Figure 4. For each event we assign a level of Satisfaction to the characters participating in it. This level will elicit emotions according to Figure 6.

   In the previous example, from the situation "*Alice started her day very early this morning*", we can get the event: "Alice wakes up very early". As we are the ones defining who is Alice, if we decide that she does not like waking up early, then the Satisfaction for this event will be NOT SATISFACTORY; otherwise the event will be SATISFACTORY.

3. **Character Preferences and Goals Definition:** Using the *PersonalityEvent Ontology* (Figure 5:B,C), we define the level of preference of the character for the physical and abstract things identified in step (2). Also, the events considered as goals are set by assigning a degree of desirability to

each potential event-goal. Finally, the level of admiration of one agent for another is established (Figure 5:G).

The character's preference for the different entities in the event will elicit: Love, Liking, Anger or Hate, or Disliking.

The character's level of admiration for other agents will elicit emotions according to Figure 6.

From the previous example we can get a *TemporalEntity* object: "very early", which can be seen as an *Instant* with a fixed time. If "waking up early" is a goal for Alice, then its desirability degree is a number between 0.7 and 1.0.

4. **Personality Definition:** Using the FFM we set the personality traits for each character. For instance, we can say that Alice has low extraversion, low agreeability, very low openness to experience, high conscientiousness, and high neuroticism.

5. **Direct Emotion Elicitation:** As a result of these two ontologies, a set of positive and negative emotions is produced. The intensities of these emotions depend on the preferences and admiration level for other agents (Figure 6).

6. **Indirect Emotion Elicitation:** At this point we use the event Satisfaction value to enhance or decrease the already obtained emotion values. For this we use the equations in Tables 1 and 2.

Table 1 indicates the relation between the event (*S, IA, NS*) and the object preference (*SG,*

G, IP, B, SB), and how positive or negative emotions are incremented or decremented by a value μ which is set by the user. The preferences scales are STRONGLYGOOD (*SG*), GOOD (*G*), INDIFFERENT (*IP*), BAD (*B*), and STRONGLYBAD (*SB*). Event satisfaction scales are SATISFACTORY(*S*), INDIFFERENT (*IA*), and NOTSATISFACTORY (*NS*).

Table 2 indicates the relation between the event and the agent admiration (*P, IAg, N*), and how positive or negative emotions are incremented or decremented by μ. Agent admiration scales are POSITIVE (*P*), INDIFFERENT (*IAg*) or NEGATIVE (*N*).

For instance, in the event "Alice was having breakfast", it the event is SATISFACTORY = 0.7 for Alice and she has a STRONGLYGOOD = 1.0 preference for "breakfast", then elicited emotions will be enhanced by $(\mu)^2$.

7. **Rules Definition:** By defining a set of rules it is possible to handle specific events and personalities to elicit different emotions in similar situations. Rules are of the form *IF THEN ELSE*. For example, a rule for the event "Alice wakes up very early" might be: *IF Action=*"wake up" *AND TemporalEntity=* very-early *THEN Emotion = Hate*

8. **Contained Events (Optional):** In case there are contained events (given by the relationship *contains*) in the main event:
   ◦ Evaluate the event satisfaction of the contained event from the main character perspective.

Table 1. Preferences: Event relationship

	SG	G	IP	B	SB
S	$(+\mu^2)Pos$	$(+\mu)Pos$	-	$(-\mu)Pos$	$(-\mu^2)Pos$
IA	-	-	-	-	-
NS	$(+\mu^2)Neg$	$(+\mu)Neg$	-	$(\pm\mu)Neg$	$(\pm\mu^2)Neg$

Table 2. Agent Admiration: Event relationship

	P	IAg	N
S	$(+\mu)Pos$	-	$(-\mu)Pos$
IA	-	-	-
NS	$(+\mu)Neg$	-	$(-\mu)Neg$ OR $(+\mu)Pos$

○ Evaluate the admiration degree of the main-character (character in the main event) for the contained-character (character in the contained event). Preferences are not evaluated in the contained event.

○ Define personality for the main-character.

○ Apply equation in Table 2 according to the resultant cases.

○ Create rules in case of refinement of emotions.

IMPLEMENTATION

To model the ontologies, the Ontology Web Language (OWL) was used (Web Ontology Working Group, 2009). Its advantage is that it provides better machine interpretability of Web content than XML, RDF, and RDF Schema (RDF-S) because it provides the formal semantics plus additional vocabulary.

With Java and JENA library (Hewlett-Packard Development Company, 2008) we were able to perform operations on them, as well as inference that was done using JENA rules. JENA is a Java framework for building Semantic Web applications. It provides a programmatic environment for RDF, RDFS and OWL, SPARQL and includes a rule-based inference engine (JENA rules). One of the advantages of Jena is that being developed in Java, it is applicable to various environments. In addition, it is open source and strongly backed up by solid documentation. Also, regardless to the schema and the used data models, Jena can simultaneously work with multiple ontologies from different sources, and it can be bound to SQL databases from different vendors.

Through a wizard interface made using Java Swing classes (Figure 7), any user can create characters and define for each of them the events, goals, preferences and admiration for other agents, which will define that character's context. This information is stored in a database, so it can be manipulated and reused to create new scenarios, or similar ones with different emotional outputs. In this way, by just assigning values for the concepts of the ontologies, the application is capable of inferring and creating the relations between

Figure 7. Interface of the context representation application

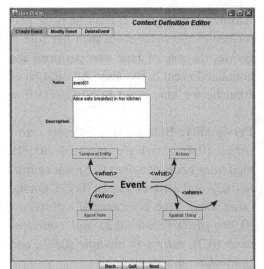
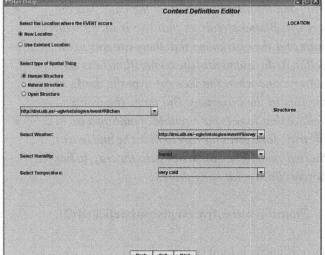

those concepts, giving as a result a set of emotions which are felt by the character. As a final goal, a database of contextual situations could be constructed, containing any kind of related data to be reused by the defined ontologies.

USE CASE

Movie Scenario

To test our model following the guidelines of previous section, we decided for a scene extracted from the Robert Aldrich's film "*What Ever Happened to Baby Jane?*" (Aldrich, 1962). Using this scenario, we intended to show that with our computational model the evaluation of the context is done automatically and the elicited emotions are the same as the ones expressed by the characters in the selected scene. This guarantees coherence between the context, the events and the emotional output.

"What Ever Happened to Baby Jane?" is a psychological thriller with some black comedy. The specific scene we are taking as example of how to produce dynamic affective states is the following (1):

Jane enters Blanche's bedroom with a closed food tray, and informs Blanche that the maid has the day off. Blanche realizes that she is alone with Jane and she also knows that there are rats in the cellar. At this moment of the scene, Blanche is very hungry, and when she sees the tray she thinks of the rats in the basement. But then, she wants to believe that Jane is not capable of putting a rat in the tray. Jane gives the tray to Blanche and leaves the bedroom. When Blanche opens the tray, to her horror, finds a rat lying there.

From this scene, five events can be elicited (2):

1.   Blanche is hungry.

2.   Jane enters Blanche's bedroom with a closed tray.

3.   Blanche is alone with Jane in the house.

4.   Blanche does not believe that Jane is capable of putting a rat in the food.

5.   Blanche opens the tray and sees the rat.

6.   Jane hears Blanche opening the tray.

These events are a simplified version of the story, but they can help us to explain how we added emotional content to them. Through the wizard of the computational model (previously explained) the user can define the context for Jane and Blanche. We will carefully examine the event 4) "Blanche does not believe that Jane is capable of putting a rat in the food".

In this case the main event is: *Blanche does not believe "something"*. That "something" is considered as a CONTAINED event, which is: "Jane is capable of putting a rat in the food". The action is "*put*" (putting a rat in the food). Then we need to apply guideline (8).

- **Event Satisfaction:** The contained event is evaluated from the perspective of the character that performs the main event: Blanche. She considers this event as NOTSATISFACTORY = 0.8, and it is not a goal.

- **Admiration Degree:** If Blanche is the performer of the main event then her role is ByMe, the role of Jane who performs the contained event is ByOther. Admiration of Blanche for Jane is set to NEGATIVE = 0.6.

- **Personality:** Blanche is *a little bit extroverted* (0.4), *extremely agreeable* (0.99), *moderately conscientious* (0.8), *not neurotic* (0.2), and *extremely open* (0.99). On the other hand, Jane is *extremely extroverted* (0.99), *disagreeable* (0.2), *not conscientious* (0.2), *extremely neurotic* (0.99), and *somewhat open* (0.6).

- **Emotion Elicitation:** Using Figure 6, we first elicit emotions using the contained-character's role (Jane, ByOther) and the contained-event satisfaction (NOT SATISFACTORY = 0.8), from the main-character's perspective (Blanche). Elicited emotion is *anger* = 0.6.

Now we need to evaluate the event using the main-character's role and contained-event satisfaction. It means, the role of Blanche (ByMe) and event Satisfaction is NOT SATISFACTORY = 0.8. Elicited emotion are *shame = 0.8* and *remorse* = 0.8.

To consider the main event satisfaction, we need to use a logic rule to decide for it. The rule is as follows:

```
IF contained-event.SatisfactionScale
= NOT SATISFACTORY
AND action = NOT "believe"
THEN main-event.SatisfactionScale =
SATISFACTORY
                 AND byMe.emotions
= pride = 0.8 OR gratification = 0.8
```

It means that as Blanche does not think that a Not Satisfactory event will occur, then it becomes Satisfactory. As we can see, elicited emotions for role ByMe are different; therefore, we select the ones obtained from the rule.

Applying the rules in Table 2, we have that satisfaction is *S* and admiration is *N*, then we use equation (-µ)*Pos*, where µ is 0.2 (set according the Neuroticism value of the character). Hence, positive emotions pride or gratification will be decreased in (0.2)*0.8 = 0.16.

The final set of emotions is: {*Anger = 0.6, Pride = 0.64, Gratification = 0.64*}. From this set we chose the ones with the greatest values.

To validate this emotional output we extracted the facial expression of Blanche, correspondent to this event in the movie scene. Then we compare it to the gratification facial expression generated

for a virtual character using the MPEG-4 standard (Arellano et al., 2008), obtaining as result a great similarity between both expressions. Due to copyright permission we cannot present the image from the film, but Figure 8 shows the facial expression of the virtual character Alice.

Table 3 presents the ontology elements associated with the selected scenes and the final emotional output of each of them. Each scene is treated as a predicate and preferences, goals, and admiration for other agents are extracted from them. After inference a set of emotions are obtained.

CONCLUSION

Context representation is a complex task that requires the definition of several aspects that influences the evaluation of what is happening

Figure 8. Expression for gratification in virtual character (Alice)

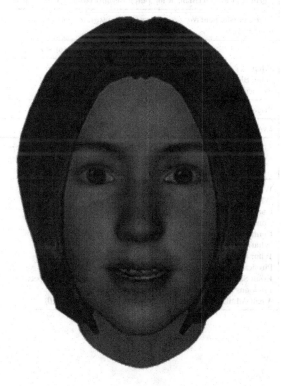

Table 3. Analysis of Events using Ontologies

Event 1: *Blanche is hungry*	
What: *is* **Who:** Blanche. Role: *OnMe* **Abstract Thing:** hunger	
Event Satisfaction: *Not Satisfactory (value = 1.0)*	**Emotions associated:** Sadness = 1.0

Event 2: *Jane enters Blanche's bedroom with a closed tray.*	
What: *enter* **Who:** Jane. Role: *ByMe* **Where:** Blanche's bedroom **Material Thing:** closed tray	
Event Satisfaction: *Satisfactory (value = 0.7)*	**Emotions associated:** Pride = 0.7

Event 3: *Blanche is alone with Jane in the house*	
What: *is* **Who:** Blanche. Role: *OnMe* (protagonist) **Who:** Jane. Role: *OnOther* **Where:** Blanche's house **Abstract Thing:** alone	
Event Satisfaction: *Not Satisfactory (value = 0.8)*	**Emotions associated:** Fear = 0.8
Agent Admiration (Blanche for Jane): *Negative (value = 0.6)*	**Emotions associated:** Anger = 0.6

Event 4: *Blanche does not believe that* "Jane is capable of putting a rat in the food"	
What: *does not believe* **Who:** Blanche. Role: *ByMe* **Contains:** "Jane is capable of putting a rat in the food" **Contained Event:** *Jane is capable of putting a rat in the food.* **What:** *put* **Who:** Jane. Role: *ByOther* **Physical Entity (Animal):** rat **Event Satisfaction:** *Not Satisfactory (value = 0.8)* (from Blanche's perspective) **Emotions associated:** Anger = 0.6 **Agent Admiration (Blanche for Jane):** *Negative (value = 0.6)*	
Event Satisfaction: *Not Satisfactory (value = 0.8)* (from Blanche's perspective)	**Emotions associated:** rules are triggered. Pride = 0.64, Gratification = 0.64

Event 5: *Blanche opens the tray and sees the rat*	
What: *see* **Who:** Blanche. Role: *ByMe* **Physical Entity (Animal):** rat	
Preferences for "rat": *Strongly Bad (value = 0.9)*	**Emotions associated:** Hate = 0.9, Fear = 0.9
Event Satisfaction: *Not Satisfactory (value = 1.0)*	**Emotions associated:** Shame = 1.0

Event 6: *Jane hears that* "Blanche opens the tray" In this case, there is a main event: *Jane hears* "something". "something" is considered as the CONTAINED event: "Blanche opens the tray". So that, the contained event is evaluated from the perspective of the character who performs the main event.	
What: *hear* **Who:** Jane. Role: *ByMe* **Goal:** This event goes with Jane's goal: to torment Blanche **Contains:** "Blanche opens the tray" **Contained Event:** *Blanche opens the tray (with the rat inside).* **What:** *open* **Who:** Blanche. Role: *ByOther* **Physical Entity (Animal):** tray (with rat) **Event Satisfaction:** *Satisfactory (value = 1.0)* (from Jane's perspective) **Emotions associated:** Joy = 1.0, Pride = 0.95 **Agent Admiration (Jane for Blanche):** *Negative (value = 1.0)*	

in that context. Without going any further, in our daily lives we can see that to evaluate one single event we consider not only what is happening, or where, or who is doing it. We also take into consideration social rules and roles that change our emotional response from one situation to another, even if evaluate the same event.

On the other hand, if we look at children, we can observe that they have the same emotional reaction to the same event, independently of social rules, culture or roles; and it does not mean that their emotions are less real than the ones felt by adults. This allows us to justify why a simpler context representation might be valid, and moreover, generic and applicable to a wide range of applications.

In this paper we have shown how to represent context using ontologies and to infer new knowledge from the relations between the context concepts. In this way we can have much more than a data storage because we can establish new relationships and therefore, create new situations using the already existing data.

To validate our ontology we have used a clip of the movie "What ever happens to Baby Jane?". The idea was to represent the events occurring in the movie clip and achieve the same emotional responses as the actresses in it. The results shown that emotions were obtained according to the real clip, as can be seen in Figure 8. Nevertheless, more validation with more examples is still needed, as well as implementation in a real application.

In future work we intend to use our context representation for interactive applications, storytelling and animation generation and to integrate other existent ontologies to enhanced the potential of our model.

AKNOWLEDGMENT

This work was subsidized by the national projects TIN2007-67993 and TIN2010-16576 from the MCYT Spanish Government. Also, thanks to Isaac Lera for his valuable help with the ontologies definition and to Miquel Mascaró Oliver for his valuable help on annotating events of the film.

REFERENCES

Aldrich, R. (Director). (1962). *What ever happened to baby Jane?* [Film]. United States: Warner Bros.

Arellano, D., Varona, J., & Perales, F. J. (2008). Generation and visualization of emotional states in virtual characters. In Computer Animation and Virtual Worlds, Special Issue: CASA'2008, 19(3-4), 259-270. doi:10.1002/cav.234

Chen, H., Perich, F., Finin, T., & Joshi, A. (2004). SOUPA: Standard ontology for ubiquitous and pervasive applications. In *First Annual International Conference on Mobile and Ubiquitous Systems: Networking and Services (MobiQuitous'04)* (pp.258-267). doi:10.1109/MOBIQ.2004.1331732

Dey, A. K., Abowd, G. D., & Salber, D. (2001). A conceptual framework and a toolkit for supporting the rapid prototyping of context-aware applications. *Human-Computer Interaction, 16*(2), 97–166. doi:10.1207/S15327051HCI16234_02

Edelstein, L. (2009). *The writer's guide to character traits*. Cincinnati, OH: Writers Digest Books.

Figa, E., & Tarau, P. (2002). The VISTA architecture: Experiencing stories through virtual storytelling agents. *SIGGROUP Bulletin, 23*(2), 27–28. doi:10.1145/962185.962196

Gangemi, A., Guarino, N., Masolo, C., Oltramari, A., & Schneider, L. (2002). Sweetening Ontologies with DOLCE. In BenjaminsR. (Ed.), *13th International Conference on Knowledge Engineering and Knowledge Management Ontologies and the Semantic Web* (pp. 166–181). London: Springer-Verlag. doi:10.1007/3-540-45810-7_18

Grüninger, M., & Fox, M. (1995). Methodology for the design and evaluation of ontologies. In: *Proceedings of the Workshop on Basic Ontological Issues in Knowledge Sharing, IJCAI-95*.

Gutiérrez, A. M., García-Rojas, A., Thalmann, D., Vexo, F., Moccozet, L., Magnenat-Thalmann, N., & Spagnuolo, M. et al. (2007). An ontology of virtual humans: Incorporating semantics into human shapes. *The Visual Computer: International Journal of Computer Graphics*, *23*(3), 207–218. doi:10.1007/s00371-006-0093-4

Hastings, J., Ceusters, W., Mulligan, K., & Smith, B. (2012). Annotating affective neuroscience data with the emotion ontology. *Proceedings of the Workshop Towards an Ontology of Mental Functioning, ICBO 2012*.

Hewlett-Packard Development Company. (2008). *Jena: A Semantic Web Framework for Java, 2008* (version 2.5.6). Retrieved October 13, 2008, from http://jena.sourceforge.net/

Hofstee, W. K., de Raad, B., & Goldberg, L. R. (1992). Integration of the big five and circumplex approaches to trait structure. *Journal of Personality and Social Psychology*, *63*(1), 146–163. doi:10.1037/0022-3514.63.1.146 PMID:1494982

Kaiser, S., & Wehrle, T. (2008). Facial expressions in social interactions: Beyond basic emotions. In Advances in Consciousness Research. (Vol. 74): Animating Expressive Characters for Social Interactions (pp. 53-69). Amsterdam, The Netherlands: John Benjamins Publishing Company.

Krummenacher, R., Lausen, H., & Strang, T. (2007). Analyzing the modeling of context with ontologies. In *International Workshop on Context-Awareness for Self-Managing Systems*. (pp. 11-22). Toronto: VDE Verlag.

Lenat, D. B. (1995). CYC: A large-scale investment in knowledge infrastructure. *Communications of the ACM*, *38*(11), 33–38. doi:10.1145/219717.219745

López, J. M., Gil, R., García, R., Cearreta, I., & Garay, N. (2008). Towards an ontology for describing emotions. In M. D. Lytras, J. M. Carroll, E. Damiani, & R. D. Tennyson (Eds.), *Proceedings of the 1st world summit on The Knowledge Society: Emerging Technologies and Information Systems for the Knowledge Society* (WSKS '08) (pp. 96-104). Berlin, Heidelberg: Springer-Verlag.

McCrae, R. R., & Costa, P. T. (1987). Validation of a five-factor model of personality across instruments and observers. *Journal of Personality and Social Psychology*, *52*(1), 81–90. doi:10.1037/0022-3514.52.1.81 PMID:3820081

Nakasone, A., & Ishizuka, M. (2006). Storytelling ontology model using RST. In *Proceedings of the IEEE/WIC/ACM international conference on Intelligent Agent Technology* (IAT '06) (pp. 163-169). Washington, DC: IEEE Computer Society. doi:10.1109/IAT.2006.114

Niles, I., & Pease, A. (2001). Towards a standard upper ontology. In *Proceedings of the international conference on Formal Ontology in Information Systems:* Vol. 2001 (pp. 2.9). New York, NY: ACM.

Obrenovic, Z., Garay, N., López, J. M., Fajardo, I., & Cearreta, I. (2005). An ontology for description of emotional cues. In J. Tao, T. Tan, & R. W. Picard (Eds.), *ACII 2005. LNCS* (Vol. 3784, pp. 505–512). Heidelberg: Springer. doi:10.1007/11573548_65

Ortony, A., Clore, G., & Collins, A. (1998). *Cognitive structure of emotions*. New York, NY: Cambridge University Press.

Scheffczyk, J., Baker, C. F., & Narayanan, S. (2006). Ontology-based reasoning about lexical resources. In N. Calzolari, A. Gangemi, A. Lenci, A. Oltramari, & L. Prévot (Eds.), *Ontologies and lexical resources for natural language processing* (pp. 1–8). Cambridge: Cambridge University Press.

Strang, T., & Popien, C. L. (2004). A context modeling survey. In *UbiComp 1st International Workshop on Advanced Context Modelling, Reasoning and Management.* (pp. 31-41). Nottingham.

Web Ontology Working Group. (2009, 27 October). *Owl 2 web ontology language. Document overview. W3C recommendation.* Retrieved September 19, 2010, from http://www.w3.org/TR/owl2-overview/

Zhang, X., Hu, B., Chen, J., & Moore, P. (2012). Ontology-based context modeling for emotion recognition in an intelligent web. *World Wide Web (Bussum), 16*(4), 497–513. doi:10.1007/s11280-012-0181-5

KEY TERMS AND DEFINITIONS

Agent: Individual that experiences the actions, interacts with the elements and is affected by the interrelations of the context.

Context: Set of actions, elements and interconnections that occur and exists around an agent.

Event: Is an action that occurs in the world where the agent lives.

Goal: State of success to be achieve by an agent.

JENA: Java framework for building Semantic Web applications.

Ontology: Structure that defines concepts and their relations in a specific domain.

Personality: Set of traits that define a person psychologically and behaviorally.

Preference: Something (or state) liked or disliked by the agent.

Role: Identity assumed by an agent in relation to peer agents and himself.

Chapter 19
Military Robotics and Emotion:
Challenges to Just War Theory

Jai Galliott
The University of New South Wales, Australia

ABSTRACT

In this chapter the author considers the complex moral interplay between unmanned systems, emotion, and just war theory. The first section examines technologically mediated fighting and suggests that through a process of moral-emotional disengagement and emotional desensitisation, any pre-existing barriers to immoral conduct in war may be reduced. Having considered the impact on the long distance warrior's capacity or willingness to adhere to jus in bello norms, the author then examines the impact on the personal wellbeing of the operators themselves. Here, among other things, the author considers the impact of being simultaneously present in contrasting environments and argue that this, if nothing else, may lead to serious transgressions of just war principles. The fourth and final section asks whether we can eliminate or relieve some of these technologically mediated but distinctly human moral problems by further automating elements of the decision making process.

INTRODUCTION

War is an all-too-human affair and will probably always require the endangerment of human lives, but military robots known as 'unmanned systems' have begun to offest the human cost of war. However, their use is not without implication for just warfare. In this chapter I examine the efficacy of unmanned systems with a particular focus on the emotional and mindset-altering dimensions of unmanned warfare and their impact on the principal war-making agents, namely unmanned systems operators. This is because many of the unintended effects of this technology cannot be attributed to the machine, but to human psychology. In the first section, I examine some problems associated with technologically mediated fighting and suggest that through a process of moral disengagement and emotional desensitisation, the barriers to immoral conduct *in* war may also be reduced. Having considered the impact on the long distance warrior's capacity or willingness to adhere to *jus in bello* norms, the second section examines the impact on the personal wellbeing of the operators themselves. Here, among other things, the impact of being simultaneously pres-

DOI: 10.4018/978-1-4666-7278-9.ch019

ent in contrasting environments is considered in arguing that this, if nothing else, may lead to serious transgressions of just war principles. In the third and final section, I consider whether we can eliminate or relieve some of these technologically mediated but distinctly human moral problems by automating elements of the decision making process. It is concluded that while greater automation certainly has the potential to alleviate some moral concerns generated by these systems, there is a strong case for keeping humans in the decision making chain, even if it involves having to make a delicate moral tradeoff between maintaining and/ or improving warfighting capability and limiting harm to noncombatants.

A BRIEF BACKGROUND TO THE PROBLEM

While it is high-level decision makers that are central to the initial decision to engage in warfare, it is the individual soldier who defends his state and society that must be most unconditional in exercising moral restraint and adhering to just war theory. Michael Ignatieff (1998) writes that more than any other of war-making agential group, it is the soldiers who actually conduct war that have the most influence on its outcomes and the ability to introduce the moral component. In his words, 'the decisive restraint on inhuman practice on the battlefield lies within the warrior himself – in his conception of what is honourable or dishonourable for a man to do with weapons' (Ignatieff 1998, p. 118). Ironically, soldiers are the primary agents of both physical violence and compassion and moral arbitration in war. As Darren Bowyer (1998) remarks, they deliver 'death and destruction one moment…[and deal] out succour to the wounded (of both sides) and assistance to the unwittingly involved civilian population, the next' (p. 276). The specific concern examined here is whether by removing soldiers from the battlefield and training them to fight via a technologically mediated proxy

we may, through a process of psycho-moral disengagement and emotional desensitisation, lower their ability or willingness to exercise restraint and compassion in warfare and adhere to the *jus in bello* principles of discrimination and proportionality. It will be argued that the employment of unmanned systems tracks unethical decision-making and/or lowers barriers to killing, endangering the moral conduct of warfare.

Most, if not all, human beings are born with what can only be described as a primitive survival instinct that, without unchecked force, would lead to a degree of violence and savagery. But in most societies, people are raised and socialised in such a way that typically leads them to hold an aversion to harming other human beings. In a military context, this socialised reluctance to kill is evidenced by recounts and statistics from earlier wars. David Grossman (1995), a self-proclaimed 'killogist' or military psychologist, writes of two World War veterans. The first confirms that many WWI infantrymen never fired their weapons and relied instead on artillery, while the second says that platoon sergeants in WWII had to move up and down the firing line kicking men to get them to fire and that they felt they were doing good if they could 'get two or three men out of a squad to fire' (Grossman 1995, p. xiv). While some have criticised his methodology, S. L. A. Marshall gave further supporting evidence in arguing from personal experience and studies conducted on firing ratios, which revealed that 'on average not more than 15 per cent of the men had actually fired at the enemy' (Marshall 2000, p. 54). He attributed this startling inhibition to kill to an 'ingrained fear of aggression' that was based on society's teaching that killing is fundamentally wrong (Marshall 2000, p. 71). For Marshall, success in combat and the welfare of the state and its people demanded that action be taken to correct or overcome this problem.

In the years following publication of the first edition of Marshall's book – that is, in those following WWII – there is evidence that Marshall's calls for corrective action were answered. The claims of very low firing rates had been replaced by very high and morally concerning firing rates. By the time of the Korean War, the American firing rate was said to be up to fifty-five percent and, in Vietnam, it was reported to be up to ninety or ninety-five percent (Meagher 2006). Some expressed doubts about these firing rates too, with some finding troops with unspent ammunition in the rear of troop formations, but they were generally satisfied that among those who actually sighted the enemy, there appeared to have been extraordinarily high and consistent firing rates (Grossman 1995). From a strictly military or operational perspective, this is a remarkable success story. In order to overcome the hesitancy to fire and kill that most people develop over time, Russel Glenn says that staff sergeants and platoon commanders watched their troops to ensure that they were actually engaging with the adversary and that in Vietnam, they listened for the steady roar of machine gun fire which indicated to them that their soldiers were unhesitatingly firing their weapons (Marshall 2000). However, this corrective action seems unlikely to account for such a radical shift in the firing ratios. The real cause for the difference in the firing rates, it could be argued, has much more to do with technology employed in later conflicts and changes in military training which, together, allowed and continues to allow, individuals to achieve a physical, emotional and/or moral distance from their enemies, thus enabling them to kill somewhat easier. It is these distances that need to be explored in more detail, as unmanned systems only further them and the disengagement and the accompanying desensitisation to a point that gives rise to unique problems affecting their operators' ability to wage discriminate and proportional warfare.

The link between physical and emotional distance, ease of aggression and waging warfare is in no way a new discovery. As Grossman (1995) writes, it has long been understood that there is a positive relationship between the empathetic and the spatial proximity of the victim and the resultant difficulty and personal trauma caused by the kill, or the morally problematic ease of killing, more generally. This relationship has been a cause for concern among anthropologists, philosophers, psychologists, theologians and, of course, soldiers themselves, who often struggle to understand their own actions. Jesse Glenn Gray (1959), an American philosophy professor whose career was interrupted by a period of service as a WWII counter-intelligence officer, wrote that unless one is caught in some sort of overwhelming murderous ecstasy where rage takes over, killing and destroying is much easier when done at a little remove and that with every foot of distance, there is a corresponding decrease in the accurate portrayal of reality. He argues that there is a point at which one's representation of the world begins to flag and another at which it fails altogether (Gray 1959). Glenn put forward this argument over fifty years ago and the concern is that unmanned systems seem to increase the relevant distances to the flagging point that he referenced or that, at worse, the advancement in unmanned systems technologies may reach a point whereby the moral inhibitions of unmanned systems operators are almost totally overcome. That is, the worry is that we have reached a morally significant point in the history of weapons development. To really understand how these weapons make it easier to kill and dampen a soldier's capacity to act ethically in war, we have to think about unmanned systems in the wider context of weapons that increase physical distance to the target and lower resistance to killing.

UNMANNED SYSTEMS: KILLING AT MAXIMUM RANGE

In painting a mental picture of this conceptual phenomenon, one must imagine a spectrum. At one end we have close range, then middle range and long range at other end. Close range, for our sake, involves any easily attributable kill at 'point-blank' range, whether with one's bare hands, an edged weapon or even a projectile weapon. According to Grossman (1995), the key factor in close range killing is the undeniable responsibility one holds for the act. John Keegan and Richard Holmes (1986) cite the story of an Israeli paratrooper during the capture of Jerusalem in 1967: 'we looked up at each other for half a second and I knew that it was up to me, personally, to kill him' (p. 266). When a soldier kills at this range, more than any other, it's an intensely vivid and personal matter (Grossman 1995, p. 115). One can see the raw emotions on their enemy's face, hear their cries and smell the gunpowder. The Israeli paratrooper mentioned above goes on to say that having shot his enemy at close range, he could see the hate on his enemy's face and that 'there was so much blood…[he] vomited, until the rest of the boys came up' (Keegan and Holmes 1986, p. 266). Combat at close proximity is an interpersonal affair, so much so that it is incredibly difficult to deny the enemy's humanity. For this reason, Grossman says, the resistance to close-range killing is 'tremendous' (Grossman 1995, p. 118). At midrange – where you can still see and engage the enemy with handgrenades, sniper rifles and so on, but usually without being able to gauge the extent of the wounds inflicted – the experience of killing changes. At this range in the spectrum, the soldier can deny responsibility for the fatal shot or blow if there are others present and participating in the act of killing. One is still located on the battlefield and can hear the gunfire and feel the stress, but the distance between adversaries makes the act of killing both physically and psychologically easier, and thus more morally troubling (Grossman 1995, p. 113).

At long range, at which one must use some sort of mechanical or electrical assistance to view potential victims (i.e., binoculars, cameras or radar), there is evidence to suggest that killing is made even easier. Among those who are least reluctant to kill are pilots, artillery numbers and missile silo attendees. Gwynne Dyer (2010, p. 57) writes that while being observed by their fellows puts pressure on them to kill (as was the case with the gunners in Vietnam), it has much more to do with the distance between them and their targets and how it acts as an emotional and moral buffer. She aptly notes that on the whole, 'gunners fire at grid references they cannot see; submarine crews fire torpedoes at 'ships' (and not, somehow, at the people in the ships); and pilots launch their missiles at 'targets'' (Dywer 2010). Grossman (1995) also reports that in his extensive career researching and reading on the subject of killing in combat, he is not aware of a single instance in which an individual operating at such long range has refused to kill. We also have numerous examples of long distance killing made easy. Dyer (2010) reminds us that in the early nineteen forties, for instance, the British Royal Airforce 'firebombed' Hamburg. Using early bomber aircraft, munitions blew in windows and doors over four square miles and resulted in a firestorm which left seventy thousand people dead, mostly women, children and the elderly (Grossman 1995). A further eighty thousand died in the firebombing of Dresden, two hundred and twenty-five thousand in Tokyo and many millions more in bombing conflicts since (Grossman 1995). If the bomber crews had to kill each of these people with a flamethrower or, as Whetham (2012) writes, slit each of their throats with a knife, the majority would be unable to do it. The awfulness of killing people at such close proximity and the emotional trauma inherent to each act, and to the collective acts, would have been of such magnitude that they simply would not have happened.

As indicated on the chart above, killing conducted with unmanned systems belongs at the very end of the long-range killing spectrum and might even be worthy of its own designation: killing at maximum range. It is reasonable to expect that at this range, killing is made most easy and morally problematic. The contention here is that there is no other tactical weapon on the battlefield today that facilitates killing with such physical and psychological ease and that it becomes a rather clinical and dispassionate matter, easing any of their operators' existing moral qualms. Noel Sharkey (2010) offers support this argument in drawing attention to reports collected by Singer. Amongst a variety of other disturbing statements, he cites one twenty-one year old soldier who talks about his acts of killing with casual indifference: 'the truth is, it wasn't all I thought it was cracked up to be. I mean, I thought killing somebody would be this life-changing experience. And then I did it, and I was like, 'All right, whatever' (Singer 2009, p. 391). Later, he says that 'killing people is like squashing an ant. I mean, you kill somebody and it's like 'allright, let's go get some pizza' (Singer 2009, p. 392). In this clinical killing environment, in which it seems reasonable to propose that some human targets are divested of their humanity, respect for *jus in bello* norms wanes. Some of those videos mentioned in the previous section serve as a demonstration. Many show raw footage of Predator strikes with people being reduced to little more than 'hot spots' or 'blips' on the screen, with operators often failing to take the necessary precautions to ensure noncombatants are protected. Again, it seems that obscuring 'targets' in this way and increasing the distance to the maximum possible, makes it easier for unmanned systems operators to kill in an indiscriminate and disproportionate fashion.

While the distances involved show the powerful role of unmanned systems in overcoming moral-emotional qualms and the socialised inhibition to killing, there are a range of other mechanisms that further this and make it even easier for systems operators to kill without regard for the consequences of their actions or *jus in bello* norms. The first additional mechanism that Grossman (1995, p. 161) explicitly notes – and the one that is most relevant to America's use of unmanned platforms, but will only mention briefly here – is cultural difference, which perpetuates racial and ethnic differences and allows warfighters to fur-

ther dehumanise the enemy. Military forces have long been trying to get their troops to think of the enemy/ies as 'inferior forms of life…as less than human' (Watson 1978, p. 250). Put simply, the further one is technologically distanced from the enemy, the easier it is to think that they are distinctly different to you in some way and the easier it is to kill them. Unmanned systems separate soldiers from the cultural environment that they would operate in if they were in the field and, in that sense, permit them to racially demonise and 'other' the enemy. Connected to cultural distance is moral distance, which involves legitimising oneself and one's cause (Grossman 1995, p. 164). Once it has been determined that the enemy is culturally inferior, it is not difficult for operators of unmanned platforms to incorrectly suppose that their counterparts are either misguided or share their leaders' moral guilt and think that this warrants waging unconstrained violence against those with the supposedly morally inferior cause (Grossman 1995, 164-7).

However, not all are convinced by the argument that unmanned systems present a moral problem in making it easier to indiscriminately and disproportionately kill. Daniel Brunstetter and Megan Braun (2011, p. 339) argue that these systems are subject to the same *jus in bello* requirements as other weapons used in war, but that their technological advantages coupled with the removal of risk to soldiers means that they should, at the least in theory, make satisfying the principles of discrimination and proportionality an easier task and perhaps make operators more reluctant to kill in situations where doubt exists as to the legitimacy of the potential victim of aggression. They say that the in the case of surveillance, at the very least, the distance or what they call 'separation factor', arguably offers an increased level of control over lethal targeting decisions and ought to actually reduce the emotional toll and unnecessary killing (Brunstetter and Braun 2011, p. 339). They regard a drone operator's ability to confer with a superior officer as being a critical factor encouraging ethical decision making in war. In some instances, this may be the case, but in others, it might be that having a mission commander overseeing the operator's actions only places additional pressure on them to fire, just as the sergeants walking the trenches of WWI aimed to encourage reluctant soldiers to kill. Christian Enemark (2013) also questions some of the assumptions relied on here. He says that there is reason to suppose that being physically absent from the battlefield is *more* conducive to discrimination (Enemark 2013). In his view, the removal of risk allows decisions to be made in a more deliberate manner and also removes anger and emotion that he thinks might otherwise lead to morally unsanctioned killings. That is, if a drone operator working from a desk in Nevada encounters the enemy, adherence to *jus in bello* protocol should improve as the operator is at little or no personal risk. It could be suggested, however, that if an operator is so emotionally removed, they are in fact likely to develop the sort disengagement referred to above or an even more morally concerning callousness.

What needs to be recognised is that the disengagement and depersonalisation of war can go so far that operators begin to lose sight of the fact that they are actually involved in real wars. It is becoming increasingly difficult to distinguish whether one is playing a video game or operating a real unmanned system with weapons that will also have very real consequences for those at which they are directed. As Nolen Gertz (2011) notes, while it should be rather clear that video games try to approximate the reality of combat insomuch as it is possible for such a medium to do so – with attempts at this reaching new levels with the designers of video games such as 'Medal of Honor' turning to former members of the military and its special forces for technical guidance – what is probably less well-known is that the military and its weapons designers often also try to approximate the reality of war gaming. Unmanned systems designers are now trying to model the controllers of these platforms to those of video game consoles or, in some cases, actually using the very same controllers, wired especially for use with these systems. Singer (2009) cites a project manager who was responsible for designing an unmanned ground vehicle and said that they modeled the controller after the PlayStation because that's what these 18-, 19-year-old Marines have been playing with pretty much all of their lives. The argument is not just that these systems create a militaristic mentality; that would be too reductive. What is being said is that recruits that are already familiar with the technology have a premediated and probably distorted idea of war. The related moral concern, of course, is that people often do things in video games that they would not do in normal life and that this may somehow carry over to the use of unmanned systems. That is, they may be unable to separate the reality from virtual reality, making them prone to launching the indiscriminate and disproportionate attacks that are characteristic of most violent video games, further supporting the argument that the increasing employment of unmanned systems tracks unethical conduct in war. As argued in the next section, this inability to separate the two worlds may also have deep psychological effects on the operators themselves, only compounding the problem posed by distancing, emotional disengagement and disindividualisation and the effect they have on adherence to *jus in bello* norms.

THE EMOTIONAL WELLBEING OF THE WARFIGHTER

In the previous section, it was argued that unmanned systems and the physical and emotional distances that they create magnify the challenges that warfighters face in applying and adhering to *jus in bello* norms. In this section, there is less focus on the mindset-altering effect or psychological impact that these systems have on the warfighting role of unmanned systems operators and more on the impact to their *personal* wellbeing, given that at both the *jus ad bellum* and *jus in bello* level, the harm incurred to one's own warfighters must be given some weight, even if it is not, or should not, be the overriding priority. Some suggest that killing via proxy does not have a significant adverse psychological or emotional effect on the distance warfighter. Lambèr Royakkers (2010), for instance, says that 'creating moral disengagement reduces or even eliminates the stress of cubicle warriors' (p. 291). Grossman (1995) also writes that in his years of reading and research on the subject of killing, he has never come across a single instance of psychiatric or psychological trauma associated with such long-range killing. Sharkey (2010, p. 372) gives further anecdotal evidence supporting these claims in citing the commander of 432nd Wing at Creech Air Force Base, who said that 'on only four or five occasions had sensor operators gone to see the chaplain or their supervisors and that this was a very small proportion of the total number of remote operators'. The reasoning here seems to follow from an idea examined in a study conducted by Michael Osofsky, Albert Bandura and Philip Zimbardo (2005), which hypothesised that the selective disengagement that similarly distancing systems or processes facilitate, allow them to perform their role and go about killing people and conducting themselves in an injurious fashion while maintaining their emotional wellbeing. However, Sparrow (2009) expresses the concern that while distancing unmanned systems operators from the risk of death and allowing them to become disengaged might be thought to reduce stress, killing by the push of a button can still be a stressful job and might actually expose operators to new, somewhat different or unexpected stressors. In this section, the argument is that something is missing from previous evaluations of what unmanned systems can reasonably achieve and that it is particularly important to understand these psychological stressors because

they will also influence moral decision-making in war and guide public opinion as to whether unmanned warfare really is an improvement over earlier forms, which links to the discussion in the first section of this chapter.

Before delving deeper into the psychological issues that affect unmanned systems operators, we must comment more generally on the burden of killing as it affects conventional warfighters in regular close and midrange warfare. As has already been mentioned, the resistance to killing at these distances can often be so extreme that it overcomes one's own innate self-preservation mechanism and the coercive force exerted by sergeants and platoon commanders in an attempt to encourage killing. Furthermore, it can override the expectations of one's peers and the more general obligation outlined in Chapter 3, that of defending the state and its otherwise vulnerable population. As such, the ordinary warfighter is put in a situation such that they cannot avoid some sort of psychological trauma because of conflicting feelings, stresses and moral obligations that are reinforced by society and a range of regulations and procedures that govern wartime conduct. It has been claimed that if the conventional soldier can overcome the socialised resistance to harm and kill individuals in close or midrange combat, he will forever be burdened by guilt. As an example, William Manchester (1979), novelist and United States Marine veteran of WWII, describes his feelings after killing a sniper in a fishing shack who was, one by one, picking off the Marines in his company: 'I shot him with a 45 and I felt remorse and shame. I can remember whispering foolishly, 'I'm sorry' and then just throwing up... I threw up all over myself. It was a betrayal of what I'd been taught since a child' (pp. 3-6). If for some reason the soldier does not kill, he has also failed to fulfil his duty to his comrades. John Early, a former mercenary and Vietnam veteran, explains that 'you're depending on him [the man next to you] for the most important thing you have, your life, and if he lets you down you're either maimed or killed. If you make a mistake, the same thing happens to him, so the bond of trust goes extremely close' (Dywer 2010, p. 34). Furthermore, the reluctant soldier is subject to the shame that comes with failing his profession, fellow citizens and state. In Grossman's (1995) words, the soldier is 'damned if he does, and damned if he doesn't' (p. 87).

For conventional soldiers, it becomes a matter of balancing the obligation to kill that is generated by the society that one serves and the comrades that one serves alongside, with the toll of guilt that inevitably follows killing in war. From their comments above, Royakkers and others seem to imply that due to the moral and emotional buffers introduced by unmanned systems, this balancing act is made significantly easier for the soldiers-turned-unmanned systems operators. If we follow Grossman's line of thought, we may even conclude that this balancing act is totally insignificant or not even a factor for these distance warriors. To make a comparison to combat at close or mid-range, it might be said that the psychological stress profile of a drone operator is much more similar to that of a higher commander, who may have some operational function, but is much more strategically focused. Unlike the average soldier, but quite like an unmanned systems operator, high level military decision makers generally do not face the same sort of risk that burdens those troops that are physically present at the frontline (Evans & Ryan 2000). Most of the time, they can go to sleep at night knowing that they are very unlikely to be bombed or mortared during their sleep; they do not have to worry that field communication lines might be cut or that resupply might not happen; and they generally are not faced with the task of retrieving the dog tags of those who have been killed in action beside them, or writing personal letters home to their loved ones (Evans & Ryan 2000).

While this may well be true, both of higher commanders and unmanned systems operators, the more relevant similarity is arguably that they both face a range of other psychological stresses that, while qualitatively different, seem to equal or surmount those faced by conventional combatants and combatant commanders. For instance, higher commanders may not have to worry about being killed by the enemy, but they too have to be concerned about the enemy's movements and how they impact operations. They may not be worried about impediments to their own progress or dangers to their own life, but they are likely to be worried about ensuring that their troops have sufficient resources to conduct their campaign, their commanders' ability to conduct operations and the views of the public and the media (Evans & Ryan 2000). Likewise, unmanned systems operators face their own unique problems. While some remote operators may be spared from the raw first-hand experience of seeing people die on the battlefield, in many ways, they may actually see more of war and its deadly outcomes than any typical soldier engaged in close or midrange warfare. There are two key reasons for this, one more convincing than the other. Firstly, while it has been argued that most of today's unmanned systems reduce targets to a 'blip' on the screen, many say that some systems have such high-resolution optics that operators can see the impact of their actions with greater clarity than most conventional airforce pilots (Kaurin 2013). Again, there is doubt about this because of the physical limitations with which optical technologies must operate, but technological developments may make this more of a concern as time passes. However, unmanned systems do improve loiter capability over conventional manned systems, meaning that an operator may observe a target for twelve or more hours before taking lethal action (Singer 2009). Thus, even if the raw footage is not particularly clear and the operator is somewhat disengaged, this extended surveillance period in which many disturbing events may unfold, has potential to be psychologically damaging, if not at the time of operation, at a later stage when the operator has had time to come to a realisation concerning what has happened and what role they have played. This is the first sort of morally relevant stress we need to be concerned about: that of witnessing traumatic events.

Another associated stress rarely mentioned in the academic literature is that related to limited participation in these events. Like a higher commander who has to exert influence on the ground via troops that he is not directly in control of, with only that information conveyed by field-based combatant commanders, a drone operator has to contend with having limited capacity to intervene or influence events that are unfolding in the combat zone. Sparrow (2009) recognises that this general concern is more significant than it perhaps seems because despite the 'hype' surrounding them, many unmanned systems are limited in the information they can relay, the force they can actually exert and the range of actions that they make possible. As mentioned in the previous chapter, it is not always the limitations of the systems themselves, but often the capacity of these systems to be utilised within particular environmental surroundings that limits adherence to just war theory and creates the psychological problem. In his first-hand account of piloting drones, Martin (with Sasser, 2010) details the anguish he experienced resulting from being unable to shape or rectify some injustices he witnessed on the battlefield. He describes how he had carefully planned to kill a group of enemy combatants and recounts the feelings he experienced when two children walked into the attack path post-missile release: 'there was nothing I could do to save them...we could only stare in abject horror as the silent missile bore down upon them' (Martin & Sasser, p. 21). The feeling of helplessness and shame that Martin tells of is compounded when it is the enemy waging the violence and one's own comrades that stand to be injured or killed. In much the same way as a missile release gone badly, an unmanned system may limit the distance warrior's moral agency in the sense of limiting their capacity to act in reference to right and wrong. In a combat scenario, this means they cannot aid fellow warfighters in the way that they could if they were physically present on the battlefield. Benjamin cites a young sensor operator who said, having witnessed the death of troops from afar, that 'it was a traumatic experience. It shocked me' (Benjamin 2012, p. 97). This experience of sitting in a peaceful country in relative safety and taking indirect action, while seeing fellow military personnel die, is one that is unique to unmanned systems operators and one that operators need time to process and understand.

Unfortunately, this time for processing potentially traumatic experiences, or lack thereof, is another problem with consequences for ethical conduct in warfare. Unmanned systems operators are under increasing operational pressure driven by cost cutting and unrealistic expectations. A recent US Air Force study revealed that one of the biggest residual sources of stress for drone operators were the long hours and frequent shift changes that occurred due to staff shortages (Chappelle, McDonald & MacMilan 2011). These staff shortages perhaps offer further anecdotal evidence confirming the concern about the stress to which these operators are exposed. Often-intense working hours and constant shift changes deny an operator time to critically reflect on their actions and prevents them from fully integrating into ordinary civilian life once they leave the base. Unmanned systems have fundamentally changed what the experience of 'going to war' is like. As Singer (2009) writes, it has given war a whole new meaning. For the last five-thousand years, when we described somebody as going to war in defence of the state – whether it be the ancient Greeks going to war against Troy or coalition forces fighting against the Iraqis in the Gulf War

– we talked about them physically going to the battlefield, putting themselves in danger, knowing that they may never come home or see their family again (Singer 2009). That is what 'going to war' has invovled for the last five millennia, but the experience of war has changed.

One US Air Force Pilot that Singer interviewed for his book describes how he would wake up in the morning, drive to the base and then spend twelve hours putting 'missiles on targets' (note the dehumanising language) before driving home again. Twenty minutes after he had been at war, 'he would be at the dinner table talking to his kids about their school work' (Singer 2009, p. 80). However, this does not mean that modern unmanned warfighters are at less psychological risk than those physically present in the battlespace. This new experience of being at war – of being simultaneously at home and at war and having to balance the two – is itself a major source of stress that distance warfighters encounter every working day. As we are only in the early stages of understanding this problem, few studies detail the psychological effects of this juxtaposition between being at peace and being at war, but Martin & Sasser (2012) hint at the significance of this problem in a powerful example given on the final page of his book. Having just killed a number of enemy combatants and destroying the building they were housed in, he recalls how on the way home to see his wife he pulled his 'car into an In-and-Out Burger, changed out of uniform, and grabbed a burger and fries. Only after I was standing in line…did I have time to reflect on what had just happened, how unreal this war truly was' (Martin & Sasser 2012, p. 306). This and the mounting civilian death toll seems to highlight that while there may be much that we do not know, the human warfighter may not yet be capable of effectively handling the dual experience of killing people at war and being at home, coping with the domestic demands of children, partners and society. Going home after a day of combat

does not necessarily afford an operator time for reflection, for few will go home and talk over the dinner table about the combatantsor noncombatants that they have killed that day. Instead, they keep it to themselves and must then find some way of dealing with the constant disjunct between military and civilian life.

In many cases, it may prove morally preferable to expose operators to these unique stresses rather than those they would experience if they were in the field themselves (Sparrow 2009). However, others seem to view it is as another eliminable problem concerning distance and that just as we have removed the warfighter from the battlefront, we should now remove the warfighter from the homefront (Gertz 2011). Subscribing to this sort of thinking, one military commentator has put forward measures that he thinks will maximise efficiency while alleviating the military-civilian disjunct (Singer 2009). These include establishing a 'communications bubble' that would see all personal phone calls to and from the control room banned and keeping units sequestered at a hotel or at barracks on a base before and after any large operation, keeping them isolated from their families and civilian lives in the hope of eliminating the accompanying troubles (Singer 2009). This may seem good operational thinking but, if anything, it merely postpones the eventual meeting of the two opposing worlds (civilians and military) and may introduce further problems affecting ethical decision making if operators come to feel unnecessarily forced apart from their families and civilian lives. The attention is best focused elsewhere. It should be realised, for instance, that distance warfighters do not benefit from the same sense of camaraderie that conventional warfighters do (Singer 2010). A squadron of drone operators is rarely together and never has the time to invest in the shared experience of the group or simply rest and recover. It may prove better to treat the stress as more of a manageable than eliminable problem, perhaps building comraderie or otherwise offering services that assist with management of the psychological stressors that come with unmanned warfare, improving operators' sense of wellbeing and ethical conduct in warfare.

Having this sort of support mechanism in place is particularly important in unmanned warfare as the proportion of inexperienced to experienced personnel is much greater than in conventional warfare and the former may not be able to cope with the emotional demands of unmanned warfighting on their own. Drone operators may be attracted to rendering military service in this form because they are familiar with the controls and the gaming experience that it replicates or simply because it seems less risky and allows them to maintain a connection with loved ones that they are reluctant to leave behind. However, many presumably do so not recognising that by fighting from the homefront, they actually cut themselves off from the support and comradeship that one finds in a typical ground unit. The perception of the distance warrior is another factor that must be taken into account, for this has bearing on the level of support that one receives from both within the military and the public. The image of the 'top gun' combat pilot has been portrayed in novels and films and it is this image that likely resonates with the military leadership and the public. Unmanned systems operators do not seem to receive the same level of gratitude for rendering public service as conventional pilots do. They do not get the welcoming home parades or the medals. The American Distinguished Flying Cross, for instance, has never been awarded to an unmanned aircraft pilot and many think this for good cause (Fitzsimmonds & Mahnken 2007). For this reason, it seems important for distance warfighters to initially establish support groups amongst themselves, particularly because our current understanding of the psychological attributes considered critical to performing well in unmanned warfare and coping with the results is at such an early stage.

All of the aspects of combat stress and trauma discussed here have the potential to profoundly impact not only the wellbeing of the warfighter, but the individual's contribution to the war effort and the aggregate contribution of arrangements of individuals that we call squadrons and military units. If we begin to understand the range of responses of unmanned systems operators, we can begin to understand how mediating warfighting technologies such as drones influence ethical conduct in warfare and then seek to make the necessary changes. As already mentioned, we do not yet have the psychological profiles that are necessary to select the most psychologically well-suited candidates for unmanned warfare and, even then, there is no guarantee that this will lead to more discriminate and proportional warfare. We also have a situation whereby political and military leaders may utilise unmanned to alter the public mindset regarding engagement in war and lower barriers to killing. For these reasons, many have suggested that we focus on technical solutions to what is a technologically mediated but largely human problem and we briefly detail some of these proposed solutions.

FUTURE TRENDS AND TECHNOLOGICAL SOLUTIONS

In the previous sections it was said that in practice, human warfighters often fail to discriminate between legitimate and illegitimate targets for at least two reasons. First, killing at maximum range temporarily reduces the humanity of one's enemy and detaches the distance warfighter from the consequences of the use of their weaponry. Second, this often results in traumatising emotional and psychological consequences for those warfighters when they eventually come to grasp their actions, which may then perpetuate further unethical conduct in wartime. Unfortunately, when it comes to trends in adherence to legal and ethical norms, the human record in adhering to the dictates of *jus in bello* principles is questionable, at best. In fact, Ronald Arkin dedicates an entire chapter in his book *Governing Lethal Behavior in Autonomous Robots* (2009) to human failings on the battlefield. He cites the US Surgeon General's report into battlefield ethics and the mental health of soldiers deployed in Operation Iraqi Freedom, which details some concerning findings. Among them were claims that: approximately ten percent of soldiers reported mistreating noncombatants; less than fifty percent agreed that noncombatants should be treated with dignity and respect; roughly fifteen percent agreed that all noncombatants should be treated as insurgents; and close to thirty percent reported facing ethical situations in which they did not know how to respond (Office of the Surgeon General 2006). Arkin (2009) suggests that with the increasing use of technology like semi-autonomous drones, the figures noted in these reports will become even more concerning and that atrocities in war will also become increasingly worse. His primary conclusion is that we cannot expect human warfighters, because of their fallible nature, to adhere to wartime standards when confronted by the horrors of the battlefield and that we ought to develop technology that extends beyond the limits of human warfighters (Arkin 2009).

In other words, his solution is not to take the moderate step of tailoring the weapons control interface to encourage ethical decision making in war, but rather to eliminate the importance of the human and human-machine interface altogether and look at how one might actually provide unmanned systems with the capacity to make ethical decisions and carryout different kinds of actions, some of them lethal. He is deeply convinced of the possibility of ethical programming that would not only meet the normative requirements of international humanitarian law and just war theory, but would ultimately surpass their requirements, writing that: 'I am convinced that they [unmanned systems] can perform more ethically than human

soldiers are capable of' (Arkin 2009, p. 36). Arkin (2009) proposes that we equip unmanned systems with an 'ethical governor', which is based on Watt's mechanical governor for the steam engine. This governor acts as a transformer or suppressor of automatically generated lethal action, so in much the same way that the mechanical governor would shut down a steam engine running too hot, the ethical governor shuts down the autonomous machine when it is about to do something unethical, such as firing too closely to civilians. But this is just one component. The second is the 'ethical behavioral control' unit, which monitors all of the systems behaviours and ensures that they evolve from within set constraints (Arkin 2009). The third is the 'ethical adaptor'. It allows the system to learn, adapt and overcome by updating the system's set of constraints (Arkin 2009). It is presumably intended to act in place of human guilt or remorse in the case of unethical conduct managing to pass the previous two components. The final component is the responsibility advisor, which ensures that in the event of a lethal action occurring, responsibility can be clearly allocated between human and machine, in the case of joint interaction (Arkin 2009).

Arkin believes that with these sub-systems working effectively together, autonomous machines would possess the capability to operate morally, ensuring that any force is delivered proportionally and with maximum discrimination between combatant and noncombatant targets. However, he does not seem to recognise that there is a difference between a machines that act in accordance with the dictates of morality and what Wendell Wallach and Colin Allen call a 'moral machine' (Wallach and Allen 2009). That is, he fails to recognise that there is a distinct difference between following rules or laws and actually being moral, in the full and proper sense of the word. While the technical acts of discriminating between targets and determining proportionality may be a necessary condition for moral conduct in war, they are not, alone, sufficient. For instance,

Andreas Matthias (2011) has said that Arkin seems to view discrimination as a mere matter of technical classification between friend and foe and between legitimate and illegitimate targets of potentially lethal military action. He reduces discrimination down to a cognitive level operation that the machine mimics. It identifies all those targets within its specified radius of operation and sorts them into various categories, combatants and noncombatants, children, wounded persons and so on. While this is an important capacity for any moral agent in war, Arkin's system does not actually establish these categories, it presupposes them. 'Individual X standing beside weapon Y is Z' (an instance of discrimination), is a straightforward classification result and there is no sort of moral deliberation involved. To ask whether it is morally right for the machine to kill Individual X standing next to Weapon Y, on the other hand, involves genuine moral evaluation. For this very reason, if no other, it seems that Arkin is incorrect in saying that his proposed system can outperform human warfighters.

Part of the problem is that Arkin takes the laws of armed conflict, rules of engagement and just war theory to be mutually compatible and translatable into a set of rules that are also compatible with his control architecture and programming language. When the principles of just war theory are viewed in this way, it is easy to mistakenly think that what is left is a technical matter of ensuring that the machinery is capable of correctly and reliably carrying them out. In reality, while many military and political leaders also portray these sources of restraint as if they were a clear and steadfast set of rules amenable to automation, each is actually a set of highly context-dependent guidelines. The law of armed conflict is, in Asaro's (2009, p. 21) words, a 'menagerie of international laws, agreements and treaties' that are open to considerable interpretation. Rules of engagement, which are devised to instruct warfighters how to act in specific situations, can also be rather vague as they are an attempt to combine legal, political

and strategic concerns on one small card and leave much up to the individual soldier. Likewise, just war theory is often presented as though it is an entirely coherent theory, when in most formulations it is necessarily, and by its very nature, a set of principles that, while setting certain values and rules of thumb, require a great deal of moral deliberation to be put to effective use. Take the *jus in bello* proportionality principle, for instance. There are a host of difficulties in operationalising this principle and in carrying out the necessary calculations in the field. As Lucas (2011) says, we do not have anything like a 'formal proportionality algorithm' and it requires weighing and comparing incommensurable goods under conditions of extreme epistemic uncertainty. How many men, women and children, for example, is it permissible to kill for a given military objective? Questions like these require a kind of moral evaluation of which Arkin's system is incapable. He might advance the more limited claim that his autonomous drones might outperform humans in classificatory tasks, but he wants to make the stronger claim that his proposed system will perform more ethically than humans.

Even if we put aside the fact that he glosses over the difference between representing morality and acting morally, both Lucas (2011) and Sparrow (2011) highlight that there is an additional conceptual problem associated with saying that an autonomous unmanned system might perform better than a human warfighter. As has already been said, one ought to be willing to concede that Arkin's proposed system might function better in classificatory tasks and thus might perform better under certain limited wartime conditions. We might discover through an empirical study, for example, that the failure rate of human warfighters confronting some specific sort of decision making scenario is ten percent or, alternatively, that they comply with the necessary legal and moral restraints ninety percent of the time. In this instance, it means that the human warfighters are fallible. Suppose that we can reliably track compliance with the relevant rules and principles. Arkin simply demands that his system perform as well or better than this ninety percent benchmark set by the human warfighter. When we send a human warfighter into battle, we expect one hundred percent compliance with the laws of war and just war theory, even though we know all to well that for those reasons stated earlier, soldiers are often statistically unlikely to meet these standards. But when human warfighters fail to do so, they are held accountable and punished. The problem with Arkin's argument is that he is effectively lowering the moral benchmark for conduct in war, which may result in further breaches of the law of armed conflict and the proportionality and discrimination principles. If we know in advance that in a particular scenario, Arkin's system will perform with less than one hundred percent compliance with the relevant laws and moral principles, it would be unethical to have it operate.

The solution may be to go beyond the sort of robotic architecture that Arkin proposes and develop systems that truly have full autonomy or what others call 'strong artificial intelligence'. That is, it might be morally preferable to develop a system that would, unlike Arkin's system that calls on a human to make certain decisions when it cannot, can create and complete its own tasks without the need for any human input, with the exception of the decision to build such a system (the human is so far removed from the loop that the level of direct influence on this sort of system is totally negligible). Such a system would display capacities that imitate or truly replicate the moral capacities of sentient human warfighters and would therefore be able to engage in the sort of moral deliberation that the laws of war and just war theory demand. There is considerable disagreement in the disciplines of artificial intelligence and philosophy as to when we can reasonably expect machines to become as capable as human warfighters on the battlefield or whether this 'strong artificial intelligence' or above human intelligence is at all possible. In 1965, Gordon

Moore, Chairman Emeritus of Intel Corporation, described 'Moore's law', which predicted the doubling of transistors on silicon chips with each new generation leading to rapid acceleration in the power of computer, and it has held true to date (Moore 1965). With this in mind, futurist Ray Kurzweil (2005) has prophesised that we will reach the 'technological singularity' – the point at which machine intelligence will surpass human intelligence – by 2045. Some are more reserved and say that while computers may exceed human intelligence in a few rather narrow domains, they will be never be as universally intelligent as is necessary for moral conduct in war. At the other end of the scale, there are those who hold no hope. Joseph Weizenbaum (1977) has famously stated that 'no other organism, and certainly no computer, can be made to confront human problems in human terms' (p. 233). The philosopher John Searle (1980) has also argued that a computer may be able to solve a complex problem, such as those in war, but without having any actual understanding of it.

Despite the fact that Weizenbaum and Searle seem to dismiss the idea of fully autonomous unmanned systems as the stuff of science fiction, it is wise to briefly consider whether they could even be a solution to immoral conduct both in resorting to war and conducting war these technological possibilities since a great deal of money is being invested toward the goal of creating them and it seems impossible to rule out their invention at this early stage. To be sure, the potential problems are many. One of the immediate concerns that surfaces about waging warfare with artificial moral agents is that they may eventually turn on human beings. Again, this might sound fantastical or highly unrealistic, but if we want to endow our unmanned systems with full moral agency (this cannot be assumed), this will involve giving them the capacity to contemplate both moral and immoral actions and it is a matter of conjecture as to what sorts of decisions autonomous military systems would make. A robot warfighter may not be motivated by sexual desire, power or dominance as human warfighters are, and may not have the same natural killer instinct, but they too may come to develop what some might claim are needs and aspirations that they will need to compete for with other agents for (Sullins 2010). There is no guarantee that these systems will not evolve into the functional equivalent of today's unethical warfighters. What is more worrying is that these systems and the moral decisions they make may become so complex that humans are incapable of understanding them. Imagine that these systems eventually become so powerful that we come to cede power to one super system and entrust it to make *jus ad bellum* decisions in lieu of human political and military leaders, a possibility taken seriously by many technological optimists given that the latter often deceive the public. The variables it would take into consideration might be so many that no human could understand whether a particular war was just or unjust. Strawser (2011) argues that with machines filling the decision-making niche that humans once did, it could eventually get to a point where there is no point to humans making personal choices at all, a situation whereby they are better off surrendering their moral agency altogether. Both war and human life could be made meaningless. Of course, while this is logically conceivable, it does not mean it is worthy of any closer examiniation. What we do need to consider is whether might be some sort of more moderate technological solution, for those above do not overcome the emotional and mind-set altering effect that is linked to unethical conduct in unmanned warfare. That is, the solution to this technologically induced human problem is not necessarily to introduce more technology. It may be that we need to find an appropriate trade-eoff between military effectiveness and harm to warfighters and human beings in general.

CONCLUSION

What has been shown in this chapter is that alongside the more technical issues that plague unmanned systems, there is a mindset-altering effect that impacts the ethical compass of our principal war-making agents. In the first section, it was demonstrated that we must be concerned with how technologically mediated fighting lowers barriers to conduct in war. It started by outlining the various killing ranges and located unmanned systems at 'maximum range', where killing is facilitated by physical and emotional distances that dehumanise and deindividualise the enemy, and concluded that this, coupled with the virtual nature of unmanned warfare, makes it significantly easier for soldiers to kill without proper respect for the *jus in bello* principles of discrimination and proportionality. In the second section, it was argued that despite some arguments to the contrary, the constant disjuncture between being at war and being at peace, and having few psychological stress management tools, further magnifies the challenges of adhering to *jus in bello* norms. Finally, it examined some technological solutions to this largely human problem and argued that we really need humans to make some wartime decisions and that we must combine our best efforts in designing weapons control interfaces and judiciously introduce autonomy to ensure support for the aims of just war theory does not wane.

ACKNOWLEDGMENT

This research has been conducted with funding support provided by the Commonwealth of Australia via Macquarie University and is derived from Galliott (forthcoming), but does not in any way represent the views of the Government or Macquarie University.

REFERENCES

Arkin, R. (2009). *Governing lethal behavior in autonomous robots*. Boca Raton: CRC Press. doi:10.1201/9781420085952

Asaro, P. M. (2009). Modeling the moral user. *IEEE Technology and Society*, 28(1), 20–24. doi:10.1109/MTS.2009.931863

Benjamin, M. (2012). *Drone warfare: Killing by remote control*. New York: OR Books.

Brunstetter, D., & Braun, M. (2011). The implications of drones on the just war tradition. *Ethics & International Affairs*, 25(3), 337–358. doi:10.1017/S0892679411000281

Chappelle, W., McDonald, K., & McMillan, K. (2011). *Important and critical psychological attributes of USAF MQ-1 predator and MQ-9 reaper pilots according to subject matter experts*. Ohio: School of Aerospace Medicine.

Dyer, G. (2010). *War: The new edition*. New York: Random House.

Fitzsimonds, J. R., & Mahnken, T. G. (2007). Military officer attitudes toward UAV adoption: Exploring institutional expediments to innovation. *Joint Forces Quarterly*, 46(3), 96–103.

Galliott, J. C. (Forthcoming). *Military robots: Mapping the moral landscape*. Farnham: Ashgate.

Gertz, N. (2011). *Technology and suffering in war*. Paper presented at Technology and Security, University of North Texas.

Gray, G. J. (1959). *The warriors: Reflections on men in battle*. New York: Harper & Row.

Grossman, D. (1995). *On killing: The psychological cost of learning to kill in war and society*. Boston: Little, Brown and Company.

Kaurin, P. (2013). Courage behind a screen. In B. J. Strawser (Ed.), Killing by remote control: The Ethics of an unmanned military. New York: Oxford University Press.

Keegan, J., & Holmes, R. (1986). *Soldiers: A history of men in battle*. New York: Viking.

Kurzweil, R. (2005). *The singularity is near: When humans transcend biology*. New York: Viking Penguin.

Lucas, G. Jr. (2011). Industrial challenges of military robotics. *Journal of Military Ethics*, 10(4), 274–295. doi:10.1080/15027570.2011.639164

Manchester, W. (1979). *Goodbye darkness: A memoir of the pacific war*. New York: Dell Publishing Company.

Marshall, S. L. A. (2000). *Men against fire: The problem of battle command*. Norman: University of Oklahoma Press.

Martin, M. J., & Sasser, C. W. (2010). *Predator: The remote-control air war over Iraq and Afghanistan: A pilot's story*. Minneapolis: Zenith Press.

Matthias, A. (2011). *Is the concept of an ethical governor philosophically sound?* Paper presented at the Tilting Perspectives: Technologies on the Stand: Legal and Ethical Questions in Neuroscience and Robotics, The Netherlands.

Meadors, T. (2011). *Virtual jus in bello: Teaching just war with video games*. Paper presented at the The Ethics of Emerging Military Technologies, University of San Diego.

Meagher, R. E. (2006). *Herakles gone mad: Rethinking heroism in an age of endless war*. Northampton: Olive Branch Press.

Moore, G. E. (1965). Cramming more components onto integrated circuits. *Electronics*, 38(8), 114–117.

Office of the Surgeon General. (2006). Mental health advisory team (MHAT) IV Operation Iraqi Freedom 05-07, Final Report. Washington, DC: United States Department of the Army.

Osofsky, M. J., Bandura, A., & Zimbardo, P. G. (2005). The role of moral disengagement in the execution process. *Law and Human Behavior*, *29*(4), 371–393. doi:10.1007/s10979-005-4930-1 PMID:16133946

Royakkers, L., & van Est, R. (2010). The cubicle warrior: The marionette of digitalized warfare. *Ethics and Information Technology*, *12*(3), 289–296. doi:10.1007/s10676-010-9240-8

Searle, J. (1980). Minds, brains, and programs. *Behavioral and Brain Sciences*, *3*(3), 417–457. doi:10.1017/S0140525X00005756

Sharkey, N. (2010). Saying 'no!' to lethal autonomous targeting. *Journal of Military Ethics*, *9*(4), 369–383. doi:10.1080/15027570.2010.537903

Singer, P. W. (2009). *Wired for war: The robotics revolution and conflict in the 21st century*. New York: The Penguin Press.

Singer, P. W. (2010). The future of war. In G. Dabringer (Ed.), *Ethical and legal aspects of unmanned systems: Interviews* (pp. 71–84). Vienna: Institute for Religion and Peace.

Sparrow, R. (2009). Building a better warbot: Ethical issues in the design of unmanned systems for military applications. *Science and Engineering Ethics*, *15*(2), 169–187. doi:10.1007/s11948-008-9107-0 PMID:19048395

Sparrow, R. (2011). Robotic weapons and the future of war. In J. Wolfendale & P. Tripodi (Eds.), *New wars and new soldiers* (pp. 117–133). Burlington: Ashgate.

Strawser, B. J. (2011). *Two bad arguments for the justification of autonomous weapons*. Paper presented at Technology and Security, University of North Texas.

Sullins, J. P. (2010). RoboWarfare: Can robots be more ethical than humans on the battlefield? *Ethics and Information Technology*, *12*(3), 263–275. doi:10.1007/s10676-010-9241-7

Wallach, W., & Allen, C. (2009). *Moral machines: Teaching robots right from wrong*. Oxford: Oxford University Press. doi:10.1093/acprof:o so/9780195374049.001.0001

Watson, P. (1978). *War on the mind: The military uses and abuses of psychology*. New York: Basic Books.

Weizenbaum, J. (1977). *Computer power and human reason: From judgement to calculation*. New York: W.H. Freeman & Company.

Whetham, D. (2012). Remote killing and drive-by wars. In D. W. Lovell & I. Primoratz (Eds.), *Protecting civilians during violent conflict: Theoretical and practical issues for the 21st century* (pp. 199–214). Aldershot: Ashgate.

KEY TERMS AND DEFINITIONS

Close Range Killing: Involves any easily attributable kill at 'point-blank' range, whether with one's bare hands, an edged weapon or even a projectile weapon.

Ethical Governor: A transformer or suppressor of automatically generated lethal action of the type wielded by unmanned systems.

Long Range Killing: Involves the use some sort of mechanical or electrical assistance to view potential victims (i.e., binoculars, cameras or radar).

Maximum Range Killing: Involves the remote operation of weaponry and a significant reduction in the number of, or the complete removal of, troops on the ground.

Midrange Killing: Involves being able to see and engage the enemy with hand grenades, sniper rifles and so on, but usually without being able to gauge the extent of the wounds inflicted.

Moral Desensitisation: A phenomenon which can reduce or even eliminate the stress of remote weapons operators by altering their comprehension or processing of sensory inputs.

Unmanned Systems: Electro-mechanical military robots that operate across land, sea and air and remove human war fighters from the battle space.

Chapter 20
The Role of Affective Computing for Improving Situation Awareness in Unmanned Aerial Vehicle Operations:
A US Perspective

Jonathan Bishop
Centre for Research into Online Communities and E-Learning Systems, Belgium

ABSTRACT

Unmanned aerial vehicles (UAVs), commonly known as drones, are a robotic form of military aircraft that are remotely operated by humans. Due to lack of situation awareness, such technology has led to the deaths of civilians through the inaccurate targeting of missile or gun attacks. This chapter presents the case for how a patented invention can be used to reduce civilian casualties through attaching an affect recognition sensor to a UAV that uses a database of strategies, tactics and commands to better instruct fighter pilots on how to respond while in combat so as to avoid misinterpreting civilians as combatants. The chapter discusses how this system, called VoisJet, can reduce many of the difficulties that come about for UAV pilots, including reducing cognitive load and opportunity for missing data. The chapter concludes that using UAVs fitted with VoisJet could allow for the reduction of the size of standing armies so that defence budgets are not overstretched outside of peacetime.

INTRODUCTION

The use of remote systems like drones, technically known as unmanned aerial vehicles (UAVs), is starting to move out of the first wave of public and media attention, and now needs to shift toward a more cohesive debate with productive and practical ends. Indeed, it has been argued that a problem with the design of existing UAVs driven by policy makers, who are not militarily

DOI: 10.4018/978-1-4666-7278-9.ch020

qualified, has been illustrative of the claim that new technological practices that aim to bridge physical distance provide a more efficient moral distance and make it difficult for people to exercise moral responsibility (Coeckelbergh, 2013). This has been associated with Internet abuse such as trolling, where people will abuse others for their own enjoyment without considering the consequences (Bishop, 2013; Bishop, 2014; Hardaker, 2013; McCosker, 2013), but should be considered a flaw that needs adjusting in current drone systems where the actions of pilots would be dehumanised. The use of UAVs by the US Government provides greater freedom in those military personnel carrying out operations on their behalf, as use of foreign military personnel and the agreement of their government will be less necessary (Byman, 2013). A greater use of UAVs also means that there will be fewer casualties arising out of improvised explosive devices (IEDs) as air-based operations provider greater safety for military personnel in this regard (Reynolds, 2013). The problem however is evident that the way UAVs are currently designed does not allow for the efficiency of operations and the safety of civilians and other non-military targets.

Uses and Limitations of UAVs in Combat Operations

The NATO forces are becoming more dependent on UAVs, and their use has been driven by the US and such policy choices have consequences, regardless of whether their military leaders believe these are right or wrong (Kean et al., 2004, p.376). Any government in the world will want to increase its national security whilst limiting loss of life to those in its military and the civilians in the localities where its military operations are engaged. However, before trying to understand the technology of UAVs and how they can be improved, it is important to understand why there is

a growing need for the US military to be allowed to use UAVs in military engagements in order to safeguard the democratic rights of Americans whom they must protect whoever is in power in the White House.

BACKGROUND

There is one thing more certain than death or taxes and that is that humans will always be in conflict with one another, regardless of which difference or transgression created that conflict. One of the longest lasting wars in history is that which is taking place in the Holy Land between those Jews that identify as Israelis and those Arabs that identify as Palestinians. During the first millennium BCE this part of the world, one might wish to call the Holy Land, was known as Israel in the Hebrew language and as Palestine in Roman Latin (i.e. they were the same place). It was only in the mid-21st century CE that there was a separation of the territories caused by meddling politicians who formed part of the United Nations. The people in the Holy Land around 900 BCE were known as the Israelites, and there were 12 Semitic tribes in total, forming part of a united kingdom. These tribes split around 820 BCE with the enthronement of the son of King Solomon, Rehoboam, who threatened "God's wrath" on the 10 tribes in the North, who have now become the Jewish Semitics (i.e. Jews) and the two tribes in the South whom supported him have now become Arabic Semitics (i.e. Arabs). These two Semitic races have been warring ever since the fall of Rehoboam and international interference has led to some of the greatest atrocities. This includes the massacre of the Jews by King Richard I in York in 1190 CE (Jones, 2000) and the same by the Hitler Government in Germany between 1933 and 1945 CE (Rees, 2005), right up to the bombing of the World Trade Center in

New York. This act of war is according to those in the FBI a direct result of political support for the Netanyahu Government by the politicians in Washington (Drezner, 2011; Kean, Hamilton, & Fitzgerald, 2004; Kean et al., 2004, p.147). The bombing of three of its sister cities (i.e. London, Madrid, Paris), in all cases by Jihads (i.e. radical Arabs), is also believed to be because of the political leadership in the US Government. The Netanyahu Government have a policy of driving out Arabs from the Holy Land with the support of Zionists (i.e. radical Jews), which is something the Jihads take exception to. The Netanyahu Government is not the first to want to drive Arabs from the Holy land to create a single country liked existed around 900 BCE, as significant attempts were made in the early Middle Ages, starting with the People's Crusade of 1096 CE right up until the Ninth Crusade ending in 1172. The Netanyahu Government's plan of mass eradication of Arabs, is to end the historical existence of the Israelites (i.e. Jews, Arabs) to create a single state made up only of so-called Israelis (i.e. Jews), with the eradication of Palestinians (i.e. Arabs). This has meant that the Western world has become less safe in relation to those countries who backed and still support the post-World War II settlement to break up the Holy Land, leaving the military to find affordable solutions to what some see a costly mistake. Indeed, it has been suggested that the US Government reassess its policy in relation to the support of the Netanyahu Government by some of its own security officials (Kean et al., 2004; Kean & Hamilton, 2006). Since the election of Nobel Peace Prize winner Barrack Obama as President in 2008, there has been a shift in the way the US Government is approaching the three millennia long war in the Holy Land (Drezner, 2011). Barrack Obama and his successors, and the US military whom they exercise control over, have a huge mess to clean up from the previous politicians in the US Government. This may come in the form of negotiating a settlement between the Zionist and Jihadist forces that threaten world peace, whether the state-led attacks of the Netanyahu Government in the case of the former, or the gruella-led attacks of Hamas and Al-Qaeda in the case of the latter. Whilst Al-Qaeda could be considered a grave threat to the peace and safety of Western nations, comparable to Japan in the Second World War, in this context one might prefer to compare Hamas to the First and Second Continental Congresses that secured US independence even though they were viewed as terrorists at one point.

The rhetoric of successive US politicians in branding anti-Zionist forces as terrorists – such as for the attacks by Jihads on the World Trade Center – has given the military political clout to enter countries where Jihadist training camps exist to counter the actions of US politicians (Mobley, 2012). These anti-Zionists seek to make further attacks against America and the allies of the US Government, such as NATO countries, because of US politicians, making life difficult for the US military, whom are tasked with protecting America, whomever is in power, and whatever their policies happen to be. The sudden rise of media-savvy Jihads supported by Western citizens, like ISIS (or ISIL, Islamic State, Al-Qaeda in Iraq), may in part be down to the empathy of these Arabs and others to the Palestinians being terrorised in their homeland (i.e. the Holy Land). Since media attention in 2014 turned towards Israeli attacks on Gaza the membership of Jihadist organisations has significantly grown. This has resulted in the State of Israel, which occupies much of the Holy Land, using UAVs in their operations as well as sporadic missile attacks designed to cause maximum destruction. It is unclear whether it is possible to have a time where all Israelites – Arabs, Jews and Gentiles – will be able to share the Holy Land in the same way Europeans move freely in the European Union.

There have been significant demands on Western military forces to take forward ground operations to deal with ISIS in Iraq, but public opinion on the issue is fragile followed the failed 2003 liberation of Iraq. The ground-led operations carried out for successive US presidents by the US military, has led to a huge number of deaths of US and other NATO military personnel, such as through IEDs, as well as civilians in the countries targeted. The innovative use of unmanned aerial vehicles (UAVs) by the military for dog-fighting as well as currently targeted drops appears to be the only effective means to hold back those anti-Zionist forces seeking to attack NATO member states, while the politicians continue to make poor policy decisions that the military, and indeed non-governmental organisations, have been left to pick up the pieces of. The current design of UAVs has led to a number of innocent civilian deaths in countries harbouring Jihadists that are military targets for NATO forces. It is therefore necessary to re-design future UAVs to take account of the need to protect civilian lives. One way to achieve this might be to add affective and augmentive sensors and software to increase the amount of information available to UAV pilots, so as to increase their situation awareness.

AN EVALUATION OF AN INVENTION FOR REDUCING HUMAN CASUALTIES IN UAV-BASED MILITARY ENGAGEMENTS: INTRODUCING VOISJET

It is clear that unmanned aerial vehicles will play an important part in defence and other military operations for the foreseeable future, but their use will have to move away from being given direction by military commanders and for more judgement on the pilots' part to be utilised. The known civilian deaths such as weddings and other social engagements, as well as unknown ones, such as where a missile may have hit the wrong person, means that the technology for assisting pilots in identifying threats and avoiding causalities needs to be improved. This section sets out how a system, known as 'VoisJet,' could be used to assist UAV pilots in correctly targeting enemy personnel, without the need for direction from military commanders.

VoisJet operates by using sensors to capture information, followed by decoding that information into a readable format by its bridge between external inputs and internal processes. The type of

Figure 1. Overview of processes for VoisJet

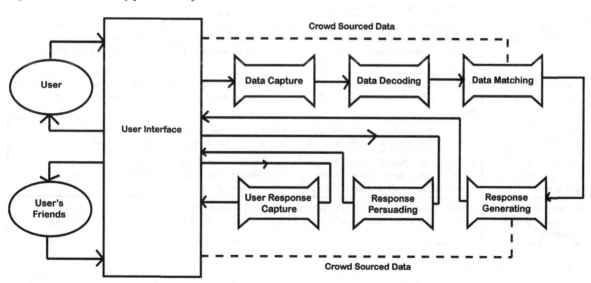

sensors used can be extended and work together to achieve an overall picture of what is going on in the area at which the pilot of a UAV has it targeted at. There will now be discussed some of the existing algorithms that could be fed into VoisJet. Systems which may make useful inputs for VoisJet are Point Clouds, which using open source libraries can filter, estimate features, and remove outliers from distorted capture, which have already been tested to be effective with UAVs (McLeod et al., 2013).

Table 1, which is drawn from Endsley, Bolte, & Jones (2010) shows many of the problems with unmanned vehicles and their aerial versions that can impair situation awareness of the pilots. This next section will be looking at the way VoisJet can improve situation awareness and thus reduce human casualties.

Reducing Poor Sensory Data, Intermittent Data, and Time-Lags in UAVs

A primary challenge in developing effective virtual reality systems is designing the human interface hardware which allows rich sensory information to be presented to users in natural ways (Rosenberg & Stredney, 1996). It has been argued that autonomic systems can provide increased manageability and higher availability by executing in an autonomous execution environment and by having rich sensory information at their disposal (Durham, Milenkovic, & Cayton, 2006). Table 1 shows that rich sensory information (visual, auditory, haptic, etc.) about the in combat operation of a UAV is essential, especially relating to the state of the UAV in the operating environment (Endsley et al., 2010). Many UAV designs result

Table 1. Limitations on situation awareness in current UVs and UAVs

Factor	Description
Poor sensory data, intermittent data, and time-lags	Rich sensory information (visual, auditory, haptic, etc.) about the in combat operation of a UV is essential, especially relating to the state of the UV in the operating environment. Many UVs result in visual or cognitive sub-optimisation, which can be fatal.
Difficulties in UV localisation	Disorientation in UVs is a common problem that seriously affects situation awareness. Being able to have a sense of localisation – where the operator is aware of what is going on in combat – is essential. Lack of situation awareness on the physical orientation and location of the vehicle can cause problems in any task that requires a special understanding of the area.
Demanding tasks in complex environments	UV operations often involve perceptually demanding tasks, especially visually, making it that more demanding. In the case of UAVs operators' visual environment is often impoverished, with object properties (e.g. surface texture and colour) as well as poor spatial and chromatic resolution of the VDU through disrupted temporal and optical flow.
Low-Level data overload and interface design	The interfaces for UVs often only provide low-level data regarding vehicle systems and parameters. Particularly with UAVs, the situation awareness of operators is poor, often because of lack of key information or poor salience.
Multitasking in UV operations	Control over UVs often require multi-tasking and systems to date have been poor at obtaining it. In terms of UAVs this has often been in the form of not being able to target accurately, leading to crashes.
Lack of support for multi-person operations	UVs and in particular UAVs may be operated based on the needs of other team members who may possess critical information on the mission context, which can add additional task loading. This includes communications with commanders at observing those on the ground.
Increased autonomy for unmanned vehicle operations	Where autonomy is added to a UV problems in acquisition and maintenance of situation awareness are multiplied when the human must "operate, monitor and supervise" those UV systems under their control.

in visual or cognitive sub-optimisation, which can be fatal (Endsley et al., 2010). Research has established that speech input is significantly better than manual input in terms of task completion time, task accuracy, flight/navigation measures, and pilot ratings in terms of UAVs (Draper, Calhoun, Ruff, Williamson, & Barry, 2003). UAVs can provide regular yet intermittent data transmission which is essential for the success of defence operations (Yang, Chen, Ammar, & Lee, 2005). VoisJet thus has an important role in reducing poor sensory data, intermittent data and time-lags. As an advice-giving agent it can process all the sensory information that the pilot is normally burdened with and also that which is absent, meaning they can make decisions based on their experience, rather than have to make do with incomplete information. The problems with time-lag, where the information collected by the UAV and presented to the operator can be removed by VoisJet through the processing being done machine-side and not by the pilot. This would enable the operator to make quicker decisions with less risk of incomplete information. One might there want to think of VoisJet like a Cloud application. The data processing is done server-side (on the UAV) and the decision-making is done client-side (by the pilot/operator).

Resolving Difficulties in UAV Localisation

Manned aerial operations are complex on their own, but in such situations fighter pilots have an awareness of the situation making it easy for judgements to be made that take account of the immediate circumstances. Traditional UAV operations can be as limiting to a fighter pilot as a PC is to a novice user, who relies on a third-party to convey information for them to be situation aware. The aim therefore should be for UAVs to provide instant access to the information a fighter pilot needs to perform the mission being asked of them. Indeed, whenever a task necessitates both local

spatial task performance and knowledge of the global environment simultaneously, the operator at present is often forced to trade off performance in one task to maintain performance in the other task, which can result in poor performance in both local and global tasks and disorientation (Yee, 2013). As can be seen in Table 1, disorientation in UAVs is a common problem that seriously affects situation awareness of operators. Being able to have a sense of localisation – where the operator is aware of what is going on in combat – is thus essential (Endsley et al., 2010). Lack of situation awareness on the physical orientation and location of the vehicle can cause problems in any task that requires a special understanding of the area (Endsley et al., 2010). Even in non-military operations it is clear that the greatest improvements in situation awareness could be achieved by adding a localisation device to the UAV (Chisholm, Cui, Lum, & Chen, 2013). Through VoisJet it will be possible for the terrain to be evaluated for threats or to ensure civilian life is not lost by mistake. For instance, reports of wedding parties being interrupted by UAV strikes firing in error can be avoided, as the situation awareness algorithms in VoisJet can let the pilot know whether someone is likely to be a civilian or combatant and the best course of action to take – such as in a hostage situation.

Improving Management of Demanding Tasks in Complex Environments

Unmanned Aerial Vehicles (UAVs) are developed to perform more demanding tasks in civic and military applications such as geological surveys, aerial photography for mapping, security and environmental monitoring (Ando, Oguchi, & Yamada, 2013). As can be seen from Table 1, UAV operations often involve perceptually demanding tasks, especially visually, making it that more demanding (Endsley et al., 2010). In the case of UAV operators, their visual environment is often impoverished, with object properties (e.g. surface texture and colour) as well as poor spatial and chromatic resolution of the VDU through disrupted temporal and optical flow (Endsley et al., 2010). With VoisJet, as fighter pilots would not need to make judgements on what something is, and would be given options about what courses of action they can take, then it could play greater emphasis on their judgement in terms of knowing what to do, as opposed to working out what is going on in such a way they lack the time to make good judgements.

Improving Low-Level Data Overload and Interface Design in UAVs

Table 1 shows that some of the interfaces for UVAs only provide low-level data regarding vehicle systems and parameters and the situation awareness of operators is often poor because of lack of key information or poor salience (Endsley et al., 2010). Low-level data for critical decision-making that is not readily available is necessary in UAVs, yet there are often demands for a single data stream that combines drone video feeds, cell phone intercepts, and targeting radar in UAVs (Gomez & Chimento, 2011). With VoisJet the most pertinent information would be available to the operator so that they have the appropriate number of options for the appropriate operating context they are in. The advancement in multi-touch technology might make it easier for pilots to access relevant information between various screens, as effortlessly as one might switch from one smartphone application to another.

Multitasking in UAV Operations

Control over UAVs often requires multi-tasking as Table 1 shows, yet to date systems have been poor at obtaining it and this often results in pilots not being able to target accurately, leading to crashes (Endsley et al., 2010). With VoisJet being based on a multi-agent system, of which one embodiment

can cope with over 250,000 action states, means the need for multi-tasking at a decision-making level could be reduced, leaving pilots to focus on operating the UAV based on their tacit experience and knowledge. As VoisJet is based around providing information and suggestions by computing several different inputs simultaneously, then it might mean that operation-specific interfaces could be designed to display that information depending on the specific goals of the pilot and the mission, of which the strategies could be varied by moving from one screen to another.

Overcoming Lack of Support for Multi-Person Operations in UAVs

As Table 1 makes evident, UAVs may be operated based on the needs of other team members who may possess critical information on the mission context, which can add additional task loading, which can included communications with commanders at observing those on the ground (Endsley et al., 2010). The advantage of VoisJet is that it can use information from the actions of one person to advise another. This need not be as simple as letting a UAV operator know whether someone is a combatant or civilian, but can also advise them in relation to other human-centred systems, like pilots of other UAVs on the same mission. Known as 'blue-on-blue' attacks, poor situation awareness can lead to pilots targeting a colleague after mistakenly thinking they are an enemy combatant. Using VoisJet would make this less likely, as the user interface for the UAV could be adjusted to make sure that the pilot is aware when a colleague is in range. As VoisJet can take into account clothing as signifying whether someone is a threat, then it would make it easier for a UAV pilot to avoid targeting an ally if they wear a specific sign to indicate their allegiances. The risk is that enemies could also use this information to either deceive as to their identity or to target those signifying their identity.

Allowing for Increased Autonomy in UAV Operations

Table 1 shows that where autonomy is added to a UAV that problems in acquisition and maintenance of situation awareness are multiplied when the human must "operate, monitor and supervise" those UAV systems under their control (Endsley et al., 2010). VoisJet would remove a lot of the cognitive load from achieving full situation awareness by making many of the calculations needed by a pilot so they can focus on using the data as opposed to having to generate it first.

The strategic and tactical component of VoisJet is based on the operational demands of those leading military operations, and can be customised to each set of circumstances. It has been argued that current concepts of operation require multiple operators for every unmanned system, a ratio will be difficult to sustain if the projected increase in use is to be believed and if the wider use of UAVs is to be realized, then a more desirable manning concept must be identified (Hughes, 2012). This is where VoisJet comes into its own – it is advanced situation awareness capability of giving pilots a set of options relating to the situation they are in, where they can exercise the judgement needed in standard aerial operations.

IMPLICATIONS AND FUTURE RESEARCH DIRECTIONS

The advantage of an invention like VoisJet is that it will make military engagements using UAVs more effective and practical, meaning military operations have more missions completed with fewest causalities. This could therefore mean that defence budgets could be cut as the money needed to train UAV pilots would be significantly reduced, as it may only be necessary to have a university education with minimal specialist training to take part in a military campaign. This would mean that military personnel would only be engaged as and when necessary as they would be working in normal jobs the rest of the time. This would have the effect of reducing the size of standing armies as the skill and training currently needed would be eliminated. The need for university graduates trained in military hacking will increase, as cyber-warfare and cyber-terrorism become the norm. The brute-force based on-the-ground operations associated with wars to date will be all-but eliminated. Ground-operations will be for specific purposes – such as interception of opposition personnel, and even then the technology that forms part of VoisJet can be used to improve the effectiveness of those engagements. Future research will have to look at how a military reduced in size and budget can improve other aspects of national security, such as expanded departments of homeland security, where those military personnel who work abroad during wartime, can be part of national security services during peacetime.

DISCUSSION

Unmanned aerial vehicles (UAVs), known in the vernacular as 'drones' are a military aircraft that looks certain to stay as a cost effective way to proceed with air-based military operations without risk to human life in terms of its pilots. Human life is at risk from such pilots however, as existing systems have major issues in terms of maintaining situation awareness. This chapter therefore has evaluated a system – called VoisJet – which can capture action-data from one person to provide information and advice to another. This can mean that UAV operators have a clear idea of what is going on around them so that they do not have to make complex calculations that increase cognitive load. VoisJet can at present cope with at least 250,000 action states, which goes way beyond what is consciously possible with the human mind, especially when operating in high pressured military engagements. The chapter has proposed means for resolving difficulties in UAV localisation as well as reducing poor sensory data, intermittent data, and time-lags in UAVs. The chapter has shown how VoisJet can allow for increased autonomy in UAV operations as well as assist with overcoming lack of support for multi-person operations in UAVs. Furthermore it shows that multitasking in UAV operations can be improved with VoisJet taking over many calculations and also how low-Level data overload and interface design in UAVs can be improved, as can the management of demanding tasks in complex environments.

It is clear that with the advancements that can be made to UAVs through VoisJet, then public policy makers will have to reconsider how they fund national security operations. The costs in terms of training military personnel would be reduced by VoisJet-based UAVs, as they could be operated by university graduates with minimal training. Thus the size of a nation's standing army could be reduced by such graduates holding other job roles during peacetime, and the more skilled personnel can be part of national security bodies, such as the FBI and CIA in the USA or the NCA in the UK.

REFERENCES

Ando, M., Oguchi, K., & Yamada, M. (2013). Exponential stabilization of quad-rotor helicopter based on exact linearization and disturbance rejection with on-line estimation of disturbances. In *2013 Proceedings of the SICE Annual Conference (SICE)*, (pp. 1180-1185). Japan.

Bishop, J. (2013). The effect of deindividuation of the internet troller on criminal procedure implementation: An interview with a hater. *International Journal of Cyber Criminology, 7*(1), 28–48.

Bishop, J. (2014). Representations of 'trolls' in mass media communication: A review of media-texts and moral panics relating to 'internet trolling'. *International Journal of Web Based Communities, 10*(1), 7–24. doi:10.1504/IJWBC.2014.058384

Byman, D. (2013). Why drones work: The case for Washington's weapon of choice. *Foreign Affairs, 92*(4), 32–43.

Chisholm, R. A., Cui, J., Lum, S. K., & Chen, B. M. (2013). UAV LiDAR for below-canopy forest surveys. *Journal of Unmanned Vehicle Systems, 1*(01), 61–68. doi:10.1139/juvs-2013-0017

Coeckelbergh, M. (2013). Drones, information technology, and distance: Mapping the moral epistemology of remote fighting. *Ethics and Information Technology, 15*(2), 87–98. doi:10.1007/s10676-013-9313-6

Draper, M., Calhoun, G., Ruff, H., Williamson, D., & Barry, T. (2003). Manual versus speech input for unmanned aerial vehicle control station operations. In *Proceedings of the Human Factors and Ergonomics Society Annual Meeting, 47*(1) 109-113. Denver, CO. doi:10.1177/154193120304700123

Drezner, D. W. (2011). Does Obama have a grand strategy: Why we need doctrines in uncertain times. *Foreign Affairs, 90*, 57.

Durham, L. M., Milenkovic, M., & Cayton, P. (2006). Platform support for autonomic computing: A research vehicle. Paper presented at the *IEEE International Conference on* Autonomic Computing, 2006 (ICAC'06), pp. 293-294. doi:10.1201/9781420009354.ch16

Endsley, M. R., Bolte, B., & Jones, D. G. (2010). *Designing for situation awareness: An approach to user-centered design.* London, UK: Taylor & Francis Group.

Gomez, E. A., & Chimento, J. (2011). Information access challenges: Data fission needs of the field expert. In *Proceedings of the 16th ICCRTS,* Québec, QC. pp. 151-160.

Hardaker, C. (2013). "Uh.... not to be nitpicky, but... the past tense of drag is dragged, not drug": An overview of trolling strategies. *Journal of Language Aggression and Conflict, 1*(1), 57–85. doi:10.1075/jlac.1.1.04har

Hughes, T. C. (2012). Sources of adaptive capacity during multi-unmanned aerial vehicle operations (Doctoral thesis). Ohio State University, USA.

Jones, S. R. (2000). The roots of antisemitism. In I. Davies (Ed.), *Teaching the Holocaust: Educational dimensions, principles and practice* (pp. 11–24). London, UK: Bloomsbury Publishing.

Kean, T. H., & Hamilton, L. H. (2006). *Without precedent: The inside story of the 9/11 commission*. New York, NY: Knopf.

Kean, T. H., Hamilton, L. H., Ben-Veniste, R., Kerrey, B., Fielding, F. F., & Lehman, J. F. et al.. (2004). *The 9/11 commission report*. New York, NY: W. W. Norton & Company.

McCosker, A. (2013). Trolling as provocation: YouTube's agonistic publics. *Convergence (London)*. . doi:doi: 1354856513501413

McLeod, T., Samson, C., Labrie, M., Shehata, K., Mah, J., Lai, P., & Elder, J. H. et al. (2013). Using video acquired from an unmanned aerial vehicle (UAV) to measure fracture orientation in an open-pit mine. *GEOMATICA, 67*(3), 173–180. doi:10.5623/cig2013-036

Mobley, B. W. (2012). *Terrorism and counterintelligence: How terrorist groups elude detection*. New York, NY: Columbia University Press.

Rees, L. (2005). *Auschwitz: The Nazis & the final solution*. New York, NY: Random House.

Reynolds, M. A. (2013). Return of the Maxim gun? Technology and empire in an age of austerity. *Global Discourse, 3*(1), 120–128. doi:10.1080/23269995.2013.807603

Rosenberg, L. B., & Stredney, D. (1996). A haptic interface for virtual simulation of endoscopic surgery. *Studies in Health Technology and Informatics, 29*, 371–387. PMID:10172846

Yang, J., Chen, Y., Ammar, M., & Lee, C. (2005). Ferry replacement protocols in sparse manet message ferrying systems. In *Proceedings of the IEEE Wireless Communications and Networking Conference* (vol. 4, pp. 2038-2044). Atlanta, GA.

Yee, A. S. (2013). An investigation of the use of real-time image mosaicing for facilitating global spatial awareness in visual search (Doctoral thesis). University of Toronto, Canada.

KEY TERMS AND DEFINITIONS

Action-Data: Information picked up by a sensor that describes what is occurring in the situation being monitored.

Autonomy: The extent to which a person can make decisions for themselves in any given operational environment.

Hamas: A group of Islamic militants who although not Jihadists are committed to using force in order to protect the Arab Semite territories from being occupied by Zionists. It can be compared to the First and Second Continental Congresses, which was a military force that existed prior to US independence and then became the US Department of Justice.

Jihadist: A person who believes that the Holy Land and other Middle East nations occupied since the Crusades should be based wholly on Islamic law and uses force rather than democratic means to achieve that.

Sensory Data: Action-data that is made available to a person for processing using their own senses and judgement.

Situation Awareness: Situation awareness refers to the extent to which someone is able to know what is going on in any given situation and the options available.

Unmanned Aerial Vehicle: An unmanned aerial vehicle (UAV) is an aircraft that is piloted by a remote operator in order to achieve a particular objective, such as to eliminate enemy combatants.

VoisJet: VoisJet is a method for assisting UAV pilots in making decisions while involved in military operations through reducing the cognitive load and other factors that can lead to errors of judgement.

Zionist: A person who believes that the Holy Land should only consist only of Jewish Semites, and use undemocratic means to exclude Arab Semites and other religious/ethic groups from that territory.

Compilation of References

Abbott, A. (2006). Neuroprosthetics: In search of the sixth sense. *Nature*, *442*(7099), 125–127. doi:10.1038/442125a PMID:16837993

Achaibou, A., Pourtois, G., Schwartz, S., & Vuilleumier, P. (2008). Simultaneous recording of EEG and facial muscle reactions during spontaneous emotional mimicry. *Neuropsychologia*, *46*(4), 1104–1113. doi:10.1016/j.neuropsychologia.2007.10.019 PMID:18068737

Adler, R. S., Rosen, B., & Silverstein, E. M. (1998). Emotions in negotiation: How to manage fear and anger. *Negotiation Journal*, *14*(2), 161–179. doi:10.1111/j.1571-9979.1998.tb00156.x

Adolphs, R., Tranel, D., Damasio, H., & Damasio, A. (1994). Impaired recognition of emotion in facial expressions following bilateral damage to the human amygdala. Nature, 372(6507), 669–672. doi:10.1038/372669a0 PMID:7990957

Aguero, J. R., & Vargas, A. (2007). Calculating functions of interval type-2 fuzzy numbers for fault current analysis. *IEEE Transactions on Fuzzy Systems, 15*(1), 31–40.

Ahn, J., Gobron, S., Silvestre, Q., Thalmann, D., & Boulic, R. (2011). *Double your face with asymmetric expression of emotions driven by a 3D emotional model.* Paper presented at the Eurographics/ACM SIGGRAPH Symposium on Computer Animation.

Ahn, J., Gobron, S., Silvestre, Q., & Thalmann, D. (2010). Asymmetrical facial expressions based on an advanced interpretation of two-dimensional Russell's emotional model. In *Proceedings of ENGAGE.*

Ajzen, I. (1985). *From intentions to actions: A theory of planned behavior* (J. Kuhl & J. Beckmann, Eds.). Berlin, Heidelberg: Springer Berlin Heidelberg; doi:10.1007/978-3-642-69746-3

Aldrich, R. (Director). (1962). *What ever happened to baby Jane?* [Film]. United States: Warner Bros.

Allwood, J. (1999). Semantics as meaning determination with semantic-epistemic operations. In J. Allwood & P. Gardenfors (Eds.), *Cognitive semantics. Meaning and cognition* (pp. 1–18). John Benjamins. doi:10.1075/pbns.55.02all

Álvarez, M., Galán, R., Matía, F., Rodríguez-Losada, D., & Jiménez, A. (2010). An emotional model for a guide robot. *IEEE Transactions on Systems, Man, and Cybernetics. Part A, Systems and Humans, 40*(5), 982–992. doi:10.1109/TSMCA.2010.2046734

Anderson, J., McRee, J., Wilson, R., & the Effective UI Team (2010). *Effective UI.* Sebastopol, CA: O'Reilly.

Ando, M., Oguchi, K., & Yamada, M. (2013). Exponential stabilization of quad-rotor helicopter based on exact linearization and disturbance rejection with on-line estimation of disturbances. In *2013 Proceedings of the SICE Annual Conference (SICE),* (pp. 1180-1185). Japan.

Andre, E., Klesen, M., Gebhard, P., Allen, S., & Rist, T. (2000). *Exploiting models of personality and emotions to control the behavior of animated interactive agents* Paper presented at the Proceedings of IWAI, Siena, Italy.

Arai, K., & Mardiyanto, R. (2011). Eye based HCI with moving keyboard for reducing fatigue effects. In *2011 Eighth International Conference on Information Technology: New Generations (ITNG)*, pp. 417–422. Retrieved from http://ieeexplore.ieee.org/xpls/abs_all.jsp?arnumber=5945272

Arellano, D., Varona, J., & Perales, F. J. (2008). Generation and visualization of emotional states in virtual characters. In Computer Animation and Virtual Worlds, Special Issue: CASA'2008, 19(3-4), 259-270. doi:10.1002/cav.234

Arkin, R. (2009). *Governing lethal behavior in autonomous robots*. Boca Raton: CRC Press. doi:10.1201/9781420085952

Arnold, M. B. (1960). *Emotion and personality*. New York: Columbia University Press.

Arnold, M. B., & Gasson, J. A. (1954). *The human person: An approach to an integral theory of personality*. Ronald Press Co.

Asada, M., Hosoda, K., Kuniyoshi, Y., Ishiguro, H., Inui, T., Yoshikawa, Y., & Yoshida, C. et al. (2009). Cognitive developmental robotics: A survey. *Transactions on Autonomous Mental Development*, 1(1), 12–32. doi:10.1109/TAMD.2009.2021702

Asaro, P. M. (2009). Modeling the moral user. *IEEE Technology and Society*, 28(1), 20–24. doi:10.1109/MTS.2009.931863

Averill, J. R. (1980). A constructivist view of emotion. In R. Harré (Ed.), *Emotion: Theory, research, and experience* (pp. 305–339). New York: Academic Press. doi:10.1016/B978-0-12-558701-3.50018-1

Averill, J. R. (1994). I feel, therefore I am: I think. In P. Ekman & R. J. Davidson (Eds.), *The nature of emotion: Fundamental questions*. Oxford: Oxford University Press.

Axelrod, R. (1986). An evolutionary approach to norms. *The American Political Science Review*, 80(4), 1095–1111. doi:10.2307/1960858

Axelrod, R. (1987). The evolution of strategies in the iterated prisoner's dilemma. In *Genetic Algorithms and Simulated Annealing* (pp. 32–41). London: Pitman.

Axelrod, R. (1997). *The complexity of cooperation*. Princeton: Princeton University Press.

Aylett, R. S. (2004). *Agents and affect: Why embodied agents need affective systems*. Paper presented at the 3rd Hellenic Conference on AI, Samos, Greece.

Bach, J. (2003) The MicroPsi Agent Architecture. In *Proceedings of ICCM-5, Universitats-Verlag Bamberg*.

Bandai. (2000) *Tamagotchi*. http://www.bandai.com

Banik, S. C., Watanabe, K., Habib, M. K., & Izumi, K. (2009). Handbook of research on synthetic emotions and sociable robotics (J. Vallverdú & D. Casacuberta, Eds.). Hershey, PA: IGI Global. doi:10.4018/978-1-60566-354-8

Banse, R., & Scherer, K. R. (1996). Acoustic profiles in vocal emotion expression. *Journal of Personality and Social Psychology*, 70(3), 614–636. doi:10.1037/0022-3514.70.3.614 PMID:8851745

Barakova, E. I., & Lourens, T. (2010). Expressing and interpreting emotional movements in social games with robots. Personal and Ubiquitous Computing, 14(5), 457–467. doi:10.1007/s00779-009-0263-2

Baron-Cohen, S. (1996). Is there a normal phase of synaesthesia in development. *Psyche*, 2(27), 223–228.

Barrett, L. F. (2006). Are emotions natural kinds? *Perspectives on Psychological Science*, 1(1), 28–58. doi:10.1111/j.1745-6916.2006.00003.x PMID:19079552

Barriga, S. D., Rodríguez, L.-F., Ramos, F., & Ramos, M. (2013). A computational model of emotional attention for autonomous agents. *Transactions on Computational Science, LNCS*, 18, 192–211.

Bartneck, C. (2002). Integrating the OCC model of emotions in embodied characters. In *Proceedings of the Workshop on Virtual Conversational*.

Bates, J., Loyall, A. B., & Reilly, W. S. (1992). Integrating reactivity, goals, and emotion in a broad agent. *Proceedings of the 14th Meeting of the Cognitive Science Society*.

Baum, L., Petrie, T., Soules, G., & Weiss, N. (1970). A maximization technique occurring in the statistical analysis of probabilistic functions of Markov chains. Annals of Mathematical Statistics, 41(1), 164–171. doi:10.1214/aoms/1177697196 doi:10.1214/aoms/1177697196

Beaudry, O., Roy-Charland, A., Perron, M., Cormier, I., & Tapp, R. (2013). Featural processing in recognition of emotional facial expressions. *Cognition and Emotion*, *28*(3), 416–432. doi:10.1080/02699931.2013.833500 PMID:24047413

Bechara, A. (2004). The role of emotion in decision-making: Evidence from neurological patients with orbitofrontal damage. *Brain and Cognition*, *55*(1), 30–40. doi:10.1016/j.bandc.2003.04.001 PMID:15134841

Bechara, A., Damasio, H., & Damasio, A. R. (2000). Emotion, decision making and the orbitofrontal cortex. *Cerebral Cortex*, *10*(3), 295–307. doi:10.1093/cercor/10.3.295 PMID:10731224

Beck, A., Hiolle, A., Mazel, A., & Cañamero, L. (2010). Interpretation of emotional body language displayed by robots. In *Proceedings of the 3rd international workshop on Affective interaction in natural environments*. New York, NY, USA: ACM. doi:10.1145/1877826.1877837

Becker, C., Nakasone, A., Prendinger, H., Ishizuka, M., & Wachsmuth, I. (2005). *Physiologically interactive gaming with the 3D agent Max*. Paper presented at the International Workshop on Conversational Informatics at JSAI-05, Kitakyushu, Japan.

Becker-Asano, C. (2008). *WASABI: Affect simulation for agents with believable interactivity* (PhD thesis). Faculty of Technology, University of Bielefeld, Germany. IOS Press (DISKI 319).

Becker-Asano, C. (2008). *WASABI: Affect simulation for agents with believable interactivity*. IOS Press.

Becker-Asano, C., & Ishiguro, H. (2011). Evaluating facial displays of emotion for the android robot Geminoid F. In *2011 IEEE Workshop on Affective Computational Intelligence (WACI)*. doi:10.1109/WACI.2011.5953147

Beira, R., Lopes, M., Praga, M., Santos-Victor, J., Bernardino, A., & Metta, G., ... Saltaren, R. (2006). Design of the robot-cub (iCub) head. In *Proceedings 2006 IEEE International Conference on Robotics and Automation*. doi:10.1109/ROBOT.2006.1641167

Belavkin, R. V., & Ritter, F. E. (2004). OPTIMIST: A new conflict resolution algorithm for ACT-R.*Proceedings of the Sixth International Conference on Cognitive Modeling*, Pittsburgh, PA.

Bell, G., Ling, D., Kurlander, D., Miller, J., Pugh, D., Skelly, T., Stankosky, A., Thiel, D., Dantzich, M.V., Wax, T. (1997). Lifelike computer characters: The Persona Project at Microsoft Research. In J. M. Bradshaw (Ed.), Software agents, (pp. 191-222). London: AAAI Press.

Benjamin, M. (2012). *Drone warfare: Killing by remote control*. New York: OR Books.

Benyon, D. (2010). *Designing interactive systems: A comprehensive guide to HCI and interaction design*. Harlow, UK: Pearson.

Ben-Ze'ev, A. (2002). Emotional intelligence: The conceptual issue. *Managing emotions in the workplace*, 164-183.

Berander, P., & Andrews, A. (2005). Requirements prioritization. In A. Aurum & C. Wohlin (Eds.), *Engineering and managing software requirements* (pp. 69–94). Berlin, Germany: Springer. doi:10.1007/3-540-28244-0_4

Biehl, M., Matsumoto, D., Ekman, P., Hearn, V., Heider, K., Kudoh, T., & Ton, V. (1997). Matsumoto and Ekman's Japanese and Caucasian Facial Expressions of Emotion (JACFEE): Reliability data and cross-national differences. *Journal of Nonverbal Behavior*, *21*(1), 3–21. doi:10.1023/A:1024902500935

Billman, G. E. (2013). Homeostasis: the dynamic self-regulatory process that maintains health and buffers against disease. In Handbook of systems and complexity in health (pp. 159–170). Springer.

Bimler, D. L., & Paramei, G. V. (2006). Facial-expression affective attributes and their configural correlates: Components and categories. *The Spanish Journal of Psychology*, *9*(1), 19–31. doi:10.1017/S113874160000593X PMID:16673619

Bishop, C. M., & Nasrabadi, N. M. (2006). *Pattern recognition and machine learning* (Vol. 1). New York: Springer.

Bishop, J. (2013). The effect of deindividuation of the internet troller on criminal procedure implementation: An interview with a hater. *International Journal of Cyber Criminology*, *7*(1), 28–48.

Bishop, J. (2014). Representations of 'trolls' in mass media communication: A review of media-texts and moral panics relating to 'internet trolling'. *International Journal of Web Based Communities*, *10*(1), 7–24. doi:10.1504/IJWBC.2014.058384

Black, M. (1993). More about metaphor. In A. Ortony (Ed.), Metaphor and thought (Second., pp. 19–41). Cambridge University Press. doi:10.1017/CBO9781139173865.004

Borod, J. C., Caron, H. S., & Koff, E. (1981). Asymmetry in positive and negative facial expressions: Sex differences. *Neuropsychologia, 19*(6), 819–824. doi:10.1016/0028-3932(81)90095-6 PMID:7329529

Borod, J. C., Haywood, C. S., & Koff, E. (1997). Neuropsychological aspects of facial asymmetry during emotional expression: A review of the normal adult literature. *Neuropsychology Review, 7*(1), 41–60. doi:10.1007/BF02876972 PMID:9243530

Borod, J. C., Koff, E., Yecker, S., Santschi, C., & Schmidt, J. M. (1998). Facial asymmetry during emotional expression: Gender, valence, and measurement technique. *Neuropsychologia, 36*(11), 1209–1215. doi:10.1016/S0028-3932(97)00166-8 PMID:9842766

Boucenna, S., Gaussier, P., Andry, P., & Hafemeister, L. (2010). Imitation as a communication tool for online facial expression learning and recognition. IROS (pp. 5323-5328). IEEE/RSJ.

Bower, G. H., Lazarus, R., LeDoux, J. E., Panksepp, J., Davidson, R. J., & Ekman, P. (1994) What is the relation between emotion and memory. In P. Ekman & R. J. Davidson, (Eds.), The nature of emotion: Fundamental questions. Series in affective science (pp. 301-318). New York: Oxford University Press.

Bower, G. H. (1981). Mood and memory. *The American Psychologist, 36*(2), 129–148. doi:10.1037/0003-066X.36.2.129 PMID:7224324

Bower, G. H. (1992). How might emotions affect memory? In S. A. Christianson (Ed.), *Handbook of emotion and memory*. Hillsdale, NJ: Lawrence Erlbaum.

Braitenberg, V., & Schüz, A. (1998). Cortical architectonics. In Cortex: Statistics and Geometry of Neuronal Connectivity (pp. 135–137). Springer.

Bratman, M. (1999). Intentions, plans, and practical reason. Cambridge University Press; Retrieved from http://books.google.com/books?hl=en&lr=&id=RhgnY0-6BmMC&oi=fnd&pg=PR9&dq=intentions+in+communication&ots=66yAtkukEd&sig=iQKmlx2ibFbmbYa-_hVFU08HYsc

Breazeal, C. (1998). A motivational system for regulating human–robot interaction. In *Proceedings of the Fifteenth National Conference on Artificial Intelligence (AAAI98)*. Madison, WI, pp. 54–61. (1998)

Breazeal, C. (2000). Regulation and entrainment in human–robot interaction. *The International Journal of Robotics Research, 21*(10–11), 883–902.

Breazeal, C. (2001). Emotive qualities in robot speech. In*Proceedings of the 2001 IEEERSJ International Conference on Intelligent Robots and Systems (IROS01)*, Maui, HI, 2001.

Breazeal, C. (2002). Emotion and sociable humanoid robots. *International Journal of Human-Computer Studies, 59*(1-2), 119–155. doi:10.1016/S1071-5819(03)00018-1

Breazeal, C. (2003). Toward sociable robots. *Robotics and Autonomous Systems, 42*(3-4), 167–175. doi:10.1016/S0921-8890(02)00373-1

Breazeal, C. L. (2004). *Designing sociable robots*. MIT press.

Breazeal, C., & Brooks, R. (2005). Robot emotion: A functional perspective. In J.-M. Fellous & M. A. Arbib (Eds.), *Who needs emotions?* New York: Oxford University Press.

Breazeal, C., & Scassellati, B. (2000). Infant-like social interactions between a robot and a human caretaker. *Adaptive Behavior, 8*(1), 49–73. doi:10.1177/105971230000800104

Broekens, J., Kosters, W., & Verbeek, F. (2007). On affect and self-adaptation: Potential benefits of valence-controlled action-selection. *Bio-inspired Modeling of Cognitive Tasks, LNCS 4527*, 357-366.

Broekens, J., DeGroot, D., & Kosters, W. A. (2008). Formal models of appraisal: theory, specification, and computational model. *Cognitive Systems Research, 9*(3), 173–197. doi:10.1016/j.cogsys.2007.06.007

Brooks, R. A., Breazeal, C., Marajanovic, M., Scassellati, B., & Williamson, M. M. (1999). The cog project: Building a humanoid robot. In C. L. Nehavic (Ed.), Computation for Metaphors, Analogy and Agents, Springer Lecture Notes in Artificial Intelligence (vol. 1562). Berlin, Germany: Springer-Verlag. doi:10.1007/3-540-48834-0_5

Brooks, R. (1986). A robust layered control system for a mobile robot. *Robotics and Automation. Journal of IEEE*, *2*(1), 14–23. doi:10.1109/JRA.1986.1087032

Brooks, R. (1986). Asynchronous distributed control system for a mobile robot. In *SPIE Conference on Mobile Robots* (pp. 77–84).

Brooks, R. (1986). A robust programming scheme for a mobile robot. In *Proceedings of NATO Advanced Research Workshop on Languages for Sensor-Based Control in Robotics*, Castelvecchio Pascoli, Italy.

Brooks, R. A. (1999). *Cambrian intelligence: the early history of the new AI*. MIT Press.

Brooks, R., Breazeal, C., Marjanović, M., Scassellati, B., & Williamson, M. (1998). The Cog project: Building a humanoid robot. In C. Nehaniv (Ed.), *Computation for metaphors, analogy, and agents* (pp. 52–87). New York: Springer.

Brown, J. E., Chatterjee, N., Younger, J., & Mackey, S. (2011). Towards a physiology-based measure of pain: Patterns of human brain activity distinguish painful from non-painful thermal stimulation. *PLoS ONE*, *6*(9), e24124. doi:10.1371/journal.pone.0024124 PMID:21931652

Brown, R., & Kulik, J. (1977). Flashbulb memories. *Cognition*, *5*(1), 73–99. doi:10.1016/0010-0277(77)90018-X

Brunstetter, D., & Braun, M. (2011). The implications of drones on the just war tradition. *Ethics & International Affairs*, *25*(3), 337–358. doi:10.1017/S0892679411000281

Bryson, J. J., & Tanguy, E. (2010). Simplifying the design of human-like behaviour: Emotions as durative dynamic state for action selection. *International Journal of Synthetic Emotions*, *1*(1), 30–50. doi:10.4018/jse.2010101603

Burell, M. (2004). Appraisal and information theory. *Comma*, *2004*(1), 55-62.

Burges, C. J. (1998). A tutorial on support vector machines for pattern recognition. *Data Mining and Knowledge Discovery*, *2*(2), 121–167. doi:10.1023/A:1009715923555

Burkhardt, F., & Sendlmeier, W. (2000). Verification of acoustical correlates of emotional speech using formant-synthesis. In *ISCA Tutorial and Research Workshop (ITRW) on Speech and Emotion*. Retrieved from http://www.isca-speech.org/archive_open/speech_emotion/spem_151.html

Burkhardt, F., Paeschke, A., Rolfes, M., Sendlmeier, W. F., & Weiss, B. (2005). *A database of German emotional speech* (pp. 1517–1520). Interspeech.

Burt, C. (1950). The factorial study of emotions. In M. L. Reymert (Ed.), *Feelings and emotions* (1st Ed.). McGraw-Hill Book Company.

Bush, G., Luu, P., & Posner, M. I. (2000, June). Cognitive and emotional influences in anterior cingulate cortex. *Trends in Cognitive Sciences*, *4*(6), 215–222. doi:10.1016/S1364-6613(00)01483-2 PMID:10827444

Butler, J. T., & Agah, A. (2001). Psychological Effects of Behavior Patterns of a Mobile Personal Robot. *Autonomous Robots*, *10*(2), 185–202. doi:10.1023/A:1008986004181

Byman, D. (2013). Why drones work: The case for Washington's weapon of choice. *Foreign Affairs*, *92*(4), 32–43.

Calder, A. J., Keane, J., Manes, F., Antoun, N., & Young, A. W. (2000). Impaired recognitiion and experience of disgust following brain injury. *Nature Neuroscience*, *3*(11), 1077–1078. doi:10.1038/80586 PMID:11036262

Calkins, S. D. (2002). Does aversive behavior during toddlerhood matter? The effects of difficult temperament on maternal perceptions and behavior. *Infant Mental Health Journal*, *23*(4), 381–394. doi:10.1002/imhj.10024

Calvo, R. A., & D'Mello, S. (2010). Affect detection: An interdisciplinary review of models, methods, and their applications. *IEEE Transactions on Affective Computing*, *1*(1), 18–37. doi:10.1109/T-AFFC.2010.1

Camras, L. A. (2011). Differentiation, dynamical integration and functional emotional development. *Emotion Review*, *3*(2), 138–146. doi:10.1177/1754073910387944

Camras, L. A., Lambrect, L., & Michel, G. (1996). Infant "surprise" expressions as coordinative motor structures. *Journal of Nonverbal Behavior, 20*(3), 183–195. doi:10.1007/BF02281955

Camras, L. A., & Shuster, M. M. (2013). Current emotion research in developmental psychology. *Emotion Review, 5*(3), 321–329. doi:10.1177/1754073913477516

Camurri, A., & Coglio, A. (1998). An architecture for emotional agents. *MultiMedia, IEEE, 5*(4), 24–33. doi:10.1109/93.735866

Cañamero, L. (1997). *A hormonal model of emotions for behavior control*. Paper presented at the 4th European Conference on Artificial Life (ECAL '97). Brighton, UK.

Cañamero, L., & Avila-Gracia, O. (2007). *A bottom-up investigation of emotional modulation in competitive scenarios*. Paper presented at the Affective Computing and Intelligent Interaction. doi:10.1007/978-3-540-74889-2_35

Cañamero, D. (1997, February). Modeling motivations and emotions as a basis for intelligent behavior. In *Proceedings of the first international conference on Autonomous agents* (pp. 148-155). ACM. doi:10.1145/267658.267688

Cañamero, L. D. (2001). Building emotional artifacts in social worlds: Challenges and perspectives. In *AAAI Fall Symposium "Emotional and Intelligent II: The Tangled Knot of Social Cognition"* Cape Cod, MA: Menlo Park, CA: AAAI Press.

Canli, T., Desmond, J. E., Zhao, Z., Glover, G., & Gabrieli, J. D. (1998). Hemispheric asymmetry for emotional stimuli detected with fMRI. *Neuroreport, 9*(14), 3233–3239. doi:10.1097/00001756-199810050-00019 PMID:9831457

Cannon, W. B. (1927). The James-Lange theory of emotions: A critical examination and an alternative theory. *The American Journal of Psychology, 39*(1/4), 106–124. doi:10.2307/1415404 PMID:3322057

Carpenter, M., Call, J., & Tomasello, M. (2005). Twelve- and 18-month-olds copy actions in terms of goals. *Developmental Science, 8*(1), F13–F20. doi:10.1111/j.1467-7687.2004.00385.x PMID:15647059

Carr, L., Iacoboni, M., Dubeau, M. C., Mazziotta, J. C., & Lenzi, G. L. (2003). Neural mechanisms of empathy in humans: A relay from neural systems for imitation to limbic areas. *Proceedings of the National Academy of Sciences of the United States of America, 100*(9), 5497–5502. doi:10.1073/pnas.0935845100 PMID:12682281

Casacuberta, D., Ayala, S., & Vallverdú, J. (2010). Embodying cognition: a morphological perspective. In J. Vallverdú (Ed.), *Thinking machines and the philosophy of computer science: concepts and principles* (pp. 344–366). Hershey, PA: IGI Global Group. doi:10.4018/978-1-61692-014-2.ch021

Casacuberta, D., & Vallverdú, J. (2014). E-Science and the data deluge. *Philosophical Psychology, 27*(1), 126–140. doi:10.1080/09515089.2013.827961

Castellano, G., Caridakis, G., Camurri, A., Karpouzis, K., Volpe, G., & Kollias, S. (2010). Body gesture and facial expression analysis for automatic affect recognition. In K. R. Scherer, T. Bänziger, & E. B. Roesch (Eds.), *Blueprint for affective computing: A sourcebook* (pp. 245–255). New York: Oxford University Press.

Castro, A., Diaz, F., & Van Boxtel, G. J. (2005). What happens to the readiness potential when the movement is not executed? *Neuroreport, 16*(15), 1609–1613. doi:10.1097/01.wnr.0000183331.51736.7f PMID:16189464

Chakraborty, A., & Konar, A. (2009). *Emotional intelligence: A cybernetic approach* (Vol. 234). Springer. doi:10.1007/978-3-540-68609-5

Chakraborty, A., Konar, A., Chakraborty, U. K., & Chatterjee, A. (2009). Emotion recognition from facial expressions and its control using fuzzy logic. *IEEE Transactions on Systems, Man and Cybernetics, Part A: Systems and Humans, 39*(4), 726–743.

Chappelle, W., McDonald, K., & McMillan, K. (2011). *Important and critical psychological attributes of USAF MQ-1 predator and MQ-9 reaper pilots according to subject matter experts*. Ohio: School of Aerospace Medicine.

Charniak, E., & Goldman, R. (1993). A Bayesian model of plan recognition. Artificial Intelligence, 64(1), 53–79. doi:10.1016/0004-3702(93)90060-O

Chauvin, Y., & Rumelhart, D. E. (Eds.). (1995). *Back-propagation: Theory, architectures, and applications*. Psychology Press.

Chen, H., Perich, F., Finin, T., & Joshi, A. (2004). SOUPA: Standard ontology for ubiquitous and pervasive applications. In *First Annual International Conference on Mobile and Ubiquitous Systems: Networking and Services (MobiQuitous'04)* (pp.258-267). doi:10.1109/MOBIQ.2004.1331732

Chen, S., Cowan, C. F. N., & Grant, P. M. (1991). Orthogonal least squares learning algorithm for radial basis function networks. *IEEE Transactions on Neural Networks*, 2(2), 302–309.

Chisholm, R. A., Cui, J., Lum, S. K., & Chen, B. M. (2013). UAV LiDAR for below-canopy forest surveys. *Journal of Unmanned Vehicle Systems*, 1(01), 61–68. doi:10.1139/juvs-2013-0017

Chomsky, N., & McGilvray, J. (2012). *The science of language. Interviews with James McGilvray*. Cambridge University Press. doi:10.1017/CBO9781139061018

Chouchourelou, A., Matsuka, T., Harber, K., & Shiffrar, M. (2006). The visual analysis of emotional actions.. *Social Neuroscience*, 1(1), 63–74 doi:10.1080/17470910600630599 PMID:18633776

Chow, C. (1970). On optimum recognition error and reject tradeoff. *IEEE Transactions on Information Theory*, 16(1), 41–46.

Christensen, H., Pacchierotti, E., & Hgskolan, K. T. (2005). Embodied social interaction for robots. In *Proceedings of the 2005 Convention of the Society for the Study of Artificial Intelligence and Simulation of Behaviour (AISB-05), Hertfordshire* (pp. 40–45).

Clark, A. (1997). *Being there – putting brain, body and world together again*. Cambridge, MA: MIT Press.

Clark, A. (1999). An embodied cognitive science? *Trends in Cognitive Sciences*, 3(9), 345–351. doi:10.1016/S1364-6613(99)01361-3 PMID:10461197

Clinical Psychology Associates of North Central Florida. P.A. (2013). *Welcome to Neuropsychology Central*. Retrieved from www.neuropsychologycentral.com

Clore, G. L. (1994). Why emotions are felt? In P. Ekman & R. J. Davidson (Eds.), *The nature of emotion: Fundamental questions*. Oxford: Oxford University Press.

Clore, G. L., & Ortony, A. (1988). The semantics of the affective lexicon. In V. Hamilton, G. Bower, & N. Frijda (Eds.), *Cognitive science perspectives on emotion and motivation* (pp. 367–397). Amsterdam: Martinus Nijhoff. doi:10.1007/978-94-009-2792-6_15

Coan, J. A., Allen, J. J., & Harmon-Jones, E. (2001). Voluntary facial expression and hemispheric asymmetry over the frontal cortex. *Psychophysiology*, 38(6), 912–925. doi:10.1111/1469-8986.3860912 PMID:12240668

Coeckelbergh, M. (2013). Drones, information technology, and distance: Mapping the moral epistemology of remote fighting. *Ethics and Information Technology*, 15(2), 87–98. doi:10.1007/s10676-013-9313-6

Cohn, J. F., Ambadar, Z., & Ekman, P. (2007). Observer-based measurement of facial expression with the facial action coding system. In J. A. Coan & J. B. Allen (Eds.), The handbook of emotion elicitation and assessment. New York: Oxford University Press.

Constantinescu, P. (1986). *Sisteme Ierarhizate. Rolul informatiei in geneza si dezvoltare [Hierarchical Systems. The role of information in genesis and development]*. Editura Academiei Republicii Socialiste Romania.

Constantinescu, P. (1990). *Sinergia, Informatia si Geneza Sistemelor [Synergy, Information and the Genesis of Systems]*. Editura Tehnica.

Cordón, O., del Jesus, M. J., & Herrera, F. (1999). A proposal on reasoning methods in fuzzy rule-based classification systems. *International Journal of Approximate Reasoning*, 20(1), 21–45. doi:10.1016/S0888-613X(00)88942-2

Cornelius, R. R. (2000). *Theoretical approaches to emotion*. Newcastle: ISCA.

Coulson, M. (2009). Expressing emotion through body movement: A component process approach. In L. Canamero & R. Aylett (Eds.), Animating expressive characters for social interaction (Advances in Consciousness Research Series; Vol. 74). Amsterdam, The Netherlands: Benjamins.

Cowie, R., & Douglas-Cowie, E. (1995). Speakers and hearers are people: Reflections on speech deterioration as a consequence of acquired deafness. In Profound Deafness and Speech Communication (pp. 510–527).

Cowie, R., Douglas-Cowie, E., Tsapatsoulis, N., Votsis, G., Kollias, S., Fellenz, W., & Taylor, J. (2001). Emotion recognition in human-computer interaction. *Signal Processing Magazine, IEEE*, 18(1), 32–80. doi:10.1109/79.911197

Craig, A. D. (2009). How do you feel–now? the anterior insula and human awareness. *Nature Reviews. Neuroscience*, 10, 59–70. doi:10.1038/nrn2555 PMID:19096369

Cristianini, N., & Shawe-Taylor, J. (2000). *An introduction to support vector machines and other kernel-based learning methods*. Cambridge University Press. doi:10.1017/CBO9780511801389

Cunningham, M. R. (1988). What do you do when you're happy or blue? Mood, expectancies, and behavioral interest. Motivation and Emotion, 12(4), 309–331. doi:10.1007/BF00992357

Cunningham, M. R. (1988). Does happiness mean friendliness?: Induced mood and heterosexual self-disclosure. Personality and Social Psychology Bulletin, 14(2), 283–297. doi:10.1177/0146167288142007

Cytowic, R. E. (1998). The man who tasted shapes. Cambridge, MA: MIT Press.

Dael, N., Mortillaro, M., & Scherer, K. R. (2012). Emotion expression in body action and posture. *Emotion (Washington, D.C.)*, 12(5), 1085–1101. doi:10.1037/a0025737 PMID:22059517

Damasio, A. (1999). *The feeling of what happens: Body and emotion in the making of consciousness* [eBook].

Damasio, A. (2005) Descartes' error: Emotion, reason, and the human brain. Penguin Books.

Damasio, A. (Ed.). (1999). The feeling of what happens: Body and emotion in the making of consciousness. Harcourt.

Damasio, A. (1994). *Descartes' error: Emotion, reason and the human mind*. New York: Grossett/Putnam.

Damasio, A. (1999). *The feeling of what happens*. London: Heinemann.

Damasio, A. (2001). Fundamental feelings. *Nature*, *413*(6858), 781–781. doi:10.1038/35101669 PMID:11677584

Damasio, A. (2005). *Descartes' error: Emotion, reason, and the human brain*. Penguin Books.

Damasio, A. R. (1994). Descartes' error: Emotion, reason and the human brain. *Journal of Neurophysiology*, 2, 29–40.

Damasio, A. R. (2004). *Looking for Spinoza: Joy, sorrow and the feeling brain*. Random House.

Daprati, E., Wriessnegger, S., & Lacquaniti, F. (2007). Kinematic cues and recognition of self-generated actions. Experimental Brain Research, 177(1), 31–44. doi:10.1007/s00221-006-0646-9 PMID:16924486

Dario, P., Guglielmelli, E., & Laschi, C. (2001). Humanoids and personal robots: Design and experiments. *Journal of Robotic Systems*. Retrieved from http://citeseer.uark.edu:8080/citeseerx/showciting;jsessionid=4942263C2202CB506C89EE4F4CEBBD6F?cid=261580

Darwin, C. (1872). The expression of the emotions in man and animals. London: Murray. (Reprinted, Chicago: University of Chicago Press, 1965.). doi:10.1037/10001-000

Darwin, C. (1965). *The expression of the emotions in man and animals*. Chicago: University of Chicago Press. (Original work published 1872)

Das, S., Halder, A., Bhowmik, P., Chakraborty, A., Konar, A., & Nagar, A. K. (2009, December). Voice and facial expression based classification of emotion using linear support vector machine. In *Second International Conference on Developments in eSystems Engineering (DESE)*, (pp. 377-384). IEEE. doi:10.1109/DeSE.2009.9

Datta, C., Kapuria, A., & Vijay, R. (2011). A pilot study to understand requirements of a shopping mall robot. In *6th ACM/IEEE International Conference on Human-Robot Interaction (HRI)* (pp 127-128). Lausanne, Switzerland. doi:10.1145/1957656.1957694

Datta, C., MacDonald, B. A., Jayawardena, C., & Kuo, I.-H. (2012). Programming behaviour of a personal service robot with application to healthcare. In GeS.S.KhatibO. CabibihanJ-J.SimmonsR.WilliamsM-A. (Eds.) *Social robotics:Proceedings of 4th International Conference, ICSR 2012, Chengdu, China*. Lecture Notes in Computer Science, 7621, 228-237. doi:10.1007/978-3-642-34103-8_23

Dautenhahn, K. (1999). Robots as social actors: aurora and the case of autism. In *Proceedings of CT99, The Third International Cognitive Technology Conference* (p. 374). San Francisco.

Dautenhahn, K. (2013). Human-Robot Interaction. In M. Soegaard & R. F. Dam (Eds.), The encyclopedia of human-computer interaction (2nd ed.). Aarhus, Denmark: The Interaction Design Foundation. Retrieved August 25, 2013 from http://www.interaction-design.org/encyclopedia/human-robot_interaction.html

Dautenhahn, K., & Sanders, J. (Eds.). (2011). Introduction. In K. Dautenhahn & J. Sanders (Eds.). New frontiers in human-robot interaction (pp. 1-5). Amsterdam, The Netherlands: John Benjamins.

Dautenhahn, K., & Werry, I. (2000). Issues of robot-human interaction dynamics in the rehabilitation of children with autism. In *Proceedings of From animals to animats, 6*, 519–528. Retrieved from http://cognet.mit.edu/library/books/mitpress/0262632004/cache/chap54.pdf

Dautenhahn, Kerstin, & Billard, A. (1999). Bringing up robots or—the psychology of socially intelligent robots: From theory to implementation. In *AGENTS '99 Proceedings of the third annual conference on Autonomous Agents* (pp. 366–367). doi:10.1145/301136.301237

Dautenhahn, K. (2007). Socially intelligent robots: Dimensions of human-robot interaction. *Philosophical Transactions of the Royal Society of London. Series B, Biological Sciences, 362*(1480), 679–704. doi:10.1098/rstb.2006.2004 PMID:17301026

Dautenhahn, K. (2007). Methodology & themes of human-robot interaction: A growing research field. *International Journal of Advanced Robotic Systems, 4*(1), 103–108.

Dautenhahn, K. (2013). Human-Robot Interaction. In M. Soegaard & R. F. Dam (Eds.), *The Encyclopedia of Human-Computer Interaction* (2nd ed.). Aarhus, Denmark: The Interaction Design Foundation.

Davidson, R. J. (2002). Activation paradigms in affective and cognitive neuroscience: Probing the neuronal circuitry underlying mod and anxiety disorders. In D. S. Charney, J. Coyle, K. Davis, & C. Nemeroff (Eds.), Neuropsychopharmacology - The Fifth Generation of Progress (pp. 373-382). Lippincott, Williams & Wilkins.

Davidson, R. J., Pizzagalli, D., Nitschke, J. B., & Kalin, N. H. (2003). Parsing the subcomponents of emotion and disorders of emotion: Perspectives from affective neuroscience. In R. J. Davidson, H. H. Goldsmith, & K. Scherer (Eds.), *Handbook of affective science* (pp. 8–24). New York: Oxford University Press.

Dawkins, R. (1988). *The selfish gene*. Oxford: Oxford University Press.

De Carolis, B., Mazzotta, I., Novielli, N., & Pizzutilo, S. (2010). Social robots and ECAs for accessing smart environments services. *Proceedings of the International Conference on Advanced Visual Interfaces, AVI '10* (pp. 275-278). Rome, Italy. doi:10.1145/1842993.1843041

de Graaf, M. M. A., & Allouch, S. B. (2013). Exploring influencing variables for the acceptance of social robots. *Robotics and Autonomous Systems, 61*(12), 1476–1486. doi:10.1016/j.robot.2013.07.007

De Lange, F. P., Spronk, M., Willems, R. M., Toni, I., & Bekkering, H. (2008). Complementary systems for understanding action intentions. *Current Biology, 18*(6), 454–457. doi:10.1016/j.cub.2008.02.057 PMID:18356050

de Rosis, F., Pelachaud, C., Poggi, I., Carofiglio, V., & De Carolis, B. (2003). From Greta's mind to her face: Modelling the dynamics of affective states in a conversational embodied agent. *International Journal of Human-Computer Studies, 59*(1-2), 81–118. doi:10.1016/S1071-5819(03)00020-X

De Sousa, R. (2012). *Emotion. Stanford Encyclopedia of Philosophy*. Retrieved from http://plato.stanford.edu/archives/spr2013/entries/emotion/

de Waal, F. (2013). The Bonobo and the Atheist. In *Search of humanism among the primates*. New York: W.W. Norton and Co.

Dehaene, S., & Changeux, J.-P. (2011). Experimental and theoretical approaches to conscious processing. *Neuron, 70*(2), 200–227. doi:10.1016/j.neuron.2011.03.018 PMID:21521609

Demuth, H., & Beale, M. (1993). *Neural network toolbox for use with MATLAB*.

Dennett, D. (1989). *The Intentional Stance*. MIT Press.

Derryberry, D. (1988). Emotional influences on evaluative judgments: Roles of arousal, attention, and spreading activation. *Motivation and Emotion, 12*(1), 23–55. doi:10.1007/BF00992471

Derrybery, D., & Reed, M. A. (2003). information processing approaches to individual differences in emotional reactivity. In R. J. Davidson, K. R. Scherer, & H. H. Goldsmith (Eds.), Handbook of affective sciences. New York: Oxford University Press.

Descartes, R. (1989). *The passions of the soul*. Hackett Publishing.

Devillers, L., Vidrascu, L., & Layachi, O. (2010). Automatic detection of emotion from vocal expression. In K. R. Scherer, T. Bänziger, & E. B. Roesch (Eds.), *Blueprint for affective computing: A sourcebook* (pp. 232–244). New York: Oxford University Press.

Dey, A. K., Abowd, G. D., & Salber, D. (2001). A conceptual framework and a toolkit for supporting the rapid prototyping of context-aware applications. *Human-Computer Interaction, 16*(2), 97–166. doi:10.1207/S15327051HCI16234_02

Di Paolo, E. A. (2003). Organismically-inspired robotics: Homeostatic adaptation and teleology beyond the closed sensorimotor loop. In K. Murase & T. Asakura (Eds.), *Dynamical systems approach to embodiment and sociality* (pp. 19–42). South Australia: Advanced Knowledge International.

Díaz, J. L. (1997). A patterned process approach to brain, consciousness, and behavior. *Philosophical Psychology, 10*(2), 179–195. doi:10.1080/09515089708573214

Dietterich, T. (2002). Machine learning for sequential data: A review. *Structural, Syntactic, and Statistical Pattern Recognition, LNCS,* (vol. 2396, pp. 1–15). Retrieved from http://link.springer.com/chapter/10.1007/3-540-70659-3_2

Dietterich, T. G. (1998). Approximate statistical tests for comparing supervised classification learning algorithms. *Neural Computation, 10*(7), 1895–1923. doi:10.1162/089976698300017197 PMID:9744903

Digman, J. M. (1990). Personality structure: Emergence of the five factor model. *Annual Review of Psychology, 41*(1), 417–440. doi:10.1146/annurev.ps.41.020190.002221

Dimberg, U., & Thunberg, M. (1998). Rapid facial reactions to emotional facial expressions. *Scandinavian Journal of Psychology, 39*(1), 39–45. doi:10.1111/1467-9450.00054 PMID:9619131

Dittrich, W., Troscianko, T., Lea, S., & Morgan, D. (1996). Perception of emotion from dynamic point-light displays represented in dance. *Perception, 25*(6), 727–738. doi:10.1068/p250727 PMID:8888304

Dorner, D. (2003). The mathematics of emotions. In *Proceedings of the Fifth International Conference on Cognitive Modeling* (pp. 75–79). Bamberg, Germany.

Dorner, D., & Hille, K. (1995). Articial souls: Motivated emotional robots. In *Proceedings of the International Conference on Systems, Man and Cybernetics* (pp. 3828–3832).

Dourish, P. (2013). Epilogue: Where the action was, wasn't, should have been, and might yet be. *ACM Transactions of Computer-Human Interaction, 20*(1).

Dourish, P. (2001). *Where the action is: the foundations for embodied interaction*. Cambridge, MA: MIT Press.

Draper, M., Calhoun, G., Ruff, H., Williamson, D., & Barry, T. (2003). Manual versus speech input for unmanned aerial vehicle control station operations. In *Proceedings of the Human Factors and Ergonomics Society Annual Meeting, 47*(1) 109-113. Denver, CO. doi:10.1177/154193120304700123

Dretske, F. (1981). *Knowledge & the flow of information*.

Dreyfus, H. L. (1992). *What computers still can't do – a critique of artificial reason*. Cambridge, MA: MIT Press.

Drezner, D. W. (2011). Does Obama have a grand strategy: Why we need doctrines in uncertain times. *Foreign Affairs*, *90*, 57.

Duffy, E. (1951). The concept of energy mobilization. *Psychological Review*, *58*(1), 30–40. doi:10.1037/h0054220 PMID:14816485

Durand, G. (1999). *The Anthropological Structures of the Imaginary*. Boombana Publications.

Durbin, R., & Willshaw, D. (1987). An analogue approach to the travelling salesman problem using an elastic net method. *Nature*, *326*(6114), 689–691comptop.stanford.edu/u/references/dw.pdf. doi:10.1038/326689a0 PMID:3561510

Durdu, A., Erkmen, I., Erkmen, A. M., & Yilmaz, A. (2011). Morphing estimated human intention via human-robot interactions. In *Proceedings of the World Congress on Engineering and Computer Science (Vol. I)*. San Francisco.

Durdu, A., Erkmen, I., Erkmen, A. M., & Yilmaz, A. (2012). Robotic hardware and software integration for changing human intentions. In T. Sobh & X. Xiong (Eds.), *Prototyping of robotic systems: Applications of design and implementation* (pp. 380–406). Hershey, PA: IGI Global; doi:10.4018/978-1-4666-0176-5.ch013

Durham, L. M., Milenkovic, M., & Cayton, P. (2006). Platform support for autonomic computing: A research vehicle. Paper presented at the *IEEE International Conference on* Autonomic Computing, 2006 (ICAC'06), pp. 293-294. doi:10.1201/9781420009354.ch16

Du, S., Tao, Y., & Martinez, A. M. (2014) Compound facial expressions of emotion. In *Proceedings of the National Academy of Sciences*, 1-9.

Dyer, G. (2010). *War: The new edition*. New York: Random House.

Edelman, G. M. (1992). *Bright air, brilliant fire: On the matter of the mind*. Basic books.

Edelstein, L. (2009). *The writer's guide to character traits*. Cincinnati, OH: Writers Digest Books.

Ekman, P., & Davidson, R. J. (1994). The nature of emotion: Fundamental questions. New York: Oxford University Press.

Ekman, P., & Friesen, W. (1974). Detecting deception from the body or face. Journal of Personality and Social Psychology, 29(3), 288–298. doi:10.1037/h0036006

Ekman, P. (1992). An argument for basic emotions. *Cognition and Emotion*, *6*(3-4), 169–200. doi:10.1080/02699939208411068

Ekman, P. (1992). Facial expressions of emotion: New findings, new questions. *Psychological Science*, *3*(1), 34–38. doi:10.1111/j.1467-9280.1992.tb00253.x

Ekman, P. (1999). Facial expressions. In T. Dalgleish & M. J. Power (Eds.), *Handbook of cognition and emotion* (pp. 301–320). New York: Wiley.

Ekman, P. (2009). *Telling lies: Clues to deceit in the marketplace, politics, and marriage*. New York, NY: W.W. Norton.

Ekman, P., & Friesen, W. V. (1969). The repertoire of nonverbal behavior: Categories, origins, usage, and coding. *Semiotica*, 49–98.

Ekman, P., & Friesen, W. V. (1978). *Facial action coding system*. Palo Alto, CA: Consulting Psychologists Press.

Ekman, P., Levenson, R. W., & Friesen, W. V. (1983). Autonomic nervous system activity distinguishes among emotions. *Science*, *221*(4616), 1208–1210. doi:10.1126/science.6612338 PMID:6612338

Ekman, P., Sorenson, E. R., & Friesen, W. V. (1969). Pan-cultural elements in facial displays of emotion. *Science*, *164*(3875), 86–88. doi:10.1126/science.164.3875.86 PMID:5773719

El Kaliouby, R., & Robinson, P. (2004). Real time inference of complex mental states from facial expressions and head gestures. In *IEEE International Conference on Computer Vision and Pattern Recognition, Workshop on Real Time Computer Vision for Human Computer Interaction*, Vol. 10, p. 154.

Electronic Arts. (2000). *The Sims*. http://thesims.ea.com/us/

Elfenbein, H. A., & Ambady, N. (2003). Universals and cultural differences in recognizing emotions. *Current Directions in Psychological Science*, *12*(5), 159–164. doi:10.1111/1467-8721.01252

Eliade, M. (2003). Mitul Reintegrarii. *Humanitas.*

Elliot, C. (1992). *The affective reasoner: A process model of emotions in a multiagent system.* Evanston: Northwestern University.

Ellsworth, P. C., & Scherer, K. R. (2003). Appraisal processes in emotion. In R. J. Davidson, K. R. Scherer, & H. Goldsmith (Eds.), *Handbook of the affective sciences* (pp. 572–595). New York, NY: Oxford University Press.

Ellsworth, P. C., & Smith, C. A. (1988). Shades of joy: Patterns of appraisal differentiating pleasant emotions. *Cognition and Emotion, 2*(4), 301–331. doi:10.1080/02699938808412702

El-Nasr, M. S., Yen, J., & Ioerger, T. R. (2000). FLAME - Fuzzy Logic Adaptive Model of Emotions. *Autonomous Agents and Multi-Agent Systems, 3*(3), 219–257. doi:10.1023/A:1010030809960

Emotiv. (n.d.). *Homepage.* Retrieved from www.emotiv.com

Endo, N., & Takanishi, A. (2011). Development of whole-body emotional expression humanoid robot for ADL-assistive RT services. *Journal of Robotics and Mechatronics, 23*(6), 969–977.

Endsley, M. R., Bolte, B., & Jones, D. G. (2010). *Designing for situation awareness: An approach to user-centered design.* London, UK: Taylor & Francis Group.

Erden, M. S., & Tomiyama, T. (2010). Human-intent detection and physically interactive control of a robot without force sensors. IEEE Transactions on Robotics, 26(2), 370–382. doi:10.1109/TRO.2010.2040202

Erickson, K., & Schulkin, J. (2003). Facial expressions of emotion: A cognitive neuroscience perspective. *Brain and Cognition, 52*(1), 52–60. doi:10.1016/S0278-2626(03)00008-3 PMID:12812804

Erk, S., von Kalckreuth, A., & Walter, H. (2010). Neural long-term effects of emotion regulation on episodic memory processes. *Neuropsychologia, 48*(4), 989–996. doi:10.1016/j.neuropsychologia.2009.11.022 PMID:19945471

Fasel, B., & Luettin, J. (2003). Automatic facial expression analysis: A survey. *Pattern Recognition, 36*(1), 259–275. doi:10.1016/S0031-3203(02)00052-3

Fellous, J. M. (2004). *From human emotions to robot emotions.* Paper presented at the AAAI Spring Symposium: Architectures for Modeling Emotion, Stanford University, CA.

Fellous, J.-M., & Arbib, M. A. (2005). Who needs emotions?: The brain meets the robot. Oxford: Oxford University Press. doi:10.1093/acprof:oso/9780195166194.001.0001

Fernald, A. (1989). Intonation and communicative intent in mothers' speech to infants: Is the melody the message? *Child Development, 60*(6), 1497–1510. doi:10.2307/1130938 PMID:2612255

Fernald, A., & Simon, T. (1984). Expanded intonation contours in mothers' speech to newborns. *Developmental Psychology, 20*(1), 104–113. doi:10.1037/0012-1649.20.1.104

Fernald, A., Taeschner, T., Dunn, J., Papousek, M., de Boysson-Bardies, B., & Fukui, I. (1989). A cross-language study of prosodic modifications in mothers' and fathers' speech to preverbal infants. *Journal of Child Language, 16*(3), 477–501. doi:10.1017/S0305000900010679 PMID:2808569

Field, T., Healy, B., Goldstein, S., Perry, S., Bendell, D., Schanberg, S., & Kuhn, C. et al. (1988). Infants of depressed mothers show "depressed" behavior even with nondepressed adults. *Child Development, 59*(6), 1569–1579. doi:10.2307/1130671 PMID:3208568

Figa, E., & Tarau, P. (2002). The VISTA architecture: Experiencing stories through virtual storytelling agents. *SIGGROUP Bulletin, 23*(2), 27–28. doi:10.1145/962185.962196

Fitzsimonds, J. R., & Mahnken, T. G. (2007). Military officer attitudes toward UAV adoption: Exploring institutional expediments to innovation. *Joint Forces Quarterly, 46*(3), 96–103.

Floreano, D., & Mattiussi, C. (2008). *Bio-inspired artificial intelligence: Theories, methods, and technologies.* Cambridge, MA: The MIT Press.

Floridi, L. (2013). *Semantic conceptions of information.* Retrieved from http://plato.stanford.edu/archives/spr2013/entries/information-semantic/

Fogassi, L., Ferrari, P., Gesierich, B., Rozzi, S., Chersi, F., & Rizzolatti, G. (2005). Parietal lobe: From action organization to intention understanding. Science, 308(5722), 662–667. doi:10.1126/science.1106138 PMID:15860620

Fogel, A. (1993). *Developing through relationships.* New York: Harvester Wheatsheaf.

Fogg, B. (2002). Persuasive technology: Using computers to change what we think and do. *Ubiquity*, 89–120. Retrieved from http://scholar.google.com/scholar?hl=en&btnG=Search&q=intitle:Computers+as+Persuasive+Social+Actors#2

Fogg, B. (1999). Persuasive technologies. *Communications of the ACM, 42*(5), 26–29dl.acm.org/citation.cfm?id=301396. doi:10.1145/301353.301396

Fong, T., Nourbakhsh, I., & Dautenhahn, K. (2003). A survey of socially interactive robots. Robotics and Autonomous Systems, 42(3-4), 143–166. doi:10.1016/S0921-8890(02)00372-X

Fong, T., Nourbakhsh, I., & Dautenhahn, K. (2003). A survey of socially interactive robots. *Robotics and Autonomous Systems, 42*(3-4), 143–166.

Fontaine, J. R. J., Scherer, K. R., Roesch, E. B., & Ellsworth, P. C. (2007). The world of emotions is not two-dimensional. *Psychological Science, 18*(12), 1050–1057. doi:10.1111/j.1467-9280.2007.02024.x PMID:18031411

Forgas, J. (1999). Mood and judgment: The affect infusion model (AIM). *Psychological Bulletin, 117*(1), 39–66. doi:10.1037/0033-2909.117.1.39 PMID:7870863

Forgas, J. (2003). Affective influences on attitudes and judgments. In K. R. S. R. J. Davidson & H. H. Goldsmith (Eds.), *Handbook of affective sciences.* New York: Oxford University Press.

Foucault, M. (2002). *The order of things.* Routledge Classics.

Fox, E. (Ed.). (2008). Emotion science: An integration of cognitive and neuroscientific approaches. Palgrave Macmillan.

Francis, A. G., Jr., Mehta, M., & Ram, A. (2009). Emotional memory and adaptive personalities. In J. Vallverdú & D. Casacuberta (Eds.), Handbook of research on synthetic emotions and sociable robotics: New applications in affective computing and artificial intelligence, (pp. 391-421). Hershey, PA: IGI Global.

Fredrickson, B. (2003). The value of positive emotions: The emerging science of positive psychology is coming to understand why it's good to feel good. *American Scientist, 91*(4), 330–335. doi:10.1511/2003.4.330

Fredrickson, B. L., & Joiner, T. (2002). Positive emotions trigger upward spirals toward emotional well-being. *Psychological Science, 13*(2), 172–175. doi:10.1111/1467-9280.00431 PMID:11934003

Freeman, W. J. (2000). *How brains make up their minds.* Columbia University Press.

Fridja, N. H. (2008). The psychologist's point of view. In M. Lewis, J. M. Haviland-Jones, & L. F. Barrett (Eds.), *Handbook of emotions* (3rd ed., pp. 68–87). New York, NY: Guilford Press.

Fries, A. B., & Pollak, S. D. (2004). Emotion understanding in postinstitutionalized Eastern European children. *Development and Psychopathology, 16*(2), 355–369. doi:10.1017/S0954579404044554 PMID:15487600

Friestad, M., & Thorson, E. (1986). Emotion-eliciting advertising: Effects on long term memory and judgment. *Advances in Consumer Research. Association for Consumer Research (U. S.), 13*(1), 111.

Frijda, N. (2008). The psychologists' point of view. In M. Lewis, J. M. Haviland-Jones, & L. F. Barrett (Eds.), *Handbook of emotions* (3rd ed.). New York: The Guilford Press.

Frijda, N. (Ed.). (1987). *The emotions (Studies in Emotion and Social Interaction).* Cambridge University Press.

Frijda, N. H. (1986). *The emotions.* Cambridge: Cambridge University Press.

Frijda, N. H. (1994). Emotions are functional, most of the time. In P. Ekman & R. J. Davidson (Eds.), *The nature of emotion: Fundamental questions.* New York: Oxford University Press.

Frijda, N. H. (Ed.). (2007). *The laws of emotion*. Mahwah, N.J.: Lawrence Erlbaum Associates.

Frijda, N. H., Kuipers, P., & Ter Schure, E. (1989). Relations among emotion, appraisal, and emotional action readiness. *Journal of Personality and Social Psychology*, *57*(2), 212–228. doi:10.1037/0022-3514.57.2.212

Frijda, N. H., & Swagerman, J. (1987). Can computers feel? Theory and design of an emotional system. *Cognition and Emotion*, *1*(3), 235–257. doi:10.1080/02699938708408050

Fussell, S. R. (2002). *The verbal communication of emotion: Interdisciplinary perspectives*. Psychology Press.

Gadanho, S. C. (2003). Learning behavior-selection by emotions and cognition in a multi-goal robot task. *Journal of Machine Learning Research*, *4*, 385–412.

Gallese, V., & Goldman, A. (1998). Mirror neurons and the simulation theory of mind-reading. *Trends in Cognitive Sciences*, *2*(12), 493–501. doi:10.1016/S1364-6613(98)01262-5 PMID:21227300

Gallese, V., Keysers, C., & Rizzolatti, G. (2004). A unifying view of the basis of social cognition. *Trends in Cognitive Sciences*, *8*(9), 398–403.

Galliott, J. C. (Forthcoming). *Military robots: Mapping the moral landscape*. Farnham: Ashgate.

Gangemi, A., Guarino, N., Masolo, C., Oltramari, A., & Schneider, L. (2002). Sweetening Ontologies with DOLCE. In BenjaminsR. (Ed.), *13th International Conference on Knowledge Engineering and Knowledge Management Ontologies and the Semantic Web* (pp. 166–181). London: Springer-Verlag. doi:10.1007/3-540-45810-7_18

Garden, M. (1970). The fantastic combinations of John Conway's new solitaire game "life". *Scientific American*, (233): 120–123.

Gazzola, V., Rizzolatti, G., Wicker, B., & Keysers, C. (2007). The anthropomorphic brain: The mirror neuron system responds to human and robotic actions. *NeuroImage*, *35*(4), 1674–1684. doi:10.1016/j.neuroimage.2007.02.003 PMID:17395490

George, J. M. (2000). Emotions and leadership: The role of emotional intelligence. *Human Relations*, *53*(8), 1027–1055. doi:10.1177/0018726700538001

Gernert, D. (2006). Pragmatic information: Historical exposition and general overview. *Mind and Matter*, *4*(2), 141–167.

Gertz, N. (2011). *Technology and suffering in war*. Paper presented at Technology and Security, University of North Texas.

Ghasem-Afhaee & Ören. (2003). Towards fuzzy agents with dynamic personality for human behavior simulation. Paper presented at SCSC, 2003.

Ghashghaei, H., Hilgetag, C., & Barbas, H. (2007). Sequence of information processing for emotions based on the anatomic dialogue between prefrontal cortex and amygdala. *NeuroImage*, *34*(3), 905–923. doi:10.1016/j.neuroimage.2006.09.046 PMID:17126037

Gibbs, R. W. Jr. (2006). *Embodiment and cognitive science*. Cambridge: Cambridge University Press.

Globus, G. G. (1992). Toward a noncomputational cognitive neuroscience. *Journal of Cognitive Neuroscience*, *4*(4), 299–300. doi:10.1162/jocn.1992.4.4.299 PMID:23968124

Goleman, D. (1995). Emotional intelligence. New York: Bantam.

Gomez, E. A., & Chimento, J. (2011). Information access challenges: Data fission needs of the field expert. In *Proceedings of the 16th ICCRTS,* Québec, QC. pp. 151-160.

Gonz, A. M. (2013). *The emotions and cultural analysis*. Ashgate Publishing.

Goodrich, M. A., & Schultz, A. C. (2007). Human-robot interaction: A survey. *Foundations and Trends in Human–Computer Interaction*, *1*(3), 203–275. doi:10.1561/1100000005

Grammer, K., & Thornhill, R. (1994). Human (Homo sapiens) facial attractiveness and sexual selection: The role of symmetry and averageness. *Journal of Comparative Psychology*, *108*(3), 233–242. doi:10.1037/0735-7036.108.3.233 PMID:7924253

Gratch, J. (2000) *Emile: Marshalling passions in training and education*. In *Proceedings of the Fourth International Conference on Autonomous Agents* (pp. 325-332), Barcelona Spain. (2000) doi:10.1145/336595.337516

Gratch, J., & Marsella, S. (2004). A domain independent frame-work for modeling emotion. *Journal of Cognitive Systems Research*, *5*(4), 269–306. doi:10.1016/j.cogsys.2004.02.002

Gray, G. J. (1959). *The warriors: Reflections on men in battle*. New York: Harper & Row.

Green, G. M. (2000). *The nature of pragmatic information. Grammatical Interfaces in HPSG*. Stanford: CSLI Publications.

Grol, M., Koster, E., Bruyneel, L., & De Raedt, R. (2013). *Effects of positive mood on attention broadening for self-related information. Psychological Research*. PubMed; doi:10.1007/s00426-013-0508-6

Grossman, D. (1995). *On killing: The psychological cost of learning to kill in war and society*. Boston: Little, Brown and Company.

Grüninger, M., & Fox, M. (1995). Methodology for the design and evaluation of ontologies. In: *Proceedings of the Workshop on Basic Ontological Issues in Knowledge Sharing, IJCAI-95*.

Gunes, H., & Pantic, M. (2010). Automatic, dimensional and continuous emotion recognition. *International Journal of Synthetic Emotions, IGI Global*, *1*(1), 68–99. doi:10.4018/jse.2010101605

Gutiérrez, A. M., García-Rojas, A., Thalmann, D., Vexo, F., Moccozet, L., Magnenat-Thalmann, N., & Spagnuolo, M. et al. (2007). An ontology of virtual humans: Incorporating semantics into human shapes. *The Visual Computer: International Journal of Computer Graphics*, *23*(3), 207–218. doi:10.1007/s00371-006-0093-4

Hager, J. C., & Ekman, P. (1983). The inner and outer meanings of facial expressions. In J. T. Cacioppo & R. E. Petty, (Eds.), Social psychophysiology: A sourcebook. New York: The Guilford Press.

Haggard, P., Clark, S., & Kalogeras, J. (2002). Voluntary action and conscious awareness. *Nature Neuroscience*. Retrieved from http://www.nature.com/neuro/journal/v5/n4/abs/nn827.html

Halder, A., Chakraborty, A., Konar, A., & Nagar, A. K. (2013, July). Computing with words model for emotion recognition by facial expression analysis using interval type-2 fuzzy sets. In *IEEE International Conference on Fuzzy Systems (FUZZ), 2013* (pp. 1-8). IEEE. doi:10.1109/FUZZ-IEEE.2013.6622543

Halder, A., Konar, A., Mandal, R., Chakraborty, A., Bhowmik, P., Pal, N. R., & Nagar, A. K. (2013). General and Interval Type-2 Fuzzy Face-Space Approach to Emotion Recognition. *IEEE Transactions on Systems, Man, and Cybernetics*.

Halder, A., Rakshit, P., Chakraborty, S., Konar, A., Chakraborty, A., Kim, E., & Nagar, A. K. (2012, June). Reducing uncertainty in interval type-2 fuzzy sets for qualitative improvement in emotion recognition from facial expressions. In *2012 IEEE International Conference on Fuzzy Systems (FUZZ-IEEE)*, (pp. 1-8). IEEE. doi:10.1109/FUZZ-IEEE.2012.6251363

Hall, E., Birdwhistell, R., & Bock, B. (1968). Proxemics. *Current Anthropology*, *9*(2/3), 83–108. doi:10.1086/200975

Ham, J., Jung, C., Park, J., Ryeo, J., & Ko, I. (2009). An artificial emotion model for visualizing emotion of characters. In *Proceedings of World Academy of Science: Engineering & Technology, 50*.

Hara, F., & Pfeifer, R. (2003). *Morpho-functional machines. The new species: Designing embodied intelligence*. Berlin: Springer. doi:10.1007/978-4-431-67869-4

Hardaker, C. (2013). "Uh.... not to be nitpicky, but... the past tense of drag is dragged, not drug": An overview of trolling strategies. *Journal of Language Aggression and Conflict*, *1*(1), 57–85. doi:10.1075/jlac.1.1.04har

Harder, P. (1999). Function, cognition, and layered clause structure. In J. Allwood & P. Gardenfors (Eds.), *Cognitive semantics. Meaning and cognition* (pp. 37–68). John Benjamins. doi:10.1075/pbns.55.04har

Hare, B., & Tomassello, M. (2005). Human-like social skills in dogs? *Trends in Cognitive Sciences*, *9*(9), 439–444. doi:10.1016/j.tics.2005.07.003 PMID:16061417

Harper, R. G., Wiens, A. N., & Matarazzo, J. D. (1978). *Nonverbal communication: The state of the art.* John Wiley & Sons.

Harper, R., Rodden, T., Rogers, Y., & Sellen, A. (2008). *Being human: Human-computer interaction in the year 2020.* Cambridge, UK: Microsoft Research Ltd.

Hartson, R., & Pyla, P. S. (2012). *The UX Book: Process and guidelines for ensuring a quality user experience.* Amsterdam, The Netherlands: Morgan Kaufmann.

Hassenzahl, M. (2013). User experience and experience design. In M. Soegaard & R. F. Dam (Eds.), *The encyclopedia of human-computer interaction* (2nd ed.). Aarhus, Denmark: The Interaction Design Foundation. Retrieved March 02, 2014, from http://www.interaction-design.org/encyclopedia/user_experience_and_experience_design.html

Hassenzahl, M., & Roto, V. (2007). Being and doing: A perspective on user experience and its measurement. *Interfaces, 72*, 10–12.

Hassenzahl, M., & Tractinsky, N. (2006). User experience – a research agenda. *Behaviour & Information Technology, 25*(2), 91–97. doi:10.1080/01449290500330331

Hastings, J., Ceusters, W., Mulligan, K., & Smith, B. (2012). Annotating affective neuroscience data with the emotion ontology. *Proceedings of the Workshop Towards an Ontology of Mental Functioning, ICBO 2012.*

Hatfield, E., Cacioppo, J., & Rapson, R. (1993). Emotional contagion. *Current Directions in Psychological Science, 2*(3), 96–99. doi:10.1111/1467-8721.ep10770953

Hauert, Ch., & Schuster, H. G. (1997). Effects of increasing the number of players and memory steps in the Iterated Prisoner's Dilemma, a numerical approach. *Proceedings of Biological Sciences, 264*(1381), 513–519. doi:10.1098/rspb.1997.0073

Hayek, F. A. (Ed.). (1999). *The sensory order: An inquiry into the foundations of theoretical psychology.* doi:10.7208/chicago/9780226321301.001.0001

Haykin, S. (1994). *Neural networks: a comprehensive foundation.* Prentice Hall PTR.

Heberlein, A. S., & Atkinson, A. P. (2009). Neuroscientific evidence for simulation and shared substrates in emotion recognition: beyond faces. *Emotion Review, 1*(2), 162–177. doi:10.1177/1754073908100441

Hegel, F., Eyssel, F. A., & Wrede, B. (2010). The social robot Flobi: Key concepts of industrial design. In *Proceedings of the 19th IEEE International Symposium in Robot and Human Interactive Communication (RO-MAN 2010).* doi:10.1109/ROMAN.2010.5598691

He, H., Ge, S. S., & Zhang, Z. (2014). A saliency-driven robotic head with bio-inspired saccadic behaviors for social robotics. *Autonomous Robots, 36*(3), 225–240. doi:10.1007/s10514-013-9346-z

Heinze, C. (2003). *Modelling intention recognition for intelligent agent systems.* The University of Melbourne, Australia. Retrieved from http://oai.dtic.mil/oai/oai?verb=getRecord&metadataPrefix=html&identifier=ADA430005

Herrera Pérez, C., & Sanz, R. (2013). Emotion as morpho-functionality. *Artificial Life, 19*(1), 133–148. doi:10.1162/ARTL_a_00086 PMID:23186348

Hess, U., & Kleck, R. E. (2005). Differentiating emotion elicited and deliberate emotional facial expressions. In P. Ekman & E. L. Rosenberg (Eds.), What the face reveals: Basic and applied studies of spontaneous expression using the facial action coding system (FACS) (2nd ed., pp. 271-286). Oxford: Oxford University Press.

Hess, U., Beaupré, M. G., & Cheung, N. (2002). Who to whom and why – cultural differences and similarities in the function of smiles. In M. Abel (Ed.), *An empirical reflection on the smile* (pp. 187–216). New York: The Edwin Mellen Press.

Hewett, T. T., Baecker, R., Card, S., Carey, T., Gasen, J., Mantei, M., . . . Verplank, W. (1996). Curricula for Human-Computer Interaction. *ACM SIGCHI Curricula for Human-Computer Interaction.* Retrieved February 26, 2014, from http://old.sigchi.org/cdg/index.html

Hewlett-Packard Development Company. (2008). *Jena: A Semantic Web Framework for Java, 2008* (version 2.5.6). Retrieved October 13, 2008, from http://jena.sourceforge.net/

Hiatt, S., Campos, J., & Emde, R. (1979). Facial patterning and infant emotional expression: Happiness, surprise and fear. *Child Development, 50*(4), 1020–1035. doi:10.2307/1129328 PMID:535426

Hjorth, B. (1970). EEG analysis based on time domain properties. *Electroencephalography and Clinical Neurophysiology, 29*(3), 306–310. doi:10.1016/0013-4694(70)90143-4 PMID:4195653

Hofstee, W. K., de Raad, B., & Goldberg, L. R. (1992). Integration of the big five and circumplex approaches to trait structure. *Journal of Personality and Social Psychology, 63*(1), 146–163. doi:10.1037/0022-3514.63.1.146 PMID:1494982

Homma, I., & Masaoka, Y. (2008). Breathing rhythms and emotions. *Experimental Physiology, 93*(9), 1011–1021. doi:10.1113/expphysiol.2008.042424 PMID:18487316

Horstmann, G. (2003). What do facial expressions convey: Feeling states, behavioral intentions, or actions requests? Emotion (Washington, D.C.), *3*(2), 150–166. doi:10.1037/1528-3542.3.2.150 PubMed doi:10.1037/1528-3542.3.2.150 PMID:12899416

Huang, C.-C., Bardzell, J., & Terrell, J. (2011). Can your pet rabbit read your email? A critical analysis of the Nabaztag Rabbit. *Proceedings of the 2011 Conference on Designing Pleasurable Products and Interfaces, DPPI '11*. Milan, Italy. doi:10.1145/2347504.2347532

Hudlicka, E. (1998). *Modeling Emotion in Symbolic Cognitive Architectures.* Paper presented at the AAAI Fall Symposium: Emotional and Intelligent I, Orlando, FL.

Hudlicka, E. (2003). *Modeling Effects of Behavior Moderators on Performance: Evaluation of the MAMID Methodology and Architecture.* Paper presented at the BRIMS-12, Phoenix, AZ.

Hudlicka, E. (2004). Two Sides of Appraisal: Implementing Appraisal and Its Consequences within a Cognitive Architecture. *AAAI Spring Symposium: Architectures for Modeling Emotion* (Vol. TR SS-04-02). Stanford University, CA: AAAI Press.

Hudlicka, E. (2007). Reasons for emotions. In W. Gray (Ed.), Advances in Cognitive models and cognitive architectures. New York: Oxford University Press. doi:10.1093/acprof:oso/9780195189193.003.0019

Hudlicka, E. (2008). Modeling the mechanisms of emotion effects on cognition. *AAAI Fall Symposium: Biologically Inspired Cognitive Architectures* (Vol. TR FS-08-04 pp. 82-86), Arlington, VA. Menlo Park, CA: AAAI Press.

Hudlicka, E. (2008). What are we modeling when we model emotion? *AAAI Spring Symposium: Emotion, Personality, and Social Behavior* (Vol. Technical Report SS-08-04, pp. 52-59), Stanford University, CA. Menlo Park, CA: AAAI Press.

Hudlicka, E. (2011). Guidelines for developing computational models of emotions. *International Journal of Synthetic Emotions, 2*(1), 26-79.

Hudlicka, E. (2014). Can computational affective models improve psychotherapy? In *Proceedings of the Workshop on Computational Models of Cognition-Emotion Interactions: Relevance to Mechanisms of Affective Disorders and Psychotherapeutic Action.* Quebec City, Quebec, Canada.

Hudlicka, E. (forthcoming). *Affective computing: Theory, methods and applications.* Boca Raton, FL: Taylor and Francis.

Hudlicka, E. (2002). This time with feeling: Integrated Model of Trait and State Effects on Cognition and Behavior. *Applied Artificial Intelligence, 16*(7-8), 1–31. doi:10.1080/08339510290030417

Hudlicka, E. (2008). Modeling the mechanisms of emotion effects on cognition. *Proceedings of the AAAI Fall Symposium on "Biologically Inspired Cognitive Architectures"* (pp. 82-86).

Hudlicka, E. (2011). Guidelines for designing computational models of emotions. *International Journal of Synthetic Emotions, 2*(1), 26–78. doi:10.4018/jse.2011010103

Huettenrauch, H., Eklundh, K., Green, A., & Topp, E. (2006). Investigating spatial relationships in human-robot interaction. In *2006 IEEE/RSJ International Conference on Intelligent Robots and Systems* (pp. 5052–5059). doi:10.1109/IROS.2006.282535

Hughes, T. C. (2012). Sources of adaptive capacity during multi-unmanned aerial vehicle operations (Doctoral thesis). Ohio State University, USA.

Iacoboni, M., & Dapretto, M. (2006). The mirror neuron system and the consequences of its dysfunction. *Nature Reviews. Neuroscience, 7*(12), 942–951. doi:10.1038/nrn2024 PMID:17115076

Ishihara, H., Yoshikawa, Y., & Asada, M. (2011). Realistic child robot "Affetto" for understanding the caregiver-child attachment relationship that guides the child development. *IEEE International Conference on Development and Learning - ICDL. 2*, pp. 1-5. Frankfurt: IEEE. doi:10.1109/DEVLRN.2011.6037346

Itoh, K., Miwa, H., Matsumoto, M., Zecca, M., Takanobu, H., & Roccella, S., … Takanishi, A. (2004). Various emotional expressions with emotion expression humanoid robot WE-4RII. In *First IEEE Technical Exhibition Based Conference on Robotics and Automation (TExCRA'04)*. doi:10.1109/TEXCRA.2004.1424983

Izard, C. E. (1993). Organizational and motivational functions of discrete emotions. In M. Lewis & J.M. Haviland (Eds.), Handbook of emotions (pp.631 - 642). New York: The Guilford Press.

Izard, C. E. (1977). *Human emotions.* NY: Plenum. doi:10.1007/978-1-4899-2209-0

Izard, C. E. (1993). Four systems for emotion activation: Cognitive and noncognitive processes. *Psychological Review, 100*(1), 68–90. doi:10.1037/0033-295X.100.1.68 PMID:8426882

Izhikevich, E. M. (2003). Simple model of spiking neurons. *Neural Networks. IEEE Transactions on, 14*(6), 1569–1572.

James, W. (1884). II. What is an emotion? *Mind, os-IX*(34), 188–205. doi:10.1093/mind/os-IX.34.188

Jenkins, O. C., Serrano, G. G., & Loper, M. M. (2007). Interactive human pose and action recognition using dynamical motion primitives. *International Journal of Humanoid Robotics, 04*(02), 365–385. doi:10.1142/S0219843607001060

Jessen, S., & Kotz, S. (2011). The temporal dynamics of processing emotions from vocal, facial, and bodily expressions. NeuroImage, 58(2), 665–674. doi:10.1016/j.neuroimage.2011.06.035 PubMed doi:10.1016/j.neuroimage.2011.06.035 PMID:21718792

Jia, H., Wu, M., Jung, E., Shapiro, A., & Sundar, S. S. (2013). When the tissue box says "Bless you!": Using speech to build socially interactive objects. *CHI '13 Extended Abstracts on Human Factors in Computing Systems, CHI EA '13* (pp. 1635-1640). Paris, France.

Jin, Y., & Meng, Y. (2011). Morphogenetic robotics: An emerging new field in developmental robotics. *Systems, Man, and Cybernetics, Part C: Applications and Reviews. IEEE Transactions on, 41*(2), 145–160.

Johnson, D.O., Cuijpers, R.H., Juola, J.F., Torta, E., S. M., Frisiello, A., Bazzani, M., Yan, W., Weber, C., Wermter, S., Meins, N., Oberzaucher, J., Panek, P., Edelmayer, G., Mayer, P., & Beck, C. (2013, November). Socially assistive robots: A comprehensive approach to extending independent living. *International Journal of Social Robotics.*

Johnson, M. (2007). *The meaning of the body: Aesthetics of human understanding.* Chicago, IL: Chicago University Press. doi:10.7208/chicago/9780226026992.001.0001

Johnstone, T., van Reekum, C. M., Hird, K., Kirsner, K., & Scherer, K. R. (2005). Affective speech elicited with a computer game. *Emotion (Washington, D.C.), 5*(4), 513–518. doi:10.1037/1528-3542.5.4.513 PMID:16366756

Jones, S. R. (2000). The roots of antisemitism. In I. Davies (Ed.), *Teaching the Holocaust: Educational dimensions, principles and practice* (pp. 11–24). London, UK: Bloomsbury Publishing.

Joshi, A. (2011). *Short essay on understanding human memory.* Retrieved 6th April, 2014, from http://www.preservearticles.com/201106087597/short-essay-on-understanding-human-memory.html

Juarez, A., Bartneck, C., & Feijs, L. (2011) Using semantic technologies to describe robotic embodiments. *Proceedings of the 6th ACM/IEEE International Conference on Human-Robot Interaction (HRI)* (pp 425-432) Lausanne, Switzerland. doi:10.1145/1957656.1957812

Jung, C. G. (1981). The archetypes and the collective unconscious (Collected Works of C.G. Jung Vol.9 Part 1) (2nd Ed.). Princeton University Press.

Jung, C. G. (1981). The development of personality (Collected Works of C.G. Jung Vol.17). Princeton University Press.

Jung, J., & Bae, S.-H. Lee, J.H., & Kim, M-S. (2013). Make it move: A movement design method of simple standing products based on systematic mapping of torso movements & product messages. *Proceedings of the SIGCHI Conference on Human Factors in Computing Systems, CHI '13* (pp. 1279-1288). Paris, France. doi:10.1145/2470654.2466168

Junghöfer, M., Elbert, T., Tucker, D. M., & Rockstroh, B. (2000). Statistical control of artifacts in dense array EEG/MEG studies. *Psychophysiology*, *37*(4), 523–532. doi:10.1111/1469-8986.3740523 PMID:10934911

Juslin, P. N., & Scherer, K. R. (2005). Vocal expression of affect. In J. A. Harrigan, R. Rosenthal & K. R. Scherer (Eds.), The new handbook of methods in nonverbal behavior research (pp. 65-135). New York: Oxford University Press.

Juslin, P. N., & Laukka, P. (2003). Communication of emotions in vocal expression and music performance: Different channels, same code? *Psychological Bulletin*, *129*(5), 770–814. doi:10.1037/0033-2909.129.5.770 PMID:12956543

Kaffman, A., & Meaney, M. J. (2007). Neurodevelopmental sequelae of postnatal maternal care in rodents: Clinical research and implications of molecular insights. *Journal of Child Psychology and Psychiatry, and Allied Disciplines*, *48*(3-4), 224–244. doi:10.1111/j.1469-7610.2007.01730.x PMID:17355397

Kaiser, S., & Wehrle, T. (2008). Facial expressions in social interactions: Beyond basic emotions. In Advances in Consciousness Research. (Vol. 74): Animating Expressive Characters for Social Interactions (pp. 53-69). Amsterdam, The Netherlands: John Benjamins Publishing Company.

Kaiser, S., & Wehrle, T. (2001). Facial expressions as indicators of appraisal processes. In K. R. Scherer, A. Schorr, & T. Johnstone (Eds.), *Appraisal processes in emotion* (pp. 285–300). New York: Oxford University Press.

Kanade, T., Cohn, J. F., & Tian, Y. (2000). Comprehensive database for facial expression analysis. *Proceeding of International Conference on Face and Gesture Recognition*, 46-53. doi:10.1109/AFGR.2000.840611

Kanungo, T., Mount, D. M., Netanyahu, N. S., Piatko, C. D., Silverman, R., & Wu, A. Y. (2002). An efficient k-means clustering algorithm: Analysis and implementation. *Pattern Analysis and Machine Intelligence. IEEE Transactions on*, *24*(7), 881–892.

Kar, R., Chakraborty, A., Saha, A., & Konar, A. (2013). Detection of true emotion or pretension: A brain-computer interface approach. In *Proceedings of National Conference on Brain and Consciousness*.

Karnik, N. N., & Mendel, J. M. (2001). Centroid of a type-2 fuzzy set. *Information Sciences*, *132*(1), 195–220. doi:10.1016/S0020-0255(01)00069-X

Kassam, K. S., Markey, A. R., Cherkassky, V. L., Loewenstein, G., & Just, M. A. (2013). Identifying emotions on the basis of neural activation. *PLoS ONE*, *8*(6), e66032. doi:10.1371/journal.pone.0066032 PMID:23840392

Kaurin, P. (2013). Courage behind a screen. In B. J. Strawser (Ed.), Killing by remote control: The Ethics of an unmanned military. New York: Oxford University Press.

Kautz, H. A., & Allen, J. F. (1986). Generalized plan recognition. AAAI, 86, 32–37.

Kawasaki, H., Adolphs, R., Kaufman, O., Damasio, H., Damasio, A. R., Granner, M., & Howard, M. A. et al. (2001). Single-neuron responses to emotional visual stimuli recorded in human ventral prefrontal cortex. *Nature Neuroscience*, *4*(1), 15–16. doi:10.1038/82850 PMID:11135639

Kean, T. H., & Hamilton, L. H. (2006). *Without precedent: The inside story of the 9/11 commission*. New York, NY: Knopf.

Kean, T. H., Hamilton, L. H., Ben-Veniste, R., Kerrey, B., Fielding, F. F., & Lehman, J. F. et al.. (2004). *The 9/11 commission report*. New York, NY: W. W. Norton & Company.

Kędzierski, J., Muszyński, R., Zoll, C., Oleksy, A., & Frontkiewicz, M. (2013). EMYS—Emotive head of a social robot. *International Journal of Social Robotics*, *5*(2), 237–249. doi:10.1007/s12369-013-0183-1

Keegan, J., & Holmes, R. (1986). *Soldiers: A history of men in battle*. New York: Viking.

Keysers, C., & Gazzola, V. (2010). Social neuroscience: Mirror neurons recorded in humans. *Current Biology, 20*(8), 353–354.

Khosrowabadi, R., Quek, H. C., Wahab, A., & Ang, K. K. (2010, August). EEG-based emotion recognition using self-organizing map for boundary detection. In *20th International Conference on Pattern Recognition (ICPR), 2010* (pp. 4242-4245). IEEE. doi:10.1109/ICPR.2010.1031

Kim, P., Feldman, R., Mayes, C., Eicher, V., Thompson, N., Leckman, J., & Swain, J. E. (2011). Breastfeeing, brain activation to own infant cry, and maternal sensitivity. *Journal of Child Psychology and Psychiatry, and Allied Disciplines, 52*(8), 907–915. doi:10.1111/j.1469-7610.2011.02406.x PMID:21501165

Kim, S. E., Kim, J. W., Kim, J. J., Jeong, B. S., Choi, E., Jeong, Y. G., & Ki, S. W. et al. (2007). The neural mechanism of imagining facial affective expression. *Brain Research, 1145*, 128–137. doi:10.1016/j.brainres.2006.12.048 PMID:17359942

Kiryazov, K., Lowe, R., Becker-Asano, C., & Ziemke, T. (2011). Modelling embodied appraisal in humanoids: Grounding PAD space for augmented autonomy. In *Proceedings of the Workshop on Standards in Emotion Modeling*.

Kishi, T., Otani, T., Endo, N., Kryczka, P., Hashimoto, K., Nakata, K., & Takanishi, A. (2012). Development of expressive robotic head for bipedal humanoid robot. In *Proceedings of IROS 2012*. doi:10.1109/IROS.2012.6386050

Kitamura, C., & Lam, C. (2009). Age-specific preferences for infant-directed affective intent. *Infancy, 14*(1), 77–100. doi:10.1080/15250000802569777

Kitayama, S., Markus, H. R., & Kurokawa, M. (2000). Culture, emotion, and well-being: Good feelings in Japan and the United States. *Cognition and Emotion, 14*(1), 93–124. doi:10.1080/026999300379003

Kleinginna, P. R. Jr, & Kleinginna, A. M. (1981). A categorized list of emotion definitions, with suggestions for a consensual definition. *Motivation and Emotion, 5*(4), 345–379. doi:10.1007/BF00992553

Klir, G. J. (Ed.). (1969). *An approach to general systems theory*. New York, N.Y.: Van Nostrand Reinhold Company.

Klüver, H., & Bucy, P. C. (1937). "Psychic blindness" and other symptoms following bilateral temporal lobectomy in Rhesus monkeys. *The American Journal of Physiology*.

Knapp, M. L. (1980). *Essentials of nonverbal communication*. Harcourt School.

Knoblich, G., & Prinz, W. (2001). Recognition of self-generated actions from kinematic displays of drawing. Journal of Experimental Psychology. Human Perception and Performance, 27(2), 456–465. doi:10.1037/0096-1523.27.2.456 PMID:11318059

Kobayashi, H., & Hara, F. (1992, September). Recognition of six basic facial expression and their strength by neural network. In *Proceedings of the IEEE International Workshop on Robot and Human Communication, 1992* (pp. 381-386). IEEE. doi:10.1109/ROMAN.1992.253857

Kobayashi, H., Ichikawa, Y., Senda, M., & Shiiba, T. (2002). Toward rich facial expression by face robot. In *Proceedings of 2002 International Symposium on Micromechatronics and Human Science*. doi:10.1109/MHS.2002.1058024

Koda, T. (1996). *Agents with faces: A study on the effect of personification of software agents* (Unpublished Master Thesis). MIT Media Lab, Cambridge.

Kohler, E., Keysers, C., Umilta, M. A., Fogassi, V., & Rizzolatti, G. (2002). Hearing sounds, understanding actions: Action representation in mirror neurons. *Science, 287*(5582), 846–848. doi:10.1126/science.1070311 PMID:12161656

Konar, A. (1999). *Artificial intelligence and soft computing: Behavioral and cognitive modeling of the human brain* (Vol. 1). CRC press. doi:10.1201/9781420049138

Konar, A. (2005). *Computational intelligence: Principles, techniques and applications*. Springer.

Koo, S., & Kwon, D. (2009). Recognizing human intentional actions from the relative movements between human and robot. In *The 18th IEEE International Symposium on Robot and Human Interactive Communication, 2009 (RO-MAN 2009)*, (pp. 939–944). doi:10.1109/RO-MAN.2009.5326127

Korb, S., Grandjean, D., & Scherer, K. (2008). Investigating the production of emotional facial expressions: a combined electroencephalographic (EEG) and electromyographic (EMG) approach. In *IEEE International Conference on computational intelligence*, pp.1-6. doi:10.1109/AFGR.2008.4813388

Kotonya, G., & Sommerville, I. (1998). *Requirements engineering: Processes and techniques.* Chichester, England: John Wiley and Sons.

Kozima, H., Nakagawa, C., & Yasuda, Y. (2005). Interactive robots for communication-care: a case-study in autism therapy. *ROMAN 2005. IEEE International Workshop on Robot and Human Interactive Communication, 2005*, pp. 341–346. doi:10.1109/ROMAN.2005.1513802

Krolak-Salmon, P., Henaff, M. A., Vighetto, A., Bauchet, F., Bertrand, O., Mauguiere, F., & Isnard, J. (2006). Experiencing and detecting happiness in humans: The role of the supplementary motor area. *Annals of Neurology*, *59*(1), 196–199. doi:10.1002/ana.20706 PMID:16261588

Krummenacher, R., Lausen, H., & Strang, T. (2007). Analyzing the modeling of context with ontologies. In *International Workshop on Context-Awareness for Self-Managing Systems.* (pp. 11-22). Toronto: VDE Verlag.

Kuhl, P. K. (2004). Early language acquisition: Cracking the speech code. *Nature Reviews. Neuroscience*, *5*(11), 831–843. doi:10.1038/nrn1533 PMID:15496861

Kuo, I.-H., Jayawardena, C., Broadbent, E., & MacDonald, B. A. (2011). Multidisciplinary design approach for implementation of interactive services: Communication initiation and user identification for healthcare service robots. *International Journal of Social Robotics*, *3*(4), 443–456. doi:10.1007/s12369-011-0115-x

Kurzweil, R. (2005). *The singularity is near: When humans transcend biology.* New York: Viking Penguin.

LaBar, K. S., & Cabeza, R. (2006). Cognitive neuroscience of emotional memory. *Nature Reviews. Neuroscience*, *7*(1), 54–64. doi:10.1038/nrn1825 PMID:16371950

Laird, J., Newell, A., Rosenbloom, P. S., & Artificial Intelligence and Psychology Project. (1987) *Soar: an architecture for general intelligence* (Paper 433). Department of Psychology.

Lakoff, G. (1993). The contemporary theory of metaphor. In A. Ortony (Ed.), *Metaphor and thought* (pp. 202–251). Cambridge University Press. doi:10.1017/CBO9781139173865.013

Lakoff, G., & Johnson, M. (1999). *Philosophy in the flesh: The embodied mind and its challenge to western thought.* Basic books.

Larsen, J. C. (2011). *Locomotion through morphosis: Development of the modular robotic toolkit-LocoKit* (Doctoral dissertation).

Laukka, P., Elfenbein, H. A., Chui, W., Thingujam, N. S., Iraki, F. K., Rockstuhl, T., & Althoff, J. (2010). Presenting the VENEC corpus: Development of a cross-cultural corpus of vocal emotion expressions and a novel method of annotating emotion appraisals. In L. Devillers, B. Schuller, R. Cowie, E. Douglas-Cowie, & A. Batliner (Eds.), *Proceedings of the LREC 2010 Workshop on Corpora for Research on Emotion and Affect* (pp. 53-57). Paris: EuropeanLanguage Resources Association.

Law, E. L.-C., Roto, V., Hassenzahl, M., Vermeeren, A. P. O. S., & Kort, J. (2009). Understanding, scoping and defining user experience: A survey approach. In *Proceedings of the SIGCHI Conference on Human Factors in Computing Systems, CHI '09.* Boston, MA, USA. doi:10.1145/1518701.1518813

Lazarus, R. S. (1984). On the primacy of cognition. *The American Psychologist*, *39*(2), 124–129. doi:10.1037/0003-066X.39.2.124

Lazarus, R. S. (1991). *Emotion and adaptation.* New York: Oxford University Press.

Lecanuet, J. P., & Schaal, B. (1996). Fetal sensory competencies. *European Journal of Obstetrics, Gynecology, and Reproductive Biology*, *68*, 1–23. doi:10.1016/0301-2115(96)02509-2 PMID:8886675

LeDoux, J. (1996). Emotional networks and motor control: A fearful view. *Progress in Brain Research, 107*, 437–446. doi:10.1016/S0079-6123(08)61880-4 PMID:8782535

LeDoux, J. E. (2000). Emotion circuits in the brain. *Annual Review of Neuroscience, 23*(1), 155–184. doi:10.1146/annurev.neuro.23.1.155 PMID:10845062

LeDoux, J. E. (2007). Emotional memory. *Scholarpedia, 2*(7), 1806. doi:10.4249/scholarpedia.1806

Lee, K. K., & Xu, Y. (2004). Modeling human actions from learning. *2004 IEEE/RSJ International Conference on Intelligent Robots and Systems (IROS), 3*, 2787–2792. doi:10.1109/IROS.2004.1389831

Lee, S., & Son, Y. (2008). Integrated human decision making model under belief-desire-intention framework for crowd simulation. *Simulation Conference, 2008 (WSC 2008)*. pp. 886–894. doi:10.1109/WSC.2008.4736153

Lee, C. M., & Narayanan, S. S. (2005). Toward detecting emotions in spoken dialogs. *IEEE Transactions on Speech and Audio Processing, 13*(2), 293–303.

Lee, T. W., Josephs, O., Dolan, R. J., & Critchley, H. D. (2006). Imitating expressions: Emotion-specific neural substrates in facial mimicry. *Social Cognitive and Affective Neuroscience, 1*(2), 122–135. doi:10.1093/scan/nsl012 PMID:17356686

Lefkoe, M. (2010). Why we have negative emotions ... and what to do about them. Retrieved from http://www.mortylefkoe.com/why-negative-emotions/

LEGO. (2001). *LEGO Mindstorms*. Retrieved from http://www.legomindstorms.com

Lenat, D. B. (1995). CYC: A large-scale investment in knowledge infrastructure. *Communications of the ACM, 38*(11), 33–38. doi:10.1145/219717.219745

Lerner, J. S., & Tiedens, L. Z. (2006). Portrait of the angry decision maker: How appraisal tendencies shape anger's influence on cognition. *Journal of Behavioral Decision Making, 19*(2), 115–137. doi:10.1002/bdm.515

Leventhal, H., & Scherer, K. R. (1987). The relationship of emotion to cognition. *Cognition and Emotion, 1*(1), 3–28. doi:10.1080/02699938708408361

Levine, L. J., & Pizarro, D. A. (2004). Emotion and memory research: A grumpy overview. *Social Cognition, 22*(5), 530-554.

Lewin, K. (1952). *Field theory in social science: Selected theoretical papers*. (D. Cartwright, Ed.). Retrieved from http://library.wur.nl/WebQuery/clc/388286

Lewis, M. D. (2005). Bridging emotion theory and neurobiology through dynamic systems modeling. *Behavioral and Brain Sciences, 28*(2), 169–194, discussion 194–245. http://www.ncbi.nlm.nih.gov/pubmed/16201458 doi:10.1017/S0140525X0500004X PMID:16201458

Liang, Q., & Mendel, J. M. (2000). Designing interval type-2 fuzzy logic systems using an SVD-QR method: Rule reduction. *International Journal of Intelligent Systems, 15*(10), 939–957. doi:10.1002/1098-111X(200010)15:10<939::AID-INT3>3.0.CO;2-G

Lim, A., Ogata, T., & Okuno, H. G. (2011). Converting emotional voice to motion for robot telepresence. *11th IEEE-RAS International Conference on Humanoid Robots (Humanoids), 2011*, (pp. 472-479).

Lim, A., Ogata, T., & Okuno, H. G. (2012). Towards expressive musical robots: A cross-modal framework for emotional gesture, voice and music. *EURASIP Journal on Audio, Speech, and Music Processing*, (1): 1–12.

Lim, A., & Okuno, H. G. (in prep.). *Emotional Contagion as a Mechanism for Basic Empathy*.

Lim, A., & Okuno, H. G. (in press). The MEI robot: Towards using motherese to develop multimodal emotional intelligence. *IEEE Transactions on Autonomous Mental Development*.

Lindblom, J. (forthcoming). *Embodied social cognition*. Berlin: Springer Verlag.

Lindblom, J., & Ziemke, T. (2003). Social situatedness of natural and artificial intelligence: Vygotsky and beyond. *Adaptive Behavior, 11*(2), 79–96. doi:10.1177/10597123030112002

Lindblom, J., & Ziemke, T. (2007). Embodiment and social interaction: implications for cognitive science. In T. Ziemke, J. Zlatev, & R. Frank (Eds.), *Body, language, and mind: Embodiment* (Vol. 1, pp. 129–162). Berlin: Mounton de Gruyter.

Lin, J. C., Wu, C. H., & Wei, W. L. (2012). Error weighted semi-coupled hidden Markov model for audio-visual emotion recognition. *IEEE Transactions on Multimedia, 14*(1), 142–156.

Lisetti, C. L., & Rumelhart, D. E. (1998, May). Facial expression recognition using a neural network. In *FLAIRS Conference* (pp. 328-332).

Lisetti, C., & Gmytrasiewicz, P. (2002). Can rational agents afford to be affectless? *Applied Artificial Intelligence, 16*(7-8), 577–609. doi:10.1080/08839510290030408

Littlewort, G. C., Bartlett, M. S., & Lee, K. (2007). Faces of pain: automated measurement of spontaneous facial expressions of genuine and posed pain. In *Proceedings of the 9th international conference on multimodal interfaces*, pp. 15–21. ACM, New York. doi:10.1145/1322192.1322198

Li, Y., Ashkanasy, N. M., & Ahlstrom, D. (2013). The rationality of emotions: A hybrid process model of decision-making under uncertainty. *Asia Pacific Journal of Management*, 1–16.

Ljung, L. (Ed.). (1987). System identification: Theory for the user. New Jersey: Prentice-Hall, Inc.

Llinás, R. R. (2001). *I of the Vortex. From neurons to Self*. Cambridge, MA: MIT Press.

Loewenstein, G., & Lerner, J. S. (2003). The role of affect in decision making. Handbook of Affective Science, 619(642), 3.

López, J. M., Gil, R., García, R., Cearreta, I., & Garay, N. (2008). Towards an ontology for describing emotions. In M. D. Lytras, J. M. Carroll, E. Damiani, & R. D. Tennyson (Eds.), *Proceedings of the 1st world summit on The Knowledge Society: Emerging Technologies and Information Systems for the Knowledge Society* (WSKS '08) (pp. 96-104). Berlin, Heidelberg: Springer-Verlag.

Loyall, A. B. (1997). *Believable agents: Building interactive personalities*. Pittsburgh, PA: CMU.

Lucas, G. Jr. (2011). Industrial challenges of military robotics. *Journal of Military Ethics, 10*(4), 274–295. doi:10.1080/15027570.2011.639164

Lungu, V. (2013). Artificial emotion simulation model and agent architecture: Extended. In *Advances in intelligent control systems and computer science* (pp. 207–221). Springer. doi:10.1007/978-3-642-32548-9_15

Lutz, C. (1988). *Unnatural emotions*. Chicago, IL: UCP.

MacFarlane, A. G. (2003). Information, knowledge and the future of machines. *Philosophical Transactions of the Royal Society of London. Series A: Mathematical, Physical and Engineering Sciences, 361*(1809), 1581-1616.

Macht, M. (2008). How emotions affect eating: A five-way model. *Appetite, 50*(1), 1–11. doi:10.1016/j.appet.2007.07.002 PMID:17707947

Mackie, J. (1974). *The cement of the universe: a study of causation*. Oxford: Clarendon.

MacLean, P. D. (1990). The triune brain in evolution: Role in paleocerebral functions. Plenum Publishing Corporation.

Maleeh, S. (2008). The conscious mind revisited (PhD thesis). University of Osnabrück, Germany.

Manchester, W. (1979). *Goodbye darkness: A memoir of the pacific war*. New York: Dell Publishing Company.

Mandal, R., Halder, A., Bhowmik, P., Konar, A., Chakraborty, A., & Nagar, A. K. (2011, June). Uncertainty management in type-2 fuzzy face-space for emotion recognition. In *2011 IEEE International Conference on Fuzzy Systems (FUZZ)*, (pp. 1902-1909). IEEE. doi:10.1109/FUZZY.2011.6007689

Mandler, G. (1984). *Mind and body: The psychology of emotion and stress*. New York: Norton.

Manera, V., Schouten, B., Becchio, C., Bara, B. G., & Verfaillie, K. (2010). Inferring intentions from biological motion: A stimulus set of point-light communicative interactions. Behavior Research Methods, 42(1), 168–178. doi:10.3758/BRM.42.1.168 PMID:20160297

Marinier, R. P. (2008). *A computational unification of cognitive control, emotion and learning* (PhD dissertation). University of Michigan, Ann Arbor, Michigan.

Marr, D. (1982). *Vision*. San Francisco, CA: Freeman.

Marsella, S., Gratch, J., & Petta, P. (2010). Computational models of emotion. In K. R. Scherer, T. Bänziger, & E. B. Roesch (Eds.), *Blueprint for Affective Computing: A sourcebook* (pp. 21–41). New York: Oxford University Press.

Marshall, S. L. A. (2000). *Men against fire: The problem of battle command*. Norman: University of Oklahoma Press.

Martin, M. J., & Sasser, C. W. (2010). *Predator: The remote-control air war over Iraq and Afghanistan: A pilot's story*. Minneapolis: Zenith Press.

Maslin, K. T., & Maslin, K. (2001). *An introduction to the philosophy of mind*. Polity Cambridge.

Mason, W. A., & Capitanio, J. P. (2012). Basic Emotions: A Reconstruction. *Emotion Review, 4*(3), 238–244. doi:10.1177/1754073912439763

Matthews, G. A., & Harley, T. A. (1993). Effects of extraversion and self-report arousal on semantic priming: A connectionist approach. *Journal of Personality and Social Psychology, 65*(4), 735–756. doi:10.1037/0022-3514.65.4.735

Matthias, A. (2011). *Is the concept of an ethical governor philosophically sound?* Paper presented at the Tilting Perspectives: Technologies on the Stand: Legal and Ethical Questions in Neuroscience and Robotics, The Netherlands.

Mazzei, D., Lazzeri, N., Hanson, D., & De-Rossi, D. (2012). HEFES: An Hybrid Engine for Facial Expressions Synthesis to control human-like androids and avatars. In *2012 4th IEEE RAS EMBS International Conference on Biomedical Robotics and Biomechatronics (BioRob)*.

McCosker, A. (2013). Trolling as provocation: YouTube's agonistic publics. *Convergence (London)*. . doi:doi: 1354856513501413

McCrae, R. R., & Costa, P. T. (1987). Validation of a five-factor model of personality across instruments and observers. *Journal of Personality and Social Psychology, 52*(1), 81–90. doi:10.1037/0022-3514.52.1.81 PMID:3820081

McLeod, T., Samson, C., Labrie, M., Shehata, K., Mah, J., Lai, P., & Elder, J. H. et al. (2013). Using video acquired from an unmanned aerial vehicle (UAV) to measure fracture orientation in an open-pit mine. *GEOMATICA, 67*(3), 173–180. doi:10.5623/cig2013-036

McNamara, C. (2005). *Field guide to consulting and organizational development: A collaborative and systems approach to performance, change and learning*. Authenticity Consulting.

Mead, R., & Matarić, M. (2011). *An experimental design for studying proxemic behavior in human-robot interaction* (Technical Report CRES-11-001). Los Angeles: USC Interaction Lab.

Meadors, T. (2011). *Virtual jus in bello: Teaching just war with video games*. Paper presented at the The Ethics of Emerging Military Technologies, University of San Diego.

Meagher, R. E. (2006). *Herakles gone mad: Rethinking heroism in an age of endless war*. Northampton: Olive Branch Press.

Meaney, M. J., & Ferguson-Smith, A. C. (2010). Epigenetic regulation of the neural transcriptome: The meaning of the marks. *Nature Neuroscience, 13*(11), 1313–1318. doi:10.1038/nn1110-1313 PMID:20975754

Mehrabian, A. (1972). *Silent messages: Implicit communication of emotions and attitudes*. Wadsworth Publishing Company.

Mehrabian, A. (1980). *Basic dimensions for a general psychological theory: Implications for personality, social, environmental, and developmental studies*. Oelgeschlager, Gunn & Hain.

Mehrabian, A. (1995). Framework for a comprehensive description and measurement of emotional states. *Genetic, Social, and General Psychology Monographs, 121*, 339–361. PMID:7557355

Mehrabian, A., & Friar, J. T. (1969). Encoding of attitude by a seated communicator via posture and position cues. *Journal of Consulting and Clinical Psychology, 33*(3), 330–336. doi:10.1037/h0027576

Mehrabian, A., & Wiener, M. (1967). Decoding of inconsistent communications. *Journal of Personality and Social Psychology, 6*(1), 109–114. doi:10.1037/h0024532 PMID:6032751

Meister, I. G., Boroojerdi, B., Foltys, H., Sparing, R., Huber, W., & Töpper, R. (2003). Motor cortex hand area and speech: Implications for the development of language. *Neuropsychologia*, *41*(4), 401–406. doi:10.1016/S0028-3932(02)00179-3 PMID:12559157

Meltzoff, A. (1995). Understanding the intentions of others: Re-enactment of intended acts by 18-month-old children. *Developmental Psychology*, *31*(5), 838–850. doi:10.1037/0012-1649.31.5.838 PMID:25147406

Mendel, J. M. (2004). Computing derivatives in interval type-2 fuzzy logic systems. *IEEE Transactions on Fuzzy Systems*, *12*(1), 84–98.

Mendel, J. M. (2007). Type-2 fuzzy sets and systems: An overview. *Computational Intelligence Magazine, IEEE*, *2*(1), 20–29. doi:10.1109/MCI.2007.380672

Mendel, J. M., & John, R. B. (2002). Type-2 fuzzy sets made simple. *IEEE Transactions on Fuzzy Systems*, *10*(2), 117–127.

Mendel, J. M., & Wu, H. (2006). Type-2 fuzzistics for symmetric interval type-2 fuzzy sets: Part 1, forward problems. *IEEE Transactions on Fuzzy Systems*, *14*(6), 781–792.

Mendel, J. M., & Wu, H. (2007). Type-2 fuzzistics for non-symmetric interval type-2 fuzzy sets: Forward problems. *IEEE Transactions on Fuzzy Systems*, *15*(5), 916–930.

Mendel, J., & Wu, D. (2010). *Perceptual computing: aiding people in making subjective judgments* (Vol. 13). John Wiley & Sons. doi:10.1002/9780470599655

Merzagora, A. C., Bunce, S., Izzetoglu, M., & Onaral, B. (2006, August). Wavelet analysis for EEG feature extraction in deception detection. In *Engineering in Medicine and Biology Society, 2006 (EMBS'06): 28th Annual International Conference of the IEEE* (pp. 2434-2437). IEEE. doi:10.1109/IEMBS.2006.260247

Miller, E. K., & Cohen, J. D. (2001). An integrative theory of prefrontal cortex function. *Annual Review of Neuroscience*, *24*(1), 167–202. doi:10.1146/annurev.neuro.24.1.167 PMID:11283309

Minsky, M. (1987). *Societies of mind*. New York, NY: Picador.

Miri, A., Daie, K., Arrenberg, A. B., Baier, H., Aksay, E., & Tank, D. W. (2011). Spatial gradients and multidimensional dynamics in a neural integrator circuit. *Nature Neuroscience*, *14*(9), 1150–1159. doi:10.1038/nn.2888 PMID:21857656

Mirolli, M., Mannella, F., & Baldassarre, G. (2010). The roles of the amygdala in the affective regulation of body, brain, and behaviour. *Connection Science*, *22*(3), 215–245. doi:10.1080/09540091003682553

Mishra, A., Yiannis Aloimonos, Y., & Fermuller, C. (2009). *Active segmentation for robotics*. Paper presented at IROS 2009. Retrieved from http://www.umiacs.umd.edu/~mishraka/downloads/iros2009_activeSeg.pdf

Mitchell, T. M. (1997). *Machine learning*. McGraw-Hill Science/Engineering/Math.

Mitra, S., & Acharya, T. (2007). Gesture recognition: A survey. *IEEE Transactions on Systems, Man, and Cybernetics, Part C: Applications and Reviews*, *37*(3), 311–324.

Miwa, H., Okuchi, T., Takanobu, H., & Takanishi, A. (2002). Development of a new human-like head robot WE-4. In *Proceedings of IEEE/RSJ International Conference on Intelligent Robots and Systems*. doi:10.1109/IRDS.2002.1041634

Mobley, B. W. (2012). *Terrorism and counterintelligence: How terrorist groups elude detection*. New York, NY: Columbia University Press.

Mohs, R. C. (n.d.). How human memory works. Retrieved 8th April, 2014, from http://science.howstuffworks.com/life/inside-the-mind/human-brain/human-memory.htm

Montebelli, A., Herrera, C., & Ziemke, T. (2008). On cognition as dynamical coupling: An analysis of behavioral attractor dynamics. *Adaptive Behavior*, *16*(2-3), 182–195. doi:10.1177/1059712308089180

Moore, G. E. (1965). Cramming more components onto integrated circuits. *Electronics*, *38*(8), 114–117.

Morecraft, R. J., Stilwell-Morecraft, K. S., & Rossing, W. R. (2004). The motor cortex and facial expression: New insights from neuroscience. *The Neurologist*, *10*(5), 235–249. doi:10.1097/01.nrl.0000138734.45742.8d PMID:15335441

Mori, T., Segawa, Y., Shimosaka, M., & Sato, T. (2004). Hierarchical recognition of daily human actions based on continuous Hidden Markov Models. In *Sixth IEEE International Conference on Automatic Face and Gesture Recognition, 2004. Proceedings.* (pp. 779–784). doi:10.1109/AFGR.2004.1301629

Mori, T., Shimosaka, M., Harada, T., & Sato, T. (2005). Time-series human motion analysis with kernels derived from learned switching linear dynamics. *Transactions of the Japanese Society for Artificial Intelligence, 20,* 197–208. doi:10.1527/tjsai.20.197

Morris, J. S., Öhman, A., & Dolan, R. J. (1998). Conscious and unconscious emotional learning in the human amygdala. *Nature, 393*(6684), 467–470. doi:10.1038/30976 PMID:9624001

Morrison, I., Mjornsdotter, M., & Olausson, H. (2011). Vicarious responses to social touch in posterior insular cortex are tuned to pleasant caressing speeds. *The Journal of Neuroscience, 31*(26), 9554–9562. doi:10.1523/JNEUROSCI.0397-11.2011 PMID:21715620

Mortillaro, M., Mehu, M., & Scherer, K. R. (2011). Subtly different positive emotions can be distinguished by their facial expressions. *Social Psychological & Personality Science, 2*(3), 262–271. doi:10.1177/1948550610389080

Mortillaro, M., Mehu, M., & Scherer, K. R. (2013). The evolutionary origin of multimodal synchronization in emotional expression. In E. Altenmüller, S. Schmidt, & E. Zimmerman (Eds.), *Evolution of emotional communication: From sounds in nonhuman mammals to speech and music in man.* New York: Oxford University Press. doi:10.1093/acprof:oso/9780199583560.003.0001

Murugappan, M., Rizon, M., Nagarajan, R., & Yaacob, S. (2010). Inferring of human emotional states using multichannel EEG. *European Journal of Scientific Research, 48*(2), 281–299.

Murugappan, M., Rizon, M., Nagarajan, R., Yaacob, S., Zunaidi, I., & Hazry, D. (2007). EEG feature extraction for classifying emotions using FCM and FKM. *International Journal of Computers and Communications, 1*(2), 21–25.

Naab, P. J., & Russell, J. A. (2007). Judgments of emotion from spontaneous facial expressions of New Guineans. *Emotion (Washington, D.C.), 7*(4), 736–744. doi:10.1037/1528-3542.7.4.736 PMID:18039042

Nagy, E., Pilling, K., Orvos, H., & Molnar, P. (2013). Imitation of tongue protrusion in human neonates: Specificity of the response in a large sample. *Developmental Psychology, 49*(9), 16–28. doi:10.1037/a0031127 PMID:23231691

Nair, S. B., Godfrey, W. W., & Kim, D. H. (2011). On realizing a multi-agent emotion engine. *International Journal of Synthetic Emotions, 2*(2), 1–27.

Nakasone, A., & Ishizuka, M. (2006). Storytelling ontology model using RST. In *Proceedings of the IEEE/WIC/ACM international conference on Intelligent Agent Technology* (IAT '06) (pp. 163-169). Washington, DC: IEEE Computer Society. doi:10.1109/IAT.2006.114

Neumann, J., & Morgenstern, O. (1944). *Theory of games and economic behavior.* Princeton: Princeton University Press.

Newell, A. (1980). Physical symbol systems. *Cognitive Science, 4*(2), 135–183. doi:10.1207/s15516709cog0402_2

Newell, A., & Card, S. K. (1985). The prospects for psychological science in human-computer interaction. *Human-Computer Interaction, 1*(3), 209–242. doi:10.1207/s15327051hci0103_1

Nezlek, J. B., Vansteelandt, K., Van Mechelen, I., & Kuppens, P. (2008). Appraisal-emotion relationships in daily life. *Emotion (Washington, D.C.), 8*(1), 145–150. doi:10.1037/1528-3542.8.1.145 PMID:18266526

Ng, G. W. (2009). *Brain-mind machinery: Brain-inspired computing and mind opening.* World Scientific. doi:10.1142/6704

Nicolescu, B. (2009). *Qu'est-ce que la realite?* Liber.

Niedenthal, P. M. (2007). Embodying emotion. *Science, 316*(5827), 1002–1005. doi:10.1126/science.1136930 PMID:17510358

Niedenthal, P. M., Barsalou, L. M., Winkielman, P., Krath-Gruber, S., & Ric, F. (2005). Embodiment in attitudes, social perception, and emotion. *Personality and Social Psychology Review, 9*(3), 184–211. doi:10.1207/s15327957pspr0903_1 PMID:16083360

Nielsen, J. (1994). Heuristic evaluation. In J. Nielsen & R. L. Mack (Eds.), *Usability inspection methods* (pp. 25–62). New York: John Wiley & Sons.

Niles, I., & Pease, A. (2001). Towards a standard upper ontology. In *Proceedings of the international conference on Formal Ontology in Information Systems:* Vol. 2001 (pp. 2.9). New York, NY: ACM.

Norman, D. A. (2004). *Emotional design- why we love (or hate) everyday things*. New York: Basic Books.

Norman, D. A. (2010). Natural interfaces are not natural. *Interaction, 17*(3), 3, 6–10. doi:10.1145/1744161.1744163

Oatley, K. (1992). *Best laid schemes: The psychology of the emotions*. Cambridge University Press.

Oberman, L. M., McCleery, J. P., Ramachandran, V. S., & Pineda, J. A. (2007). EEG evidence for mirror neuron activity during the observation of human robot action: Toward an analysis of the human qualities of interactive robots. *Neurocomputing, 70*(13-15), 2194–2203. doi:10.1016/j.neucom.2006.02.024

Obrenovic, Z., Garay, N., López, J. M., Fajardo, I., & Cearreta, I. (2005). An ontology for description of emotional cues. In J. Tao, T. Tan, & R. W. Picard (Eds.), *ACII 2005. LNCS* (Vol. 3784, pp. 505–512). Heidelberg: Springer. doi:10.1007/11573548_65

O'Brien, J. S., & Sampson, E. L. (1965). Lipid composition of the normal human brain: Gray matter, white matter, and myelin. *Journal of Lipid Research, 6*(4), 537–544. PMID:5865382

Ochsner, K. N., Bunge, S. A., Gross, J. J., & Gabrieli, J. D. E. (2002). Rethinking feelings: An fMRI study of the cognitive regulation of emotion. *Journal of Cognitive Neuroscience, 14*(8), 1215–1299. doi:10.1162/089892902760807212 PMID:12495527

Office of the Surgeon General. (2006). Mental health advisory team (MHAT) IV Operation Iraqi Freedom 05-07, Final Report. Washington, DC: United States Department of the Army.

Ogata, T., & Sugano, S. (2000). Emotional communication robot: WAMOEBA-2R emotion model and evaluation experiments. In *Proceedings of the International Conference on Humanoid Robots*, 2000.

Oh, J., Hanson, D., Kim, W., Han, Y., Kim, J., & Park, I. (2006). Design of android type humanoid robot Albert HUBO. In *Proceedings of the 2006 IEEE/RSJ International Conference on Intelligent Robots and Systems* (pp. 1428–1433). doi:10.1109/IROS.2006.281935

Oh, K., & Kim, M. (2010). Social attributes of robotic products: Observations of child-robot interactions in a school environment. *International Journal of Design, 4*(1), 45–55.

Okada, S., Kobayashi, Y., Ishibashi, S., & Nishida, T. (2010). Incremental learning of gestures for human–robot interaction. *AI & Society, 25*(2), 155–168. doi:10.1007/s00146-009-0248-8

O'Reilly, W. S. N. (1996). *Believable social and emotional agents* (Unpublished Ph.D. Thesis). Carnegie Mellon University, Pittsburgh, PA.

O'Rorke, P., & Ortony, A. (1994). Explaining emotions. *Cognitive Science, 18*(2), 283–323. doi:10.1207/s15516709cog1802_3

Orozco, J., Rudovic, O., Gonzàlez, J., & Pantic, M. (2013). Hierarchical on-line appearance-based tracking for 3D head pose, eyebrows, lips, eyelids and irises. *Image and Vision Computing, 31*(4), 322–340. doi:10.1016/j.imavis.2013.02.001

Ortony, A. (2002). On making believable emotional agents believable. In R. Trappl, P. Petta & S. Payr (Eds.), Emotions in humans and artifacts (pp. 189-211). Cambridge, MA: The MIT Press.

Ortony, A. (Ed.). (2003). On making believable emotional agents believable. In R. P. Trapple, (Ed.), Emotions in humans and artefacts. Cambridge, MA: MIT Press.

Ortony, A., Clore, G. L., & Collins, A. (1988). The cognitive structure of emotions. New York: Cambridge University Press. doi:10.1017/CBO9780511571299

Ortony, A., Norman, D., & Revelle, W. (2005). Affect and proto-affect in effective functioning. In J. M. Fellous & M. A. Arbib (Eds.), Who needs emotions? New York: Oxford University Press. doi:10.1093/acprof:oso/9780195166194.003.0007

Ortony, A. (1990). *The cognitive structure of emotions.* Cambridge University Press.

Ortony, A. (1993). Metaphor, language, and thought. In A. Ortony (Ed.), *Metaphor and thought* (pp. 1–16). Cambridge University Press. doi:10.1017/CBO9781139173865.003

Ortony, A., Clore, G., & Collins, A. (1998). *Cognitive structure of emotions.* New York, NY: Cambridge University Press.

Ortony, A., & Turner, T. J. (1990). What's basic about basic emotions? *Psychological Review, 97*(3), 315–331. doi:10.1037/0033-295X.97.3.315 PMID:1669960

Osgood, C. E. (1962). Studies of the generality of affective meaning systems. *The American Psychologist, 17*(1), 10–28. doi:10.1037/h0045146

Osgood, C. E. (1964). Semantic differential technique in the comparative study of cultures. *American Anthropologist, 66*(3), 171–200. doi:10.1525/aa.1964.66.3.02a00880

Oshni Alvandi, E., & Akbari Dehaghi, M. (2008). Karl Popper and evolutionary concept of epistemology. *Philosophical Investigation (Journal of Faculty of Letters and Humanities), 51*(205).

Osofsky, M. J., Bandura, A., & Zimbardo, P. G. (2005). The role of moral disengagement in the execution process. *Law and Human Behavior, 29*(4), 371–393. doi:10.1007/s10979-005-4930-1 PMID:16133946

Pacchierotti, E., Christensen, H. I., & Jensfelt, P. (2005). Human-robot embodied interaction in hallway settings: a pilot user study. In *ROMAN 2005. IEEE International Workshop on Robot and Human Interactive Communication, 2005.* (pp. 164–171). doi:10.1109/ROMAN.2005.1513774 doi:10.1109/ROMAN.2005.1513774

Padgham, L., & Taylor, G. (1997). A system for modelling agents having emotion and personality. In Intelligent Agent Systems Theoretical and Practical Issues (pp. 59–71). Springer.

Palm, G., & Glodek, M. (2013). Towards emotion recognition in human computer interaction. In Neural nets and surroundings (pp. 323–336). Springer.

Panskepp, J. (1998). *Affective neuroscience: The foundations of human and animal emotions.* New York: Oxford University Press.

Pantic, M., & Bartlett, M. S. (2007). *Machine analysis of facial expressions* (pp. 377–416). Viena, Austria: I-Tech.

Pantic, M., & Rothkrantz, L. J. (2003). Toward an affect-sensitive multimodal human-computer interaction. *Proceedings of the IEEE, 91*(9), 1370–1390. doi:10.1109/JPROC.2003.817122

Pantic, M., & Rothkrantz, L. J. M. (2000). Automatic analysis of facial expressions: The state of the art. *Pattern Analysis and Machine Intelligence. IEEE Transactions on, 22*(12), 1424–1445.

Papez, J. (1995). A proposed mechanism of emotion. 1937. *The Journal of Neuropsychiatry and Clinical Neurosciences, 7*(1), 103–112. doi:10.1176/jnp.7.1.103 PMID:7711480

Park, J.-C., Kim, H.-R., Kim, Y.-M., & Kwon, D.-S. (2009). *Robot's individual emotion generation model and action coloring according to the robot's personality.* Paper presented at the The 18th IEEE International Symposium on Robot and Human Interactive Communication (RO-MAN 2009). doi:10.1109/ROMAN.2009.5326128

Parlangeli, O., Guidi, S., & Caratozzolo, M. C. (2013). A mind in a disk: The attribution of mental states to technological systems. *Work (Reading, Mass.), 41*, 1118–1123. PMID:22316869

Partala, T., & Kallinen, A. (2012). Understanding the most satisfying and unsatisfying user experiences: Emotions, psychological needs, and context. *Interacting with Computers, 24*(1), 25–34. doi:10.1016/j.intcom.2011.10.001

Patel, S., Scherer, K. R., Björkner, E., & Sundberg, J. (2011). Mapping emotions into acoustic space: The role of voice production. *Biological Psychology, 87*(1), 93–98. doi:10.1016/j.biopsycho.2011.02.010 PMID:21354259

Patterson, M. L., Powell, J. L., & Lenihan, M. G. (1986). Touch, compliance, and interpersonal affect. *Journal of Nonverbal Behavior, 10*(1), 41–50. doi:10.1007/BF00987204

Paulos, E., & Canny, J. (1998). Designing personal tele-embodiment. In *IEEE Internetional Conference on Robotics and Automation, 1998* (pp. 3173–3178). Retrieved from http://ieeexplore.ieee.org/xpls/abs_all.jsp?arnumber=680913

Pedregosa, F., Varoquaux, G., Gramfort, A., Michel, V., Thirion, B., & Grisel, O. et al.. (2011). Scikit-learn: Machine learning in Python. *Journal of Machine Learning Research, 12*, 2825–2830.

Pelachaud, C., & Poggi, I. (2002). Subtleties of facial expressions in embodied agents. *The Journal of Visualization and Computer Animation, 13*(5), 301–312. doi:10.1002/vis.299

Penfield, W., & Rasmussen, T. (1950). *The cerebral cortex of man; a clinical study of localization of function.* New York, N.Y: The Macmillan Company.

Perkel, D. H. (1993). *Computational neuroscience: Scope and structure.* Paper presented at the Computational Neuroscience.

Pessoa, L. (2008). On the relationship between emotion and cognition. *Nature Reviews. Neuroscience, 9*(2), 148–158. doi:10.1038/nrn2317 PMID:18209732

Peter, C., & Herbon, A. (2006). Emotion representation and physiology assignments in digital systems. *Interacting with Computers, 18*, 139–170.

Peters, E. (2006). The functions of affect in the construction of preferences. In S. Lichtenstein & P. Slovic (Eds.), *The construction of preference,* (pp. 454-463). Cambridge University Press.

Petrantonakis, P. C., & Hadjileontiadis, L. J. (2010). Emotion recognition from brain signals using hybrid adaptive filtering and higher order crossings analysis. *IEEE Transactions on Affective Computing, 1*(2), 81–97.

Petrantonakis, P. C., & Hadjileontiadis, L. J. (2010). Emotion recognition from EEG using higher order crossings. *IEEE Transactions on Information Technology in Biomedicine, 14*(2), 186–197.

Petrariu, A. M. (2012). *Niveluri de Realitate în sistemele sociale.* Babes-Bolyai.

Pfeifer, R., & Scheier, C. (1997). Sensory—motor coordination: The metaphor and beyond. *Robotics and Autonomous Systems, 20*(2–4).

Pfeifer, R., & Scheier, C. (1999). *Understanding intelligence.* Cambridge, MA: MIT Press.

Phansalkar, V. V., & Sastry, P. S. (1994). Analysis of the back-propagation algorithm with momentum. *IEEE Transactions on Neural Networks, 5*(3), 505–506. doi:10.1109/72.286925 PMID:18267819

Phelps, E. A. (2004). Human emotion and memory: Interactions of the amygdala and hippocampal complex. *Current Opinion in Neurobiology, 14*(2), 198–202. doi:10.1016/j.conb.2004.03.015 PMID:15082325

Picard, R. (1995, November) *Affective computing* (Technical Report 321). MIT Media Laboratory, Perceptual Computing Section.

Picard, R. (1997). *Affective computing.* Cambridge, MA: The MIT Press. doi:10.1037/e526112012-054

Picard, R. W. (2003). What does it mean for a computer to "have" emotions? In R. Trappl, P. Petta, & S. Payr (Eds.), *Emotions in Humans and Artifacts.* Cambridge, MA: The MIT Press.

Plutchik, R. (1982). A psychoevolutionary theory of emotions. *Social Science Information/sur les sciences sociales.*

Plutchik, R. (1962). *The emotions: Facts, theories and a new model.* Random House.

Plutchik, R. (1984). Emotions: A general psychoevolutionary theory. In K. R. Scherer & P. Ekman (Eds.), *Approaches to emotion.* Hillsdale, N.J.: Erlbaum.

Plutchik, R. (2002). *Emotions and life: Perspectives from psychology, biology, and evolution.* Washington, DC: American Psychological Association.

Plutchik, R., & Conte, H. R. (Eds.). (1997). *Circumplex models of personality and emotions.* American Psychological Association.

Poel, M., Rieksopden Akker, N. A., van Kesteren, A. J. (2002). Learning emotions in virtual environments. In R. Trappl (Ed.), Cybernetics and Systems 2002, (pp. 751-755). Vienna: Austrian Society for Cybernetic Studies.

Poggi, I. (2001). Signals and meanings of gaze in animated faces. In Language, Vision and Music (pp. 133–144). John Benjamins.

Poggi, I., & Pelachaud, C. (2000). Performative facial expressions in animated faces. In J. Cassell, J. Sullivan, S. Prevost, & E. Churchill, (Eds.), Embodied conversational agents. Cambridge: MIT Press.

Poggi, I. (2006). *Le parole del corpo. Introduzione alla comunicazione multimodale.* Carocci.

Pohl, A., Anders, S., Schulte-Ruther, M., Mathiak, K., & Kircher, T. (2013). Positive Facial Affect – An fMRI Study on the involvement of insula and amygdala. *PLoS ONE, 8*(8), e69886. doi:10.1371/journal.pone.0069886 PMID:23990890

Port, R. F., & Van Gelder, T. (1995). Mind as motion: Explorations in the dynamics of cognition. Cambridge, MA: The MIT Press.

Port, R. F., & Van Gelder, T. (Eds.). (1995). *Mind as motion: Explorations in the dynamics of cognition.* MIT Press.

Poundstone, W. (1992). *Prisoner's dilemma.* New York: Doubleday.

Prendinger, H., Descamps, S., & Ishizuka, M. (2002). Scripting affective communication with life-like characters in Web-based interaction systems. *Applied Artificial Intelligence, 16*(7-8), 519–553. doi:10.1080/08839510290030381

Prendinger, H., Saeyor, S., & Ishizuka, M. (2004). MPML and SCREAM: Scripting the bodies and minds of life-like characters. In H. Prendinger & M. Ishizuka (Eds.), *Life-like characters: Tools, affective functions, and applications.* Berlin: Springer. doi:10.1007/978-3-662-08373-4_10

Pressman, R. S. (2000). *Software engineering: A practitioner's approach* (5th ed.). London: McGraw Hill.

Press, W. H., & Dyson, F. J. (2012) Iterated prisoner's dilemma contains strategies that dominate any evolutionary opponent. In *Proceedings of the National Academy of Sciences* (109), 10409–10413.

Prinz, J. (2004). Embodied emotions. In *Thinking about feeling*, (pp. 44-58).

Prinz, J. J. (Ed.). (2004). Gut reactions: A perceptual theory of emotion. Oxford: Oxford University Press.

Prinz, J. J. (2004). *Gut reactions: A perceptual theory of emotion.* Oxford University Press.

Proceedings of the 5th ACM/IEEE International Conference on Human-Robot Interaction, Osaka. (2010). Retrieved from http://hri2010.org/

Purves, D., Cabeza, R., Huettel, S. A., LaBar, K. S., Platt, M. L., & Woldorff, M. G. (2013). *Principles of cognitive neuroscience* (2nd ed.). Sinauer Associates Inc.

Pylyshyn, Z. (1984). *Computation and cognition.* Cambridge, MA: The MIT Press.

Qingji, G., Kai, W., Haijuan, L., (2008). A robot emotion generation mechanism based on PAD emotion space: Research on robot emotion. In *IFIP Advances in Information and Communication Technology, Vol. 288, Intelligent Information Processing IV* (pp. 138-147). Boston: Springer.

Ramachandran, V.S. (2000). Mirror Neurons and imitation learning as the driving force behind "the great leap forward" in human evolution. *Edge, 69*.

Ramachandran, V. S. (2004). *A brief tour of human consciousness.* New York: Pi Press, Pearson Education.

Raudys, S., & Duin, R. P. W. (1998). Expected classification error of the Fisher linear classifier with pseudo-inverse covariance matrix. *Pattern Recognition Letters, 19*(5-6), 385–392. doi:10.1016/S0167-8655(98)00016-6

Rees, L. (2005). *Auschwitz: The Nazis & the final solution.* New York, NY: Random House.

Reeves, B., & Clifford Nass, C. (2003, January). The media equation: How people treat computers, television, and new media like real people and places (CSLI Lecture Notes). Stanford, CA: Center for the Study of Language and Information.

Reeves, B., & Nass, C. (1996). *The media equation: how people treat computers, television, and new media like real people and places.* Cambridge: Center for the Study of Language and Information Publication.

Reilly, W. S. N. (2006). *Modeling what happens between emotional antecedents and emotional consequents* Paper presented at the ACE 2006, Vienna, Austria.

Reilly, W. S., & Bates, J. (1992). *Building emotional agents.*

Reilly, W. S. R. (1996). *Believable social and emotional agents*. Pittsburgh, PA: CMU.

Reisenzein, R., Studtmann, M., & Horstmann, G. (2013). Coherence between emotion and facial expression: Evidence from laboratory experiments. Emotion Review, 5(1), 16–23. doi:10.1177/1754073912457228

Reisenzein, R. (1994). Pleasure-arousal theory and the Intensity of Emotions. *Journal of Personality and Social Psychology*, 67(3), 525–539. doi:10.1037/0022-3514.67.3.525

Reisenzein, R. (2001). Appraisal processes conceptualized from a schema-theoretic perspective: Contributions to a process analysis of emotions. In K. R. Scherer, A. Schorr, & T. Johnstone (Eds.), *Appraisal processes in emotion: Theory, methods, research*. NY: Oxford University Press.

Reisenzein, R., Hudlicka, E., Dastani, M., Gratch, J., Hindriks, K. V., Lorini, E., & Meyer, J.-J. Ch. (2013). Computational modeling of emotion: Toward improving the inter- and intradisciplinary exchange. *IEEE Transactions on Affective Computing*, 4(3), 246–266. doi:10.1109/T-AFFC.2013.14

Reynolds, M. A. (2013). Return of the Maxim gun? Technology and empire in an age of austerity. *Global Discourse*, 3(1), 120–128. doi:10.1080/23269995.2013.807603

Ribeiro, T., & Paiva, A. (2012). The illusion of robotic life: principles and practices of animation for robots. In *Proceedings of the seventh annual ACM/IEEE international conference on Human-Robot Interaction*. New York, NY: ACM. doi:10.1145/2157689.2157814

Ritter, F. E., & Avramides, M. N. (2000). *Steps towards including behavior moderators in human performance models in synthetic environments*. The Pennsylvania State University.

Ritter, F. E., Reifers, A. L., Klein, L. C., & Schoelles, M. J. (2007). Lessons from defining theories of stress for cognitive architectures. In W. Gray (Ed.), *Advances in Cognitive Models and Cognitive Architectures*. New York: Oxford University Press. doi:10.1093/acprof:oso/9780195189193.003.0018

Rizzolatti, G., Fadiga, L., Fogassi, L., & Gallese, V. (2002). From mirror neurons to imitation: facts and speculations. In A. N. Meltzoff & W. Prinz (Eds.), The imitative mind – development, evolution, and brain bases (pp. 247–266). Cambridge: Cambridge University Press. doi:10.1017/CBO9780511489969.015

Rizzolatti, G., & Craighero, L. (2004). The mirror-neuron system. *Annual Review of Neuroscience*, 27(1), 169–192. doi:10.1146/annurev.neuro.27.070203.144230 PMID:15217330

Roberts, C., & Kleiner, A. (1999). Five kinds of systems thinking. The dance of change (pp. 96-106). New York: Double-Day.

Robins, B., Dautenhahn, K., Boekhorst, R., & Billard, A. (2005). Robotic assistants in therapy and education of children with autism: Can a small humanoid robot help encourage social interaction skills? *Universal Access in the Information Society*, 4(2), 105–120. doi:10.1007/s10209-005-0116-3

Roederer, J. G. (2003). On the concept of information and its role in nature. *Entropy*, 5(1), 3–33. doi:10.3390/e5010003

Roederer, J. G. (2005). *Information and its role in nature*. Springer.

Roether, C., Omlor, L., Christensen, A., & Giese, M. (2009). Critical features for the perception of emotion from gait. *Journal of Vision*. Retrieved from http://jov.highwire.org/content/9/6/15.short

Roseman, I. J. (2001). A model of appraisal in the emotion system. In K. R. Scherer, A. Schorr, & T. Johnstone (Eds.), Appraisal processes in emotion: Theory, methods, research. New York: Oxford University Press.

Roseman, I. J., & Smith, C. A. (2001). Appraisal theory: Overview, assumptions, varieties, controversies. In K. R. Scherer, A. Schorr, & T. Johnstone (Eds.), Appraisal processes in emotion: theory, methods, research. New York: Oxford University Press.

Roseman, I., & Evdokas, A. (2004). Appraisals cause experienced emotions: Experimental evidence. *Cognition and Emotion*, *18*(1), 1–28. doi:10.1080/02699930244000390

Rosenberg, L. B., & Stredney, D. (1996). A haptic interface for virtual simulation of endoscopic surgery. *Studies in Health Technology and Informatics*, *29*, 371–387. PMID:10172846

Ross, A., & Jain, A. (2003). Information fusion in biometrics. *Pattern Recognition Letters*, *24*, 2115–2125.

Royakkers, L., & van Est, R. (2010). The cubicle warrior: The marionette of digitalized warfare. *Ethics and Information Technology*, *12*(3), 289–296. doi:10.1007/s10676-010-9240-8

Rozin, P. (2003). Introduction: Evolutionary and cultural perspectives on affect. In R. J. Davidson, K. R. Scherer, & H. H. Goldsmith (Eds.), *Handbook of affective sciences*. New York: Oxford University Press.

Rumelhart, D. E., Hinton, G. E., & Williams, R. J. (1985). *Learning internal representations by error propagation (No. ICS-8506)*. California University of San Diego La Jolla, Institute For Cognitive Science.

Russell, J. (2003). Core affect and the psychological construction of emotion. *Psychological Review*, *110*(1), 145–172. doi:10.1037/0033-295X.110.1.145 PMID:12529060

Russell, J. A. (1980). A circumplex model of affect. *Journal of Personality and Social Psychology*, *39*(6), 1161–1178. doi:10.1037/h0077714

Russell, J. A. (2009). Emotion, core affect, and psychological construction. *Cognition and Emotion*, *23*(7), 1259–1283. doi:10.1080/02699930902809375

Russell, J. A., Bachorowski, J. A., & Fernández-Dols, J. M. (2003). Facial and vocal expressions of emotion. *Annual Review of Psychology*, *54*(1), 329–349. doi:10.1146/annurev.psych.54.101601.145102 PMID:12415074

Russell, J. A., & Bullock, M. (1986). On the dimensions preschoolers use to interpret facial expressions of emotion. *Developmental Psychology*, *22*(1), 97–102. doi:10.1037/0012-1649.22.1.97

Russell, J. A., & Fernandez-Dols, J. M. (1997). *The psychology of facial expression*. New York: Cambridge University Press. doi:10.1017/CBO9780511659911

Russell, J. A., Lewicka, M., & Niit, T. (1989). A cross-cultural study of a circumplex model of affect. *Journal of Personality and Social Psychology*, *57*(5), 848–856. doi:10.1037/0022-3514.57.5.848

Russell, J. A., & Mehrabian, A. (1974). Distinguishing anger and anxiety in terms of emotional response factors. *Journal of Consulting and Clinical Psychology*, *42*(1), 79–83. doi:10.1037/h0035915 PMID:4814102

Russell, J., & Barrett, L. F. (1999). Core affect, prototypical emotional episodes, and other things called emotion: Dissecting the elephant. *Journal of Personality and Social Psychology*, *76*(5), 805–819. doi:10.1037/0022-3514.76.5.805 PMID:10353204

Russell, J., & Mehrabian, A. (1977). Evidence for a three-factor theory of emotions. *Journal of Research in Personality*, *11*(3), 273–294. doi:10.1016/0092-6566(77)90037-X

Sabatini, M. J., Ebert, P., Lewis, D. A., Levitt, P., Cameron, J. L., & Mirnics, K. (2007). Amygdala gene expression correlates of social behavior in monkeys experiencing maternal separation. *The Journal of Neuroscience*, *27*(12), 3295–3304. doi:10.1523/JNEUROSCI.4765-06.2007 PMID:17376990

Sacks, O. (1985). The disembodied lady. In *The man who mistook his wife for a hat and other clinical tales*. USA: Summit Books.

Saini, P., de Ruyter, B., Markopoulos, P., & van Breemen, A. (2005). Benefits of social intelligence in home dialogue systems. In M.F. Costabile & F. Paternò (Eds.) *Human-Computer Interaction -INTERACT 2005: Proceedings IFIP TC13 International Conference, Rome, Italy*. Lecture Notes in Computer Science, 3585, 510-521. doi:10.1007/11555261_42

Saint-Georges, C., Chetouani, M., Cassel, R., Apicella, F., Mahdhaoui, A., Muratori, F., & Cohen, D. et al. (2013). Motherese in interaction: At the cross-road of emotion and cognition? (A systematic review). *PLoS ONE, 8*(10), e78103. doi:10.1371/journal.pone.0078103 PMID:24205112

Saldien, J., Goris, K., Vanderborght, B., Vanderfaeillie, J., & Lefeber, D. (2010). Expressing emotions with the social robot Probo. *International Journal of Social Robotics, 2*(4), 377–389. doi:10.1007/s12369-010-0067-6

Sander, D., Grandjean, D., & Scherer, K. R. (2005). A systems approach to appraisal mechanisms in emotion. *Neural Networks, 18*(4), 317–352. doi:10.1016/j.neunet.2005.03.001 PMID:15936172

Sanz, R., Hernandez, C., & Sanchez-Escribano, M. G. (2012). Consciousness, action selection, meaning and phenomenic anticipation. *International Journal of Machine Consciousness, 4*(2), 383–399. doi:10.1142/S1793843012400227

Sanz, R., Sanchez-Escribano, M. G., & Herrera, C. (2013). A model of emotion as patterned metacontrol. *Biologically Inspired Cognitive Architectures, 1*(2), 2013.

Sato, E., Yamaguchi, T., & Harashima, F. (2007). Natural interface using pointing behavior for human–robot gestural interaction. *IEEE Transactions on Industrial Electronics, 54*(2), 1105–1112 doi:10.1109/TIE.2007.892728

Sauter, D., Panattoni, C., & Happé, F. (2013). Children's recognition of emotions from vocal cues. *The British Journal of Developmental Psychology, 31*(1), 97–113. doi:10.1111/j.2044-835X.2012.02081.x PMID:23331109

Schank, R. C., & Abelson, R. P. (1977). *Scripts, plans, goals and understanding: an inquiry into human knowledge structures*. Hillsdale, NJ: Lawrence Erlbaum.

Scheffczyk, J., Baker, C. F., & Narayanan, S. (2006). Ontology-based reasoning about lexical resources. In N. Calzolari, A. Gangemi, A. Lenci, A. Oltramari, & L. Prévot (Eds.), *Ontologies and lexical resources for natural language processing* (pp. 1–8). Cambridge: Cambridge University Press.

Scherer, K. (2001). Appraisal processes in emotion: Theory, methods, research. (Series in Affective Science). New York: Oxford University Press.

Scherer, K. (2003). Vocal communication of emotion: A review of research paradigms. Speech Communication, 40(1-2), 227–256. doi:10.1016/S0167-6393(02)00084-5 doi:10.1016/S0167-6393(02)00084-5

Scherer, K. R. (2001). Appraisal considered as a process of multievel sequential checking. In K. R. Scherer, A. Schorr, & T. Johnstone (Eds.), Appraisal Processes in Emotion: Theory, Methods, Research. New York: Oxford University Press.

Scherer, K. R. (2001). Appraisal considered as a process of multi-level sequential checking. In K. R. Scherer, A. Schorr, & T. Johnstone (Eds.), Appraisal processes in checking emotion: Theory, methods, research (pp. 92-120). Oxford University Press.

Scherer, K., Schorr, A., & Johnstone, T. (2001). Appraisal processes in emotion: theory, methods, research. New York: Oxford University Press.

Scherer, K. R. (1984). Emotion as a multicomponent process: A model and some cross-cultural data. In P. Shaver (Ed.), Review of personality and social psychology: Vol. 5. *Emotions, relationships and health* (pp. 37–63). Beverly Hills, CA: Sage.

Scherer, K. R. (1992). Emotions are biologically and socially constituted: A response to Greenwood. *New Ideas in Psychology, 10*(1), 19–22. doi:10.1016/0732-118X(92)90043-Y

Scherer, K. R. (1994). Toward a concept of ''modal'' emotions. In P. Ekman & R. J. Davidson (Eds.), *The nature of emotion: Fundamental questions* (pp. 25–31). New York: Oxford University Press.

Scherer, K. R. (2000). Emotions as episodes of subsystem synchronization driven by nonlinear appraisal processes. In M. D. Lewis & I. Granic (Eds.), *Emotion, development, and self-organization*. New York: Cambridge University Press. doi:10.1017/CBO9780511527883.005

Scherer, K. R. (2001). Appraisal considered as a process of multilevel sequential checking. In K. R. Scherer, A. Schorr, & T. Johnstone (Eds.), *Appraisal processes in emotion: Theory, methods, research* (pp. 92–120). New York: Oxford University Press.

Scherer, K. R. (2005). What are emotions? And how can they be measured? *Social Sciences Information. Information Sur les Sciences Sociales*, *44*(4), 695–729. doi:10.1177/0539018405058216

Scherer, K. R. (2009). The dynamic architecture of emotion: Evidence for the component process model. *Cognition and Emotion*, *23*(7), 1307–1351. doi:10.1080/02699930902928969

Scherer, K. R. (2009). Emotions are emergent processes: They require a dynamic computational architecture. *Philosophical Transactions of the Royal Society of London. Series B, Biological Sciences*, *364*, 3459–3474. PMID:19884141

Scherer, K. R. (2010). The component process model: Architecture for a comprehensive computational model of emergent emotion. In K. R. Scherer, T. Bänziger, & E. B. Roesch (Eds.), *Blueprint for affective computing: A sourcebook* (pp. 47–70). New York: Oxfor University Press.

Scherer, K. R., & Brosch, T. (2009). Culture-specific appraisal biases contribute to emotion dispositions. *European Journal of Personality*, *288*(3), 265–288. doi:10.1002/per.714

Scherer, K. R., & Ceschi, G. (2000). Criteria for emotion recognition from verbal and nonverbal expression: Studying baggage loss in the airport. *Personality and Social Psychology Bulletin*, *26*(3), 327–339. doi:10.1177/0146167200265006

Scherer, K. R., Clark-Polner, E., & Mortillaro, M. (2011). In the eye of the beholder? Universality and cultural specificity in the expression and perception of emotion. *International Journal of Psychology*, *46*(6), 401–435. doi:10.1080/00207594.2011.626049 PMID:22126090

Scherer, K. R., & Ellgring, H. (2007). Are facial expressions of emotion produced by categorical affect programs or dynamically driven by appraisal? *Emotion (Washington, D.C.)*, *7*(1), 113–130. doi:10.1037/1528-3542.7.1.113 PMID:17352568

Scherer, K. R., & Grandjean, D. (2008). Facial expressions allow inference of both emotions and their components. *Cognition and Emotion*, *22*(5), 789–801. doi:10.1080/02699930701516791

Scherer, K. R., Mortillaro, M., & Mehu, M. (2013). Understanding the mechanisms underlying the production of facial expression of emotion: A componential perspective. *Emotion Review*, *5*(1), 47–53. doi:10.1177/1754073912451504

Scherer, K. R., Schorr, A., & Johnstone, T. (2001). *Appraisal processes in emotion: Theory, methods, research*. New York: Oxford University Press.

Scherer, K. R., Shuman, V., Fontaine, J. R. J., & Soriano, C. (2013). The GRID meets the Wheel: Assessing emotional feeling via self-report. In *Components of emotional meaning: A sourcebook*. Oxford: Oxford University Press. doi:10.1093/acprof:oso/9780199592746.003.0019

Scherer, K. R., Wranik, T., Sangsue, J., Tran, V., & Scherer, U. (2004). Emotions in everyday life: Probability of occurrence, risk factors, appraisal and reaction pattern. *Social Sciences Information. Information Sur les Sciences Sociales*, *43*(4), 499–570. doi:10.1177/0539018404047701

Scheutz, M. (2004). Useful roles of emotions in artificial agents: A case study from artificial life. In *Proceedings of the 19th National Conference on Artifical Intelligence* (pp. 42–47). Retrieved from http://kiosk.nada.kth.se/kurser/kth/2D1381/AAAI104ScheutzM.pdf

Scheutz, M., Schermerhorn, P., & Kramer, J. (2006). The utility of affect expression in natural language interactions in joint human-robot tasks. In *HRI '06 Proceedings of the 1st ACM SIGCHI/SIGART Conference on Human-Robot Interaction* (pp. 226–233). doi:10.1145/1121241.1121281 doi:10.1145/1121241.1121281

Scheutz, M. (2011). Architectural roles of affect and how to evaluate them in artificial agents.[IJSE]. *International Journal of Synthetic Emotions*, *2*(2), 48–65. doi:10.4018/jse.2011070103

Schmidt, C., Sridharan, N., & Goodson, J. (1978). The plan recognition problem: An intersection of psychology and artificial intelligence. Artificial Intelligence, 11(1-2), 45–83. doi:10.1016/0004-3702(78)90012-7

Schmidt, S., & Färber, B. (2009). Pedestrians at the kerb–Recognising the action intentions of humans. Transportation Research Part F: Traffic Psychology and Behaviour, 12(4), 300–310. doi:10.1016/j.trf.2009.02.003

Schmidt, K. L., Liu, Y., & Cohn, J. F. (2006). The role of structural facial asymmetry in asymmetry of peak facial expressions. *Laterality*, *11*(6), 540–561. doi:10.1080/13576500600832758 PMID:16966242

Scholtz, J. (2003). Theory and evaluation of human robot interaction. In *Proceedings of the 36ᵗʰ Hawaii International Conference of System Sciences (HICSS'03), Vol. 5*. doi:10.1109/HICSS.2003.1174284

Schon, D. (1993). Generative metaphor: A perspective on problem-setting in social policy. In A. Ortony (Ed.), *Metaphor and thought* (pp. 137–163). Cambridge University Press. doi:10.1017/CBO9781139173865.011

Schroder, M., Baggia, P., Burkhardt, F., Pelachaud, C., Peters, C. & Zovato, E. (2011). *EmotionML – an upcoming standard for representing emotions and related states.*

Schroeter, C., Mueller, S., Volkhardt, M., Einhorn, E., Huijnen, C., van den Heuvel, H., van Berlo, A., Bley, A., & Gross, H-M. (2013). Realization and user evaluation of a companion robot for people with mild cognitive impairments. In *IEEE International Conference on Robotics and Automation (ICRA)* (pp. 1153-1159). Karlsruhe, Germany.

Schwarz, G. (1978). Estimating the dimension of a model. *Annals of Statistics*, *6*(2), 461–464. doi:10.1214/aos/1176344136

Schwarz, N., & Clore, G. L. (1988). How do I feel about it? The information function of affective states. In K. Fiedler & J. P. Forgas (Eds.), *Affect, cognition, and social behavior* (pp. 44–62). Toronto: Hogrefe.

Searle, J. (1980). Minds, brains, and programs. *Behavioral and Brain Sciences*, *3*(3), 417–457. doi:10.1017/S0140525X00005756

Sebe, N., Lew, M. S., Cohen, I., Garg, A., & Huang, T. S. (2002). Emotion recognition using a cauchy naive Bayes classifier. In *Proceedings of the 16th International Conference on Pattern Recognition, 2002.* (Vol. 1, pp. 17-20). IEEE. doi:10.1109/ICPR.2002.1044578

Sedikides, C. (1992). Mood as a determinant of attentional focus. Cognition and Emotion, 6(2), 129–148. doi:10.1080/02699939208411063

Sehaba, K., Sabouret, N., & Corruble, V. (2007). *An emotional model for synthetic characters with personality* Paper presented at the Affective Computing and Intelligent Interaction (ACII), Lisbon, Portugal. doi:10.1007/978-3-540-74889-2_81

Selic, B. (2003). The pragmatics of Model-Driven development. *IEEE Software*, *20*(5), 19–25. doi:10.1109/MS.2003.1231146

Sevdalis, V., & Keller, P. E. (2010). Cues for self-recognition in point-light displays of actions performed in synchrony with music. Consciousness and Cognition, 19(2), 617–626. doi:10.1016/j.concog.2010.03.017 PMID:20382037

Sexton, R. S., Dorsey, R. E., & Johnson, J. D. (1999). Optimization of neural networks: A comparative analysis of the genetic algorithm and simulated annealing. *European Journal of Operational Research*, *114*(3), 589–601. doi:10.1016/S0377-2217(98)00114-3

Shannon, C. E. (2001). A mathematical theory of communication. *Mobile Computing and Communications Review*, *5*(1), 3–55. doi:10.1145/584091.584093

Sharkey, N. (2010). Saying 'no!' to lethal autonomous targeting. *Journal of Military Ethics*, *9*(4), 369–383. doi:10.1080/15027570.2010.537903

Shimosaka, M., Mori, T., Harada, T., & Sato, T. (2005). Marginalized bags of vectors kernels on switching linear dynamics for online action recognition. In *International Conference on Robotics and Automaiton* (pp. 72–77). doi:10.1109/ROBOT.2005.1570582

Shivakumar, G., & Vijaya, P. A. (2011), Human emotion recognition from facial images using feed forward neural network with batch back propagation algorithm. In *International Conference on Data Engineering and Communication Systems-2011* (ICDECS 2011), Bangalore, pp. 198-203.

Shivakumar, G., & Vijaya, P. A. (2013). An improved artificial neural network based emotion classification system for expressive facial images. Lecture Notes in Electrical Engineering (vol. 258, pp. 243-253). Berlin: Springer.

Shivakumar, G., Vijaya, P. A., & Anand, R. S. (2007). Artificial neural network based cumulative scoring pattern method for ECG analysis. *IEEE International Conference on Advances in Computer Vision and Information Technology,* pp. 451-457.

Shivakumar, G., & Vijaya, P. A. (2009). Face recognition system using back propagation artificial neural network. *International Journal of Computer Science and Information Technology, 1*(1), 68–77.

Shivakumar, G., & Vijaya, P. A. (2011). Analysis of human emotions using galvanic skin response and finger tip temperature. *International Journal of Synthetic Emotions, 2*(1), 15–25. doi:10.4018/jse.2011010102

Shivakumar, G., & Vijaya, P. A. (2012). Emotion recognition using finger tip temperature: First step towards an automatic system. *International Journal of Computer and Electrical Engineering, 4*(3), 252–255. doi:10.7763/IJCEE.2012.V4.489

Shiv, B., Loewenstein, G., & Bechara, A. (2005). The dark side of emotion in decision-making: When individuals with decreased emotional reactions make more advantageous decisions. *Brain Research. Cognitive Brain Research, 23*(1), 85–92. doi:10.1016/j.cogbrainres.2005.01.006 PMID:15795136

Shute, B., & Wheldall, K. (1989). Pitch alterations in British motherese: Some preliminary acoustic data. *Journal of Child Language, 16*(3), 503–512. doi:10.1017/S0305000900010680 PMID:2808570

Siemer, M., Mauss, I., & Gross, J. J. (2007). Same situation--different emotions: How appraisals shape our emotions. *Emotion (Washington, D.C.), 7*(3), 592–600. doi:10.1037/1528-3542.7.3.592 PMID:17683215

Sigelman, C. K., & Rider, E. A. (2010). *Life span human development*. CengageBrain.

Silke, A., Heinzle, J., Weiskopf, N., Ethofer, T., & Haynes, J.-D. (2011). Flow of affective information in communicating brains. *NeuroImage, 54*(1), 439–446. doi:10.1016/j.neuroimage.2010.07.004 PMID:20624471

Simon, H. A. (1967). Motivational and emotional controls of cognition. *Psychological Review, 74*(1), 29–39. doi:10.1037/h0024127 PMID:5341441

Singer, P. W. (2009). *Wired for war: The robotics revolution and conflict in the 21st century*. New York: The Penguin Press.

Singer, P. W. (2010). The future of war. In G. Dabringer (Ed.), *Ethical and legal aspects of unmanned systems: Interviews* (pp. 71–84). Vienna: Institute for Religion and Peace.

Singer, T. (2004). Empathy for pain involves the affective but not sensory components of pain. *Science, 303*(5661), 1157–1162. doi:10.1126/science.1093535 PMID:14976305

Sloman, A. (2011). What's information, for an organism or intelligent machine? How can a machine or organism mean.

Sloman, A. (1987). Motives, mechanisms, and emotions. *Cognition and Emotion, 1*(3), 217–233. doi:10.1080/02699938708408049

Sloman, A. (2001) *Varieties of affect and the CogAff architecture schema*. In *Proceedings of the AISB'01 Symposium on Emotion, Cognition, and Affective Computing*. York, UK2001.

Sloman, A., Chrisley, R., & Scheutz, M. (2005). The architectural basis of affective states and processes. In J.-M. Fellous & M. A. Arbib (Eds.), *Who needs emotions?* New York: Oxford University Press. doi:10.1093/acprof:oso/9780195166194.003.0008

Smetacek, V., & Mechsner, F. (2004). Making sense. Proprioception: Is the sensory system that supports body posture and movement also the root of our understanding of physical laws? *Nature, 432*(7013), 21. doi:10.1038/432021a PMID:15525964

Smith, C. A., & Kirby, L. (2000). Consequences require antecedents: Toward a process model of emotion elicitation. In J. P. Forgas (Ed.), Feeling and Thinking: The role of affect in social cognition. New York: Cambridge University Press.

Smith, C. A., & Kirby, L. D. (2001). Toward delivering on the promise of appraisal theory. In K. R. Scherer, A. Schorr, & T. Johnstone (Eds.), Appraisal Processes in Emotion. New York: Oxford University Press.

Smith, C. A. (1989). Dimensions of appraisal and physiological response in emotion. *Journal of Personality and Social Psychology*, *56*(3), 339–353. doi:10.1037/0022-3514.56.3.339 PMID:2926633

Smith, C. A., & Kirby, L. D. (2004). Appraisal as a pervasive determinant of anger. *Emotion (Washington, D.C.)*, *4*(2), 133–138. doi:10.1037/1528-3542.4.2.133 PMID:15222849

Smith, C. A., & Scott, H. S. (1997). A componential approach to the meaning of facial expressions. In J. A. Russell & J. M. Fern (Eds.), *The psychology of facial expression* (pp. 229–254). Paris, France: Editions de la Maison des Sciences de l'Homme. doi:10.1017/CBO9780511659911.012

So, J. (2013, 12 31). Can robots fall in love, and why would they? *The Daily Beast*. Retrieved April 7, 2014, from http://www.thedailybeast.com/articles/2013/12/31/can-robots-fall-in-love-and-why-would-they.html

Soken, N. H., & Pick, A. D. (1992). Intermodal perception of happy and angry expressive behaviors by seven-month-old infants. *Child Development*, *63*(4), 787–795. doi:10.2307/1131233 PMID:1505240

Sokol, S. (1978). Measurement of infant visual acuity from pattern reversal evoked potentials. *Vision Research*, *18*(1), 33–39. doi:10.1016/0042-6989(78)90074-3 PMID:664274

Soleymani, M., Lichtenauer, J., Pun, T., & Pantic, M. (2012). A multimodal database for affect recognition and implicit tagging. *IEEE Transactions on Affective Computing*, *3*(1), 42–55.

Solomon, R. C. (1993). *The passions: Emotions and the meaning of life* (Rev. ed.). Indianapolis: Hackett.

Sonnemans, J., & Frijda, N. H. (1994). The structure of subjective emotional intensity. *Cognition and Emotion*, *8*(4), 329–350. doi:10.1080/02699939408408945

Sparrow, R. (2009). Building a better warbot: Ethical issues in the design of unmanned systems for military applications. *Science and Engineering Ethics*, *15*(2), 169–187. doi:10.1007/s11948-008-9107-0 PMID:19048395

Sparrow, R. (2011). Robotic weapons and the future of war. In J. Wolfendale & P. Tripodi (Eds.), *New wars and new soldiers* (pp. 117–133). Burlington: Ashgate.

Spivey, M. (2007). *The continuity of mind*. Oxford University Press New York.

Staller, A., & Petta, P. (1998). *Towards a tractable appraisal-based architecture for situated cognizers*. Paper presented at the 5th International Conference of the Society for Adaptive Behaviour (SAB'98): Grounding Emotions in Adaptive Systems Workshop, Zurich, Switzerland.

Sternberg, R., Tourangeau, R., & Nigro, G. (1993). Metaphor, induction and social policy: The convergence of macroscopic and microscopic views. In A. Ortony (Ed.), *Metaphor and thought* (pp. 277–303). Cambridge University Press. doi:10.1017/CBO9781139173865.015

Strand, M., Oram, M. W., & Hammar, Å. (2013). Emotional information processing in major depression remission and partial remission: Faces come first. *Applied Neuropsychology*, *20*(2), 110–119. doi:10.1080/09084282.2012.670159 PMID:23397997

Strang, T., & Popien, C. L. (2004). A context modeling survey. In *UbiComp 1st International Workshop on Advanced Context Modelling, Reasoning and Management*. (pp. 31-41). Nottingham.

Strasser, E., Weiss, A., & Tscheligi, M. (2012). Affect misattribution procedure: An implicit technique to measure user experience in HRI. In *Proceedings of the Seventh Annual ACM/IEEE International Conference on Human-Robot Interaction HRI '12* (pp. 243-244). Boston, Massachusetts, USA.

Strawser, B. J. (2011). *Two bad arguments for the justification of autonomous weapons*. Paper presented at Technology and Security, University of North Texas.

Sullins, J. P. (2010). RoboWarfare: Can robots be more ethical than humans on the battlefield? *Ethics and Information Technology*, *12*(3), 263–275. doi:10.1007/s10676-010-9241-7

Sun, R., & Zhang, X. (2004). Top-down versus bottom-up learning in cognitive skill acquisition. In Proceedings of the 24th Annual Conference of the Cognitive Science Society (2002), pp. 63-89. doi:10.1016/j.cogsys.2003.07.001

Sutcliffe, A. (2002). *User-centred requirements engineering: Theory and practice*. London: Springer. doi:10.1007/978-1-4471-0217-5

Suzuki, K., Camurri, A., Ferrentino, P., & Hashimoto, S. (1998). Intelligent agent system for human-robot interaction through artificial emotion. In *SMC'98 Conference Proceedings of the 1998 IEEE International Conference on Systems, Man, and Cybernetics* (Vol. 2, pp. 1055–1060). doi:10.1109/ICSMC.1998.727828

Svensson, H., Lindblom, J., & Ziemke, T. (2007). Making sense of embodied cognition: simulation theories of shared neural mechanisms for sensorimotor and cognitive processes. In T. Ziemke, J. Zlatev, & R. Frank R. (Eds.), Body, language, and mind: Embodiment (vol. 1, pp. 241-270). Berlin: Mouton de Gruyter.

Syrdal, D. S., Otero, N., & Dautenhahn, K. (2008). Video prototyping in human-robot interaction: Results from a qualitative study. In *Proceedings of the 15th European conference on Cognitive ergonomics: the ergonomics of cool interaction, ECCE '08*. Madeira, Portugal. doi:10.1145/1473018.1473055

Tahboub, K. (2005). Compliant human-robot cooperation based on intention recognition. In *Proceedings of the 2005 International Symposium on Intelligent Control*. (pp. 1417–1422). IEEE. Retrieved from http://ieeexplore.ieee.org/xpls/abs_all.jsp?arnumber=1467222 doi:10.1109/.2005.1467222

Tahboub, K. A. (2006). Intelligent human–machine interaction based on dynamic Bayesian networks probabilistic intention recognition. Journal of Intelligent & Robotic Systems, 45(1), 31–52. doi:10.1007/s10846-005-9018-0

Takayama, L., & Pantofaru, C. (2009). Influences on proxemic behaviors in human-robot interaction. In *2009 IEEE/RSJ International Conference on Intelligent Robots and Systems* (pp. 5495–5502). doi:10.1109/IROS.2009.5354145

Talarico, J. M., LaBar, K. S., & Rubin, D. C. (2004). Emotional intensity predicts autobiographical memory experience. *Memory & Cognition*, *32*(7), 1118–1132. doi:10.3758/BF03196886 PMID:15813494

Taylor, J. G., & Fragopanagos, N. F. (2005). The interaction of attention and emotion. *Neural Networks*, *18*, 353–369.

Terada, K., & Ito, A. (2010). Can a robot deceive humans? In *2010 5th ACM/IEEE International Conference on Human-Robot Interaction (HRI)*, pp. 191–192. doi:10.1109/HRI.2010.5453201

Terada, K., Shamoto, T., Mei, H., & Ito, A. (2007). Reactive movements of non-humanoid robots cause intention attribution in humans. In *IEEE/RSJ International Conference on Intelligent Robots & Systems* (pp. 3715–3720). doi:10.1109/IROS.2007.4399429

Thellefsen, T., Thellefsen, M., & Sørensen, B. (2013). Emotion, information, and cognition, and some possible consequences for library and information science. *Journal of the American Society for Information Science and Technology*, *64*(8), 1735–1750. doi:10.1002/asi.22858

Thomas, F., & Johnston, O. (1995). *The illusion of life: Disney animation*. Disney Editions.

Thrun, S. (2004). Toward a framework for human-robot interaction. *Human-Computer Interaction*, *19*(1), 9–24. doi:10.1207/s15327051hci1901&2_2

Tian, Y. L., Kanade, T., & Cohn, J. F. (2005). Facial expression analysis. In *Handbook of face recognition* (pp. 247–275). Springer New York. doi:10.1007/0-387-27257-7_12

Tomkins, S. S. (1995). *Exploring affect: The selected writings of Silvan S Tomkins*. Cambridge University Press. doi:10.1017/CBO9780511663994

Tottenham, N., Hare, T. A., Millner, A., Gilhooly, T., Zevin, J., & Casey, B. J. (2011). Elevated amygdala response to faces following early deprivation. *Developmental Science*, *14*(2), 190–204. doi:10.1111/j.1467-7687.2010.00971.x PMID:21399712

Trainor, L. J., Austin, C. M., & Desjardins, R. N. (2000). Is infant-directed speech prosody a result of the vocal expression of emotion? *Psychological Science*, *11*(3), 188–195. doi:10.1111/1467-9280.00240 PMID:11273402

Tritton, T., Hall, J., Rowe, A., Valentine, S., Jedrzejewska, A., Pipe, A. G., . . . Leonards, U. (2012). Engaging with robots while giving simple instructions. In G. Herrmann, M. Studley, M. Pearson, A. Conn, C. Melhuish, M. Witkowski, J-H.n Kim & P. Vadakkepat (Eds.) *Advances in Autonomous Robotics: Joint Proceedings of the 13th Annual TAROS Conference and the 15th Annual FIRA RoboWorld Congress, Lecture Notes in Computer Science, Vol. 7429*, (pp. 176-184). doi:10.1007/978-3-642-32527-4_16

Trovato, G., Kishi, T., Endo, N., Hashimoto, K., & Takanishi, A. (2012). Evaluation study on asymmetrical facial expressions generation for Humanoid Robot. In *2012 First International Conference on Innovative Engineering Systems (ICIES)*. Alexandria, Egypt. doi:10.1109/ICIES.2012.6530858

Trovato, G., Zecca, M., Kishi, T., Endo, N., Hashimoto, K., & Takanishi, A. (2013). Generation of humanoid robot's facial expressions for context-aware communication. *International Journal of Humanoid Robotics*, *10*(1). doi:10.1142/S0219843613500138

Tsai, J. L. (2007). Ideal affect: Cultural causes and behavioral consequences. *Perspectives on Psychological Science*, *2*(3), 242–259. doi:10.1111/j.1745-6916.2007.00043.x

Tsuchiya, N., & Adolphs, R. (2007). Emotion and consciousness. *Trends in Cognitive Sciences*, *11*(4), 158–167. doi:10.1016/j.tics.2007.01.005 PMID:17324608

Turkle, S. (2012). *Alone together: Why we expect more from technology and less from each other*. Basic Books.

User Experience. UX Design (2010). UX Design Defined. *User Experience. UX Design*. Retrieved February 26, 2014, from http://uxdesign.com/ux-defined

User Experience. UX Design. (2010). UX Design Defined. *User Experience. UX Design*. Retrieved February 26, 2014, from http://uxdesign.com/ux-defined

Vallverdú, J., & Casacuberta, D. (2008) The panic room. On synthetic emotions. In A. Briggle, K. Waelbers, & P. Brey (Eds.), Current issues in computing and philosophy, (pp. 103-115). The Netherlands: IOS Press.

Vallverdú, J., & Casacuberta, D. (2009) Modelling hardwired synthetic emotions: TPR 2.0. In J. Vallverdú & D. Casacuberta, (Eds.), Handbook of Research on Synthetic Emotions and Sociable Robotics: New Applications in Affective Computing and Artificial Intelligence, (pp. 103-115). Hershey, PA: IGI Global. doi:10.4018/978-1-60566-354-8.ch023

Vallverdú, J. (2009). Computational epistemology and e-science. A new way of thinking. *Minds and Machines*, *19*(4), 557–567. doi:10.1007/s11023-009-9168-0

Vallverdú, J. (2014). What are simulations? An epistemological approach. *Procedia Technology*, *13*, 6–15. doi:10.1016/j.protcy.2014.02.003

Vallverdú, J., Casacuberta, D., Nishida, T., Ohmoto, O., Moran, S., & Lázare, S. (2013). From computational emotional models to HRI. *International Journal of Robotics Applications and Technologies*, *1*(2), 11–25. doi:10.4018/ijrat.2013070102

Vallverdú, J., Shah, H., & Casacuberta, D. (2010). Chatterbox challenge as a test-bed for synthetic emotions. *International Journal of Synthetic Emotions*, *1*(2), 57–86.

Valstar, M., Mehu, M., Pantic, M., & Scherer, K. R. (in press). Meta-analysis of the first facial expression recognition and analysis challenge. *IEEE Transactions on Systems, Man, and Cybernetics*. PMID:22736651

Van Breemen, A., Yan, X., & Meerbeek, B. (2005). iCat: an animated user-interface robot with personality. In *Proceedings of the fourth international joint conference on Autonomous agents and multiagent systems*. New York, NY, USA: ACM. doi:10.1145/1082473.1082823

Van der Perre, G. et al.. (2014) *Conference on human-robot interaction.*

Van Gelder, R. S., & Borod, J. C. (1990). Neurobiological and cultural aspects of facial asymmetry. *Journal of Communication Disorders*, *23*(4-5), 273–286. doi:10.1016/0021-9924(90)90004-I PMID:2246383

Vanderborght, B., Simut, R., Saldien, J., Pop, C., Rusu, A. S., Pintea, S., . . . David, D. O. (2012). Using the social robot probo as a social story telling agent for children with ASD. Interaction Studies: Social Behaviour and Communication in Biological and Artificial Systems, 13(3), 348–372. doi:10.1075/is.13.3.02van

Varela, F. J., Thompson, E., & Rosch, E. (1991). *The embodied mind: Cognitive science and human experience.* Cambridge, MA: MIT Press.

Velásquez, J. D. (1997). *Modeling emotions and other motivations in synthetic agents.* Paper presented at the AAAI/IAAI.

Velásquez, J. D. (1998). *When robots weep: emotional memories and decision-making.* Paper presented at the Proceedings of the National Conference on Artificial Intelligence.

Velásquez, J. D. (1999). *An emotion-based approach to robotics.* Paper presented at the IROS. doi:10.1109/IROS.1999.813010

Vijaya, P. A., & Shivakumar, G. (2013). Galvanic skin response: A physiological sensor system for affective computing. *International Journal of Machine Learning and Computing*, *3*(1), 31–34. doi:10.7763/IJMLC.2013.V3.267

Vinayagamoorthy, V., Gillies, M., Steed, A., Tanguy, E., Pan, X., Loscos, C., & Slater, M. (2006). *Building expression into virtual characters.* Paper presented at the Eurographics Conference State of the Art Report.

Viterbi, A. (1967). Error bounds for convolutional codes and an asymptotically optimum decoding algorithm. IEEE Transactions on Information Theory, 13(2), 260–269. doi:10.1109/TIT.1967.1054010

Vlasenko, B., & Wendemuth, A. (2009). Heading toward to the natural way of human-machine interaction: the NIMITEK project. In *IEEE International Conference on Multimedia and Expo, 2009. ICME 2009.* (pp. 950–953). doi:10.1109/ICME.2009.5202653

von Bertalanffy, L. (1950). An outline of general system theory. *The British Journal for the Philosophy of Science*, *1*(2), 134–165. doi:10.1093/bjps/I.2.134

Wada, K., Shibata, T., Saito, T., & Tanie, K. (2004). Effects of robot-assisted activity for elderly people and nurses at a day service center. In *Proceedings of the IEEE* (Vol. 92, pp. 1780–1788). doi:10.1109/JPROC.2004.835378

Wadlinger, H., & Isaacowitz, D. (2006). Positive mood broadens visual attention to positive stimuli. *Motivation and Emotion*, *30*(1), 89–101doi:10.1007/s11031-006-9021-1 PMID:20431711

Wallace, B. (2007). *The mind, the body, and the world: Psychology after cognitivism?* Imprint Academic.

Wallach, W., & Allen, C. (2010). *Moral machines: Teaching robots right from wrong.* New York: Oxford University Press.

Wallbott, H. G. (1998). Bodily expression of emotion. European Journal of Social Psychology, 28(6), 879–896. doi:10.1002/(SICI)1099-0992(1998110)28:6<879::AID-EJSP901>3.0.CO;2-W

Walters, M. L., Oskoei, M. a., Syrdal, D. S., & Dautenhahn, K. (2011). A long-term human-robot proxemic study. In IEEE, RO-MAN 2011 (pp. 137–142). doi:10.1109/RO-MAN.2011.6005274

Wang, E., Lignos, C., Vatsal, A., & Scassellati, B. (2006). Effects of head movement on perceptions of humanoid robot behavior. In *Proceeding of the 1st ACM SIGCHI/SIGART Conference on Human-Robot Interaction - HRI '06* (p. 180). New York: ACM Press. doi:10.1145/1121241.1121273

Wang, Z., Mülling, K., Deisenroth, M. P., Ben Amor, H., Vogt, D., Schölkopf, B., & Peters, J. (2013). Probabilistic movement modeling for intention inference in human-robot interaction. The International Journal of Robotics Research, 32(7), 841–858. doi:10.1177/0278364913478447

Wang, S., Liu, Z., Lv, S., Lv, Y., & Wu, G. (2010). A natural visible and infrared facial expression database for expression recognition and emotion inference. *IEEE Transactions on Biometrics Compendium, 12*(7), 682–691. doi:10.1109/TMM.2010.2060716

Watanabe, A., Ogino, M., & Asada, M. (2007). Mapping facial expression to internal states based on intuitive parenting. *Journal of Robotics and Mechatronics, 19*(3), 3–15.

Watson, D., Clark, L. A., & Harkness, A. R. (1994). Structures of personality and their relevance to psychopathology. *Journal of Abnormal Psychology, 103*(1), 18–31. doi:10.1037/0021-843X.103.1.18 PMID:8040477

Watson, D., & Tellegen, A. (1985). Toward a consensual structure of mood. *Psychological Bulletin, 98*(2), 219–235 psycnet.apa.org/journals/bul/98/2/219/. doi:10.1037/0033-2909.98.2.219 PMID:3901060

Watson, P. (1978). *War on the mind: The military uses and abuses of psychology*. New York: Basic Books.

Web Ontology Working Group. (2009, 27 October). *Owl 2 web ontology language. Document overview. W3C recommendation*. Retrieved September 19, 2010, from http://www.w3.org/TR/owl2-overview/

Webb, T., & Sheeran, P. (2006). Does changing behavioral intentions engender behavior change? A meta-analysis of the experimental evidence. *Psychological Bulletin, 132*(2), 249–268. doi:10.1037/0033-2909.132.2.249 PMID:16536643

Wehrle, T. (1995). *The Geneva Appraisal Theory Environment (GATE)* [Unpublished computer software]. Switzerland: University of Geneva.

Wehrle, T., & Scherer, K. R. (2001). Toward computational modelling of appraisal theories. In K. R. Scherer, A. Schorr, & T. Johnstone (Eds.), *Appraisal processes in emotion: Theory, methods, research* (pp. 92–120). New York: Oxford University Press.

Weiss, A., Bernhaupt, R., Laukes, M., & Tscheligi, M. (2009). The USUS evaluation framework for human-robot interactions. *Proceedings of the symposium on new frontiers in human-robot interaction, AISB 2009* (pp. 158–165). Edinburgh, Scotland.

Weiss, A., Bernhaupt, R., & Yoshida, E. (2009). Addressing user experience and societal impact in a user study with a humanoid robot. In *Proceedings of the Symposium on New Frontiers in Human-Robot Interaction, AISB2009* (pp. 150-157).

Weiss, X., Bernhaupt, X., & Tscheligi, C. (2011). The USUS framework. In K. Dautenhahn & J. Saunders (Eds.), *New frontiers in human-robot interaction* (pp. 89–110). Amsterdam, The Netherlands: John Benjamins.

Weizenbaum, J. (1977). *Computer power and human reason: From judgement to calculation*. New York: W.H. Freeman & Company.

Weizsäcker, C. F., & von Weizsäcker, C. F. (1985). *Wahrnehmung der Neuzeit*. Deutscher Taschenbuch Verlag.

Werner, L. A. (2002). Infant auditory capabilities. *Current Opinion in Otolaryngology & Head & Neck Surgery, 10*(5), 398–402. doi:10.1097/00020840-200210000-00013

Werry, I., Dautenhahn, K., Ogden, B., & Harwin, W. (2001). Can social interaction skills be taught by a social agent? The role of a robotic mediator in autism therapy. *Computer Technology: Instruments of Mind, 2117*, 57–74. Retrieved from http://link.springer.com/chapter/10.1007/3-540-44617-6_6

Whetham, D. (2012). Remote killing and drive-by wars. In D. W. Lovell & I. Primoratz (Eds.), *Protecting civilians during violent conflict: Theoretical and practical issues for the 21st century* (pp. 199–214). Aldershot: Ashgate.

Wicker, B., Keysers, C., Plailly, J., Royet, J. P., Gallese, V., & Rizzolatti, G. (2003). Both of us disgusted in my insula: The common neural basis of seeing and feeling disgust. *Neuron, 40*, 655–664.

Wilensky, R. (1983). *Planning and understanding: A computational approach to human reasoning*. Retrieved from http://www.osti.gov/energycitations/product.biblio.jsp?osti_id=5673187

Wilson, A. D., & Golinka, S. (2013). Embodied cognition is not what you think it is. *Frontiers in Psychology*, *4*(58), 1–13.

Wilson, R. A., & Keil, F. C. (1999). *The MIT encyclopedia of the cognitive sciences* (Vol. 134). MIT Press.

Wilson, R. A., & Keil, F. C. (Eds.). (1999). *The MIT encyclopedia of cognitive sciences*. Cambridge, MA: MIT Press.

Witzany, G. (2010). Biocommunication and natural genome editing. *World Journal of Biological Chemistry*, *1*(11), 348.

Wolfram, S. (2002). *A new kind of science*. Champaign, IL: Wolfram Media, Inc.

Wong, F. S. (1991, November). Fastprop: A selective training algorithm for fast error propagation. In *1991 IEEE International Joint Conference on Neural Networks* (pp. 2038-2043). IEEE. doi:10.1109/IJCNN.1991.170635

Wood, J. V., Saltzberg, J. A., & Goldsamt, L. A. (1990). Does affect induce self-focused attention? Journal of Personality and Social Psychology, 58(5), 899–908. doi:10.1037/0022-3514.58.5.899 PMID:2348375

Wu, H., & Mendel, J. M. (2002). Uncertainty bounds and their use in the design of interval type-2 fuzzy logic systems. *IEEE Transactions on Fuzzy Systems*, *10*(5), 622–639.

Wu, H., Wu, Y., & Luo, J. (2009). An interval type-2 fuzzy rough set model for attribute reduction. *IEEE Transactions on Fuzzy Systems, 17*(2), 301–315.

Xu, Q., Li, L., & Wang, G. (2013). Designing engagement-aware agents for multiparty conversations. In *Proceedings of CHI 2013* (pp. 2233-2242). Paris, France.

Xu, Q., Ng, J., Cheong, Y. L., Tan, O., Wong, J. B., Tay, T. C., & Park, T. (2012). The role of social context in human-robot interaction. *Southeast Asian Network of Ergonomics Societies Conference (SEANES)*, Langkawi, Kedah.

Yamato, J., Ohya, J., & Ishii, K. (1992). Recognizing human action in time-sequential images using hidden Markov model. In *Proceedings 1992 IEEE Computer Society Conference on Computer Vision and Pattern Recognition* (pp. 379–385). IEEE Computer Society Press. doi:10.1109/CVPR.1992.223161

Yanco, H. A., & Drury, J. (2004). Classifying human-robot interaction: an updated taxonomy. *IEEE International Conference on Systems, Man and Cybernetics 2004, Vol. 3* (pp. 2841-2846).

Yang, J., Chen, Y., Ammar, M., & Lee, C. (2005). Ferry replacement protocols in sparse manet message ferrying systems. In *Proceedings of the* IEEE *Wireless Communications and Networking Conference* (vol. 4, pp. 2038-2044). Atlanta, GA.

Yeasin, M., Bullot, B., & Sharma, R. (2006). Recognition of facial expressions and measurement of levels of interest from video. *IEEE Transactions on Multimedia*, *8*(3), 500–507. doi:10.1109/TMM.2006.870737

Yee, A. S. (2013). An investigation of the use of real-time image mosaicing for facilitating global spatial awareness in visual search (Doctoral thesis). University of Toronto, Canada.

Yokoyama, A., & Omori, T. (2010). Modeling of human intention estimation process in social interaction scene. *International Conference on Fuzzy Systems*, 1–6. doi:10.1109/FUZZY.2010.5584042

Young, J. E., Sung, J. Y., Voida, A., Sharlin, E., Igarashi, T., Cristensen, H. I., & Grinter, R. E. (2011). Evaluating human-robot interaction: Focusing on the holistic interaction experience. *International Journal of Social Robotics*, *3*(1), 53–67. doi:10.1007/s12369-010-0081-8

Yu, H., & Wilamowski, B. M. (2011). Levenberg-Marquardt training. *The Industrial Electronics Handbook*, *5*, 1–15.

Zadeh, L. A. (1965). Fuzzy sets. *Information and Control*, *8*(3), 338–353. doi:10.1016/S0019-9958(65)90241-X

Zborowski, M. (1969). *People in pain.* San Francisco: Jossey-Bass, Inc. Publications.

Zeelenberg, M., Nelissen, R. M., Breugelmans, S. M., & Pieters, R. (2008). On emotion specificity in decision making: Why feeling is for doing. *Judgment and Decision Making, 3*(1), 18–27.

Zeki, S., & Romaya, J. P. (2008). Neural correlates of hate. *PLoS ONE, 3*(10), e3556. doi:10.1371/journal.pone.0003556 PMID:18958169

Zeng, Z., Pantic, M., Roisman, G. I., & Huang, T. S. (2009). A survey of affect recognition methods: Audio, visual, and spontaneous expressions. *IEEE Transactions on Pattern Analysis and Machine Intelligence, 31*(1), 39–58. doi:10.1109/TPAMI.2008.52 PMID:19029545

Zhang, D., Cungen, C., Young, X., Wang, H., & Pan, Y. (2005). A survey of computational emotion research. In T. Panayiotopoulos et al. (Eds.), LNAI 3661, (p. 490). Berlin; Heidelberg: Springer-Verlag.

Zhang, X., Hu, B., Chen, J., & Moore, P. (2012). Ontology-based context modeling for emotion recognition in an intelligent web. *World Wide Web (Bussum), 16*(4), 497–513. doi:10.1007/s11280-012-0181-5

Zhao, J., & Kearney, G. (1996). Classifying facial emotions by backpropagation neural networks with fuzzy inputs. In *Proceedings of the International Conference on Neural Information Processing* (Vol. 1, pp. 454-457).

Ziemke, T. (2003). What's that thing called embodiment? In AltermanR.KirschD. (Eds.), *Proceedings of the 25th Annual Meeting of the Cognitive Science Society* (pp. 1305-1310). Mahwah, NJ: Lawrence Erlbaum.

Ziemke, T. (2008). On the role of emotion in biological and robotic autonomy. *Bio Systems, 91*(2), 401–408. doi:10.1016/j.biosystems.2007.05.015 PMID:17714857

Ziemke, T., & Lowe, R. (2009). On the role of emotions in embodied cognitive architectures: From organisms to robots. *Cognitive Computation, 1*(1), 104–117. doi:10.1007/s12559-009-9012-0

Zimmermann, H. J. (1992). *Fuzzy set theory and its applications second* (Revised Ed.). Kluwer Academic Publishers.

Zowghi, D., & Coulin, C. (2005). Requirements elicitation: A survey of techniques, approaches, and tools. In A. Aurum & C. Wohlin (Eds.), *Engineering and managing software requirements* (pp. 21–46). Berlin, Germany: Springer. doi:10.1007/3-540-28244-0_2

About the Contributors

Jordi Vallverdú, Ph.D., M.Sci., B.Mus, B.Phil is Tenure Professor at Universitat Autònoma de Barcelona (Catalonia, Spain), where he teaches Philosophy and History of Science and Computing. His research is dedicated to the epistemological, ethical and educational aspects of Philosophy of Computing and Science and AI. He is Editor-in-chief of the *International Journal of Synthetic Emotions (IJSE)*, and as a researcher is member of the IACAP, Convergent Science Network of Biomimetic and Biohybrid systems Net member, member of the Spanish Society of Logic, Methodology and Philosophy of Science, member of the GEHUCT (Grup d'Estudis Interdisciplinaris sobre Ciència i Tecnologia) research project, member of the TECNOCOG (Philosophy, Technology and Cognition Research Group), member of EUCogIII, Main researcher of SETE (Synthetic Emotions in Technological Environments), and Expert of the Biosociety Research (European Commission). He has written 8 books as author or editor. In 2011 he won a prestigious Japanese JSPS fellowship to conduct his research on computational HRI interfaces at Kyoto University. He was keynote at ECAP09 (TUM, München, Germany), EBICC2012 (UNESP, Brazil) and SLACTIONS 2013 (Portugal). - See more at: http://orcid.org/0000-0001-9975-7780#sthash.rhvZw6l3.dpuf.

***

Beatrice Alenljung is a senior lecturer in informatics at the School of Informatics, University of Skövde, Sweden. She graduated with the degree of Doctor of Philosophy from Linköping University, Sweden, in 2008 within informatics. Dr. Alenljung also holds a Ph.Lic (2005) in Informatics from Linköping University, an MSc in Informatics and a BSc in Systems Analyses, both from the University of Skövde. Her research interests include user experience design (UXD), human-computer interaction (HCI) (ranging from more traditional information technology to social robots), requirements engineering (RE), decision support systems (DSS), and simulation-enhanced learning environments. The human-centered perspective is the main thread of her research.

Ebrahim Oshni Alvandi has earned his Bachelor of Art degree in linguistics from Tabriz PNU University, Tabriz, Iran. He received his Master of Science degree in Philosophy of Science and Mind from IAU, Tehran, Iran. In his master degree, he has majored in philosophy of cognitive sciences and artificial intelligence. He is currently a HDR researcher in Psychological Studies Lab of Monash University, Gippsland campus, Australia. During HDR period of study and research, Ebrahim works on a cognitive model of emotional agency for telecounselling. His research interests focus on cognitive and informational modelling of emotions, cyber psychology and engineering psychology. Additionally, he has published his research at international journals including *Synthesizing Human Emotion in Intelligent Systems and Robotics*, published by IGI Global, Hershey, USA.

Diana Arellano is an R&D Engineer at the Institute of Animation of the Filmakademie Baden-Württemberg, Germany. In 2004 and 2008 she received her Bachelor and Master degrees in Computer Sciences from the University Simon Bolivar, Venezuela. In 2012, she obtained her PhD at the University of the Balearic Islands (UIB), Spain, where she developed a system that made use of ontologies and facial animations to represent the real and emotional context of virtual characters. At the Filmakademie she is involved with more artistic projects that deal with emotions and research on autism. She is a member of ACM SIGGRAPH and ACM SIGGRAPH International Resources Committee.

Andra Băltoiu received a B.Sc. in Systems Engineering from the Politehnica University of Bucharest with a thesis on the possibilities of representing the dynamics of human figurative thinking in a control systems approach. She is currently taking a M.Sc. program in Intelligent Control Systems at the Faculty of Automatic Control and Computers of the same University. Her research interests focus on modeling emotions and cognition, the dynamics of non-linear systems, data mining and pattern recognition. She works as Research Assistant at the National Institute for Sport Research, exploring the relationship between information, control and human performance.

Jonathan Bishop is an information technology executive, researcher and writer. He is the founder of the companies that form part of the Crocels Community Media Group, and founded the Centre for Research into Online Communities and E-Learning Systems in 2005 from which the group is named. Jonathan's research generally falls within human-computer interaction, and he has numerous publications in this area, such as on Internet trolling, gamification, Classroom 2.0, and multimedia forensics. In addition to his BSc(Hons) in Multimedia Studies and various postgraduate degrees, including in law, economics and computing, Jonathan has served in local government as a councillor and school governor, as well as having contested numerous elections. He is also a fellow of numerous learned bodies, including BCS - The Chartered Institute for IT, the Royal Anthropological Institute, and the Royal Society of Arts. Jonathan has won prizes for his literary skills and been a finalist in national and local competitions for his environmental, community and equality work, which often form part of action research studies. In his spare time Jonathan enjoys listening to music, swimming and chess.

Cătălin Buiu is Professor and Head of the Natural Computing and Robotics Lab at the Politehnica University of Bucharest, Department of Automatic Control and Systems Engineering. Professor Buiu has primarily taught courses in Cognitive Robotics, Modeling of Biological Processes, Bioinformatics, and Natural Computing. His current research interests include swarm robotics, membrane systems, models of emotions, bioinformatics, and educational technologies. He has authored/participated in several successful national and international grants. Prof. Buiu's publications include papers in international journals and conference proceedings. He is Academic Editor at PLOS ONE.

David Casacuberta is a philosophy of science professor in the Universidad Autònoma de Barcelona (Spain). He has a PhD in Philosophy and a master degree in "Cognitive sciences and Language". His current line of research is twofold: 1) The cognitive, cultural and social impact of new media; 2) Philosophical foundations of Artificial Intelligence, especially those related to the "3rd generation of cognitive sciences" such as enactive artificial intelligence, artificial emotions, morphological computing and social robots. He is a member of The Spanish Society of Logic, Methodology and Philosophy of Science.government, The consolidated research group GEHUCT (Grup d'Estudis Interdisciplinaris sobre Ciència i Tecnologia), and the research project TECNOCOG (Philosophy, Technology and Cognition Research Group) financed by the Spanish government. He works for Transit Projectes as project manager and scientific coordinator for the EU Project E-learning for E-inclusion (www.el4ei.net) under the E-learning program. He is also a member of the Spanish think-tank edemocracia (www.edemocracia.com) devoted to the study on how ICT can improve democratic processes such as voting and participation. He is also the secretary of the Spanish chapter of Computer Professionals for Social Responsibility (www.cpsr.org) and the Spanish representative in the International Coalition European Digital Rights (http://www.edri.org/).

Aruna Chakraborty received the M.A. degree in cognitive science and the Ph.D. degree on emotional intelligence and human–computer interactions from Jadavpur University, Calcutta-700032, India, in 2000 and 2005, respectively. She is currently an Associate Professor in the Department of Computer Science and Engineering, St. Thomas' College of Engineering and Technology, Calcutta. She is also a Visiting Faculty of Jadavpur University, Calcutta-700032, India, where she offers graduate-level courses on intelligent automation and robotics, and cognitive science. She, with her teacher Prof. A. Konar, has written a book on *Emotional Intelligence: A Cybernetic Approach*, which has appeared from Springer, Heidelberg, 2009. She is also co-editing a book with Prof. A. Konar on *Advances in Emotion Recognition*, which is shortly to appear from Willey Interscience. She serves as an Editor to the *International Journal of Artificial Intelligence and Soft Computing*, Inderscience, U.K. Her current research interest includes artificial intelligence, emotion modeling, and their applications in next-generation human–machine interactive systems. She is a nature lover, and loves music and painting.

Aydan M. Erkmen received her B.Sc. from Bogazici Univ.Turkey in Electrical Eng double majoring in Math, M.Sc. in ECE from Drexel University, USA, and Ph.D. in Info Tech & Engineering from George Mason University, USA. She is full professor in Electrical Eng. Middle East Tech University Turkey. Her research interests include rescue robotics, robot hands, cognitive robotics, and multi-robots networks. She served 2 terms in IEEE RAS Admin Committee; was IEEE RAS vice president 2000 to 2003; was till 2010 associate editor of *Int. Journal of Robotics & Automation*; since 2009, she has been Editor in SpringerVerlag-Paladyn *Journal of Behavioral Robotics*. She served 3 years in editoral board of IEEE RAS Magazine. She was vice president for industrial funds at TUBITAK Scientific & Tech Research Council of Turkey, the FP6 national coordinator till 2002, and IST NCP till 2003. She served 3years as Vice Dean of the Engineering Faculty. Since 2009, she has served in EURON George Giralt Award Committee.

Jai Galliott is an applied ethicist and military theorist. After a brief stint in the military, Jai completed a PhD on the ethics and politics of drone use in the armed forces. He has taught in a range of classes at undergraduate and Master's level, including Practical Ethics, Business and Professional Ethics, Bioethics and Biotechnology and Violence and Conflict in World Politics. He has published widely on the topic of ethics and emerging technologies and is Lead Editor of Ashgate's Emerging Technologies, Ethics and International Affairs book series. He is also author of *Military Robots: Mapping the Moral Landscape*.

O. Can Görür is an electrical and electronics engineer who has research interests in human-robot interactions, sociable assistant robotics, human intention and emotion estimations, and cognitive robotics. He received his B.Sc in 2011 and M.Sc on robotics in 2014 from Electrical and Electronics Eng. Dept. in Middle East Tech University of Turkey. He did his master thesis on human intention and emotion engineering under the supervision of Prof. Aydan M. Erkmen. During his graduate student times, he also worked as a hardware engineer in a defense company called Aselsan for 2 years and then started working as a software engineer in a software company called AnelArge for one year till the end of his master's study. He is now a researcher at an institution called GT-ARC and he is a Ph.D candidate at Technische Universität Berlin of Germany.

Anisha Halder received the B.Tech. degree in Electronics and Communication Engineering from the Haldia Institute of Technology, Midnapore, India, and the M.E. degree in Control Engineering from Electronics and Telecommunication Engineering Department, Jadavpur University, Kolkata, India, in 2007 and 2009 respectively. She has recently submitted her Ph.D. thesis named "A Computational Approach to Multimodal Emotion Recognition" under the guidance of Prof. Amit Konar and Dr. Aruna Chakraborty at Jadavpur University. Her principal research interests include artificial intelligence, pattern recognition, cognitive science, and human–computer interaction. She is the author of over 30 papers published in top international journals and conference proceedings.

Carlos Herrera was born in Caceres, Spain. He received his Bachelor in Mathematics from the Universidad Complutense de Madrid (1996). He holds a PhD in "The synthesis of emotion in artificial agents" from Glasgow Caledonian University (2006), and a postgraduate diploma in Philosophy from the University of Glasgow (2005). He has worked for IBM UK (1996-1998) and as a part-time lecturer at Glasgow Caledonian University (1998-2006). He has worked as a postdoctoral research in cognitive science (Skovde, Sweden 2006-07) and in cognitive robotics (University of Ulster, 2007-2009), and held a Marie Curie grant at the Universidad Politécnica de Madrid (2011- 2014), within the Autonomous Systems Laboratory. He has also trained in dance and worked as an ensemble member at the Echo Echo Dance Theatre Company (2007-2009), and has produced a number of short videos and films.

Eva Hudlicka is a Principal Scientist and President of Psychometrix Associates, in Amherst, MA, Visiting Lecturer at the School of Computer Science, University of Massachusetts-Amherst and Adjunct Associate Professor at Hampshire College. Her primary research focus is the development of computational models of emotion-cognition interactions. Prior to founding Psychometrix in 1995, she was a Senior Scientist at BBN in Cambridge, MA. Dr. Hudlicka is an Associate Editor of the *International Journal of Synthetic Emotions*, member of the Editorial Board of the *International Journal of Machine Consciousness* and the Oxford Series on Cognitive Models and Architectures, and was a member of the National Research Council committee on "Behavioral Modeling and Simulation". Dr. Hudlicka has authored numerous journal and conference articles and book chapters. She received her BS in Biochemistry from Virginia Tech, MS in Computer Science from The Ohio State University, and PhD in Computer Science from the University of Massachusetts-Amherst.

Shashi Shekhar Jha received his Bachelor of Engineering degree in Information Technology from Shri Vaishanav Institute of Technology and Science, Indore, India in 2010. Presently he is pursuing his doctoral degree in Computer Science and Engineering at the Department of Computer Science and Engineering at the Indian Institute of Technology Guwahati, Guwahati, India. He has been awarded the Tata Consultancy Services (TCS) fellowship under the TCS Research Scholar Program. He is a graduate student member of IEEE. His current research interests include Multi-Mobile Agent based systems, Bio-inspired Algorithms, Synthetic Emotions, Machine Learning, etc.

Reshma Kar completed her B.E. in Information Technology from North Eastern Hill University, Shillong in 2010. She received her M.E. degree from National Institute of Technology, Agartala in 2012. She is currently pursuing her PhD degree at Jadavpur University under the joint guidance of Dr. Amit Konar and Dr. Aruna Chakraborty. Her current research interests include EEG Analysis, Emotion Recognition Artificial Intelligence and Human-Computer Interactions. She has also authored publications in reputed national and international conferences.

Amit Konar received the B.E. degree from Bengal Engineering and Science University (B.E. College), Howrah, India, in 1983 and the M.E. Tel E, M. Phil., and Ph.D. (Engineering) degrees from Jadavpur University, Calcutta-700032, India, in 1985, 1988, and 1994, respectively. In 2006, he was a Visiting Professor with the University of Missouri, St. Louis. He is currently a Professor with the Department of Electronics and Tele-communication Engineering (ETCE), Jadavpur University, where he is the Founding Coordinator of the M.Tech. program on intelligent automation and robotics. He has supervised fifteen Ph.D. theses. He has over 200 publications in international journal and conference proceedings. He is the author of eight books, including two popular texts: *Artificial Intelligence and Soft Computing* (CRC Press, 2000) and *Computational Intelligence: Principles, Techniques and Applications* (Springer, 2005). He serves as the Associate Editor of *IEEE Transactions on Systems, Man and Cybernetics, Part-A,* and *IEEE Transactions on Fuzzy Systems*. His research areas include the study of computational intelligence algorithms and their applications to the various domains of electrical engineering and computer science. Specifically, he worked on fuzzy sets and logic, neurocomputing, evolutionary algorithms, Dempster–Shafer theory, and Kalman filtering, and applied the principles of computational intelligence in image understanding, VLSI design, mobile robotics, pattern recognition, brain-computer interfacing and computational biology. He was the recipient of All India Council for Technical Education (AICTE)-accredited 1997–2000 Career Award for Young Teachers for his significant contribution in teaching and research.

Angelica Lim received her B.Sc. in Computing Science from Simon Fraser University, and her M.Sc. and Ph.D. in Informatics from Kyoto University in 2014. She currently works for Aldebaran Robotics in France, and has previously interned at Google, Honda Research Institute Japan, and I3S-CNRS, France. Since 2006, she has been engaged in robotics and artificial intelligence, and is currently interested in signal processing, machine learning and developmental robotics for intelligent systems, particularly in the field of emotions. She was a Guest Editor for the *International Journal of Synthetic Emotions*, and has received various awards including CITEC Award for Excellence in Doctoral HRI Research (2014), NTF Award for Entertainment Robots and Systems at IROS 2010, and the Google Canada Anita Borg Scholarship (2008). She is a contributor to IEEE Spectrum Automaton Robotics Blog, and is a member of the IEEE.

Jessica Lindblom (School of Informatics, Informatics Research Centre, SWEDEN) is a senior lecturer in cognitive science at the School of Informatics, University of Skövde, Sweden. She graduated with the degree of Doctor of Philosophy from Linköping University, Sweden in 2007 within Cognitive Systems. Dr. Lindblom also holds an MSc (2001) in Informatics and a BSc (2000) in Cognitive Science, both from the University of Skövde. Her research interests include social aspects of embodied and situated cognition and its implications for socially interactive technology, ranging from Human-Robot Interaction (HRI) to Human-Computer Interaction (HCI) and User Experience Design (UXD). Her research projects currently centre on cognitive load and interruption management in information systems as well as farmers' decision-making and the implementation of agricultural decision support systems.

Marcello Mortillaro is Senior Research Associate at the Swiss center for Affective Sciences at the University of Geneva. His research interests include vocal, facial, and bodily expression of emotions, as well as appraisal constituents of emotions. His work has a specific focus on the integration of multimodal nonverbal expressions, both in terms of production and recognition, and affective computing. He is also interested in developing applications based on fundamental emotion research and coordinated several projects aimed at assessing emotional and affective reactions in real world scenarios.

Ben Meuleman received a master's degree in Experimental Psychology and a master's degree in Statistical Data Analysis from the University of Ghent. He is currently working as a Ph.D. candidate at the Swiss Center for Affective Sciences. The project concerns the computational modeling of appraisal theory of emotion, supervised by Klaus Scherer and Agnes Moors. The goal of this project is to advance the understanding of emotion production processes using methods from statistical machine learning.

Atulya K. Nagar holds the Foundation Chair, as Professor of Computer and Mathematical Sciences, at Liverpool Hope University and is Head of the Department of Mathematics and Computer Science. A mathematician by training, Professor Nagar possesses multi-disciplinary expertise in Natural Computing, Bioinformatics, Operations Research and Systems Engineering. He has an extensive background and experience of working in Universities in the UK and India. He has been an expert reviewer for the Biotechnology and Biological Sciences Research Council (BBSRC) grants peer-review committee for Bioinformatics Panel and serves on Peer-Review College of the Arts and Humanities Research Council (AHRC) as a scientific expert member. He has coedited volumes on Intelligent Systems, and Applied Mathematics; he is the Editor-in-Chief of the *International Journal of Artificial Intelligence and Soft Computing (IJAISC)* and serves on editorial boards for a number of prestigious journals as well as on International Programme Committee (IPC) for several international conferences. He received a prestigious Commonwealth Fellowship for pursuing his Doctorate in Applied Non-Linear Mathematics, which he earned from the University of York in 1996. He holds BSc (Hons.), MSc, and MPhil (with Distinction) from the MDS University of Ajmer, India. Prior to joining Liverpool Hope, Prof. Nagar was with the Department of Mathematical Sciences, and later at the Department of Systems Engineering, at Brunel University, London.

Shivashankar B. Nair is a Professor in the Department of Computer Science and Engineering at the Indian Institute of Technology Guwahati, (IIT-G) Guwahati, India. He obtained his Masters' and doctoral degrees in Engineering from Amravati University, Amravati, India, in 1988 and 1998 respectively. He was awarded the Korean Brain Pool Professorship in 2008-'09, to work on Emotional Robotics at the Hanbat National University, Daejeon, S. Korea. He is a member of IEEE and ACM. His research interests include Emotion based control, Bio-inspired Systems, Artificial Immune Systems and Mobile Agents.

Hiroshi G. Okuno received his B.A. and Ph.D from the University of Tokyo in 1972 and 1996, respectively. He worked for NTT, JST, Tokyo University of Science, and Kyoto University. He is currently a professor at the Graduate Program for Embodiment Informatics, Waseda University, and a professor emeritus, Kyoto University. He is currently engaged in computational auditory scene analysis, artificial intelligence and robot audition. He received various awards, including 2013 Award of Minster of Education, Culture, Sports, Science and Technology, the Best Paper Awards of JSAI in 1991 and Advanced Robotics in 2014, the Best Paper Awards of IEA/AIE-2001, 2005, 2010, and 2013, and IEEE/RSJ IROS-2010 NTF Award for Entertainment Robots and Systems. He co-edited "Computational Auditory Scene Analysis" (CRC Press, 1998), and "New Trends in Applied Artificial Intelligence" (Springer, 2007). He is a fellow of IEEE and JSAI (the Japanese Society for Artificial Intelligence), and a member of AAAI, ACM, ASA, RSJ, IPSJ, JSSST and JCSST.

Francisco Perales obtained his BSc. in Computer Sciences at the UAB (1986) and his PhD. in Computer Sciences at the UIB (1993). He specializes in the field of Computer Graphics, Computer Vision and its applications. He has over 100 publications in Computer Vision, User Interfaces and Neuroscience. Perales actively participates in national and European R&D projects in Multimodal Interfaces and Intelligent Agents. He is reviewer in international journals and is a member of ACM-SIGGRAPH, IEEE, IAPR y EUROGRAPHICS. He is Senior member of IEEE and General Co-chair of AMDO (Articulated Motion and Deformable Objects) and IAPR, which is organized every two years at the UIB. He holds a Bachelor in Medicine (DEA) and he is currently pursuing his PhD in Neuro-rehabilitation using BCI and Neurofeedback.

María Guadalupe Sánchez-Escribano is Automation and AI-Robotics Engineer by degree and Master. She is researcher in Systems Engineering and Cognitive Systems and PhD Student. Previously specialized in Computer Vision and Image Processing. She received the Degree in Electrical Engineering from the Universidad Politécnica de Madrid in September 2003 while working in different multinational companies. In October 2006, she received the Degree in Automatic and Electronic Engineering from the same university and joined the group of Intelligent Control as a Computer Vision researcher. Once she joined the group, she studied the Master in Robotics and Automation obtaining an MSc in Robotics and Automation in May 2009. Afterwards, she joined the group of ASLab - Autonomous System Laboratory of the Universidad Politécnica de Madrid (www.aslab.org) where she is currently working. Once here, she started PhD studies, while working as a researcher and lecturer. Her research areas include the fields of model driven development, artificial emotions, autonomous engineering systems, data analysis, control algorithms and image processing.

Ricardo Sanz was born in Tomellosa, Spain in 1963. He got a degree in electrical engineering (1987) and a Ph.D. in robotics and artificial intelligence (1990). Since 1991, he has been a member of the Department of Automatic Control at the Universidad Politecnica de Madrid, Spain. Now he is professor in Automatic Control and Systems Engineering. His main research interests focus around control architectures for intelligent systems, being involved in research lines on autonomous control, software technologies for complex, distributed controllers, real-time artificial intelligence, cognitive systems, bio-inspired controllers and philosophical aspects of intelligence. He has been associated editor of the *IEEE Control Systems Magazine* and chairman of the OMG Control Systems Working Group and the IFAC Technical Committee on Computers and Control. He is also associated editor of the *International Journal of Machine Consciousness* and the *Biologically Inspired Cognitive Systems Journal*. Since 2004 he is the coordinator of the UPM Autonomous Systems Laboratory, Spain.

Klaus R. Scherer is an honorary professor of emotion psychology at the University of Geneva and directs the Geneva Emotion Research Group. His major research interest is the further theoretical development and empirical test of his Component Process Model of Emotion (CPM), specifically the modeling of appraisal-driven processes of motor expression and physiological reaction patterns, as well as the reflection of these processes in subjective experience. Other major research foci are the study of the expression of affect in voice and speech, and applied emotion research.

G. Shivakumar obtained his B.E. Degree in Instrumentation from University of Mysore, India and M.Tech. from Indian Institute of Technology, Kharagpur, India. Presently he is doing doctoral degree with Visvesvaraya Technological University, Belgaum, India. Currently, he is working as an associate professor in the Department.

Saurabh K. Singh completed his Bachelor of Technology degree in Information Technology from Dr. K.N. Modi Institute of Engineering and Technology, Modinagar, Gaziabad, India, in 2011. He received his Masters' degree in Computer Science and Engineering from the Indian Institute of Guwahati, Guwahati, India in 2013. He is currently working as Software Development Engineer with Microsoft India Development Centre in Hyderabad, India. His research interests include Artificial Intelligence, Bio-Inspired Algorithms and Synthetic emotions for Robots.

Atsuo Takanishi is a Professor of the Department of Modern Mechanical Engineering, Waseda University and a concurrent Professor and the director of the HRI (Humanoid Robotics Institute), Waseda University. He received the B.S.E. degree in 1980, the M.S.E. degree in 1982 and the Ph.D. degree in 1988, all in Mechanical Engineering from Waseda University. His current researches are related to Humanoid Robots and its applications in medicine and well-being. He is a member of Robotics Society of Japan (a board member in 1992 and 1993), Japanese Society of Biomechanisms, Japanese Society of Mechanical Engineers, Japanese Society of Instrument and Control Engineers and Society of Mastication Systems (a major board member from 1996 to current), IEEE and other medicine and dentistry related societies in Japan.

Gabriele Trovato is Visiting Researcher in CTI Archer and lecturer of Human-Robot Interaction in UNICAMP in Campinas, Brazil; and Research Associate of Waseda University, Tokyo, Japan. He received his M.S. degree in Computer Engineering from the University of Pisa, Italy, in 2008, and Ph.D. degree in Biorobotics from Waseda University, in 2014. As Research Assistant for the Global Robot Academia program in Japan, Gabriele Trovato was the president of the organising committee of the Italy-Japan Workshop 2012 and co-organiser of the other years. He has been Visiting Researcher in Karlsruhe Institute of Technology, in Germany; in Egypt-Japan University of Science and Technology, in Alexandria, Egypt; in Carnegie Mellon University, in Pittsburgh, USA; and in Eindhoven University of Technology, in the Netherlands. His research interests include Human-Robot Interaction, with focus on culture related aspects, artificial emotions in humanoid robotics, and robot design.

Javier Varona received the Ph.D. degree in Computer Engineering from the Universitat Autonoma de Barcelona, Barcelona, Spain, in 2001. He is Professor in the Mathematics and Computer Science Department at University of Balearic Islands, Islas Baleares, Spain. His research interests include computer vision and human–computer interaction. He is the leader of a Spanish government funded research project on vision-based interaction for rehabilitation (TIN2010-16576 and TIN2012-35427).

P.A. Vijaya received her M.E. and Ph.D. degree from the Department of CSA, I.I.Sc., Bangalore, India. She is currently working as Professor in the Department of E&C Engineering at BNMIT, Bangalore, INDIA. She has around 50 research publications in international journals/conferences. She has been involved in the organization of a number of workshops, symposiums and refresher courses. She is also a reviewer for a number of journals of National and International repute. Her main research interests are in pattern recognition, image processing, embedded systems, operating systems and computer architecture.

Index

V

Virtual Characters 366-367, 369, 371
VoisJet 404, 407-412, 414

W

Word Description 299-300, 306, 311, 313
WOZ 191, 194, 196, 199, 202

Z

Zionist 406, 414

Printed in the United States
By Bookmasters